PRACTICAL
LOSS CONTROL
LEADERSHIP

Frank E. Bird, Jr.
and
George L. Germain

Published by
Institute Publishing
(A Division of International Loss Control Institute)
4546 Atlanta Highway, P.O. Box 1898
Loganville, Georgia 30249

Foreword

Now, as never before in the history of the industrial age, management faces an overwhelmingly complex situation in its efforts to prevent and control occupational injury and illness, property damage (including fire and explosion), security breaches, pollution and product liability.

This complexity has come about because of advances in technology, the increasing role of government and government agencies, increasing awareness on the part of individuals and communities of human rights, occupational health problems, environmental problems and the economic constraints of the past few years.

This complex environment is here to stay and because it is, it is imperative that management understand and accept its role in making the workplace as safe and healthy as possible as well as preventing and controlling all other associated losses. I'm happy to note that dedicated people at all levels recognize this fact and have taken steps to assume their portion of the responsibility for safety and health. I cannot stress too strongly that productivity and quality are inextricably interrelated with workplace safety and health in particular and loss control in general. All, and management in particular, must look at their operations as a whole, made up of dynamic relationships. Efforts expanded in loss control have a positive impact throughout the organization.

Not only does a systematic, committed approach to all forms of loss control impact favourably on the profitability of an enterprise, it has also a human impact in the reduction of pain and suffering, increased awareness of and commitment to management goals, better morale and a more stable workforce.

This book is designed as a guide for all levels in an organization in their efforts to address the issues just mentioned. The Industrial Accident Prevention Association of Ontario commends the application of its principles to the professional management and control of losses everywhere.

James V. Findley
Executive Vice President and General Manager
Industrial Accident Prevention Association
Ontario, Canada

Preface

Effectiveness. Efficiency. Excellence. These words and concepts permeate current literature, courses and discussions. They are defined in nearly as many different ways as the number of people who write and talk about them. For practical purposes, the definitions seem to boil down to these:

- Effectiveness - doing the right things.
- Efficiency - doing things right.
- Excellence - efficiently meeting effective goals, both short term and long range.

We believe that this book can help you improve the effectiveness, efficiency and excellence of your management system for safety/loss control... and for quality, production and cost control. In essence, it can help improve your management system. Improved quality, production and cost control go hand-in-hand with improved safety and loss control. And they all depend on how the system is managed.

The reason behind our belief is that the book's concepts, practices, techniques and tools reflect what leading organizations around the free world have done, and are doing, to get their results. Spanning three decades, we have had the good fortune to work with tens of thousands of managers in hundreds of organizations to distill the contents of this book. The ideas and applications are tried, tested and proven. Put them to work and they will work for you.

It's impossible to give adequate thanks to all who contributed so much to producing this book. But we sincerely appreciate their help, without which there would not be this book. Special thanks go to:

Raymond L. Kuhlman, for his work on "Accident/Incident Investigation" and "Planned Inspections."

Dr. Robert M. Arnold, for the chapter on "Occupational Health."

George D. Stevenson, for the chapter on "Fire Loss Control."

Dr. M. Douglas Clark, for the chapter on "Managing The Troubled Employee." But more than that, for the countless hours of editing, coordinating, researching and refining.

Finally, we thank the many friends-clients-customers who have responded positively to our previous publications. We trust that you will also respond positively to this one... as the state-of-the-art in practical loss control leadership.

Frank E. Bird, Jr.
George L. Germain

CONTENTS

Foreword

Contents   Page

Contents	Page

CHAPTER 1

THE MODERN EVOLUTION OF SAFETY MANAGEMENT

History is philosophy teaching by examples.
— Dionysius

INTRODUCTION

It is as true of safety management as it is of any other significant field of study: full understanding and appreciation of the present requires comparison with the past. This chapter's purpose is to aid such understanding and appreciation.

People often long for "the good old days." But their yearning is only for the real or imagined positive parts of the past. In safety and health, for instance, what were the "good old days" really like? In terms of one critical indicator, accidental deaths, *Figure 1-1* shows that death rates for all accidents were more than twice as high in 1912 as they were in 1983 and that the rate for non-motor vehicle deaths was nearly four times as high.

Many things are vastly different now than they were then, For instance, in the early 1900's

- the Industrial Revolution was in its infancy
- equipment was not designed with operator safety in mind
- machines were unguarded
- people were unskilled and untrained
- work hours were much longer
- general cultural and educational levels were lower
- employers were less employee-oriented
- employees had more fatalistic attitudes
- safety studies and laws were sparse.

With this background in mind, let's examine the evolution of safety management in terms of these three aspects: 1) evolution of laws, 2) evolution of safety activism factors, and 3) evolution of management concepts.

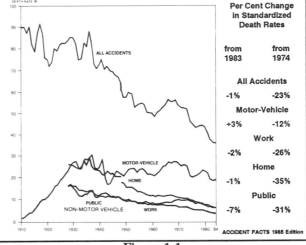

Trends in accidental death rates

Between 1912 and 1984, accidental deaths per 100,000 population were reduced 52 percent from 82 to 39. The 76 percent reduction from 79 to 19 in the nonmotor-vehicle death rate was offset in part by the sixfold increase in the motor-vehicle death rate from 3 to 20. The reduction in the overall rate during a period when the nation's population more than doubled has resulted in 2,500,000 fewer people being killed accidentally than would have been killed if the rate had not been reduced.

	Per Cent Change in Standardized Death Rates	
	from 1983	from 1974
All Accidents	-1%	-23%
Motor-Vehicle	+3%	-12%
Work	-2%	-26%
Home	-1%	-35%
Public	-7%	-31%

ACCIDENT FACTS 1985 Edition

Figure 1-1

EVOLUTION OF LAWS

Findlay and Kuhlman, in *Leadership In Safety,* provide the following historical perspective regarding legal developments.

Babylonian Law

Contrary to the opinion of many, safety is not a new management responsibility. It can be found throughout recorded history. In ancient Babylon, for example, the "Code of Hammurabi" (*Figure 1-2*) prescribed punishment of overseers for injuries suffered by workers. For instance, if a worker lost an arm due to an overseer's negligence or oversight, the overseer's arm was taken — to match the worker's loss.

A. If a builder build a house for a man and do not make its construction firm and
   the house which he has built collapse and cause the death of the owner of
   the house - that builder shall be put to death
B. If it cause the death of the son of the owner of the house - they shall put
   to death a son of that builder.
C. If it cause the death of a slave of the owner of the house - he shall give to
   the owner of the house a slave of equal value.
D. If it destroy property, he shall restore whatever it destroyed, and because
   he did not make the house which he built firm and if collapsed, he shall
   rebuild the house which collapsed at his own expense.
E. If a builder build a house for a man and do not make its construction meet
   the requirements and a wall fall in, that builder shall strengthen the
   wall at his own expense.

Translated by R.F. Harper.
"Code of Hammurabi" p. 83 - seq.

**From The Code of Laws of HAMMURABI (2200 BC)
King of Babylonia**

Figure 1-2

English Law

England's first Factory Act, introduced in 1802, laid out general standards of heating, lighting, ventilation, and work hours. It was intended primarily to stop the widespread abuse of poor children imported into the textile factory districts. It was a pioneer effort. But, unfortunately, it was misunderstood and ignored by factory managers and was inadequately enforced by inspectors and local magistrates, due to strong pressures from influential people. So, as the years went by, progressively restrictive laws were passed to deal with specific hazards (such as the Explosives Act of 1875) and with general hazards (such as the Safety and Health Act of 1974).

German Law

At times, safety laws were also politically motivated. To stem the rise of Communism in Imperial Germany in the 1880's, as well as to respond to increasing dissatisfaction of workers with hazardous workplace conditions, the Chancellor introduced the world's first workers' compensation law. German industrialists, spurred by warnings in the writings of Karl Marx, endorsed the act. In doing so, they expressed some of the first recorded concerns by executives for safety in the workplace as a vital contribution to the well-being of the business.

North American Law

In Canada and the United States, events followed much the same course. Workers were pressed into long hours at uncomfortable, dangerous machines. In desperation, they sought solutions through unified efforts and violent reactions. Brought into conflict with both social values and prevailing laws, they succeeded in changing both. Laws were passed to set up standards and establish inspections. Lack of compliance by managers, and lackadaisical enforcement by government agencies, led to even more stringent and comprehensive laws.

Other aspects of the situation have been of considerable benefit to management leaders. In Ontario, Canada, a government commission was appointed in 1910 to study compensation laws throughout the world. The commission concluded that the cost of compensation should be considered an expense of production or service, and that every employee should have the right to compensation for injury without having to resort to the courts. The Ontario Workmen's Compensation Act of 1915 incorporated these provisions for the first time. It also provided for employers' associations with the express purpose of advancing accident prevention. Nineteen such organizations federated in 1917 to charter the Industrial Accident Prevention Association of Ontario. This progressive association has worked diligently and successfully in helping employers to help themselves improve safety in the workplace.

In the United States, early laws (starting in 1887 in Massachusetts) provided for factory inspectors, work hours, and machine guarding requirements. Typically, enforcement and compliance were weak, which led to more stringent laws. Also, common law began to be altered in the worker's favor.

One historic study with an enormous influence at the time is known as the Pittsburgh Survey. It was completed in Allegheny County, Pennsylvania, in 1909, and revealed that 526 fatal industrial accidents occurred in that county alone during 12 months of 1906-1907. The study further revealed that over 50 percent of the surviving widows and children were left with no source of income. It was calculated that only 30 percent of the settlements received exceeded $500. This same report stated that there were 30,000 fatal industrial injuries in the United States in 1909.

The Pittsburgh Survey prompted rapid passage of state compensation laws, beginning in Wisconsin in 1911. The enactment of similar laws in several other states resulted in a 1912 safety congress under the sponsorship of the Association of Iron and Steel Electrical Engineers. A second congress, held in New York in 1913, established what is now known as the National Safety Council. This organization has made monumental contributions in safety research and promotion.

Lead or Be Led

The years since these initial safety movements have seen North American society change from independent businesses and private lives to an interdependent society. Business and social activities which were once considered separate and private now are regarded as interwoven and public. Constraints on business organizations will increase unless their managers provide sound safety leadership — responsible protection of people, equipment, materials and environment.

What lessons can we learn from this aspect of history? When managers proved unresponsive to the well-being of people and the environment, we saw reaction and intervention. Collective bargaining for basic welfare considerations and wide-ranging safety and health legislation are factors that clearly attest to this. Look at these examples

- The U.S. Occupational Safety and Health Act of 1970
- The Consumer Product Safety Act of 1972
- The Ontario Industrial Safety Act of 1972
- The Toxic Substances Control Act of 1976
- The Report of the Royal Commission on the Health and Safety of Workers in Mines, Government of Ontario, 1976
- The U.S. Mine Safety and Health Act of 1977
- The act regarding the Occupational Health and Occupational Safety of Workers, enacted by the Ontario Legislature in 1979
- The Resource Conservation and Recovery Act, reauthorized and expanded in 1984.

These are typical of laws to ensure safety, after managers (at least in the eyes of workers and consumers) neglected to meet their full leadership responsibilities. The challenge to management is clear. Safety through leadership is more fulfilling, more rewarding, more economical, and more successful than safety by work group imposition or by governmental interven-

tion. Initiative and positive leadership can control the erosion of management's freedom to manage.

EVOLUTION OF SAFETY ACTIVISM FACTORS

Many factors influence the decisions of modern managers regarding safety and health. Some of them are quite recent in origin. *Figure 1-3* shows nine major factors. Let's take a quick look at each of them (as presented by Findlay and Kuhlman, *Leadership In Safety*).

Unions

In many countries, collective bargaining has played a role in workplace safety improvements for many years. Union influence has been exerted not only in direct negotiations, but also through financing or supporting of safety and health research, lobbying for safety and health legislation, and backing of liability suits filed by union members. Today's union activity in safety and health is greater than ever before.

Consumers

Consumerism is more recent as a significant influence on safety and health management. Its goals may be clustered under a concern for "quality of life." As Alvin Toffler observed in *The Adaptive Corporation*, "Corporate retorts to the New Consumerism based on traditional economic arguments cut no ice — for the very good reason that the movement's goals are a saner, more civilized society, not necessarily a richer one."

Consumerism has emphasized growing concerns over dangers to people from manufactured products. Many products with formerly widespread common use have been banned or severely restricted. Food additives, appliances, sleepwear, furniture and even soft drink containers have all been the targets of restrictions or bans. In the case of the containers, for instance, the suspicion of birth defects arising from use of acrylonitrile in a plastic bottle resulted in the Monsanto Company's closure of four plants, the layoff of 1,000 workers, a profit reduction of fifteen million dollars, and a projected one-year sales loss of one hundred million dollars.

Courts

The editors of *Business Insurance* magazine have observed that the rise in consumerism has brought along with it an almost unrestrained tendency to sue for injury, aggravation or even affront. In the United

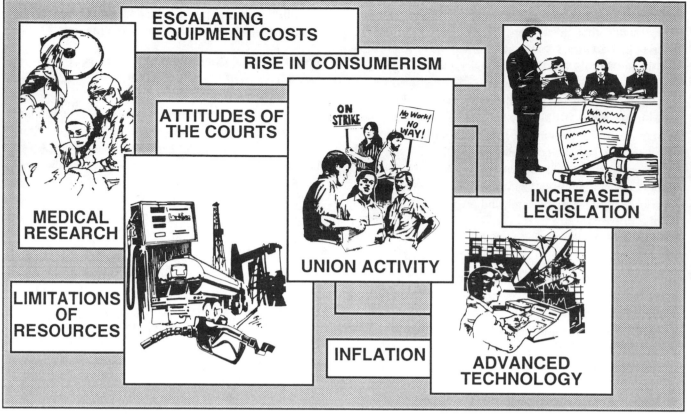

Figure 1-3

States, sympathetic juries have responded to these suits with astronomical awards, even though plaintiffs are sometimes motivated by greed rather than suffering. The snowballing consequences in business losses, insurance premiums and court costs borne through tax dollars, have virtually gotten out of hand. Safety management leadership can be a critical factor in regaining control.

Technology

Technology has created a need for extensive, dynamic safety programs. In the past 50 years, scientists and engineers have developed more new equipment and processes than were developed in the preceding thousands of years. Many tasks are becoming increasingly complex and demanding and the potential consequences of errors more costly. Also, it has been shown that virtually total safety is possible... *if* one is able and willing to pay the price in resources. The space program, for example, was highly successful, quite safe (about 99.9%), and extremely expensive.

The psychological effect of these advances has been greater insistence on safety where risks had previously been assumed. People now feel that things can and should be safe. As a result, management decision-making has been broadened to encompass the potential applications of sophisticated techniques, such as a

system safety analysis and a concern for the entire useful life of a product.

In brief, technological progress suggests these two vital considerations for management leaders: first, potential safety and health problems are being generated faster than ever before; second, no problem in the workplace is too big or complex to master through professional management.

Workforce Changes

The character of the workplace has undergone great changes in the last decade. Regulations requiring employment opportunity without bias, as well as the economic need to have an added earner in the family, have brought more women into work environments which were once exclusively male precincts. Other regulations require the employment of the handicapped within their limitations. In addition, today's workers tend to be better educated and informed, and they expect more of their jobs than just a livelihood.

Each of these factors introduces new demands and new challenges for safety management.

Laws

In addition to making the laws discussed earlier, legislative bodies have responded to the actions of individuals, courts, and influence groups. They have started inquiries and hearings, or made new laws and standards where they perceived a need or desire. For example, twenty-four hour compensation, including equal compensation for on-the-job and off-the-job accidents, already in effect in New Zealand, is being considered in other countries. Many jurisdictions are revising workers' compensation laws to expand their application and their scope.

Laws now also fix liability for disposal of materials which may at some future date affect the environment. Other laws require the study of environmental or human impact during the design and development of products. These are just a few of the legislative constraints on business. They pose a real challenge to business leaders.

Inflation

Materials shortages brought about by expansion of business have contributed to inflationary trends. These shortages, combined with increased costs of labor, energy, and insurance, have caused both capital and replacement equipment costs to go sky high.

Managers find that costs of premature replacement of equipment damaged or destroyed by accident are far greater than the depreciation reserves started when the old equipment was bought. Costs can be reduced if equipment can be made to last longer — to serve at least its expected life. Consequently, accident control takes on added importance for executives.

Replacements for fire losses have even greater impact. Of businesses in North America which suffered severe fire losses in the last ten years, 43% never reopened their doors. An additional 28% failed within two years. These business failures were due to two simple facts. First, the insurance did not cover the cost of replacement: equipment, materials and buildings had been insured at an initial, or even a depreciated cost. Second, since insurance and the safety program were separated, management had not considered the consequences of *property damage* and *business interruption* as accidental loss.

Progressive executives and supervisors are showing greater interest in the broad concept of safety management, and are working diligently to solve the problems aggravated by rampant inflation.

Medical Research

A relatively recent and widespread cause of concern has been the toxic substances that create health hazards in the workplace. For many years, industry has con-

ducted research on the effects of these toxic substances, and industrial standards organizations have recommended controls and exposure limits. But general lack of management response has led governmental groups to take over standards-setting as a logical addition to their own research and enforcement. Also, medical researchers, both those in governmental agencies and those working on governmental grants, are focusing their attention more and more on physical and health hazards in the workplace. Research is helping to define limits on exposures in those cases where problems can be avoided by limiting the amount or duration of exposure. More importantly, research is identifying substances and by-products which have irreversible effects and, in some cases, are carcinogenic. The enlarged list of diseases which may be work-related presents an enlarged list of liabilities possibly causing harm to workers' physical and/or mental health.

PVC is an example that most people have heard about. Until 1974, vinyl chloride gas was used in the production of over half of the plastic products produced, and was hardly thought of as dangerous. No one fainted or developed a rash when it was used. Then it was found to cause a rare form of cancer of the liver, which could not be diagnosed until it had reached an incurable stage. Human exposure had to be prevented. Again, management had to decide how best to control the problem highlighted by medical research.

The consequences of new facts found through medical research have sometimes been swift and drastic. Governmental control has abruptly closed down many primary product lines, dictating a total change in the objectives of the affected businesses. In many cases, research findings have also dictated expensive recalls of products when user experience has revealed hazards not acceptable to the people, or the legislators who represent them. These kinds of potential consequences are among the many reasons managers must exert safety leadership.

Energy

A final influence on safety and loss control responsibility is the efficient use of energy — and control of its loss or waste. Energy resources have become critical in a large part of the world. Where energy is limited, and even where it is not, costs are rising rapidly. Energy loss affects the supply of equipment and materials needed to make the product or provide the service. Energy loss increases production costs. Energy loss results in failure to fill orders on time, which leads to loss of future sales.

The control of energy loss contributes to an urgent national need while it brings these kinds of benefits to your business: 1) controls costs in a time of spiraling prices; 2) controls downtime due to shortages of fuel and power; and 3) keeps you more competitive, both at home and abroad.

Unions - Consumers - Courts - Technology - Workforce Changes - Laws - Inflation - Medical Research - Energy; these have brought us a long way since the turn of the century! They have spawned professional safety organizations and more enlightened management practices; a broadening of safety concepts to include health factors and property damage, as well as traumatic injury; and much better measures for the prevention and control of losses. But there is still much more to be done... and these strong forces are still pushing for further progress.

EVOLUTION OF MANAGEMENT CONCEPTS

This century has witnessed a tremendous safety management evolution from the infamous "sweat shops" of the early 1900's, through treating safety strictly as injury prevention up to loss control as an integrated management responsibility. Emphasis has broadened from "engineering" to "management"; safety specialists have advanced from "inspectors" to "directors"; and benefits have come from a *management approach* which integrates safety, quality, production and cost control.

The Early 20th Century

During the early part of this century, the Industrial Revolution brought about extensive use of power machinery: machines were designed with little or no consideration for operator safety; available labor was untrained and unskilled in the use of the new, unguarded machines; power sources were changing rapidly from manpower and horsepower to steam, electricity and internal combustion; workdays of 11-13 hours increased exposure to accident potential; facilities for emergency care were horribly inadequate and medical help was seldom available. As a result, death and disability rates were at record high levels.

Figure 1-4

Workers Casting The 24-Ton Anchor For The Brooklyn Bridge

Naturally, attention began to focus on injuries, disabilities and deaths. To the extent that it existed, *safety was primarily injury-oriented.* Worker compensation laws were passed, adding to the emphasis on the prevention of injuries.

Corrective measures were primarily engineering-oriented. The predominant management style was F.W. Taylor's stop-watch and slide-rule school of "scientific management." Managers tended to consider work as an impersonal exchange of labor for money — a unit of pay for a unit of work. "Bosses" tended to rule "hired hands" with an iron fist. Maximum production was the big objective. Safety was low on management's motivational scale.

Here are some of the landmark publications and organizations associated with this period of the safety management evolution:

1906 - U.S. Steel Corporation started a company "safety campaign" that claimed a reduction of 43.2 percent in its serious and fatal accidents by 1912.

1911 - American Society of Safety Engineers founded.

1912 - "First Cooperative Safety Congress," Association of Iron and Steel Electrical Engineers, Princeton University Press, 1912.

1913 - Formation of what is now known as the National Safety Council.

1917 - Industrial Accident Prevention Association (IAPA) formed in Ontario, Canada.

1928 - American National Standards Institute (ANSI) founded.

1931 - Heinrich, H.W., *Industrial Accident Prevention,* McGraw-Hill, New York, 1931.

1938 - American Conference of Government Industrial Hygienists (A.C.G.I.H.) organized.

1938 - New York University's Center for Safety Education started.

1939 - American Industrial Hygiene Association organized.

The Mid-Century Years

The evolution toward integration of safety into a professional management system experienced many significant advances in the mid-1900's (forties, fifties and sixties). Slowly but surely, leaders in the field began to broaden management's mental picture of "safety" and how best to achieve it. Books and journal articles began to emphasize safety *management,* a *systems* approach to accident prevention and control, and management *professionalism.*

Some of the landmark publications and organizations associated with this period of the evolution are as follows:

1943 - Blake, Roland, *Industrial Safety,* Prentice-Hall, Inc., Englewood Cliffs, NJ.

1949 - Canadian Society of Safety Engineers (CSSE) founded.

1951 - Cutter, Walter A., Ph.D., "Organization and Functions of the Safety Department," American Management Association, New York.

1958 - DeReamer, R., *Modern Safety Practices*, John Wiley & Sons, Inc., New York.

1959 - Cutter, W.A., Ph.D., and Wilkenson, T.H., "Toward the Profession of Safety Program Management," *National Safety News*, October.

1960 - American Board of Industrial Hygiene organized.

1961 - Bird, Frank E., Jr., "Damage Control, A New Horizon in Accident Prevention," *National Safety News,* October.

1962 - System Safety Society founded.

1963 - Certified Industrial Hygienist (C.I.H.) program implemented.

1963 - Simonds, R.H. and Grimaldi, J.V., *Safety Management,* Richard D. Irwin, Inc., Homewood, Illinois.

1963 - U.S. Department of the Interior formally announced that it had initiated a new program based on system safety.

1964 - Allen, Louis A., *The Management Profession*, McGraw-Hill Book Company, New York.

1965 - Pope, W.C. and Creswell, T.J., "A New Approach to Safety Programs Management," *ASSE Journal*, August.

1965 - Tarrants, W.E., Ph.D., "The Professional Development of the Safety Engineering Field," *ASSE Journal*, February.

1966 - Bird, Frank E., Jr. and Germain, George L., *Damage Control*, American Management Association, Inc.

1967 - The first Total Loss Control course, taught by Frank E. Bird, Jr., in Naples, Florida.

1968 - Canadian Safety Council organized.

1968 - National Safety Management Society chartered.

1969 - Certified Safety Professional program implemented.

1969 - Bird, Frank E., Jr., "Incident Recall," *National Safety News*, October.

This period witnessed a clear movement beyond the strictly injury-oriented concept of safety toward a broader accident-oriented approach. Definitions of *accident* included property damage, and the definition of *safety* evolved from "freedom from injuries" toward "control of accidental loss."

SAFETY — THE CONTROL OF ACCIDENT LOSS

Safety professionals and operating managers increasingly recognized that it was neither economically feasible nor administratively practical to prevent all accidents, or to create a risk-free environment. The concept of *management control* began to develop as part of a professional management approach to safety. This control concept recognizes the importance not only of preventing accidents but also of minimizing loss when accidents do occur.

During this period, *damage control* provided a logical bridge from "injury-oriented" safety programs to "accident-oriented" programs (as depicted in *Figure 1-5*). More and more people recognized not only that accidental damage is extremely expensive, but also

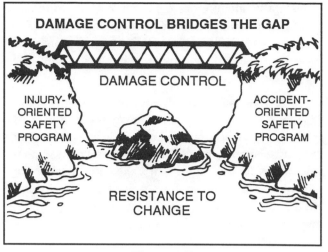

Figure 1-5

that damage accidents have significant potential for injuring and killing people.

Starting in the 1950's, Lukens Steel Company led the way to industrial property damage control. After about a decade of development and success, their program was published in 1966 by the American Management Association as the book *Damage Control* by Bird and Germain. Billing it as "a new horizon in accident prevention and cost improvement," the AMA said:

> *Damage Control* is the first book published on a totally new approach to plant safety that places the emphasis on *all* accidents — not just those resulting in injury. It describes a practical injury and cost reduction program developed by the Lukens Steel Company to reduce potential injuries, improve product quality, and heighten employee morale.

Notice the emphasis not only on safety but also on cost reduction, quality, and morale. They could also have included productivity, as did the authors of the British Iron and Steel Federation report on their study of Lukens' damage control system (see *Figure 1-6* for more details). This is one of the early studies proving the positive correlations among safety, quality, productivity and cost control.

The Lukens program led to visits, speeches, articles, and seminars. Interest spread to many companies in many countries. In recent years, the escalating costs of repairing and replacing damaged tools, machines, materials, and facilities has motivated even greater management interest and involvement in total accident control. Today, damage control is recognized as a vital

EXCERPTS FROM THE 1964 REPORT ON THE LUKENS STEEL COMPANY DAMAGE CONTROL SYSTEM, BY HARRY VAN DER VORD (BRITISH IRON AND STEEL FEDERATION) AND WILLIAM J. SHAW (BRITISH IRON AND STEEL RESEARCH ASSOCIATION)

It was apparent to us very early in our visit that the Damage Control Scheme had the whole-hearted support of management... not only because injury-prevention and cost-control were worthwhile aims in themselves; but because the objects of the scheme were entirely consistent with the Company's wider philosophy of efficient management. *Safety, Quality, Productivity and Cost Control were regarded as the four main avenues of approach to the single objective of efficient operations. It was the belief at Lukens that these four aims were not conflicting but complementary; that they ought not be pursued independently but as an inseparable part of a united effort.* The damage severity rates were regarded as one index of efficiency but the Company also maintained other indices which would make interesting study in conjunction with the damage and injury rates. These other indices were:

-A percentage figure for plate quality control.
-A percentage figure for orders shipped on time.
-A "work performance" index.

The last of the above is a measure of work accomplished in relation to a goal. Goals are based on standard units of manpower output — time and tonnage — and the index is derived by dividing total standard hours by actual hours and expressing the answer as a percentage of goal.

Serious injuries have been halved since 1960, as also has the damage severity... The correlation between these injury and damage rates over the five years is significant but only at the 10% level. When further figures become available it may be, however, that a stronger relation will be shown. It is by no means impossible that a further reduction in injury rates may be achieved when the Damage Control Scheme reaches what may be described as the "second wind" stage, and long range preventive measures take effect.

The correlations between Damage Severity and the indices A, B and C (described above) were also calculated and in each case were significant at the 5% level. In other words, there is a close association between improvement or deterioration as shown in the Damage Control figures and as reflected in the other indices of efficiency. This is an interesting finding and bears out the view held at Lukens that *the Damage Control Scheme, far from interfering with production and the delivery of orders on time, is an inseparable part of the total effort for efficiency.*

Figure 1-6

part of safety/loss control by leading organizations around the world. In turn, accident control is recognized as a vital part of integrated management — for safety, for quality, for productivity and for cost control.

The Past Two Decades

This might be characterized as the "international" era of safety/loss control management evolution, in which the professional management approach spread rather rapidly around the free world. This is evident in many of the following landmark publications, programs and organizations associated with this period.

1968 - Frank E. Bird, Jr. introduced the Total Loss Control profile at the Insurance Company of North America.

1970 - Bird, Frank E., Jr., and Schlesinger, Lawrence, "Safe Behavior Reinforcement," *ASSE Journal,* June.

1970 - Fletcher, John A., and Douglas, Hugh M., *Total Environmental Control,* National Profile Limited, Toronto.

1970 - National Institute of Occupational Safety and Health (NIOSH) created.

1970 - Pope, W.C., "Computers in Safety Management," *National Safety News,* May.

1973 - Johnson, W.G., *The Management Oversight and Risk Tree — MORT,* prepared for the U.S. Atomic Energy Commission, U.S. Government Printing Office.

1973 - Miller, C.O., "Safety Related to Management," *Selected Readings in Safety,* Academy Press, Macon, Georgia.

1974 - Mehr, Robert L., and Hedges, Bob A., *Risk Management Concepts and Applications,* Richard D. Irwin, Inc., Homewood, Illinois.

1974 - International Loss Control Institute (ILCI) founded.

1974 - Bird, F.E., Jr., *Management Guide To Loss Control,* Institute Press, Loganville, Georgia.

1975 - Canadian Registered Safety Professional (CRSP) program implemented.

1976 - International Safety Rating System started by the International Loss Control Institute and the Industrial Accident Prevention Association of Ontario, Canada.

1976 - Lowrance, William W., *Of Acceptable Risk: Science and the Determination of Safety,* William Kaufmann, Inc., Los Altos, California.

1976 - Bird, Frank E., Jr., and Loftus, Robert G., *Loss Control Management,* Institute Press, Loganville, Georgia.

Around the world, more and more managers progressed from the "employee carelessness" view of accident to emphasis on inadequacies in the management system.

The concept of *management control* as a primary pathway to safety was put to work. The essence of a control system being used around the world is summarized by the acronym ISMEC:

I - *Identification* of work. Specifying the program elements and activities to achieve desired results.

S - *Standards.* Establishing performance standards (criteria by which methods and results will be evaluated).

M - *Measurement.* Measuring performance; recording and reporting work in progress and completed.

E - *Evaluation.* Evaluating performance as measured and compared with established standards; appraising work and results.

C - *Correction.* Regulating and improving methods and results by constructively correcting substandard performance and commending desired performance.

Along with this concept, some have shifted away from the relatively narrow terms "unsafe acts" and "unsafe conditions" to the broader "substandard practices" and "substandard conditions." This line of thinking has three distinct advantages: 1) it avoids "pointing fingers" at people and the associated blame-fixing; 2) it relates practices and conditions to *standards* — bases for measurement, evaluation and correction; and 3) it broadens the scope of coverage from accident control to *loss control,* relating to safety, quality, production and costs.

This type of emphasis gradually shifted the thoughts and actions of many people *away from* the finger-pointing, witch-hunting, blame-fixing approach, *toward* the mutual problem-solving approach; *away from* the belief that 85% (or more) of accidents are caused by unsafe acts, *toward* the belief that most accidents involve both unsafe acts and unsafe conditions; *away from* the conviction that the basic causes of most accidents are within the control of workers, *toward* the conviction that the basic causes of most accidents can be controlled only by management.

During this era, managers of leading organizations gained a greater grasp of the integrated nature of safety, quality, productivity and cost control — and a realization that problems in all these areas are solved by the same management techniques. Before this broadened perception, safety was not among the most powerful day-to-day motivators of management action. As expressed by Robert Rogers, President, Texas Industries, Inc.:

> I think it is important for you to know what the typical C.E.O. thinks about items that are important to him and how he feels about items that are important to the organization. Safety is not one of these items. It ranks very low on the totem pole. Why? It ranks low because the C.E.O. is interested in cost, he is interested in productivity and he is interested in return on investment.

The view he was commenting on has been well supported by extensive opinion polls and feedback from managers from all over the free world. For example, the International Loss Control Institute obtained feedback from thousands of management conferees who ranked the following as upper management motivators:

A. Provide personal satisfaction
B. Improve labor relations
C. Enhance public relations
D. Increase production rate
E. Give legislative compliance
F. Improve product quality
G. Reduce injury rate
H. Improve operating costs
I. Increase job pride
J. Reduce liability potential
K. Improve customer relations

Typically, H, D and F (costs - production - quality) ranked first, second and third; while G (reduce injury rate) ranked seventh and J (reduce liability potential) ranked ninth.

Subsequent opinion polls show that these rankings often change significantly after the implementation of modern safety/loss control management programs. Then, it is not unusual for the safety items to be ranked close to the top. Even those managers who had not taken part in the earlier polls, but who had experienced their company's modern safety management approach, tended to rank safety as high as number two and to put it on a par with costs, production and quality. Also, we begin to see and hear more statements such as the following one by Raymond H. Marks, President, Tenneco Chemicals, Inc.:

> Safety and loss control are an important part of the executive suite. No longer second-class citizens, loss prevention and profit performance have become synonymous... How often do we get the chance to demonstrate our innate concern for the health and well-being of our fellow humans, while at the same time we improve our profit performance? Think about it — total loss control programming is sound business planning, the best of both worlds under one roof.

J.B. Reid, President of the Carbon Products Division of Union Carbide Corporation, put it this way:

> Having lived with safety as a integral part of the way we manage our business, I know that the benefits of having a good safety program far outweigh the costs. In fact, it is difficult to imagine a system that could adequately address all other aspects of managing a business and ignore safety. After all, the discipline required to control costs and quality is exactly the same as that required to control safety and health. Whether we think in terms of cost/benefit or simply our duty to see that employees are protected... safety pays.

Lester A. Hudson, President and Chief Operating Officer at Dan River, Inc., expressed much the same thought:

> At Dan River, safety is seen as an opportunity to improve overall management... the most valuable fringe benefit of considering safety an operational strategy has been the general improvement in line management's ability to manage all aspects of their total jobs.

"Signs of the times" included the tremendous popularity of the *Management Guide to Loss Control,* written for operating management and published in 1974. Used by tens of thousands of supervisors and executives, both in management conferences and home study programs, this book helped to move managers to the leading edge of practical loss control. Emphases included:

- application of *professional management* principles to safety, as well as production, quality and cost control
- the *new* cause-and-effect sequence, spotlighting "lack of management control" as the first step toward losses
- application of the I-S-M-E-C system of *management control* to all types of loss incidents — involving people, property, productivity and profitability
- broadening the view from "unsafe" to *substandard*
- going beyond symptoms (unsafe/substandard practices and conditions) to get at *basic causes* (in people, in the work, in the management system)
- recognition of the fact that the *basic causes* of problems or downgrading incidents — be they matters of safety, quality, cost or production — are the same
- broadening the view from the "safe way" to the *right way* (safe—high quality—productive—cost effective)
- recognition that the primary way to improve safety (and/or production; quality; costs) is to *improve the management system*

Those organizations whose managers have applied these guidelines have achieved impressive results, as shown below. The injury rates referred to are based on the number of lost-workday accidents per 200,000 man hours.

- Petrochemical corporation, exploration and production — injury rate reduced from 3.1 to .5 in three years
- Twenty mining companies — injury rate (weighted average) reduced from 5.2 to 3.8 in six months
- Meat products plant — injury rate reduced from 12.7 to 2.4 in three years
- Forest products corporation — injury rate reduced from 19.97 to 10.52 in two years
- Paper products plant — injury rate reduced from 20.9 to 2.2 in three years

- 2,397 firms in the province of Ontario, Canada — 20% reduction in accident rate in three years
- Livestock feed lot company — injury rate reduced from 27 to 3.4 in three years
- Stevedoring operation — injury rate reduced from 34 to 5.8 in two years
- Steel division — injury rate reduced from 105 to 9.3 in five years

Another example involves a merit award for productivity. In 1980, the Mine Safety Division of the Chamber of Mines of South Africa received a certificate of merit from the National Productivity Institute in recognition of *productivity improvement* resulting from the introduction of a new *safety* management system. A substantial drop in accident frequencies with corresponding savings in costs, time and production shifts, as well as improved employee morale were all attributed to the implementation of the program. It is proof positive that safety and productivity go hand in hand. The graph shown in *Figure 1-7* displays the results achieved by one mine in the program.

One manufacturing corporation with 80 plant locations made a comparison of accident costs between the plants which scored the highest on a safety manage- ment audit and those which scored the lowest. The 17 plants with the most complete safety programs had accident costs of $.087 per man hour. The 19 plants with the least complete programs had costs of $.235 per man hour, almost three times as high. The other plants also showed a direct correlation between the level of safety programming and amount of accident costs. It should be noted that these costs are real, not hypothetical. They are actually on the books — and come right off "the bottom line."

The Years Ahead

What is most likely to occur regarding management of safety and health during the remainder of the 20th century? Although predicting in print is an open invitation to contention, there are some trends which strongly suggest the direction in which management is headed. The following fourteen are almost certain:

1. Increasing numbers of both company and union leaders will help employees to realize that "safety" is not an absolute; that there are degrees of safety; that a situation is "safe" to the degree that it is at an acceptable level of risk.

2. The trend will continue away from looking for accident "culprits" to looking for "causes"; away from a focus on symptoms to a focus on basic causes; away from blaming employees to improving the management system.

3. Laws and regulations will increasingly make managers, at all levels, collectively and individually accountable for managing control of safety and health risks.

4. There will be a growing movement away from treating safety as a separate aspect of working and managing, toward treatment of safety as part of *the right way;* a movement...

    FROM THESE:
    - Job Safety Instruction
    - Job Safety Analysis
    - Job Safety Procedure
    - Safety Tipping

    TO THESE:
    - Proper Job/Task Instruction
    - Proper Job/Task Analysis
    - Standard Task Procedure
    - Key Point Tipping

3 Year Study

Plant Availability Up 13%

Degree of Safety Total Mine Up 27%

Production Output Up 40%

Tons per Employee Up 15%

Machine Availability Up 4%

Total Accident Frequency Rate Down 57%

Disabling Injury Frequency Rate Down 87%

Labor Turnover Rate Down 57%

NOT TO SCALE

Figure 1-7 Results from a comprehensive program

FROM THESE:
- Job Safety Observation
- Job Safety Orientation
- Safe Behavior Reinforcement
- Personal Safety Contact

TO THESE:
- Planned Job/Task Observation
- Proper Job Orientation
- Positive Performance Reinforcement
- Personal Task Contact

5. For both workers and managers, performance appraisal, feedback, and merit systems will be based more and more on specific standards and measurement of performance to those standards.

6. Safety activism factors such as consumerism, union interest and medical research will continue to exert significant pressures for effective management of safety, health and environmental hazards.

7. There will be a greater recognition of the fact that the humane and the economic aspects of safety/loss control need not be in opposition; that safety (like quality and production) must be cost-effective; that we can take better care of people by taking better care of the business.

8. Greater attention will be given to preactive control, to close calls or near-accidents, to techniques such as incident recall and accident imaging which enable the identification and evaluation of hazards prior to a loss.

9. The system approach to management will grow; there will be added emphasis on the integrated management approach to safety, quality, production and costs; and factors such as the following will be seen as common to all four aspects:

- attitudes   - process   - materials
- skill   - structures - substances
- knowledge   - machines
- fitness   - equipment

10. Human factors engineering will play a large role in safety/loss control management; more will be done to adapt work and the workplace to worker characteristics, rather than forcing workers to adapt to error-prone environments.

11. There will be steady and significant growth of union-management collaboration, spearheaded by cooperative leadership activities for safety and health; increased employee participation in planning and problem solving; and more attention given to quality of work life.

12. Auditing of the management system will become a universally accepted part of the professional management approach.

13. Greater numbers of programs will be based on the recognition that performance excellence requires management excellence (as depicted in *Figure 1-8*).

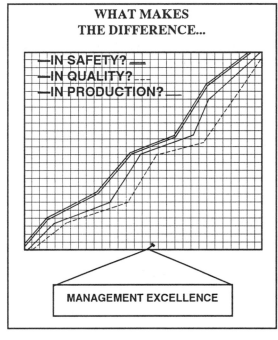

Figure 1-8

14. Greater numbers of managers will realize that a modern, well-managed safety/loss control program maintains the basic foundation of a complete management system; that it is the only discipline within a company that systematically accomplishes this goal if it is managed with such intent.

CORE CONCEPTS IN REVIEW

1. The legal system can and does have a significant impact on managing for employee health and safety. Workers' compensation laws are a prime example. History shows that when managers seem unresponsive to the well-being of people and the environment, they can expect social reaction and legal intervention. The challenge to management is clear. Safety through leadership is more economical and more successful than safety by work group imposition or by government intervention. Initiative and positive leadership can control the erosion of management's freedom to manage.

2. The new safety activism includes more than the laws of the land. The following factors seem significant:

   a. **union** interest and activity for safety and health
   b. the growing awareness and agitation of **consumers**
   c. the attitude of the **courts** and the size of liability awards
   d. modern **technology**, with its accelerating pace and accompanying possibility of generating potential safety and health problems faster than ever before
   e. changes in **work force**
   f. **laws** regarding safety, occupational health, workers' compensation, hazardous materials and environmental pollution control
   g. the impact of **inflation** on cost factors such as medical insurance, fire insurance, workers' compensation, and repair or replacement of damaged items
   h. **medical research,** producing vastly increased knowledge and awareness of what's harmful in our modern environment
   i. the increasing need for the efficient use of **energy** sources

3. This century has seen a tremendous safety **management change**. We have progressed from the infamous "sweat shops" of the early 1900's, through treating safety strictly as injury prevention, up to total loss control and toward an integrated (safety - quality - production - cost) management approach.

4. The integration of safety into a professional management system saw many significant advances in the mid-1900's (forties, fifties and sixties). Slowly but surely, leaders in the field began to broaden management's mental picture of "safety" and how best to achieve it. Books and journal articles began to emphasize safety **management,** a **systems** approach to accident prevention and control, and management **professionalism.** This period witnessed a clear movement beyond the strictly injury-oriented concept of safety toward an **integrated management system concept.**

5. The 70's and 80's might be characterized as the **international era** of safety/loss control management change, in which the professional management approach spread rather rapidly around the free world and successes were freely shared. Around the world, more and more managers progressed from the "employee carelessness" view of accidents to emphasis on inadequacies in the management system, e.g., inadequate programs, inadequate standards and inadequate management of compliance with standards.

Consequences of the safety and health evolution include:

1. This emphasis gradually shifted the thoughts and actions of many people **away from** the finger-pointing, blame-fixing approach, toward the mutual problem-solving approach; **away from** the belief that 85% (or more) of accidents are caused by unsafe acts, **toward** the belief that most accidents involve both unsafe acts and unsafe conditions; **away from** the conviction that the basic causes of most accidents are within the control of workers, **toward** the conviction that the basic causes of most accidents can be controlled only by management.

2. The concept of **management control** as a primary means to safety (along with production, quality and cost effectiveness) was put to work by many managers, in many companies, in many countries. ISMEC (Identification of Work - Standards - Measurement - Evaluation - Correction and Commendation) became widely recognized as the essence of a control system.

3. Results from around the world clearly show that effective safety/loss control management not only reduces fatalities, injuries and property damage, but also improves production, quality and cost control The trend is now toward an integrated management system and management excellence.

KEY QUESTIONS

1. True or False? During most of this century, the trend of accident death rates has been downward.

2. The world's first workers' compensation law was enacted in: a) Germany; b) England; c) Canada; d) United States.

3. In what year was the Industrial Accident Prevention Association of Ontario chartered?

4. What is now known as the National Safety Council was formed in what year?

5. List at least six of the nine discussed safety activism factors.

6. How is inflation related to the need for increased attention to safety management?

7. True or False? During the 20th century, safety emphasis has broadened from "management" emphasis to "engineering" emphasis.

8. True or False? During the early part of this century, safety was primarily injury-oriented.

9. The American Society of Safety Engineers was founded in: a) 1901; b) 1911; c) 1921; d) 1931.

10. Heinrich's *Industrial Accident Prevention* was first published in: a) 1901; b) 1911; c) 1921; d) 1931.

11. True or False? The evolution toward integration of safety into a professional management system experienced many significant advances in the mid-1900's.

12. In what year was the System Safety Society founded? The National Safety Management Society? The Certified Safety Professional program?

13. During the mid-century years, the definition of *safety* evolved from "freedom from accidents" to _____ of _____ loss.

14. List the five major aspects of a modern management control system.

15. What makes damage control a natural bridge from an injury-oriented safety program to an accident-oriented safety program?

16. The *Damage Control* book was published in: a) 1946 b) 1956; c) 1966; d) 1976.

17. The 1970's and 1980's could be characterized as the _____ era of safety/loss control management evolution.

18. In what year was the International Loss Control Institute founded?

19. In what year was the International Safety Rating System started?

20. True or False? Opinion polls show that safety normally tends to be high on management's motivational scale.

21. True or False? There is increasing recognition of the fact that the *basic causes* of problems or downgrading incidents — be they matters of safety, quality, cost or production — are the same.

22. The primary way to improve safety is to improve the m_____ s_____.

23. Results show that effective safety/loss control management not only reduces fatalities, injuries and property damage but also improves p_____, q_____ and c_____ control.

PRACTICAL APPLICATIONS SUMMARY

S - For Supervisors
E - For Executives
C - For Safety/Loss Control Coordinators

	S	E	C
1. Profit from the past. Use the present to create a better (safer, more productive, higher quality) future.	x	x	x
2. Collaborate with union leaders on significant aspects of safety and health leadership.	x	x	x
3. Establish a policy for employee involvement in quality and workplace factors such as safety and health.		x	
4. Encourage and coordinate significant employee involvement activities for safety and health in own area of responsibility.	x		
5. Advise and assist operating managers regarding effective application of employee involvement principles and practices.			x
6. Teach and practice the concept of safety as "control of accidental loss."	x	x	x
7. Ensure that safety programs and activities include adequate emphasis on damage control as well as injury control (i.e., on "accident" control).	x	x	x
8. Identify and evaluate loss exposures in own area of responsibility.	x		
9. Develop safety/loss control plans and programs.		x	x
10. Apply professional management skills to implementation of safety/loss control program activities.	x	x	x
11. Teach and practice the philosophy that refrains from the "employee carelessness" view of accidents and emphasizes inadequacies in the management system i.e., inadequate programs, inadequate standards, and inadequate management of compliance with standards.	x	x	x
12. Use the concept of management control (I-S-M-E-C) as a primary pathway to safety.	x	x	x
13. Treat safety on an equal basis with cost, production and quality.	x	x	x
14. Teach and practice the fact that the basic causes of problems or downgrading incidents (be they matters of safety, quality, cost or production) are the same.	x	x	x
15. Treat safety not as a separate aspect of working and managing, but as part of *the right way* of working and managing.	x	x	x
16. Give adequate attention to preactive control, to close calls or near-accidents.	x	x	x
17. Use the Principle of Management Results as a constant guide: "a leader tends to secure most effective results through others by performing the management work of planning, organizing, leading and controlling."	x	x	x
18. Let your words and deeds reflect your belief that performance excellence requires management excellence.	x	x	x

CHAPTER 2

THE CAUSES AND EFFECTS OF LOSS

"All things are hidden, obscure and debatable if the cause of the phenomena be unknown, but everything is clear if this cause be known."
— Louis Pasteur

INTRODUCTION

Most managers do not understand how much accidents and other loss-producing events really cost. Wearing the blinders of traditional thinking in the area of accidents, they are likely to see only the costs of medical treatment and workers' compensation. What is worse, they may accept these as the inevitable costs of "doing business," or assume that accident costs are borne by the insurance carrier. Even fewer managers understand that the same factors which are creating accidents are also creating production losses as well as quality and cost problems. To understand the causative factors of accidents is to take a giant step in the control of all losses.

The safety records of leading organizations prove that accidents are *not* the inevitable cost of getting the work done. Also, insurance companies are not charitable organizations. The amounts they pay out, plus their administrative costs and profits, are charged back to the insured in higher premiums based on the accident experience of each organization. In addition, it has been demonstrated by numerous organizations that the cost of medical insurance and workers' compensation, as large as they are, are only a small part of the real costs of accidents.

However, more is involved than just understanding the costs of accidents and the sizeable negative impact on profit or services rendered. A proper understanding of accident causation is critical to the development of appropriate controls. For instance, managers who believe that most accidents are caused by "carelessness" are likely to resort to punishment or incentive programs to get people to be "more careful." A very likely result is that accident problems are covered up rather than solved. Managers who believe that accidents are "freak" occurrences are likely to attempt to protect themselves by buying more insurance, only to discover that it rarely, if ever, pays for the full losses involved.

The purpose of this chapter is to provide managers with a better understanding of the real causes and costs of accidents and other losses, and a functional framework for analyzing their sources and controlling their effects. The forward-thinking managers will recognize that the causes of accidents are the same as the causes of many other types of loss.

PRACTICAL DEFINITIONS

To understand the sequence of events that can lead to a loss, it is essential to understand what one is trying to prevent or control. An ACCIDENT may be defined as *an undesired event that results in harm to people, damage to property or loss to process.* It is usually the result of contact with a substance or a source of energy (chemical, thermal, acoustical, mechanical, electrical, etc.) above the threshold limit of the body or structure.

In terms of persons, contact may result in a cut, burn, abrasion, fracture, etc. or in an alteration of or interference with a normal body function (cancer, asbestosis, drowning, etc.) as shown in *Figure 2-1*. In terms of property, it may result in fire, breakage, distortion, etc., as shown in *Figure 2-2*. There are three important aspects of this definition.

> **Accident - an undesired event that results in harm to people, damage to property or loss to process.**

First, it doesn't limit the human results to "injury," but says "harm to people." This includes both injury and illness, as well as adverse mental, neurological or systemic effects resulting from an exposure or circumstances encountered in the course of employment (ANSI Z16.2-1962, Rev. 1969). For simplification, the words "injury" and "illness" will be used hereafter, depending on which best defines the harm to people.

Second, this definition does not confuse "injury" with "accident." They are not the same. Injuries and illnesses result from accidents. But not all accidents result in injuries or illnesses. This distinction is critical to significant progress in safety and health. The occurrence of the accident itself is controllable. The severity of an injury that results from an accident is often a matter of chance. It depends upon many factors, such as dexterity, reflexes, physical condition, the portion of the body injured, etc; as well as the amount of energy exchanged, what barriers were in place, whether or not protective equipment was worn, etc. This distinction between accidents and injuries lets us direct our attention to accidents, rather than just to the injuries they might cause.

Third, if the event results in property damage or process loss alone, and no injury, it is still an accident. Often, of course, accidents result in harm to people, property *and* process. However, there are many more property damage accidents than injury accidents. Not only is property damage expensive, but damaged tools, machinery and equipment often lead to further accidents. Also, analysis of the more frequently occurring property damage accidents provides more information for guidance in the work of prevention and a clearer understanding of the causes of accident problems. Safety programs which ignore accidental property damage ignore far more accident data than they

INJURIES CAUSED BY DELIVERY OF ENERGY IN EXCESS OF LOCAL OR WHOLE-BODY INJURY THRESHOLDS		
Type of energy delivered	Primary injury produced	Examples and comments
Mechanical	Displacement, tearing, breaking, and crushing, predominantly at tissue and organ levels of body organization	Injuries resulting from the impact of moving objects such as bullets, hypodermic needles, knives, and falling objects; and from the impact of the moving body with relatively stationary structures, as in falls and plane and auto crashes. The specific results depends on the location and manner in which the resultant forces are exerted. The majority of injuries is in this group.
Thermal	Inflammation, coagulation, charring, and incineration at all levels of body organi- zation	First-, second-, and third-degree burns. The specific result depends on the location and manner in which the energy is dissipated.
Electrical	Interference with neuro- muscular function and coagulation, charring, and incineration at all levels of body organization	Electrocution, burns, interference with neural function as in electroshock therapy. The specific result depends on the location and manner in which the energy is dissipated.
Ionizing radiation	Disruption of cellular and sub-cellular components and function	Reactor accidents, therapeutic and diagnostic irradiation, misuse of isotopes, effects of fallouts. The specific result depends on the location and manner in which the energy is dissipated.
Chemical	Generally specific for each substance or group	Includes injuries due to animal and plant toxins, chemical burns, as from KOH, Br_2, F_2, and H_2SO_4, and the less gross and highly varied injuries produced by most elements and compounds when given in sufficient dose.

Source: D. W. Clark and B. MacMahon, *Preventive Medicine*, Boston, 1967. (Courtesy Little, Brown and Company)

Figure 2-1

TYPICAL EXAMPLES OF PROPERTY DAMAGE

Figure 2-2

analyze, a serious obstacle to effectiveness in either reducing injuries or controlling costs.

Here are some examples of accidents:

A mechanic was working in the grease pit in a repair shop. Due to the cold weather the doors and windows were closed. A nearby vehicle was left with the engine running. The mechanic was overcome by carbon monoxide, a substance which interferes with the blood's ability to transfer oxygen.

An electrician was working on a high voltage machine while it was "hot" to save time. The screwdriver slipped and shorted between two contact points. The resulting explosion severely burned the electrician, damaged the control box and shut down part of the manufacturing process.

An instrument technician was carrying a fluid-flow indicator from the shop where it had been calibrated to the area where it would be installed. When he slipped on an oily spot on the floor he was able to regain his balance, but the indicator was dropped and damaged beyond repair.

All three of these events were accidents: the first because it resulted in injury; the second because it resulted in injury, property damage and process loss; and the third because it resulted in property damage.

Another term frequently used in safety and health is the word INCIDENT. As related to safety, occupational health and fire, the incident is usually referred to as the "near accident" or the "near miss." William G. Johnson, author of the widely acclaimed book, *MORT Safety Assurance Systems,* states that the incident is similar to an accident, but without injury or damage. He goes on to state that incidents are enormously important to safety. An incident with high potential for harm (HIPO) should be investigated as thoroughly as an accident. In this context, then, an incident is *an undesired event which, under slightly different circumstances, could have resulted in harm to people, damage to property or loss to process. Here is an example:*

A night shift maintenance worker found an electric lift truck parked in an aisle instead of at the charging bay. He drove the lift truck to the bay, but on slowing down to enter he found the brakes to be quite sluggish. He quickly reversed the controls and simply bumped the battery charging set, causing no apparent damage. Under slightly different circumstances, this incident could have resulted in extensive damage to the lift truck and charging set as well as injury to the driver.

A number of companies with more sophisticated programs refer to every undesired event as an incident to permit a broader loss control coverage in their programs. Certain no-loss events are referred to as high potential in order that the same special attention be paid to them as to serious loss-producing events. This definition of incident includes accidents, near-accidents, security breaches, production or quality losses or near-losses, etc.

Both of the following definitions are necessary and will be used. The context will make clear which one is intended.

INCIDENT

- an undesired event which, under slightly different circumstances, could have resulted in harm to people, damage to property or loss to process.

- an undesired event which could or does result in a loss.

DO OCCUPATIONAL DISEASES HAVE CAUSES COMMON TO ACCIDENTS?

There are many reasons for the growing concern about occupational diseases. The list of substances which can cause cancer or other diseases gets longer each year. Many of these substances were once considered safe, and significant numbers of workers were exposed to them. Often the results of such exposures are not known for a long time, and by the time they are known, the damage is irreversible.

In our definition of an accident, we said that it was the result of contact with a substance or source of energy above the threshold limit of the body or structure. The human body has tolerance levels or injury thresholds for each substance or form of energy. Generally, the harmful effects of a single contact, such as a cut, fracture, sprain, amputation, chemical burn, etc., are regarded as injuries. The harmful effects of repeated contacts, such as tenosynovitis, cancer, liver damage, hearing loss, etc., are

regarded as illnesses (it is recognized that illnesses can also result from a single contact).

Accidents result from contact with a substance or source of energy above the threshold limit of the body or structure.

The critical point which must be made is that both have a common factor: contact with a substance or energy source above the local or whole-body threshold. Ultimately, both have the same controls: the prevention of the contact or its reduction to a level where no harm is done. Both involve the same steps: identification of exposures, evaluation of the severity and probability of occurrence, and the development of appropriate controls. This is not to minimize the specialized knowledge required to deal with occupational health problems. An entire chapter of this book is devoted to these. An effective safety and health program must be comprehensive enough to deal with all accidents and incidents, whether the result is injury, illness, property damage or near-miss.

SAFETY - Control of accidental loss

A third important definition is of the word SAFETY. It is usually defined as freedom from accidents or the condition of being safe from pain, injury or loss. However, a more functional definition is *control of accidental loss*. This definition relates to injury, illness, property damage and loss to process. It includes both preventing accidents and keeping losses to a minimum when accidents do occur. It also related to the function of control in the management system.

A Landmark Safety Study

The study described below will further help the reader understand why accidents that result in property damage should be given a great deal of attention.

In 1969, a study of industrial accidents was undertaken by one of the authors of this text, then the Director of Engineering Services for the Insurance Company of North America. An analysis was made of 1,753,498 accidents reported by 297 cooperating companies. These companies represented 21 different industrial groups, employing 1,750,000 employees who worked over 3 billion man hours during the exposure period analyzed. The study revealed the following ratios in the accidents reported:

For every reported major injury (resulting in death, disability, lost time or medical treatment), there were 9.8 reported minor injuries (requiring only first aid). For the 95 companies which further analyzed major injuries in their reporting, the ratio was one lost time injury per 15 medical treatment injuries.

Forty-seven percent of the companies indicated that they investigated all property damage accidents and eighty-four percent stated that they investigated major property damage accidents. The final analysis indicated that 30.2 property damage accidents were reported for each major injury.

Part of the study involved 4,000 hours of confidential interview by trained supervisors on the occurrence of incidents that under slightly different circumstances could have resulted in injury or property damage.

In referring to the 1-10-30-600 ratio (*Figure 2-3*), it should be remembered that this represents accidents and incidents reported and not the total number of accidents or incidents that actually occurred.

As we consider the ratio, we observe that 30 property damage accidents were reported for each serious or disabling injury. Property damage accidents cost billions of dollars annually and yet they are frequently misnamed and referred to as "near accidents." Ironically, this line of thinking recognizes the fact that each property damage situation could probably have resulted in personal injury. This term is a hold-over from earlier training and misconceptions that led supervisors to related the term "accident" only to injury.

The 1-10-30-600 relationships in the ratio indicate quite clearly how foolish it is to direct our major effort at the relatively few events resulting in serious or disabling injury when there are so many significant opportunities that provide a much larger basis for more effective control of total accident losses.

It is worth emphasizing at this point that the ratio study was of a certain large group of organizations at a given point in time. It does not necessarily follow that the ratio will be identical for any particular occupational group or organization. That is not its intent. The significant point is that major injuries are rare events and that many opportunities are afforded by the more frequent, less serious events to take actions to prevent the major losses from occurring. Safety leaders have also emphasized that these actions are most effective when directed at incidents and minor accidents with a high loss potential.

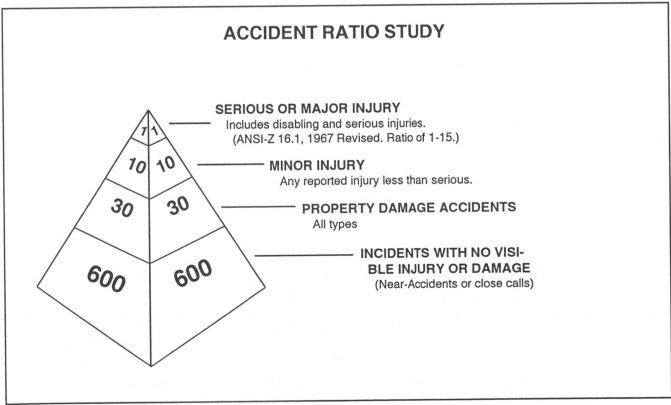

ACCIDENT RATIO STUDY

SERIOUS OR MAJOR INJURY
Includes disabling and serious injuries.
(ANSI-Z 16.1, 1967 Revised. Ratio of 1-15.)

MINOR INJURY
Any reported injury less than serious.

PROPERTY DAMAGE ACCIDENTS
All types

INCIDENTS WITH NO VISIBLE INJURY OR DAMAGE
(Near-Accidents or close calls)

Figure 2-3

LOSS CAUSATION MODELS

Numerous accident and loss causation models have been introduced during recent years. A large percentage are complex and difficult for many to understand and remember. While the loss causation model shown in *Figure 2-4* is relatively simple, it contains the necessary key points that enable the user to understand and retain the critical few facts important to the control of the vast majority of accidents and loss and management problems. It is current and consistent with what safety and loss control leaders throughout the world are saying about accident and loss causation.

Remembering the critical few points illustrated in the model will enable the user to recall many more of the details presented throughout this book.

Loss

The result of an accident is *loss* (pictured in *Figure 2-5*). As reflected in our accident definition, the most obvious losses are harm to people, property or process. Implied and important related losses are "performance interruption" and "profit reduction." So there are losses involving people, property, process and ultimately, profit.

Once the sequence has occurred, the type and degree of loss are somewhat a matter of chance. The effect may range from insignificant to catastrophic, from a scratch or dent to multiple fatalities or loss of a plant. The type and degree of loss depend partly on fortuitous circumstances and partly on the actions taken to minimize loss. Actions to minimize loss at this stage of the sequence include prompt and proper first aid and medical care, fast and effective firefighting, prompt repair of damaged equipment and facilities, efficient implementation of emergency action plans and effective rehabilitation of people for work.

Nothing is more important or more tragic than the human aspects of accidental loss: injury, pain, sorrow, anguish, loss of body parts or functions, occupational illness, disability, death. The best known way to minimize these is to use both the humane aspects and the economic aspects to motivate control of the *accidents* that lead to the losses.

Whether or not people are hurt, accidents do cost money — and lots of it! And the injury or illness costs are a relatively small part of the total costs; *Figure 2-6* summarizes the best available information on these costs.

Conscientious, cost-minded managers do not take this information lightly. While it is true that the injury-related costs at the tip of the iceberg can be very significant destroyers of profit, they are dwarfed in significance by the costs under the surface — which range from at least six to fifty-three times as much! Any organization which determines the cost of its accident losses only in terms of injuries and occupational illnesses (e.g., workers' compensation) is looking at only a small fraction of its identifiable costs. *Figure 2-7* lists many of these costs, which come straight out of profit. Save a dollar in accident costs and you add a dollar to profit.

Figure 2-8 illustrates the importance and the potential for profit improvement through loss control. Add this to the overriding human element and you have the best of both worlds — protection of profits, process, property and PEOPLE. This is why it is so essential to understand and use the accident cause and effect sequence.

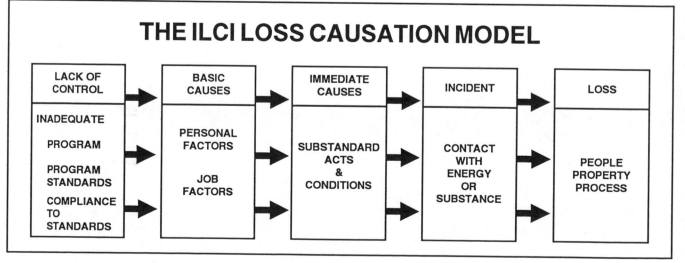

THE ILCI LOSS CAUSATION MODEL

LACK OF CONTROL	BASIC CAUSES	IMMEDIATE CAUSES	INCIDENT	LOSS
INADEQUATE PROGRAM PROGRAM STANDARDS COMPLIANCE TO STANDARDS	PERSONAL FACTORS JOB FACTORS	SUBSTANDARD ACTS & CONDITIONS	CONTACT WITH ENERGY OR SUBSTANCE	PEOPLE PROPERTY PROCESS

Figure 2-4

ACCIDENT RESULTS

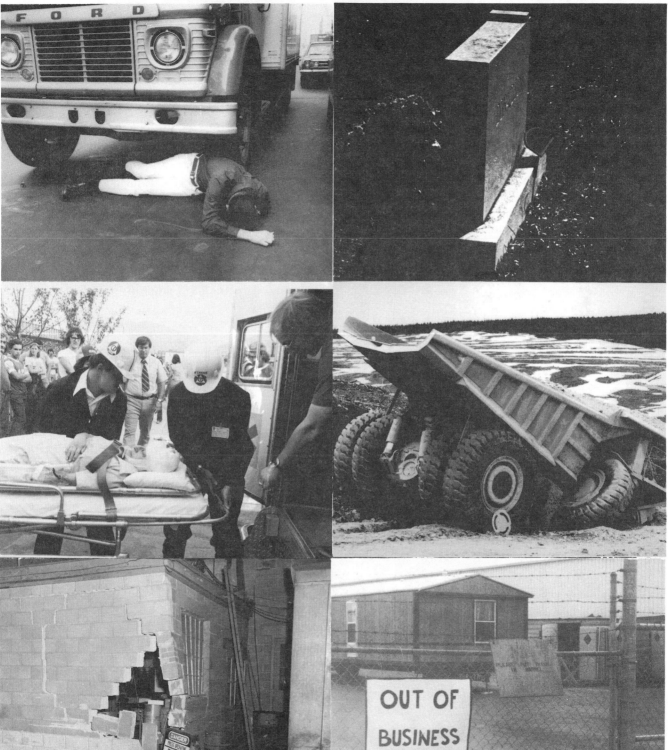

Figure 2-5

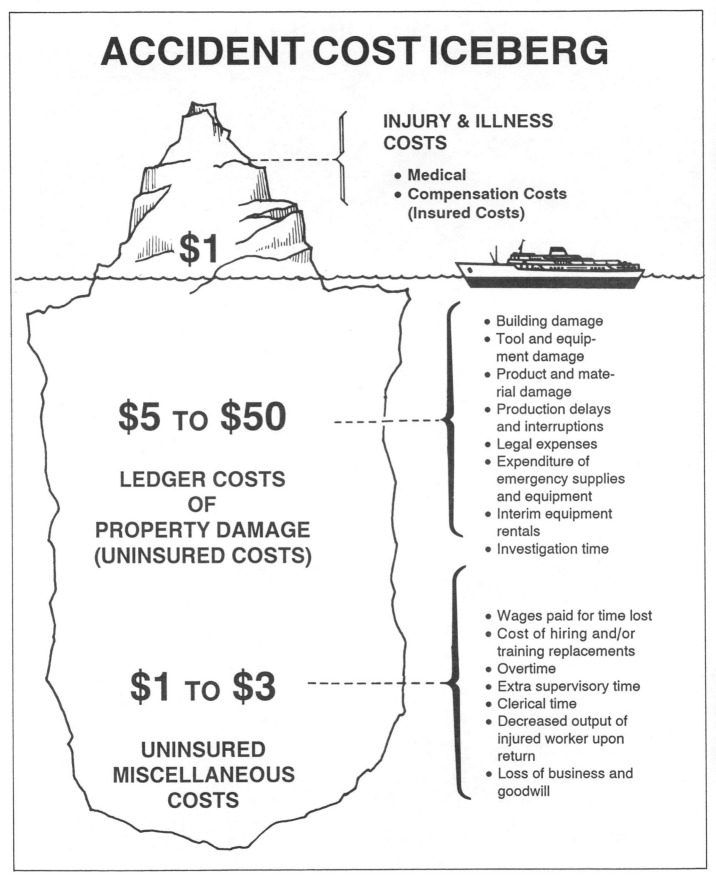

ACCIDENT COST ICEBERG

INJURY & ILLNESS COSTS

- Medical
- Compensation Costs (Insured Costs)

$1

$5 TO $50

LEDGER COSTS OF PROPERTY DAMAGE (UNINSURED COSTS)

- Building damage
- Tool and equipment damage
- Product and material damage
- Production delays and interruptions
- Legal expenses
- Expenditure of emergency supplies and equipment
- Interim equipment rentals
- Investigation time

$1 TO $3

UNINSURED MISCELLANEOUS COSTS

- Wages paid for time lost
- Cost of hiring and/or training replacements
- Overtime
- Extra supervisory time
- Clerical time
- Decreased output of injured worker upon return
- Loss of business and goodwill

Figure 2-6

LOSSES FROM ACCIDENTS

Injured Worker Time

(1) Productive time is lost by injured employee and is not reimbursed by worker's compensation.

Co-Worker Time

(2) Time is lost by co-worker at the scene, as well as when assisting the injured to dispensary or ambulance.

(3) Time is lost through sympathy or curiosity, and work interruption at time of injury and later from discussing the case, telling similar stories, swapping opinions of cause, grumbling, etc.

(4) Incidental lost time results from cleanup, collecting donations to aid the employee and his or her family, review hearings, etc. The cost of other employee overtime required to accomplish the injured employee's work and the time spent by Safety organization personnel on the accident should be included.

Supervisor Time

Supervisor time charged to the accident should include:

(5) Assisting injured employee.

(6) Investigating accident cause, i.e., initial investigation, follow-up, research on prevention, etc.

(7) Arranging for work continuance, getting new material, rescheduling.

(8) Selecting and training new employee, including obtaining applicants, evaluating candidates, training new employees or transferred employee.

(9) Preparing accident reports, i.e., injury reports, property damage reports, incident reports, variance reports, vehicle accidents, etc.

(10) Participating in hearings on accident case.

General Losses

(11) Production time is lost due to upset, shock, or diverted interest of workers, slowdown of others, discussion by others - "did you hear..." (applies to employees of other units not included in item 3, above).

(12) Losses result from work stoppage of machines, vehicles, plants, facilities, etc., and can be either temporary or long term and affect related equipment and schedules.

(13) The injured employee's effectiveness is often reduced after return to work, from work restrictions, reduced efficiency, physical handicaps, crutches, splints, etc.

(14) Loss of business and goodwill, adverse publicity, problems in obtaining new hires, etc., are common general losses.

(15) Legal expenses arise from compensation hearings, liability claims handling, etc., that involve contractor legal services, rather than the insurance carrier legal expense that appears in direct costs.

(16) Cost can increase for insurance reserves and tax multipliers which are, respectively, small annual percentages of the gross incurred losses, and taxes based upon the dollar value of losses, that are tied up in reserves.

(17) Miscellaneous additional items should be included which may be unique to particular operations and are appropriate to specific accident cases.

Property Losses

(18) Expenditures of emergency supplies and equipment.

(19) Cost of equipment and materials above use derived and salvage.

(20) Material cost of repair and replacement parts.

(21) Time cost of equipment repair and replacement in terms of productivity lost and delay of scheduled maintenance on other equipment.

(22) Cost of corrective actions other than repair.

(23) Obsolescence losses of spare parts in stock for the equipment destroyed.

(24) Pro-rata cost of rescue and emergency equipment.

(25) Production lost during period of employee reaction, investigation, clean-up, repair, and certification.

Other Losses

(26) Penalties, fines, citations levied.

Figure 2-7

IN TIMES OF KEEN COMPETITION AND LOW PROFIT MARGINS, LOSS CONTROL MAY CONTRIBUTE MORE TO PROFITS THAN AN ORGANIZATION'S BEST SALESMEN.

It is necessary for the salesman of a business to sell an additional $1,667,000 in products to pay the costs of $50,000 in annual losses from injury, illness, damage or theft, assuming an average profit on sales of 3%. The amount of sales required to pay for losses will vary with the profit margin.

YEARLY INCIDENT COSTS	PROFIT MARGIN				
	1%	2%	3%	4%	5%
$ 1,000	100,000	50,000	33,000	25,000	20,000
5,000	500,000	250,000	167,000	125,000	100,000
10,000	1,000,000	500,000	333,000	250,000	200,000
25,000	2,500,000	1,250,000	833,000	625,000	500,000
50,000	5,000,000	2,500,000	1,667,000	1,250,000	1,000,000
100,000	10,000,000	5,000,000	3,333,000	2,500,000	2,000,000
150,000	15,000,000	7,500,000	5,000,000	3,750,000	3,000,000
200,000	20,000,000	10,000,000	6,666,000	5,000,000	4,000,000
SALES REQUIRED TO COVER LOSSES					

This table shows the dollars of sales required to pay for different amounts of costs for accident losses, i.e., if an organization's profit margin is 5%, it would have to make sales of $500,000 to pay for $25,000 worth of losses. With a 1% margin, $10,000,000 of sales would be necessary to pay for $100,000 of the costs involved with accidents.

Figure 2-8

Incident/Contact

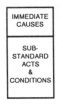

This is the event that precedes the "loss" — the contact that could or does cause the harm or damage. When potential causes of accidents are permitted to exist, the way is always open for a contact with a source of energy above the threshold limit of the body or structure. As an example, a flying or moving object involves kinetic energy which transfers to the body or structure it hits or contacts. If the amount of energy transferred is too much, it causes personal harm or property damage. This is true not only of kinetic energy but also electrical energy, acoustic energy, thermal energy, radiant energy and chemical energy.

Here are some of the more common types of energy transfers, as listed in the American Standard Accident Classification code (ANSI Z16.2-1962, Rev. 1969).

- Struck against (running or bumping into)

- Struck by (hit by moving object)

- Fall to lower level (either the body falls or the object falls and hits the body)

- Fall on same level (slip and fall, tip over)

- Caught in (pinch and nip points)

- Caught on (snagged, hung)

- Caught between (crushed or amputated)

- Contact with (electricity, heat, cold, radiation, caustics, toxics, noise)

- Overstress/overexertion/overload

As will be discussed more fully in the next chapter, thinking of the accident in terms of a contact and energy exchange helps to structure thinking about means of control. Control measures that alter or absorb the energy can be taken to minimize the harm or damage at the time and point of contact. Personal protective equipment and protective barriers are common examples. A hard hat, for instance, does not prevent contact by a falling object, but it could absorb and/or deflect some of the energy and prevent or minimize injury. Other control measures at the contact stage include substitution of a less harmful chemical or a less volatile solvent; reduction of the amount of energy released, such as keeping the shower water below the scalding level, or putting governors on engines to limit their speed; modifying a hazardous surface by rounding off sharp edges or padding the point

of contact; and reinforcing the object (column, truck bed, floor) or body (muscles) so that is has a higher threshold limit.

When substandard conditions are permitted to exist (such as unguarded machine tools) or substandard acts are allowed (such as cleaning with gasoline), there is always the potential for contacts and energy exchanges which harm people, property and/or process.

Immediate Causes

The "immediate causes" of accidents are the circumstances that immediately precede the contact. They usually can be seen or sensed. Frequently they are called "unsafe acts" (behaviors which could permit the occurrence of an accident) and "unsafe conditions" (circumstances which could permit the occurrence of an accident).

Modern managers tend to think a bit broader, and more professionally, in terms of *substandard practices and substandard conditions* (deviations from an accepted standard or practice). This line of thinking has distinct advantages: 1) it relates practices and conditions to a *standard,* a basis for measurement, evaluation and correction; 2) it somewhat minimizes the finger-pointing stigma of the term "unsafe act"; and 3) it broadens the scope of interest from accident control to *loss control,* encompassing safety, quality, production, and cost control.

Some people advocate substituting the word *error* (e.g., management error, operational error, maintenance error, engineering error) to identify management responsibility. There is a vast amount of research and error removal information from quality control research that is being increasingly used for managing losses. But the term "error" is often misunderstood as "blame." As everyone knows, blame leads to defensive behavior and safety problems get disguised rather than solved. Also, an increasing number of safety leaders confirm the results from research in quality control that 80% of the mistakes (substandard/unsafe acts) that people make are the result of factors over which only management has control. This significant finding gives a completely new direction of control to the long-held concept that 85-96% of accidents result from the unsafe acts or faults of people. This new direction of thinking encourages the progressive manager to think in terms of how the management system influences human behavior rather than just on the unsafe acts of people. Thus, the term "substandard" seems more acceptable, more useful and more professional.

Substandard practices and conditions usually are seen in one or more of the following forms:

SUBSTANDARD PRACTICES

1. Operating equipment without authority
2. Failure to warn
3. Failure to secure
4. Operating at improper speed
5. Making safety devices inoperable
6. Removing safety devices
7. Using defective equipment
8. Using equipment improperly
9. Failing to use personal protective equipment properly
10. Improper loading
11. Improper placement
12. Improper lifting
13. Improper position for task
14. Servicing equipment in operation
15. Horseplay
16. Under influence of alcohol and/or other drugs

SUBSTANDARD CONDITIONS

1. Inadequate guards or barriers
2. Inadequate or improper protective equipment
3. Defective tools, equipment or materials
4. Congestion or restricted action
5. Inadequate warning systems
6. Fire and explosion hazards
7. Poor housekeeping; disorderly workplace
8. Hazardous environmental conditions; gases, dusts, smokes, fumes, vapors
9. Noise exposures
10. Radiation exposures
11. High or low temperature exposures
12. Inadequate or excessive illumination
13. Inadequate ventilation

Thorough applications of the MORT (Management Oversight and Risk Tree) system of loss causation analysis have repeatedly shown that a substandard physical condition exists for nearly every substandard practice in accident causation. A vast number of these conditions involve poor ergonomic design of machines, equipment and the work environment. Safety leaders recognize that many of these conditions would not be easily recognized by the supervisory investigator. Those who review investigation reports and engineers who design the machines and the

workplace must be ever mindful of these facts.

It is essential to consider these practices and conditions only as immediate causes or *symptoms*, and to do a thorough job of diagnosing the diseases behind the symptoms. If you only treat the symptoms, they will occur again and again. You need to answer the questions:

> ...*Why* did that substandard practice occur?
> ...*Why* did that substandard condition exist?
> ...*What* failure in our supervisory/management system permitted that practice or condition?

If you dig deep enough, the answers will point the way to more effective control. To solve loss control performance problems, you must get at the basic or root causes.

Basic Causes

Basic causes are the diseases or real causes behind the symptoms; the reasons why the substandard acts and conditions occurred; the factors that, when identified, permit meaningful management control. Often, these are referred to as root causes, real causes, indirect causes, underlying or contributing causes. This is because the immediate causes (the symptoms, the substandard acts and conditions) are usually quite apparent, but it takes a bit of probing to get at basic causes and to gain control of them.

Basic causes help explain why people perform substandard practices. Logically, a person is not likely to follow a proper procedure. Likewise, the operator of equipment requiring precise and skillful handling will not operate it efficiently and safely without the chance to develop skill through guided practice. The same idea applies to maintaining skill through frequent practice. What professional team would ever win a game without practice? It is equally logical that poor quality of work and substantial waste will result from placing a person with faulty eyesight on a job where good vision is critical for proper performance. Similarly, a person who is never told the importance of a job is unlikely to be motivated to a high degree of pride in his or her work.

Basic causes also help explain why substandard conditions exist. Equipment and materials which are inadequate or hazardous will be purchased if there are not adequate standards, and if compliance with standards is not managed. Unsafe structures and work process layouts will be designed and built if there are not adequate standards and compliance for design and construction. Equipment will wear out and produce a substandard product, create waste or break down and cause an accident if that equipment is not properly selected, properly used and properly maintained.

Just as it is helpful to consider two major categories of immediate causes (substandard practices and substandard conditions), so is it helpful to think of basic causes in two major categories:

PERSONAL FACTORS
- Inadequate capability
  - Physical/Physiological
  - Mental/Psychological
- Lack of knowledge
- Lack of skill
- Stress
  - Physical/Physiological
  - Mental/Psychological
- Improper motivation

JOB FACTORS (WORK ENVIRONMENT)
- Inadequate leadership and/or supervision
- Inadequate engineering
- Inadequate purchasing
- Inadequate maintenance
- Inadequate tools, equipment, materials
- Inadequate work standards
- Wear and tear
- Abuse or misuse

Basic causes are shown in more detail in *Figure 2-9*, which gives specific examples of each cause.

BASIC CAUSES OF LOSS

PERSONAL FACTORS

- **Inadequate Physical/Physiological Capability**
  - inappropriate height, weight, size, strength, reach, etc.
  - restricted range of body movement
  - limited ability to sustain body positions
  - substance sensitivities or allergies
  - sensitivities to sensory extremes (temperature, sound, etc.)
  - vision deficiency
  - hearing deficiency
  - other sensory deficiency (touch, taste, smell, balance)
  - respiratory incapacity
  - other permanent physical disabilities
  - temporary disabilities

- **Inadequate Mental/Psychological Capability**
  - fears and phobias
  - emotional disturbance
  - mental illness
  - intelligence level
  - inability to comprehend
  - poor judgment
  - poor coordination
  - slow reaction time
  - low mechanical aptitude
  - low learning aptitude
  - memory failure

- **Physical or Physiological Stress**
  - injury or illness
  - fatigue due to task load or duration
  - fatigue due to lack of rest
  - fatigue due to sensory overload
  - exposure to health hazards
  - exposure to temperature extremes
  - oxygen deficiency
  - atmospheric pressure variation
  - constrained movement
  - blood sugar insufficiency
  - drugs

- **Mental or Psychological Stress**
  - emotional overload
  - fatigue due to mental task load or speed
  - extreme judgment/decision demands
  - routine, monotony, demand for uneventful vigilance
  - extreme concentration/perception demands
  - "meaningless" or "degrading" activities
  - confusing directions
  - conflicting demands
  - preoccupation with problems
  - frustration
  - mental illness

- **Lack of Knowledge**
  - lack of experience
  - inadequate orientation
  - inadequate initial training
  - inadequate update training
  - misunderstood directions

- **Lack of Skill**
  - inadequate initial instruction
  - inadequate practice
  - infrequent performance
  - lack of coaching

- **Improper Motivation**
  - improper performance is rewarding
  - proper performance is punishing
  - lack of incentives
  - excessive frustration
  - inappropriate aggression
  - improper attempt to save time or effort
  - improper attempt to avoid discomfort
  - improper attempt to gain attention
  - inappropriate peer pressure
  - improper supervisory example
  - inadequate performance feedback
  - inadequate reinforcement of proper behavior
  - improper production incentives

JOB FACTORS

- **Inadequate Leadership and/or Supervision**
  - unclear or conflicting reporting relationships
  - unclear or conflicting assignment of responsibility
  - improper or insufficient delegation
  - giving inadequate policy, procedure, practices or guidelines
  - giving objectives, goals or standards that conflict
  - inadequate work planning or programming
  - inadequate instructions, orientation and/or training
  - providing inadequate reference documents, directives and guidance publications
  - inadequate identification and evaluation of loss exposures
  - lack of supervisory/management job knowledge
  - inadequate matching of individual qualifications and job/task requirements
  - inadequate performance measurement and evaluation
  - inadequate or incorrect performance feedback

- **Inadequate Engineering**
  - inadequate assessment of loss exposures
  - inadequate consideration of human factors/ergonomics
  - inadequate standards, specifications and/or design criteria
  - inadequate monitoring of construction
  - inadequate assessment of operational readiness
  - inadequate monitoring of initial operation
  - inadequate evaluation of changes

- **Inadequate Purchasing**
  - inadequate specifications on requisitions
  - inadequate research on materials/equipment
  - inadequate specifications to vendors
  - inadequate mode or route of shipment
  - inadequate receiving inspection and acceptance
  - inadequate communication of safety and health data
  - improper handling of materials
  - improper storage of materials
  - improper transporting of materials
  - inadequate identification of hazardous items
  - improper salvage and/or waste disposal

- **Inadequate Maintenance**
  - inadequate preventive
    - ...assessment of needs
    - ...lubrication and servicing
    - ...adjustment/assembly
    - ...cleaning or resurfacing

- inadequate reparative
  - ...communication of needs
  - ...scheduling of work
  - ...examination of units
  - ...part substitution

- **Inadequate Tools and Equipment**
  - inadequate assessment of needs and risks
  - inadequate human factors/ergonomics considerations
  - inadequate standards or specifications
  - inadequate availability
  - inadequate adjustment/repair/maintenance
  - inadequate salvage and reclamation
  - inadequate removal and replacement of unsuitable items

- **Inadequate Work Standards**
  - inadequate development of standards
    - ...inventory and evaluation of exposures and needs
    - ...coordination with process design
    - ...employee involvement
    - ...inconsistent standards/procedures/rules
  - inadequate communication of standards
    - ...publication
    - ...distribution
    - ...translation to appropriate languages
    - ...reinforcing with signs, color codes and job aids
  - inadequate maintenance of standards
    - ...tracking of work flow
    - ...updating
    - ...monitoring use of standards/procedures/rules

- **Wear and Tear**
  - inadequate planning of use
  - improper extension of service life
  - inadequate inspection and/or monitoring
  - improper loading or rate of use
  - inadequate maintenance
  - use by unqualified or untrained people
  - use for wrong purpose

- **Abuse or Misuse**
  - condoned by supervision
    - ...intentional
    - ...unintentional
  - not condoned by supervision
    - ...intentional
    - ...unintentional

Figure 2-9 continued

Basic causes are the origins of substandard practices and conditions. However, they are not the beginning of the cause and effect sequence. What starts the sequence, ending in loss, is "lack of control."

Lack of Control

```
LACK OF
CONTROL

INADEQUATE
PROGRAM
PROGRAM
STANDARDS
COMPLIANCE
TO
STANDARDS
```

Control is one of the four essential management functions: plan, organize, lead, control. These functions relate to any manager's work, regardless of level or title. Whether the function is administration, marketing, production, quality, engineering, purchasing or safety, the supervisor/leader/manager must plan, organize, lead and control to be effective.

The person who manages professionally knows the safety/loss control program; knows the standards; plans and organizes work to meet the standards; leads people to attain the standards; measures performance of self and others; evaluates results and needs; commends and constructively corrects performance. This is *management control.* Without it, the accident sequence begins and triggers the continuing causal factors that lead to loss. Without adequate management control, the accident cause and effect sequence is started and, unless corrected in time, leads to losses.

There are three common reasons for lack of control: 1) inadequate program, 2) inadequate program standards, and 3) inadequate compliance with standards.

Inadequate Program - A safety/loss control program may be inadequate because of too few program activities. While the necessary program activities vary with an organization's scope, nature, and type, significant research and the experience of successful programs in many different companies and countries show the activities in *Figure 2-10* (next page) to be the common elements of success. Many organizations around the world use these as a blueprint for building an adequate safety/loss control management program.

Inadequate Program Standards - A common cause of confusion and failure is standards that are not specific enough, not clear enough and/or not high enough. Below is an example of ten simple standards adopted by a major corporation. Standards such as these let people know what is expected of them and permit meaningful measurement of how well they perform in relation to the standards. Adequate standards are essential for adequate control.

Inadequate Compliance With Standards - Lack of compliance with existing standards is a common reason for lack of control. In fact, most managers agree that this is the single greatest reason for failure to control accident loss. This almost unanimous agreement explains the emphasis found throughout this book on measurements of quantity and quality of efforts in the program.

Correcting these three common reasons for lack of control is a critical management responsibility. Developing an adequate program and standards is an *executive* function, aided by supervisors. Maintaining compliance with standards is a *supervisory* function, aided by executives. It's a management team effort all the way. (The next chapter discusses details of this management control function).

---

1 Every member of management will ensure that:
Each employee has had a thorough initial review of all rules related to his job and that he knows and understands them. He will also make sure that a complete review of all rules is held with each employee on an annual basis and take such action to make sure that all rules are enforced.

2 Every member of management will ensure that:
Any unsafe practice or condition reported to him by an employee is promptly placed in the hazard report system and followed up promptly. He will conduct and record the results of a formal inspection of the entire physical plant area under his reponsibility not less than once every two months and develop a system to make sure that all critical parts in his area are inspected as necessary or required.

3 Every member of management will ensure that:
Each employee received well-planned, proper job instruction (PJI) with every new or different job assigned to him and that safety tips are given frenquently during routine contacts on a day-to-day basis.

4 Every member of management will ensure that:
Each new employee receives an adequate, complete indoctrination to his job on all aspects of safety and efficiency before being permitted to work... and that several follow-up contacts are made with him during his probationary period to determine that he knows and is following all required standards.

5 Every member of management will ensure that :
Each employee under his management attends a weekly safety meeting that has been properly planned and presented by the member.

6 Every member of management will ensure that:
All employees know, understand and practice the principles of good housekeeping and that the "order" of his area of responsibility reflects this desired goal at all times.

7 Every member of management will ensure that:
All employees are properly issued required protective equipment and motivated to wear it as prescribed at all times.

8 Every member of management will ensure that:
Every accident resulting in personal injury or property damage is promptly and efficiently investigated with results reported on the supervisor's report form before the end of the turn on which the accident occurred.

9 Every member of management will ensure that:
Each employee in his charge is recognized frequently on a personal basis when he demonstrates behavior that is safe or desired... and that his recognition should reflect the supervisor's personal enthusiasm, constant interest and deep concern for the safety and welfare of his employees.

10 Every member of management will ensure that:
His personal example of safe behavior sets the best possible pattern to follow for everyone with whom he comes in contact.

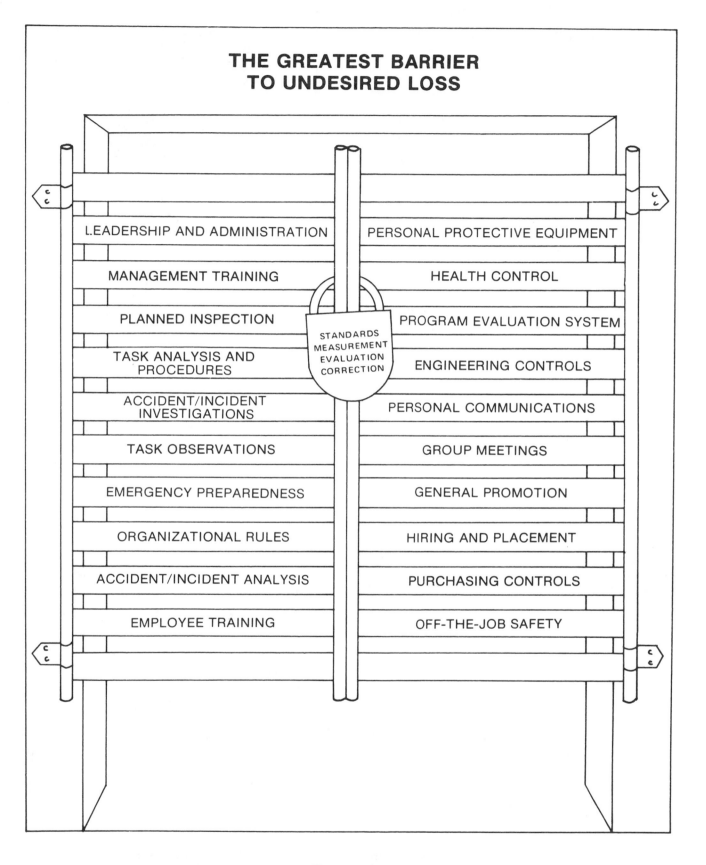

**THE GREATEST BARRIER
TO UNDESIRED LOSS**

LEADERSHIP AND ADMINISTRATION

PERSONAL PROTECTIVE EQUIPMENT

MANAGEMENT TRAINING

HEALTH CONTROL

PLANNED INSPECTION

PROGRAM EVALUATION SYSTEM

STANDARDS
MEASUREMENT
EVALUATION
CORRECTION

TASK ANALYSIS AND
PROCEDURES

ENGINEERING CONTROLS

ACCIDENT/INCIDENT
INVESTIGATIONS

PERSONAL COMMUNICATIONS

TASK OBSERVATIONS

GROUP MEETINGS

EMERGENCY PREPAREDNESS

GENERAL PROMOTION

ORGANIZATIONAL RULES

HIRING AND PLACEMENT

ACCIDENT/INCIDENT ANALYSIS

PURCHASING CONTROLS

EMPLOYEE TRAINING

OFF-THE-JOB SAFETY

Figure 2-10

MULTIPLE SOURCES-CAUSES-CONTROLS

Management leaders have written thousands of articles through the years on the complex nature of the errors and problems that lead to losses in the business world. A combination of factors or causes comes together under just the right circumstances to bring out these undesired events. Seldom, if ever, is there a single cause of any management problem, including those involved with safety, production, or quality.

As complex as the problem may sound, tremendous achievements (such as those in aerospace) have proved beyond doubt that it is possible to prevent or control the causes of accident loss. While the enormous resources put into the aerospace program may not be available to everyone, there is well-documented evidence that high levels of success can be achieved by the average businessman. For example, one recent study projected mathematically that the national disabling injury rate could be cut 75% if the average businessman would apply those safety program activities used by leaders in general industry. Available information has led management personnel to accept the following conclusions:

1. The incidents that downgrade our businesses are caused: they don't just happen.

2. The causes of loss can be determined and controlled.

In order to better understand the circumstances which lead to the causes of undesired incidents, it would be helpful to consider the four major elements or subsystems in the total business operation that provide their sources. These four elements would include: (a) people, (b) equipment, (c) materials and (d) environment.

All four of these elements (shown in *Figure 2-11*) must relate or interact properly with each other or problems may be created which could lead to loss. Let's examine each of these elements briefly:

PEOPLE - This element includes management, employees, contractors, customers, visitors, suppliers, the public, the human element. Experience shows that the human element is involved in a large proportion of accident/incident causes. However, "people" does *not* simply mean "the employees who are involved in the incidents." The old concept that 85%, or more, of accidents are caused by the faults of workers will come under more and more critical analysis in the light of modern knowledge and experience. The "people" fac-

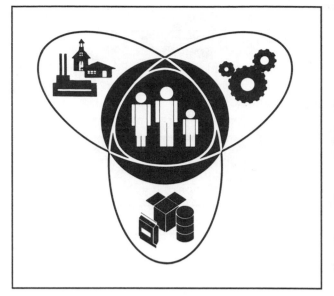

Figure 2-11

tor includes, for example...

> ...the executives who establish company policies, procedures, practices, standards and related aspects of the "company climate"
> ...the engineers and designers who create the workplace environment in which workers must work
> ...those who manage the preventive maintenance systems, to keep tools, machines and equipment in good, safe working condition
> ...the managers who select, hire and place specific people in specific jobs
> ...the supervisors who orient, inform, instruct, motivate, guide, coach and lead employees

As indicated earlier, there is increasing evidence that at least 80% of the mistakes people make involve

> "**Prescription without diagnosis is malpractice, whether it be in medicine or management.**"
> **Karl Albrecht**, *Organization Development*

things that only *management* can do something about. Managing the people element, and the interactions of people with the other elements of the system, is a major means of effective control.

EQUIPMENT - This element includes all the tools and machines that people work near and with: fixed machines, vehicles, materials handling devices, hand tools, protective equipment, personal gear, and so on. These items that people work with are a tremendous source of potential injury and death. As such, they have long been a target for laws concerning mechanical safeguarding and operator training. More recently, this concern has expanded to include greater emphasis on ergonomics or *human factors engineering.* This involves designing work and the workplace to fit the capabilities of human beings — their sizes, reaches, ranges of movement, perceptual capabilities, response patterns, stress limits and so on. Failure to recognize these substandard physical conditions in the past usually led to the classification of accident causes as "unsafe practices." The major goal is to design the equipment and environment to make the "people functions" more natural and comfortable, and to prevent confusion, fatigue, frustration, overloading, errors and accidents.

Again, this points out the need for managers to consider all four subsystems of the total organizational system, and especially the interactions among these subsystems.

MATERIALS - This element includes raw materials, chemicals and other substances that people use, work with and process. They are another major source of accident loss. In many companies, material handling injuries account for 20 to 30 percent of all their injuries. Likewise, much property damage involves materials that spilled, corroded, burned or exploded.

This subsystem has gained greater management attention in recent years, prompted by society's increased emphasis on occupational health. Rarely do we find a modern manager who is unaware of Material Safety & Health Data Sheets and safe handling practices for hazardous materials. No manager is doing a satisfactory job of controlling accident losses unless he or she is effectively managing the safe, proper handling of materials.

ENVIRONMENT - This element includes all parts of the surroundings; buildings and enclosures that surround people, equipment and materials; fluids and air which surround other elements; chemical hazards such as mists, vapors, gases, fumes and dusts; weather and atmospheric phenomena; biological hazards such as molds, fungi, bacteria and viruses; and physical conditions such as light noise, heat, cold pressure, humidity and radiation.

This subsystem of the business organization represents the source of causes of an ever-increasing number of diseases and health-related conditions. It not only is involved in accidents and occupational illness problems, but also in other losses such as absenteeism, poor quality products and services, and loss of produc-

tivity. Of course, more and more attention must be given to the external or public environment that can be so adversely affected by air, stream and soil pollution from the occupational establishment.

The four major elements or subsystems in the total organizational system (People, Equipment, Material, Environment), individually or in their interactions, are the major sources of causes that contribute to accidents and other loss-producing events. All four should be carefully considered when investigating such incidents and especially, when developing and implementing corrective and preventive measures. Effective managers manage the total system.

The Concept of Multiple Causes

Among the practical principles of professional management is the Principle of Multiple Causes: *problems and loss-producing events are seldom, if ever, the result of a single cause.* This is an essential principle for safety/loss control management. One should never assume that there is a single cause of an accident of incident.

W.G. Johnson, Former General Manager of the National Safety Council and author of *MORT Safety Assurance Systems,* said it like this: "Accidents are usually multi-factoral and develop through relatively lengthy sequences of changes and errors." (One of his examples is shown in *Figure 2-12*). His following comment adds support to the Principle of Multiple

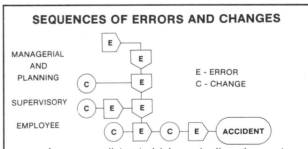

SEQUENCES OF ERRORS AND CHANGES

A man was distracted (change), slipped on wet sealer (error), and fell from sloping roof (accident). He had not tied off to a safety harness (error) because he was hurrying to finish after delay by a safety meeting on falls (change).

The supervisor was new (change), he had no written procedure for job (error), and he conducted no pre-job review or briefing (error).

When the building, previously slated to be torn down, was continued in service (change), the engineer ordered a roofing job but failed to comply with a previous accident recommendation to provide a cable for tie-off (error).

Intermediate supervision failed to assist new supervisor or audit work order preparation methods. Management failed to specify audit, monitoring, assistance to supervisor, and written procedures.

Figure 2-12

Causes: "MORT analysis of serious accidents typically shows on the order of 25 specific factors and 15 systemic failures, many of them linked in causal or temporal sequence." This complexity of events leading to loss can, in one way, be viewed quite positively. It shows that there are many opportunities to intervene or interrupt the sequence — and thus control the loss.

Experience shows that a majority of accidents involve both substandard practices and substandard conditions. And these are only *symptoms*. Behind the symptoms are the *basic causes,* the personal factors and job factors which led to the substandard acts and conditions. Even after uncovering all of these causes, there is more to be done. Then one should determine what *deficiencies in the management system* (e.g., poor hiring and placement, lack of training, inadequate maintenance) permitted or caused those personal and job factors. In effect, there are three levels of causes: (a) immediate causes, (b) basic causes and (c) lack of management control factors.

It is good to keep in mind that, while we must try to identify every possible cause of a problem, we should give the greatest amount of attention to those with the greatest potential of loss severity and the greatest probability of recurrence. This is essential to effective control.

CAUSATION EXPRESSED WITH DOMINOES

Dominoes have been widely used to convey the principles of accident prevention and loss control. H.W. Heinrich's original domino sequence was a classic in safety thinking and teaching for over 30 years in many different countries. Since dominoes have been used for so long by so many as a classic illustration in accident causation, their application in *Figure 2-13* has been updated to reflect the direct management relationship with the causes and effects of accident loss. Also, arrows are incorporated to show the *multilinear interactions* of the cause and effect sequence.

Three Stages Of Control

The model not only reflects multiple causes but also multiple opportunities for control. These opportunities can be grouped into three major categories or stages of control: 1) pre-contact, 2) contact, and 3) post-contact.

Pre-Contact Control: This is the stage that includes everything we do to develop and implement a program to avoid the risks, prevent the losses from occurring, and plan actions to reduce loss if and when contacts occur.

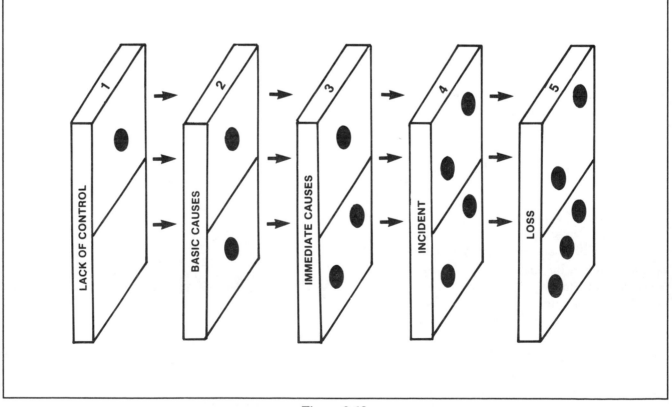

Figure 2-13

Pre-contact control is the most fruitful stage. This is where we develop an optimum program, establish optimum standards, maintain effective performance feedback, and manage compliance with performance standards. The goal here is the PREVENTION part of control. Pre-contact control is the goal of most of this book.

Contact Control: Accidents usually involve contact with a source of energy or substance above the threshold limit of the body or structure. Many control measures take effect at the point and time of contact, by reducing the amount of energy exchange or harmful contact. For example:

- substitution of alternate energy forms or less harmful substances
  - electric motors instead of shafts and belts
  - higher flash point substances or non-flammable materials
  - less toxic solids, liquids, vapors and gases
  - lifting and materials handling devices to replace "backbreaking" manual labor
- reducing the amount of energy used or released
  - prohibiting running within the workplace
  - low voltage or low pressure equipment
  - reduced temperatures in hot water systems
  - use of materials which do not require high processing temperatures
  - roadway bumper pads to slow down in-plant traffic speeds
  - speed governors on vehicles
  - control of vibration and other noise-producing phenomena
  - screens, shades and tints to reduce excess heat, light and glare
- placing barricades or barriers between the source of energy and the people or property
  - personal protective equipment or devices
  - skin creams and lotions
  - fire walls
  - explosion bunkers
  - enclosures or insulation for noise-emitting machines, for heat and cold, for electricity and for radiation
  - filters for removing toxic elements from the air
- modifying contact surfaces
  - padding points of contact
  - adding bumper guards to building columns in materials handling areas
  - rounding off the corners and edges of work benches, counters, furniture and equipment

- smoothing rough surfaces or sharp edges of equipment and materials
- removing debris, potholes and other damage exposures from vehicular surfaces
- strengthening the body or structure
  - weight control and physical conditioning
  - immunization vaccines
  - drug treatments to improve blood clotting of hemophiliacs, etc.
  - reinforcement of roofs, floors, columns, docks, platforms, materials handling equipment, load-bearing surfaces, etc.
  - reinforcing the structures of vehicles for impact resistance
  - case hardening of machine tool parts such as cutting edges

The contact stage is where the incident occurs that may or may not result in loss, depending on the amount of energy or substance involved. Effective controls keep the exchange at a minimum, resulting in minor rather than major losses, and "close calls" rather than accident losses. These measures do not prevent the contacts or incidents, but they do contribute significantly to the control of losses.

Post-Contact Control: After the accident or "contact," the extent of losses can be controlled in many ways, such as:

- implementation of the emergency action plans
- proper first aid and medical care for people
- rescue operations
- fire and explosion control
- removal of damaged equipment, materials and facilities from use until repaired
- prompt repair of damaged equipment, materials and facilities
- prompt ventilation of the air-polluted workplace
- effective cleanup of spills
- compensation claims control
- liability claims control
- salvage and waste control measures to reclaim all possible value from damaged items
- prompt and effective rehabilitation of injured workers to a productive life

Post-contact controls do not prevent the accidents, but they minimize the losses. They can mean the difference between injury and death, between reparable damage and total loss, between a complaint and a lawsuit, between business interruption and business closing.

CORE CONCEPTS IN REVIEW

Safety is control of accidental loss which relates to accidents, to the losses caused by accidents and to the control function in the management system.

A modern definition of "accident" is: an undesired event that results in harm to people, damage to property or loss to process. It is usually the result of a contact with a substance or source of energy above the threshold limit of the body or structure.

From a strictly safety perspective, an **"incident"** is an event which, under slightly different circumstances, could have resulted in harm to people, damage to property or loss to process. In the broader loss control definition, it refers to an event which could or does result in a loss.

The 1-10-30-600 ratio study shows how foolish it is to direct total efforts at the relatively few events that result in serious or disabling injuries, when for every one of these there are many other occurrences (minor injuries, property damage and near-accidents) that provide a much larger base for more effective control of accidental loss.

Three critical avenues to better control of accidental loss are the following methods:

1. **Develop an adequate program.** Ensure that the management system adequately incorporates sufficient, program activities (such as those shown in the top section of *Figure 2-14*).

2. **Establish adequate program standards.** Specify who must do what (and when) for safety/loss control. Ensure that standards are high enough, specific enough and clear enough.

3. **Maintain compliance with standards.** Communicate, educate, motivate and lead the way to proper performance.

People, equipment, material and environment (P-E-M-E) are four major subsystems of the total organization which must interact properly to obtain effective safety, quality, production and cost control. These subsystems are four major sources of loss — and four major sources of control.

Accidental loss is seldom, if ever, the result of a single cause. A majority of accidents involve both substandard practices and substandard conditions. And these are only **symptoms**.

1. **Basic causes** are the personal factors and job factors which cause or permit the substandard acts and conditions.

2. Behind these causes are the deficiencies in the management system.

3. Thus, there are three levels of causation:
   a. immediate causes
   b. basic causes
   c. lack of management control factors

Modern thinking and experience regarding the causes of accidental loss are reflected in the loss causation model and the new domino sequence. **Modern loss causation models** reflect these ideas:

a. multiple causes concept
b. multilinear interactions of causes and effects
c. multiple opportunities for control (pre-contact, contact and post-contact)

KEY QUESTIONS

1. In writing, define the following terms:
   a) safety
   b) accident
   c) incident

2. True or False? In modern thinking, an event must involve human harm to be properly called an accident.

3. Most accidents involve _____
   with a substance or source of _____
   above the threshold limit of the body or structure.

4. What are the correct labels for the four tiers of the 1-10-30-600 ratio?

5. What are the words on each of the five dominoes in the new cause and effect sequence?

6. Name four primary areas of loss from accidents which are also four primary areas of control.

7. True or False? The costs of accidental injury and illness are from five to fifty times the costs of uninsured property damage.

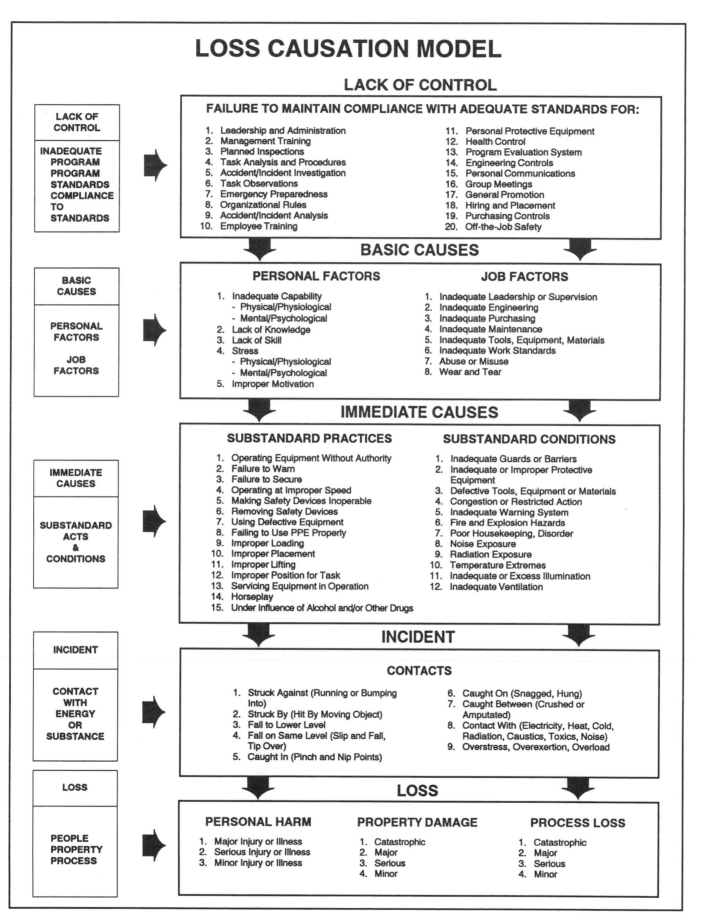

LOSS CAUSATION MODEL

LACK OF CONTROL

LACK OF CONTROL

INADEQUATE PROGRAM PROGRAM STANDARDS COMPLIANCE TO STANDARDS

FAILURE TO MAINTAIN COMPLIANCE WITH ADEQUATE STANDARDS FOR:

1. Leadership and Administration
2. Management Training
3. Planned Inspections
4. Task Analysis and Procedures
5. Accident/Incident Investigation
6. Task Observations
7. Emergency Preparedness
8. Organizational Rules
9. Accident/Incident Analysis
10. Employee Training
11. Personal Protective Equipment
12. Health Control
13. Program Evaluation System
14. Engineering Controls
15. Personal Communications
16. Group Meetings
17. General Promotion
18. Hiring and Placement
19. Purchasing Controls
20. Off-the-Job Safety

BASIC CAUSES

BASIC CAUSES

PERSONAL FACTORS

JOB FACTORS

PERSONAL FACTORS

1. Inadequate Capability
   - Physical/Physiological
   - Mental/Psychological
2. Lack of Knowledge
3. Lack of Skill
4. Stress
   - Physical/Physiological
   - Mental/Psychological
5. Improper Motivation

JOB FACTORS

1. Inadequate Leadership or Supervision
2. Inadequate Engineering
3. Inadequate Purchasing
4. Inadequate Maintenance
5. Inadequate Tools, Equipment, Materials
6. Inadequate Work Standards
7. Abuse or Misuse
8. Wear and Tear

IMMEDIATE CAUSES

IMMEDIATE CAUSES

SUBSTANDARD ACTS & CONDITIONS

SUBSTANDARD PRACTICES

1. Operating Equipment Without Authority
2. Failure to Warn
3. Failure to Secure
4. Operating at Improper Speed
5. Making Safety Devices Inoperable
6. Removing Safety Devices
7. Using Defective Equipment
8. Failing to Use PPE Properly
9. Improper Loading
10. Improper Placement
11. Improper Lifting
12. Improper Position for Task
13. Servicing Equipment in Operation
14. Horseplay
15. Under Influence of Alcohol and/or Other Drugs

SUBSTANDARD CONDITIONS

1. Inadequate Guards or Barriers
2. Inadequate or Improper Protective Equipment
3. Defective Tools, Equipment or Materials
4. Congestion or Restricted Action
5. Inadequate Warning System
6. Fire and Explosion Hazards
7. Poor Housekeeping, Disorder
8. Noise Exposure
9. Radiation Exposure
10. Temperature Extremes
11. Inadequate or Excess Illumination
12. Inadequate Ventilation

INCIDENT

INCIDENT

CONTACT WITH ENERGY OR SUBSTANCE

CONTACTS

1. Struck Against (Running or Bumping Into)
2. Struck By (Hit By Moving Object)
3. Fall to Lower Level
4. Fall on Same Level (Slip and Fall, Tip Over)
5. Caught In (Pinch and Nip Points)
6. Caught On (Snagged, Hung)
7. Caught Between (Crushed or Amputated)
8. Contact With (Electricity, Heat, Cold, Radiation, Caustics, Toxics, Noise)
9. Overstress, Overexertion, Overload

LOSS

LOSS

PEOPLE PROPERTY PROCESS

PERSONAL HARM

1. Major Injury or Illness
2. Serious Injury or Illness
3. Minor Injury or Illness

PROPERTY DAMAGE

1. Catastrophic
2. Major
3. Serious
4. Minor

PROCESS LOSS

1. Catastrophic
2. Major
3. Serious
4. Minor

Figure 2-14

8. Name five or six types of energy that may be involved in accidental loss.

9. True or False? Personal protective equipment prevents incidents.

10. Why are the terms "substandard practices" and "substandard conditions" more functional than "unsafe practices" and "unsafe conditions?"

11. Substandard practices and conditions should be treated as _____ rather than basic causes.

12. What are the two primary categories of basic causes? Give several examples of each.

13. Name three common reasons for "lack of control."

14. List ten or twelve elements of successful safety/loss control programs.

15. Why are program standards important?

16. What is the Principle of Multiple Causes? Why is it important in safety/loss control management?

17. We should give the greatest amount of attention to those causal factors with the greatest potential of l_____ severity and the greatest probability of r_____.

18. Explain the "multilinear interactions" concept regarding the loss causation model.

19. Name the three stages of control and give several examples of each.

PRACTICAL APPLICATIONS SUMMARY

S – For Supervisors
E – For Executives
C – For Safety/Loss Control Coordinators

	S	E	C
1. Develop and communicate the organization's safety and health philosophy, basic concepts and functional definitions.	x	x	x
2. Develop, implement and improve the organization's safety and health management program and standards.	x	x	x
3. Include accident causes and effects concepts in management training activities.		x	x
4. Include accident causes and effects concepts in employee training programs, group meetings and personal contacts.	x	x	x
5. In the inspection program, emphasize not only the substandard conditions but also the basic causes behind them.	x	x	x
6. In the job observation program, emphasize not only the substandard practices but also the basic causes behind them.	x	x	x
7. In accident/incident analyses, include immediate causes, basic causes, and lack of management control factors.	x	x	x
8. Maintain compliance with the safety and health program standards.	x	x	x
9. In all pertinent program activities, ensure that "lack of management control" factors are adequately considered along with immediate and basic causes.	x	x	x
10. Emphasize near-accidents as well as accidents.	x	x	x
11. Manage control at all three stages: pre-contact, contact and post-contact.	x	x	x

CHAPTER 3

MANAGEMENT CONTROL OF LOSS

"The most valuable fringe benefit of considering safety an operational strategy has been the general improvement in line management's ability to manage *all* aspects of their total jobs. Believe me, this is not just mere rhetoric... It is a proven fact."
— Lester A. Hudson, President and Chief Operating Officer, Dan River, Inc.

INTRODUCTION

Loss Control is a vital part of every manager's job, at every organizational level. To be done effectively, it requires a professional management approach. Three major reasons for this are: 1) managers are responsible for the safety and health of others, 2) managing safety provides significant opportunities for managing costs, and 3) safety/loss control management provides an operational strategy to improve overall management.

Managers Are Responsible For The Safety And Health Of Others

A manager's responsibility for productivity and profitability is substantial. But responsibility for the safety and health of employees is awesome! Machines, materials and market strategies can be explained in terms of facts and figures. But there simply is no way to satisfactorily explain to a grief-stricken family their loved one's death, loss of sight or permanent disability. A dollar loss on the balance sheet is temporary, and can be regained through better management. But there is no way to regain the human losses which result from accidents. The life, the body part, the normal functioning are lost forever.

Being human, managers have the human tendency to rationalize regarding accident causes; to focus on the "careless" or "unsafe" acts of employees; and to avoid blaming themselves. But, as Dr. W. Edwards Deming (renowned quality consultant) and other management specialists have discovered, only 15% of a company's problems can be controlled by employees — while 85% can be controlled only by management. In other words, most safety problems are management problems.

Managing Safety And Other Loss-Related Areas Provides Significant Opportunities For Managing Costs

Accidents are expensive. Obvious cost items include workers' compensation, medical insurance, damage to equipment and product, downtime, repairs, replacements, lawsuits and liability. Other significant costs include investigation time, costs of hiring and/or training replacements, lost productivity, overtime, extra supervisory time, clerical time and loss of business and goodwill.

> "Minimizing loss is as much improvement as maximization of profit."
> — Louis Allen

Traditionally, safety has been considered as an expense, as a cost of doing business. However, many modern managers now see and treat it as an investment — an investment with significant returns, both humane and economic. As one chief executive put it:

We are now looking at safety expenditures as opportunities — opportunities which are considered just as important and just as potentially profitable as production-oriented investments or the introduction of a new product line.

More effective safety programs, aimed at the control of all losses, produce greater profitability by reducing costs.

Safety/Loss Control Management Provides An Operational Strategy To Improve Overall Management

Leaders around the world are increasingly recognizing that a well-managed safety program provides an operational strategy to improve overall management. This is not a new concept. It was expressed almost 50 years ago by H.W. Heinrich, a pioneer in safety management thinking, in his influential book, *Industrial Accident Prevention.* He wrote, "Methods of most value in accident prevention are analogous with methods required for the control of the quality, cost and quantity of production." At that time, Heinrich's thoughts in this regard were not given the attention they deserved because of the overwhelming need to reduce the injury rates. But in recent years a significant number of major organizations have discovered that applying the tools and techniques described in these chapters has given them not only increased safety, but also measurable improvements in efficiency, quality and productivity.

Chapter Objective

The need to know what professional management is — its characteristics, principles and functions — is not only a basic need of most managers but is also at the base of most of their problems. Without exaggeration, one of the biggest needs throughout the world among organizations that have not attained the desired levels of loss control performance is this matter of managing the work necessary to get the desired job done efficiently and effectively.

> "The first duty of business is to survive and the guiding principle of business economics is not the maximization of profit—it is the avoidance of loss." **Peter Drucker**

This chapter presents highlights of professional management characteristics, principles and functions as evolved from the experience of leading managers and management consultants and trainers. The primary objective is to help managers effectively manage control of loss, in areas such as those shown in *Figure 3-1*. Application of these principles and practices will help reach not only desired safety and loss control goals, but also desired goals for quality, productivity and cost

---

SOME MAJOR TARGETS FOR THE LOSS CONTROL PROGRAM

1. **On-the-job injury and illness**
2. **Off-the-job injury and illness**
3. **Fire and explosion**
4. **General property damage**
5. **Shrinkage and theft**
6. **Absenteeism**
7. **General and administrative liability**
8. **Product liability**
9. **Alcohol and other drug abuse**
10. **Natural catastrophic loss**
11. **Violations of legislation**
12. **Environmental abuse**
13. **Disorder**
14. **Wasteful behavior**
15. **Other avoidable waste**
16. **Management system inadequacies**

Figure 3-1

effectiveness.

Loss Control Management Goals

The following general loss control management goals, when properly achieved, will minimize the chance of a major or catastrophic loss for any organization with high risks.

Loss Control Management Goals

1. Identify all loss exposures
2. Evaluate the risk in each exposure
3. Develop a plan
4. Implement the plan
5. Monitor

Most important to the achievement of these goals is the identification of all exposures facing an organization. This is the only way to identify the critical few exposures that could result in major or catastrophic loss if not controlled. There are numerous ways to accomplish this such as through the use of exposure or risk inventories, reviews of all business activities including flow charts, annual reports, purchasing, sales and marketing materials, etc.

However, one of the most effective ways to identify the majority of accidental exposures on an ongoing basis is to implement a modern safety and health/loss control program, and effectively manage its control.

The remainder of this chapter and book gives the insight necessary to take a giant step in that direction.

Specific Professional Vocabulary

Just as doctors and lawyers have their own professional vocabulary, so do managers. Because management is a distinct profession, it has many specialized terms with specific meanings. In many cases, the functional meanings of such terms are not found in the dictionary. Functional definitions evolve from experience. They become a sort of shorthand for effective communication among members of the profession, e.g., the management profession. Of course, the professional should always be cautious about how he or she uses that "shorthand" when communicating with people outside of the profession.

There also are technical terms specific to the loss control aspects of managing. Many of these are introduced and explained in various chapters of this book. While operating managers do not need to become safety specialists, they do need to know terms such as these:

- *Loss* - avoidable waste of any resource.

- *Risk* - chance of loss.

- *Hazard* - a condition or practice with the potential for accidental loss.

- *Safety* - control of accidental loss.

- *Loss Control* - anything done to reduce loss from the pure risks of business. It includes:

  1. The prevention of loss exposures.
  2. The reduction of loss when loss-producing events occur.
  3. The termination or avoidance of risk.

- *Loss Control Management* - the application of professional management skills to the control of loss from the risks of business. The major targets are shown in *Figure 3-1*.

The professional supervisor/manager keeps up with current, functional meanings of terms in the pertinent professions, uses them effectively, and helps others to understand and use them effectively. Essentially, true communication is what one does to share the same meaning, to achieve mutual understanding. This requires "being on the same wavelength" regarding the meanings of the terms used in the communication process.

Identification Of Required Work

A characteristic of the "pro" in any field is that he or she understands which activities will get the required results and which will be ineffective. Professional managers know, from training and experience, what they and their employees must do to get the job done in the proper way. Not having this knowledge, or not applying it, results in frustration, waste and confusion for all concerned.

No organization has to start from scratch in identifying and classifying the work required for optimum results in managing safety and loss control. Analysis of successful programs around the world has already identified most of it. Based on such analysis, 20 program elements or activities for management work have been identified. (See *Figure 3-2*)

For managers to be able to say, "I am managing my loss control work in a professional way," they should know which elements of their own organization's program apply to them and what specific work they must do in each of those elements. These work responsibilities may be spelled out in job descriptions, procedures manuals and/or standard practices. But, regardless of where or how the performance standards are identified, supervisors must know what those standards are. Completing the worksheet shown as *Figure 3-3* could be a quick check of how well you know the performance standards for your responsibilities in this critical area. (It includes spaces for adding activities you perform that are not on the list.)

Measurement of Work Performance

Almost anyone can measure the output of an organization - whether it be in tons, units, sales, services, etc. However, a professional manager must know and be able to measure the inputs required to get those results. This is one difference between a manager and a clerk. In safety, in the past, almost all of the measurements were of the outputs of the program—reduced injuries and injury-related costs. However, these figures can be kept by any reasonably competent clerk. It requires professional management skills to be able to measure the inputs into the program which determine the outputs. Professional managers can measure their own work performance and that of the people who report to them. For example, a supervisor may be conducting only 60% of the group meetings required by the organization's standards, or doing 75% of the required job instruction. Employees may be complying with protective equipment requirements only 80% of the time or adjusting a machine to the correct tolerance only 92% of the time.

A good analogy might compare the business manager's use of measurements with that of the sports coach. The good coach is very much interested in measurements of results of consequences (the score of the game), but the way he or she wins games is by measuring the performance of the players — and coaching for improvement. Likewise, in the business world, supervisors and higher managers are very much interested in measurements of results (numbers of accidents, amount of downtime and lost time, etc.). But they also recognize that it takes input to get output, and that input depends on the performance of the team members. Only by knowing people's performance in each area of the program can supervisors take appropriate action before losses occur. In effect, management actions can be predictive and preactive rather than reactive and after-the-loss.

Meaningful measurement of performance is such an important characteristic of the professional manager that we are going to discuss it in greater detail later in this chapter.

Fundamental Truths or Principles

Almost every management discipline has certain fundamental truths or principles that guide the general actions of the professional.

Henri Fayol (1841-1925) was one of the early distinguished contributors to the management movement who emphasized the need for these leadership principles in his writings as early as 1916.

The following have been selected as those deemed to have special value during the implementation of any program or project. Most of them have continued value as a leader strives for never-ending improvement.

1. *The Principle of Reaction to Change* - **People accept change more readily when it is presented in relatively small amounts**. Introduce change in steps that are not too big at one time. Be sure to plan for handling the likely resistance to change. Keep

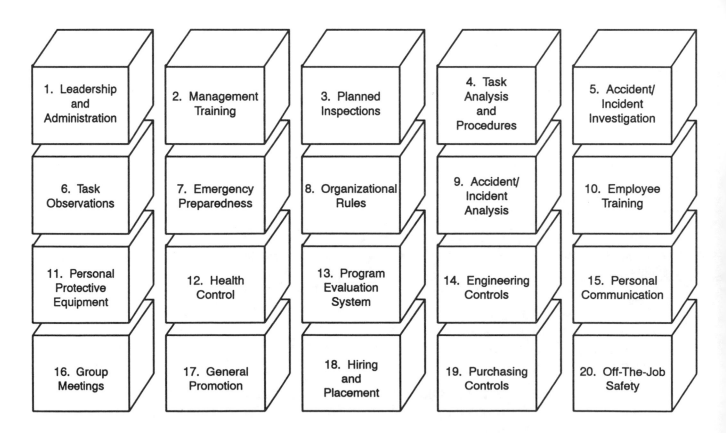

Figure 3-2: THE MANAGEMENT WORK FOR LOSS CONTROL SUCCESS

LOSS CONTROL MANAGEMENT

WORKSHEET FOR SUPERVISORS

ACTIVITY	PART OF OUR PROGRAM? YES – NO DON'T KNOW	CLEAR STAND-ARDS FOR MY PERFORMANCE? YES – NO DON'T KNOW
1. Communicate and reinforce safety/loss control policy		
2. Set the leadership example for subordinates		
3. Take the supervisory orientation program		
4. Complete the supervisory training programs		
5. Conduct planned general inspections		
6. Audit the critical parts inspection program in my area		
7. Audit the preventive maintenance program in my area		
8. Implement and monitor pre-use equipment checkouts		
9. Prepare a critical job/task inventory		
10. Analyze critical jobs/tasks and prepare procedures or practices		
11. Use job/task procedures and practices for instructing, observing and coaching		
12. Investigate accidents		
13. Investigate close calls		
14. Determine basic causes of accidents		
15. Follow-up investigations with corrective and preventive actions		
16. Perform planned job/task observations		
17. Use observation information in performance discussions		
18. Include emergency preparedness in safety meetings and safety contacts		
19. Coordinate fire drills, evacuation exercises, and emergency team activities in the department		
20. Cover rules in orientation of new and transferred workers		
21. Conduct annual rules review for workers		
22. Enforce rules consistently		
23. Reinforce rule compliance with positive recognition		
24. Serve on loss control project teams		
25. Inventory the training needs of our people		
26. Use training to improve workers' present skills and to prepare them for upgrading		
27. Explain and enforce personal protective equipment standards		
28. Promote PPE conservation		
29. Reinforce compliance with PPE requirements		
30. Teach safe handling practices for hazardous substances		
31. Ensure adequate first aid facilities & equipment		
32. Report unsafe aspects of purchased items		
33. Report unsafe aspects of new or changed tools, machines and methods		
34. Orient new and transferred employees		
35. Give proper job instruction		
36. Use effective coaching & tipping techniques		
37. Conduct group meetings with workers		
38. Actively promote safety facts, figures, posters, publications, contests, etc.		
39. Communicate personnel placement problems to those who hire and place people		
40. Analyze safety records and reports for lessons to be learned		
41. Include off-the-job safety in group meetings and personal contacts		
42. Encourage people to share their off-the-job safety experiences		
43.		
44.		
45.		
46.		

Figure 3-3

people well informed of pending changes and the reasons for them; emphasize the benefits of the change for the people involved; get people to participate in the planning as much as is feasible and build from the known to the new.

2. *The Principle of Behavior Reinforcement* - **Behavior with negative effects tends to decrease or stop; behavior with positive effects tends to continue or increase.** A key to motivational success is to identify the desired behaviors critical to safety-quality or production and to give repeated immediate positive recognition when their performance is recognized. Repeated positive reinforcement of desired actions will make the right way so attractive that the individual will have less desire to take the substandard or unsafe way. The need for sincere recognition is among the most basic powerful psychological hungers which people have. When that need is not met in legitimate ways (positive behavior reinforcement), people will tend to stop trying as hard or attempt to get recognition through unacceptable means (horseplay, rule violations, showing off, etc.).

3. *The Principle of Mutual Interest* - **Programs, projects and ideas are best sold when they bridge the wants and desires of both parties.** Supervisors who are best at "selling" programs or ideas are those who clearly establish a bridge or connection of values between what "the company" wants and what the workers want. They seek out the benefits of the idea or program for the individual workers, and build upon them, honestly and persistently. In other words, "you scratch my back and I'll scratch yours."

4. *The Principle of Point of Action* - **Management efforts are most effective when they focus at the point where the work is actually done.** Most of the day-to-day action takes place on the floor, in the shop, in the field - where people provide the service or make the product. Thus, front-line supervisors are the point of management control for safety, quality, production and costs. The more quickly they can identify variances, determine their significance and do something about them, the more effective control becomes.

5. *The Principle of Leadership Example* - **People tend to emulate their leaders.** Most people want to please their leaders, and do so by following their behavioral example. Attitudes and influence, like waterfalls, flow downward. At all levels of manage-

ment, the attitudes and actions of leaders is one of the most powerful motivational forces in the world.

6. *The Principle of Basic Causes* - **Solutions to problems are more effective when they treat the basic or root causes.** Whether we relate this to items detected on planned inspections, to causes of accidents during investigations, or to quality and production problems, the meaning is the same. We can't cure the disease by treating only the symptoms. We must find out why the symptoms exist, the basic causes behind them, the real problems.

7. *The Principle of the Critical/Vital Few* - **The majority (80%) of any group of effects is produced by a relatively small (20%) number of causes.** For example, a critical few operations are involved in a large portion of the accidents; a critical few people present a large portion of the performance problems; and a critical few types of loss incidents causes a large portion of the losses. The management professional tries to identify the critical factors, and to concentrate efforts on them. This gives the greatest return on the investment of time, money, and other resources.

8. *The Principle of the Key Advocate* - **It is easier to persuade decision makers when at least one person within their own circle believes in the proposal well enough to champion the cause.** This is known as "lobbying" in political circles. Recognition of this principle should be part of the planning strategy for any important presentation to "sell" an idea or program. Win at least one strong advocate who will support your proposal to the group. The positive persuasive power of such a champion may make the difference between rejection and acceptance.

9. *The Principle of Minimum Commitment* - **It is easier to gain approval and commitment for a portion of a system than the entire project or program.** When implementation steps are chosen with care, each subsequent approval toward the complete plan or project becomes an easier exercise. This again highlights the need for having a well organized overall plan to take you step-by-step from where you are to where you want to be.

10. *The Principle of System Integration* - **The better new activities are integrated into existing systems, the higher the chance of acceptance and success.** The implementation of new ideas and activities usually carries the idea of extra work or requirements. The probability of acceptance is great-

ly increased when the new is incorporated into or linked with an existing program or system, i.e. incorporating the safe way into the standard job/task procedure rather than creating an extra job/task safety procedure.

11. *The Principle of Involvement* - **Meaningful involvement increases motivation and support.** In doing this, supervisors ask their people for suggestions, recommendations, and advice in matters that affect their work. They develop a mutual interest, a climate of collaboration and cooperation. Such participation is packed with motivational power. People tend to develop a feeling of ownership and support of what they helped to create. This power is evident in shift safety teams, loss control project teams, quality circles, and other forms of participative problem-solving teams. Supervisors who use this principle effectively develop mutual interest, mutual motivation, and mutual respect. Effective leaders periodically inventory the level of participation and ownership they develop in others.

12. *The Principle of Multiple Causes* - **Accidents and other problems are seldom, if ever, the result of a single cause.** The systematic problem solver resists the temptation to jump to conclusions, to take the first piece of plausible evidence as the cause, to take hasty action. Nearly every problem has a variety of contributing causes. Most loss incidents, for example, involve both immediate causes (substandard practices and substandard conditions) and basic causes (personal factors and job factors). The management professional tries to identify all possible causes of the loss problem at hand, then gives the greatest attention to those with the most potential to actually control the problem.

A MANAGEMENT CONTROL SYSTEM

Henri Fayol mentioned earlier as a pioneer in management thinking, defined the functions of management in 1916 as: Forecasting and Planning, Organizing, Commanding, Coordinating and Controlling.

Over the years other great management thinkers made minor adjustments to that list of functions. Forecasting and coordinating have been combined into other functions. Commanding has been replaced with directing or leading. These changes reflect the changing role of management through the years. Today the functions of management are listed by many organizations as:

Planning
Organizing
Leading/Directing
Controlling

It is the fourth function that we want to zero in on. First, a word of clarification. "Controlling" is not treating people as puppets. As a matter of fact it is not something we do to people at all. Instead, it is something we do to the work process. It is like the control loop in a process, which monitors temperature or pressure etc., and makes adjustments to the process to keep it within certain pre-determined levels. A simple example is a thermostat which monitors the temperature in a room and turns the heating/cooling system off and on to keep it at a preset level. Management control is the same process but is applied to work processes. There are five progressive steps that lead to control of an activity for management. These are summarized by the acronym I-S-M-E-C.

Figure 3-4 shows the system in more detail, including a program loop, and a program development growth loop. Let's examine each section.

Identification of Work

If you don't care where you are going, any road will get you there. But when you *do* care where you are

---

ACTIVITIES FOR MANAGING CONTROL

I- *Identification* of work. Specifying the program elements and activities to achieve desired results.

S- *Standards.* Establishing performance standards (criteria by which methods and results will be evaluated).

M- *Measurement.* Measuring performance; recording and reporting work in progress and completed.

E- *Evaluation.* Evaluating performance as measured and compared with established standards; appraising work and results.

C- *Commendation and Correction.* Regulating and improving methods and results by commending desired performance and constructively correcting substandard performance.

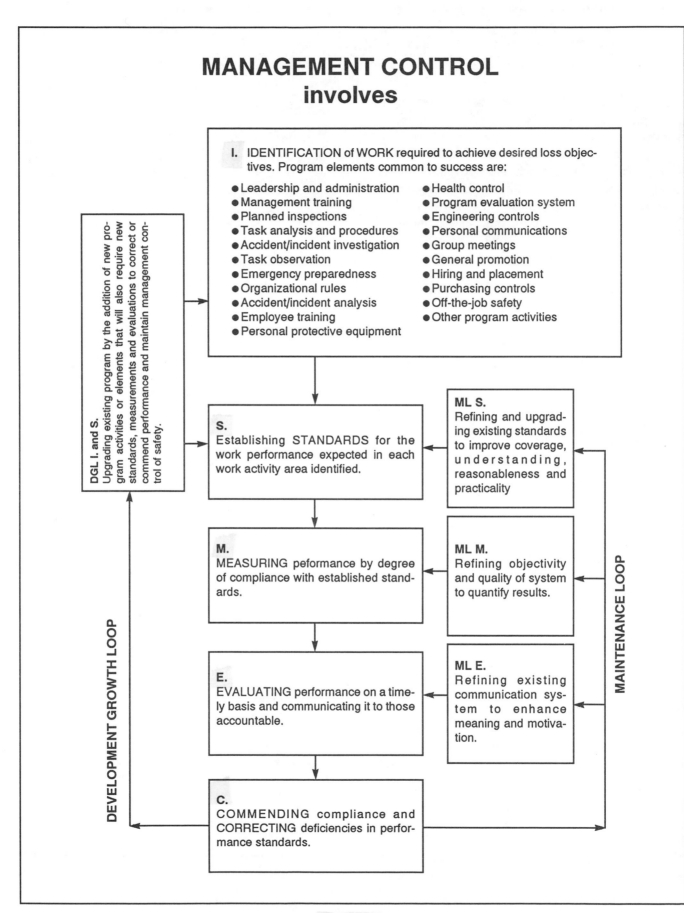

MANAGEMENT CONTROL
involves

I. IDENTIFICATION of WORK required to achieve desired loss objectives. Program elements common to success are:

- Leadership and administration
- Management training
- Planned inspections
- Task analysis and procedures
- Accident/incident investigation
- Task observation
- Emergency preparedness
- Organizational rules
- Accident/incident analysis
- Employee training
- Personal protective equipment
- Health control
- Program evaluation system
- Engineering controls
- Personal communications
- Group meetings
- General promotion
- Hiring and placement
- Purchasing controls
- Off-the-job safety
- Other program activities

DGL I. and S.
Upgrading existing program by the addition of new program activities or elements that will also require new standards, measurements and evaluations to correct or commend performance and maintain management control of safety.

S.
Establishing STANDARDS for the work performance expected in each work activity area identified.

ML S.
Refining and upgrading existing standards to improve coverage, understanding, reasonableness and practicality

M.
MEASURING peformance by degree of compliance with established standards.

ML M.
Refining objectivity and quality of system to quantify results.

E.
EVALUATING performance on a timely basis and communicating it to those accountable.

ML E.
Refining existing communication system to enhance meaning and motivation.

C.
COMMENDING compliance and CORRECTING deficiencies in performance standards.

DEVELOPMENT GROWTH LOOP

MAINTENANCE LOOP

Figure 3-4

going, you want to take the best route. The experience of others who have successfully made the trip can provide the map to help you plan, organize and lead the way to control of accidental loss.

There have been a number of significant studies made to determine the components of successful safety and health programs. The results of these studies have been reported in the *Journal of Safety Research* and publications of the Businessmen's Roundtable. Some studies were done by governmental agencies, such as the National Institute of Occupational Safety and Health and others by major universities, such as the University of Nebraska and Stanford University. A major study was also done by the Industrial Accident Prevention Association of Ontario, Canada.

These studies, and the practical experience they reflect provide the best guide for identifying the activities which get the desired results. One such guide is the list of 20 program elements shown in the first box of the management control model, *Figure 3-4*. These activities, when properly done, have been repeatedly proven to achieve optimum results, not only for safety and loss control but also for quality, production and cost control.

Most organizations cannot immediately put major emphasis on every one of the program elements, nor would it be wise to attempt it. Many start with a 10-point program or a 12-point program and gradually build up to the full-grown program of the leaders. Other organizations will use the list of 112 activity areas shown in *Figure 3-5* as a sort of "shopping list" to pick those critical activities which will help them most at their particular stage of program growth. Thus, *Figure 3-5* provides a blueprint for program development in identifying the work to be done.

Standards

Measurement involves comparison with standards. Without adequate standards, there can be no meaningful measurement, evaluation or correction of performance. You should have specific, clear, demanding standards for all program elements and for all major work activities identified. Following are sample standards from several program elements. (*Figure 3-6*).

Good standards are tests of performance. They not only enable improvement of the organization's appraisal of program and individual performance, but also permit each supervisor to guide, appraise and correct his or her own performance. The effectiveness of the remaining three steps to control (measuring,

evaluating, correcting and commending) depends completely on step #2, the development of good STANDARDS.

Measurement

As leading management consultants have emphasized: *you cannot manage what you cannot measure*. The heart of management control is measuring performance in quantifiable, objective terms. But many managers do not measure safety/loss control performance this way, because they haven't been taught how. About the only "safety" measurements they know about are accident consequences such as "frequency rates" and "severity rates." These measurements may enable meaningful comparisons between the accident performance of an organization for a given period of time and the performance of that *same* organization for a like period of time under similar circumstances. However, for managing a program, they have serious limitations. They are the most abused and misused measurements of "safety" and are subject to many variables and forms of manipulation. But their greatest weakness is that they are after the fact and reactive. In effect, they are measurements of "unsafety," and tell you nothing about the nature of your problems or what to do about them. As Charles E. Gilmore pointed out in an address at the National Safety Congress:

> **What is the sense in measuring if the loss must occur before you can act? That's reaction, not control.**

The measurements referred to in I-S-M-E-C are measurements of control, which come before the accidents and losses. They are measurements which answer the question. "How well are we doing our work for safety and health/loss control?"

To work well, these require prior establishment of specific standards. The measurements reflect accomplishments as a percentage of standard. For example, if your standard requires weekly inspections by each supervisor, but you conduct only three in a given month, you are a 75% performer regarding that specific standard. If one of your standards requires all employees to wear hard hats at all times within your department, but random observations show that 15% of them are not wearing the protection at any given time, your department's level of performance to that standard is 85%. Or, if a standard calls for each supervisor to prepare two Critical Task Procedures each quarter, and you prepare only five for the whole year, your performance to that standard is 62.5%.

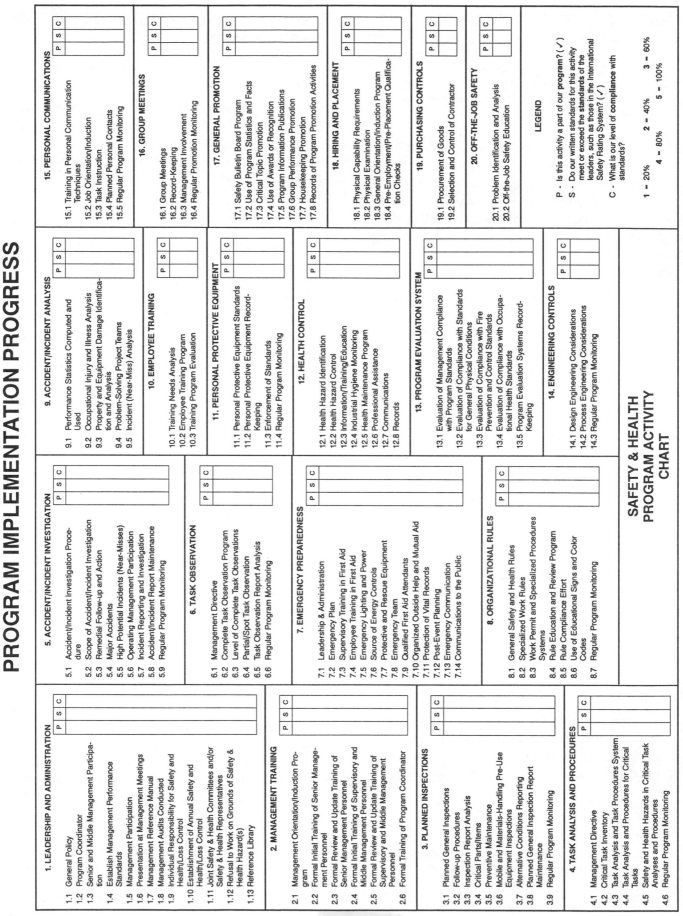

Figure 3-5

SAMPLE PERFORMANCE STANDARDS

... The Plant Manager will include safety as a significant part of the agenda at all monthly general management meetings.

... The safety performance of each member of management will be evaluated annually by the manager's immediate supervisor and will be an important part of the annual job performance appraisal process.

... Annual safety performance objectives will be established by each member of management during the fourth quarter. These objectives will be oriented to program development and improvements in program performance.

... All new members of management will be given safety and health program orientation during the first week of work assignment by their immediate supervisor.

... Shift supervisors will conduct planned general inspections not less than every two months.

... To ensure accuracy the critical parts and items lists will be reviewed and updated annually by shift foremen.

... The list of critical tasks will be reviewed and updated annually by team leaders for every occupation under their control.

... Every standard task procedure or practice will be reviewed and updated appropriately by the supervisor involved at least annually, and whenever a question is raised about the task because of a process change, accident or high potential loss incident.

... Every accident resulting in occupational illness or injury, regardless of how trivial, and all property damage accidents involving $500 or more of loss will be properly investigated on the company accident investigation form by the front-line supervisor during the shift in which the event occurred.

... Department heads will be involved in an at-the-scene investigation of all major injuries (potential or actual lost time), all major property damage accidents ($15,000 or more loss) and all major environmental spills (quantities in excess of reportable limits) during the same shift of the event's occurrence. Plant managers will hold a follow-up review of all major accidents within 48 hours of their occurrence.

... Specialized safety rules for all positions will be reviewed annually by group leaders and foremen for those occupations under their control. Team assignments and completion dates for this task will be established by department heads.

... A review of relevant rules will be conducted and recorded not less than annually for each employee.

... A personal protective equipment needs inventory of each occupation will be carried out annually by the foreman with recommendations made to the safety and industrial hygiene department.

... The warehouse manager will carry out an analysis of non-disposable personal protective equipment every six months and distribute the report to foremen, department heads and the loss control manager.

... Quarterly audits of personal protective equipment compliance will be made by the loss control coordinator with reports forwarded to department heads and front line foremen.

... Each new or transferred employee will receive a formal job indoctrination prior to the start of work activity and a follow-up review within thirty (30) days by their immediate supervisor. Required forms to guide the supervisor and record actions in these important activities will be completed and forwarded as indicated by the personnel assistant.

... Each employee will receive proper job instruction (PJI) by their supervisor for each new or different job assigned prior to being required to perform that job. When applicable, a standard job procedure or practice will be utilized in this instruction.

... Each supervisor will give key point tips on critical aspects of jobs when assigning work to workers during the normal workday personal contacts, at a frequency such that every worker will receive at least one key point tip per week.

... A short group meeting of at least 10 minutes on a critical loss control subject will be held with all workers weekly at all plant locations by their front-line supervisor.

Figure 3-6

THE SUPERVISOR WHO EFFECTIVELY MANAGES CONTROL OF LOSS...

... Identifies and understands the management work (planning, organizing, leading, controlling) that he or she must do for optimum results

... Identifies, clarifies, and specifies the work that his or her people must do for optimum results

... Understands and applies the performance standards for his or her job

... Effectively communicates to his or her people the performance standards for their work

... Uses performance measurements to gauge and guide his or her own performance

... Measures, as objectively as possible, the performance of his or her people

... Evaluates what must be done to reach and/or maintain the performance standards for his or her own job

... Determines what his or her people must do to reach and/or maintain the performance standards for their work

... Uses measurement, evaluation and feedback information to keep his or her own performance up to par

... Coaches his or her people to keep their performance up to par

---

Figure 3-7: A Profile of Performance on Supervisory Loss Control Management

Evaluation

Evaluation of performance is simply determining to what degree a standard or standards have been met. This is usually expressed, as shown above, as a percentage. This enables you to *know* which standards are being met and which aren't, what is working well and what isn't, what deserves commendation and what needs constructive correction.

Commendation and Constructive Correction

This approach to performance evaluation enables good performance to be objectively identified and given appropriate commendation. Top executives should set the tone for positive behavior reinforcement throughout the organization. All members of management, especially front line supervisors, should be trained in and apply the motivational power of giving recognition and reinforcement to proper job performance.

This approach also enables substandard performance to be identified and corrected before accidents and other losses occur. A variety of constructive corrective measures may be used, many of which involve:

- Better communication of goals, objectives and standards to be sure they are understood.

- More effective training to enable a person to carry out the goals, objectives and standards.

- Increased and improved performance feedback so people won't have to guess where they stand.

- Improved procedures and work methods which help to remove frustration, hazards and meaningless activity.

- Improved recognition for desired behavior to communicate that it really matters.

- Punishment as a last resort, but done in a way that communicates your genuine concern.

Most of this book is devoted to discussion of how to do these things.

Measuring Program Performance

Measuring and evaluating program performance is a vital function of management control. Its significant value has been emphasized repeatedly by leaders throughout management literature.

Periodically, perhaps once a year, the entire safety and health/loss control program should be measured for compliance to standards. This may be done by staff professionals, by operating management, or by a combination of both. According to the size of the organization and the type of program evaluation, it can be done by an individual or a team.

There is also a need for more frequent measurements of certain aspects of critical program activities such as the quantity and quality of planned inspections (see *Figure 3-8* for an evaluation method for planned inspections), the quantity and quality of investigations conducted, the degree of protective equipment compliance, the quantity and quality of group meetings, the level of housekeeping, etc. These are usually measured every two or three months to provide feedback to appropriate managers at all levels with a barometer of performance. The indicators which are measured can be changed periodically to verify that critical program objectives, established as a result of the comprehensive evaluation, are being achieved. The results of these measurements can be a source of pride of performance or they can motivate corrective action to get a critical program activity back on target.

The results of these regular bi-monthly or quarterly measurements can be reported on a summary form such as *Figure 3-9*.

"Performance measurement and motivation are almost synonymous."
— Dan Petersen

"What gets measured gets done. Putting a measure on something is tantamount to getting it done. It focuses management attention on that area. Information is simply made available and people respond to it."
— Thomas J. Peters and Robert W. Watterman, Jr.
In Search of Excellence

"Every player is given a performance grade on every play of every game."
— Don Shula

"When you can measure what you are speaking about, and express it in numbers, you know something about it; but when you cannot express it in numbers, your knowledge is of a meager and unsatisfactory kind: it may be the beginning of knowledge, but you have scarcely, in your own thoughts, advanced to the state of science."
— Lord Kelvin, 1883
Scottish Physicist

"Unfortunately, most measures presently used in the safety field require loss-type accidents to occur with a certain degree of severity before identification of accident problems is possible."
— Dr. W.E. Tarrants

INSPECTION REPORT SCORING WORKSHEET

Department _____

Area _____

Inspector(s) _____

Evaluator _____

Evaluation Date _____

Date of Inspection _____

FACTOR	POSSIBLE	AWARDED
Thoroughness of Inspection	20	
Hazards Accurately Classified	10	
Clear Description and Location of Each Item	10	
Effectiveness of Remedial Actions	20	
Clear Responsibility for Remedial Actions	15	
Follow-Up Data Recorded	15	
Timeliness of Report	10	
TOTAL	100	

Comments:

Figure 3-8

SAFETY PERFORMANCE RATING

Quarter   **Year**

MAJOR UNIT	1	2	3	4	5	6	7	8	9	10	11	12	13	PF	TQ	TYD	PF

PROGRAM ACTIVITIES EVALUATED

1. Pre-use equipment inspections compliance
2. Planned general inspections
3. Task Analysis and procedures
4. Accident/Incident Investigations
5. Task Observations
6. Rule compliance and review
7. PPE Compliance
8. Group meetings
9. Housekeeping
10.
11.
12.
13.

TQ   This quarter
TYD   This year to date
LY   Last Year
PF   Performance position

Figure 3-9

CORE CONCEPT IN REVIEW

The professional management approach means exercising the management **functions** and **activities** that prevent accidents and minimize losses. It involves planning, organizing, leading, directing and controlling efforts to:

1. Identify all loss exposures.
2. Evaluate the risk of each exposure.
3. Develop plans and programs for control.
4. Manage implementation and control of the plans and programs.
5. Monitor and improve the whole process.

Safety's primary goal is control of accidental loss. The essence of a management control system in use around the world is summarized by I-S-M-E-C:

I - Identification of work. Specifying the program elements and activities to achieve desired results.

S - Standards. Establishing performance standards (criteria by which methods and results will be evaluated).

M - Measurement. Measuring performance; recording and reporting work in progress and completed.

E - Evaluation. Evaluating performance as measured and compared with established standards; appraising work and results.

C - Commendation and Correction. Regulating and improving methods and results by commending desired performance and constructively correcting substandard performance.

A **management principle** is a brief statement of "the wisdom of the ages" on a particular subject. The following principles have been found especially useful in effective implementation of a safety/loss control management program:

1. The Principle of Reaction to Change
2. The Principle of Behavior Reinforcement
3. The Principle of Mutual Interest
4. The Principle of Point of Action
5. The Principle of Leadership Example
6. The Principle of Basic Causes
7. The Principle of the Critical/Vital Few
8. The Principle of the Key Advocate
9. The Principle of Minimum Commitment
10. The Principle of System Integration
11. The Principle of Involvement
12. The Principle of Multiple Causes

KEY QUESTIONS

1. True or False? Managing the control of loss is as much the supervisor's job as it is the chief executive's job.

2. What are the four major functions of management?

3. Define safety.

4. What is the difference between "loss control" and "loss control management"?

5. List the five goals of loss control management.

6. What can managers do to minimize resistance to change from their people?

7. Explain the Principle of Basic Causes.

8. Name this principle: "Programs, projects and ideas are best sold when they bridge the wants and desires of both parties."

9. Discuss the implications of the Principle of Point of Action and the Principle of the Key Advocate.

10. What acronym stands for "management control"? What do each of the letters mean?

11. Name at least 10 of the 20 program elements in the International Safety Rating System.

12. Give several examples of objective, measurable standards.

13. True or False? Accident frequency rates and severity rates are the best measurements of safety management performance.

14. Explain the "maintenance loop" and the "development growth loop" of the management system.

15. What are the steps in developing a management performance audit?

16. Why should measurement of quality be used as well as measurements of quantity?

PRACTICAL APPLICATION SUMMARY

S - For Supervisors
E - For Executives
C - For Safety/Loss Control Coordinators

		S	E	C
1.	Develop and communicate a policy statement reflecting management's commitment to safety, loss control and/or risk management.		x	
2.	Refer to and practice the policy regularly.	x	x	x
3.	Appoint a specific person as safety/loss control coordinator.		x	
4.	Conduct a thorough inventory and evaluation of loss exposures.	x	x	x
5.	Develop an optimum program which identifies the elements and activities to implement the policy.	x	x	x
6.	Establish adequate standards for each element of the program.	x	x	x
7.	Establish techniques and tools for measuring consequences, causes and control of incidents/accidents.		x	x
8.	Coordinate and communicate regular, representative measurements and periodic, comprehensive audits of program performance.			x
9.	Use measurement data for performance feedback and coaching.	x	x	x
10.	Apply enforcement (constructive correction) and reinforcement (commendation) techniques to maintain compliance with performance standards.	x	x	x
11.	Personally participate in program activities such as training, communication, inspection, investigation and general promotion.	x	x	x
12.	Issue a safety/loss control reference manual to guide all levels of management on matters of program policy, procedures and practices.		x	
13.	Specify safety/loss control responsibilities in all job descriptions of management personnel; provide appropriate copy to each person.		x	x
14.	Integrate safety/loss control performance into the performance appraisal and review for each member of management.		x	x
15.	Establish annual safety/loss control objectives for the total organization and each significant segment.	x	x	x
16.	Maintain the program by refining existing standards, measurements and performance evaluations and feedback.		x	x
17.	Broaden and improve the program by upgrading existing standards and/or adding program elements, work activities and standards.		x	x
18.	Ensure a systematic approach to control of accidental loss by carefully considering people, equipment, materials and environment, at the post-contact, contact and pre-contact stages.	x	x	x

CHAPTER 4

ACCIDENT/INCIDENT INVESTIGATION

"On the occasion of every accident that befalls you, remember to turn to yourself and inquire what power you have to turn it to use."
— Epictetus, 60-120 A.D.

INTRODUCTION

Some type of accident investigation is a part of almost every safety program. Yet, the purpose for doing investigations is often poorly understood. As a result, they can degenerate into finger-pointing, blame-fixing and fault-finding exercises which seldom determine the real reasons for what happened or arrive at any effective solutions to the problems involved. Even when the purpose is properly defined, investigations are often poorly done. Perhaps the greatest reason for this is not understanding the many real values to be gained. Effective investigations can:

1. **Describe what happened.** Thorough investigations can sift through sometimes conflicting evidence and arrive at an accurate statement of what really happened.

2. **Determine the real causes.** The sad fact is that a large percentage of investigations are so superficial as to be useless. Because real causes are not identified, there is little or no return on the investment of the time spent doing them.

3. **Decide the risks.** Good investigations provide the basis for deciding the likelihood of recurrence and the potential for major loss — two critical factors in determining the amount of time and money to spend on corrective action.

4. **Develop controls.** Adequate controls to minimize or eliminate a problem can only come from a sound

investigation which has truly solved the problem. Otherwise, the problem will appear again and again but with different symptoms.

5. **Define trends.** Few accidents and incidents are truly isolated events. When a significant number of good reports are analyzed, emerging trends can be identified and dealt with.

6. **Demonstrate concern.** Accidents give people vivid pictures of threats to their well-being. It is assuring to see a prompt, objective investigation in process. Good investigations aid employee relations.

WHAT TO INVESTIGATE

Common sense tells us that any serious loss should be investigated promptly and thoroughly. This includes injury, occupational illness, damage, spill, fire, theft, vandalism, etc. Many people will have interest in such losses and their effects on the organization. Suffering, cost, liability and lost production cause concern. Such losses also point to serious deficiencies in the management system which need to be corrected.

If we think about it, any accident or incident with a *potential* for a serious loss points out the same deficiencies. This was shown in the incident ratio study described in Chapter 2. The cause factors make the incident occur. The severity of the actual loss in each event is often a matter of chance. The loss may vary according to very slight differences in circumstances. So, the practical approach is to investigate every accident and incident to evaluate the loss potential. Then, investigate high potential incidents and accidents in depth to allow adequate control of the problem. Each organization, of course, has to define what losses and potential losses are significant to its resources, its people and its public relations.

WHO SHOULD INVESTIGATE

Which supervisors or other managers should make investigations? Designating the investigator or investigating team is a critical first step. As with any type of problem solving, the person with the most interest in the problem is the obvious first choice. The person with a vital interest finds solutions that work. There is also another important consideration in the choice of the investigator. The person must be able to stay objective. The findings have to be truthful and relevant or the problem isn't really solved.

Let's look at the possible choices: the supervisors, other managers and the staff.

The Line Supervisors

Supervisors are busy people with lots to do. Is it reasonable for them to be involved in investigations? Absolutely! Most of their time is spent in problem solving. Investigating incidents and accidents is not only their responsibility, it is their *right*. Let's look at why this is so:

1. **They have a personal interest.** Supervisors are responsible for specific work and work areas. Incidents affect the work output, quality, cost and every other aspect of the jobs they have to get done. They must deal with the absence of people who are injured or ill, the lack of equipment which has been damaged and the shortage of materials which have been spilled or wasted.

2. **They know the people and conditions.** They plan the use of resources daily. They make some of the decisions that affect selection, training, standards and schedules. They know what things influenced other decisions. They already know much of the information that an investigator has to seek.

3. **They know best how and where to get the information needed.** They know their people. They know "who knows what." They have set up communications with other work groups. They know what records are kept and where they are. They can get accurate information about an incident, or the underlying problem, quickly.

4. **They will start or take the action.** They can determine what will work and what won't, and why. They will follow through better if they are involved in the decisions on remedial actions. It makes good sense for them to be involved from the start so they can do better in the end.

5. **They benefit from investigating.** When the procedure lets the supervisor start the investigation, it has several benefits:

   a. **It shows concern.** Supervisors who do conscientious investigations of accidents and incidents give clear evidence of their concern for people. Failure to do so can create serious morale problems.

   b. **It increases productivity.** Incidents, investigation activities, emergency actions and remedial actions interrupt work. When supervisors do these things efficiently, it minimizes the interruptions. When they do investigations well, it prevents future interruptions.

   c. **It reduces operating costs.** Injuries, absences, damage, waste and the other effects of accidents all cost time and money. Effective investigations spell accident prevention, which in turn spells lower net operating costs, with benefits for everyone.

   d. **It shows that supervisors have control.** People go to the managers *who have control* with their problems and ideas. They follow the instructions of those who are really in charge. Studies of leading organizations also show that people who work for supervisors who are "in control" take greater pride in their work. Upper managers also look for subordinates who have demonstrated control in their responsibilities.

The Middle Managers

Sometimes investigations require participation by middle- or higher-level managers. Typical situations are when:

1. **There is a major loss or a high potential incident.** The seriousness of some situations takes them beyond the supervisor's hands. It would be unfair

to ask supervisors to solve problems beyond their level of knowledge. Also, major losses might get the attention of the government, the public, executives or owners, who should be met by higher-ranking managers.

2. **The circumstances cross into other supervisors' areas.** Accidents, as a rule, should be investigated by the lowest-level manager with authority over the entire operation involved.

3. **The remedial actions have a broad scope or significant costs.** In such cases, it is simply a matter of needing a greater authority to develop the most effective and practical actions. At times a supervisor will start an investigation only to discover that other operational areas could be affected. Then it is appropriate that the investigation responsibility be passed up to a higher level.

In all of these situations, the line supervisors can still give valuable assistance. They can be included as members of investigation teams to make the most of their knowledge and abilities.

Staff Personnel

Occasionally, special knowledge is needed in an investigation. This could be because of a new process, suspected equipment failure, use of hazardous materials, or a complex situation. Parts of the information may need to be obtained or analyzed by a technical expert. Such experts then become *advisors* to the investigators. The problems are still operational ones. So, the people to solve the problem are still the managers at the appropriate levels. Safety personnel are included in the group as technical staff advisors.

BUDGETING TIME FOR INVESTIGATIONS

Where does any manager get the time to make thorough investigations? The time used in investigation is part of the cost of an accident. If that is true, then why spend that time and add the cost? It's not an easy decision. We have to work toward minimizing the costs of accidents. Following Louis Allen's *Principle of Future Characteristics,* the accidents will occur over and over unless there is good investigation to remedy the *basic* causes. Managers simply have to take the time, understanding that, in the long run, inadequate investigations will cost them even more time.

STEPS IN INVESTIGATION

There are a lot of things that have to be done when an accident occurs. These include: care for the injured, prevent secondary accidents like fires and explosions, look over the scene, interview witnesses, check equipment and records, analyze causes, write reports, take corrective actions and get people back to work. All vary with the situation. They also vary with the loss potential. No investigation method can be applied without thought and variation. Successful investigation programs, however, show that some things are common to every good investigation. These are reflected in the flow chart in *Figure 4-1.* They are:

1. **Respond to the emergency promptly and positively.** On seeing or being told of an incident, the supervisor should go to the scene immediately. Take charge and give specific instructions to specific people. Keep those who aren't needed out of the area. Decide if emergency care or damage control are needed; and if people should be evacuated or put back to work. Estimate the loss potential and decide who else should be notified.

2. **Collect pertinent information about the incident.** Ask yourself some fundamental questions: What appears to have happened? Who should be interviewed? What equipment, tools, materials, or people are missing that should be there? What is there that shouldn't be? What things might have failed or malfunctioned? What do you need to know about training, repair, maintenance and other things that are in records?

3. **Analyze all significant causes.** Go through the domino sequence given in Chapter 2. Identify first the damage and injuries. Then define the energy contacts, and the substandard actions and conditions that allowed the contact. Finally, trace the job and personal factors for each action and condition. Sort out what you know, what you need to find out and what you can assume in view of the loss potential.

4. **Develop and take remedial actions.** Systems may need to be shut off or locked out to keep another incident from occurring right away. Barriers may need to be put up. Spills or leaks may need to be cleaned up. Work orders may need to be written. Recommendations may need to be developed for engineering changes, purchase requisitions or some program activity development. Some of these may

Incident Investigation Flow Chart

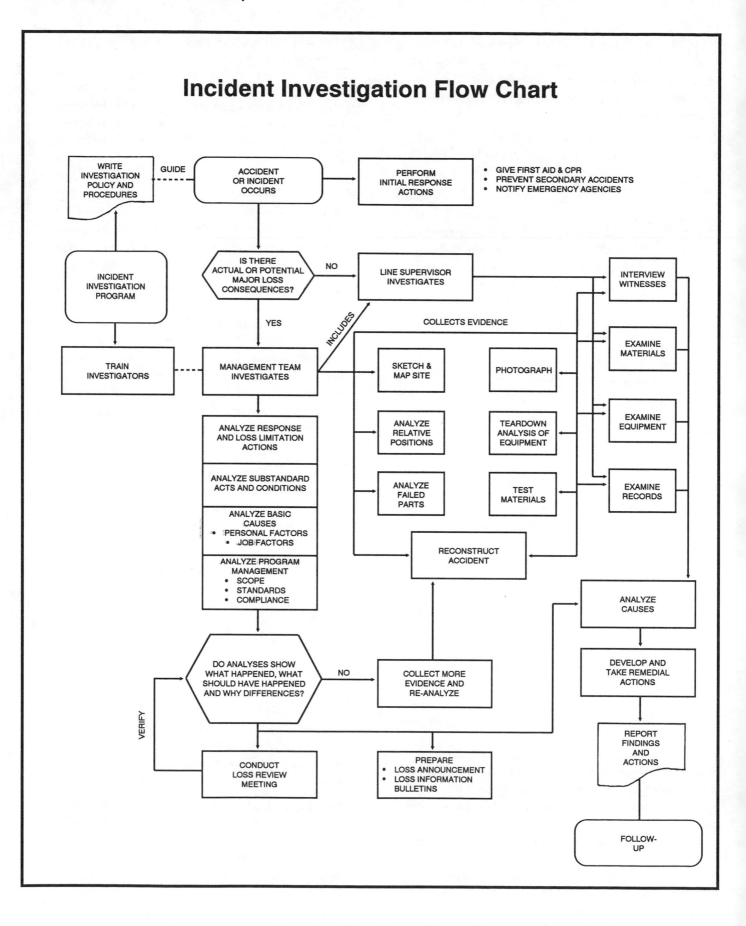

Figure 4-1

need approval for funding, hiring or personnel transfer.

5. **Review findings and recommendations.** Every investigation should be reviewed at the next higher level of management. This is for several reasons. One is to verify that the problem has been defined and solved. Another is to decide who else should know about it. A third is to analyze why the safety program has not given adequate control of the hazard.

6. **Follow through on the effectiveness of the actions.** This is to see that the intended actions are completed. It is also to see that the actions don't have unexpected, undesired effects. After the initial furor over an incident, things are often forgotten as other problems arise. Follow-through is needed for the investigation to be effective.

GET PROMPT REPORTING

Supervisors have to know about accidents before they can be very effective in investigating them. Conscientious supervisors can investigate every accident reported to them and still not have much of the safety picture. Studies have shown that, in the average organization, many incidents with loss potential are never reported. Many, in fact, are hidden to avoid investigation. Results-oriented supervisors realize that they can get the full value from investigation, as a problem-identifying and solving activity, only if people report all incidents as well as accidents to them. To encourage reporting, supervisors need to understand why people often don't report accidents and incidents.

Reasons for Failure to Report

Extensive research and experience indicate that the reasons below are the ones most commonly given by employees for not reporting accidents:

1. **Fear of discipline.** Many people see investigation as faultfinding rather than fact-finding. No one is perfect, and people fear they might get punished for some contributory negligence. While good discipline is always needed, punishment is only a small part of discipline. Good supervisors know that substandard actions are only symptoms of the problem. They don't use their people as scapegoats. But the fact remains that many supervisors haven't been well trained in how to manage people. Their reaction is to criticize and punish, so people keep things from them.

2. **Concern about the record.** The average person doesn't want to spoil the safety record of the group. When group recognition and awards programs are based on accident-free records, the programs discourage good reporting. No one wants to be the person who spoiled the records with some minor injury, damage or incident.

3. **Concern about reputation.** People don't want to be labeled as accident-prone or as a dangerous worker by their supervisors or peers. They try to avoid bringing such negative attention to themselves. The employee who has an incident may feel responsible for it and decide to just be more careful next time.

4. **Fear of medical treatment.** It's surprising how many people dread simple medical care. Many lose fingers, toes or even die because they waited too long to get treatment. Others fear that when they go for simple treatment some major disorder will be found. As a result, their injuries never get reported.

5. **Dislike of medical personnel.** Some people don't want to be treated by certain medical personnel because of sex or personality. This might also be due to a previous experience, or to distorted stories of bad treatment.

6. **Desire to avoid work interruption.** Most employees have a sincere interest in getting the job done. They don't want to stop things to get medical aid or to repair damage.

7. **Desire to keep personal records clear.** Many individual recognition programs and performance appraisals are based on accident-free records. Incident analyses often include personal data. People who don't fully understand these things see reporting incidents as giving themselves black marks and threatening their own job security.

8. **Avoidance of red tape.** Many have heard people say, "Why, you have to answer two dozen questions just to get a band-aid!" Or, people are asked to fill out long forms on incidents they report. Inconvenience is a sure way to stop getting reports, but not to stop accidents.

9. **Concern about the attitude of others.** People value their good relationships with their peers and supervisors. Often, they feel that reporting an inci-

dent would be "telling on" another employee. That would threaten the relationship.

10. **Poor understanding of importance.** Often, people don't see any immediate, positive action after they report problems. They see this as a lack of care. So, they decide not to do anything either. This happens when there is little or no communication on the benefits of incident and hazard reporting, or on the progress of remedial actions.

This list of reasons was developed from various studies. Some employees interviewed in those studies truly believed that they had helped the company by not reporting their accidents.

How to Get Incidents/Accidents Reported

Another outcome of the studies was a guide for supervisors which gives six ways to prompt incident reporting. They are:

1. **React in a positive way.**
   If information can be utilized to prevent or control future incidents that could be of major or even catastrophic dimension, let the worker know the contribution his information is making. If reactions are handled properly and positively, the experience of sharing valuable predictive and preventive data will create an atmosphere of cooperation ... and not of interrogation.

2. **Give more attention to loss control performance.**
   Talk about things like good housekeeping, following safety rules and practices and use of personal protective equipment regularly with the work group. Make more objective records of individuals' compliance, and coach the people on these. The good athletic coach wins games by measuring and improving each individual's skills on specific plays. He realizes that skill improvement gets the desired score. Likewise, improvements in program activities get low accident rates.

3. **Recognize individual performance promptly.**
   Learn to pay more attention to people's actions and practices that contribute to accident prevention. Commend people when they perform to the standards. Give praise as often as criticism. Develop pride in performance instead of fear of failure.

4. **Develop awareness of the value of incident information.**
   Use group meetings and personal contacts to give feedback. Tell people how incidents reported were used to improve safety for everyone. Use these cases as illustrations in employee orientations and training.

5. **Show personal belief by action.**
   Make sure that problems are followed up. There is always something that can be done right away. Do it. Then keep checking on work orders, education, materials, equipment purchases, etc. Verify that the corrective measure works as planned. Check that it is still in use a month later. Show people by your actions that you truly believe in the importance of their incident reports.

6. **Make mountains out of molehills!**
   Emphasize near-accidents and minor accidents, especially those with high potential. Praise good examples whenever possible. Encourage workers to share good examples verbally in group meetings. Publicize preventive actions on bulletin boards and in company newsletters.

SUPERVISOR'S INITIAL ACTIONS

The success of an investigation often comes in the first few moments. A lot of critical things happen in quick order. On the bad side, a lot can be done in these same moments to distort information and doom the investigation to failure. A supervisor who is trained adequately can both reduce the extent of the loss and get the investigation started properly. In a brief time the supervisor can get evidence that might take others days to get.

A supervisor's initial actions vary for every accident. The person on the scene must be the judge of what is critical. These steps are guidelines to apply as appropriate:

1. **Take control at the scene.**
   Incidents make people act differently. They are curious and they want to help. Often they are irrational and do more harm than good. Unless a senior manager is there, the supervisor needs to take charge, directing and approving everything that is done.

2. **Ensure first aid and call for emergency services.**
   People's lives and their well-being come first. If medical help is not close by, give urgently neces-

sary first aid or ensure that it is done. Have someone call for help. Be specific. Tell what service to call, where the telephone is, and where the number can be found. Every telephone should have emergency numbers posted on or close to it to help get prompt response.

3. **Control potential secondary accidents.**
The explosion that follows a puncture, the collapse that follows an impact, the absentminded action that follows a minor trauma are common examples. Secondary accidents are usually even more serious because the normal controls over the loss exposure have been weakened by the incident. Positive, temporary actions need to be taken after quick, but careful, thought of the consequences.

4. **Identify sources of evidence at the scene.**
Things can change quickly and information lost forever. Items can be moved during emergency response or attempt at rescue work. People leave the scene. They take equipment and materials with them. Light, ventilation, sound and other conditions change. Supervisors need to notice these things while taking other initial actions.

5. **Preserve evidence from alteration or removal.**
If there seems to be a significant loss potential, good investigation is more important than getting back to work. Supervisors have authority to keep things from being moved. They should also keep people away from the accident site so nothing is disturbed before they get to look it over.

6. **Investigate to determine the loss potential.**
It's easy to see how badly people are hurt and property is damaged. That's important, but what *could* happen is vital to future loss prevention. Supervisors should make a prompt appraisal of how bad the incident could have been and how likely it is to occur again. Then they can decide if the investigation is over their heads.

7. **Notify appropriate managers.**
Some managers may need just a courtesy notification. Others may need to be on the scene right away. This varies with everything from management philosophy to the process or materials involved. A notification procedure provides guidelines for these decisions.

GATHERING INFORMATION

A lot of information is available on every accident and incident. The supervisor's problem is to find and concentrate on the most important. A few sources will usually give supervisors what they need to know.

Get "The Big Picture" First

It's always a good idea to look over the scene and the environment around it. This gives a mental picture as you seek and discuss information. "The big picture" is an orientation to what elements of people, equipment, materials and environment are involved. From these, questions that need to be answered will come to mind. As information is gathered, the pieces start to fit into place in the picture. A few minutes of visual orientation gives supervisors a better idea of where to start and what information to seek. This saves a lot of hours later on.

Interviewing Witnesses

A witness is anyone who knows something related to what happened. Some are eyewitnesses who saw the incident happen. Others are the people involved. Still others are people who designed facilities, ordered materials, trained operators, etc. A few questions should identify who these various witnesses are. Experience has shown that it is best to start with eyewitnesses and the people involved. These are the most likely to know details of what happened. They are also the most likely to forget these details if not questioned promptly. The first details from these witnesses give the supervisor the symptoms of the problem. They are the starting point on the path to basic causes.

The Interview

People's memories as well as their willingness to talk can be affected by the way they are questioned. Here again, experience has shown a method that usually works best.

1. **Interview separately.**
Each interview should be as private as possible. A courteous explanation that each person will be given a chance to talk will usually be accepted without taking offense. No one is a perfect observer or has instant recall. Separate interviews are important to keep people from influencing each other's memories. When there are significant differences of opinion, follow-up interviews may be needed. That doesn't make the individual interview invalid.

2. Interview in an appropriate place.

If the incident site is not dangerous or uncomfortable, interview on the spot. Being at the scene, the witness can look around to help him or her remember details. If the site isn't appropriate, a private room or corner may be used. The place should let the supervisor and witness talk as two people on equal levels. Too often, the busy supervisor calls the witness to his or her desk and the interview deteriorates to an interrogation or cross-examination.

3. Put the person at ease.

This is to help "free up" the person's mind. It is critical to the successful interview. The person may be physically hurt, or may be anxious or fearful. Or, some personal problem, like a spouse waiting in the parking lot, may be occupying the person's mind. Usually, a simple, sincere inquiry about the person's condition is enough. That should be followed with a brief assurance that the purpose of the investigation is to find and correct the basic problems. A friendly, understanding manner can work miracles in setting up an atmosphere for a cooperative discussion. Don't overlook body language! Don't threaten the person by standing over or too close to him.

4. Get the individual's version.

Start the interview with, "Would you please tell me about...?" Let the person tell things as he or she remembers them. Don't interrupt unless the comments get off the subject. Don't make value judgments like, "that sure was the wrong thing to do!"

5. Ask necessary questions at the right time.

These can be used to prompt more detail in comments, or to seek answers to questions that came to mind while looking at the site or listening to the witness. Avoid asking questions in a way that leads the witness, puts the witness on the defensive or can be answered simply "yes" or "no." These types of questions don't prompt a person's memory. They distort the evidence. Near the end of the interview you may want to ask some control questions. Ask what attracted the person's attention to the incident. Also ask a few questions that you know the answer to. These can help evaluate whether a person really saw what happened and also his or her powers of observations.

6. Give the witness some feedback.

Put key points into your own words and repeat them. This has several values. First, it assures that you understood what was said. Second, it gives the witness a chance to correct a detail. Third, it provides *active* listening by interviewer and witness. It also gives the witness a chance to collect thoughts.

7. Record critical information quickly.

Make notes of key points. You can't remember everything accurately. Seeing you taking notes assures the witness that you really are interested. Avoid using recorders. They make people uncomfortable. If needed for legal purposes, ask the witness to write a statement, after the interview. Or, you can make a statement from the interview and ask the witness to sign it.

8. Use visual aids.

If you aren't interviewing on-site, use sketches, blueprints, models or instant-print photographs. These help witnesses sort out relevant facts in their minds.

9. End on a positive note.

Thank the person for time and effort. If some facts given are particularly useful, let the witness know. Ask for ideas on how similar incidents can be prevented. Give credit and feedback when ideas are used.

10. Keep the line open.

Tell the witness to talk to you if he or she thinks of anything else. No piece of information is too small to be considered. Follow up with questions if there are conflicts between different witnesses' comments.

Reenactment

During an investigation, a supervisor might ask workers to show what they mean or how it happened. This is asking for trouble. A demonstration can help visualize the incident; but, too often, it results in a repeated injury or in turning a minor incident into a serious loss. That happens often enough to justify a few comments.

Incident reenactment should be used only:

1. **When the information cannot be gained in another way.**

2. **When it is vital to the development of remedial actions.**

3. **When it is absolutely necessary to verify critical facts about the incident.**

When circumstances justify a reenactment, the following methods may help control the dangers:

1. Have the best qualified person available observe the reenactment and stop it if advisable, or if things are questionable.

2. Have the worker first explain, step by step, what happened — **tell but not show.** This is to help give you and the observer insight into the events leading up to the incident.

3. Be sure that things are shut down, locked out, blanked off, bled off, propped up, etc., as appropriate, to control any source of energy that might be involved.

4. Have the worker go through the motions only, as he or she retells the event step-by-step. Make sure the worker understands that nothing is to be touched or operated.

5. Have the worker act out the accident up to, but not including, that last step before the accident occurred. Make sure he or she understands that this is to be slow motion, step-by-step. The worker tells what the step is, the observer approves it and you tell the worker it is all right to do it. Each time, before approving, confirm that this was not the last step. This step-by-step method will reduce the chance of another accident, as well as aid in understanding what happened.

6. Stop the reenactment just as soon as you get the information you need.

Before starting a reenactment, make sure that the person is emotionally fit to cooperate and will respond to your instruction. Ask if there is any objection to doing a reenactment. When there has been a severe loss or a close call, people often become upset. They may be preoccupied and not be able to control their actions.

Sketches and Maps

Drawings help other people visualize what happened. Sketches document important information. The location of people involved, and of key facilities and equipment, can be noted with simple sketches of the site. These don't have to be works of art. A simple sketch takes only a few minutes. It can save a lot of time later when interviewing the witness, analyzing the causes, or writing the report. Keep the sketch simple. Include only key things that are factors in the incident. Label them clearly.

For major accidents, a scale map may be needed. Accurate drawings are useful for legal purposes. For these, careful measurements must be made at the accident site. Graph paper can be used to draw the site to scale. Each item should be measured from at least two reference points to document its exact position.

Equipment Examination

A good basic investigation requires a look at the tools, equipment and materials that people were using. Often, people's actions were prompted by worn or improper equipment. The supervisor doesn't have to be a technical expert to do this. A good supervisor knows what people need to do the job productively and safely. There are standards for usable condition, for guards, safety features, hazard warning labels, etc. Check for these. If things don't look right, you may need to ask a technical expert from engineering or safety to look at them also.

Records Check

Logs, schedules, personnel training records and other files have information that can help identify the basic causes of problems. These are seldom at the scene of an accident, so supervisors often overlook them. While there are many possible sources of information in records, a few convenient ones will give supervisors most of what they need. For example:

1. **Training records.** When a person hasn't followed a safety rule, hasn't used the right procedure or equipment, etc., check to see if the person ever got appropriate job instruction.

2. **Maintenance logs/records.** When equipment appears to be worn out or previously damaged, check to see if there was proper service and repair.

3. **Schedules.** When people are trying to operate and service equipment at the same time, or there are other activities going on that cause congestion or interference, check to see if there is schedule planning.

4. **Job procedures and practices.** Unclear or out-of-date procedures can lead to improper actions. Check if there were current standards for the job being done.

Accident Photography

Photos of accident scenes are very useful. They can reveal much about an accident and save hours of note-taking and drawing. They can also be useful to illustrate reports and save time in writing. Also, they are useful in employee training. Most supervisors won't have cameras convenient to use. However, upper managers should make plans for photographs of major losses and of incidents and minor accidents with serious loss potential. Three tips for more useful photographs of safety problems are:

1. Photograph the scene from all sides. This helps orient people to the incident.

2. Use a long/medium/close-up sequence. First, take a photo to show the general scene. Then move in to show the equipment or work station. Then get a close-up of the deficiency or damage you want to show. Put a pencil or other object of known size in the close-up to give correct perspective. This method lets the pictures tell their own story.

3. Get the correct exposure. Know how to set the cameras, to use the flash and to get light readings. If you haven't practiced using the camera, make good notes and sketches in case the pictures don't turn out well.

Material Failure Analysis

Sometimes part of the problem is in the failure of equipment or structures. Again, these are cases with high loss potential. They are investigated by an upper manager, and usually with technical assistance. Overloading, material defects, improper construction, inadequate servicing and other forms of abuse leave clues. Supervisors can learn to recognize the clues most likely to be found in their work area. That helps make sure such parts get saved for a technical examination.

ANALYZING ACCIDENT/INCIDENT CAUSES

Chapter 2 gave the causes of accidents and incidents in the causation model. Even if you learned those by heart you still need an analysis method. Otherwise, as you look over the information you've gathered, you'll pick the few most obvious causes. These will usually be some of the substandard actions and conditions. You'll have found the symptoms but not the problems.

A causal factor outline can help you do a better job of cause analysis, and also make it easier.

Causal Factor Outline

This is simply writing down causal factors that tie together. It's much like you'd organize notes for a safety talk or staff meeting.

1. Write down each loss. Make a list of the injuries, illnesses, damages, spills, etc. You'll need to list these for your investigation report, so this serves a double purpose. To make it a little easier, put each loss at the top of a sheet of memo paper.

2. Under each loss, write all the contacts with forms of energy or substances that were responsible for the loss. Then write down any inadequate post-contact controls of loss. For example:

   Hand amputated
   palm punctured by screwdriver blade
   wound not cleaned

   Leave several lines of space beneath each factor for further listings of causes.

3. Under each contact factor, list the substandard actions and conditions that created it. To continue the same example:

   Palm punctured by screwdriver blade
   wrong size screwdriver used
   screwdriver blade worn
   no pilot hole for screw made in hard material
   holding screw with palm exposed
   reusing dulled screw
   rushing to complete job at end of shift
   and

   Wound not cleaned
   no plant nurse
   no plant medical station
   no first aid kits on job site
   supervisor did not give first aid
   employee washed hand in locker room
   employee decided to treat wound at home

4. Under each substandard action or condition list all the basic causes which prompted it. To continue the example further:

   Wrong size screwdriver used
   inadequate tool selection—no assessment to tool needs
   inadequate work standards—no published standards on safe tool use

inadequate knowledge—no basic education on tool selection and use

inadequate leadership—no identification of loss exposures

Here we've seen how one loss branched into one contact and one inadequate post-contact control factor. These, in turn, branched into 12 symptoms and, if pursued, would branch into about 30 basic causes. With each basic cause identified it is now possible to select, within the constraints of time and budget, what corrections will do the most to prevent not only that specific accident but also ones similar to it. *Figure 4-7* (at the end of this chapter) lists the 14 categories of personal factors and job factors and their specific aspects.

5. During the managerial review of the investigation, the next level manager should carry the analysis one more step — an examination of the program, its standards and compliance with those standards. This helps bridge this gulf between a systematic examination of basic causes and an exploration of the program activities which might have prevented them.

TAKING REMEDIAL ACTIONS

There are many ways to take care of each basic cause. Some ways lower the likelihood of the incident occurring. Others reduce the potential severity of the injury or damage. Each possible action also has a different degree of effect, a different reliability, a different cost, and different side effects. These are discussed in detail in the chapter on inspections.

Temporary Actions

As they respond to and investigate incidents, supervisors should keep in mind the question, "What can I do right now to keep this from happening again?" Most temporary actions correct only the symptoms — the substandard actions and conditions. There's nothing wrong with that. It's a good place to start and it needs to be done. The worn-out tool needs to be replaced; the hole needs to be covered or filled; the guard needs to be replaced; the cluttered floor needs to be cleaned up. But supervisors must remember that, while necessary, these aren't the final actions. They don't remedy the basic problems.

Temporary actions can also begin to deal with basic causes. For example, if there's a lack of knowledge, give some immediate re-instruction. One doesn't have to wait until the training program is revised. Good temporary actions give sort of a one-two punch.

Permanent Actions

Permanent actions are needed to truly solve the problem. These remedy the personal factors and job factors of the basic causes. They also treat the oversights and omissions in programs, standards and compliance. Of course, time and materials are usually needed. So, the action plan usually starts with recommendations to upper managers.

A **risk evaluation** will help guide the investigator in making practical recommendations. The degree of risk in a particular situation is a combination of its potential severity and its likelihood of occurrence. The **potential severity** of an accident or incident is not determined just by what happened. It is determined by what the consequences are likely to be if it happens again. This is because an undesirable event that produced only minor loss may have the potential for major loss should it happen again. For instance, a grinding wheel that exploded may have produced only a minor loss, but it has the realistic potential to cause a major injury or a fatality as well as significant property damage. Therefore, it has high **potential** severity. **Probability of recurrence** is determined by asking how likely the accident or incident is to occur again if no corrective action is taken.

Thus, each recommendation should be guided by the risk involved in the situation and how much the recommended action reduces it. Accidents and incidents which have a high severity potential and high likelihood of happening again will receive more extensive corrective action than those with a low severity potential and a low likelihood of ever occurring again. Corrective actions that significantly reduce one or both of these factors, i.e., make it less likely to recur or reduce the severity if it does recur, are of greater value than corrective actions which have small impact on these factors. Risk evaluation is a critical tool in making decisions and setting priorities.

WRITING THE INVESTIGATION REPORT

The report puts the investigation all together in a brief summary. It communicates the critical facts to people who have to act on them. It makes a record which has many uses in the loss control program. Also, it gives feedback to help appraise supervisor's performance in problem solving.

A Standard Form

Most organizations have a standard investigation report form. A sample modern form is shown in *Figure 4-2*. Using a standard form has several benefits:

1. It raises all the basic questions that should be answered by the investigation. These are: What was the loss? What were the causes? What is the loss potential? What happened? Where? How? What was done to control the loss exposures? What needs to be done? Is the report complete and accurate?

2. It provides consistency in data reported. That aids managers' reviews. It prompts sharing of information with others in the organization. Finally, it allows analysis for trends and that helps program management.

3. It provides follow-up on action plans. It gives the status of actions in one convenient record.

4. A well-designed form also accommodates investigations of all types of losses. The simpler the form, the better it meets this goal.

Writing a Good Report

One doesn't have to be a literary wizard to write a good investigation report. All you need to do is communicate. The key to that is to be clear and simple. Use words that are common, short and specific. Some tips for writing the main sections of the report are:

1. **Identifying information.** Fill in all spaces. This gives details, so use specific words and numbers.

2. **Evaluation.** What was the real potential for loss (not just what happened)? If no corrective action is taken, how often could it be expected to occur?

3. **Description.** Tell what you have decided actually happened: what actions led up to the incident, the contact and what was done post-contact to reduce the loss.

4. **Cause analysis.** List the symptoms (the substandard actions and conditions) and the basic causes (the job and personal factors). Give a few words explaining each cause. In listing basic causes, list first those that made the greatest contribution to the accident.

5. **Action plan.** Write first in a short sentence or a few words what was done right away. Then write your recommendations. Put them in the same order as the basic causes so they will be easier to follow. If the recommendations call for work orders, purchase requests or other things set up in a company format, write these out and attach them. Make it easy for the senior manager to approve your ideas.

Timely Reporting

It's critical to start an investigation as soon as possible. It's just as important to get the report written and submitted promptly. Investigators forget details just as quickly as witnesses. Studies have shown that the most complete reports, with the best cause analyses, were those written as soon as the investigations were finished. Prompt reports also help get information to other supervisors who can then use it to prevent similar incidents.

In most cases, supervisors' reports should be submitted to middle management within one work day of the incident. If tests are needed or some information isn't available right away, a temporary report should be made. An amended report can be made when the information is ready. The quality of the prompt report usually pays for the effort of amending it later.

REPORT REVIEWS

Every investigation report should be reviewed by the next level manager. This is for several reasons.

1. It allows an objective pair of eyes to look at the findings and recommendations. The reviewer may spot it when the supervisor has jumped to a conclusion that is not supported by the facts. The reviewer can also notice when thoughts and reasonings are not explained well.

2. It prompts thoroughness and accuracy. The middle manager doesn't know all the facts. But, in reviewing the report, he or she can sense when something doesn't seem quite right for the circumstances.

3. It prompts sharing of the report information. Middle managers know the entire operation well. They can perceive when other supervisors might have the same problems. They can also pass ideas along quickly or adapt them to other operations.

INVESTIGATION REPORT

REPORT QUALITY SCORE

1. COMPANY OR DIVISION Western Box Company		2. DEPARTMENT Sheet and Paint			
3. LOCATION OF INCIDENT #2 Shipping Dept. South Wall, Col. 20B		4. DATE OF INCIDENT 4/18/19—	5. TIME 3:20 / PM	6. DATE OF REPORT 4/18/19—	(20)

IDENTIFYING INFORMATION

INJURY OR ILLNESS		PROPERTY DAMAGE	OTHER ACTUAL OR POTENTIAL LOSS
7. INJURED'S NAME Robert K. Berry		14. PROPERTY DAMAGE Three machine guards	18. TYPE
8. PART OF BODY upper l. leg	9. DAYS LOST 13	15. NATURE OF DAMAGE Badly bent	19. COST
10. NATURE OF INJURY OR ILLNESS Compound fracture		16. COST 125.00 / ESTIMATED ACTUAL 110.00	20. NATURE OF LOSS
11. OBJECT EQUIPMENT SUBSTANCE INFLICTING HARM Misc. parts on floor		17. OBJECT/EQUIPMENT/SUBSTANCE INFLICTING DAMAGE Worker falling on parts	21. OBJECT/EQUIPMENT/SUBSTANCE RELATED
12. OCCUPATION Painter	13. EXPERIENCE 8 Years	22. PERSON IN CONTROL OF ACTIVITY AT TIME OF OCCURRENCE Robert K. Berry	(10)

RISK

EVALUATION OF LOSS POTENTIAL IF NOT CORRECTED	23. LOSS SEVERITY POTENTIAL ☒MAJOR ☐SERIOUS ☐MINOR	24. PROBABILITY OF OCCURRENCE ☐FREQUENT ☒OCCASIONAL ☐SELDOM	(5)

DESCRIPTION

25. DESCRIBE HOW THE EVENT OCCURRED

Bob was reaching out with a paint brush while standing on the third rung from the top of a 20' ladder section, the top section of a 40' extension ladder. He was attemptimg to paint a small unpainted area of the oxygen pipe running along the south wall of the #2 shipping department. He lost his balance as the bottom of the ladder started slipping and fell approximately 10' to the top of a pile of miscellaneous parts and machine guards piled on the floor.

(15)

CAUSE ANALYSIS

26. IMMEDIATE CAUSES: WHAT SUBSTANDARD ACTIONS AND CONDITIONS CAUSED OR COULD CAUSE THE EVENT?

Attempting to reach too far. Ladder positioned at too great an angle, probably due to disorderly storage under the pipe. The ladder did not have safety shoes and was not tied off to the pipe since the tie-off rope was missing. Also, Bob was not using his safety belt.

27. BASIC CAUSES: WHAT SPECIFIC PERSONAL OR JOB FACTORS CAUSED OR COULD CAUSE THIS EVENT? CHECK ON BACK, EXPLAIN HERE.

A check indicates that Bob's last review of ladder rules and standard practices was over 3 years ago. There are no recorded job observations in Bob's file and his record is free of disciplinary actions. Ladder inspections have been informal in the past unless picked up in general inspections. The ladder section was not stenciled with the required warning against using it alone.

(15)

ACTION PLAN

28. REMEDIAL ACTIONS: WHAT HAS AND/OR SHOULD BE DONE TO CONTROL THE CAUSES LISTED?

1. Rule and standard practice review with painters will be completed within 30 days. 2. All ladders were inspected immediately after the accident and a monthly ladder inspection will be made and recorded thereafter. 3. A paste-in rule is being prepared requesting painters to inspect their equipment daily before use and to date and sign the attached tab. 4. Our department is meeting with Carl Doan of "Safety This Week" to institute a planned job observation program. 5. A separate report on housekeeping is being prepared.

(30)

29. SIGNATURE OF INVESTIGATOR Ann Greene		30. FOLLOW-UP: CIRCLE NUMBER FOR TEMPORARY, X OUT FOR FINAL ACTION/DATE		
31. SIGNATURE OF REVIEWER Jim Stone	32. DATE 4/18/19—	1. ___ 2. ✗ 4/18/19—	3. ___ 4. ✗ 4/21/19—	5. ___ 6. ___

TOTAL SCORE ___

(5)

Figure 4-2

CAUSE CHECKLIST

26A. CODING OF IMMEDIATE CAUSES: CHECK ALL APPLICABLE

SUBSTANDARD ACTIONS
- [ ] 1. Operating equipment without authority
- [ ] 2. Failure to warn
- [ ] 3. Failure to secure
- [ ] 4. Operating at improper speed
- [ ] 5. Making safety devices inoperable
- [ ] 6. Removing safety devices
- [ ] 7. Using defective equipment
- [ ] 8. Using equipment improperly
- [ ] 9. Failing to use personal protective equipment properly
- [ ] 10. Improper loading
- [ ] 11. Improper placement
- [ ] 12. Improper lifting
- [ ] 13. Improper position for task
- [ ] 14. Servicing equipment in operation
- [ ] 15. Horseplay
- [ ] 16. Under influence of alcohol and/or other drugs

SUBSTANDARD CONDITIONS
- [ ] 1. Inadequate guards or barriers
- [ ] 2. Inadequate or improper protective equipment
- [ ] 3. Defective tools, equipment or materials
- [ ] 4. Congestion or restricted action
- [ ] 5. Inadequate warning system
- [ ] 6. Fire and explosion hazards
- [ ] 7. Poor housekeeping; disorder
- [ ] 8. Hazardous environmental conditions; gases, dusts, smokes, fumes, vapors
- [ ] 9. Noise exposures
- [ ] 10. Radiation exposures
- [ ] 11. High or low temperature exposures
- [ ] 12. Inadequate or excess illumination
- [ ] 13. Inadequate ventilation

27A. CODING OF BASIC CAUSES:

PERSONAL FACTORS
- [ ] 1. Inadequate capability
- [ ] 2. Lack of knowledge
- [ ] 3. Lack of skill
- [ ] 4. Stress
- [ ] 5. Improper motivation

JOB FACTORS
- [ ] 1. Inad. leadership/ supervision
- [ ] 2. Inad. engineering
- [ ] 3. Inad. purchasing
- [ ] 4. Inad. maintenance
- [ ] 5. Inad. tools/equipment
- [ ] 6. Inad. work standards
- [ ] 7. Wear and tear
- [ ] 8. Abuse or misuse

33. TYPE OF CONTACT
- [ ] 1. Struck against
- [ ] 2. Struck by
- [ ] 3. Caught in
- [ ] 4. Caught on
- [ ] 5. Caught between
- [ ] 6. Slip
- [ ] 7. Fall on same level
- [ ] 8. Fall to below
- [ ] 9. Overexertion

CONTACT WITH:
- [ ] 10. Electricity
- [ ] 11. Heat
- [ ] 12. Cold
- [ ] 13. Radiation
- [ ] 14. Caustics
- [ ] 15. Noise
- [ ] 16. Toxic or noxious substances

CODING FOR INCIDENT ANALYSIS
- 1. LOCATION [ ]
- 5. TIME OF DAY [ ]
- 8. INJURY TYPE [ ]
- 10. SEVERITY [ ]
- 11. AGENCY [ ]
- 12. OCCUPATION [ ]
- 13. EXPERIENCE [ ]
- 16. PROPERTY TYPE [ ]
- 18. COST [ ]
- 19. AGENCY [ ]
- 26. SUBSTD. ACTIONS [ ] [ ]
- 26. SUBSTD. CONDTS. [ ] [ ]
- 27. PERSONAL FACTORS [ ] [ ]
- 27. JOB FACTORS [ ] [ ]

REVIEW

34. REVIEWER'S REACTIONS TO THE INVESTIGATOR'S ANALYSIS OF THE BASIC CAUSES OF THIS ACCIDENT AND THE REMEDIAL ACTIONS DIRECTED AT POSSIBLE INADEQUACIES IN THE PROGRAM, ITS STANDARDS OR COMPLIANCE TO THE STANDARDS.

_____

_____

_____

_____

_____

35. SIGNATURE	36. TITLE	37. DATE

SKETCH OF SITE INVOLVED/CONTINUATION OF EXPLANATION: LIST NUMBER OF REPORT ITEM BEING CONTINUED

Figure 4-2 (Continued)

4. It carries the analysis from the findings of basic causes through the identification of inadequacies in programs, standards and compliance. Realistically, supervisors are reluctant to criticize the organization's program. The next level manager can provide the follow-through needed for an effective program.

5. It provides an opportunity for the middle manager to apply his or her greater experience and wider knowledge to the solution of the problems revealed by the accident.

6. It provides an opportunity to give appropriate commendation to supervisors who do good investigations or to give specific guidance in how to improve performance in this critical area.

Measurement of Report Quality

As a report is reviewed by the next level manager, its quality will naturally be evaluated. Also, in many organizations the safety professional will use a measurement system like the one illustrated in *Figure 4-3*. The measurement is made by dividing the report into sections and setting value factors for each section. The report is rated as follows:

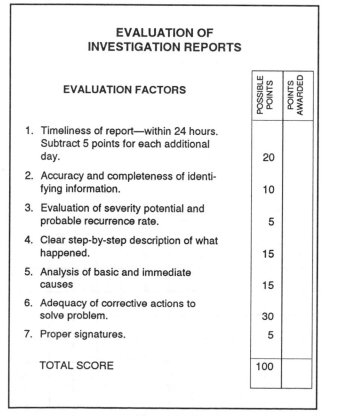

EVALUATION OF INVESTIGATION REPORTS

EVALUATION FACTORS	POSSIBLE POINTS	POINTS AWARDED
1. Timeliness of report—within 24 hours. Subtract 5 points for each additional day.	20	
2. Accuracy and completeness of identifying information.	10	
3. Evaluation of severity potential and probable recurrence rate.	5	
4. Clear step-by-step description of what happened.	15	
5. Analysis of basic and immediate causes	15	
6. Adequacy of corrective actions to solve problem.	30	
7. Proper signatures.	5	
TOTAL SCORE	100	

Figure 4-3

1. **Identifying information.** Give the report up to 10 points if all boxes are filled in and the information seems to be accurate.

2. **Loss potential evaluation.** Give up to 5 points for a correct evaluation of how bad the loss could have been, and how often the incident could occur if nothing is done about the causes.

3. **Description.** Give the report up to 15 points on clarity. Does the description tell what happened? It should tell, step-by-step, the actions, conditions and decisions that led to the incident. It should describe the energy contact. It should say what emergency care and damage control followed.

4. **Cause analysis.** Give the report up to 15 points for listing and describing all significant immediate causes and basic causes. Allocate about 5 points for substandard actions and conditions, and about 10 points for personal and job factors. The cause statement should say what each basic cause was and why it existed. For example, "a lack of knowledge of how to lock out a machine because the procedure was overlooked in the job training lesson plan."

5. **Remedial action plan.** Give up to 30 points on the adequacy of temporary actions taken and the suitability of recommendations. The actions should correct the substandard practices and conditions which are symptoms of the problem. Most of the reviewer's interest, and most of the points given, should go to solutions to the personal factors and job factors.

6. **Timeliness of reporting.** Give 20 points if the report is submitted within one workday after the incident. Subtract 5 points for each day late, down to a score of 0 if four days late.

7. **Signatures.** Give 5 points if the report is properly dated and signed.

This method of report reviews helps to objectively identify good reports for commendations, specify deficiencies for improvement and point out supervisors' problem-solving weaknesses for personal counseling.

UPPER MANAGEMENT ACTIONS

Several critical actions in investigation must come from a member of higher management. Without these actions, investigations have very little real effect. From upper managers come budgets, priorities, special reviews and program changes.

Assessing Priorities

Every day there are demands for use of the organization's people, property and financial resources. Remedial actions requested in investigation reports compete with the other needs. The estimated loss potential gives a good basis for setting priorities for actions, whether done by the supervisor's work crew or through work orders, purchase orders or contracts. The highest priority should go to remedial actions for undesired events with a major/frequent risk evaluation. Reports with this combination of ratings should be routed to appropriate upper managers for their attention to the remedial actions.

Sharing Accident and Incident Information

One of the most valuable actions by middle and upper managers is the wide sharing of accident and incident information. As with communicable diseases, the symptoms of safety problems are not isolated in small areas of the organization. Many supervisors will have the same potential problems because the symptoms are spread through the organization. The upper managers know what employees are doing and what they have to work with. When accidents are reported adequately, these managers can quickly perceive similar problems and prompt actions before there are other losses.

A tool for information sharing is the Accident/Incident Announcement. A typical form for this is shown in *Figure 4-4*. The form gives critical information about the incident. It tells managers what common problems to look for. It is brief and to the point. This saves reading time and avoids misunderstanding. Copies of reports should not be sent out in place of reviews. Reports contain a lot of record detail and findings which cloud the message. The loss review form can be used by an incident investigation team or a reviewer to give information that should be shared. It can also be made up for a senior manager to direct critical actions throughout the organization. Another use is an action memo for follow-up discussion at a management meeting.

Accident/incident information can be promptly shared with employees by means of bulletin boards or in meetings. A prompt announcement following a major loss or a high potential incident has several benefits. It helps employee relations by giving the facts before the "rumor mill" produces distortions of them. It points out general safety problems so that responsible management and/or other employees can take general actions, as indicated by the information available at that time, to avoid similar problems. Also, it increases safety awareness by reinforcing information given in employee orientation and training programs.

Assessing Program Inadequacies

Another task for the middle or upper manager reviewing the report is to assess why the safety program failed to control the loss. This is taking the analysis to the final step. It is rather unrealistic to expect a line supervisor to critique the program set by upper management. It must be established whether each basic cause was due to an inadequate program, inadequate standards or inadequate compliance with the standards.

Personal Involvement on the Scene

A common practice in the organizations that have effective loss control programs is to have the department head go immediately to the scene of any major accident, regardless of the time of day. This has several purposes and benefits:

1. It demonstrates management's interest in the protection of employees and property.

2. It provides the authority needed for decisions to shut down major operations for the investigation or because of dangers existing in the area.

3. It gives access to the resources of people and equipment that may be needed for an investigation team.

4. It gives upper management knowledge of the facts and circumstances.

Formal Investigation Reviews

After accidents or incidents with either a major loss or a major loss potential, a department head or higher-level executive may hold a loss review meeting. Such a meeting can have several major benefits. It helps ensure that the investigation and remedial actions are adequate. Line managers from the supervisor up are included to give their reports or findings and actions. Representatives from groups such as safety, personnel, engineering, purchasing and maintenance are usually invited to review what happened from their functional point of view.

ACCIDENT/INCIDENT ANNOUNCEMENT

☒ PERSONAL INJURY ☒ PROPERTY DAMAGE ☐ PROCESS LOSS	LOCATION #2 Shipping Dept. South Wall Col. 20B		
	DEPARTMENT/DIVISION Sheet and Paint		DATE 4/8/19—

NATURE OF LOSS

APPARENT NATURE AND EXTENT OF INJURY, DAMAGE, PROCESS LOSS OR POTENTIAL LOSS:

Compound fracture of upper left leg.
Three machine guards badly bent.

DESCRIPTION OF INCIDENT

INFORMATION AVAILABLE AT THIS TIME:

Employee was reaching out with a paint brush while standing near the top of a 20 ft. section of an extension ladder. He lost his balance as the bottom of the ladder started slipping and fell approximately 10 feet to a pile of machine guards and spare parts stored beneath where he was working.

APPARENT CAUSES

CAUSES APPARENT AT THIS TIME:

It seems apparent that the worker was reaching from the ladder which may have contributed to the ladder leg's slipping. Since the upper section of the extension ladder was being used, it was not equipped with safety feet. Additional factors would seem to have contributed to loss results. Interviews are incomplete at this time.

Figure 4-4

Another major benefit is that a review meeting provides an opportunity to look at the entire safety and loss control program. Depending on the frequency of reviews for a particular organization, there may be evidence of deterioration of the management system and need for an analysis of the whole program. Other available barometers of general safety performance should be examined as an important aspect of the review.

A typical agenda for a loss investigation review meeting is:

1. **Briefing on the accident.** The supervisor or senior member of the investigation team describes the accident, explains the findings of immediate and basic causes and presents the action plan.

2. **Remedial actions status.** Beginning with the supervisor, operational managers report in turn on concurrence with the action plan and give the status of actions they have taken or started. Actions needing approval of the senior manager, or needing staff action or funding, are highlighted.

3. **Discussions and questions.** Meeting participants examine actions taken and other possible measures.

4. **Directions and priorities.** The senior manager conducting the meeting gives decisions on additional actions to be taken and on priorities for actions not yet completed.

5. **Incident review report.** Prepare a summary of the investigation review with statements of actions to be taken. Distribute to appropriate managers for action and feedback. See *Figure 4-5* for an example.

6. **Program analysis.** It may be appropriate to delve into the effectiveness of the safety program itself. Questions can be raised about the adequacy of the program, it standards and compliance to standards.

7. **Follow-up.** Actions directed by the senior manager are followed up with progress reports to review committee members.

DATA ANALYSIS

Even after methodical investigation and careful review, there is still another way to get more information out of accidents and incidents. That way is to analyze certain data for trends. Trend analyses can unmask problems. They can show, for instance, that large numbers of incidents involve the use of certain materials or equipment, involve people with certain levels of experience, or occur at certain times of the workday. Chapter 2 cited a study which shows that there were 600 near-accidents for every accident in the study. Within that large number of incidents are trends pointing to the serious loss exposures.

Common Categories for Analysis

There are many subjects for incident/accident analysis. The ones chosen will depend on several factors: the staff capability to work up analyses, the training in the use of analyses that will be given to managers and the overall level of risk. Some of the common or most useful categories are:

1. **Accident frequency and severity rates by organization and department.** These numbers show how many accidents occur, or how many days are lost, per base number of days worked. They show the history of accidents and give the trend from year to year. That is important; but overall, the only truth they tell is who is honestly reporting accidents. Other data on degree or risk is needed before these numbers are meaningful.

2. **Accident trends by cause factor.** More useful for positive action are compilations of the number of times each of the basic factors is a cause. The major basic cause factors are given in the first column of the cause analysis chart in Chapter 2. When the majority of causes fall into a few categories it gives clues to trends. For example, a number of "Lack of Knowledge" factors indicates that there may be a deficiency in the training program.

3. **Accidents by experience level of people involved.** Large numbers of accidents involving inexperienced people can point toward complacency, initial training, review training or employee development problems.

4. **Incidents by time of day or time into work shift.** Groups of numbers can show periods of inadequate supervision, fatigue or inadequate rest periods.

5. **Injuries and damage by the agency of the accident.** These data can show what materials or tools are inflicting the most harm on people and property.

MAJOR INCIDENT REVIEW

LOCATION #2 Shipping Dept. South Wall Col. 20B	DEPARTMENT/DIVISION Sheet and Paint
DATE OF ACCIDENT/INCIDENT 4/8/19—	DATE OF REVIEW 4/11/19—

NATURE OF LOSS

NATURE AND EXTENT OF ACTUAL OR POTENTIAL LOSS TO PERSONS OR PROPERTY (INCLUDE COSTS OF PROPERTY LOSS)

Compound fracture of upper left leg.
Three machine guards badly bent - $110.00

DESCRIPTION

DESCRIPTION OF ACCIDENT/INCIDENT (WHO, WHAT, HOW)

Employee was reaching out with a paint brush while standing near the top of a 20 ft. extension ladder section. He lost his balance as the bottom of the ladder started slipping and fell approximately 10 feet to the floor.

CAUSES

WHY DID THE ACCIDENT/INCIDENT OCCUR?

The ladder was improperly positioned (too far out from support) and was not tied off. Because it was the top section of an extension ladder, it did not have safety feet. Employee reached beyond normal arm's reach and the ladder slid out from under him. Improper storage of machine guards and spare parts contributed to the placement of the ladder.

CONTROL

ACTION TO PREVENT RECURRENCE. INFORMATION FOR ORGANIZATION – WIDE ATTENTION.

Since ladders are used widely throughout the company and by employees and their family members off the job as well, it is suggested that all items on the attached ladder safety checklist be reviewed with everyone during the next 30 days and that the safe practices booklet for ladder safety be reissued to everyone. Physical and mechanical items related should be checked by each area supervisor within the next 48 hours and all deficiencies corrected during this same time. The use of ladder tie-off and safety belts on and off the job should be given special emphasis. Provision for the purchase of off-the-job safety belts and tie-off lanyards is being established with our safety store and should be given on-going wide publicity.

MEMBERS

REVIEW MEMBERS

Paul T. Jenings	Richard P. Bowen
R.L. Simons	Donald M. Chance

REVIEW CHAIRMAN	DATE	PRESIDENT	DATE
John N. Babcock	4/11/19—	J. R. Carter	4/11/19—

Figure 4-5

6. **Accident trends by categories of inadequacies in programs, standards and compliance.** These enable the correlation of accident rates with program performance and provide critical information on actual program effectiveness.

Figure 4-6 shows an analysis summary which gives a comprehensive review of trends. Such information is most valuable in program management.

Use of Computer Systems

The computer enables us to quickly analyze large amounts of information. It makes it possible for managers to have a lot of useful data condensed into useful summaries. The usefulness of the information provided by the computer is dependent upon the quality of data put into it and the quality of the program used to process it. Some organizations ask supervisors to encode all the incident data as they prepare the report. Lacking both the training and the time to do this properly, the supervisors frequently miscode the data. They quickly learn that some code numbers will be accepted without question. The data thus entered are inaccurate and the analysis meaningless. It may even be harmful, as it can lead people into wrong decisions.

A supervisor can keep tallies of simple data for his or her own area. That will be quite helpful in spotting problems. Data for comprehensive trend analysis, however, should be encoded by clerical people trained to be accurate and given enough time to do the encoding properly. Then the analyses will be meaningful and reliable in pointing out problem areas. Several loss management information systems have been developed for incident analysis. A simplified coding for investigation report data is on the back of the Investigation Report Form shown as *Figure 4-2*. Organizations can and should adapt programs to give managers useful data.

Actions by Management

Whatever their form, accident and incident analyses must be used to be effective. The incidents show loss exposures that were not adequately identified and controlled. The analysis gives managers a second chance.

The management environment tends to be consistent throughout an organization. It is built with policies and programs. The analysis reveals the flaws in the environment. It tells each manager what can happen.

Analyses should be studied carefully. Look at each category and the trends shown. Don't ask if the same things could occur in your area. They can and will. Instead, ask:

1. Where could they occur? Where are the energy contacts and other factors possible?
2. How could they occur? In what way will the basic causes indicated lead to accidents in your area?
3. What needs to be done? What is the loss potential and what can be done? Where is help needed?
4. What do senior and subordinate managers need to be told? What do the trends show you that can help others define all the potentially serious problems?

PREPARATION FOR EFFECTIVE INVESTIGATIONS

The various actions we have discussed can bring many benefits to a manager and to the organization, but only if they are done well. Good investigation depends on good planning. To help make investigations more effective, some organizations with effective programs have the following:

Investigation Policy

A good investigation program starts with a clear policy. The policy should state the importance of incident investigation and the benefits gained from prompt, thorough investigation. It should specify what accidents and incidents are to be investigated and the criteria for determining whether a loss potential is significant. These are usually expressed in terms of days lost and cost of repair or replacement.

Responsibility

The program should specify to whom each type of accident and incident is reported so it will be investigated adequately. Training is provided to all who will be involved so they can perform their tasks properly.

Resources

Many items are needed for investigations. These start with simple things like forms and note pads. They go all the way up to testing laboratories and equipment to clean up accident sites. Finally, they include people for review committees and data analyses. Each of these resources must be planned and budgeted to be available when needed. Equip-

Incident Analysis Summary

LOSSES		INCIDENTS		IMMED. CAUSES		BASIC CAUSES		INADEQUATE CONTROL				
TYPE	NO.	TYPE	NO.	TYPE	NO.	TYPE	NO.	PROGRAM ELEMENTS	P	S	C	

LOSSES — TYPE

INJURY/ILLNESS
FIRST AID
MEDICAL TREATMENT
LOST WORKDAY
FATAL
PART OF BODY HARMED
HEAD
EYE
HEARING
RESPIRATORY
TRUNK
DIGESTIVE TRACT
ARM
HAND
FINGER
LEG
KNEE
ANKLE
FOOT
TOE
SKIN

PROPERTY
MINOR (LESS THAN $100)
SERIOUS ($100-$999)
MAJOR ($1,000-$9,999)
CATASTROPHIC (OVER $10,000)

TYPE PROPERTY DAMAGED
BUILDING
FIXED EQUIPMENT
MOTOR VEHICLE
TOOLS
MATERIALS
MATERIALS HANDLING EQUIPMENT

PROCESS LOSS
MINOR (LESS THAN $100)
SERIOUS ($100-$999)
MAJOR ($1,000-$9,999)
CATASTROPHIC (OVER $10,000)

INCIDENTS — TYPE

STRUCK AGAINST
STRUCK BY
FALL TO LOWER LEVEL
FALL ON SAME LEVEL
CAUGHT IN
CAUGHT ON
CAUGHT BETWEEN
OVEREXERTION
OVERSTRESS
CONTACT WITH
HEAT
COLD
FIRE
ELECTRICITY
CHEMICAL-CAUSTIC
CHEMICAL-TOXIC
NOISE
PRESSURE
RADIATION

IMMED. CAUSES — TYPE

SUBSTANDARD PRACTICES
OPERATING WITHOUT AUTHORITY
FAILURE TO WARN
FAILURE TO SECURE
IMPROPER SPEED
MADE SAFETY DEVICE INOP.
USED DEFECTIVE EQUIPMENT
USED EQUIPMENT IMPROPERLY
DID NOT USE PROT. EQUIPMENT
SERVICED EQUIP. IN OPERATION
ADJUSTED EQUIP. IN OPERATION
HORSEPLAY
UNDER DRUG/ALCOHOL INFLUENCE

SUBSTANDARD CONDITIONS
INADEQUATE GUARDS
INADEQUATE PROT.
DEFECTIVE EQUIP.
CONGESTION
INADEQUATE WARNING SYSTEM
FIRE HAZARD
EXPLOSION HAZARD
REACTIVE CHEMICAL
HAZARDOUS ATMOSPHERE
NOISE
RADIATION
ILLUMINATION
VENTILATION
POOR HOUSEKEEPING

BASIC CAUSES — TYPE

PERSONAL FACTORS
PHYSICAL INCAPACITY
MENTAL INCAPACITY
LACK OF KNOWLEDGE
LACK OF SKILL
PHYSICAL STRESS
PSYCHOLOGICAL STRESS
IMPROPER MOTIVATION

JOB FACTORS
INADEQUATE LEADERSHIP/SUPERVISION
INADEQUATE ENGINEERING
INADEQUATE PURCHASING
INADEQUATE MAINTENANCE
INADEQUATE TOOLS/EQUIPMENT/MATERIALS
INADEQUATE WORK STANDARDS
WEAR AND TEAR
ABUSE OR MISUSE

INADEQUATE CONTROL — PROGRAM ELEMENTS

LEADERSHIP AND ADMINISTRATION
MANAGEMENT TRAINING
PLANNED INSPECTIONS
TASK ANALYSIS AND PROCEDURES
ACCIDENT/INCIDENT INVESTIGATION
TASK OBSERVATIONS
EMERGENCY PREPAREDNESS
ORGANIZATIONAL RULES
ACCIDENT/INCIDENT ANALYSIS
EMPLOYEE TRAINING
PERSONAL PROTECTIVE EQUIPMENT
HEALTH CONTROL
PROGRAM EVALUATION SYSTEM
ENGINEERING CONTROLS
PERSONAL COMMUNICATIONS
GROUP MEETINGS
GENERAL PROMOTION
HIRING AND PLACEMENT
PURCHASING CONTROLS
OFF-THE-JOB SAFETY

P = INADEQUATE PROGRAM
S = INADEQUATE STANDARDS
C = INADEQUATE COMPLIANCE

Figure 4-6

ment planning can range from simply having clipboards with forms and pencils available to supervisors, to extensive investigator's kits.

Procedure

Perhaps the most important part of investigation planning is developing an organization procedure. This tells everyone how things are to be done when an incident occurs. Incidents don't happen every day. When they do, people need aids to help them do the right things in the correct order. They need to know how to get emergency assistance, who to report the incident to, how to go about the investigation, what reports are needed and how to prepare them and what follow-through actions are to be taken.

Accidents cost. When one occurs, people and organizations pay a price. The only thing they can get for that price is the information which has already been paid for, information which can help prevent similar losses in the future. It's up to the organization, and its managers, if they want to get it and use it.

CORE CONCEPTS IN REVIEW

Accident/incident investigation should be part of every safety program. Effective investigations can:

1. Describe what happened
2. Determine the real causes
3. Decide the risks
4. Develop controls
5. Define trends
6. Demonstrate management's concern

Line supervisors should conduct most investigations.

1. They have a personal interest in the people and workplace involved.

2. They know the people and conditions.

3. They know how best to get the information needed.

4. They are the ones who implement most remedial actions.

5. They are held accountable for what happens in their areas. Staff personnel and higher level managers take part in major loss cases and those where specialized knowledge is needed.

Reasons why people may not report accidents:

1. Fear of consequences.
2. Concern about the safety record.
3. Lack of understanding of the importance of complete reporting.

Basic ways to get better reporting are to:

1. Communicate
2. Educate
3. Train employees on the need for reporting and why it is so critical

4. React in a positive way to timely reporting

Following are six major phases of effective investigation, with key point guidelines for each:

1. **Respond to the emergency promptly and positively**
   a. Take control at the scene
   b. Ensure first aid and call for emergency services
   c. Control potential secondary accidents
   d. Identify sources of evidence at the scene
   e. Preserve evidence from alteration or removal
   f. Investigate to determine loss potential
   g. Decide who should be notified

2. **Collect pertinent information**

   a. Get "the big picture" first
   b. Interview witnesses separately
   c. Interview on-site whenever feasible
   d. Put the person at ease
   e. Get the individual's version
   f. Ask questions at the right time
   g. Give the witness feedback of your understanding
   h. Record (in writing) critical information quickly
   i. Use visual aids
   j. Use reenactment sparingly and carefully
   k. End on a positive note
   l. Keep the communication line open

3. **Analyze and evaluate all significant causes**

   a. Use the cause and effect (domino) sequence
   b. Make a causal factor outline
   c. Cover immediate causes or symptoms (substandard acts and conditions)
   d. Cover basic or underlying causes (personal factors and job factors)

e. Determine the critical few specific causes

f. Cover deficiencies in the management system (inadequate program, inadequate standards, inadequate compliance with standards)

4. **Develop and take remedial actions**

   a. Consider alternative controls
   b. Lower the likelihood of occurrence
   c. Reduce the potential severity of loss
   d. Take temporary actions immediately
   e. Take permanent actions as soon as possible
   f. Document with written report

5. **Review findings and recommendations**

   a. Have every report reviewed by the next higher level manager

b. Measure the quality of the reports and coach for improvement

6. **Follow through**

   a. Conduct investigation review meetings
   b. Monitor timely implementation of remedial/preventive actions
   c. Analyze data for trends
   d. Profit from prompt and positive changes based on reviews, analysis and experience

Accidents are costly in both human and economic terms. When they occur, people and organizations pay a steep price. Effective investigation is the only known way to get something for the price you have paid — better safety from this day forward.

KEY QUESTIONS

1. List at least four significant values gained from effective investigations.

2. List at least three reasons why line supervisors should be involved in investigations.

3. Under what circumstances should middle and upper managers actively participate in the investigation?

4. True or False? When safety/loss control staff members participate in investigations, they should serve as advisors to the line management investigators.

5. What are the six major steps in investigation?

6. True or False? Supervisors can conscientiously investigate every accident reported to them and still not have much of the safety picture.

7. List at least six reasons why people fail to report accidents.

8. True or False? One of the ways to promote effective incident reporting is to react in a positive way to effective reporting.

9. True or False? The immediate actions of a well-trained supervisor at the site of an accident can gain evidence that might take others days to get through accident reconstruction.

10. Investigators should appraise not only the actual losses but also the _____ losses.

11. True or False? The only important witnesses are the eyewitnesses.

12. True or False? Witnesses should be interviewed as a group, to save time and get all information as quickly as possible.

13. List at least six of the ten guidelines for interviewing witnesses.

14. True or False? Because showing is usually better than telling, investigators should use accident reenactment whenever possible.

15. Name several types of records that may provide useful investigation information.

16. True or False? Typically, there is only one important causal factor involved in the accident.

17. True or False? In many accidents/incidents the loss potential is much more important than the actual loss which occurred.

18. Temporary remedial actions tend to treat the s_____; permanent actions should remedy the _____ causes.

19. In the "Analysis of Basic Causes: Questions for the Investigator," what are the five categories of Personal Factors? The seven categories of Job Factors?

20. List five major sections of a good investigation report form.

21. List at least three reasons why every incident report should be reviewed by the next higher level of management.

22. True or False? The quality of investigation reports is not measurable.

23. List several benefits of personal involvement by upper managers in major accident investigations.

24. List at least four common categories of incident data analysis factors.

25. True or False? A good investigation program starts with a clear policy and procedure.

THE USE OF SCAT

Scat is a new tool that can be used following a high-potential accident or incident investigation as a check on the thoroughness of the investigative process. Its suggested use is for those accidents or incidents involved with major loss or those that under slightly different circumstances could have been. Taking the time required to increase safety assurance that major loss or catastrophe will not recur is a valuable expenditure of time.

S C A T ©

SYSTEMATIC CAUSAL ANALYSIS TECHNIQUE

PERSONAL FACTORS: Inadequate Capability

N

Was some person's **lack of physical or mental capability** or the lack of aptitude for the job a factor? If no, proceed to **Lack of Knowledge.**

If yes or uncertain:

1. Was the person given a pre-placement medical examination?

2. Was the examination based on a job safety and health physical capability requirements survey?

3. Was the person given a pre-placement aptitude test? Or, if not, was the person's qualification for the job verified with previous employers or by observation?

4. Did a pre-placement interview and orientation include a review of the work conditions and requirements such as the handling of hazardous materials, work in high places or confined spaces, etc.?

5. Was the pre-placement orientation based on a loss exposures inventory?

6. If the person had a lack of physical or mental capability, was workplace modification to compensate for this condition considered?

7. Was the person closely supervised during a probationary period to identify any lack of aptitude or any physical or mental incapability to do the job safely?

8. Did the person get a follow-up medical examination on critical items of physical capability within an appropriate period and not more than four years, if such re-examination was dictated by a potential disability?

If there were any Inadequate Capability factors as indicated by any circles being checked for the above questions, analyze:

Does the Hiring and Placement program element include adequate examination and evaluation of each person's basic capability to perform the job safely? Or, does it include provisions to modify the workplace or the activity to accommodate personnel with permanent or temporary incapacities?

If the program includes this element and these activities, are the standards adequate to define the control measures and the level of job performance necessary to identify the exposures and control the risks?

If the program and standards are adequate, why were those standards not complied with?

What is the additional loss potential due to inadequate program, standards and compliance?

If uncertain on any of these questions, you may need to examine additional evidence.

If all of the squares were checked, this may not be a cause factor

Answer each question yes, uncertain or no by marking the appropriate box, triangle or circle. A marked circle indicates a possible Causal Factor.

Figure 4-7

PERSONAL FACTORS : Lack of Knowledge

[N]

Was the lack of knowledge on how to perform the task safely a factor? If no, proceed to **Lack of Skill.**

If yes or uncertain:

[Y] [?] (N) 1. Was the person given a general orientation on the organization's safety program?

[Y] [?] (N) 2. Was the person given a work-site safety orientation?

[Y] [?] (N) 3. Was the work-site orientation based on a loss exposure inventory?

[Y] [?] (N) 4. Did the person receive formal training for his/her job, to include safe work methods, procedures, practices and rules?

[Y] [?] (N) 5. Did the person get on-the-job instruction in the specific task related to the incident?

6. Was this instruction given or reviewed within the past:

[1] **1 year**

[2] **2 two years**

(3) **3 three years**

[Y] [?] (N) 7. Did the person get formal review training on the critical parts of the job within the past three years?

[Y] [?] (N) 8. Did the person get update education related to the task involved through safety contacts, job coaching or safety meetings within the past year?

[Y] [?] (N) 9. Was the person given clear task assignment stating what was to be done, the hazards involved, and the safe practices to follow?

[Y] [?] (N) 10. Was the person performing a job that is listed on the critical job inventory?

If not, should the job be added to the inventory?

[Y] [?] (N) 11. Had the person supervising the activity received management training in safety?

◯——— If there were any Lack of Knowledge factors as indicated by any circles being checked, analyze:

Do the Employee Training, Personal Communications and Group Meetings elements of the program include adequate education to develop and update each person's knowledge of how to perform their job safely and how to act in abnormal or emergency situations?

If the safety program includes these elements and the activities, are the standards adequate to define the control measures and the level of performance needed to identify the exposures and control the risks?

If the program elements and standards are adequate why were the standards not complied with?

What is the additional loss potential due to inadequate program, standards and compliance?

▽——— If uncertain on any of these questions, additional examination of evidence may be needed.

▢——— If all of the squares were checked, this may not be a cause factor.

PERSONAL FACTORS : Lack of Skill

N

Was the lack of skill to do the job safely a factor? If no, proceed to **Stress.**

If yes or uncertain:

Y ? N   1. Was the task taught by someone who had been trained in how to give proper job instruction?

Y ? N   2. Was the "Motivate-Tell and Show-Test-Check" method of instruction used?

Y ? N   3. Was the person given adequate supervised practice to develop the skill needed to perofrm the task safely?

Y ? N   4. Did the person perform the task often enough, since initial training, to maintain the ability to do it safely?

Y ? N   5. If not performing the task regularly, was the person given supervised practice or review before being assigned to do the task?

Y ? N   6. Could the task be simplified or mechanized to preclude the need for high operator skill, within reasonable cost and time?

○——— If there were any Lack of Skill factors as indicated by any circles being checked, analyze:

Do the Employee Training, Health Control and Personal Communications elements of the program include adequate instruction and supervised practice to develop the skills needed to perform safely in critical situations?

If the program includes these elements and activities, are the standards adequate to define the control measures and the level of performance needed to identify the exposures and control the risks?

If the program elements and standards are adequate, why were the standards not complied with?

What is the additional loss potential due to inadequate program, standards, and compliance?

▽——— If uncertain on any of these questions, additional examination of evidence my be needed.

☐——— If all of the squares were checked, this may not be a cause factor.

PERSONAL FACTORS : Stress

N

Was physical or mental stress a factor in the incident? If no, proceed to **Improper Motivation.**

If yes or uncertain:

N ? Y   1. Was the person suffering any temporary illness that created personal stress or decreased sensory abilities?

N ? Y   2. Was the person using any medications or under the influence of any drugs, including alcohol?

N ? Y   3. Were there any recent significant changes in the job (consider tools, equipment, materials, pace, environment, etc.)?

N ? Y   4. Was the task load, pace or duration high enough to physically or mentally fatigue the person?

N ? Y   5. Was the person subject to threshold limits of:

     – vibration
     – noise
     – heat or cold
     – oxygen deficiency
     – chemicals or contaminants
     – atmospheric pressure changes

N ? Y   6. Were the person's movements constrained, were abnormal body positions required or were there other ergonomic stresses?

N ? Y   7. Did the potentially hazardous nature of the task cause mental fixation on the hazards?

N ? Y   8. Were any personal or family situations causing mental preoccupation?

N ? Y   9. Was the person required to make extreme or difficult judgments often while doing the task?

N ? Y   10. Were there activities or conditions at the site which might have causes distractions?

Y ? N   11. Did the signs, color-coded items and systems controls follow human factors standards to prompt normal perception and response?

○——— If there were any Stress factors as indicated by any circles being checked, analyze:

Do the Health Control, Engineering Controls and Task Observations elements of the program include adequate activities to identify and control the effects of stress-producing situations?

If the program includes these elements and activities, are the standards adequate to define the control measures and the level of performance needed to identify the exposures and control the risks?

If the program elements and standards are adequate, why were the standards not complied with?

What is the additional loss potential due to inadequate program, standards and compliance?

▽——— If uncertain on any of these questions, additional examination of evidence may be needed.

□——— If all of the squares were checked, this may not be a cause factor.

PERSONAL FACTORS : Improper Motivation

N

Was motivation to perform improper activities or to not perform critical activities a factor? If no, proceed to **Job Factors.**

If yes or uncertain:

Y	?	N	1. Was the person recognized regularly and frequently when he/she did satisfactory or better work?
N	?	Y	2. Did the person get more of the supervisor's attention from poor work or unsafe actions than from proper performance?
Y	?	N	3. Was the importance of the task involved, and the need for its safe completion, explained to the person?
N	?	Y	4. Did safe and proper performance on the job prompt any ridicule, contempt or other negative reactions from other employees?
N	?	Y	5. Did the person perceive any personal benefits, such as saving time/effort on an opportunity to socialize with others, in not following the prescribed safe work method, procedure, practice, or rule?
N	?	Y	6. Were there any physical or psychological obstacles or inconveniences encountered in safe performance of the task involved in the incident?

If there were any Improper Motivation factors as indicated by any circles being checked, analyze:

Do the Employee Training, Personal Communications and General Promotion (Incentives) elements of the program include adequate activities to identify and control the sources of improper motivation?

If the program includes these elements and activities, are the standards adequate to define the control measures and the level of performance needed to identify the exposures and control the risks?

If the program elements and standards are adequate, why were the standards not complied with?

What is the additional loss potential due to inadequate program, standards and compliance?

If uncertain on any of these questions, additional examination of evidence may be needed.

If all the squares were checked, this may not be a cause factor.

JOB FACTORS : Inadequate Leadership and Supervision

N

Was inadequate leadership of safety program activities a factor? If no, proceed to **Inadequate Engineering.**

If yes or uncertain:

Y ? N 1. Was there a written safety policy and was it well known to managers and employees in the area involved?

Y ? N 2. Were program activities that would have prevented the accident, or reduced the loss, in the current year's objectives?

N ? Y 3. Was control of the loss exposure affected by limited budgeting of personnel, equipment, materials, or other financial support?

Y ? N 4. Was responsibility for control of the loss exposure related to the accident assigned to a specific person or position, and was sufficient authority given to enable effective control?

Y ? N 5. Did the responsible person have management training in safety related to the type of loss exposure?

Y ? N 6. Was the exposure identified in a loss exposure inventory, and its potential evaluated correctly?

Y ? N 7. Was the exposure and its control measures discussed at a management meeting within the past 12 months?

Y ? N 8. Does the safety program reference manual provide adequate guidance on measures that would control the type of accident?

Y ? N 9. Does the reference library include sufficient background information on controlling the type of loss exposure, and data on sources of appropriate program supplies or safety equipment?

Y ? N 10. Was program management, related to measures that would control the loss exposure, audited and evaluated within the past 12 months?

Y ? N 11. Was management at each level from the line supervisor to the area where the incident occurred up to the senior manager, appraised on his or her safety performance within the past 12 months?

○— If there were any inadequate Leadership Factors as indicated by circles being checked, analyze:

Do the Leadership and Administration, and the Management Training elements of the program include adequate activities to ensure that planning, organizing, leading, and controlling of safety are effectively incorporated into the organization management program?

If the program includes this element and these activities, are the standards adequate to ensure that loss exposures are identified and their potential effect evaluated, and appropriate actions taken to control significant exposures?

If the program and standards are adequate, why were the standards not complied with?

What is the additional loss potential due to inadequate program, standards or compliance?

▽— If uncertain on any of these questions, additional examination of evidence may be needed.

☐— If all of the squares were checked, this may not be a cause factor.

JOB FACTORS : Inadequate Engineering

[N]

Was inadequate design of the facility or process line equipment, or inadequate incorporation of safety devices during fabrication, a factor? If no, proceed to **Inadequate Purchasing.**

If yes or uncertain:

Y ?/ (N) 1. Were hazard assessments made during the conceptual stage of the facilities involved?

Y ?/ (N) 2. Were the hazards revealed by this accident identified in the preliminary hazard analysis?

Y ?/ (N) 3. Were the effects of operations that interface with the process considered in the hazard analysis?

Y ?/ (N) 4. Were all appropriate standards, codes and past accident reports researched to establish criteria for design of the facility?

Y ?/ (N) 5. Were controls for the hazards incorporated into the facility design?

Y ?/ (N) 6. Did the safety staff coordinate on the design?

Y ?/ (N) 7. Were the safety criteria specified to the contractor?

Y ?/ (N) 8. Were pre-construction conferences held with contractors and did agendas for these conferences include safety specifications and safety during construction?

Y ?/ (N) 9. Was the facility examined to ensure that safety criteria had been followed before acceptance of the facility?

Y ?/ (N) 10. Were the initial operations of the system supervised closely for overlooked hazards?

Y ?/ (N) 11. Were any modifications made to the original plant and were those modifications assessed for hazards during the modification design?

○——— If there were any Inadequate Engineering Factors as indicated by circles being checked, analyze:

Do the Purchasing Controls and Engineering Controls elements of the program include adequate activities to ensure that hazards potentially encountered during experimental, construction, operation and disposal phases are assessed; that safety codes and standards are researched, that past experience is evaluated; and that appropriate safety criteria are incorporated into design and construction of facilities and equipment?

If the program includes this element and these activities, are the standards adequate to identify the exposures and define the controls needed to ensure a safe system?

If the program and standards are adequate, why were the standards not complied with?

What is the additional loss potential due to the inadequate program, standards, or compliance?

▽——— If uncertain on any of these questions, additional examination of evidence may be needed.

□——— If all of the squares were checked, this may not be a cause factor.

JOB FACTORS : Inadequate Purchasing

N

Was inadequate purchasing, management of materials or disposal of scrap, waste, or obsolete items a factor? If no, proceed to **Inadequate Maintenance.**

If yes or uncertain:

Y ? N   1. Were safety standards and safety devices researched and specified to vendors of tools and equipment, and to contractors that built the facilities involved in the incident?

Y ? N   2. Were the safety and health aspects of the materials used, as related to the accident, researched and were safety data sheets obtained before purchase?

Y ? N   3. Were the materials selected the safest ones that could be obtained?

Y ? N   4. Did the safety staff coordinate on requests for purchase of the tools, equipment and materials involved in the incident?

Y ? N   5. Were safety information and instructions on equipment and materials communicated to the supervisor of the area?

Y ? N   6. Were the hazardous material labels on materials, safety placards on tools, etc. kept intact and legible?

Y ? N   7. Were appropriate methods of handling, and personal protective equipment, used when unloading, moving, storing and issuing the materials, as pertinent to the accident?

Y ? N   8. Were materials and equipment stored properly prior to use to prevent deterioration or instability?

Y ? N   9. Were hazardous properties of waste, scrap, and unserviceable or obsolete equipment identified so proper disposal methods could be followed?

○——— If there were any Inadequate Purchasing Factors as indicated by circles being checked, analyze:

Do the Purchasing Controls and Planned Inspections elements of the program include adequate activities to ensure that the safest possible equipment and materials are obtained, that hazards are identified and the control measures are upheld during transportation, handling, use and disposal?

If these elements and activities are included in the program, are the standards adequate to ensure that potential hazards are identified before items are purchased or facilities are constructed, and that risks are controlled throughout the life of facilities, equipment and materials?

If these elements and activities are adequate, why were the standards not complied with?

What is the additional loss potential due to the inadequate program, standards or compliance?

▽——— If uncertain on any of these questions, you may need to examine additional evidence.

☐——— If all of the squares were checked, this may not be a cause factor.

JOB FACTORS : Inadequate Maintenance

[N] Was premature failure or malfunction of equipment or structures a factor? If no, proceed to reparative maintenance section below.

If yes or uncertain:

[Y] [?] (N) 1. Have service manuals, planned use and government codes been checked to assess the need for preventive maintenance?

[Y] [?] (N) 2. Was a maintenance schedule written?

[Y] [?] (N) 3. Were adequate time and priority given to preventive maintenance?

[Y] [?] (N) 4. Was all preventive maintenance conducted according to the schedule?

[Y] [?] (N) 5. Were written maintenance instructions, or adequate verbal instructions, given to the mechanics?

[Y] [?] (N) 6. Was preventive maintenance work regularly audited for proper completion?

[Y] [?] (N) 7. Are lubrication and service points readily accessible?

[Y] [?] (N) 8. Are the specified lubricants or approved substitutes used?

[Y] [?] (N) 9. Were parts assembled correctly?

[Y] [?] (N) 10. Were adjustable parts set to correct specifications?

[Y] [?] (N) 11. Are assembly and adjustment or parts made to clearly written standards in technical manuals or procedures?

[Y] [?] (N) 12. Are appropriate parts cleaned and resurfaced as required?

If any of the above questions were answered NO, Inadequate Preventive Maintenance was a factor.

If uncertain on any of these questions, this is a potential area for additional evidence examination.

If all questions were answered YES, Preventive Maintenance may not be a cause factor.

[N] Were any parts replacements or equipment repairs a factor? If no, proceed to **Inadequate Tools and Equipment.**

If yes or uncertain:

[Y] [?] (N) 1. Were the defects or deficiencies adequately described in a written repair work order?

[Y] [?] (N) 2. Was the mechanic given adequate written or verbal instruction on the repair(s) made?

[Y] [?] (N) 3. Was adequate time and assistance scheduled for the repair work?

[Y] [?] (N) 4. Was the equipment checked for proper operation on completion of the repair?

[Y] [?] (N) 5. Was the repair checked by a skilled craftsman or mechanical inspector?

[Y] [?] (N) 6. Were specified parts or approved substitutes used?

If any of the above questions were answered NO, Inadequate Reparative (or On-Call) Maintenance was a factor.

If Uncertain on any of these questions this is a potential area for additional evidence examination.

If all questions were answered YES, Reparative Maintenance may not be a cause factor.

If Inadequate Maintenance Factors were indicated by circles being checked, analyze:

Do the Engineering Controls, Purchasing Controls and Planned Inspections elements of the program include adequate research of requirements for maintenance?

Do the Job Analysis and Procedures, and Personal Communication elements include adequate development and communication of maintenance instructions?

If the safety program includes these elements and the activities referenced in the questions in this section, are the standards adequate to define the control measures and the level of performance needed to identify the loss exposures and control the risks?

If the program standards were adequate, why were those standards not complied with?

What is the additional loss potential due to this lack of compliance?

JOB FACTORS : Inadequate Tools and Equipment

N

Were inadequate or unsuitable tools, machines or vehicles a factor? If no, proceed to **Inadequate Work Standards.**

If yes or uncertain:

Y ? (N)   1. Were the tools used in activities related to the accident correct for the task, as specified in instruction manuals and safety standards?

N ? (Y)   2. Were the tools or equipment worn beyond limits for safe and proper use?

N ? (Y)   3. Were adequate numbers of correct tools and parts, in proper condition, available for the task?

Y ? (N)   4. Were tool issue or storage areas convenient and well organized so the proper tools could be readily obtained?

Y ? (N)   5. Was there a procedure for prompt repair, adjustment, sharpening and other maintenance of tools and equipment to help keep them in safe condition?

Y ? (N)   6. Had defective tools involved in the accident been replaced and salvaged or otherwise made inaccessible, or marked to prevent unintentional use until refurbished?

Y ? (N)   7. If defective equipment was involved, had it been shut down and locked out, and tagged or marked to prevent its use until it was repaired or replaced?

Y ? (N)   8. Had the equipment defects been reported to supervision?

○   If there were any Inadequate Tools and Equipment Factors, as indicated by circles being checked, analyze:

Do the Purchasing Controls, Engineering Controls, Personal Protective Equipment and Planned Inspections elements of the program include adequate selection, supply, inspection, maintenance and disposal to ensure that usable, safe tools and equipment are provided, and to identify defective items and remove them from use?

If these elements and activities are included in the program, are the standards adequate to ensure that proper, safe tools and equipment are used?

If the program and standards are adequate, why were the standards not complied with?

What is the additional loss potential due to the inadequate program, standards or compliance?

▽   If uncertain on any of these questions you may need to examine additional evidence.

□   If all of the squares were checked, this may not be a cause factor.

JOB FACTORS : Inadequate Work Standards

N

Were inadequate methods, procedures, practices or rules a factor? If no, proceed to **Wear and Tear.**

If yes or uncertain:

1. Were safe methods for the process involved developed along with system equipment and were these methods communicated to area managers and to employee trainers?

2. Was the task involved in the incident listed on the critical task inventory?
   If not, should it be added to the inventory?

3. Was a written procedure for the task available and used?

4. Was the procedure correct and current?

5. Had the procedure been reviewed and updated within the past 12 months?

6. Was the procedure based on a proper task analysis?

7. Were safe work practices for the general type of work involved in the incident published and available to supervisors and employees?

8. If there was no procedure or practice, was there a safety rule to identify or control the hazard?

9. Was the rule published and distributed to affected employees?

10. Was the rule reinforced with a sign or notice in the work area?

11. Was the method, procedure, practice or rule consistent with other instructions?

If there were any Inadequate Work Standards Factors as indicated by circles being checked, analyze:

Do the Engineering Controls, Task Analysis and Procedures and Organizational Rules elements of the program include adequate activities to ensure the study of work activities and the development of methods, procedures, practices or rules when engineering controls or safeguards are not in use?

If these elements and activities are included in the program, are the standards adequate to ensure that methods, procedures, practices or rules are used as appropriate to the hazard and the evaluated degree of risk?

If the program and standards are adequate, why were the standards not complied with?

What is the additional loss potential due to the inadequate program,, standards, or compliance?

If uncertain on any of these questions, you may need to examine additional evidence.

If all the squares were checked, this may not be a cause factor.

JOB FACTORS : Wear and Tear

N

Was a deteriorated condition of tools, equipment or facilities a factor? If no, proceed to **Abuse and Misuse.**

If yes or uncertain:

N ? Y
1. Was the tool, equipment or facility used in a different way than as anticipated when it was purchased or built?

N ? Y
2. Was the equipment or facility used beyond normal service life?
If so, was it refurbished or overhauled to compensate for wear?

Y ? N
3. Was the equipment overloaded, operated at excessive speed, temperature or pressure or operated in any other abnormal ways?

N ? Y
4. Were substitute lubricants, operating fluids or fuels used in the equipment?

N ? Y
5. Were outside contractors or others who were not trained and supervised by the organization allowed to use tools, equipment or facilities?

Y ? N
6. Were inspection and maintenance activities increased as equipment got older or as use rate was increased?

If there were any Wear and Tear Factors as indicated by circles being checked, analyze:

Do the Planned Inspections and Task Observations elements of the program include adequate activities to detect and compensate for wear and tear, and to prevent abnormal wear?

If these elements and activities are included in the program, are the standards adequate to identify exposures and to define the measures that will control the risks of equipment malfunction or facility failure due to wear and tear?

If the program and standards are adequate, why were the standards not complied with?

What is the additional loss potential due to the inadequate program, standards or compliance?

If uncertain on any of these questions, you may need to examine additional evidence.

If all the squares were checked, this may not be a cause factor.

JOB FACTORS : Abuse or Misuse

N

Was a deteriorated or damaged condition of equipment or facilities due to abuse or misuse a factor? If no, skip this section.

If yes or uncertain:

N ? Y
1. Were wrong tools, equipment or facilities used for convenience or due to a misunderstanding of the correct item to use?

N ? Y
2. Was the wrong tool, equipment or facility used intentionally due to personal preference based on past work methods?

N ? Y
3. Was overloading, operating at excessive speed, temperature or pressure or other abusive treatment done in response to management directive to increase output without full study of the effects?

N ? Y
4. Was the damage to or deterioration of equipment or facilities the result of actions of employees during an employee dispute, or of outsiders in a protest demonstration of some act of civil disobedience?

Y ? N
If so, were emergency measures taken to protect equipment and facilities as much as possible?

N ? Y
5. Was the damage to or deterioration of equipment or facilities the result of storms or other acts of nature?

Y ? N
If so, were emergency measures taken to protect people and property as much as possible?

Y ? N
6. Did supervisors take all reasonable measures to guard against abuse or misuse of tools, equipment and facilities?

Y ? N
7. Did the security program provide adequate surveillance of property during periods when areas were unsupervised?

○——— If there were any Abuse or Misuse Factors as indicated by circles being checked, analyze:

Do the Planned Inspections, Task Observations and Emergency Preparedness elements of the program include adequate activities to detect abuse or misuse of tools, equipment and facilities and to control the risks of accidents due to abusive damage or wear?

If these elements and activities are included in the program, are the standards adequate to identify exposures to abuse or misuse, and to define measures that will control the extent of losses?

If the program and standards are adequate, why were the standards not complied with?

What is the additional loss potential due to the inadequate program, standards or compliance?

▽——— If uncertain on any of these questions, you may need to examine additional evidence.

☐——— If all the squares were checked, this may not be a cause factor.

PRACTICAL APPICATIONS SUMMARY

S - For Supervisors
E - For Executives
C - For Safety/Loss Control Coordinators

	S	E	C
1. Issue investigation policy/procedures/practices		x	
2. Communicate, enforce and reinforce investigation policy/procedures/practices	x	x	x
3. Recommend improvements in investigation policy/procedures/practices	x	x	x
4. Allot adequate resources (time, money, equipment) for effective investigations		x	
5. Educate employees on the importance of accident/incident reporting and investigation	x	x	x
6. Make your behavior show that you believe accident/incident reporting and investigation really are important	x	x	x
7. Emphasize investigation in job orientation, job instruction, group meetings, personal contacts, performance discussions and coaching	x		
8. Maintain contacts with emergency services such as medical, paramedical, fire department, police, utilities, bomb disposal and poison control		x	x
9. Cooperate for effective investigations	x	x	x
10. Release accident information to the mass media		x	x
11. Coordinate activities of "outside investigators" required in some situations		x	x
12. Ensure adequate investigator training for all supervisors		x	x
13. Take supervisory investigator training and recommend training program improvements	x		
14. In deciding how extensive the investigation should be, consider not only the actual loss incurred but also the realistic loss potential	x	x	x
15. Use a positive approach to counteract the common reasons why people do not report accidents and do not cooperate fully in investigations	x	x	x
16. Make your behavior show that you believe investigation is a mutual problem-solving process, rather than a blame-fixing inquisition	x	x	x
17. Recognize and reinforce those who do a good job of reporting accidents and close calls and who cooperate fully in investigations	x	x	x
18. Dig beneath immediate causes to unearth basic causes and deficiencies in the management system	x	x	x
19. Provide proper forms as a guide to problem-solving investigations		x	x
20. Complete investigation forms and/or reports properly	x		
21. Do a thorough job of reviewing supervisory investigation reports and coaching for improvement		x	x

22.	Follow up the implementation of remedial action plans	x	x	x
23.	Ensure a system for measuring the quantity and quality of investigations		x	x
24.	Use the measurement results as a coaching aid toward better investigations and reports		x	x
25.	Promote an organized follow-up system to ensure that all remedial actions listed on major or high potential accidents/incidents are taken		x	
26.	Conduct investigation review meetings		x	
27.	Issue major loss announcements, loss information bulletins, and major incident reviews		x	
28.	Conduct incident data analyses		x	x
29.	Periodically audit the effectiveness of the investigation program and communicate the results to all levels of management			x
30.	Use audit results as a blueprint for investigation program improvement	x	x	x

CHAPTER 5

INCIDENT RECALL AND ACCIDENT IMAGING

"Growing risk factors require a more comprehensive approach to hazard management than our wealth and isolation have permitted in the past."
— Jerome Lederer

INTRODUCTION

The crash of a DC-10 at Chicago's O'Hare Airport stunned the country by the number of lives lost and the seemingly simple cause of not following an established mechanical procedure. The narrowly averted meltdown of a nuclear reactor at Three Mile Island resulted in such a mass of new regulations that the added cost of similar facilities soared into the billions of dollars. The sinking of the off-shore drilling platform, Ocean Ranger, off the Grand Banks of Canada led to an extensive review of all aspects of safety in offshore petroleum operations. In December 1984, the most tragic industrial accident in recorded history occurred in Bhopal, India. As a result of the release of a highly toxic chemical, more than 2,000 people died. Hundreds of others were blinded and otherwise permanently disabled. The flood of litigation which followed led some to doubt the very survival of a major international corporation.

Jerome Lederer, Director of the Office of Manned Space Flight Safety for NASA at the time of the early moon landings, said this in one of his speeches:

This nation was built on risk. Personal risk in tackling the wilderness, financial risk in business, risks in exploring the scientific unknown, enormous engineering risks, management risks.

We shall continue to take risks of greater magnitude than in the past. But the consequences of failure are becoming less permissible. The political, social, as well as economic and personal, risks that now accompany our ventures can have enormous repercussions when failure occurs.

These potential repercussions became realities when the space shuttle Challenger exploded less than a minute after launch, killing all seven astronauts and producing days of national mourning and a congressional investigation. That investigation revealed that there were indications of potential problems which might have predicted the disaster had they been properly analyzed.

For these and other reasons that have multiplied the potential losses associated with major and catastrophic losses, it is increasingly important to be able to predict their potential causes before they occur.

Accident statistics are not in themselves a reliable indicator of the degree of risk in a particular operation. Just because an organization has a favorable frequency rate today does not mean that it cannot have a disaster tomorrow. A recent study, "Success and Failure in Accident Prevention," was done in the United Kingdom by the Accident Prevention Advisory Unit of the Health and Safety Executive. This extensive study concluded:

Any simple measurement of performance in terms of accident frequency rate or accident incidence rate is not seen as a reliable guide to the safety performance of an undertaking. The report finds there is no clear correlation between such measurements and the work conditions, in injury potential, or the severity of injuries that have occurred.

There is a serious need for tools to enable organizations to identify and control the potential causes of major and catastrophic losses, which often are not preceded by smaller accidents whose causes can be analyzed for preventive values. Major or catastrophic losses often have a different sequence of causal events than do minor losses. These comparatively rare accidents provide too frequently only a small amount of useful preventive data. The results of studies such as the extensive accident ratio study *(Figure 5-1)*, show that there are far more incidents than there are accidents.

Incident recall and accident imaging are two techniques which have proven effective in getting at the much larger amount of data found in the more numerous incidents and potential accidents. They also provide means of utilizing the vast untapped knowledge of potential loss causes that exists in the work force. They make use of the knowledge, experience and observation of a far larger number of people who have direct contact with and knowledge of identifiable loss causes. In addition, the use of these tools has significant positive effects on those involved. It taps the enormous power of participation and allows people to respond to four of the most powerful words in any language, "I need your help."

The following list of reasons why employees do not report accidents was discussed in the chapter on accident investigation:

Fear of Discipline
Concern About the Record
Concern About Reputation
Fear of Medical Treatment
Dislike of Medical Personnel
Desire to Avoid Work Interruption
Desire to Keep Personal Record Clear
Avoidance of Red Tape
Concern About the Attitude of Others
Poor Understanding of Importance

It can readily be seen that most of these do not apply to reporting incidents, making it much easier for the interviewer to obtain useful information. In addition, when reporting incidents, people are often able to point to quick thinking and action on their part that prevented

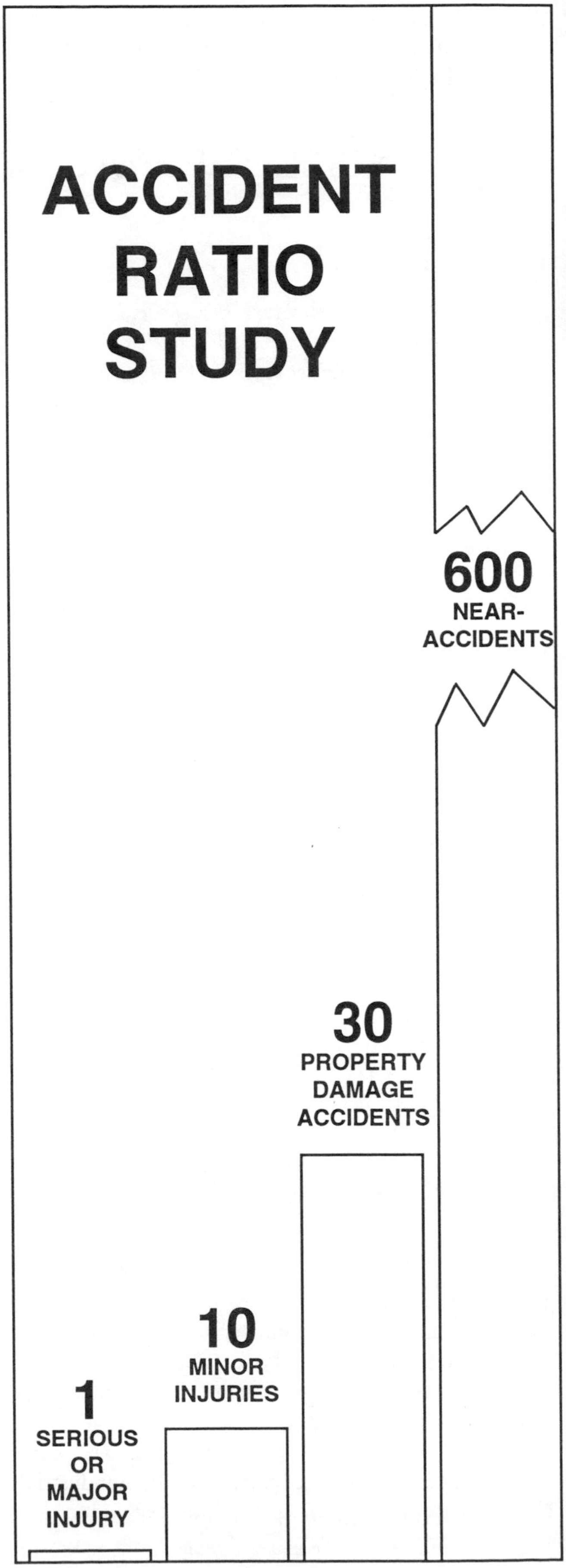

ACCIDENT RATIO STUDY

600 NEAR-ACCIDENTS

30 PROPERTY DAMAGE ACCIDENTS

10 MINOR INJURIES

1 SERIOUS OR MAJOR INJURY

Figure 5-1

the near-miss from being an accident. This taps the person's pride of performance in accident prevention. Accident imaging taps this same pride of performance in being able to foresee problems even before they result in a near-miss.

ORIGINS OF INCIDENT RECALL

During the last half-century, attempts have been made to systematically gather and learn from near-accidents. One approach was used in the Aviation Psychology Program of the U.S. Army Air Force during the Second World War. Because more planes were being lost in flight training than in combat, an attempt was made to survey human factors problems in the use and operation of aircraft equipment. The approach was simple: **interviewers asked a large number of pilots whether they had ever made, or seen anyone else make, an error** in reading or interpreting an aircraft instrument, detecting a signal or understanding instructions. Here is a verbatim example of an incident description obtained:

> It was an extremely dark night. My co-pilot was at the controls. I gave him instructions to take the ship, a B-25, into the traffic pattern and land. He began letting down from an altitude of 4,000 feet. At 1,000 feet above the ground I expected him to level off. Instead, he kept right on letting down until I finally had to take over. His trouble was that he had misread the altimeter by 1,000 feet. The incident might seem extremely stupid, but it was not the first time I have seen it happen. Pilots are pushing plenty of daises today because they read their altimeter wrong while letting down on dark nights.

> (P.M. Fitts and R.E. Jones, "Psychological Aspects of Instrument Display. I. Analysis of 270 'Pilot Error' Experiences in Reading and Interpreting Aircraft Instruments." Dayton, Ohio: *U.S. Air Force Memorandum Report* TSEAA-694-12A, 1947.)

This approach of gathering a **large number of incidents** and examining them to **detect patterns** is called the Critical Incident Technique. It was also tested several times in industry by accident researchers. The Division of Accident Research of the Bureau of Labor Statistics in Washington, D.C., conducted one of the more recent studies at an industrial site, to evaluate the usefulness of this technique as a method of identifying potential accident causes and to develop procedures for its practical application.

The results of the study, reported by this reliable government research group, were:

A. The critical incident technique dependably reveals causal factors in terms of errors and unsafe conditions which lead to industrial accidents.

B. The technique is able to identify causal factors associated with both injurious and non-injurious accidents.

C. The technique reveals a greater amount of information about accident causes than presently available methods of accident study, and provides a more sensitive measure of total accident performance.

D. The causes of non-injurious accidents, as identified by the critical incident technique, can be used to identify the sources of potentially injurious accidents.

E. Use of the critical incident technique to identify accident causes is feasible.

However, there was still a major weakness - the foundation of the technique was the analysis of numerous incidents for trends of common causal characteristics. Smaller organizations in particular might not have enough to analyze for patterns or the staff to do the analysis. Because they have even fewer accidents, they may be unaware of their real exposures to major losses. In addition, a technique based on analysis of accumulated data does not place a timely importance on single high potential incidents. In the 1960's, these weaknesses were overcome by a modification in the Critical Incident Technique.

As reported by Frank E. Bird, Jr. and Harold O'Shell in the *National Safety News* (October 1969) of the National Safety Council, the modified approach was called Incident Recall. While it is still desirable to collect as many incidents as possible, the new approach requires that **each** incident be evaluated to determine its **potential** to cause a major loss and its **probability** of occurrence. This approach made use of the thoughts of another seasoned safety pioneer, W.W. Allison, who had also successfully guided large organizations in determining and dealing with high-potential incidents and accidents. It was confirmed later by William G. Johnson in his influential book, *MORT - System Safety Assurance.*

Incident recall can be conducted in a variety of ways. These can be divided into two categories, planned and informal. They can be used separately or in combination to reinforce the desired results.

THE PLANNED INCIDENT RECALL INTERVIEW

The basic objective of the planned incident recall interview is to gain the willing cooperation of the employees being interviewed in freely relating as many high potential incidents as they can recall. Since the success or failure of the program depends so much on the interviews, it is important to understand several important factors that could have a major impact on the results of the technique.

Front-line Supervisors as Interviewers

Generally speaking, selected and trained supervisors are preferred as interviewers. While they may not have the ability to interview as well as certain staff specialists or those with in-depth psychological training, they do have certain important characteristics. In addition, learning to do good incident recall interviews can help develop other valuable management leadership skills.

The major reasons why select supervisors are the most recommended interviewers for general incident recall applications are identical to those that make them the most practical investigators of accidents:

1. They have a special interest to protect.

2. They know the most about people and conditions.

3. They frequently know how to get the information better than outsiders.

4. They or their colleagues will be initiating the action anyway.

However, in those situations where an organization is permeated and restricted by past practices and is accustomed (or required) to handling reports of substandard practices with a view of discipline or punishment, interviews by supervisory personnel may be impractical or impossible. In such situations certain approved staff personnel, or even outside or independent consultants, could conduct interviews. Sometimes these persons, because of their professional backgrounds, can guarantee anonymity and ensure that the negativity of the past is overcome.

One large high-risk company found that the benefits of a limited trial were significant enough to justify a full-time staff interviewer utilizing incident recall on a continuous basis. His scope includes periodic plant-wide incident recall as well as more frequent application in high risk areas. For most organizations, this may not be practical. In climates unfavorable to the applica-tion of incident recall through select supervisors, the emphasis should be on adjusting attitudes and preparing people for program application at a future time. With complete upper management support, a sound policy, adequate training and follow-up, an incident recall program can effectively be administered through regular supervisory channels. Just the indirect benefits from a positive management response to volunteered information on problems can justify the time and effort spent on such a program.

Privacy Preferred

Since the interview requires a good degree of concentration, interruptions can have a damaging effect upon the results. Best results are achieved in a location where there will be as few interruptions as possible. It should be pointed out that excessive noise can be just as disturbing as the telephone or other interruptions. These can be minimized by planning. Failure to achieve anticipated results in recall has sometimes been traced to the interview location. Recall is difficult while standing in a busy shop area next to an operating machine or while sitting on an uncomfortable locker room bench. Also, it conveys that this activity is not very important.

An office, where both the supervisor and the employee can sit comfortably in relative freedom from unnecessary outside noise, is generally best. People also tend to be more self-conscious about such conversations conducted in the view of their fellow workers. It should also be kept in mind that the employee's complete cooperation sometimes depends on the importance that is placed on ability to recall. The interview location can have a very positive effect by demonstrating the importance that management places on this special exercise.

Selection of People to be Interviewed

While the selection method could vary with the specific technique being employed, there is a general practice that can be recommended. Whenever the supervisor is using a recall technique that will involve a group of employees, it is best to use a system of selection that enables them to understand why specific people are being interviewed. For example, they could be selected by alphabetical order of their last names or by numerical order of their organization's personnel number identification. This type of selection places everyone on notice that they will get their chance in fair order, and it tends to minimize unnecessary guessing by employees as to why certain people get such attention from the interviewer.

An orderly system of selection is also best because interviews are probably not everyday occurrences. This alone tends to focus special attention on the person being interviewed. Exceptions to this general rule would be where the planned recall interview is being used as a problem-solving tool with a relatively small group of people on a specific job or occupation. Interviews would then be restricted to the smaller groups, or individuals, as the case may be. The others quickly understand exceptions when there is some logical explanation - as there would obviously be in these cases.

Adjusting Interview Time

The time required to conduct a planned recall interview will also vary with the particular method used. Just as with worker selection, there are several recommended general practices relative to the required time when the supervisor is utilizing a recall technique that will eventually involve everyone in a group. The immediate objective of the recall exercise is to obtain clear, accurate descriptions of incidents. Once this important objective has been fulfilled, the interviewer can determine the need to obtain any additional information on cause analysis or remedy. Many incidents recalled may have little or no potential for serious or major loss. In effect, they are not high potential (HIPO) incidents. Likewise, the probability of recurrence may be negligible for a considerable number. In most cases, it is best to use the available time getting the incidents reported. The interviewers can always make one or more personal follow-up contacts at a later mutually convenient time. This is not meant to demean the important role the employee can play in assisting the interviewer to determine the causes and remedies of high potential incidents. It is merely suggested as the most practical way to use the time available to the best advantage.

Experience has proven that a well-planned recall interview can be conducted in from 10 to 20 minutes, depending on the experience of the interviewer. The first few recall interviews would naturally take longer, in order to establish the special rapport which is necessary for effective recall. Subsequent interviews with the same person might require less time, since experience and knowledge reinforced by previous confidential disclosures would encourage and facilitate an easier exchange of information.

When incident recall is being applied to problem-solving, select proven interviewers could be used and the time involved may be dependent on the dimension of loss involved. Organizations recognizing the potential values of this technique have, on occasion, permitted extended periods of planned time with certain employees whose special knowledge could help provide answers to costly problems.

No-Fault Assurance a Must

As has been pointed out so often in training on accident investigation, many employees have been conditioned through experience to associate blame-fixing and fault-finding with the reporting of accidents. This well-founded association is one of the biggest reasons that many accidents are never reported by the people who could furnish the best information on the prevention of similar and even more serious occurrences in the future. The decision to use the planned incident recall interview in an organization's safety or loss control program should only be made if no-fault, no-discipline assurance can be given to every person participating. This type of confidential disclosure decision is, of course, made by top management before the program is ever introduced. In fact, it is so critical that a written policy, assuring no-fault confidential disclosure, signed by a chief executive, should be a must. The reason for its need must be thoroughly understood by every member of management or the program will be doomed to failure.

Experienced professionals feel so strongly about the importance of this point to the success of the program that they usually make putting a name on the incident report the option of the person reporting the incident. Actual experience in diverse types of organizations has proven repeatedly that any indication of fault-finding or discipline for information revealed through the incident recall interview system will close off the flow of vital information faster than any other single factor. The big question that must be answered by the organization and interviewers is simply, "Am I willing to give positive no-fault assurance to everyone involved in a planned recall interview, in exchange for an abundance of information that could be of value in preventing future losses?"

Most organizations that adopt the planned interview technique with its no-fault assurance policy also require confidentiality unless it is otherwise deemed best by mutual agreement of the supervisor and the employee being interviewed. This important aspect of the planned recall interview demands the highest degree of leadership maturity possessed by the supervisor or interviewer. It is this type of experience that will reinforce and strengthen the skills of those involved.

Preparation for Interviews

One of the first things the supervisor or other interviewer should do in preparation for the interview is to review personal facts and information that could acquaint him or her with anything that might be helpful in putting the employee at ease and stimulating participation in the recall exercise. This background will enable the supervisor to personalize comments and demonstrate the type of interest and relationship that encourages a spirit of cooperation.

It is easy to understand that employee transfers, replacements for illness and vacations, seasonal layoffs and other factors such as interviewer selection, would make it difficult for every interviewer to know this information in depth without preparation and possible help from others.

Another very important step is to prepare a checklist of potential sources of accidents involving the job of the employee to be interviewed. The same checklist can be used with others on the same job who will be interviewed at a later date. The checklist will assist the interviewer to stimulate the recall of incidents if it doesn't come easily. Experience has also proven that suggestions of specific areas of thought are great stimulators of recall.

Like priming a pump, one word or thought is frequently all that is needed to stimulate the recall of incidents that may be quite removed from the suggestion, yet can be brought back to mind by association with a familiar word or thought. The job description, job analysis or procedures and safety rules are excellent sources of items for the recall aid checklist. *Figure 5-2* shows a typical checklist that might be prepared as a tool to aid recall for crane operators.

The supervisor or interviewer should recognize that the only purpose of the checklist is to prime the pump (the memory) and not to be a complete guide for recall. The checklist may not even be necessary with certain people, but the good interviewer will always have it ready if recall does not come freely.

Conducting the Interview

In the final analysis, the success of the entire program rests on the incident recall interview itself. The rewards for effective application are too great to jeopardize success by not following the necessary guidelines established by experience and success. Generally speaking, the step-by-step procedure described in this section should be followed in every recall interview. After the first interview has been conducted with everyone in the group, the interviewer will certainly modify the details, but the general format must remain the same to produce the most effective

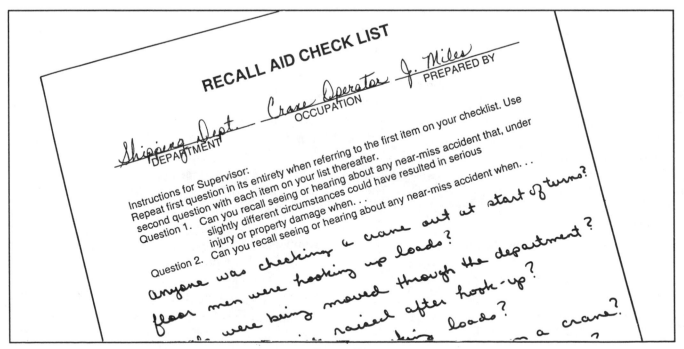

Figure 5-2

results. The quotation below was taken from an interview with a general plant manager who had introduced a planned incident recall program throughout his organization. This interview was conducted several months after a broad program had been introduced, and the questioner had inquired as to whether or not he would do anything differently if he had to introduce the program over again. His answer was:

> Yes, there are little things we've learned. For example, the importance of insisting that the initial training instructions be accepted on faith that recall will only work effectively when a proper rapport with the employee is established. We have had instances when supervisors have deviated from the original instructions, and just as we warned in advance during the training, recall was not as effective as with those supervisors who followed the recommended interview technique. The importance of the supervisor's checklist cannot be overemphasized.

The important step-by-step procedure that the interviewer must follow is described below:

1. **Put the employee at ease.** One of the best ways to create the favorable rapport necessary for good recall is to talk briefly about the employee's work, family or a subject discovered in advance to be of interest. Advance planning is vital to this important effort. Make sure you use his or her first name rather than the last. Be friendly, warm, cheerful, sympathetic and sincere. Emphasize the fact that you need and want his or her help. This step appeals to the basic psychological needs of the average person and motivates cooperation.

2. **Explain the purpose and state the importance of recall.** Don't keep the employee waiting. Tell him or her what incident recall is. (While most supervisors or interviewers will have explained the program to groups involved, in advance, there are usually several in every group that didn't get the word or didn't hear it properly.) Remind the person of the great aerospace successes because people were able to predict potential system failures in advance. Explain how major catastrophes such as those which have occurred in recent years might have been prevented by the use of this technique. This is what incident recall will do. Try to create a desire to be part of a program that can play an extremely important

role in the correction of problems that could cause major injury or death, or inflict extensive damage to equipment or property.

While the interviewer's comments can vary on subsequent occasions and may not require as much detail, keep in mind that motivation varies in its intensity, and an appropriate reminder of the important contribution the employee can make would always be in order. At this point, the interviewer is appealing to needs for acceptance and accomplishment, and desire for self-respect and status. Creating recognition of the real value and importance of the employee's role in accomplishing the objectives of the program can make a big difference in willingness to cooperate.

3. **Give assurance that recall will not result in blame-fixing or fault-finding and can be strictly confidential.** While every step in the recall routine is important, this is probably more important than others. The degree of recall the interviewer achieves on the first attempt is usually directly related to the ability to convince the employee that the conversation is privileged. There may be value in showing a copy of the no-fault confidential assurance policy signed by the chief executive. The supervisor should point out that the only purpose of recall is to aim at the facts related to near-injury/damage accidents. Depending on the organization's policy, the interviewer or supervisor can emphasize this point by letting the person choose whether or not his or her name should be placed on any form being used. The employee should be reminded that only by his or her willingness to share information with others will his or her name ever be associated with the incidents discussed. The no-fault assurance position of the organization, mentioned earlier, should be utilized throughout this part of the recall interview. Emphasis can be placed on the fact that a select group of supervisors or other interviewers are being used because of their special training and dedication to the policy.

4. **Point out that recall benefits everyone - the organization, the department, the employee and his or her family.** Explain that fewer injuries and less damage mean less lost time from work, less downtime of equipment and greater safety for the young men and women coming into the operation. Fewer accidents mean increased operating efficien-

cy, which results in an improved business climate, conducive to increased profit and job security that benefit everyone.

5. **Explain the use of the recall aid checklist.** Show the employee the checklist you have developed. Point out that you have selected aspects of his or her work activity that you believe could have had some involvement in near-accidents. Explain that the list was designed as an aid to remembering or recalling incidents he or she has seen or heard about, and that it need not be used if he or she can recall without it. The interviewer could explain that the words in the checklist provide associations with experiences stored in the memory that become unlocked when some key word or phrase is heard. If the recall goes well without this help, don't spoil a good thing. Lay the list aside and pursue the employee's own line of recall. Always have the list available for the next person who may need it, and add to it as recall or experience give you additional items. This casual, no-secrets approach also gives the person confidence in the interviewer.

6. **Apply recall, using the checklist.** Simply ask the employee to recall each near-accident he or she can remember seeing or hearing about that, under slightly different circumstances, could have resulted in major injury, property damage or catastrophe. Use the recall checklist to help. With each incident recalled, be sure to determine how many times he or she has seen or heard of its occurrence. This information will help determine the probable recurrence rate of this incident and serve as a guide to the urgency and extent of action necessary. Explain that the primary purpose of the interview is not to determine why the incident happened or what to do about it, as important as that is. Politely advise, if necessary, that you plan to come back to these aspects another time. It is extremely important to get all of the incidents reported in the time that is allotted for recall.

Experience has proved that people will sometimes report accidents during incident recall that were not previously reported. Whenever this happens, treat it in the same manner as the near-injury/damage incidents being reported. As a matter of fact, the same principles for recalling incidents can be used for the recall of accidents that resulted in unreported injuries or costly property damage.

7. **Ask questions to fill in the gaps.** Try to avoid interrupting the train of thought. Whenever possible, let the person complete the description of what happened. But do ask questions at the appropriate time, if necessary, to clarify important points or to clearly identify the incident.

8. **Review your understanding of the incident.** Repeat your understanding of each incident, just to make sure your information is accurate. Again, make sure your approach is tactful. Be warm and friendly during the review. Correct your detailed notes on any changes made in your understanding of the incident.

9. **Discuss causes and remedies if time permits.** Time permitting, and depending on the completion of the recall of incidents, you may want to invite the employee's valued opinion on the possible causes, as well as any suggested remedy or control. If you plan a later contact for this information say when the contact will be made. Prompt follow-up contacts, as much or more than anything else, give people a genuine feeling of contributing and being needed. Remedial action may frequently involve getting help from several other sources, just as it does in accident investigation. The most important thing of all is to get the record of incidents that will identify potential serious losses before they occur.

10. **Express your sincere thanks for the employee's cooperation.** Never fail to feed one of the deepest desires of every person - to know his or her contribution has been helpful. Be sincere and honest in whatever reaction is given, but always be sure to underline your personal appreciation with a thank-you. The interviewer who believes the employee has been helpful and who fully grasps the importance of the information being given is best able to convey appreciation.

Figure 5-3 shows several examples of actual incidents which were reported to supervisors during planned incident recall interviews. The value of obtaining information of this type to control future occurrences of similar events should be obvious.

INCIDENTS RECALLED THROUGH PLANNED INTERVIEWS

- While sweeping railroad switches during a snowstorm, a trackman caught his foot between a flat rod and a railroad tie. His helper had gone ahead to sweep other switches. The trackman could not get his foot released and he noticed the engine approaching. He screamed to attract the brakeman's attention. The brakeman saw him in time and stopped his train 10 feet away.

- Employee reported catching the heel of her shoe in a crack on one of the stair treads at the top of the front stairs in the main office. She caught the guard rail and narrowly missed falling down the stairs.

- An employee was working on top of a vertical mill. A crane passed over, knocking off his hard hat. Fortunately, it was only the hat and not the individual under it.

- Instructions were issued to change from gas to oil fuel because there was a shortage of gas due to the cold weather. In pulling the gas burner out and in the process of installing the oil burner, the employee had his face close to the fitting while trying to line up the burner. There was a backfire, causing smoke and fire to come out the end of the tube and almost burning the employee.

- Lift truck operator attempted to start a lift truck that was parked near a local floor heating unit. He had trouble starting it, so he opened up gas valve on propane tank to release condensation and in doing so, the gas hit the heating unit, causing flames to strike the man. Luckily he was not burned.

- The mail delivery boy tripped over the packing boxes at the top of the stairway on the landing platform outside the shipping room and nearly fell headlong down the stairs.

- The electrician approached a buffing machine in the shop with the intent of changing an indicator lamp. He opened circuit breaker marked "Buffer." But this switch was for lighting only — not for drive motor on same. As he turned to work on the machine, he barely missed walking into the buffer wheel at full speed, because operator last using this machine failed to turn buffer off. This was a surprise to the electrician, and certainly a near miss.

- A heavy piece of lumber came down off the high roof on Building "H" and narrowly missed one of the office girls walking across to the cafeteria.

- A bridge wheel packing box fell off crane going between JBT office and Charlie Bowan's office and nearly ran into the awning window that was opened into walkway.

- Safety lights were turned on and switch tagged out. Two men were replacing parts on the scrap transfer car on the floor. Overhead crane operator picked material up from the car with men working under it; they could have been mashed and easily killed.

- The bottom roll in a pile of carpets moved out of position, causing the whole pile to come down rolling across the aisleway about 11:50 a.m. yesterday. Some of those rolls weighed about a ton and could have caught several people if the incident had occurred a few minutes later.

- A maintenance man was working under a machine which had not been locked out. Another employee — unable to see the maintenance man — closed the switch and started the machine. Fortunately, at that instant, the maintenance man's hands were away from the moving parts of the machine.

- A tow motor was backing up in a comparatively dark area of a warehouse. The tow motor brushed against an employee who had been taking a short-cut through the building to get to the canteen.

Figure 5-3

Making Out The Report

Most organizations using planned incident recall interviews require the submission of an individual report form on each incident with high potential for major injury or damage, within a 48- to 72-hour period following the recall. This gives the interviewer an opportunity to follow up and complete the cause analyses and remedial recommendations with the person interviewed (or others if indicated). Detailed notes are usually made during the incident recall interview, with the final incident description written on the report form immediately following the interview, while all facts remain clear in the interviewer's mind.

The step-by-step procedure for conducting the interview has proven so important to effective recall that many organizations print it on top of a special supervisor's incident recall report form to serve as a guide and reminder during the interview. (See *Figure 5-4*.) This special form, including the interview procedure, is most frequently used during the introductory stages of the program. While "Incident Recall" requires an additional form, experience has proven its value. It assures good results and minimizes the tendency to shortcut and not properly apply the proven step-by-step method described. Most organizations eventually use one form, such as the one shown in *Figure 5-5*, for reporting both incidents and accidents.

Since there is usually some permissible lag time between the interview and the completion of the supervisor's report, another special form (such as shown in *Figure 5-6*) is sometimes required to be submitted within 24 hours of the interview. This latter form provides loss control personnel with a record that enables them to measure whether or not program goals are being achieved, and gives them a tool to follow up completion of individual incident report forms.

PRACTICAL APPLICATIONS OF FORMAL INCIDENT RECALL TECHNIQUES

There are several ways that formal incident recall interviews can be used to significant advantage in a loss control program. Specific applications that have proved of special value are briefly discussed below:

High-risk area applications. Perhaps the most significant values are in those locations known to possess a high-risk potential. The frequency of the interviews would be determined by the level of risk. The three factors in evaluating the level of risk would be the probable amount of loss if the undesired event occurred, the likelihood of its occurrence, and the frequency with which the exposure occurs. An extremely high level of risk, such as might be present in a large explosives plant or in certain petro-chemical operations, could completely justify a full-time person to conduct incident recall interviews or its regular use by selected supervisors and/or staff interviewers.

Problem-solving on an area or job basis. Planned recall interviews can be directed at the identification and solution of specific potential accidents or known accidents or problems where adequate causal informa-

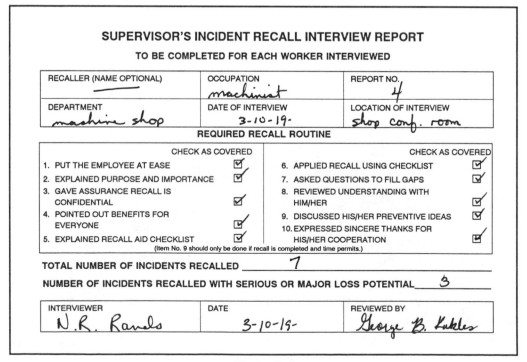

Figure 5-6

INCIDENT RECALL REPORT

COMPANY OR BRANCH Baldwin Works	DEPARTMENT-SHIFT Manufacturing 3-11	RECALL REPORT NO. 3
PERSON INTERVIEWED (NAME USE OPTIONAL) George P. Stall	OCCUPATION Operator A	DATE OF INTERVIEW Feb. 15, 19—

REQUIRED ROUTINE

CHECK AS COVERED

1. PUT THE EMPLOYEE AT EASE .... ☒
2. EXPLAINED PURPOSE AND IMPORTANCE .... ☒
3. GAVE ASSURANCE RECALL IS CONFIDENTIAL .... ☒
4. POINTED OUT BENEFITS FOR EVERYONE .... ☒
5. EXPLAINED RECALL AID CHECK LIST .... ☒

CHECK AS COVERED

6. APPLIED RECALL USING CHECK LIST .... ☒
7. ASKED QUESTIONS TO FILL GAPS .... ☒
8. REVIEWED UNDERSTANDING WITH HIM/HER .... ☒
9. DISCUSSED HIS/HER PREVENTIVE IDEAS .... ☒
10. EXPRESSED SINCERE THANKS FOR HIS/HER COOPERATION .... ☒

(Item No. 9 should only be done if recall is completed and time permits.)

RISK

EVALUATION OF LOSS POTENTIAL IF NOT CORRECTED	LOSS SEVERITY POTENTIAL ☒ MAJOR ☐ SERIOUS ☐ MINOR	PROBABILITY OF OCCURRENCE ☐ FREQUENT ☒ OCCASIONAL ☐ SELDOM

DESCRIPTION

DESCRIBE HOW THE EVENT OCCURRED AND EMERGENCY ACTIONS.

Recaller was riding maintenance scooter downhill from the #2 power station when the brakes failed to operate causing the vehicle to run wild going down entire hill between buildings and across main street, just missing a collision with an automobile traveling north. Maintenance personnel determined that the brake bands were worn substantially beyond normal wear.

CAUSE ANALYSIS

IMMEDIATE CAUSES, WHAT SUBSTANDARD ACTIONS AND CONDITIONS CAUSED OR COULD CAUSE THE EVENT?

Maintenance records verified that a substandard brake condition caused the mechanical failures involved. The recaller indicated that a pre-use check of the brakes was not made at the start of the work turn. A personal check indicates that only about 20% of operators are completing their pre-use equip. check forms.

BASIC CAUSES, WHAT SPECIFIC PERSONAL OR JOB FACTORS CAUSED OR COULD CAUSE THIS EVENT? CHECK ON BACK. EXPLAIN HERE.

Lack of knowledge by operators of the critical importance of pre-use checks. A system to determine that operators of this equipment are checking critical parts prior to use is not working. In addition, these vehicles are not getting to the garage on schedule for the required quarterly inspection and routine maintenance check.

ACTION PLAN

REMEDIAL ACTIONS, WHAT HAS BEEN AND/OR SHOULD BE DONE TO CONTROL THE CAUSES LISTED?

1. I have requested our shop clerk to notify me each day before 9 a.m. of any scheduled operator that has not turned in his pre-use equipment check form. 2. The clerk will also compile each operator's conformance to this pre-use check on a monthly report. 3. Scooter rules have been reissued to all operators with special instructions on rule #10. 4. Charles Wright, garage supervisor, will recommend a notification system for identifying, with colored stickers, which vehicles need inspection.

SIGNATURE OF INVESTIGATOR *Charles Reed*		FOLLOW-UP: CIRCLE NUMBER FOR TEMPORARY, X OUT FOR FINAL ACTION DATE.
SIGNATURE OF REVIEWER *Joe Smith*	DATE 2/18/19—	X 2/15/19— X 2/15/19— 5. _____ X 2/15/19— ⓪ 2/15/19— 6. _____

Figure 5-4

INVESTIGATION REPORT

REPORT QUALITY SCORE

1. COMPANY OR DIVISION South Bend Works	**2. DEPARTMENT** Electric	

3. LOCATION OF INCIDENT Extreme South End bay #2, bldg.4	**4. DATE OF INCIDENT** 2/10/19—	**5. TIME** AM ⊘(PM) 2:30	**6. DATE OF REPORT** 2/10/19—

____(20)

INJURY OR ILLNESS		PROPERTY DAMAGE	OTHER ACTUAL OR POTENTIAL LOSS
7. INJURED'S NAME		**14. PROPERTY DAMAGE**	**18. TYPE** Near Miss
8. PART OF BODY	**9. DAYS LOST**	**15. NATURE OF DAMAGE**	**19. COST** —
10. NATURE OF INJURY OR ILLNESS		**16. COST** ESTIMATED ACTUAL	**20. NATURE OF LOSS** Near fall from overhead
11. OBJECT/EQUIPMENT/SUBSTANCE INFLICTING HARM		**17. OBJECT/EQUIPMENT/SUBSTANCE INFLICTING DMG.**	**21. OBJECT/EQUIPMENT/SUBSTANCE RELATED** Crane bridge parking brake
12. OCCUPATION	**13. EXPERIENCE**	**22. PERSON IN CONTROL OF ACTIVITY AT TIME OF OCCURRENCE.** Unknown at present	

____(10)

RISK	EVALUATION OF LOSS POTENTIAL IF NOT CORRECTED	**23. LOSS SEVERITY POTENTIAL** ☒ MAJOR ☐ SERIOUS ☐ MINOR	**24. PROBABILITY OF OCCURRENCE** ☐ FREQUENT ☒ OCCASIONAL ☐ SELDOM

____(5)

25. DESCRIBE HOW THE EVENT OCCURRED.

Recaller was sent to adjust hoist brake on crane. After pulling main switch in cab, he proceeded to top of crane to adjust brake. As he started to perform job, crane started to drift down track. Crane operator depressed bridge brake pedal to stop crane causing recaller to lose his balance and almost fall off crane; only ladder that extends about 3 feet above crane prevented him from falling to ground.

____(15)

26. IMMEDIATE CAUSES: WHAT SUBSTANDARD ACTIONS AND CONDITIONS CAUSED OR COULD CAUSE THE EVENT?

The bridge parking brake did not set when main switch was pulled open. The recaller should have checked to be sure the brake was set before going on the bridge. Also, he should have been wearing the required safety belt to avoid falling.

27. BASIC CAUSES: WHAT SPECIFIC PERSONAL OR JOB FACTORS CAUSED OR COULD CAUSE THIS EVENT? CHECK ON BACK. EXPLAIN HERE.

Improper motivation to follow existing rules. Inadequate knowledge of the best way to do these inspections. The brake had not been adjusted by maintenance personnel. Proper inspection would have discovered this need. Records show that it was also not adjusted on the turn following the incident.

____(15)

28. REMEDIAL ACTIONS: WHAT HAS AND OR SHOULD BE DONE TO CONTROL THE CAUSES LISTED?

1. I reinstructed my crew at our weekly meeting to make sure parking brake is set and working before going on top of crane. 2. Also have improved my job instruction when assigning work. 3. Have recommended a change in the method of parking brake inspection. 4. My entire crew has been equipped with the new type safety belts and lanyards for 100% wear with regular work pants. 5. The related rules have been completely reviewed with all employees.

____(30)

29. SIGNATURE OF INVESTIGATOR *Smli Brown*	**30. FOLLOW-UP: CIRCLE NUMBER FOR TEMPORARY X OUT FOR FINAL ACTION DATE.**
	X 2/10/19— ② 2/10/19— X 2/10/19—
31. SIGNATURE OF REVIEWER *Brad Johnson* **32. DATE** 2/12/19—	X 2/10/19— X 2/10/19— 6. _____

____(5)

Figure 5-5

TOTAL SCORE _____

tion may be lacking. Since many unreported accidents and incidents of a similar type are probably occurring, the interviewer can use the incident recall technique, with its confidential disclosure atmosphere, to obtain additional information that could be helpful in developing a solution to a specific problem. One such problem solved through the recall technique involved the damaging of end gates in railroad cars used by a manufacturer to transport bulk materials. Accident reports were grossly inadequate in revealing causal information of any significant value. Recall by equipment operators identified many occurrences of near damage and actual damage to the end gates by operators who were using methods they knew could be improved by establishing a simple procedure that had never been recognized by management. The common practice of the operator was to lower unloading devices into the cars by yard crane and move them back and forth to scoop up materials. This practice was causing the heavy devices to strike or nearly strike the end gates with every movement. The simple procedure that evolved was to lower unloading devices at the end of the car and always lift them at the car's mid-point. A standard job procedure for this job, with a reasonable frequency of planned observations, reduced the costs of end gate replacement 82% for this company.

The majority of supervisors will recognize the general problem-solving value of the incident recall technique, but special problems of unusual loss dimension deserve the best interviewers possible. Staff professionals or selected supervisors, who have proven their skill at recall, are generally considered to be the best interviewers for these important assignments.

Use in the termination interview. An employer of several thousand short-term employees per year in a high-risk industry found that a good application of planned incident recall is with employees upon termination. Previously they had simply asked departing employees if they had any suggestions for the improvement of safety, quality or production. This approach received an average of 75 to 100 suggestions per year. The first year of incident recall interviews with this same group brought reports of more than 2,000 incidents with high potential for major injury or property damage that had not been previously reported. This application of incident recall made a major contribution to the continued improvement of safety and health conditions for the organization.

While the average employee being given a close-off interview prior to lay-off or termination is certainly not overjoyed, he or she does generally want to ensure the possibility of return, or at least a positive recommendation for a future job. By utilizing the planned interview, a supervisor or other person using the recall exercise can be more certain that an abundance of helpful accident prevention information can be gained.

Plant-wide applications. High-risk organizations sometimes require that supervisors or other interviewers conduct formal interviews with people throughout the organization. Some organizations do this on a *periodic* basis. Interviews are scheduled at a reasonable rate, using a random sampling technique. Then the program is interrupted for a pre-determined time before starting the routine again. During the interview period, the program is reinforced by sharing information about the successes which were achieved in high potential incident reporting as a result of the interviews.

Other organizations use formal incident recall interviews plant-wide on a *continuous* basis. Because of the supervisory planning and effort required to do an effective job, an objective is usually established of 2-4 incident recall interviews per month. This enables the supervisor to have recall with an average-size work group of 15 several times each year. Management groups have come to recognize that the benefits to be derived from this program are too great to risk losing them through the improperly-conducted interviews that can result when objectives are not realistic. The number of incidents that will be reported through a program utilizing this reasonable rate of interviews will far exceed the number of accidents voluntarily reported through normal program channels. As mentioned earlier, continuous plant-wide application could also be conducted by a special staff professional. This may be in conjunction with a program directed through general supervision or in lieu of such a program. This approach generally requires excellent cooperation between the special interviewer, the supervisor of the area and the employees involved.

Considerable thought should be given before starting a continuous program of formal incident recall on a plant-wide basis. Proper application of this technique requires considerable interviewing time and administrative paperwork. The risks involved in the operation should be carefully evaluated in order to make a good cost-benefit decision on the breadth of application. Generally speaking, the applications mentioned earlier are the best, and continuous plant-wide applications in general business or industrial operations are not recommended.

INFORMAL INCIDENT RECALL TECHNIQUES

Organizations have developed a variety of ways to get incidents recalled through informal techniques. Here are several of the most common:

Group Meetings

A number of supervisors have made it a practice to conclude each safety meeting with a request for incidents that those attending might have experienced themselves or be aware of. Also, the value of reporting near-misses can be the subject of an entire meeting, with examples of those previously reported and the potential losses which have been avoided.

There are at least two values of using group meetings to encourage incident recall. One, of course, is in the actual incidents reported and the steps taken to ensure that near-misses don't become "hits." The second value is in a greatly heightened safety consciousness of those involved and the knowledge gained from the experience of others.

The good supervisor will keep incident reports brief and make sure that any group comments are always conducted in a positive way. Reporting what the person did to avert the accident is one of the best ways to accomplish this.

General Management Meetings

Some organizations have reinforced this practice by including a call for reports of high-potential incidents at general management meetings. This practice also serves to alert managers of other areas to incidents with a high loss potential and to bring to bear on the problem the diverse perspectives of people other than those directly involved. It also allows upper level managers to model the appropriate behaviors involved with incident reporting and thus reinforce the importance of this whole program activity.

Personal Contacts

A significant number of organizations have a program of planned personal contacts between a supervisor and each of his or her people. This is conducted on an individual, one-to-one basis. (See the chapter, "Personal Communications," for more detail of how these work.) Although it is a simple matter, it can be a highly productive use of the time to conclude each of these personal contacts with a request for reports of incidents. This personal approach appeals to the individual who might be embarrassed to speak up in a group setting.

Written Reports

Figure 5-7 is a form to allow and encourage people to submit written reports of near-accidents. These forms can be made available at time-clock stations, change rooms, break areas, etc. They should be accompanied by a locked box into which they can be deposited.

NEAR-ACCIDENT REPORT

NEAR-ACCIDENT. Use this section to report events that, under slightly different circumstances, could have resulted in injury to persons or damage to plant equipment/materials/environments. This is your chance to help us stop an accident before it has a chance to "get" someone or something.

I,_____witnessed a near-accident on_____in the_____department.
    (name is optional)   (date)

Here's what happened:

_____

_____

_____

I think this could have injured/damaged _____
                                  (person, object, material, environment)

if _____
                  (different circumstances)

I recommend the following actions _____

_____

Put your completed form in one of the collection boxes or submit it to your supervisor.

Figure 5-7

Posters and Publications

Leading safety organizations around the world have now recognized the value of incident recall and reporting. Posters and other publications (such as *Figure 5-8*) as well as films are available. These serve to publicize, teach and reinforce the value of the program.

Regardless of the techniques employed, the three most important practices by the supervisor to stimulate the employee's desire to voluntarily report incidents on a continuous basis are: the frequency of communication that encourage reporting, immediate behavior recognition of those who report incidents, and prompt effective action to control their recurrence.

Limitations of Incident Recall

While there is little doubt that the use of incident recall has benefits that outweigh its shortcomings, it is only proper to indicate the potential limitations of the technique. Several have been briefly mentioned previously:

1. While "incidents" occur much more frequently than loss-producing accidents, they too, are rela-

NEAR-ACCIDENTS ARE WARNINGS!

Figure 5-8

tively infrequent events. It is a false assumption to believe that an incident recall system will replace those program activities such as observation and inspection, that detect substandard practices at an even earlier stage in the cause and effect sequence.

2. Since incidents are "near-accidents" that occurred in the past, the investigator cannot see or examine the circumstances and evidence that led to the occurrence. Most of the related information must be obtained from the recaller, who may have limited or biased knowledge of what really happened, or may have caused the happening. While there are sometimes ways to check what really happened, we must largely rely on the memory of the recaller for our data.

3. Neither incident nor accident recall information will necessarily tell us the causes that led to their occurrence, or the possible controls. Interviewers frequently place too much value on the limited knowledge revealed by one witness or one knowledgeable person when, in reality, this should be the beginning of a search for as many facts as possible to determine the real causes.

4. Incident recall is no panacea for the accident problem. It is simply another useful tool to add to your arsenal of program activities. The value received from its application will be a direct function of the planning and effectiveness with which the program is introduced and applied.

ACCIDENT IMAGING

Another practical technique for identifying the potential causes of major accidents or catastrophes is accident imaging, sometimes called accident simulation or accident scenarios. **Accident imaging is the act of visualizing in one's mind that combination of variable factors that could come together under the right circumstances to cause a major accident.** It is more than hazard reporting. Usually when someone reports a hazard he or she has in mind an accident that could occur because of it. Hazard reports usually describe a condition, with the visualization of one or two causes that could result in the hazard being involved in an accident loss. Accident imaging, on the other hand, describes a sequence of a larger group of events or circumstances, specifying person, place, equipment, substance, actions, timing, etc., that could come together under certain circumstances to result in a loss. With all its values, hazard reporting fails to adequately identify the multiple causes and circumstances that combine to produce the interactions that result in the accident.

Quite frequently, people have recognized the multiple causes and circumstances that could be involved with a potential accident or loss before it occurred, but were not properly motivated to report them. This is precisely the objective of this important new technique.

Accident imaging and simulation have been successfully used in a wide variety of situations. Among these are prevention and identification of computer fraud and institutional embezzlement, hospital risk management, disaster planning for natural disasters, predicting and preventing grain explosions and avoidance of maritime collisions, rammings and groundings. Its use in industry has enabled the prediction and prevention of potential major losses and catastrophes. Because of the tremendous increase in risks involved with new technology as well as the rapid growth in the number and size of claims associated with losses, it will become even more important in the future.

Consider the following situations:

1. The pilot of a Phantom jet is in a simulated battle situation. The safety bolts which would prevent his Sidewinder missiles from firing have been removed. However, the ground crew failed to put tape over the master arms switch, which controls the electric circuit to the missiles, to stop it being applied accidentally. This was because there was no tape in stock. As a part of the training exercise, he intercepts two other jets; and in the split-second excitement of the moment, he forgets about the missing tape. When he turns on his cockpit camera to record the simulated kill he also fires the missile, shooting down a $15,000,000 jet fighter whose pilot fortunately bailed out. Enough circumstances involved with this situation could have been imaged to prevent or control it. Instead, it actually happened.

2. Early each morning a narrow-gauge railroad, taking a load of explosives to a major construction project, goes through a chemical storage area. Periodically, there is a delay and it comes through at lunchtime just as a large group of people are emerging from a nearby building. It is a known fact that the gear boxes on the cars are not always properly lubricated. As a result, they occasionally freeze up, the wheels drag, and the heat is transmitted up through the frame of the car. The result is an explosion in the middle of the chemical storage area with multiple fatalities to the office workers. The circumstances involved could have been imaged. Instead, a very similar accident really happened.

3. Two employees are repairing a loose flange and double plate on a belt-loading spout in a major export elevator tunnel in preparation for loading a ship. Because of poor housekeeping, considerable dust has accumulated. One of the employees bumps the spout while the other is drilling with a hand drill. Dust is shaken loose into suspension where it is ignited by the arcing motor brushes. The resulting explosion travels down the tunnel, up the elevator leg, and through the gallery. Two employees die and the elevator is destroyed. This accident did not happen because the circumstances were imaged and preventive action was taken to ensure that it did not.

Introducing the Program

Like any other new activity, accident imaging must be properly introduced, explained, and promoted. An explanation such as the following might be used to introduce the program:

> We are introducing a new technique called accident imaging in our safety program. It involves getting everyone to visualize the things that could come together under certain circumstances to cause a major accident or other loss. Almost everyone has at one time or another visualized an accident that could happen. Accident imaging is not just hazard reporting. It is visualizing the combination of people/equipment/materials and environmental factors that could come together at a particular point in time to result in a major accident loss. I want you to think about accidents or losses that you can visualize that might have happened. I'll contact you in the near future to ask you to tell me about any accidents you have visualized or imaged.

The program can be promoted in a variety of ways, like using a poster such as was shown in *Figure 5-8*, employee publications, bulletin boards, training sessions, group meetings and personal contacts.

How the Program Works

The seven steps of the accident imaging technique are shown in *Figure 5-9*. They are:

Step 1: Description. Think beyond the accidents and near-accidents which have happened to those that *could* happen if certain acts or conditions occurred. Most often this does not involve "flights of fancy." In any work force there are those who have already imaged accidents which realistically could occur. With

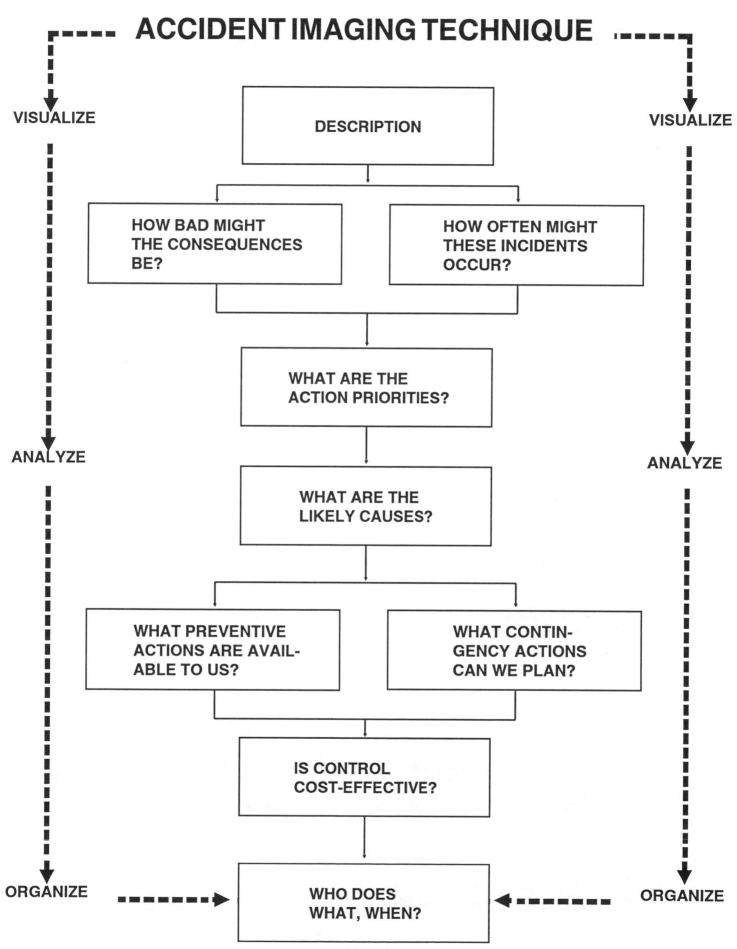

Figure 5-9

the right approach this valuable information can be yours for the asking. Here is one that was actually imaged:

> The damper on the exhaust vent of the waste furnace where we burn scrap rubber (in a tire plant) froze up one night because of the buildup of carbon. The maintenance employee climbed up a nearby make-shift scaffolding to free it up by shaking it. Because of the distance between the scaffold and the vent pipe, he had to stretch way over. He lost his balance and fell 20 feet into a pool of toxic liquids at the base of the furnace. He lost consciousness because of his injuries and drowned in the sump pool.

You can do accident imaging by yourself, with one other person or in group sessions with people in similar jobs. There may be some organizations and situations where group brainstorming will help to get accidents imaged. People in a group setting may, of course, be reluctant to describe imaged accidents that involve improper actions of their colleagues. On the positive side, you have the value of one person's thoughts stimulating the thinking of others in the group. People will be reminded of other realistically known situations and circumstances. For successful brainstorming, it is important to withhold evaluation until as many accidents as possible are imaged. Too early an evaluation can close off the process. You can stimulate the imagination, if necessary, by considering a variety of questions, for instance, questions built around P-E-M-E.

> **PEOPLE** - What contacts are present that could cause injury, illness, stress or strain? Could the worker be caught in, on or between? Struck by? Fall from? Fall into? What practices are likely to downgrade efficiency, quality, safety or productivity?

> **EQUIPMENT** - What circumstances and situations are presented by the tools, machines, vehicles or other equipment? What equipment emergencies are most likely to occur? How might the equipment cause loss of efficiency, quality, safety or productivity?

> **MATERIAL** - What potential accidents are presented by chemicals, raw materials, or products? What are the specific problems involving materials handling? How might materials cause loss of efficiency, quality, safety or productivity?

> **ENVIRONMENT** - What are the potential losses from housekeeping and disorder? What are

the potential problems from sound, lighting, heat, cold, ventilation or radiation? How might environmental factors cause loss of efficiency, quality, safety or productivity?

Step 2: Evaluation. After generating descriptions of potential accidents, evaluate each of them in terms of: (1) if this accident should happen, how bad are the losses likely to be; (2) how likely is the accident to happen; and (3) what is the cost of control? These are the first three questions in the Guide to Management Risk Decisions shown in *Figure 5-10*.

Step 3: Priorities. Use the evaluation results to rank each accident imaged in order of priority. If you let the group help you do this, you will minimize the possibility of a person feeling that his or her contribution has been slighted or arbitrarily ruled out.

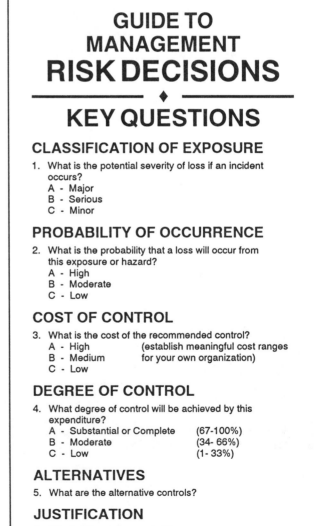

GUIDE TO MANAGEMENT
RISK DECISIONS
♦
KEY QUESTIONS

CLASSIFICATION OF EXPOSURE

1. What is the potential severity of loss if an incident occurs?
   A - Major
   B - Serious
   C - Minor

PROBABILITY OF OCCURRENCE

2. What is the probability that a loss will occur from this exposure or hazard?
   A - High
   B - Moderate
   C - Low

COST OF CONTROL

3. What is the cost of the recommended control?
   A - High   (establish meaningful cost ranges
   B - Medium   for your own organization)
   C - Low

DEGREE OF CONTROL

4. What degree of control will be achieved by this expenditure?
   A - Substantial or Complete   (67-100%)
   B - Moderate   (34-66%)
   C - Low   (1-33%)

ALTERNATIVES

5. What are the alternative controls?

JUSTIFICATION

6. Why is this one suggested?

Figure 5-10

Step 4: Causal Analysis: Imaged accidents which have high potential should be further analyzed to determine their causes. You might even want to evaluate them further using the Investigation Report form in *Figure 5-5* as a guide. The list of basic causes in the chapter, "Causes and Effects," will also be helpful.

Step 5: Action Plans. Based on the causal analysis, develop plans which include both **preventive** actions (those which will keep the accident from happening) and **contingency** actions (those which will minimize losses in case the accident does occur).

Step 6: Cost-Effectiveness. Now comes the time to decide: "Is the control worth the cost?" This is where you calculate the cost of the resources required for the loss control actions, and weigh that cost against the value of control. Three key questions to answer are:
1. How widely can the controls be applied?
2. How much will the controls cost?
3. How effective will the controls be?

Step 7: Accountabilities. For the cost-effective measures, convert the action plans into work. Determine who is to do **what,** and **when.** Communicate responsibilities and maintain accountabilities.

Major Applications of Accident Imaging

There are several major applications of accident imaging which have proven to be valuable. Among these are:

1. With individual workers from groups doing work which is known to have high risks.

2. Brainstorming in group sessions to image accidents.

3. Brainstorming in group sessions of people with interrelated work activities to further develop and analyze basic descriptions of high potential accidents already imaged.

4. Group brainstorming sessions with special groups of staff or supervisory personnel.

5. Accidents imaged reports (*Figure 5-11*) to be placed in a special report box.

6. Use in termination interviews.

REPORT OF ACCIDENT IMAGED OR NEAR-ACCIDENT

ACCIDENT IMAGED - Use the space below to report an accident you have visualized in your mind that could result because of the acts of people, conditions and/or circumstances that could come together to result in a major accident involving harm to people, property damage or process loss.

NEAR-ACCIDENT (INCIDENT) - Use the space below to report events that you have seen or heard about that under slightly different circumstances could have resulted in major injury, property damage or process loss.

Please check as appropriate:
Accident imaged _____ Near-accident _____

Describe the event and the actual or potential circumstances related:

I think this could have injured/damaged _____
(persons, objects, materials, environment)

if _____
(different circumstances)

I recommend the following actions:

DATE _____   NAME (OPTIONAL) _____

Put your completed form in one of the collection boxes or submit to your supervisor.

Figure 5-11

116 - Practical Loss Control Leadership

Helpful Hints for Planned Accident Imaging Interviews

Here are some guidelines for accident imaging interviews which have been gleaned from successful programs:

1. Selected front-line supervisors can be used as facilitators or interviewers.
2. Management at all levels should participate in various ways to lend their important support.
3. Imaging discussions conducted at the location or site facilitate visualizing and remembering. They also enable better involvement and contribution by the interviewer/facilitator.
4. A proper understanding of the accident imaging technique is essential to effective participation.
5. While no-fault assurance and confidentiality are not absolutely necessary, having such a policy enables its use if it becomes important.
6. No-fault assurance and confidentiality are especially useful when accident imaging is combined with incident recall.
7. Advance notification and information about the program (usually a week or so) is important to workers' effective participation.
8. Interviews with individuals should be conducted at the designated time and place.
9. Imaging is especially useful with individuals and groups whose work activities are interrelated.
10. Imaging can be a successful means of involving people from the engineering and research disciplines in the safety and health/loss control program.

Other Applications

Other applications of accident/incident imaging are as unlimited as your imagination. For starters, here are some examples:

- In training programs, trainees can develop their own descriptions of potential accidents for use in case study and role-playing exercises.
- Use a role-play exercise in which a disgruntled employee unloads to a supervisor about "all the safety and health things that could go wrong around here" ... and how the supervisor reacts.
- Quality circles, loss improvement project teams, and other problem-solving teams can invest some of their time and talent in "potential problem analysis," rather than simply reacting to past problems.
- Based on inspections, you can stimulate the imaging

process by posing questions such as, "What kinds of accidents do you think that condition (or practice) could lead to?"
- In participative emergency preparedness planning, ask employees to develop "worst case scenarios" for their own areas of the organization. Then get their ideas on prevention and control. This application is of such great value that it is almost a must for high-risk organizations.
- In safety meetings for off-the-job safety, have people develop scenarios of accidents that could happen in and around their homes. Use the scenarios for analysis of control measures. Discuss how the basic controls are the same on and off the job.
- In a safety promotion program, use enlarged photographs with the caption. "What kinds of accidents could this cause?" In meetings and contacts, follow up with, "What things can be done to prevent such accidents?" For job/task analyses, ask employees to describe "what could go wrong" at each step of the job/task. Use these descriptions in developing control measures.
- When giving job instruction on a critical assignment, ask the employee to "describe the loss incidents that could occur at this critical point." Use the results in coaching and tipping.
- Stimulate people to think about specialized aspects of safety/loss control by asking them to "describe several accidents that could happen because of inadequate purchasing controls" (or engineering controls, or medical controls, or hiring controls). Use these scenarios for discussion, analysis and preventive action.
- Related to investigations, ask people to describe what could have happened under slightly different circumstances. Use these scenarios as thought-joggers for additional control measures.
- As part of a safety theme campaign (on protective equipment or rules compliance, for instance) ask people to submit descriptions of "accidents that haven't happened yet, but could, because of non-compliance." Use these in a contest or in other parts of the program.

Program Benefits

Here are some of the numerous benefits from the use of accident imaging:

1. It is even more "before-the-fact" than incident recall.
2. The higher the risks, the more checks and balances are required. This is another check and balance for

high-risk situations.

3. It is another proven means of gaining employee participation in the safety and health program.
4. It is participative management at its best.
5. It provides an excellent opportunity to express appreciation to those who have contributed their thoughts.

Leading safety practitioners and thinkers fully agree that the higher the risks, the more checks and balances should exist. The higher the risks involved with specific areas of an operation or the overall operation, the more organized, regular and systematic the incident recall and accident imaging that should be used.

CORE CONCEPTS IN REVIEW

Increasing risk factors and the increasing consequences of failure make it even more important to predict and control the causes of major accidents before they occur. Accident statistics alone are not adequate for this purpose. Two successfully used techniques are incident recall and accident imaging.

Incident Recall is a modification of an approach called the Critical Incident Technique.

1. The Critical Incident Technique is based on gathering a **large number** of incidents and examining them **to detect patterns**.

2. Incident recall requires that **each incident be**

evaluated to determine its **potential** to cause a major loss and its **probability** of occurrence.

Planned incident recall interviews can be conducted by selected and trained supervisors, qualified staff personnel or outside specialists.

1. **Confidentiality** and no-fault assurance are critical to the program's success and should be established in a special **policy statement** from senior management.
2. The interviews should be done in privacy. The primary purpose is to get as many **high potential incidents** recalled as possible.
3. The interview time can be adjusted to deal with **causes and prevention** as well.

Guidelines for conducting interviews are:

1. Put the employee at ease.
2. Explain the purpose and importance of recall.
3. Give no-fault and confidentiality assurance.
4. Point out the benefits.
5. Explain the recall aid checklist.
6. Apply recall, using the checklist as needed.
7. Ask questions to fill in the gaps.
8. Review your understanding of the incident.
9. Discuss causes and remedies if time permits.
10. Express sincere thanks.

Formal incident recall should include:

1. High-risk areas
2. Problem solving
3. Termination interviews
4. Plant-wide applications for high-risk organizations.

Informal incident recall can be used in:

1. Group meetings
2. General management meetings
3. Personal contacts
4. Written incident reports

Accident Imaging is the act of **visualizing** in one's mind that combination of variable factors that could come together under the right circumstances to cause **a major accident.** Its usefulness has been proven in a wide variety of applications. Like any other program activity, accident imaging must be properly introduced, explained and promoted.

The seven steps involved in accident imaging are:

1. Descriptions of accidents that could happen if certain acts and conditions occurred
2. Evaluation of potential severity, probability and cost of control
3. Establishing priorities
4. Causal analysis
5. Action plans
6. Cost-effectiveness
7. Accountabilities

Among the major applications of accident imaging are:

1. Individuals doing high-risk work
2. Brainstorming in group sessions
3. Accident imaged reports
4. Termination interviews

> **THE HIGHER THE RISKS, THE MORE CHECKS AND BALANCES SHOULD EXIST. INCIDENT RECALL AND ACCIDENT IMAGING ARE TWO PROVEN TECHNIQUES.**

KEY QUESTIONS

1. What's the main thought behind the statement, "Accidents are our enemies, but close calls can be our friends"?

2. Define "incident."

3. Explain the 1-10-30-600 ratios.

4. Why can we not rely on accident statistics alone to predict future losses?

5. How does the Critical Incident Technique differ from the Incident Recall Technique?

6. What are three of the important factors that could have a major impact on the results of an incident recall program?

7. List the ten steps in conducting an incident recall interview.

8. State in your own words what accident imaging is.

9. How does accident imaging differ from hazard reporting?

10. What are the seven steps of the accident imaging technique?

11. Which three of the applications of accident imaging will be most useful to you?

12. What does it mean, "the higher the risks, the more checks and balances should exist"?

PRACTICAL APPLICATIONS SUMMARY

S - For Supervisors
E - For Executives
C - For Safety/Loss Control Coordinators

	S	E	C
1. Establish a "no-fault assurance" policy regarding incidents reported in the incident recall program.		x	
2. Ensure that the no-fault policy is complied with in practice.	x	x	x
3. Establish performance standards and responsibilities for incident recall activities.		x	
4. Develop forms, instructions, and procedures (if required) to aid incident recall and imaging activities.			x
5. Perform incident recall responsibilities in compliance with standards.	x	x	x
6. See that incident recall and imaging concepts are included in training programs for workers and for members of management.		x	x
7. Develop recall aid checklists.	x		
8. Conduct incident recall interviews with workers.	x		
9. Use incident recall in management meetings.		x	
10. Participate in critical incident investigations.	x	x	x
11. Follow up incident investigations with prevention and control measures.	x	x	
12. See that incident recall interviews are tried and evaluated in the exit interview process.		x	x
13. Integrate incident recall and imaging concepts into safety promotion activities.	x	x	x
14. Appraise and audit incident recall performance to the established standards.		x	x
15. Use incident recall and imaging techniques in a variety of formal and informal ways, to get more complete participation in more complete accident/loss control.	x	x	x

CHAPTER 6

PLANNED INSPECTIONS

"To look is one thing. To see what you look at is another. To understand what you see is another. To learn from what you understand is something else. But to act on what you learn is all that really matters."
— Winston Churchill

INTRODUCTION

Inspection is one of the best tools available to find problems and assess their risks *before* accidents and other losses occur. A well-managed inspection program can meet goals such as these:

1. **Identify potential problems** that were not anticipated during design or task analysis. Standards overlooked during design, and hazards not discovered during job/task analysis, become more apparent when inspecting the functioning workplace and workers.

2. **Identify equipment deficiencies.** Among the basic causes of problems are normal wear and tear and abuse or misuse. Inspections help managers find out if equipment is getting worn to a substandard condition, is inadequate in capacity or has been used improperly.

3. **Identify improper employee actions.** Since inspections cover both conditions and practices, they help managers spot substandard methods and practices that have loss potential.

4. **Identify effects of changes** in processes or materials. Processes frequently change from the original design. As different materials become available, or as original materials are restricted, changes are made. The changes occur gradually and their total, cumulative effects may go unnoticed. Inspections give managers regular opportunities to concentrate on current materials, and current problems... to see what's going on.

5. **Identify inadequacies in remedial actions.** Remedial actions are usually taken for a specific problem. If they are not adequately developed, they can cause other problems. If they are not adequately implemented, the original problem recurs. Inspections give follow-up and feedback regarding how well the remedial actions are working.

6. **Provide management self-appraisal information.** The inspection is an excellent opportunity for appraising management performance. It is a means for disciplined examination of the way things are being managed, giving you a picture of:

   - Well-conditioned equipment *or* key items that are about to break down
   - Efficient layout *or* congestion and poor use of space
   - Tools in order *or* scattered where they must be searched out when needed
   - Materials ready for use *or* buried behind and under things where they have to be dug out
   - Safe work areas *or* ones with slip and trip hazards, unprotected points of operation, sharp points or edges, health hazards and so on
   - Clean work areas *or* ones that will require shutdown and cleanup the next time an executive or a customer is scheduled to visit.

7. **Demonstrate management commitment** through visible activity for safety and health. Any manager worthy of the title, whether supervisor or executive, checks regularly to see that people have the things

they need to get the job done. Commonly, the "things" are job knowledge, equipment and materials, as well as a safe and healthful workplace.

Inspection-detection-correction activities are hard to beat as ways of showing employees that their safety and health are important. When the executive makes regular safety tours, when the middle manager makes general inspections and when the supervisor does informal and formal inspections, people know that others care. They are prompted to do their own part, to be involved in the safety program; they take pride in the work they do, in their safety and productivity.

The objective of this chapter is to help managers at all levels effectively meet these seven goals.

NEEDS FOR INSPECTION

Loss exposures are created by the day-to-day activities in any type of organization. Equipment and facilities do wear out. At some point, wear and tear makes the risk of accidents too high. Inspections are needed to detect such exposures in a timely manner. They also provide feedback on whether equipment purchasing and employee training are adequate. Also, conditions change. People, equipment, materials and the environment are constantly changing. Some changes remove previous hazards, others create new ones. A prominent management philosophy is that "all problems result from changes." Inspections focus on these changes and help identify and solve problems.

Safety and health legislation requires organizations to provide employees with a reasonably safe and healthful place to work. The company and the manager who fail to meet legislated standards are subject to increasingly expensive liability, citations, fines and imprisonment. Effective inspections vastly improve management's assurance of freedom from such penalties.

Accidents stop work. Hazards and clutter slow people down. Unsafe conditions in the workplace, or unsafe practices of fellow employees, bother people and impair their performance. The person who has to give half his mind and one eye or one hand to self-protection has only 50 percent left to give the job. Even low risks, if they seem to be ignored by management, can be irritating to employees. The irritations may fester into grievances. Inspections are opportunities to find and treat these problems early, before they become big ones.

Two broad categories are "informal" inspections and "planned" inspections. Both are important. Both are discussed below, with major emphasis on the category named in the chapter title... planned inspections.

INFORMAL INSPECTIONS

This type comes so naturally that it needs very little explanation. It is simply the purposeful awareness of people as they go about their regular activities. Properly promoted and utilized, it can spot many potential problems as changes occur and work progresses.

Informal inspections also have limitations. They are not systematic. They miss things that take extra effort to find. Managers constantly have things on their minds. Preoccupied, they don't perceive what they are seeing. They may notice a few specific loss exposures, but not the total picture. They may forget to follow-up. To overcome this problem, some managers carry a pocket notebook with memory ticklers — notes of problem items to check on and remedial actions to take. Then they cross the items out as they are corrected.

Some companies have formalized the informal inspection a bit. Because of recent laws that permit workers to call for government inspections and unusually high court awards for failure to correct hazards that resulted in injury, they require records of all items reported by workers, as well as significant items noticed by supervisors and other managers. Some use a pocket size record for convenience along the lines of the one shown in *Figure 6-1*. A record file of these forms has several values:

1. It provides a better system to ensure that supervisors take action.

2. It documents company interest in safety and encourages reporting back to employees, keeping them informed.

3. It keeps upper managers and safety staff informed of problems and concerns.

4. It provides data for trend analysis.

5. It serves as a barometer of employee safety awareness and morale.

The informal inspections in which employees notice defects, unsafe conditions and unsafe practices are very valuable. Employees are often the first to see things occur. If educated on hazard recognition, they can be very effective in identifying loss potentials. In any case, employees who see substandard conditions should report them to their supervisors. A positive approach is to have the employee report the condition verbally. The supervisor writes out a condition report, like *Figure 6-1,* in the employee's presence. The program works even better when the employees are also

---

CONDITION REPORT

TO __Dave Roberts__ SUPT. DATE ISSUED __2/8/19—__

LOCATION & DESCRIPTION OF CONDITION AND/OR PRACTICE

Leak in roof causes rain water to run over floor in N.W. corner weld shop. Dangerous to welders in bad weather.

CONDITION DISCUSSED WITH __Charlie Downs__ DEPT. SUPV.

SIGNED __D Baldwin__

PERSON INITIATING REPORT

REMEDIAL ACTION __Roofers patched area__ believed to have problems. M. Washke to check during next rainstorm.

CONDITION CORRECTED __corrected__ __2/11/19—__ DATE

SIGNED __D. K. Roberts__ SUPERINTENDENT

PREPARE FORM IN TRIPLICATE
1ST COPY SEND TO SAFETY DEPT.
2ND COPY SEND TO DEPT. HEAD TO RETAIN
3RD COPY SEND TO DEPT. HEAD FOR SIGNATURE AND FORWARDING TO SAFETY DEPT.

Figure 6-1

---

told, after evaluation, what the supervisor intends to do about the problem, and is kept informed on remedial actions as they are planned, budgeted and taken... or why action is denied or delayed. Another approach is to have a substandard condition report box conveniently located for anyone to use as a means to submit a written report on a condition needing attention.

PLANNED INSPECTIONS

As valuable as informal inspections are, they are not enough. They do not meet all needs for inspection. There are also critical needs for Planned Inspections — such as critical parts/items inspections, housekeeping evaluations, general inspections and upper manager safety and health tours.

CRITICAL PARTS/ITEMS INSPECTIONS

Anyone who has ever worked around cranes that were lifting heavy loads knows the importance of thorough inspection of cables and slings. Many have used a high-rise building elevator and wondered how recently the cables had been checked. Others have driven over a long, high bridge and wondered when cables and support points got their last rust check and painting. Most people are aware that there are many parts and items whose failure could lead to catastrophes. **Critical parts or items may be defined as the components of machinery, equipment, materials, structures or areas more likely than other components to result in a major problem or loss when worn, damaged, abused, misused or improperly applied.** If currently in use, it is a critical part; if in storage, it is a critical item. For instance, a grinding wheel is a critical part when on the grinder, but is a critical item when in storage because it requires special care.

Every good manager is concerned with these parts/items. Looking out for things that could cause the biggest problems is logical and prudent. Sharp supervisors can quickly tell you the parts and items that are most likely to fail or malfunction, and what kind of losses are likely. Effective inspection programs make sure that all these parts/items are identified, evaluated and kept in proper condition.

No supervisor or manager should leave these inspections to chance. They must manage the system to prevent losses due to critical parts/items. That involves taking an inventory, setting up inspection schedules and auditing the inspections.

Making an inventory. As reflected in *Figure 6-2,* this includes a comprehensive listing of all areas, structures, machines, equipment, materials and substances for the organization — and determination of their critical parts and items. This is best accomplished by teams of knowledgeable people. Many of these will come to mind by giving them some thought. Others may have to be researched a good bit. Consideration should be given to such things as loss history, potential for loss, maintenance experience and accident history. Incident reports, maintenance records, manufacturers' guide books and servicing instructions and interviews with employees can all help track down the critical parts. Examples might be: safety devices, guards, controls, work or wearpoint components, electrical and mechanical components, fire hazards, etc. Consider those parts and/or exposures most likely to develop unsafe conditions due to stress, wear, impact, vibra-

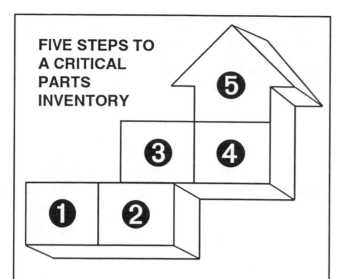

FIVE STEPS TO A CRITICAL PARTS INVENTORY

1. Categorize everything the company owns, such as machinery, equipment, structures, substances, materials and areas.

2. Delineate areas of responsibility considering physical and operation arrangements and assign responsibilities within each area.

3. List all objects in each category (machines, equipment, structures, materials, etc.) for each area. Use existing inventories such as accounting inventories, purchasing logs, insurance ledgers and storage and stockroom inventories.

4. Compile the list, and from it identify all critical parts/items using a team approach.

   A. Team members might be front-line managers, operators, manufacturer's reps., loss control specialists, occupational health specialists.
   B. Helpful tools might include loss records, maintenance records, operator's manual, training manuals, safety publications, job procedures.
   C. Identify the critical few parts or items that will likely result in a major problem if they fail.

5. List all parts on appropriate record system if not already on one.

   A. Identify the piece of equipment, structure, etc.
   B. Identify the critical parts/items.
   C. Indicate what to inspect.
   D. Identify who does the inspection and at what frequency.

Figure 6-2

tion, heat, corrosion, chemical reaction, misuse, etc.

A worksheet which could be used for development of a critical parts inventory is shown in *Figure 6-3*.

Recordkeeping. Appropriate records are essential to the proper functioning of the system. The form shown in *Figure 6-4* has been widely used. Components which have been identified as critical are copied from the worksheet into the first column. The second column contains the specific conditions for which one should inspect each part of component. Use words like: jagged, sharp-edged, crooked, splintery, broken, mutilated, frayed, worn, deteriorated, corroded, leaking, explosive, flammable, vibrating, missing, loose, inoperative, deficient, slipping, unstable, decomposed, defective, excessive, littered, gaseous, rotted, spillage, etc. Give the most precise definition possible. Describe how to identify the hazard and measure its severity whenever possible.

Answering "conditions to look for" leads to two other questions, "How often could the substandard condition occur?" and "Who is best qualified to detect it?" Inspection needs to be done at a frequency that will detect a problem before failure or other loss occurs, but not so often as to waste time or to replace the part or service it long before needed. Here you might use such words as: before use, before issue, when serviced, daily, weekly, monthly, bi-monthly, quarterly and yearly.

Some substandard conditions are best detected by a trained person. Others require that the item be disassembled before it can be examined, and are likely to be done by a mechanic or maintenance specialist. Some are easily detected by the operator or user. In each case, the most knowledgeable person for whom it is practical to do the inspection should be held responsible for doing it.

Monitoring the critical parts inspections assures the supervisor that the failure or malfunction will be prevented. This is aided by the record cards. Periodically, the supervisor can spot check a representative sample of the inspections, to be sure the system is working as it should. It's well worth the small amounts of time and effort it takes, since these are the *critical parts or items* — the ones whose failures result in major losses.

A basic cause of many losses is normal wear and tear. Proper servicing, adjustment or replacement reduces wear, and controls premature failures. This essential activity does not eliminate the need for critical parts inspections of machinery and equipment. Preventive maintenance usually involves servicing,

CRITICAL PARTS OR ITEMS INVENTORY

SPECIFIC ITEM _____

(MACHINE, EQUIPMENT, SUBSTANCE, MATERIAL, STRUCTURE, AREA)

_____ _____

DEPARTMENT   LOCATION   INVENTORIED BY: APPROVED BY:

COMPONENTS CONSIDERED CRITICAL	REASONS FOR CRITICAL CLASSIFICATION	CRITICAL?	
		NO	YES

Figure 6-3

CRITICAL PARTS OR ITEMS RECORD CARD

SPECIFIC ITEM _____

(MACHINE, EQUIPMENT, SUBSTANCE, MATERIAL, STRUCTURE, AREA))

_____   _____

DEPARTMENT   LOCATION OF ITEM

CRITICAL PARTS	PRIMARY THINGS TO LOOK FOR	INSPECTION FREQUENCY	INSPECTION RESPONSIBILITY

Note: A part when stored may become a critical item; especially if it needs special care or attention, e.g., grinding wheel, scaffold lumber, chemical substance. In such case, the critical item should be listed on the top of the card and again listed with pertinent information across all columns; even though there may then be only one item on the card.

Figure 6-4

adjusting or replacing equipment. Unless a critical parts/items inventory has been taken to identify and evaluate potential safety, quality and production loss exposures resulting from parts failures, a preventive maintenance program alone is incomplete. If a proper critical parts/items inventory has been made, a preventive maintenance program could be designed with inspection of many critical parts/items, which would complement the parts/items program. An effective critical parts/items program should also include areas, structures, substances and materials, as well as machinery and equipment (such as sling chains and fire doors). They are made to detect and correct impending failures or malfunctions which could cause serious losses. Both are vital to control losses. Each complements the other. Neither negates the need for the other.

Pre-use equipment checks. A type of critical parts/items inspection worthy of special note is pre-use checks. Many types of equipment have systems such as controls, emergency controls, lights, brakes, etc. that are vital to safe operation. These systems can be

damaged or become substandard between normal maintenance schedules. For such equipment, pre-use checks are an important method of loss control. Most organizations find that a simple record form (see example in *Figure 6-5*) aids considerably in making the system work effectively.

Motor vehicles, materials handling equipment such as lift trucks and cranes and motorized equipment are typical examples of items that should be checked before use. These checks are usually made at the start of a work shift, for assurance of safe operation during the shift. The operator usually makes the pre-use check and submits the form to the supervisor who monitors the system to ensure that it is working properly. How to do a pre-use check is an important part of the operator's training and coaching by the supervisor.

HOUSEKEEPING EVALUATIONS

"Housekeeping" evaluations are a vital part of effective general planned inspections. This includes both *cleanliness* and *order.* Many managers and safety

```
PRE-USE EQUIPMENT CHECK
          OF
     MOTOR VEHICLE
```

_____   _____
TYPE OF EQUIPMENT   EQUIPMENT I.D. NO.

ITEMS TO CHECK:	OK	NOT OK	COMMENTS:
OIL LEVEL			
WATER			
BATTERY (WATER LEVEL)			
FUEL			
LIGHTS			
BRAKES			
FIRE EXTINGUISHER			
GAUGES (OR WARNING LIGHTS)			
ENGINE OIL PRESSURE			
ENGINE TEMPERATURE			
AMMETER			
TIRE INFLATION			

ADDITIONAL COMMENTS:
_____
_____
_____
_____
_____

*DAMAGE REPORTING: Any damage to this equipment present at the start of this day's work is noted in space below.
_____
_____
_____
_____

_____   _____
OPERATOR'S SIGNATURE   DATE

Figure 6-5

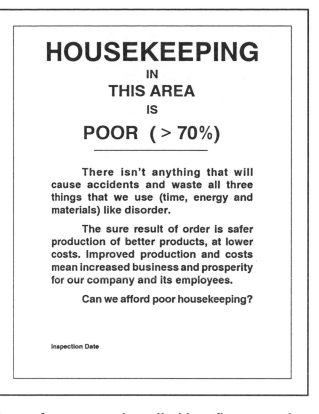

HOUSEKEEPING
IN
THIS AREA
IS
POOR (> 70%)

_____

There isn't anything that will cause accidents and waste all three things that we use (time, energy and materials) like disorder.

The sure result of order is safer production of better products, at lower costs. Improved production and costs mean increased business and prosperity for our company and its employees.

Can we afford poor housekeeping?

Inspection Date

know of ever went to the wall without first accumulating a vast pile of dirt. The dirt and all that goes with it, untidy thinking and methods, helped to cause that failure. The first thing I would do would be to clean that business up."

HOUSEKEEPING
IN
THIS AREA
IS
FAIR (70-80%)

_____

There isn't anything that will cause accidents and waste all three things that we use (time, energy and materials) like disorder. The sure result of order is safer production of better products at lower costs. Improved production and costs mean increased business and prosperity for our company and its employees.

Can we afford to be just fair in safety, quality or service?

Inspection Date

specialists feel these are so important that they agree that the First Law of Good Work is, as Harry Myer put it, "be clean and orderly."

Dirt and disorder are enemies of safety, quality, productivity and cost effectiveness. The legendary Henry Ford was once asked, "What would you do if you were called upon to take charge of a business that had failed?" His response was, "No business I

Here's another executive opinion regarding the prime importance of housekeeping:

It does not matter what you are doing, if there is dirt and disorder in your department, your costs are still higher than they should be and — this may surprise you — but somebody can come into your department and, even if he does not know a single thing about your work, if he can put the place in order he will lower your costs of production.

Inspections provide excellent opportunities to seek out signs of disorder such as these:

- Cluttered and poorly arranged areas
- Untidy and dangerous piling of materials
- Items that are excess, obsolete or no longer needed
- Blocked aisleways
- Material stuffed in corners, on overcrowded shelves, in overflowing bins and containers
- Tools and equipment left in work areas instead of being returned to tool rooms, racks, cribs or chests
- Broken containers and damaged material
- Materials gathering dirt and rust from disuse
- Excessive quantities of items
- Waste, scrap and excess materials that congest work areas
- Spills, leaks and hazardous materials creating safety and health hazards

Two key questions that inspectors should ask about items they are not sure of are 1) Is this item necessary? and 2) Is it in its proper place? These tie in with this tried, tested, proven and practical definition of order:

A PLACE IS IN ORDER WHEN THERE ARE NO UNNECESSARY THINGS ABOUT AND WHEN ALL NECESSARY THINGS ARE IN THEIR PROPER PLACES

"NO" IN THIS SENTENCE MEANS NONE! - NOT ANY! - NOT EVEN ONE!

It means more than clean. It means more than neat. It means that things are *where they ought to be* for maximum productivity - quality - safety - cost control. It brings benefits such as these:

- **Eliminates accidental injury and fire causes**
- **Prevents wasted energy**
- **Maintains greatest use of precious space**
- **Keeps stores' inventory at a minimum**
- **Helps control property damage and waste**
- **Guarantees good shop appearance**
- **Encourages better work habits**
- **Impresses customers and others**
- **Reflects a well run shop**

Many organizations put special emphasis on cleanliness and order by having housekeeping contests,

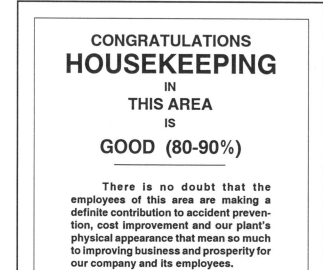

HOUSEKEEPING RATING FORM

RATING

AREA _____ DATE INSPECTED _____ INSPECTOR _____

INSTRUCTIONS:
Circle the appropriate score under the ITEM RATINGS opposite the item being evaluated. Place circled score in the score column. Add ratings for your total score.

A place is in order when there are no unnecessary things about and when all necessary things are in their proper places.

ITEM RATINGS

	NO CREDIT	VERY POOR	POOR	FAIR	GOOD	EXCELLENT	SCORE
MACHINERY AND EQUIPMENT							
a. Must be clean and free of unnecessary material or hangings	0	.5	1	1.5	2	3	
b. Must be free of unnecessary dripping of oil or grease	0	1	2	3	4	5	
c. Must have proper guards provided and in good condition	0	1.5	2.5	3.5	5	7	
STOCK AND MATERIAL							
a. Must be properly piled and arranged	0	1.5	3	4.5	6	8	
b. Must be loaded safely and orderly in pans, cars and trucks	0	1.5	2.5	3.5	5	7	
TOOLS							
a. Must be properly stored	0	1	2	3	4.5	6	
b. Must be free of oil and grease when stored	0	.5	1	1.5	2	3	
c. Must be in safe working condition	0	1	2	3	4.5	6	
AISLES							
a. Must be provided to work positions, fire extinguishers, fire blankets and stretcher cases	0	1	2	3	4.5	6	
b. Must be safe and free of obstructions	0	1	2	3	4.5	6	
c. Must be clearly marked	0	.5	1	1.5	2	3	
FLOORS							
a. Must have surfaces safe and suitable to work	0	1	2.	3	4.5	6	
b. Must be clean, dry and free of refuse, unnecessary material, oil and grease	0	1	2	3	4.5	6	
c. Must have an adequate number of receptacles provided for refuse	0	.5	1	1.5	2	3	
BUILDINGS							
a. Must have walls and windows that are reasonably clean for operations in that area and free of unnecessary hangings	0	.5	1	1.5	2	3	
b. Must have lighting systems that are maintained in a clean and efficient manner	0	.5	1	1.5	2	3	
c. Must have stairs that are clean, free of materials, well lit, provided with adequate hand rails and treads in good condition	0	1	2	3	4	5	
d. Must have platforms that are clean, free of unnecessary materials and well lit	0	.5	1	2	3	4	
GROUNDS							
a. Must be in good order, free of refuse and unnecessary materials	0	2	4	6	8	10	

TOTAL SCORE

Figure 6-6

awards and recognition. Based on standards, such as the examples shown in *Figure 6-6,* integrated into a rating form, contests can stimulate housekeeping competition among departments and/or with each department's past performance. Some organizations provide performance feedback and recognition by means of departmental placards which summarize the housekeeping evaluation as poor, fair, good or excellent. This section has several examples of such a placard for posting in a conspicuous spot.

> **Order is the first step in doing anything right and if you cannot manage the order of your department, you cannot manage your department.**

GENERAL INSPECTIONS

The general inspection is a planned walk-through of an entire area. It is comprehensive. Inspectors look at anything and everything to search out loss exposures. Some of the advantages of these inspections are that:

1. Inspectors devote full attention to the inspection. It is not done as something incidental to operational work.

2. Inspectors prepare their eyes to be observant and their minds to be perceptive.

3. Checklists are used as guides to ensure that a thorough inspection has been made.

4. Inspectors look outside normal eye level. They look into closed rooms and compartments, and at equipment not in use. They look around, behind, beneath and above the operating activity.

5. Reports of findings and recommendations are made to increase hazard awareness, corrective actions and accident prevention measures.

General inspections are often made on a frequency ranging from monthly to quarterly, sometimes more often, sometimes less. Optimum frequency depends on the types and degrees of hazards and loss exposures, as well as the rate at which things change in the operating area. Changes in people, equipment, materials and environmental factors create unknown situations. The general inspection is a vital tool for detection. It should be done often enough to keep abreast of changes. Yet, there should be enough time between inspections to allow action on findings.

When the chances of loss are high, inspections can help keep control. In such cases, proper condition of equipment, full use of safeguards and following set procedures are vital. Frequent general inspections add assurance that the risks are under control.

Line supervisors usually do the general inspections. This is logical and proper. They have primary interest in and responsibility for efficient and safe operation. They usually have better working knowledge of jobs and the people doing them than anyone else. They should also have full knowledge of the safety and health standards. If they don't, the solution is not to have someone else do their management work for them, but to give them the management development training they need to do it well themselves. Supervisors also have the authority to correct some of the problems on the spot, and to budget resources for prompt, practical actions of others. They most likely will be held accountable for seeing that corrective actions are taken and followed through.

Middle and upper managers should also take part in planned inspections and "safety and health tours" from time to time. This is an excellent way to keep in touch with what's happening at the point of control and also to visibly show their safety interest and commitment. These are not comprehensive inspections for all substandard conditions and practices. Rather they are walk-throughs of an area specifically to observe critical or especially important safety and health items. It gives them an opportunity to contribute their experience and perspective to especially knotty problems and to reinforce positive practices in an area.

Team inspections may involve various levels of management, both operating and staff. They also may involve union representatives and/or non-union employees. Inspection teams often are used for specific emphasis, for special problems, to minimize individual limitations or bias and as an inspector training and development process. They may include specialists such as quality control, personnel, safety, damage control, environmental health, fire loss control, security, maintenance and so on... as advisors or coaches. One of their best uses is for a periodic physical conditions audit in which they evaluate the actual physical conditions to determine how well the inspection program is actually working.

STEPS OF INSPECTION

While there are many types of inspections, the procedure for each is similar. The steps are: prepare, inspect, develop remedial actions and take follow-up actions. These are applied in varying degrees, according to the type of inspection.

Prepare

Adequate preparation includes emphasis on a positive approach, pre-inspection planning, application of checklists, review of previous inspection reports and gathering of inspection tools and materials.

Start with a positive attitude. One of the most modern concepts in good inspection techniques is to make sure you give adequate attention to the things that show high compliance with standards. Get mentally prepared to look not only for what is wrong but also what is *right*. Be ready to comment on and note good conditions and practices. People who look only for mistakes get grudging response at best. Nothing will do more than praise to perpetuate good work.

Plan the inspection. Regardless of the area or equipment, a person will do a better inspection if prepared. The first step in planning is to define the area of responsibility. Every part of the facility, and every piece of mobile equipment should be someone's responsibility. Plant maps and equipment lists are often used for this. The plant map also aids drawing out an inspection route. A planned route helps divide the inspection time better, so areas get appropriate coverage. A floor plan layout can be useful to show the route of materials flow and also to identify factors such as accident sites, airborne health hazard locations and hazardous materials storage areas.

Determine what to look at. Once the boundaries have been set, the next step is to determine what to look at. The broad categories shown in *Figure 6-7* may help the new supervisor get started on a general or housekeeping inspection.

Know what to look for. Knowing what to look *at* is not enough. Inspectors must also know what to look for. It's not enough to say "in safe condition." The specific size, type material, color, placement, etc. that makes for a safe condition needs to be determined. Standards or inspection guide books will give this information.

Sometimes the substandard condition or practice to look for needs to be stated. In these cases, the usual practice is to give a few descriptive words.

Some common ones are:

bent	kinked	sharp-edged
broken	littered	slippery
corroded	loose	spilled
decomposed	missing	stalled
excessive	mutilated	splintery
frayed	leaking	unstable
greasy	noisy	vibrating
jagged	protruding	worn

Make checklists. The checklist is a necessary tool for the inspection. It is as important to the inspector as the wrench is to a mechanic. General and specific inspection checklists are available from many sources. They range up to hundreds of pages in length. Carrying such a list on an inspection would be like carrying the entire maintenance shop to a job site to replace a mounting bolt.

Some checklists, like those a manufacturer might provide for a machine, are tailored to the job. In most cases, the checklist will have to be made up or adapted to suit the situation. But, once made, its usefulness will repay the time and effort many times over. It is especially helpful to people who are inspecting areas other than their own. It can also be a good thought-jogger in their own areas.

In planning the inspection, we identified the facilities, equipment, materials and processes in the area to be inspected. From this start, we can go to general checklists and take the items that apply. Put these on a few pages and we have a tailored checklist—a custom made tool that will help assure that all appropriate items are looked at. Once made, a checklist needs only to be kept up to date, added to, and deleted from as things change and experience dictates.

However, inspectors should guard against relying only on the checklist. It is to be used as a guide and not regarded as the definitive statement of everything that might possibly be found.

Review previous inspection reports. A scan through previous inspection reports is the transition from planning to inspecting. The new inspection is a chance for follow-up. Past reports might also suggest some critical subjects for attention, such as:

1. Items that have been repeated problems because basic causes have not been corrected.

GENERAL PHYSICAL CONDITIONS

1. **Electrical fixtures:** wiring, cords, grounds and connections.

2. **Mechanical power transmission:** condition and guarding.

3. **Machine guarding:** nip points, cutting and shear edges, presses, rotating parts and gear devices.

4. **Walking and working surfaces:** guarding and condition.

5. **Compressed gas cylinders:** segregation in storage, weather protection and restraints.

6. **Flammables:** storage, ventilation and working supply.

7. **Exits:** marking, visibility, lighting and unobstructed access.

8. **Deluge showers and eye baths:** water flow, temperature and drainage.

9. **Ladders and climbing devices:** condition, storage and proper use.

10. **Hand tools:** condition, storage and proper use.

11. **Materials handling equipment and lifting devices:** condition, proper use and storage.

12. **Scrap and refuse:** accumulation, removal, storage and disposal.

13. **Aisleways and storage stacks:** accessibility, marking, adequate dimensions.

14. **Stacking and storage:** location, segregation, stability, damage, protection.

15. **Tag-out and lock-out:** adequacy, use and condition of tags and lock-out devices.

FIRE PREVENTION AND CONTROL

1. **Fire detection and alarm systems:** installation, adequacy of coverage and service testing.

2. **Sprinkler systems:** clearance for type storage, adequacy of pressure and flow volume of water or chemical supply and maintenance.

3. **Fire evacuation:** exit route maps, personnel training and emergency drills.

4. **Portable extinguishers:** correct type, and mounting, locating signs and guides, unrestricted accessibility and maintenance of serviceability.

5. **Fire prevention:** adequacy of housekeeping, waste disposal and flammable materials work controls.

6. **Fire containment:** fire control doors and seals, ventilation controls.

7. **Fire notification:** telephone and alternate systems for notification of fire team and outside services.

8. **Fire services:** hose outlets, valves and water supply adequate, compatible with local fire unit equipment and tested for serviceability.

9. **Fire equipment:** color coding, signs and access, compliance with governmental standards.

ENVIRONMENTAL HEALTH

1. **Caustic, corrosive and toxic materials:** container labels, storage, disposal and spill clean-up.

2. **Ventilation:** of toxic fumes, vapors, mists, smoke and gases.

3. **Noise exposure:** measurement and controls.

4. **Radiation exposure:** measurement and controls.

5. **Temperature extremes:** measurement and controls.

6. **Hazardous substances:** information to affected employees.

7. **Illumination:** surveys and controls.

8. **Human factors engineering:** surveys and controls

9. **Personal protective equipment:** selection, location and compliance.

10. **External environmental protection:** evaluations and actions.

Figure 6-7

2. Areas or equipment omitted from the last inspection because they were out of operation.

3. Items that were becoming marginal.

4. Remedial actions that were questionable as to effect.

5. Critical parts to be randomly sampled.

Any of these critical subjects should be added to the top of the checklist. That helps make sure they are examined thoroughly. It also documents follow-up actions.

Get tools and materials. Getting off to a good start gives a positive atmosphere to an inspection or tour. People believe in the person who comes prepared. Here are the types of items generally found useful for routine inspection purposes:

1. Appropriate clothing: personal attire suitable for the area and any climbing, crawling, or other movement necessary. Clothes should not be loose or create any hazard, such as static sparks from some synthetic fabrics.

2. Personal protective equipment: all items that people in the work area are required or encouraged to wear; pre-fitted and in proper condition.

3. Checklists: to guide the inspection.

4. Writing materials: report forms, note or graph paper, clipboard and pencil or pen. A clear plastic bag to cover the clipboard in rainy weather.

5. Measuring instruments: tape measure to check standard dimensions and appropriate test instruments for the area and inspection.

6. Flashlight.

7. Camera: suggested as an aid to middle management teams, for documenting commendable and substandard areas and items.

Inspect

Here are some key points that will help make inspection more effective:

1. **Refer to the map and checklist.** Cover the area systematically. Be thorough. Follow the planned route so you give each area the appropriate attention and look at the appropriate items. Without checklists, people often become interested in the process and fail to see the problems.

2. **Accent the positive.** Make brief notes or tallies of what you have looked at and found satisfactory. Compute a percentage of compliance for each type of item. Be alert to items which you can commend.

3. **Look for off-the-floor and out-of-the-way items.** Without endangering yourself or others, make sure you get a complete picture of the whole area. Look in closed rooms and cabinets. Ask operators to start up machines not in use (but in workable condition). It's usually items outside normal operations that cause problems. Spend a good amount of time looking for the things that might be missed in routine supervision and informal inspections.

4. **Take immediate temporary actions.** When any serious risk or danger is found, do something right away. See that the proper supervisor shuts down operations if the dangers are out of control. Put up barriers to isolate hazards. The action should be appropriate to the risk, but should always lower the risk or correct the problem. If a senior manager or outside inspector is doing the inspection, the area supervisor should make sure the discrepancy is properly understood and is valid, then respond promptly.

5. **Describe and locate each item clearly.** Write down a concise simple description of the problem. Give an exact location. Use established names and markings to pinpoint locations. Photograph to aid the written descriptions, but always write a full description on the spot. Don't rely on memory or even on abbreviated notes. Also, remember that other people may need to locate the item in your absence.

6. **Classify the hazards.** A technique used to achieve spectacular loss control success in the aerospace program is the classification of loss potential for all systems. This classification system has been modified by many organizations into a practical and valuable management tool. It is particularly valuable when used as a communications tool in the reporting of substandard practices and conditions. One of the most apparent benefits is the establishment of priorities. It enables managers to give priority, in the budgeting of personnel and material resources, to the most significant problems.

These hazard classifications can be used to describe the loss potential of a condition or practice observed.

Class A Hazard — A condition or practice likely to cause permanent disability, loss of life or body part and/or extensive loss of structure, equipment or material.

- Example 1 — a barrier guard missing on a large press brake for a metal shearing operation.
- Example 2 — a maintenance worker servicing a large sump pump in an unventilated deep pit, with the gasoline motor running.

Class B Hazard — A condition or practice likely to cause serious injury or illness, resulting in temporary disability or property damage that is disruptive but not extensive.

- Example 1 — slippery oil condition in main aisleway.
- Example 2 — broken tread at bottom of office stairs.

Class C Hazard — A condition or practice likely to cause minor, non-disabling injury or illness or non-disruptive property damage.

- Example 1 — a carpenter handling rough lumber without gloves.
- Example 2 — a strong rancid odor from cutting oil circulating in the bed of a large lathe.

By using this classification system, the inspectors put remedial action planning into proper perspective for themselves and others. They also help themselves by motivating the rapid action of others to correct the more serious hazards. In addition, they focus attention on control of the critical areas that require the greatest concentration of time, effort and resources.

When introducing a system of hazard classification, some organizations have found that a few people abuse the system to get attention for pet projects. The good supervisor, however, recognizes that the classifications are based on objective professional judgment, and that other qualified management people will also carefully evaluate any hazard considered to be an "A" because of the grave implications. The abuser who overuses the "A" classification quickly loses support for all work requests. It benefits everyone when supervisors use their best possible judgment and make accurate classifications.

7. **Report items that seem unnecessary.** There is nothing that will pay off the time spent on inspec-

tions faster than the relocation or salvage of excess material and equipment. Putting materials where they are needed, or exchanging them for resources that are needed helps control costs. Freeing valuable floor or storage space in the area where the items were removed becomes an extra bonus. Removing congestion and possibly interference, makes work more efficient and safer.

8. **Determine the basic causes of substandard actions and conditions.** The work is only started when the discrepancies are found. The same things will occur over and over again unless the basic causes of the problems are uncovered. Answer the question, "Why?" *Why* does the substandard condition exist? *Why* did the person perform in a substandard manner? Dig out the basic causes (personal factors and job factors) behind the symptoms (substandard practices and conditions). Never accept a remedial action without answering the question, "Does it address the basic causes?"

Develop Remedial Actions

It's not enough to find the substandard actions and conditions, or even the basic causes behind them. You have to do something about them to prevent the losses. Cleaning up leaks and spills, reinstalling guards, removing materials or waste from operating areas and similar actions are only treating the symptoms. These actions do not correct the basic problems. Permanent remedial actions are needed to maintain loss control.

There are many possible remedial actions for any problem. They vary in cost, in effectiveness and in the method of control. Some reduce the chance of occurrence. Some reduce the severity of loss when the incident occurs. If remedial actions have any universal characteristics, it's that they do not achieve *total* control. Some risk remains unless the activity is stopped and removed — fully.

A manager can make a better decision on a proposed action if certain critical factors are looked at systematically. As shown in *Figure 6-8,* six of them are:

1. The potential severity of loss
2. The probability of a loss occurrence
3. The cost of control
4. The likely degree of control
5. Control alternatives
6. Justification for this control measure.

GUITO
RISK DECISIONS

◆

KEY QUESTIONS

CLASSIFICATION OF EXPOSURE

1. What is the potential severity of loss if an incident occurs?
   A – Major
   B – Serious
   C – Minor

PROBABILITY OF OCCURRENCE

2. What is the probability that a loss will occur from this exposure or hazard?
   A – High
   B – Moderate
   C – Low

COST OF CONTROL

3. What is the cost of the recommended control?
   A – High   (establish meaningful cost ranges
   B – Medium   for your own organization)
   C – Low

DEGREE OF CONTROL

4. What degree of control will be achieved by this expenditure?
   A – Substantial or Complete   (67-100%)
   B – Moderate   (34- 66%)
   C – Low   (1- 33%)

ALTERNATIVES

5. What are the alternative controls?

JUSTIFICATION

6. Why is this one suggested?

Figure 6-8

Other factors can enter into the consideration of the remedial actions. Among these are the extent to which the remedial action will benefit other loss controls, or the beneficial side effects, the possible adverse effects and political or social factors. These can also be coded, to maintain a systematic framework for making risk decisions and selecting remedial/preventive controls.

Take Follow-up Actions

The best remedial action ideas are of little value if they aren't completed or if they don't work out as planned. For these reasons, follow-up action is needed. The person responsible for the inspection should also take the follow-up

initiative. The follow-up can include performing or checking the following.

1. Ensuring appropriate commendation for individuals or groups for their work in keeping their areas orderly and safe

2. Writing the work order for the memorandum directing the action to be taken

3. Monitoring the programming and budgeting of the people and materials needed to complete the action

4. Verifying that the action is started on schedule; taking problems to the appropriate authority

5. Monitoring the actions during development, construction and/or modifications, to ensure that they meet the intents and specifications or reviewing revisions in the actions

6. Certifying the adequacy of the completed action; examining the facility or equipment, evaluating the training, reviewing the procedure, etc

7. Final review after the action has been in use for some time to verify that it is being used as intended, has no unforeseen adverse effects and has the expected effectiveness and reliability.

Special attention should be given to recurring hazards. People making repeated inspections of areas or equipment often find repeats of the items judged substandard on previous inspections. This is a serious situation, because it means the problem has been there all along. Everyone is getting another chance to prevent a loss — but there might not be any more chances!

People responding to inspections often overlook the fact that incidents have multiple causes. They should expect to trace each substandard act or condition found on the inspection to several basic causes. Each probably has a combination of personal factors and job factors as the basic or underlying causes. One or more of these multiple causes has been overlooked or uncorrected following the previous inspections. Simply doing more of the remedial action that was taken the first time will probably have little effect. More extensive analysis of causes will be needed, as well as additional remedial actions to control the multiple causes.

THE INSPECTION REPORT

Writing a report is another vital part of an inspection. The report is the means by which we communicate information and avoid time-wasting duplication effort.

1. The supervisor's inspection report gives middle and upper managers feedback on area safety problems. It helps them make better decisions on equipment, materials and people needed. It also helps make decisions on needs in all program elements, such as purchasing controls, training, protective equipment and workplace design.

2. Copies of reports, or information taken from them, distributed appropriately can share information that can help identify similar problems in other areas.

3. The written report, with classification of hazards, communicates information about substandard conditions and practices better than verbal advisories. The written report prompts people to remember what they have to do, and to do it.

4. The report documents all actions so efforts aren't repeated over and over, or so multiple actions aren't taken on the same basic cause. Uncoordinated corrective actions often conflict and are wasteful.

5. The report prompts follow-up actions and gives continuity between inspections.

Criteria For Report Forms

An inspection report form for any type of inspection should meet criteria such as these:

1. Identify the area or item inspected

2. Prompt all the appropriate actions

    a. Observations of the substandard practices and conditions
    b. Classification of the degrees of hazard or risk
    c. Remedial actions and recommendations
    d. Assignment of responsibility for action
    e. Follow-up on action taken
    f. Completion and verification of remedial actions

3. Provide sufficient space to write required information if desired

4. Provide for managerial review of the report

5. Allow use of the back of the form. Some organizations use this space for recording such things as spot task observations (see Chapter 8) made during the inspection.

Figure 6-9 shows a general inspection report form which meets these criteria.

Preparation Tips

Organizations with effective inspection programs have found the following common keys to good reports.

1. Write clearly. The report must be readable or it has no value. Supervisor's and operator's inspection reports need to be written clearly. The items should be complete but concise, so careful writing or printing isn't a burden. Typing usually isn't required as these reports are made in only a few copies. The clerical cost of typing usually isn't justified. If carefully written, the initial write-up can also serve as the final report. This saves people the time of rewriting. Because management team reports get wider distribution, they should be typed.

2. Leave space after each item so that the analysis of basic causes and the remedial actions can be written under the finding. This again saves rewriting and helps keep all related information together for easy follow-up.

3. Write commendations on a separate page and put them at the front of the report. This isn't sugar-coating the pill. It identifies the strengths that can be used to build up the rest of the program.

4. Consecutively number each item on the report (1, 2, 3, etc.) to help separate and identify them.

5. Copy all open items from the last report at the beginning of the new report. Note the action taken to date and remaining to be completed. Revise the recommendations and hazard classifications as appropriate. Precede the item number with an asterisk (*). Doing this makes the report a complete picture, and readily identifies repeat items.

6. Follow each item number with a letter showing the hazard classification; i.e., 1B, 2A, 3C, etc.

7. To help assess the status of action on items, additional coding can be used. The number group can be circled to show that some temporary action was taken. An X can be drawn across the number when remedial actions have been completed and verified. The action taken, in both cases, should be noted in the space left after the written description of the item.

ITEM NUMBER	HAZARD CLASS	

INSPECTION REPORT

DEPARTMENT	Machine Shop
INSPECTOR(S)	Bob Mettner, Paula St. John
AREA INSPECTED	Plant #2
REVIEWER	John Sharp
TYPE OF REPORT (INITIAL, FOLLOW-UP, FINAL)	~~Initial~~ Final
DATE(S)	~~8/3/19..~~ 8/31/19..
QUALITY SCORE	86%

ITEMS DETECTED — ACTIONS TAKEN — DATES —

Item	Class	Description
*①(X)	A	6/10/19—, guard missing - cutting head machine #2046. N.E. corner bay #2 bldg. B.
*2(X)	C	6/16/19—, door at south end bldg. 2 warped, hard to open. WO issued to carpenter shop, work scheduled for 7-22.
*3(X)	B	7/8/19—, heavy accumulation of oil and trash under main motor in bldg. 2 pump house. Cleaned out Aug. 20, discussion with workers all turns, permanent signs posted.
4	B	Two pallets of chemical 265 in yard, column B14. Directions warn against outside storage. Reported to R. Jones - area supervisor. Pallets moved to inside storage Aug. 6.
5	A	Major building column P32 is receiving severe damage from bulldozer operation cellar bldg. 4. WO issued for concrete barricade base Aug. 12, meeting held with all operators on major damage.
6(X)	A	Seven leaks in natural gas line between columns A1 and A2 in north bay, bldg. 2. Strong odor of gas in entire area. G. Sutter, area foreman roped area off. Gas dept. called. Leaks repaired Aug. 6.
7(X)	C	Sharp edge on latch - tool shanty door bldg. 2. Maintenance worker filed surfaced Aug. 7.
(8)	B	Compressed air pipe N side of truck door, E end press shop damaged. Guard or relocation could prevent major loss. WO issued 8-9 for permanent striped metal guard - hazard striped board wired to pipe Aug. 10.
9		Two empty whiskey bottles found in empty locker #15 - washroom bldg. 1. Plant protection notified 8-6, request area sup. to permit observation before discussing.

NOTATIONS:
*-Indicates item detected previously   0-around a number indicates intermediate action   X-over a number indicates item corrected.

Figure 6-9

These codings take only a few minutes for managers to learn. They give the status of each item at a glance to anyone making a follow-up. An additional way to aid follow-up is to color code the page. Put a small piece of red plastic tape at the top or edge of a report with items still uncorrected. When all items on the page have been completed and verified, cover the red tape with a piece of green tape. A quick glance through a file shows the pages to look at closely.

8. Simplify follow-up reports. People's time can be saved if a form like that shown in *Figure 6-10* is used. This follow-up report quickly gives the next level manager a status summary. It also gives space for comments on items where assistance is needed.

Report Filing

Reports properly filed and readily available continue to serve the organization. They will, of course, be used for reference until follow-up is completed. Working files can help area and functional managers keep up on work to be done. Central files can help all managers assess the safety status and the performance of managers in various areas.

Files document what has been done to date. Their use can keep people from "re-inventing the wheel" and taking actions that are unproductive. They can also be valuable for research on safety problems when developing facilities and processes. There are several other uses, including verification of the safety program in labor relations meetings, in pre-governmental inspection conferences, and in litigation proceedings.

There should be two differing files of inspection reports. One should be a complete master file for central reference in program administration. The other should be a working file, with each supervisor, as an aid to follow-up actions. At times a middle manager may have use for working files of subordinate supervisors' reports. However, the more files there are, the greater chance that information will not be posted consistently. An additional type of working file is that for pre-use inspections. In these cases, the working files should be near the vehicle or equipment.

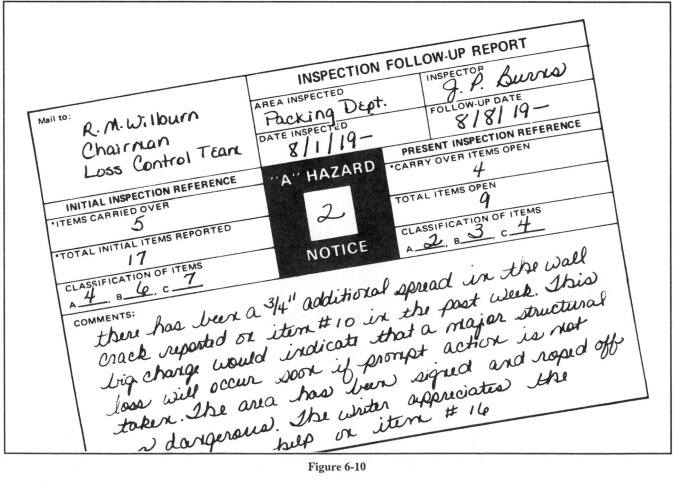

Figure 6-10

Report Quality Measurement

The inspection report can tell the manager several stories. First, it can tell whether the inspectors have adequate education in the various aspects of inspection, such as hazard recognition, basic cause analysis or remedial action planning. Second, it can tell whether the inspection was adequately planned, by the depth or superficiality of the findings. Third, it can tell if time was adequate and equally apportioned, by the grouping of items reported and whether the tone of the inspection is carried throughout the report.

The basic process of report quality measurement is to break the report down into items of interest and then assign relative value factors to each of these items. For the inspection report shown in *Figure 6-9* this breakdown might be as shown on the worksheet in *Figure 6-11*.

UPPER MANAGEMENT ACTIONS

Inspection is a program element where management involvement is critical. The activities of operators and supervisors have to be emphasized and supported. Certain executive roles have to be fulfilled. In return, these give upper managers feedback on the control of risks involved in operations. Added payback comes from the effects a well run program has on employee motivation and on customer relations. Inspection activities of managers are highly visible to the employees. Hazardous appearing and disorderly work places are often and correctly, viewed as evidence of poor management.

As in any program activity, there are certain functions that can be done effectively only by upper managers. Other functions belong to line supervisors and middle managers. The roles of upper managers in inspection programs are to:

1. **Budget resources.** Supervisors and employees need time and equipment to do inspections effectively. Some corrective actions cost little in time or material; others can be quite expensive. These must be provided in the programming of operating activities. If resources aren't provided, people know that the upper manager really has little concern for inspections — or for safety and health. Pre-use inspections won't be done if crews are waiting on the equipment operator. Critical parts inventories, loss exposure inventories, inspection plans, area inspection checklists and inspections won't be done unless the time and emphasis are provided.

2. **Set program standards.** State how often inspections of each type are to be performed, who is to inspect, what reports are required and how often follow-up is expected. Standards help the good managers set their pace to the requirements.

INSPECTION REPORT SCORING WORKSHEET

FACTOR	POSSIBLE	AWARDED	COMMENTS
Thoroughness of inspection	20		
Hazards Accurately Classified	10		
Clear Description and Location of Each Item	10		
Effectiveness of Remedial Actions	20		
Clear Responsibility For Remedial Action	15		
Follow-Up Data Recorded	15		
Timeliness of Report	10		
TOTAL	100		

Figure 6-11

3. **Set objectives related to inspections.** Aid subordinates in completing inspection plans, checklists, critical parts inventories, etc. by setting these as objectives with middle and line managers, and by reviewing them as they are completed.

4. **Provide adequate management and employee training.** Make sure that managers and employees are educated on hazard recognition and appropriate inspection methods, techniques and records keeping.

5. **Monitor the status of the inspection program.** Have middle managers give periodic input on inspections performed, numbers of items in each hazards classification found and numbers of remedial actions completed in the period. Or, have managers rotate assignments to make these program status evaluations.

6. **Direct program audits.** Have periodic audits of program management compliance made by members of management and conduct an audit review meeting to discuss the results and actions to be taken.

7. **Make safety and health tours.** Tours by senior and middle managers provide visible evidence of interest, involvement and commitment. As used here, tour means a management walk-through specifically to observe critical or especially important safety and health items (not a comprehensive inspection for all substandard conditions and practices). It can be persuasive visible evidence of management's involvement in, and support of, the safety and health/loss control program. It also serves to educate managers regarding program needs. Some managers find such tours tie in nicely with their needs to check on high risk activities, examine persistent problems, follow through on remedial actions and better understand problems beyond the capability or responsibility of front line supervisors. Tours of this type also provide excellent opportunities for managers to give recognition and reinforcement of good performance in meeting standards for proper conditions and practices.

The executive safety tour should be scheduled and publicized well in advance. This gives employees and supervisors time to prepare. It lets them take care of the problems they can handle by themselves. It also lets them get facts in order for areas where they need help. The safety manager helps executives prepare for the tour by making up a checklist based on past accidents, loss potentials, current problems *and* current accomplishment in the area to be toured. Maximum program promotion value should be gained before, during and after the tour.

Additional actions which most organizations have found of great benefit are reviews of inspection reports, reviews of high loss potentials and inspection program evaluations.

Every planned inspection report should be reviewed at the next higher level of management. This review has several purposes:

1. To ensure that the scope and quality of inspections is adequate, and meets program standards.

2. To assess the possibilities of problems, similar to those reported, in other areas of the organization.

3. To approve the remedial actions that require resources outside the authority of the managers who made the inspections.

4. To assess the need for help in completing the actions to be taken.

Every organization should have a system to ensure that high potentials are communicated to upper managers. The hazard classification system is an excellent tool for such a system. Every item classified as an "A" hazard should be examined carefully. If the rating potential is true, the reviewer should consider who else needs to know about the problem right away. Depending on the item, the reviewer may "flag" it on the report and send it to the senior manager. In some cases, the reviewer may write a memo on the item, adding his or her comments and suggestions.

An increasing number of organizations find it useful to evaluate periodically the inspection program itself to ensure that standards are being complied with. The information for this evaluation can be compiled by a staff person from the inspection reports and shown on a form such as *Figure 6-12*. This gives senior managers a quick overview of compliance to program standards.

Inspections are essential activities in the control of accidental losses. The inspection is an opportunity for the manager to find and correct problems before losses occur. An effective inspection program requires detailed planning, careful observation of facilities and activities, clear communication on findings and follow-up to make sure that all remedial actions are completed and effective. But the many benefits make it a most worthwhile investment.

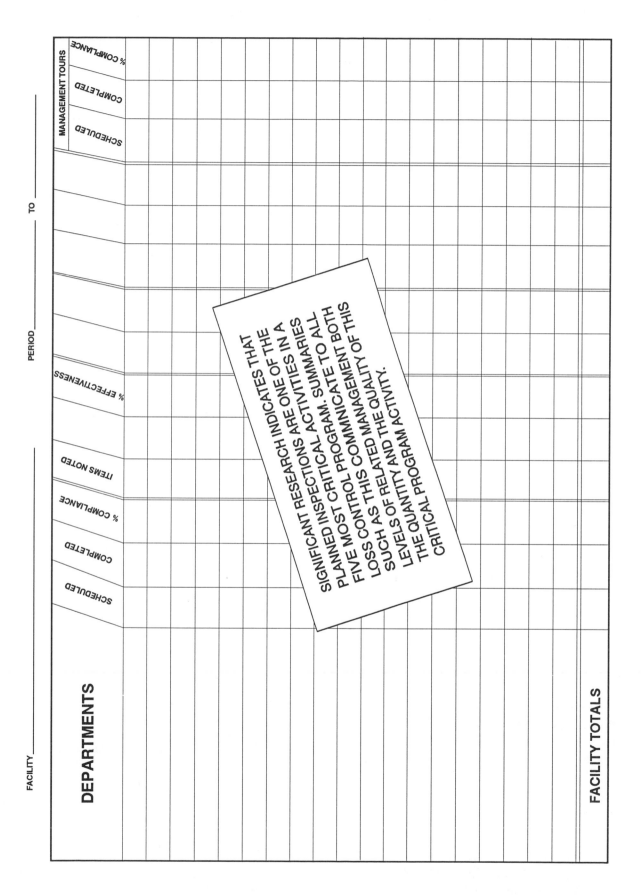

PLANNED INSPECTIONS SUMMARY

FACILITY _____ PERIOD _____ TO _____

DEPARTMENTS

SCHEDULED | COMPLETED | % COMPLIANCE | ITEMS NOTED | % EFFECTIVENESS

MANAGEMENT TOURS
SCHEDULED | COMPLETED | % COMPLIANCE

FACILITY TOTALS

SIGNIFICANT RESEARCH INDICATES THAT PLANNED INSPECTIONS ARE ONE OF THE FIVE MOST CRITICAL ACTIVITIES. SUMMARIES OF THIS CONTROL PROGRAM COMMUNICATE TO ALL LEVELS OF MANAGEMENT BOTH THE QUALITY OF THIS RELATED QUANTITY AND THE PROGRAM ACTIVITY. SUCH AS THIS CRITICAL LOSS CONTROL ACTIVITY.

Figure 6-12

CORE CONCEPTS IN REVIEW

Inspection is one of the oldest, most widely used and best ways to detect and correct potential losses... before they occur. Inspection-detection-correction activities are hard to beat as ways of showing employees that the company considers their safety and health vitally important.

Inspections are needed because **nothing is completely risk free.**

1. Things wear out
2. Conditions change
3. People are not perfect
4. Managers have moral and legal responsibilities for a safe and healthful workplace

Two broad categories are **informal** inspections and **planned** inspections. Two major types of the latter are "general planned inspections" and "critical parts/items inspections." Each plays a vital role in effective inspection systems.

1. **Informal inspection** is done as people go about their regular activities.

2. The **general inspection** is a planned walk-through of an entire area, a comprehensive look at anything and everything to search out loss exposures.

3. **Critical parts/items inspections** focus on the components of machinery, equipment, materials, structures or areas likely to result in a major problem or loss when worn, damaged, abused, misused or improperly applied.

Front-line supervisors do the majority of the general planned inspections. However, middle and upper managers, and sometimes employees, should also take part in team inspections. Senior and middle managers also should conduct "safety tours" — walk-throughs specifically to observe especially important safety and health items.

"Housekeeping" evaluations are a vital part of effective general planned inspections. They concentrate on both **cleanliness** and **order**.

Two key questions that inspectors should ask about items they are not sure of are:

1. Is this item necessary?
2. Is it in its proper place?

Many professional management authorities agree that, **"If you cannot manage the housekeeping of your department, you cannot manage your department."**

Every good manager is concerned with critical parts/items, the things that could cause the biggest problems. Managing the system to prevent losses caused by these parts and items involves making a critical parts inspection inventory, establishing inspection responsibilities and schedules and auditing the inspections.

Inspection steps and activities can be summarized as follows:

1. **Prepare**

   a. Start with a positive attitude
   b. Plan the inspection
   c. Prepare checklists
   d. Know what to look for
   e. Review previous inspection reports
   f. Get tools and materials

2. **Inspect**

   a. Use floor plan and checklist
   b. Accent the positive
   c. Look for off-the-floor and out-of-the-way items
   d. Take necessary temporary actions
   e. Describe and locate each item clearly
   f. Classify the hazards
   g. Report items that seem unnecessary
   h. Determine the basic causes of substandard actions and conditions

3. **Develop Remedial Actions**

   a. Consider potential severity of loss
   b. Evaluate the probability of a loss occurrence
   c. Weigh various control alternatives
   d. Assess the likely degree of control to be achieved
   e. Determine the cost of control
   f. Justify the recommended control if major expenditures are involved

4. **Take Follow-Up Actions**

   a. Issue work order
   b. Monitor the budgeting of resources
   c. Ensure timely actions
   d. Monitor activity progress
   e. Check the effectiveness of implemented controls
   f. Give ample credit where credit is due

5. **Prepare Inspection Report**

   a. Write clearly
   b. Consecutively number the items

c. Classify each hazard

d. Leave space to add basic causes and remedial actions for each item

e. Use codes for open items from previous reports, intermediate actions taken and remedial actions completed

f. Emphasize commendations

g. Forward copies and maintain files

Inspections and reports can be improved significantly by measuring the quality of the reports and coaching for improvement.

Management involvement, at all levels, is essential to an effective inspection system. Some specific ways managers can motivate good inspection methods are shown in *Figure 6-13*.

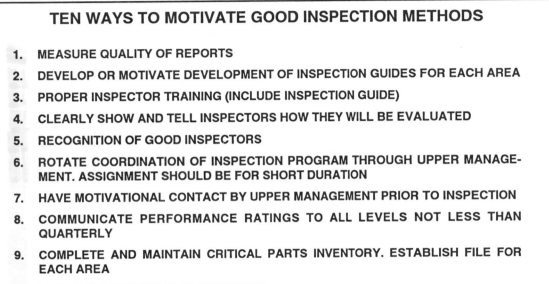

TEN WAYS TO MOTIVATE GOOD INSPECTION METHODS

1. MEASURE QUALITY OF REPORTS

2. DEVELOP OR MOTIVATE DEVELOPMENT OF INSPECTION GUIDES FOR EACH AREA

3. PROPER INSPECTOR TRAINING (INCLUDE INSPECTION GUIDE)

4. CLEARLY SHOW AND TELL INSPECTORS HOW THEY WILL BE EVALUATED

5. RECOGNITION OF GOOD INSPECTORS

6. ROTATE COORDINATION OF INSPECTION PROGRAM THROUGH UPPER MANAGEMENT. ASSIGNMENT SHOULD BE FOR SHORT DURATION

7. HAVE MOTIVATIONAL CONTACT BY UPPER MANAGEMENT PRIOR TO INSPECTION

8. COMMUNICATE PERFORMANCE RATINGS TO ALL LEVELS NOT LESS THAN QUARTERLY

9. COMPLETE AND MAINTAIN CRITICAL PARTS INVENTORY. ESTABLISH FILE FOR EACH AREA

10. USE PHOTOGRAPHY IN POSITIVE WAY

Figure 6-13

KEY QUESTIONS

1. Inspection is primarily a _____ control measure: a) post-contact b) contact c) pre-contact.

2. True or False? Inspections cover both conditions and practices.

3. Inspection and detection are wasted efforts without c_____.

4. List at least three limitations of informal inspections.

5. When a company uses a "Condition Report," it typically is used in connection with _____ inspections. a) information b) formal c) both "a" and "b" d) neither "a" nor "b".

6. Define "critical parts or items."

7. True or False? Developing a critical parts/items inventory is best accomplished by a team of knowledgeable people.

8. Who should conduct critical parts/items inspections?

9. The "Critical Parts Record Card" has four columns for essential information. What are the column headings?

10. True or False? A preventive maintenance list and a critical parts/items list are essentially the same.

11. "Housekeeping" includes both cleanliness and _____.

12. A place is in _____ when there are no

_____ things about and when all _____ things are in their proper places.

13. List several advantages of planned general inspections.

14. Why should line supervisors do most of the general inspections?

15. What are the four major steps of a general planned inspection?

16. In preparing for general inspections, why should you review previous inspection reports?

17. Define "Class A Hazard." Class B. Class C.

18. Effective remedial/preventive actions require determination of b_____ causes.

19. List at least three benefits of written inspection reports.

20. List at least three benefits of measuring the quality of inspection reports.

21. List at least five important inspection activities for upper managers.

PRACTICAL APPLICATIONS SUMMARY

S - For Supervisors
E - For Executives
C - For Safety/Loss Control Coordinators

		S	E	C
1.	Set inspection program standards and objectives.		x	
2.	Allot adequate resources (time, money, equipment) for effective inspection activities.		x	
3.	Ensure adequate inspection training throughout the organization.		x	
4.	Conduct periodic safety and health tours.		x	x
5.	Direct program audits and monitor the status of the inspection program.		x	x
6.	Review inspection reports.		x	
7.	Issue procedure to assure follow-up of inspection findings and correction of items in order of priority.		x	
8.	Prepare inspection aids and checklists.	x		x
9.	Conduct general planned inspections.	x		
10.	Determine basic causes of substandard actions and conditions.	x	x	
11.	Prepare critical parts/items inventories.	x		
12.	Prepare critical parts/items record cards.	x		
13.	Monitor how well the critical parts/items inspection activities (including pre-use inspections) meet the standards.	x	x	
14.	Measure the quality of inspection reports.		x	x
15.	Conduct informal inspections.	x	x	x
16.	Prepare "Condition Reports."	x		
17.	Monitor housekeeping evaluations, contests, awards and recognition.		x	x
18.	Coordinate inspections for training and development purposes.			x
19.	Monitor how well the hazard classification system is used.		x	x
20.	Follow-up recommended remedial/preventive actions.	x	x	
21.	Periodically analyze general inspection reports to identify repetitive items and their basic or underlying causes.	x	x	x
22.	At least annually, evaluate the adequacy of inspection checklists, critical parts/items inventories and inspection forms and procedures.	x	x	x
23.	Accentuate the positive findings and results of inspections.	x	x	x
24.	Periodically evaluate the frequency of inspections against program standards, and the quality of inspections for major units of the organization; communicate findings in writing to all levels of management.			x

CHAPTER 7

JOB/TASK ANALYSIS AND PROCEDURES

"We undermanage work and overmanage workers."
— Peter Drucker

INTRODUCTION

Job/task analysis is a critical program activity, not only for the safety and health of workers but also for the safety and health of the organization itself. Today's marketplace for goods and services will not long tolerate the survival of organizations which continue to do things simply because that's the way they have always been done. There is enormous pressure to reduce costs while at the same time improving quality. In addition, humanitarian and liability concerns require greater levels of safety, both for those who do the work as well as for the customer or client. The single most useful tool to meet these objectives is to systematically analyze the work which is done and to establish appropriate procedures or practices to ensure that it is consistently done the proper way.

Several previous methods of doing this have been only partially successful. The time and motion study technique was responsible for major advances in efficiency. It also experienced certain negative side effects. One was to continue to do the wrong thing, only do it quicker. Another has been the alienation of the people who do the work from the work being done. Time and motion studies have often left workers feeling that they were regarded as little more than unthinking human robots who could only be motivated by money. As a result, the vast store of knowledge and experience that workers possessed about better ways of doing things was seldom utilized and at times deliberately rejected. The consequences have included high accident rates, loss of markets, loss of jobs, unnecessary labor relations problems and at times, plant closings.

Another method with some question as to its complete success has been job safety analysis. This approach frequently examines the work only from the perspective of safety and health. It has resulted in safer work. But it has also resulted in duplication of effort and paperwork, with safety procedures, quality procedures, efficiency procedures, etc. Because job procedures which deal only with safety are not related to the primary purpose for doing the work, they tend to get ignored in the face of other pressures.

The technique described here systematically analyzes the work from the perspective of safety, quality and efficiency, all at the same time. Thus, it deals with all of these critical concerns in today's marketplace. This approach actually gives greater assurance of the safety aspects. Without such an integrated approach, changes can be made in the production or quality areas which have a negative impact on the safety and health aspects. Also, because it facilitates input from the people who actually do the work, this technique is completely in tune with the current emphasis on employee involvement and participative management. The result is procedures and practices which are more valuable, more useful and more likely to be used by all concerned.

The correct use of this technique requires a proper understanding of the terms involved.

- JOB/TASK - a segment of work, a specific work assignment, a set of actions required to complete a specific work objective. The work objective is called "job" by many people and "task" by many others. For the sake of simplicity and consistency, we will use *task* most of the time.

- PROCEDURE - a step-by-step description of "how to proceed," from start to finish, in performing a task properly.

- PRACTICE - a set of positive guidelines helpful to the performance of a specific type of work that may not always be done in a set way.

Practices are particularly useful for persons in the trades, crafts, maintenance and materials handling. The purpose is to provide written guidelines or advisory tips to avoid major problems that have historically occurred with certain types of work. For instance, replacing an electric motor may be done differently in different situations and thus may not lend to being proceduralized. However, locking the disconnect switch in the "off" position, tagging it and testing to ensure that the motor is really de-energized is a required practice to avoid the major problems that have historically occurred with this type work. The details of loading a semi-trailer with a forklift will vary according to what is being loaded. However, ensuring that the lift truck is in proper operational condition and that trailer wheels are chocked and that the dock plate is firmly in place is a required practice. The distinction between procedures and practices is made to help avoid attempts to proceduralize tasks which really cannot be proceduralized and thus have an end product which is not practical.

Properly done, procedures and practices are among the most valuable tools imaginable for such important activities as job orientation - task instruction - task observation - group meetings - employee coaching - accident/incident investigation - skill training.

Because of the extensive time required to develop good practices or procedures, and because it requires the cooperation of persons from various areas, a written directive or letter stating management's position on this subject is valuable for establishing the proper climate for maximum cooperation. This communication not only should show that management supports this activity wholeheartedly, but also should re-emphasize the major potential benefits for all areas of the operation.

The objective of this chapter is to aid supervisors, executives and program coordinators in applying a systematic, practical approach to preparing and using Task Procedures and/or Work Practices. This approach involves these nine aspects:

1. **Inventory the tasks**
2. **Identify the critical tasks**
3. **Break tasks down into steps or activities**
4. **Pinpoint loss exposures**
5. **Make an efficiency check**
6. **Develop controls**
7. **Write procedures or practices**
8. **Put to work**
9. **Update and maintain records**

The first seven steps in this process are illustrated with examples from a concentrator mill. Here, ore is mixed with water to make a slurry and ground to a fine consistency, first in a huge rod mill and then in one of six smaller ball mills. A rod mill contains a number of 10-foot steel rods, each weighing about 350 pounds, which crush the ore. The ball mills contain steel balls, each slightly smaller than a bowling ball, which grind the ore to fine particles. It is then fed to cyclone pumps, which use centrifugal force to separate the fine materials from the coarse. The coarse particles are sent back to be reground and the "fines" are fed through a series of tanks where different reagents cause each desirable ore to bind to air bubbles and be floated off from the waste. The particle size monitor samples and records the size of the ground particles of ore being fed into the flotation system. As such, it serves as an early warning of grinding problems which, if undetected at this point, will clog the remainder of the system and make it impossible to separate the various ores. The concentrated ore (in this case lead, tin, zinc, silver and gold) is sent by railcar to a smelter where the remaining impurities are burned off.

The process itself is relatively simple and can be reproduced in a small laboratory. Although the size of the actual equipment involved is enormous, the process requires delicate balances to avoid losing thousands of dollars an hour in valuable ore. Other loss exposures include: injury (electrical shock, caught in or on heavy equipment, slips and falls, back injury, etc.); poor quality of final product; production delays that are expensive because failure of any part of the process affects other stages; and equipment damage.

This example was chosen primarily because it is a "process" operation, that is, tasks involved are not done in isolation but are interdependent with a larger, ongoing process. Because the basics apply to operations that involve processing metals, forest and agricultural products, information (data, records, reports, claims, etc.), food, petroleum and chemical stocks, as well as assembly work, most readers will be able to understand and identify with it. The specific task illustrated is simple enough to follow but complicated enough to demonstrate the real challenge and satisfaction that can come with developing proper procedures or practices for critical tasks.

INVENTORY THE TASKS

The first step in developing an inventory of the critical tasks is to make a systematic list of all occupations. Here is a list of occupations from the concentrator mill itself:

OCCUPATION INVENTORY

1. **Grinding Operator**

2. **Stacker**
3. **Flotation Operator**
4. **Assistant Flotation Operator**
5. **Tin Plant Operator**
6. **Filter Floor Operator**
7. **Loading Shed Operator**
8. **Reagent Operator**
9. **Bagger**
10. **Operator, Sink and Float**
11. **Transportation Operator**

The second step in developing a critical task inventory is to divide each occupation into tasks so that each task can be scrutinized to determine whether it is critical. Supervisors and workers can do this together as a team by thinking about the work, by referring to Job or Position Descriptions (general statements of what the occupation or work title involves). It should be noted that general responsibilities and relationships which are normally included in a position charter or job description are not tasks and should not be listed as such. Another source of information is industry-wide job classification guides which list the jobs/tasks normally done by people in various job classifications. Observing and talking with those who do the work provides an excellent opportunity to apply the principle of participation by getting the involvement and help of those who will be most affected - the work group. For example, a team of people who do similar work could develop the inventory for that work. It is critical that this list be absolutely complete and include not only the tasks that a person normally does but also the tasks that they might be called on to do in unusual situations. Experience has repeatedly proved that the latter category is a major source of accident loss. A safety study by J. Saari, of the Finland Institute of Occupational Safety, concluded that:

> **Most accidents occur in a work area to which a worker is unaccustomed, and during a task that is not a worker's usual task.**

The tasks can be inventoried on a form which is shown partially filled out in *Figure 7-1*. This page shows only the first 11 tasks of the Chief Grinding Operator. Other tasks would be listed on additional copies of the same form.

IDENTIFY THE CRITICAL TASKS

A question that comes up early in the program is, "Which tasks should we thoroughly analyze and describe?" Some organizations do them all. However, most organizations realize some practical problems with this approach. For instance, the amount of time and effort required to analyze every task in the company may be formidable. Let's say, for example, that your company had 50 different occupations or work titles, with an average of only 20 specific tasks each. This means (allowing for duplication) there are probably more than 800 tasks to analyze. Another problem is keeping the procedures and practices up-to-date, which can also require an enormous amount of time. You can minimize the effort involved and maximize the results by applying the principle of the critical few and concentrating your analysis program on the critical tasks.

All tasks with a history of loss, whether personal injury, property damage, quality or production loss, should be classified according to their criticality. Since the program is predictive rather than reactive, it is also vital to include the tasks having a potential for major loss even though there is no history of such. In order to do this the following questions should be asked:

(a) Can this task, if not done properly, result in major loss while being performed?
(b) Can this task, if not done properly, result in major loss after having been performed?
(c) How serious is the loss likely to be? (What is the severity of injury, cost of damage or cost of quality or production loss likely to be? Are other persons or departments likely to be affected?)
(d) What is the expected frequency of occurrence?

CRITICAL TASK INVENTORY WORKSHEET

Grinding Operator	Grinding	4/18/19—
OCCUPATION OR TITLE	DEPARTMENT	INVENTORY DATE(S)
Mel Douglas	Elizabeth Bromley	Bill Livingston
INVENTORIED BY	REVIEWED BY	REVIEWED BY

TASKS OR ACTIVITIES	LOSS EXPOSURES	RISK EVALUATION				PROGRAM NEEDS				
LIST ALL TASKS OR ACTIVITIES NORMALLY DONE OR THAT MIGHT BE DONE BY A PERSON IN THIS OCCUPATION	CONSIDER SAFETY, HEALTH, DAMAGE, FIRE, QUALITY, PRODUCTION PROBLEMS, ETC. CONSIDER PEOPLE, EQUIPMENT, MATERIALS AND ENVIRONMENT INTERACTIONS	SEVERITY	REPETITIVE-NESS	PROBABILITY	CRITICAL TASK	PROCEDURES	PRACTICES	SKILL TRAINING	SPECIAL RULES	INDUSTRIAL HYGIENE REVIEW
Operate Pumps										
Operate Ball Mill										
Operate Cyclones										
Operate Conveyor Belts										
Operate Drum Feeder										
Operate Rod Mill										
Stop and Start Complete Grinding Circuit										
Operate Particle Size Monitor										
Charge Ball Mill										
Charge Rod Mill										
Hose Down and Clean Up Work Areas										

CONSIDER PAST HISTORY AND POTENTIAL FOR BIG LOSS

Figure 7-1

Frequency of occurrence is governed by a number of factors, of which the most important are:

(a) The number of times the task is performed in the organization in a specific time period (repetitiveness).

(b) The chance that there will be loss as a result of performing the task (probability of loss).

It must be recognized that there are many degrees of criticality and, in fact, every task worth doing is critical to some degree. Thus, a system which develops a scale of criticality is likely to result in fewer differences of opinion than one which merely classifies the task as critical or not critical. It is suggested that the above factors be converted into three scales relating to severity, repetitiveness and probability of loss. Although some subjective judgment is still required, the fact that each factor is given due considera-

tion results in a more consistent and logical classification of tasks according to criticality.

Severity (the first evaluation column) is derived from the costs of the losses being incurred or the loss most likely to be incurred as a result of wrong performance of the task. In many cases a whole range of losses could occur but only the most likely result is considered, e.g., if a wrong vessel entry procedure results in an accident, it is more likely to be serious than not, while a wrong shoveling technique is more likely to result in a small loss than a large loss. A scale of from zero to six, such as the following, is suggested:

0 - No injury or illness, or a quality, production or other loss of less than $100.

2 - Minor injury or illness without lost time, non-disruptive property damage or a quality,

production or other loss of $100 to $1000.

4 - A lost time injury or illness without permanent disability, or disruptive property damage, a quality, production or other loss of more than $1,000 but not exceeding $5,000.

6 - Permanent disability or a loss of life or body part, and/or extensive loss of structure, equipment or material. Quality, production or other losses exceeding $5,000.

These descriptions and evaluations of severity, as well as the number of points on the scale, can be varied to suit different requirements.

Repetitiveness (the second evaluation column) can be assessed from the following table (*Figure 7-2*), according to a scale of one to three:

Number of persons performing task	Number of times task is performed by each person		
	Less than daily	Few times per day	Many times per day
Few	1	1	2
Moderate number	1	2	3
Many	2	3	3

Figure 7-2

The **probability** of loss occurring each time a particular task is performed (the third evaluation column) is influenced by the following factors:

(a) Hazardousness, i.e., how inherently dangerous is the task?

(b) Difficulty, i.e., how prone to quality, production or other problems is the task?

(c) Complexity of the task.

(d) The chance that there will be loss if the task is improperly performed.

These factors are not evaluated separately but they should all be borne in mind. The key question is, "How likely is it that things will go wrong as a result of the performance of this task?" Since, for the sake of simplicity, only the most likely loss is considered when evaluating severity, it follows that only the probability of that particular loss should be considered.

A scale of from -1 to +1 is used as follows:

-1 = Less than average probability of loss
 0 = Average probability of loss
+1 = Greater than average probability of loss

The points allotted to each of the three factors are then added to indicate a scale of criticality ranging from 0 to 10. It is, in effect, an order of priority. Management may decide that all tasks allotted less than say 3 points will be disregarded from a loss control point of view and not be listed as critical tasks, while tasks allotted 8 or more points will be regarded as the most critical tasks, requiring immediate attention.

There are several ways of evaluating the criticality of tasks. The method shown here has been successfully used. The A-B-C Risk Evaluation System discussed in Chapter 6. "Planned Inspections," could also be used.

The "Loss Exposures" section is completed at the same time as the evaluation. Here the specific major loss exposures are indicated, providing clarification and justification of the evaluations given.

The completed worksheet is shown in *Figure 7-3*. This worksheet also shows the determination of whether a task procedure or a set of task practices would best serve the overall purposes of this program activity. At times this can be determined when the tasks are evaluated. At other times further analysis of the tasks is required before making this decision. Some tasks require only a few special rules to adequately control the loss exposures. Also, whether or not skill training is required can be decided and recorded on the form. These important considerations are recorded here because the completed form will serve as a checkpoint to determine progress in dealing with the tasks that have been inventoried and evaluated. It can also become the basis for identifying tasks for the observation program.

A special word is in order about new or unknown tasks. Each time a supervisor is presented with the challenge to get a new task off to a flying start with a minimum of delays or problems, he or she is faced with the question, "What's the best way to be sure I do what the boss wants?" Whenever a new task is recognized as critical, by the same judgment exercise we have

CRITICAL TASK INVENTORY WORKSHEET

OCCUPATION OR TITLE: Grinding Operator
DEPARTMENT: Grinding
INVENTORIED BY: Mel Douglas
REVIEWED BY: Elizabeth Bromley
INVENTORY DATE(S): 4/18/19–
REVIEWED BY: Bill Livingstone

TASKS OR ACTIVITIES — LIST ALL TASKS OR ACTIVITIES NORMALLY DONE OR THAT MIGHT BE DONE BY A PERSON IN THIS OCCUPATION	LOSS EXPOSURES — CONSIDER SAFETY, HEALTH, DAMAGE, FIRE, QUALITY, PRODUCTION PROBLEMS ETC. CONSIDER PEOPLE, EQUIPMENT, MATERIALS AND ENVIRONMENT INTERACTIONS	RISK EVALUATION				PROGRAM NEEDS				
		SEVERITY	REPETITIVE-NESS	PROBABILITY	CRITICAL TASK	PROCEDURES	PRACTICES	SKILL TRAINING	SPECIAL RULES	INDUSTRIAL HYGIENE REVIEW
Operate Pumps	Back injury from lifting plugs. Too much flow will overload secondary grinding circuit, casuing balls to "wash" and poor grind	4	1	0	5			✓		
Operate Ball Mill	Injury from mechanical scoop. Exposure to cyanide and lime. Injury from rotating screen. Poor grinding here will cause clogs and poor separation of various ores.	6	1	0	7	✓		✓		✓
Operate Cyclones	Ruptured lines can cause injury. Too fast a speed will send coarse ore into the system.	4	2	0	6			✓		
Operate Conveyor Belts	Injury from caught between roller and belt, particularly tail roller, from cleaning plug-ups while belt is running. Overloading will cause spills & belt damage.	4	1	+1	6			✓		
Operate Drum Feeder	Oversize feed will loosen or damage wrappers, break pins and cause choke-ups.	4	1	0	5			✓		
Operate Rod Mill	Since all product goes through the rod mill, proper oil and grease is critical. Due to its size, the rod mill is more prone to problems than the ball mills.	6	1	+1	8	✓		✓		
Stop and Start Complete Grinding Circuit	The proper timing and sequence of start-up for equipment involved is critical.	6	1	+1	8	✓		✓		
Operate Particle Size Monitor	If monitor malfunctions, grinding problems may not be detected until whole system is affected.	6	2	0	8	✓		✓		
Charge Ball Mill	If ball level is not maintained, poor grind results.	2	1	-1	2					
Charge Rod Mill	Back injury from lifting worn rods from below feet from spinning screen. Possible fall with major injury. Hand and finger injury. Poor grind will overload ball mills.	2	1	0	3					
Hose Down and Clean Up Work Areas	Operation of high pressure water hoses around high voltage motors presents exposure to electrocution and motor damage.	6	1	0	7		✓		✓	

Figure 7-3

been discussing here and in other chapters, it should become a target for analysis with or without any known history of loss. The same type of logic should be applied to tasks that are different from any we have ever done or tasks that we really don't know much about. The method for doing an analysis on this type of task would be different in most cases than the technique normally used on an established task, and will be discussed later in this chapter. As a general rule of thumb, treat all new tasks as critical until proven otherwise.

Since the task, "Operate Particle Size Monitor," received a task criticality evaluation of "8," and since it is a fairly simple one, it will be used to illustrate the next step.

BREAK TASK DOWN INTO STEPS

Every task can be broken down into the sequence of steps required to do it. There is usually a particular order of steps that is best to do the task most effectively, and it is this orderly sequence of steps that will eventually become the basis for the task procedure. Each step should then be examined to determine what loss exposures it presents. Every aspect of the task, including safety, quality and production, should be considered.

We could define the "task step" as one segment of the total task where something happens to advance the work involved. This doesn't mean that we list every tiny detail on our breakdown. For instance, the first 5 steps in the task, "Operate Particle Size Monitor," are:

Step 1. Inspect equipment
Step 2. Look for sand buildup in cyclone box
Step 3. Hose out air eliminator
Step 4. Close drain valve
Step 5. Open fresh water valve

Selecting the right steps in doing a task analysis is critical to the end result. When the task is first observed, write down **everything** that you see the person do. After the loss exposures are identified, you can go back and combine things or eliminate unnecessary detail. In trying to do a good job, the average supervisor is prone to have too many detailed steps. These become difficult to use for practical purposes of teaching a worker the essential steps you want him or her to remember. Let's look at the start of a listing of task steps that can quickly be recognized as being too fine a breakdown.

Step 1. Inspect equipment
Step 2. Open cyclone box
Step 3. Look for sand buildup
Step 4. Remove buildup if necessary
Step 5. Close cyclone box
Step 6. Remove air eliminator cover

It's quite obvious that this breakdown is much too detailed, and it's not too difficult to visualize the final length if we continued in this manner. The difficulty a worker would have in remembering such details makes the approach impractical.

On the other hand, let's consider the breakdown that takes the opposite extreme and doesn't provide enough steps to be of significant value.

Step 1. Inspect equipment
Step 2. Turn on monitor
Step 3. Inspect hourly
Step 4. Cut a sample hourly

As we look at this breakdown, which could be considered too general, it's obvious that many steps were missed that could involve any one or all of the areas of safety, quality and production.

To illustrate the most efficient way to do the task, the breakdown must include all major steps that are critical to doing the task right but exclude those that would probably not present major problems if they were not highlighted. The decision to include or not include steps can also follow the thinking used in selecting the task to begin with. "Could it be a critical step if done wrong?"

Experience shows that many tasks will break down into ten to fifteen key steps. Certain tasks might justify a greater number of key steps. Each task must be evaluated on its own needs. The key to the prevention of losses from injury, property damage, quality problems or production losses is the supervisor's judgment in selecting the task steps deemed critical to this goal.

Figure 7-4 shows all the steps of the task, "Operate Particle Size Monitor," and includes inspection, sampling, and shutdowns.

IDENTIFY LOSS EXPOSURES

After breaking the work down into its significant steps or critical activities, analyze each one to determine the loss exposures involved with that particular step in doing the task. This is another opportunity for employee participation to gain the benefits of their knowledge and experience.

In pinpointing these loss exposures (such as in the

TASK ANALYSIS WORKSHEET

Plant/Division	Task Analyzed
Concentrator	Operate Particle Size Monitor

Department	Date Completed
Grinding	5/14/19—

Occupation	Completed By
Grinding Operator	E. Bromley

Approvals

Signature	Function	Date
W. Livingstone	Engineering	5/18/19—
R. Hagan	Supervisor	5/16/19—
R. Swinehart	Supervisor	5/23/19—

No.	Significant Steps or Critical Activities	Loss Exposures (Safety - Quality - Production)	Efficiency Check? YES	NO	RECOMMENDED CONTROLS
1	Inspect equipment	Equipment damage, poor readings	✓		Follow checklist
2	Look for sand buildup in cyclone box	Equipment failure will force coarse particles into system	✓		Clean any accumulation
3	Hose out air eliminator	Damage to air eliminator from sand	✓		Clean any accumulation
4	Close drain valve	Water spills, electric shock	✓		Close drain valve
5	Open fresh water valve	Inadequate flow of water will cause plugups	✓		Clear water filter
6	Clear sensor pump	Hand injury from wrench slipping	✓		Shut down before cleaning / Use special cleaning tool
7	Ensure sensor is in place	Poor reading	✓		Replace if missing
8	Put safety system on automatic	Damage from low water pressure	✓		Put on automatic
9	Ensure that sample screens are clear in cyclone overflow box	Poor readings	✓		Visually inspect. Clean any accumulation
10	Start Particle Size Monitor		✓		Pull stop/start button
11	Ensure adequate water pressure	Automatic shut down of system	✓		Ensure at least 60 psi
12	Allow tank to fill	Overflow, clogs, system shutdown	✓		Listen for safety water in cycle off and on
13	Place sample screen in slurry	Inadequate vacuum	✓		Look for normal vacuum of 17+ inches
14	Adjust sample intake flow valve for normal slurry level	Overflow or inadequate flow of slurry, slips and falls to surface	✓		Allow 5 minutes to stabilize

Figure 7-4

No.	Significant Steps or Critical Activities	Loss Exposures (Safety - Quality - Production)	Efficiency Check? YES	Efficiency Check? NO	RECOMMENDED CONTROLS
15	Start sample cutter	Damage to cutter	✓		Ensure cutter is free to move
16	Start 470 & 470A pumps	Overflow, slips and falls	✓		Start in proper sequence
17	Visually inspect every hour	Increased damage and injury potential from equipment about to fail	✓		Visually inspect every hour
18	Cut a sample every hour	Poor readings	✓		Move cutter from side to side through flow. Do not hold in center of flow.
19	For emergency shutdown	Equipment damage, spillage production delay	✓		Shut off feed, shut down equipment. Arrange for repairs.
20	Power failure shutdown	Much greater damage than that which caused the shutdown.	✓		Determine reason for shutdown. Obtain permission before re-starting
21	Shut down particle size monitor	Overflow, hardened slurry in system	✓		Open drain valve, press the start/stop button. Flush system with water

Figure 7-4

middle column of *Figure 7-4*), carefully consider each of these four subsystems (P-E-M-E) within the total system. Ask questions such as these:

1. People
    a. What contacts are present that could cause injury, illness, stress or strain?
    b. Could the worker be caught in, on or between? Struck by? Fall from? Fall into?
    c. What practices are likely to downgrade safety, productivity or quality?
2. Equipment
    a. What hazards are presented by the tools, machines, vehicles or other equipment?
    b. What equipment emergencies are most likely to occur?
    c. How might the equipment cause loss of safety, productivity or quality?
3. Material
    a. What harmful exposures are presented by chemicals, raw materials or products?
    b. What are the specific problems involving materials handling?
    c. How might materials cause loss of safety, productivity or quality?
4. Environment
    a. What are the potential problems of housekeeping and order?
    b. What are the potential problems of sound, lighting, heat, cold, ventilation or radiation?
    c. How might environmental factors cause loss of safety, productivity or quality?

When things do go wrong, they result in losses. Identifying specific loss exposures is a key step in more effective loss prevention and control.

MAKE AN EFFICIENCY CHECK

In the extensive research for his influential book, *MORT - Systems Safety Analysis*, William G. Johnson discovered that unidentified change is a causative factor in most accidents. Changes in the workplace may include one or more of the following: schedule, sequence of activities, personnel, methods, materials, tools, equipment, machinery, specifications, priorities, etc. Many, if not most, of these changes are beneficial or intended to be. But when changes are not recognized and compensated for, there is increased chance of accidents. Consider the following facts discovered in accident investigations:

• Laboratory workers were using chemicals they had brought from home.

• The regular worker was absent and no one told his replacement about the new setting on the machine.
• During renovation the oxygen and nitrous oxide lines leading into the surgical suite were cross-connected, leading to the death of a surgery patient.
• The new lubricant that was supposed to reduce maintenance time by one-fourth failed, causing irreparable damage to the shaft and bearings and setting fire to the packing materials.
• The new raw material was to be processed at a much lower temperature to save energy costs. Operation at the previous temperature setting led to an explosion.
• Removal of an easily clogged filter in a hot acid line, in an efficiency move, led to a clogged valve and indicator. The overpressurized line ruptured, severely burning two workers.

On the other hand, needed changes are sometimes not made to keep pace with new methods and materials or simply with better ways of doing things. This can allow inefficiencies to creep into any organization over a period of time. Samuel Walter Foss expressed this in a delightful manner nearly a century ago in his poem, "Path of the Calf" (*Figure 7-5*).

PATH OF THE CALF
Samuel Walter Foss, 1895

One day through the primeval wood
A calf walked home as good calves should;
But made a trail all but bent askew,
A crooked trail as all calves do.
Since then three hundred years have fled.
And I infer the calf is dead.
But still he left behind his trail
And thereby hangs my moral tale.
The trail was taken up next day
By a lone dog that passed that way;
And then a wise bell wether sheep
Pursued the trail o'er vale and steep,
And drew the flock behind him, too,
As good bell wethers always do.
And from that day o'er hill and glade
Through those old woods a path was made.

The years passed on in swiftness fleet.
The road became a village street;
And this, before men were aware,
A city's crowded thoroughfare.
And soon the central street was this
Of a renowed metropolis;
And men two centuries and a half
Trod in the footsteps of that calf.
Each day a hundred thousand tout
Followed this calf about
And o'er his crooked journey went
The traffic of a continent.
A hundred thousand men were led
By one calf near three centuries dead.
They followed still his crooked way,
And lost one hundred years a day;
For thus such reverence is lent
To well established precedent.

For men are prone to go it blind
Along the calf-paths of the mind.
And work away from sun to sun
To do what other men have done.

Figure 7-5

Many supervisors and workers find the efficiency check to be the most rewarding part of the whole task analysis process. It's a great opportunity to work together to...

... make work easier and safer

... reduce wasted time, space, energy and materials

... improve quality and productivity

... make best use of tools, machines and equipment

... make best use of employees' knowledge, skills and abilities

The improvements from this one step alone, the efficiency check, have often more than paid for all the time and effort invested in the entire task analysis process. In fact, for some organizations, the savings have exceeded the costs of the entire safety and health program for that period of time. The program coordinator who systematically maintains control that this is being done, and with proper records maintained has taken a giant step in demonstrating the value of the safety and loss control program, both now and in the future. When it is considered that the primary purpose of task procedures is as a guide to training, it becomes even more important that they show the most efficient methods lest inefficiencies be permanently entrenched in an organization.

> **Once upon a time business was conducted according to the rules of an established game complete with its old boy network, which said, "do whatever you do - better." As a result, we just got better at what we did and never evaluated what we were doing in the first place. Now that the fat is gone, it is more important to do the right thing, which means constantly challenging our existing methods and approaches.**
> **— Art McNeil**

Essentially, making an efficiency check is a matter of asking the right questions and seeking satisfactory answers. The old stand-by Who-Where-When-What-Why-How questions can be a good starting point. For instance, you can ask questions such as the following about *each* significant step or critical activity:

- Who is best qualified to do it?
- Where is the best place to do it?
- When should it be done?
- What is the purpose of this step?
- Why is this step necessary?
- How can it be done better?

You can also analyze work in terms of four major management goals (Cost - Production - Quality - Safety). The interfaces of these four subsystems and four goals provide the following sixteen areas of questioning for a thorough efficiency check:

1. **Cost-People:** Could we control costs by having better trained people? By better utilization of people? Through more effective motivation?

2. **Cost-Equipment:** Could we control costs by having different tools, machines or equipment? By using present equipment more effectively?

3. **Cost-Material:** Can less expensive or less scarce material be used? How can we reduce waste of material?

4. **Cost-Environment:** Can we save money through better housekeeping? Order? Layout? Lighting? Atmosphere?

5. **Production-People:** How can we reduce lost time? Increase manpower efficiency? Make it easier for people to be more productive?

6. **Production-Equipment:** How can we minimize damage and downtime? What tools - machines - equipment can we provide to increase productivity?

7. **Production-Material:** How might materials be handled or transported more efficiently? What other materials might aid productivity?

8. **Production-Environment:** Can we improve production through better lighting, layout, cleanliness and order? Through better work climate or conditions?

9. **Quality-People:** What knowledge and skills are critical for quality performance? Could we improve quality through better selection, placement, training, coaching and key point tipping?

10. **Quality-Equipment:** What tools - machines - equipment could we provide to ensure optimum quality? Could we improve maintenance operations to get closer tolerances and better quality?

11. **Quality-Material:** What different materials might boost quality? Would it be helpful to make material quality checks earlier or more frequently?

12. **Quality-Environment:** Is quality affected by dirt, dusts or smoke? By solvents, vapors, mists, fumes

or gases? By lighting, temperature or ventilation?

13. **Safety-People:** What are the potential hazards that could harm people? What are the critical needs for rules, for task instruction, and for task observation?

14. **Safety-Equipment:** What are the potential hazards that could cause equipment damage, fire or explosion? How can we make better use of safety devices, protective equipment, preventive maintenance and pre-use equipment inspection?

15. **Safety-Material:** How can we eliminate or control exposure to hazardous materials? How can we improve training in safe handling practices? How can we best prevent waste and damage of raw materials and products?

16. **Safety-Environment:** How can we improve housekeeping (cleanliness and order) to control accident losses? What can we change in the work environment to improve safety?

Figure 7-6 is a review of the efficiency check.

EFFICIENCY CHECK REVIEW

I. Answer basic questions about each job step.

- WHO should do it?
- WHERE should it be done?
- WHEN should it be done?
- WHAT is its purpose?
- WHY is it necessary?
- HOW can it be done better?

II. Answer specific subsystem questions about each job step.

PEOPLE

- What are the potential hazards that could harm people?
- What are the critical needs for rules, for job instruction and for job observation?
- What knowledge and skills are critical for quality performance?
- Could we improve quality through better selection, placement, training, coaching and key point tipping?
- How can we reduce lost time? Increase manpower efficiency? Make it easier for people to be more productive?
- Could we control costs by having better trained people? By better utilization of people? Through more effective motivation?

MATERIAL

- How can we eliminate or control exposure to hazardous materials?
- How can we improve training in safe handling practices?
- How can we best prevent waste and damage of raw materials and products?
- What different materials might boost quality?
- Would it be helpful to make material quality checks earlier or more frequently?
- How might materials be handled or transported more efficiently?
- What other materials might aid productivity?
- Can less experience or less scarce material be used?
- How can we reduce waste of material?

EQUIPMENT

- What are the potential hazards that could cause equipment damage, fire or explosion?
- How can we make better use of safety devices, protective equipment, preventive maintenance and pre-use equipment inspection?
- What tools - machines - equipment could we provide to ensure optimum quality? To increase productivity?
- Could we improve maintenance operations to get closer tolerance and better quality?
- How can we minimize damage and downtime?
- Could we control costs by having different tools, machines or equipment? By using present equipment more effectively?

ENVIRONMENT

- How can we improve housekeeping (cleanliness and order) to control accident losses?
- What can we change in the work environment to improve safety?
- Is quality affected by dirt, dusts or smoke? By solvents, vapors, mists, fumes or gases? By lighting, temperature or ventilation?
- Can we improve production through better lighting, layout, cleanliness and order? Through better work climate or conditions?
- Can we save money through better housekeeping? Order? Layout? Lighting? Atmosphere?

III. S-C-O-R-E by brainstorming.

- SIMPLIFY all necessary details
- COMBINE details where practical
- ORGANIZE for safety - quality - productivity - cost control
- REARRANGE to get better sequence
- ELIMINATE all unnecessary details

Figure 7-6

Here are seven major ways to make improvements indicated in the Efficiency Check:

1. **Improve procedures** - eliminate or reduce the loss potential by changing the way the job/task is performed. Examples: add a pre-use inspection with a checklist; use dollies for all loads over 25 pounds.

2. **Improve the work environment** - eliminate or reduce loss potential by better design, better lighting, less noise, better layout, less stress, better ventilation, less discomfort and so on.

3. **Improve work methods** - eliminate or reduce loss potential by making major methods changes. For instance, replace a hand-shoveling, wheelbarrow-carrying operation with a conveyor.

4. **Reduce the exposure frequency** - reduce loss potential by reducing the number of exposures to potential hazards. Keep to a minimum the number or length of times that hazardous operations must be performed.

5. **Improve communication** - increase people's potential for loss control in terms of awareness, input, knowledge, understanding and feedback.

6. **Improve training** - increase people's potential for loss control by increasing their skill or proficiency.

7. **Improve motivation** - increase people's desire to control losses by providing effective incentives and reinforcements.

Here are some savings which have resulted from the "efficiency check" step of task analysis:

- Provided adequate storage for materials stored in the ground areas of the main production shop. Improper storage and handling of materials such as brick, insulation materials, timber and cardboard had resulted in damage or loss of materials valued at approximately $3,100 per month.

- Reduced time lost in locating precision tools. Designed and built portable tool cart that enabled users to remove and replace tools conveniently in less time. Savings of $157,000.

- Installed insulating brick on bottoms of pre-heaters to reduce downtime when furnaces are down for repairs or rebuild ... decreasing cleanout time by 40%.

- Reused gland rings, used in blending machines that produce wire insulation, for a savings of $38,000 a year.

- Wrapped manuals sent by a government agency in plastic shrink wrap rather than paper bags, for a savings of $11,000 per year.

- Sixty-nine proposals have been implemented and have resulted in verifiable savings of approximately $280,000; as well as improvements in material flow, safety, communications and customer relations.

This kind of information should be recorded and communicated whenever measurable results in cost reductions occur as a result of task analysis. This information serves at least three values: (1) it demonstrates rather quickly the enormous value of the program; (2) it provides a basis for recognition by upper management of those persons who achieve good results; and (3) it provides motivation to all involved to go ahead and make the changes necessary to get the desired results. *Figure 7-7* is another example of the benefits gained from the efficiency check. *Figure 7-8* shows a form for reporting the improvements which can come from the efficiency check.

THERE IS A BETTER WAY

There's always a better way of doing things. For example: The Riverside Plant does a lot of "buffing" ... a process of knocking off the rough spots on metal castings by using a rag wheel. The old operation was like this:

1. Operator leaned over and picked up one casting from a box on the floor and to the right side of the buffing machine
2. Operator held the casting against the buffing wheel until the operation was completed
3. After inspecting the process, operator leaned over and placed the finished casting in a box on the floor and to the left of the buffing machine.

After an "Efficiency Check," the operator now:

1. Pre-arranges the supply of castings on a table at the same height as the buffing machine
2. Holds the casting against the buffing wheel until the operation is completed
3. Inspects the process and pushes the finished casting to the left of the rag wheel, into the throat of a chute which is connected to a box on the floor.

SOME ADVANTAGES OF THE NEW METHOD:

1. Time used for picking up and depositing castings reduced 80%
2. Reduced potential for "back problems"
3. Less fatigue
4. Less floor space required for buffing operation
5. Increased productivity
6. Cost improvement
7. Improved supervisor-worker relations.

Figure 7-7

JOB/TASK PROCEDURE
EFFICIENCY IMPROVEMENT REPORT

<table>
<tr><td rowspan="4">LOCATION</td><td>PLANT/DIVISION
Concentrator</td><td>DEPARTMENT
Grinding</td><td>OCCUPATION
Grinder Operator</td><td>TASK
Operate Particle
Size Monitor</td></tr>
<tr><td>DATE
5/18/19—</td><td>SUBMITTED BY
S. Bentley</td><td>ANNUAL COST SAVINGS
$4,017.00</td><td>APPROVED BY
K. Brown</td></tr>
</table>

DESCRIPTION OF CHANGES AND BENEFITS

Clearly describe all changes/efficiency improvements made or that will be made as a result of the efficiency check.

Previously the sensor pump had to be removed from the monitor for clearing when it was clogged. This had to be done an average of 4 times a day and took about 10 minutes to remove, clear and replace. Also, because the operator would occasionally try to remove it without shutting down, there was serious potential for hand injury. Manipulating the wrench in such tight quarters frequently led to wrench slippage and a bruised hand.

Clearly describe all benefits (direct and indirect) that have occurred or will occur because of these changes.

The new procedure uses a special fitting which allows the pump to be cleared while still mounted. This only takes about one minute and the operator's hand is never in danger. Also, it eliminates the annoyance and hand bruises from using the wrench for disassembly and assembly. The equipment should still be shut down to avoid damage but if for any reason it is not there is no danger of injury.

COMPUTATION OF SAVINGS

Clearly describe method used to compute and measure costs, being sure to include implementation cost.

Ten Minutes Previously x 4 Times Daily	= 40 Minutes
One Minute Now x 4 Times Daily	= 4 Minutes
Time Savings (Daily)	= 36 Minutes
Time Savings Yearly - 350 Days x 36 Minutes	=12,600 Minutes
	= 210 Hours

Hours Per Year	=	210
Labor Costs	=	19.50
Labor Savings Per Year	=	$4,095
Less Cost of Fabricating New Tool		78
Annual Savings First Year		$4,017

Figure 7-8

DEVELOP CONTROLS

This is what it's all about. After analyzing the work and the potential problems, and making the efficiency check, you have what you need to develop the recommended controls (final column of the Task Analysis Worksheet, *Figure 7-4*). Controls are the actions and precautions that will prevent the potential losses from occurring and will ensure that the work is performed with maximum efficiency. Remember that the controls should be directed primarily at the person or persons doing the task by telling them what they are to do to avoid or eliminate the loss exposures. Ideas for controls will naturally have been generated throughout the efficiency check and related discussions. Recording them on the worksheet is a fairly simple formality.

WRITE EITHER TASK PROCEDURE OR WORK PRACTICE

Figure 7-9 shows the task procedure for "Operate Particle Size Monitor." Notice several features of it. (1) It starts with a statement of the purpose and importance of the task. This is included both for motivational purposes and to increase understanding and thereby retention and conformance. (2) It presents a step-by-step description of "how to proceed." (3) It expresses the steps in a positive "what to do" way rather than a long list of "don'ts." (4) Again, to improve understanding, retention and conformance, the reasons "why" are given for key steps. (5) It is printed in a simple, functional format. Since procedures are primarily teaching and learning tools, they must be clear, concise, correct and complete.

As mentioned earlier, not all tasks can or should be proceduralized. This is particularly true of tasks in the trades, crafts, maintenance and materials handling which may be done a little differently each time they are done. It is also true of tasks where the final result is what is important and how the person achieves that is pretty much left up to her or him. For tasks of this nature, practices are more functional and useful.

Guidelines for preparing functional practices are:

1. Present positive guidelines for correct performance, plus pertinent rules and regulations.

2. Sometimes not limited to a specific task, but deal with a fairly wide range of work activities (e.g., using a chain saw, entering confined spaces, handling explosives, locking out equipment).

3. Especially useful for occupations in which workers perform a large number of tasks infrequently or where specific tasks are hard to proceduralize because the way they are done varies greatly with the specific situation.

4. Suggested areas of emphasis in Work Practices are...

   a. **Motivation** - explain why the worker should comply with the standard practice. Relate to the worker's own welfare. Build a bit of pride.

   b. **Special Problem Sources** - point out the most probable sources of problems; the things to which special attention should be paid.

   c. **Clothing and Personal Protection** - specify required clothing and equipment, the conditions under which it is required and the reasons for its use.

   d. **Special Devices and Equipment** - emphasize proper use of special guards, barriers, switches, locks and emergency equipment.

   e. **Emergency Procedures** - refer to the procedures for cases of fire, explosion, flooding and other catastrophies. Specify emergency first aid equipment and practices, emergency shutdown procedures and reporting requirements.

   f. **Critical Rules and Regulations** - reinforce the most important rules by including them in the Work Practices. Keep them as short and simple as possible; give the reasons for the rules; and focus on the "critical few."

   g. **Positive, Proper Practices** - highlight the things that the worker can do to ensure efficient, safe, productive results. Keep the "thou shalt nots" to a minimum. Accentuate the positives.

   h. **Summary Statement** - summarize the most important points. Give a "prescription" for positive action. Zero in on the benefits of proper performance.

The following excerpt from the Smoky Mountain National Park's Work Practices for "Wood Craftsman and Carpenter" shows how motivation can be emphasized:

Restoration of historical structures, built long before the advent of safe work practices, in part takes the craftsman back to those dangerous times. Accidents took more American pioneers'

STANDARD TASK PROCEDURE

ISSUED TO _____

Operate Particle Size Monitor   **June 20, 19—**
            TASK   DATE

Grinding   **Grinding Operator**
DEPARTMENT   OCCUPATION

TASK PURPOSE AND IMPORTANCE

The particle size monitor analyzes the grind and density of the final grinding product. The trends are recorded on chart recorders. The result is a record of representative samples of the total day's grind.

The proper adjustment of the entire grinding and flotation process is dependent upon accurate sampling techniques. Errors and malfunctions can be responsible for many thousands of dollars of wasted ore, materials and efforts. Some of the equipment involved is easily damaged if not properly operated and regularly inspected.

The major steps are outlined in their proper order. Key points to remember follow each job step. All steps and key points must be followed in sequence to achieve maximum efficiency and avoid losses.

1. **INSPECT EQUIPMENT FOR DEFECTS**

   a) To avoid equipment damage and poor readings, visually inspect the following equipment for defects and make any necessary corrections before startup.
      1) Look for sand buildup in cyclone box and clean any accumulation.
      2) Hose out the air eliminator.

   b) Close drain valve to avoid spillage and possible falls or electric shock.

   c) Open main fresh water valve and clear water filter to assure adequate flow of water.

   d) Shut down and clear sensor pumps and ensure that sensor is in place. Use special cleaning tool to avoid disassembly of pump and possible hand injury.

   e) Put water system safety switch on automatic to avoid damage from low water pressure.

   f) Visually inspect the sample screen in the cyclone overflow box and clean any accumulation to avoid poor readings.

2. **START PARTICLE SIZE MONITOR**

   a) Pull start/stop button on control box to start.

   b) Ensure that water pressure is at least 60 psi to avoid automatic shutdown of system.

   c) Allow tank to fill until the sensor section is full at which point the safety water will automatically turn off. The safety water may cycle off and on.

   d) Place the sample screen in the slurry. The vacuum should rise to normal (17+ inches).

   e) Adjust sample intake flow valve for normal tank slurry level - allow 5 minutes to stablize to avoid overflow or starving the system.

3. **START SAMPLE CUTTER**

   To avoid damage to cutter, ensure that it is free to move.

4. **START 470 AND 470A PUMPS**

   To avoid overflow start 470 pump first.

5. **HOURLY INSPECTION**

   a) Visually inspect all equipment every hour to avoid increased damage and injury potential from failed equipment and to ensure proper sampling.

   b) Key items to look for are:
      1) The vacuum seal should be cool to the touch.
      2) There should be only slight vibration of the air eliminator
      3) The ball in the flow indicator should be at the top of the sight glass.

6. **HOURLY SAMPLE**

   a) Cut a sample every hour off the east and west cyclone overflow by moving the sample cutter through the flow from side to side.

   b) To avoid poor readings do not hold the cutter in the center of the flow.

7. **EMERGENCY SHUTDOWN**

   a) When the following conditions occur the equipment must be shut down immediately to avoid further damage, spillage and production delays:
      1) Hot drive assembly bearings
      2) Holes in feed lines or discharge lines
      3) Water in drive motors
      4) Sanding of sumps
      5) Excessive vibration or air eliminator.

   b) For any of these conditions:
      1) Shut off feed
      2) Shut down the equipment
      3) Arrange for repairs.

   c) In case of power failure:
      1) To avoid much greater damage than that which caused the shutdown and to avoid possible electric shock, determine reason for loss of power.
      2) Obtain permission before restarting any part of the process to avoid possible serious injury to anyone who might be working on the system.

8. **SHUTDOWN**

   a) To avoid overflow open the drain valve before pressing the start/stop button.

   b) To avoid the slurry setting up in the system flush the system with water.

STANDARD TASK PROCEDURE

I have received the Standard Job Procedure on this date. It has been explained to me, and the importance to following it has been stressed.

RECEIVED BY _____

DATE _____   SUPERVISOR _____

Figure 7-9

lives than all the hostile elements put together. It is a challenge to your skill as a craftsman to accurately restore these priceless structures as well as maintain the equally priceless health and safety of yourself, your fellow employees and the visitors to our Park... These safe work practices are designed to help you, and your fellow craftsmen and apprentices, meet this challenge.

The booklet then covers practices under the headings: Order - Clothing and Dress - Personal Protective Equipment - Ladders - Scaffolding - Roof Repair Practices - Historical Structure Restoration Practices - Hand Tool Use - Power Tool Use - General Safe Working Practices. And it does all of this very concisely!

Figure 7-10 shows excerpts from a set of general work practices for electricians. By taking the time to develop Task Procedures and Work Practices for the critical work activities in your area of responsibility, you will save a great deal of time in the long run. They provide carefully thought out guidance, based on the best available knowledge, of the correct way to do critical tasks in the most efficient way.

It should be noted again the most organizations call both practices and procedures by one name or the other. Other organizations refer to both as "work methods," "standard operating procedures" or other terms. What you call them is not terribly important. It is important to understand that some tasks can and should be proceduralized. Others either cannot or should not be proceduralized. The purpose is to be able to give people written guidelines for doing critical jobs in the most efficient way.

"Most accidents occur in a work area to which a worker is not accustomed, and during a task that is not a worker's usual task. A worker primarily needs information on how to perform his job, and only secondarily on how to do the job safely."
— J. Saari, Safety Study
   Finland Institute of Occupational Safety

STANDARD TASK PRACTICES FOR ELECTRICIANS

1. GENERAL

   a. Only persons qualified by training and familiar with the construction and operation of the apparatus, and the hazards involved, shall be allowed in those areas of open wiring, exposed and live switches, breakers, conductors, etc., as found in substations and generating rooms. Foremen shall be responsible for determining which persons are so qualified. Warning signs must be installed at the entrance to such areas.

   b. Before starting work, a thorough survey shall be made by the workman to determine all the hazards present and to see that all necessary safeguards are provided to protect himself, other workmen and equipment.

   c. Before starting work, safeguards such as danger signs, roped off space, etc., shall be used.

   d. In all cases where the work is hazardous and is being performed on or close to live conductors or apparatus, at least two workmen shall work together. When it is necessary for one workman to leave for any reason, all such work shall be discontinued until both are again present.

   e. It is the responsibility of the person to whom the instructions are given to account for all persons in his group before leaving the job at quitting time, for meals, or for any other reason.

   f. Before starting work on live circuits on poles, rubber blankets or shields shall be placed over adjacent, intervening and ground wires or grounded structures for protection while working on selected wires.

   g. Rubber mats or other suitable insulating material shall be used for protection while working on live circuits or when operating high tension switches.

   h. While working on all wires, cables, or apparatus, electricians should realize that when there is voltage on a circuit, current can flow to ground and therefore, precautions shall be taken to keep their bodies properly insulated.

Figure 7-10

PUT TO WORK

It is hard to find more practical supervisory management tools than Task Procedures and Work Practices. Here are seven key ways you can put them to work.

1. **Employee orientation** - One of the first things new employees want to know is what work they will be doing. Copies of procedures and practices are useful for explaining this to them in a general way. You might want to give them copies to study before you start proper task instruction.

2. **Proper task instruction** - Written procedures and practices are of tremendous value in helping leaders meet their basic responsibility for teaching others how to do their jobs/tasks properly (correctly - quickly - conscientiously - safely).

3. **Planned task observation** - Written work procedures and practices enable supervisors to systematically analyze how well worker performance meets the necessary standards.

4. **Personal contacts, coaching and tipping** - Written task procedures and work practices are an abundant source of practical points for supervisors to emphasize in their personal contacts with workers and in their vital leadership skills of "coaching" (the day-to-day actions taken by the supervisor, designed to stimulate a subordinate to improve) and "tipping" (the organized process of giving employees helpful hints, suggestions, reminders or tips about key quality, production, cost, of safety points in their work).

5. **Safety talks** - When everyone in the group performs the task or is directly affected by it, written procedures and practices provide supervisors with excellent information to emphasize in their group meetings ("Safety Talks" - "Toolbox Meetings" - "Tailgate Sessions").

6. **Accident/incident investigation** - Written descriptions of the work help supervisors do a thorough job of investigating accidents and incidents, analyzing whether the work was being done as it should be, where the process went wrong, and what kinds of changes could lead to better control.

7. **Skill training** - By showing specifically and systematically what the work is, written Task Procedures and Work Practices improve the efficiency and effectiveness of training programs for equipment operators and other skilled workers.

It takes some time and effort to prepare procedures and practices, but when you put them to work the returns on your investment are highly profitable — in terms of:

• Greater efficiency, safety and productivity

• Better results in job/task instruction, job/task observation, coaching, tipping, safety talks, investigation and skill training

• Optimum protection of people, property, process, productivity and profitability.

UPDATE AND MAINTAIN RECORDS

Analyzing and describing the proper way to perform critical tasks is so vital to any organization that systematic documentation is a must. Each supervisor should keep track of progress with a card or sheet along the lines of the "Critical Job/Task Procedures and Practices Record" shown as *Figure 7-11*. These records provide a master reference regarding the status for each critical task in each occupation or work title — an indispensable tool for management control.

Tools as valuable as work procedures and practices should not be allowed to become obsolete. Each one should be reviewed for possible updating at a stipulated period of time, usually annually. They should also be reviewed whenever a high-potential incident or serious loss occurs and whenever significant changes are made in or related to the task.

Since Standard Task Procedures are developed to establish the one proper way to do a particular task, it is important that every area which will be affected by them has an opportunity for input and final approval. The Summary Report shown in *Figure 7-12* provides space for the necessary documentation of key facts connected with the development and approval of task procedures. It is usually circulated by the program coordinator as the cover sheet for the completed task procedure. The signatures and evaluations are added as it moves from person to person. It is another assurance of quality in the critical program activity.

Painter OCCUPATION	CRITICAL TASK RECORD	Service DEPARTMENT
CRITICAL JOBS	**BASIS FOR LISTING**	**INITIAL (I) UPDATE (UD) HISTORY**
1.Mixing paints	Potential for big loss (health) Past waste experience. Quality problems with mix errors	I 7/6/- P.R.B. UD 8/6/- J.R.J
2.Glazing a window	Past history waste Past injury experience	I 7/6/- P.R.B. UD 7/10/- P.R.B.
3.Rigging a scaf-fold	Past history injury & property damage. Potential fire loss	I 5/14/- P.R.B. UD 9/10/- P.R.B.
4.Placing an upright ladder	Past history of injury Potential for major injury	I 6/8/- P.R.B. UD 8/10/- P.R.B.
5.Spraying interior walls	Potential for major illness Big waste potential Major fire & explosion hazard	I 4/6/- P.R.B. UD 6/10/- J.R.C.
6.Painting machinery	Potential for major injury Potential for machine damage	I 6/12/- J.R.C. UD 9/15/- P.R.B.

Figure 7-11

USE THE BEST ANALYSIS TECHNIQUE

Two basic approaches to task analysis are "analysis by observation and discussion" and "analysis by discussion alone." Whenever feasible, you should use the "observation and discussion" technique, in which you actually see the person, the equipment, the materials, the surroundings and the process.

Here are twelve steps involved in analysis by observation.

1. Select several good workers who are willing to share their knowledge and experience.

2. Gain cooperation by explaining what is being done and assuring that it is the work, not the worker, which is being evaluated.

3. Observe the task being done by one of the selected workers and record an initial breakdown.

4. Check this breakdown with the worker for accuracy, thus encouraging the worker to share knowledge and experience.

5. Repeat steps 2-4 with another worker if appropriate. Record the basic steps of the task breakdown. It usually helps to start each statement with an action verb, such as set, adjust, start, remove and so on.

6. Identify the loss exposures for each significant step or critical activity.

7. Make an efficiency check of each significant step or critical activity.

8. Develop recommended controls, stating them in brief positive sentences which tell what to do to eliminate or avoid the loss exposures and how to do the work most efficiently.

9. Write the Task Procedure or Practice.

10. Contact other interested groups such as safety and quality control for their suggestions and approval. Revise, if necessary.

11. Distribute the procedure or practice to the appropriate people and put it to work.

12. Reinforce it by frequent reference and use in orientation, task instruction, planned task observation, coaching, tipping, safety talks, accident/incident investigation and skill training.

> A special variation of the observation technique involves the use of a special camera and spaced photography (for prints, slides or videotape). You and the worker can analyze the pictures in detail and develop descriptions of what is involved. Then you have not only the job/task breakdown, but also the makings of a good training tool.

Coordinator's Summary Report For Standard Job/Task Procedure

Organization _____   Location _____

Occupation _____   Task _____

1. Task analysis and task procedure completed by persons contributing or supplying information:

_____   _____
Name   Title

_____   _____
Name   Title

_____   _____
Name   Title

2. The task analysis was done by: Observation _____   Discussion _____

3. If discussion method is checked, please explain why observation method was not used.

4. Give names of workers observed, or if discussion method was used, give names of persons contributing:

_____   _____
Name   Occupation

_____   _____
Name   Occupation

_____   _____
Name   Occupation

_____   _____
Name   Occupation

_____   _____
Name   Occupation

_____   _____
Name   Occupation

5. Was an efficiency check made for each task step and related loss exposure?   Yes _____   No _____

6. List all changes as a result of the efficiency check on reverse side and indicate the benefits to be derived. Attach an efficiency improvement report for each efficiency change.

7. What plans have been made to implement the efficiency changes/improvements? Attach details.

8. The following task procedures and reviews were made, based on a score of 1-100. Scoring included: 1. evaluation of technical content for reviewer's area of interest, 2. adequacy of coverage and 3. quality of communication for end user.

Production	Job Title	Score
Quality	Job Title	Score
Environmental Health	Job Title	Score
Safety/Loss Control	Job Title	Score
Maintenance	Job Title	Score
Signature & Title	Dept./Area	Score

Approved ☐
Not Approved ☐

Evaluator's Score

9. Comments by reviewers related to evaluation score.

Figure 7-12

When it is not feasible to observe the work, do an "analysis by discussion alone." This could be for a new task that is not yet being done; for one at a location so remote that a visit is impractical; or for one that is done infrequently but is so critical it is not wise to wait. In such cases:

- Get together the most knowledgeable people available to you (holding one or more meetings with some or all of these people, as appropriate).
- Explain the purpose and approach.
- Determine the significant steps or critical activities.
- Complete steps 6-12 as above.

Both approaches make good use of the management Principle of Participation: "Motivation to accomplish results tends to increase as people are given opportunity to participate in matters affecting those results." Participation is important in *analysis by observation and discussion* (especially steps 2, 4 and 10) and in *analysis by discussion alone.* Even when staff specialists do the analyses, a vital key to success is the active involvement of supervisors and workers. Effective participation may well make the difference between failure and success in developing and implementing work procedures and practices.

CORE CONCEPTS IN REVIEW

Task Procedures and Practices play a big part in achieving proper performance — **the key to effective results** in safety, quality, productivity and cost control. **Procedures are step-by-step** descriptions of how to proceed in performing **a task** properly. **Practices are guidelines** for performing a specific **type of work** properly.

A systematic approach to preparing and using procedures and practices involves these eight aspects:

1. **Inventory the tasks.** List all the tasks in each occupation or job title.

2. **Identify the critical tasks.** Consider such factors as:
   a. the severity of the potential losses
   b. how frequently the task is performed
   c. the probability of loss when the task is performed.

Concentrate on critical jobs or tasks.

3. **Break work down into steps or activities.** Do a breakdown which identifies the significant steps or critical activities.

4. **Identify loss exposures.** For each significant step or critical activity, pinpoint what could go wrong. Consider all subsystems, such as people - equipment - material - environment.

5. **Make an efficiency check.** For each significant step or critical activity, ask and answer enough questions to determine whether or not it is being done the best way. Consider people, equipment, material, environment, cost, production, quality and safety.

6. **Develop controls.** Specify the actions and precautions that will prevent the potential losses from

occurring and will ensure that the work is performed with maximum efficiency.

7. **Write either a Task Procedure or Practice.** Use guidelines such as these:
   a. Procedures
      (1) Present a step-by-step description of "how to proceed."
      (2) Express in a positive "what to do" way as much as possible.
      (3) Tell "why" whenever feasible.
      (4) Use a simple, easy-to-follow format.
   b. Practices
      (1) Present positive guidelines for proper performance, plus pertinent rules and regulations.
      (2) Generally, are not limited to a specific task, but deal with a fairly wide range of work activities.
      (3) Are especially useful for occupations in which workers perform a large number of jobs infrequently or where specific tasks are hard to proceduralize because the way they are done varies greatly with the specific situation.
      (4) Emphasize motivation, special problem sources, clothing, personal protection, special devices and equipment, emergency procedures, critical rules and regulations, positive practices and summary suggestions.

8. **Put to work.** Use the tremendous tools you have developed for orientation, proper task instruction, planned task observation, coaching, tipping, safety talks, accident/incident investigation and skill training.

9. **Documentation and follow-up** of progress **are important.** Someone should keep track of progress with a "Critical Job/Task Procedure and Practices Record." The coordinator should keep track of overall progress of the program.

Two basic approaches are:

1. Analysis by observation and discussion
2. Analysis by discussion alone

Analysis by observation and discussion is normally best. It involves these twelve steps:

1. Select workers to observe
2. Explain the process
3. Observe and record the initial task breakdown
4. Check initial breakdown with worker
5. Repeat steps 2-4 with another worker, if appropriate
6. Identify loss exposures
7. Make an efficiency check
8. Develop recommended controls
9. Write the procedure or practice
10. Contact special interest groups
11. Distribute procedure or practice to users
12. Reinforce practical applications

When observation is not feasible, analysis by discussion alone may be done. This involves:

1. Getting together the most knowledgeable people available to you
2. Explaining the purpose and approach
3. Determining the significant steps or critical activities by discussion
4. Completing steps 6-12 as above.

It is difficult to think of any management tool with more potential payoff than well-developed and well-used work procedures and practices.

KEY QUESTIONS

1. What is the unified or integrated approach to job/task procedures or practices?

2. Why is it important?

3. What is the basic difference between procedures and practices?

4. What are the nine main aspects of a systematic approach to preparing and using procedures and practices?

5. Why should supervisors inventory the tasks in their areas of responsibility?

6. Which tasks should be analyzed first?

7. What is a "critical" job or task?

8. Why is the "efficiency check" important?

9. What are the seven major ways to improve efficiency?

10. What is meant by "controls?"

11. What are six major practical applications for written procedures and practices?

12. Who should keep records of progress in the task analysis program?

13. What are the two basic approaches to task analysis? Which is usually best?

14. How might a camera be used in task analysis?

15. Who should be involved in analysis by discussion?

16. Who should establish program policy?

17. Who should advise, assist and audit management's program performance?

18. Who should make most use of procedures and practices?

PRACTICAL APPLICATIONS SUMMARY

S - For Supervisors
E - For Executives
C - For Safety/Loss Control Coordinators

		S	E	C
1.	Issue directives or letters backing the program for task analyses, procedures and practices.		x	
2.	Establish objectives for accomplishments of analyses, initial procedures and practices and updates.	x	x	
3.	Provide suitable forms and techniques for analyses, procedures and practices.			x
4.	Inventory the tasks.	x		
5.	Determine critical tasks.	x		x
6.	Do task breakdowns.	x	x	
7.	Pinpoint potential problems.	x		
8.	Make efficiency checks.	x		
9.	Develop controls.	x		
10.	Draft procedures and practices.	x		
11.	Approve procedures and practices.		x	x
12.	Distribute procedures and practices to users.	x		x
13.	Stimulate use of written procedures and practices.	x	x	
14.	Use written procedures and practices in orientation, proper task instruction, planned task observation, coaching, tipping and safety talks.	x		
15.	Use written procedures and practices in accident/incident investigation and in skill training.	x	x	x
16.	Update procedures and practices.	x		
17.	Maintain central files of procedures and practices.			x
18.	Maintain program progress records.	x		x
19.	Advise and assist people in carrying out the overall program.			x
20.	Ensure proper related training for all management people.			x
21.	Audit performance to the established standards and objectives.			x
22.	Issue quarterly progress reports.			x
23.	Reinforce practical applications of procedures and practices.			x

CHAPTER 8

PLANNED JOB/TASK OBSERVATION

"We do not expect a machine to operate efficiently without proper break-in, preventive maintenance, regular observation, close attention and required corrective actions. Nor should we expect a person to perform properly without similar attention."
- G. L. Germain

INTRODUCTION

One quality which sets top supervisors apart from others is their knowledge of what is going on in their areas of responsibility. This knowledge causes upper managers to react with expressions like, "Ask Jack, he'll know what the problem is," or "Get Ida's opinion, she knows what is going on." They realize that front-line supervisors must know what is going on to get the work done properly.

The best way to find out how well a person does a particular job or task is to observe him or her doing it. This is what job/task observation (or performance observation) boils down to... personally observing the performance of your people. It is a sure way to know whether or not critical jobs are being performed according to standards, or whether there are better ways that everyone should be using.

The importance of identifying and evaluating changes in the ways people do critical jobs/tasks cannot be overstated. There is abundant evidence that undetected change in the workplace is a major source of causal factors that contribute to a high percentage of accidents. These changes can slip into the workplace unnoticed and unevaluated until problems result from them. Also there are beneficial changes that occur as people discover better ways of doing things. The key is to be certain that change is detected and evaluated to determine its full potential for good or bad.

Planned observation is a tool for observing conditions and practices in an organized and systematic way. It enables you to know with a high level of confidence how well people are performing specific jobs or tasks. It enables you to ...

- pinpoint practices that could cause accidents, injuries, damage, inefficiency and waste
- determine specific needs for coaching and training
- learn more about the work habits of your people
- check the adequacy of existing job/task methods and procedures
- follow-up on the effectiveness of recent training
- give appropriate on-the-spot constructive correction
- spotlight specific behaviors for recognition and reinforcement

The purposes of this chapter are to differentiate between "seeing" and "observing," to discuss various types of job/task observation, to emphasize the five key steps of planned observation and to highlight the practical benefits of performance observation. By "job/task" we

> **Job/Task - a segment of work, a specific work assignment, a set of actions required to complete a specific work objective.**

mean a segment of work, a specific work assignment, a set of actions required to complete a specific work objective (called "job" by many people and "task" by many others). For the sake of simplicity and consistency, we will use *task* throughout the rest of this chapter.

"SEEING" VS. "OBSERVING"

The difference between seeing and observing is not only a key to effective performance observation, it is also an important difference between effective supervisors and not-so-effective ones. *Seeing* has to do with looking at, experiencing through the eyes, using the sense of sight. Essentially, it is a physiological process.

Observing is more of a psychological process. It means to consider carefully, to regard with attention so as to learn something. It means seeing with sufficient care to be able to give an account of conditions and behavior. Observing is not limited to the sense of sight. It means to perceive or identify through various senses (e.g., vision, hearing, taste, smell, touch). Observing includes noticing and noting and understanding the significance of what you observe.

Observation skills usually require development. Any supervisor who has conducted an accident investigation with several witnesses has dealt with the problem of reconciling several versions of the same event. This is because what we see is often determined by previous experiences and by present conditions. For instance, a herpetologist may see a snake as a thing of rare beauty; others may see it as a thing of repulsive horror. A starving person may see the same snake as a source of food. Our perceptions can also be distorted by our point of view, our surroundings or the surroundings of what we are looking at (see *Figure 8-1*).

The following guidelines can help you learn to be a better observer.

1. Force yourself to concentrate. Prepare yourself to observe.

2. Get rid of distractions - clear your mind.

3. Get the big picture - don't get lost in unimportant details.

4. Make a conscious effort to remember what you see.

5. Avoid interruptions.

6. Be sure you understand the intention of the actions you see - don't "jump the gun."

7. Don't let preconceived ideas about the person or the task distort what you see.

8. Don't fall victim to the "satisfaction of search" syndrome.

PERCEPTUAL FLUCTUATIONS AND ILLUSIONS

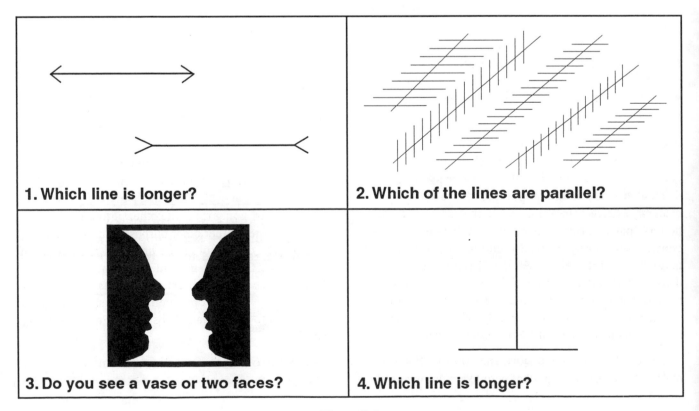

1. Which line is longer?

2. Which of the lines are parallel?

3. Do you see a vase or two faces?

4. Which line is longer?

Figure 8-1

The last guideline requires a bit of explanation. It comes from the field of medicine, particularly in reading X-rays and making diagnoses. "Satisfaction of search" refers to the tendency to find only what one is looking for and not look any further. As a result an equally or more serious condition may be overlooked. An unwary supervisor may see only what he or she expected to see, stop observing at that point and miss factors of equal or even greater significance.

Planned observation then, can be considered as a psychological process involving:

- *Intention* - observing on purpose, with specific goals in mind
- *Attention* - concentrating the powers of observation on the task at hand
- *Detection* - noticing and noting details; observing all important conditions and behavior
- *Comprehension* - mentally figuring out the significance of what is observed
- *Retention* - making mental notes and written notes; stamping observations into the mind long enough to put them to work for performance improvement.

Job observation can put real *vision* into supervision.

INFORMAL OBSERVATION

Casual

If you are like most supervisors, you are on the go, checking things out, contacting people, covering your area. This gives you thousands of chances to use your ears and eyes, to hear and see what's happening. Incidental to your main purpose of the moment, you probably notice things like what the new worker is doing, a piece of equipment that doesn't sound right, a worker not wearing protective equipment or a critical task being performed excellently. This incidental looking and listening provides an alert supervisor with valuable information and insight, either for immediate use in correcting and commending people or for storing in mental files for future use.

The key to incidental performance observation is to make a *habit* of noticing what people are doing as you go from place to place. Remind yourself to use that "travel time" productively. Build your reputation as a supervisor who is alert, who knows what's going on, who cares and coaches.

Intentional

This is still informal, but a step beyond the incidental. It's where something motivates you to pause and deliberately observe how a person handles part of a task. Perhaps your path crosses the work area of a person who is relatively new to the job. So you stop briefly and notice how he or she is doing. And you may take the time to give a training tip or to commend a good aspect of performance. Or you may notice a habitual risk-taker, and take time to let him or her see that you are interested in the way the job is being done. Or you may happen upon an especially hazardous job being done, so you take a few minutes to see how it goes. Thus you add valuable information to your mental reservoir... to use in contacting, communicating and coaching.

Do You See When You Look?

Read this sentence:

FINISHED FILES ARE THE RESULT OF YEARS OF SCIENTIFIC STUDY COMBINED WITH THE EXPERIENCE OF YEARS

Now count aloud the F's in the square above. Count them **only once**. Do not go back and count them again. See the next page for the actual number.

Limitations

While informal observations are necessary and helpful, they don't give you all of the observation data you need. Informal observations are somewhat haphazard and miss a great deal. They take place only where you happen to be going for some other purpose... and your mind is more on that other purpose than on the observation. They are likely to be brief and hurried. Being unplanned, they may not attend to the most critical tasks that should be observed. Informal observations may miss certain people, certain areas, certain work important to performance observation and review activities.

Informal observations are good, but they are not enough.

PLANNED OBSERVATION

Planned observations are not done as a sideline to some other activity. They require preparation, undivided concentration and adequate time to do a thorough job. A planned task observation is a systematic supervisory activity which justifies the time it takes by the benefits it brings... benefits such as improved quality and productivity, fewer injuries and damage, better morale and motivation, less scrap and waste, improved performance and profitability.

Planned observations are to human performance what planned inspections are to physical conditions. They are a basic and vital management activity for observing and evaluating the degree to which things are up to desired standards. They provide essential

---

COUNT THE F'S

There is really no "catch or trick" - the sentence actually contains six "F's." If you found six your power of observation ranks as "genius"; observing five shows you "on the ball"; finding four indicates "average alertness." If you observed and counted only three (or less) you're definitely not seeing when you look.

---

feedback information regarding job placement, orientation, training, on-the-job instruction and supervisory communication and contacts.

Planned observation is gaining worldwide attention as one of the most fundamental and valuable supervisory management tools available. As put by an experienced front-line supervisor, in an organization which has used planned task observations for over five years, "You haven't completed your job of teaching someone how to do a job until you *know* that person *knows* the proper way you *think* you taught him." Planned observation not only lets you know whether the employee knows, but also lets you know whether or not he or she can *do* it.

The steps of a planned observation are:

1. **Preparing**
2. **Observing**
3. **Discussing**
4. **Recording**
5. **Following-up**

PREPARING

As in every significant activity, appropriate planning means the difference between a hit-or-miss approach and a systematic method which assures that the full

benefits are obtained from an investment of time and energy. The many benefits from a job/task observation program fully justify taking the slight additional time to establish a means of systematic coverage. This involves establishing yearly and quarterly objectives for the number of observations to be made as well as determining which tasks and which people will be observed.

Deciding Which Tasks To Observe

A reminder of what we mean by "job" or "task" might be helpful...

> ... a segment of work, a specific work assignment, a set of actions required to complete a specific work objective (called "job" by some and "task" by others).

Examples are hooking up a crane lift, installing a switch, analyzing a sample in a laboratory, preparing a purchase order and changing a split-rim tire in a maintenance shop.

Since a complete planned observation does take time, it is usually not practical for every supervisor to do them for every worker on every task. Some tasks need more attention than others; have more potential for major loss if done improperly; are more critical to safety, quality and productivity. To make best use of the time you invest in your observation activities, concentrate on the critical tasks.

A "Critical Job/Task Inventory" (shown and described in Chapter 7, Job/Task Analysis and Procedures) is very valuable for this purpose. If you already have one, you can put it to good use here. If you don't have one, you should develop it. You should find such a list very helpful not only for planned observation, but also for task analysis and for employee training. In using the inventory, always consider a "new" job as "critical," until proven otherwise.

The focus of the observation program is on observing critical tasks, i.e., the work being done. However, at the same time we also want to consider the people doing the tasks we observe being done.

Deciding Who To Observe

In the long run, you should conduct planned observations for all your people. This does not mean the same number of observations and the same amount of time and attention to each person. But it does mean that everyone is included. Otherwise, some will feel picked on, some will feel left out, and you will not get the total performance picture you need for most effective leadership.

Keeping people well informed of the purpose of the program helps to prevent misunderstanding and related problems. Most of them will readily accept the fact that some people and some tasks deserve or require more observation and coaching than others. For example, it is fairly easy to see the need for priority in cases such as the following.

EMPLOYEES NEW TO THE WORK - New hires generally need more attention, training, observation and coaching than experienced employees do. Everything is new to them: their co-workers, the equipment and facilities, the procedures and practices, the rules and regulations, their whole environment. They are anxious to make a good impression. They are forming their early and lasting impressions of the work, the company and you the supervisor. Whether their performance is outstanding or poor, it is reinforced each time it is repeated. Planned observation of their performance on all critical tasks is your best insurance that their future performance will be on the positive side of the ledger.

Studies support common sense regarding how important it is to instruct, observe and coach new workers. For instance, Levitt and Parker reach seven major conclusions in their research study ("Reducing Construction Accidents — Top Management's Role," *Journal of the Construction Division*, ASCE, September, 1976). One of the seven conclusions is:

> Managers should provide for the training of newly-hired workers, stressing safe work-methods and job hazards. Statistics from the study indicate very strongly (99.9% certainty) that such training will significantly reduce accident costs.

The U.S. Bureau of Labor Statistics announced that, of all the injuries reported to them in a recent year, 48% were to workers who were in their first year on the job.

Remember, too, that *new to the work* means more than just new hires. Priority for observation should also be given to the person who is not new to the organization, but *is* new to this particular job or task. A task may also be relatively "new" to the person who does it very infrequently. Where work techniques change quite rapidly, it adds to the probability that someone should be considered a "new worker" when it comes to priority for observation. And don't overlook the person who has transferred from another area or department. Even though that person comes with a good reputation as a worker, don't be blinded to the need for performance observation. You need to know how well the person performs *this* work, in *this* department, with *this* equipment and with *these* standards.

POOR PERFORMERS - One of the greatest satisfactions for any supervisor is helping the worker with a reputation as a poor performer improve to a point where his or her work is making a positive, recognized contribution. Many of the reasons why people perform poorly become evident when time is taken to systematically analyze the problem. This is exactly what planned task observation can often do. The time required for observation is more than justified when you consider the time wasted due to the defects, delays, damage and rework caused by poor performance. When you have poor performers in your group, you need to find out *why* their work is not up to par. Planned observation is one of your best tools for analyzing their performance proficiencies and deficiencies. A complete turnabout often results from the instructing-observing-coaching process. Pride in job performance frequently accompanies observation feedback which has given the poor performer understandable reasons and realistic steps toward improvement.

It is easy to see that problems are amplified when critical work is in the hands of poor performers. There is no question that this situation requires priority attention for planned observation.

RISK-TAKERS - Some people seem always ready to take a chance, to violate safety rules and practices in hope of saving a little time or effort, and to do things "their own way" even though it's not the best and safest way. They may get away with such behavior so long that it becomes habitual. People around them shake their heads in wonder that something drastic hasn't happened, and say that the person sure has been "lucky" so far!

There should be little doubt that risk-takers deserve planned observation priority, *before* accidents and related losses occur. Risk-takers often have incomplete knowledge or awareness of what they are doing. Task observation will often reveal to the worker a dimension or value that changes the whole perspective. The fact that substandard practices also influence others should increase your motivation to do something about the problem. Planned observation will give you knowledge and perspective to make proper decisions regarding training needs, as well as insight that could help improve your overall relationships with these workers.

WORKERS WITH ABILITY PROBLEMS - There are many physical, mental, or emotional problems, known or suspected, that cause questions about a worker's ability to do a job. These problems could range from drug abuse or alcoholism to areas involving visual acuity or muscular coordination. Planned observation is one of the few tools that can give you some direction in such difficult situations.

In some cases, your observations and follow-up may show that the person simply cannot be trained to do that job properly. The solution may be *redesign* or *reassign*: either redesign the work to fit the worker's abilities, or reassign the person to work which is better suited to his or her abilities. In other cases, your observations may show that, with proper guidance, the person *can* learn to do the job correctly and safely. Regardless of the findings, planned observations serve as a good basis for decision-making that could otherwise be based on something less than the best available information.

OUTSTANDING PERFORMERS - If asked, "Who needs planned task observation the least?" you might be tempted to answer, "Those who are doing the best job." Fully experienced, capable, and dependable employees are left on their own much too often, because we take their past performance for granted. However, there are at least three good reasons to observe good performers.

First, and most important, the best workers may be using techniques and methods that could help others do their work more efficiently. Thorough observation and evaluation may show them to be of significant value, worth communicating to other workers. Wise supervisors do not ignore the resources that can help them most — the people whose expertise can help solve many problems and bring better quality, productivity and safety.

The second important reason for giving observation priority to outstanding performers is that, too long ignored, they may drift into substandard practices and habits. To avoid this, even highly skilled and experienced airline pilots receive occasional check rides, which are one form of task observation.

A third reason to include good performers in your observation program is because it offers an excellent opportunity for commendation. There is always the danger that the best workers will become "invisible people" in an organization, in comparison with the time and attention given to those whose performance creates problems. A planned task observation program contains built-in opportunities to reinforce the better performers.

People are not equal in their needs for task observation. Priority considerations should be given to (1) employees new to the work, (2) poor performers, (3) risk-takers, (4) workers with ability problems and (5) outstanding performers. Though you should conduct planned observations for all of your people, you should gear the number and spacing of your observations to specific situations and individual needs.

Scheduling Planned Observations

Scheduling is another vital part of preparing for observations. Properly done, observations require a significant time commitment. They are too important to be put off until "one of these days." Planned observations should be part of your planned, scheduled activities.

In this scheduling, keep in mind that you want to observe certain people doing certain (critical) tasks and to include every employee in the observation program. A guide such as shown in *Figure 8-2* not only can serve as a useful record of your planned observation activity, but also can help you make the best choices regarding who to observe, doing what and when.

To use the form shown in *Figure 8-2*, begin by listing the critical jobs/tasks done in your area across the top, under the A, B, C, etc. The form may be made as wide as necessary to accommodate the number of critical tasks. Using the guidelines given above, think of the tasks that have been the source of major loss (safety, quality, productivity) in the past. Add those that have the potential for major loss even though they have not caused one yet. Continue the list by including those which have a series of smaller problems frequently associated with them. Add those tasks that are fairly new or which involve a new process, equipment, machinery, raw material, specifications, etc. You are now well on your way to a good list.

Under the heading, "Individuals," list all of the people in your area of responsibility. Then go across the page one name at a time and place an "X" above the dotted line at each task that person might do. When an observation is made of a certain person performing a particular task, place the date of the observation under the dotted line.

Suppose, for example, that you are thinking about observing employee #6 performing task "D." A quick

COMPLETE OBSERVATION SCHEDULE GUIDE

DEPARTMENT

SUPERVISOR

INDIVIDUALS	CRITICAL JOB/TASKS										
	A	B	C	D	E	F	G	H	I	J	ADD ADDITIONAL COLUMNS AS NEEDED
1											
2											
3											
4											
5											
6											
7											
8											
9											
10											
11											
12											
13											
14											
15											
16											
17											
18											
19											
20											

For each person listed in the numbered rows, put an "X" above the dotted line to show which critical job/tasks that person performs. Below the dotted lines, enter the date of the last complete observation conducted for that person and that job/task.

Figure 8-2

glance at your record shows that you did this observation about eleven weeks ago. Then you see that you have never observed employee #17 doing critical task "J" and may decide on that for your next observation.

Reviewing Key Facts

Check your records and notes to refresh your mind about both the person and the task to be observed. Review the results of past observations for this person to determine if there are items to be followed up. If there is a written task procedure or work practice review that to refresh your awareness of the key points of the task. You might want to take the task procedure or practice with you. Some supervisors attach a page to the procedure for notes about the performance of each significant step or critical activity. Others take with them an abbreviated version of the procedure. However you do it, have something on which to record detailed notes about the observation. These will be most useful in preparing for your discussion with the person observed.

Can you do a planned observation if no written procedure or practice exists? Sure. Although it's better to have one, you can get along without one. Even in the absence of written procedures, there are commonly accepted standards for performing most work. Without the written procedure or practice you may have more disagreement about "the best way" to do it. However, you can use the areas of disagreement as a basis for clarifying the performance standards and eventually, getting them put into written form.

In summary, preparing for planned observations involves these four activities: 1) deciding who to observe, 2) deciding which tasks to observe, 3) scheduling the observations and 4) reviewing key facts.

To Tell Or Not To Tell?

The question often arises, "Should I or should I not tell the person that I am doing the planned observation?" As with so many other questions, the answer is, "It depends..." In this case it depends on whether you want to know how well the person *can do* the job, or how the person *does* the job.

If you want to know how well the person can do the job, tell him or her that you are going to do the observation. Also tell why. With this awareness, most employees will try to do their best. Under these circumstances, you can be quite certain that mistakes or substandard practices mean lack of knowledge or skill... and that the solutions require communication, coaching, training and/or guided practice.

If you have a good reason for wanting to know how the person normally does the job, you do *not* tell him or her that you are going to do the observation. But be careful how you go about doing it. Don't sneak around or hide. That would be a sure way to be branded as a "snoopervisor" or "spy," thereby losing the respect of your workers and associates. Instead, try to do the observation indirectly — incidental to some other supervisory activity in the area such as checking records or controls, etc. Whenever possible, it is desirable to have other people about, in order to have one's presence blend into the group.

When you find that a person does not do the job properly, but you know from other observations that he or she *can*, then you know that training is not the solution. The problem most likely is one of feelings - attitudes - motivation. If so, the solution requires performance management techniques such as constructive discipline and positive behavior reinforcement.

Typically, you tell the worker that you are going to conduct a planned observation, especially if it's a "complete" one. In fact, in keeping with the motivational power of participative management, you might want to tell the person well in advance of the scheduled observation... and have a pre-observation discussion. Such a discussion could improve understanding of the program's purpose, strengthen relationships with the worker, highlight key factors for observation and replace fear or suspicion of observation with pride of participation.

OBSERVING

Practical Guideposts

Stay Out Of The Way - It's important to stay far enough from the worker that you do not interfere with job activities nor with equipment actions or material flow. But it's also important to be in a spot from which you can clearly see all important details of the work. Frequently there are little things that people do (or fail to do) that can make the difference between top quality and defects or between safety and a serious accident. Do your best to strike a balance between the worker's need for plenty of room to do the job properly and your need to see everything the job involves.

Minimize Distractions - If at all possible, stay outside the worker's direct line of vision. Otherwise you may distract his or her attention from the task at hand. Don't interrupt with questions, suggestions or admonitions... unless you see a serious accident or loss in the making. Try to let the person perform the whole operation without interruption. Hold the questions, the discussion, the coaching for later.

Focus Your Attention - Since you have done all the preparation and have scheduled your time for the observation, it makes sense to get the most out of it that you can. Give it your undivided attention. Keep your eyes and ears open. Be alert to "the little things" that might make a big difference.

Relate what the person does to the proper task procedure. Whenever some aspect of performance does not fit what the procedure calls for, note it for follow-up. Ask yourself whether it is as good as, poorer than or better than the generally accepted standard. Don't let your note-taking distract your observation. Use key words rather than details, and stop taking notes if it can't be done without disturbing your focus of attention. Write things out as soon as possible after the direct observation.

DISCUSSING

Immediate Feedback

Whenever possible, talk with the worker immediately following the observation. If there is no natural break immediately, find out when there will be so you can come back then. In this feedback contact, do at least these four things:

1. Thank the person for helping with the planned observation program for better efficiency, productivity and safety.

2. Ask questions and review any points necessary to make sure you understand all vital aspects of what you observed.

3. For any worker behavior requiring immediate correction, give on-the-spot feedback and instruction.

4. For exemplary behavior, give on-the-spot recognition and reinforcement.

If it was a complete observation, also let the person know that you will have a more complete discussion after you review and analyze your notes, your observations and related data.

Preparing For The Performance Discussion

Good preparation involves completing your notes, evaluating what you observed, and reviewing related performance information. As you organize your thoughts and notes, remember that procedures are not always updated each time an operational change takes place. You may not have seen what you thought you would see, according to the written procedure or practice, because changes in the task have been made but not yet show in the written procedures or practices. The employee may be doing the work properly, in accordance with verbal instructions which have not yet been recorded.

> "He hath strange places cramm'd with observation, the which he vents in mangled forms."
> Shakespeare, "As You Like It."

Another important possibility to keep in mind when you have observed the job being done differently from what's in writing is that the worker has developed a better way to do it. In such cases, you may want to discuss it with your supervisor, your colleagues and other key people, to see if it should be incorporated into the written procedures and practices. Naturally, this would then be a significant item of commendation during the performance discussion.

Adequate preparation for the performance discussion also involves reviewing previous observations, follow-ups and related performance information.

RECORDING

To enable thorough observations, good performance discussions and desired documentation, you need some basic written information. A form along the lines of *Figure 8-3* can be very helpful. It can help in preparing for a good performance discussion; in conducting systematic follow-up; and in keeping good records of who was observed, doing which tasks, when. These records may also be measured and evaluated as evidence of your level of performance in this critical area of supervisory management.

Looking at *Figure 8-3*, items 1 through 11 provide essential information for record and reference purposes. Items 4 and 5 may also give a clue to why certain actions were observed.

Items 12 through 15 reflect the basic purposes of the planned observation. They lie at the heart of the observation, the analysis, the performance discussion and the follow-up.

Items 16 through 18 have special significance and tie-in with the powerful concepts of job pride development. It is important to remember that the planned observation, like the incident investigation, is not a blame-fixing, fault-finding expedition. Its purpose is to find out how well the worker performs the job. When observation and evaluation show a high level of performance, it's only logical that the person should be recognized for that performance. There may be nothing you can do to more emphatically encourage continued proper performance than to reinforce desired behavior.

Item 19 can be of great importance. It provides the basis for discussion, not only with the worker but also with colleagues, higher managers and other key personnel, regarding potential changes of methods, equipment, materials, environmental factors and/or written standards, procedures and practices.

Items 20 and 21 provide additional necessary data for effective documentation and follow-up purposes.

While hardly anyone likes "paperwork," documentation is becoming increasingly important in today's world. Doing a good job with required paperwork is one of the marks of the truly professional supervisory manager. And that paperwork serves as a permanent record of the professional's leadership accomplishments.

FOLLOWING-UP

Follow-up is a critical factor in whether the time you invest in planned observation is wasted or well-used. Your preparing, observing, discussing and recording can all go down the drain if you do not follow-up fully. Suppose, for instance, that the observation highlighted a need to change an existing procedure or to provide certain retraining or education for the worker. Your follow-up activity not only should ensure that this gets done in a timely manner, but also should include scheduling and doing a follow-up observation to verify the effectiveness of the change.

For best results, keep your corrective coaching and re-instruction as positive as possible. For example, rather than saying, "You did that tape measurement wrong, here's the right way to do it!" a more positive approach would be, "I noticed how you did that measurement with your tape; let me show you how to do it more easily and avoid the likelihood of misreading." And always try to tell the "why" of a suggestion or procedure... why it's important, what it does, its benefits.

One of the fastest, surest ways to lose the respect of your people is to fail to do what you said you would do. Likewise, one of the best ways to earn and keep the respect of your people is to always keep your word — do what you said you would.

Another important part of follow-up is making sure the employee lives up to his or her end of the "contract." A *promise* is not *performance*. Follow-up includes seeing whether or not the person has done what he or she agreed to do — whether performance is up to par. If the person has *not* done what he or she agreed to do, by the time it was supposed to be done, take the action you said you would take. If appropriate, discuss the lack of improvement, the reasons for it and the specifics of a new "contract." If the person *has* fulfilled the "contract," give full credit for it. In fact, whenever the person's performance improves, even part way toward the goal, recognize the achievement and encourage continued improvement.

Establish planned objectives for regular follow-up on all critical tasks, and all employees on the "high priority" list for planned observations. Without effective follow-up, you will be working in the dark, never knowing whether your efforts are paying off or how well. Proper follow-up gives you the confidence that only comes when you really know what's going on in your area of responsibility. It also enables you to provide upper management with tangible proof of the benefits from this time investment.

> **Complete Task Observation is a systematic process built around these five activities: 1) preparing, 2) observing, 3) discussing, 4) recording and 5) following-up. It is a proven technique which enables a supervisor to know whether or not a worker is performing all aspects of a specific task with maximum efficiency. Maximum efficiency means greater and safer production at lower costs. This can only mean increased prosperity for any organization using this tool.**

PLANNED TASK OBSERVATION REPORT

1. NAME Edward Riley		2. CHECK NO. 369	3. DEPARTMENT Labor dept.
4. OCCUPATION laborer	5. JOB OBSERVED waxing floor	6. DATE 3/15/19—	7. TYPE OF OBSERVATION ☐ INITIAL ☐ FOLLOW-UP
8. TIME WITH COMPANY 3 years	9. TIME ON PRESENT JOB 3 mos.	10. NOTIFICATION ☒ TOLD IN ADVANCE	☐ NOT TOLD IN ADVANCE

11. REASON FOR OBSERVATION

☐ JOB PROCEDURE/ PRACTICE UPDATE   ☐ ACCIDENT REPEATER   ☐ INCAPACITATED WORKER ☐ TRAINING FOLLOW-UP   ☐ EXPERIENCED WORKER CHECK

JOB OBSERVATION

12. Could any of the practices or conditions observed result in property damage or personal injury? ☒ Yes ☐ No	13. Were the methods and practices observed the most efficient and productive? ☐ Yes ☒ No
14. Did the practices you observed comply with all of the applicable standards that exist for this task or job? ☐ Yes ☒ No	15. Could any of the practices you observed have a detrimental effect upon the quality of the product? ☐ Yes ☒ No

16. Describe clearly below any practices or conditions related to items above that deserve compliment or correction.

1. Worker had equipment and supplies well organized, especially in their positioning at the work area. He was very systematic in clearing furniture and used prescribed dollies. 2. He did not use color coded stickers required. I interrupted the worker since wax has an organic base and he did not ask me to check the ventilation as required on checklist. 3. All other steps were according to the checklist; except for failure to use the non-slip pullovers on his shoes and the color code marking for furniture. 4. Since he was aware of being observed, his conscientious manner of work during the observation appeared to be his natural way of doing that job. 5. He did an excellent job of roping off area and placing caution and no smoking signs. 6. The major need for correction was obviously the worker's failure to use the required checklist.

17. Have you properly complimented and/or reinstructed the worker on these observations? ☒ Yes ☐ No	18. Should a follow-up observation of this worker or task be made in the near future? ☒ Yes ☐ No

19. Describe any standard procedure, method or equipment you observed.

20. Supervisor/Observer	21. Check No. 41686	22. Department Labor

Follow-Up Action

A follow-up observation was made on 3/22. Worker used the required checklist and followed all items on it. I thanked him for his good work and encouraged him to continue it.

Figure 8-3

PARTIAL OR SPOT OBSERVATION

The partial or spot observation is a planned observation of a portion of the task, e.g., a significant step, a critical activity or a portion of the work that is convenient to observe at the time. Here are some of the benefits of partial or spot observations:

- They enable observation coverage of more tasks and more employees in a given amount of time.

- They provide a broader base of performance appraisal and discussion information.

- They enable planned observations that would not otherwise be done, because of the time factor.

- They provide a greater number of opportunities for meaningful coaching, based on specific, observable job performance.

- They furnish additional checks on the adequacy of procedures, practices, training and on-the-job instruction.

The steps for doing spot observations are similar to those for complete observations: preparing - observing - discussing - recording - following-up. However, they may be somewhat simplified and shortened.

In *preparing*, you still decide who to observe, decide which work activities to observe, schedule your observations and review key facts to help you do effective observations. However, for spot observations, you can make a more intensive effort to ensure that all employees receive a certain number of observations within a given time frame; and that a greater variety of work activities are covered.

For *observing*, there may not be as great a need to tell the worker about the pending observation or to discuss it beforehand. In fact, from the worker's viewpoint, these may appear to be no different than the informal observations that occur so frequently.

The main difference is that a spot observation is planned so that it focuses on critical steps of doing the task. The practical guidelines for observing still apply: stay out of the way - minimize distractions - focus your attention.

Regarding *discussing*, you should give immediate feedback when performance is poor enough to justify on-the-spot coaching or good enough to justify on-the-spot commendation. You should also incorporate the results of spot observations into your periodic performance discussions.

The *recording* can be quite simple. *Figure 8-4* shows both sides of a pocket card that can be used to record a number of observations as well as personal contacts.

Following-up is always important. For instance, make sure that your performance discussions with the individual include reference to specific performance factors noted during spot observations. Also, whenever observations suggest a need for coaching, training, counselling, changing procedures, etc., note it in your records and take action as soon as possible.

PLANNED OBSERVATION BENEFITS

When planned job/task observations are properly conducted, they provide major benefits to you and your organization. Perhaps the most direct and obvious benefit is knowing what your people know about the proper way to do their jobs. This feedback gives you excellent information on the effectiveness of training programs and job instruction, and the adequacy of existing job/task procedures. It provides a solid base of information for effective performance discussions. You and your workers may learn a lot about critical jobs in the cooperative observation relationship. You are likely to identify and correct substandard practices before potential losses become actual losses. You also identify good work habits and related worker contributions to efficiency, safety and productivity — thus gaining valuable opportunities for positive reinforcement of desired behavior. A continuous planned observation program promotes a continuous awareness of the importance of each worker in reaching the goals of your department, and the organization as a whole. The overall result is better performance due to pride of performance... and effective leadership.

PERSONAL CONTACT RECORD

DATE	EMPLOYEE	SUBJECT DISCUSSED

Outside

SPOT OBSERVATION PROMOTER

1 PREPARE 2 OBSERVE 3 DISCUSS 4 RECORD 5 FOLLOW-UP

SPOT

PERSONAL COPY FOR
_____

FOR THE PERIOD OF

PLANNED OBSERVATION HELPS YOU TO ....

...pinpoint practices that could cause accidents, injuries, damage, inefficiency and waste.

...determine specific needs for coaching and training.

...learn more about the work habits of your people.

...check the adequacy of existing job/task methods and procedures.

...follow-up on the effectiveness of recent training.

...give appropriate on-the-spot constructive correction.

...spotlight specific behaviors for recognition and reinforcement.

...establish a solid base for performance appraisal and discussion.

Supervisor's Performance Observation Technique

SPOT OBSERVATIONS

DATE	EMPLOYEE	CR	NC	ACTIVITY OBSERVED AND COMMENTS	CM	CC
TOTALS						

Inside

LEGEND: CR = Critical Activity   NC = Non-Critical Activity   CM = Commendation Given   CC = Constructive Correction

Figure 8-4

CORE CONCEPTS IN REVIEW

Job/task observation is a valuable tool to help you, as a supervisor, meet your greatest responsibility — getting optimum performance from every person in your work group. Types of observation that you can use to good advantage are **informal** and **planned**.

Key activities in **planned observations** are preparing, observing, discussing, recording and following-up.

1. **Preparing** includes deciding who to observe, deciding which tasks to observe, scheduling the observations and reviewing key facts before making each observation.

2. For the **observing** phase, some practical guideposts are to stay out of the worker's way, minimize distraction and focus your attention solely on the observation.

3. **Discussing** includes two main parts:

   a. **Immediate feedback,** in which you thank the person for his or her help, clarify unclear parts of what you observed, give appropriate on-the-spot correction and commendation and let the person know when you will have a more complete discussion.

   b. A more complete **performance discussion,** using a planned approach.

4. **Recording** your observations gives you better observations, better performance discussions and better documentation.

5. Optimum results also require **follow-up,** both of what you agreed to do and what the employee agreed to do.

Properly done, an ongoing program of planned observation helps you to...

1. **Pinpoint** practices that could cause accidents, injuries, damage, inefficiency and waste

2. **Determine** specific needs for coaching and training

3. **Learn** more about the work habits of your people

4. **Check** the adequacy of existing job/task procedures and methods

5. **Follow-up** on the effectiveness of recent training

6. **Give** appropriate on-the-spot correction

7. **Spotlight** specific behaviors for recognition and reinforcement

KEY QUESTIONS

1. True or False? Job/Task Observation can properly be thought of as "performance observation."

2. List at least five specific goals of the observation process.

3. How can you distinguish "observing" from "seeing"?

4. Name two types of informal observation.

5. List at least three limitations of informal observation.

6. Name two types of planned observation.

7. List the five major activities in planned observations.

8. Name several categories of workers who deserve priority consideration for planned observation.

9. Why should outstanding performers be included in the planned observation program?

10. True or False? To make best use of the time you invest in task observation activities, you should emphasize critical tasks.

11. True or False? Typically, you should conduct task observations without telling the worker in advance.

12. List three practical guideposts to guide the observer during the observation.

13. Name several things that should be done in the immediate feedback contact.

14. In evaluating and discussing an employee's work, focus on p_____, not p _____.

15. How can you end a performance discussion on a positive note?

16. Why should you keep records of planned observations and performance discussions?

17. Whose activities should be included in the follow-up?

18. In comparison with complete observations, list at least three benefits of partial or spot observations.

19. List the five major steps to partial or spot observations.

20. List at least three major benefits of a planned observation program.

PRACTICAL APPLICATIONS SUMMARY

S - For Supervisors
E - For Executives
C - For Safety/Loss Control Coordinators

	S	E	C
1. Issue a policy statement regarding the task observation program and stressing its importance for accident control		x	
2. Ensure that supervisors are trained in performance observation techniques.		x	
3. Establish objectives for the annual number of complete task observations to be made on critical tasks for which there are set procedures and/or practices.		x	
4. Establish annual objectives for the number of partial or spot observations to be made.		x	
5. Prepare and/or use a Critical Task Inventory in preparing for planned observations.	x		
6. Meet or beat the objectives for planned complete task observations.	x		
7. Meet or beat the objectives for partial or spot task observations.	x		
8. Conduct frequent informal task observations.	x		
9. Prepare task observation reports.	x		
10. Review task observation reports.		x	x
11. Emphasize the results of task observations in performance discussions with the people observed.	x		
12. Follow-up the observations and discussions to ensure that both the employee and the organization carry out the actions agreed to.	x	x	
13. Respond promptly to supervisors' inquiries regarding questionable areas involved with established procedures.		x	
14. Measure and evaluate the degree of compliance to complete task observation objectives.		x	x
15. Measure and evaluate the degree of compliance to partial or spot observation objectives.		x	x
16. Evaluate the quality of complete task observations for major units within the organization.		x	x
17. Communicate findings of program effectiveness, in writing, to all pertinent levels of management.		x	x
18. Recognize and reinforce good planned observation performance by organizational units and individual supervisors.		x	

CHAPTER 9

GROUP MEETINGS

You may know your subject, but you have to keep in mind that your audience is coming in cold. So start by telling them what you're going to tell them. Then tell them. Finally, tell them what you've already told them. I've never deviated from that axiom.
— Lee Iacocca

INTRODUCTION

This chapter focuses on selected aspects of a fascinating, but sometimes frustrating, process related to most of our problems and our progress... the vital process of communication. Specifically, the chapter includes highlights of...

- the basic psychology of communication

- guiding principles for communicating

- the importance of group communications

- a training program known for improving the talks given by supervisors to their work groups

- practical tips about presentation aids

- upper management's role in group communication.

No attempt is made to cover all (or even most) aspects of the group communication process. The aim is simply to present enough information to help supervisors understand the basics and to improve their skill in communicating with groups.

BASIC PSYCHOLOGY OF COMMUNICATION

Feelings, emotions and attitudes tend to make clear communication a considerable challenge. We communicate with our "hearts" as much as we do with our "heads." Communication is not simply logical; it is psychological.

It involves not only logic, facts, figures, the brain, the mind but also feelings, attitudes, emotions... the whole person. For instance, if you like the person who is speaking, you will tend to accept what that person says more readily and more positively than you would accept a similar message from someone you detest. You tend to give different meaning to a comment from "the boss" than you would give to a similar comment coming from a co-worker. You are very likely to interpret things said by a beautiful woman differently than you would interpret the same thoughts coming from a bum. The very same words (such as, "Go jump in the lake") can have different meanings, depending on whether they are said jokingly, matter-of-factly or angrily.

Communication is a two-way process that involves the sending and receiving of symbols, signs or signals (words, pictures, things, actions). It is speaking and listening, writing and reading, behaving and observing behavior. Its goal is to achieve understanding. Perhaps this is the simplest, most practical, easiest-to-remember definition:

COMMUNICATION is what we do to GIVE and GET UNDERSTANDING

Figure 9-1: Communication Defined

Clear communication (giving and getting understanding) is not necessarily "doin' what comes naturally." It must be worked at. It involves give-and-take. It requires concentration. It depends as much (maybe more) on feelings as it does on facts. But it can be learned. There are known principles of clear communication and there are some down-to-earth, practical techniques that have proven themselves. They will work. Let's explore some of them.

GUIDING PRINCIPLES

Management principles which have stood the test of time emphasize the importance of good communication. Let's explore some of them.

- **The Information Principle: Effective communication increases motivation.**

When people understand clearly the results they are trying to accomplish and how they contribute to those results, motivation increases. In addition, a supervisor who makes a sincere effort to keep people informed is telling them, "I think you are important... I want to be sure you know what's going on."

Alexander Cohen's review of research on successful safety programs identified seven significant factors. One of them is "Close contact and interaction between workers, supervisors and management, enabling open communications on safety as well as other job-related matters." A significant part of this communication can occur in well-managed group meetings.

To be most efficient and effective, these meetings must be conducted well. Supervisors must know how to talk to groups; how to make group presentations; how to communicate (give and get understanding) with the whole team.

Three more of the proven principles of professional management relate directly to communication:

- **The Distortion Principle: The more levels a communication goes through, the more distorted it becomes.**

The more people involved in the line of communication, the greater the probability of distortion, delay and loss of meaning. When a message is communicated from one person to another, each human brain and tongue that relays the message tends to change it. Unintended meaning may be added, or the original sense may be changed. As communications are transmitted through several levels of an organization, each person tends to "hedge" the message with safeguards as he passes it on, and to add "CYA" (Cover Your Anatomy) thoughts. The direct, face-to-face communication of group meetings can help overcome line loss.

- **The Psychological Appeal Principle: Communication that appeals to feelings and attitudes tends to be more motivational than that which appeals only to reason.**

We tend to think with our emotions. If you want a person to grasp your meaning, find an emotional peg upon which to hang that understanding. Even if your message is factual and impersonal, people will listen and understand better if you introduce the idea by relating it to their personal interests, their desires, their families, their jobs. The way we feel about things strongly affects the way we think about them. A sincere emotional appeal can produce understanding and action most quickly and effectively.

- **The Utilization Principle: The sooner and more often an idea or skill is put to work, the better it is learned and remembered.**

If we hear something and understand it, our possession of the information tends to be temporary - unless we do something to use it. Once the new thought is applied, it starts to become "our own," to become a permanent part of us. To make a communication your own, use it. To help other people understand and remember your communicated ideas, help them put those ideas to work. Application converts ideas into action, and gets results. Meetings held early in the day and early in the week not only get the day and week started off right, they also allow time for application of the important message conveyed in the meeting.

THE IMPORTANCE OF GROUP COMMUNICATIONS

Today's supervisor is a key member of management, and should use a "professional management" approach. Reduced to basics...

PROFESSIONAL
MANAGEMENT

is
Getting Results
Through
Other People
by

• COMMUNICATING

• MODELING

• EMPOWERING

• REINFORCING

• COACHING

which are
THE BEDROCKS
Of Supervisory Management

Figure 9-2: Bedrocks of Supervisory Management

In this management work, nothing is more important than communication. The planning, the organizing, the leading, the controlling that supervisors must do... all demand "giving and getting understanding" (communication). It takes only a moment's reflection to see that a supervisor's effectiveness rests largely on communication skills. Plans can be acted upon, organizations can be made effective, leadership can be exercised, controls can be maintained, only if supervisors can convey their understanding of these things to others — and can understand what others are trying to convey to them.

Effective group meetings serve a number of basic management purposes:

• They are often the only way that management can be sure that everyone has received a critical message in the most timely way.

• They create a cooperative climate through participation and group interaction.

• They help give everyone the same attention and exposure to information.

• They give the person conducting the meeting practice in improving communications and human relations skills.

• They help build that person's image as a leader in the minds of the team members.

DISCUSSION LEADING PROCEDURES AND METHODS

The following four-step discussion leading procedure is an effective one:

1. Introduce the subject, topic, question or concept for discussion

2. State the subject, topic, question or concept

3. Establish key points of explanation or answer

4. Summarize or conclude the discussion.

This procedure is described in *Figure 9-3*, which also summarizes how it can be used for each of the following four discussion leading methods.

• Lecture and discussion method

• Question and answer discussion method

• Pro and con discussion method

• Small group discussion method

Lecture and Discussion Method

The leader describes, explains, demonstrates and so on; while the conferees listen, take notes and ask questions. The leader is the key figure and does most of the talking. This method is most applicable when the topic to be covered involves matters that are new and unfamiliar to the conferees, and when the key points of the topic might not be readily developed through free discussion. It is an efficient way to reveal factual information unknown to the group, such as accident statistics, details of new procedures, or definitions of terms.

In addition to its suitability to certain kinds of topics (those that call for giving information), this method gives the leader the advantage of having more control over the meeting. You can pace the presentation to fit a time schedule. You can direct the group's thinking. You can present ideas in the order you have planned. You can use predetermined examples and aids. You can defer questions until you are ready for them. This kind of control usually means that the session is more likely to be carried off as planned.

But the lecture and discussion method has at least one serious weakness - it tends to be mostly "lecture" and little "discussion." And most people are not good listeners. They tend to become restless, bored, sleepy and inattentive when expected to listen for too long a period. How soon this occurs depends somewhat on the nature of the topic and the skill of the leader.

METHODS

PROCEDURE	LECTURE & DISCUSSION	QUESTION & ANSWER	PRO & CON	SMALL GROUP
Introduce the subject, topic question or concept for discussion.	Stimulate the group's interest and create a desire or need to know. The instructor gives a brief introduction describing generally what the instruction will cover. Ties the new topic in with previous training topics, when there is such a relationship. Prepare the group for the method you will use.			
State the subject, topic question or concept.	Example: "Let's see, then, what are the six most common conflicts between the desire for safety and other desires?"	Example: "What do you see as some of the relationships between effective job instruction and safety performance?"	Example: "Should we or should we not give a safety tip with every task assignment? Why?"	Example: "OK, now each sub-group has 15 minutes to come up with suggested weekly safety talk titles and visual aids for the next 2 months."
Establish key points of explanation or answer.	You, the leader, do most of the answering of the question or explanation of the concept. You may use outlines, audiovisual aids and handouts.	You draw the key answer points out of the group. Call on both volunteers and others. Rephrase their responses if necessary. Jot key words and phrases on board or pad.	You remain impartial and stimulate people to voice their opinions for or against the issue and to support their opinions with reasoning. Record two lists — one "pro" and one "con."	You turn the assigned sub-groups loose to develop and record their answer key points. Then get them to reassemble and report... and you record the total results.
Summarize or conclude the discussion.	Present a summary (a brief review of the main points in the explanation or answer) or a conclusion (a generalization based on the facts or opinions brought out during discussion). When it's practical, get the group to formulate the conclusion, using leading questions if necessary. Tie in with the recorded key point words and phrases. Pull it all together.			

Figure 9-3: DISCUSSION LEADING PROCEDURE AND METHODS

Nevertheless, this method normally should be supplemented by others of more active discussion and participation.

Question and Answer Discussion Method

With some topics there may be good reason to believe that the key points are known to the group as a whole, although no one person may know all of the separate points of the answer. In other words, the answers are there, waiting to be brought out. As the discussion leader, you are merely the catalyst or facilitator who brings the answers out of the group. You use skillful questioning and guidance to promote active participation and, in effect, help the group members tell each other the answers.

Pro and Con Discussion Method

Some topics invite arguments for or against a certain proposition. For example, the topic question may be, "Should operators be permitted to adjust machine guards?" Such topics are well suited to getting the group involved in an active discussion of the pro's and con's. The method is very simple. As leader, your role is to stimulate people to voice their opinions for or against the issue posed by the topic question... and to support their opinions with reasoning. You assume an impartial role during the discussion to avoid discouraging participants from expressing their opinions. Through the skillful use of questions, you try to get all the arguments for and against out in the open so that the group can evaluate them and draw a conclusion.

Small Group Discussion Method

The discussion methods described above focus on the leader. He or she is always part of the discussion serving an active role in guiding or controlling it.

The small group method permits you, the leader, to remove yourself from the discussion. You divide the large group into several smaller groups, perhaps 4-7 people each. You give the discussion question to the groups and turn them loose to develop the key points or answers on their own. Have each small group pick someone to jot down ideas developed through the discussion, and serve as group reporter. After a given period of time (perhaps five, ten or twenty minutes), get the people to reassemble. Then call on each reporter in turn to give one point in answer to the topic question... continuing from group to group until all points have been picked up and recorded on the pad or chalkboard.

This method can be applied as an alternative for the Pro and Con Method and the Question and Answer Method. Instead of leading a large group discussion as described in those methods, you divide them into small groups and proceed with the Small Group Method.

For variety and effectiveness, you normally should use two or more of these discussion leading methods in each meeting or training session. That is, you may get certain points across by Lecture and Discussion, and get more active group involvement on other points by using the Question and Answer, Pro and Con and/or Small Group Methods.

MEETING LEADERSHIP SKILLS

Nothing is more vital to effective meetings than what the leader does to plan to communicate, to prepare — before the meeting occurs.

PLANNING includes pinpointing the objectives of the meeting, developing the agenda and deciding what's necessary for fulfilling the agenda and objectives. You may find it helpful to draw a few lines on a piece of paper and use headings like the following to organize your thoughts:

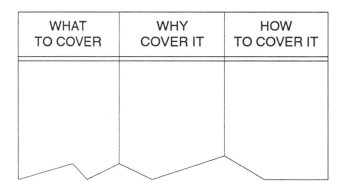

WHAT TO COVER	WHY COVER IT	HOW TO COVER IT

In some cases, it will be helpful to use a more complete meeting planning worksheet, along the lines shown in *Figure 9-4*.

Good advance COMMUNICATION helps to ensure a good meeting. Whenever practical, the leader should send an agenda to all who are expected to attend. This should show the meeting's purpose, time, place and subjects. Often it will be helpful to state briefly what is expected of those who attend. Also, distribute the agenda ahead of time, giving them time to arrange their schedules and to prepare for the meeting.

MAINTAINING MOMENTUM. Unless it is strictly a "telling" type of meeting, you can keep it

Meeting Planning Worksheet

Meeting Subject: _____

_____

Scheduled For: _____

(Time)   (Date)

To Be Attended By: _____ _____

_____ _____ _____

_____ _____ _____

General Purpose of Meeting:

_____

_____

Desired End Result(s) To Be Achieved At The Meeting (The Meeting Objectives. What the meeting is to accomplish.)
(The situation desired to be in place when the meeting is over.)

_____

_____

_____

_____

_____

Planning Detail: (Messages to be passed on. Information desired. Decisions to be made. Activity to be assigned. What is to be avoided.)

_____

_____

_____

_____

_____

_____

_____

_____

Meeting Area Arranged? ☐ **Checked?** ☐   **Agenda Prepared?** ☐ **Distributed?** ☐

Do all participants know the answers to these questions?

☐ What are the objectives of the meeting?

☐ What contributions do you expect me to make?

☐ How do you suggest I prepare for the meeting?

Figure 9-4

going by putting to work the Principle of Involvement:

Meaningful involvement increases motivation and support.

Most effective meetings promote participation. Meeting leaders encourage participation in various ways such as asking people for their observations, opinions or reactions; giving specific assignments; using buzz groups; asking for volunteers; responding positively to conferee questions and comments; getting responses to scenarios and reinforcing the good contributions that people make to the meeting.

The art of asking questions is especially important in promoting participation and keeping a meeting moving in the right direction. *Figure 9-5* summarizes many key aspects of this critical meeting leadership skill.

For the leader, PREPARATION includes ensuring the availability of the meeting place and all necessary supplies (pencils, pads, name cards, etc.), equipment (easels, screens, projectors, etc.), and audio-visual aids (charts, displays, slides, tapes, etc.). If you are going to give a talk during the meeting, preparation also includes getting ready to do this well. A good system you can use is explained and illustrated in a later section, "Safety Talk Technique."

During The Meeting

Essentially, the meeting leader's job is to 1) get it going, 2) maintain momentum and 3) bring it to a stop.

GET IT GOING. You owe it to those who are there to start on time. You can start the meeting by thanking the people for coming; referring to the written agenda; introducing the pertinent subject, topic, concept or question; and if you have one, making your presentation sincerely and skillfully.

- GUIDE FOR ALL MEETINGS -

To deal with the problems on the table, you must know how to work with the people around it.

Another useful skill is the ability to handle sticky situations or problem participants. Here are some helpful guidelines for working with various types of meeting participants.

The Arguer - against everything; tries to trip up the leader; disagrees with key points made by others; professional heckler.

- Keep your cool. Help group members keep theirs, too.

- Use questions, such as "Why do you say that?" - "Are there other possibilities?" - "Do you think everybody feels that way?" - "What's the other side of the coin?"

- Give the person enough rope to form his or her own noose, and let the group reaction handle it. Quickly move the program along.

- Get a show of hands: "How many of you see it that way?" - "How many of you see it some other way?"

- Find honest merit in one of his or her points; express your agreement and/or get the group to agree.

- Talk to the person between meetings; try to find out what's bugging him or her; try to win cooperation.

The Pessimist - emphasizes the negative; complains about details; displays pet peeves.

- Help him or her see that others in the group view the same variables positively.

- Encourage him or her to see the brighter side: Ask, "Is it totally hopeless, or is there something we can salvage out of the situation?"

- Point out that some things are beyond the control of the group and there is nothing to be gained from concentrating on them.

- Tell the person you will discuss the matter with him or her privately, later.

- Ask for the person's suggestions concerning what can be done to improve the situation.

- For valid complaints, adjust the adjustable; correct the correctable; thank the person for aiding the improvement.

The Jokester - treats things lightly; delights in puns, jokes and stories; tries to take center stage, to stay in the spotlight.

- The Art of Asking Questions -

I keep six honest serving men
(They taught me all I knew);
Their names are What and Why and When
and How and Where and Who.

-Rudyard Kipling

Six Question Types

1. Open questions: invite a true expression of opinion and feelings; show the other person that you are interested and want to understand; cannot be answered "yes" or "no."

2. Factual questions: seek data, information, facts; sometimes require only "yes" or "no" answer.

3. Leading questions: suggest the desired answer.

4. Controversial questions: stimulate new thoughts: challenge traditional concepts.

5. Provocative questions: stimulate new thoughts: challenge traditional concepts.

6. Directive questions: direct the discussion toward positive factors toward perceived areas of agreement.

Examples

1. What do you think of the...?
Why do workers...?
When should discipline...?
How can operators prevent...?

2. How many lost time accidents did our department have last quarter?
Did you receive the new rule booklets?

3. Don't you agree that this is excess absenteeism?

4. Is a desire for safety inborn or learned?

5. "A thing is safe if its risks are judged to be acceptable."
What's your reaction to this concept?

6. How much time do you think this corrective action will save in your area?

Six Questioner Techniques

1. Ask a specific person: to start a reluctant group responding, or to stimulate a non-participant. Don't embarrass the person; ask questions he or she can readily respond to.

2. Ask the group: to let the participative members help keep the ball rolling; to learn more about the group's thinking.

3. Ask for a show of hands: to stimulate listener response; to determine the group's experience or reaction.

4. Ask for an example: to promote participation; to emphasize a point or principle; to bring out "real life" incidents to which the group can relate.

5. Redirect the discussion: to get it back on the track.

6. Redirect the question: to stimulate group centered dynamics (even though you may later summarize the responses, relate to research results and/or give your own answer).

Examples

1. Sam, based on your 17 years of experience, how would you say preventive maintenance is related to safety?

2. How would you define or describe safety? What does it mean to you?

3. How many of you are aware that we have an Employee Assistance Program? Let's see the hands, please.

4. Can you tell us about a near-accident that had a high potential for major loss?

5. How does that tie in with the meeting objectives? Which point on the agenda does this relate to?

6. Member A asks the leader, "Do you think carelessness is the biggest cause of accidents? Leader asks Member A, "What do you think?" Or, leader asks the group, "What do some of you think about that?"

Figure 9-5

- Sober him or her up a bit with a challenging question or serious assignment.
- Emphasize the meeting objectives, agenda and time constraints.
- Thank him or her for the remarks that help to emphasize key points; let him or her know when the remarks are inappropriate; ignore some comments.

The Know-It-All - may try to monopolize the conversation; shows symptoms of the "I" disease (I did this, I did that, I... I... I...); doesn't seem open to learning more.

- Use small group discussions, call on specific people, and use related group dynamics to promote everyone's adequate participation.
- Build the confidence of the rest of the group so they will not be intimidated by this person; encourage appropriate reactions.
- Ignore or downplay superfluous statements and give the individual credit for good contributions.

The Clam - the non-participant; the loner; may be bashful, inarticulate, insecure, or timid; may be bored; may feel superior.

- Ask direct questions; encourage discussion of the familiar ("You've had lots of safety committee experience. What do you see as the committee's strongest points and weakest points?").
- Promote participation by special assignments (e.g., timer, buzz group recorder/reporter, visual aid assistant).
- Reinforce participation by expressing honest appreciation; by restating and re-emphasizing key points made by relating to those points in later discussion.

The Rambler - gets off base, misses the point; makes irrelevant comments.

- Refocus his or her attention by ignoring the irrelevant and restating the relevant; use leading questions to steer back onto track.
- Keep the meeting objectives, agenda and timetable in the forefront.
- Offer to discuss other matters with the person outside the meeting time.
- Assume responsibility ("I'm afraid I must have led you astray; here's what I meant we should discuss...").

But don't get the wrong idea! These types (Arguer - Pessimist - Jokester - Know-It-All-Clam-Rambler) are the extremes. They do not represent the vast majority of meeting members. Most people will do their best to make meetings successful. Some will be tremendously helpful, for example...

The Initiator - gets the discussion going when others are having trouble; participates without monopolizing; stimulates others to participate effectively.

The Conciliator - has a knack for smoothing things over; minimizes potential problems of personality conflicts among individuals; provides a rational, calming influence.

The Creative Thinker - gives things a new twist; brings out relationships and implications that are unique; stimulates others to look at things with a fresh viewpoint.

The Skillful Questioner - knows when and how to use questions; gives others the opportunity to make their points by responding to questions raised; makes significant points by asking the right questions at the right time.

The Summarizer - organizes information quickly and concisely; summarizes where we've been and where we're headed; highlights key points; helps keep discussion on the right track.

The Positive Participant - pays attention; takes meaningful notes; makes significant contributions; asks pertinent questions; reveals insights and practical applications.

As a meeting leader, recognize these types (Initiator - Conciliator - Creative Thinker - Skillful Questioner - Summarizer - Positive Participant), be thankful for them, and use them well.

BRING IT TO A STOP. Skilled meeting leaders do not let a meeting peter out. They summarize the meeting's accomplishments and relate them to the objectives. They highlight the action steps to be taken. They thank people for their participation. And they end on time.

After The Meeting

The meeting leader's job doesn't end when the

meeting ends. He or she still has at least four critical tasks to perform:

1. See that meeting minutes and/or reports are prepared quickly and distributed properly.

2. Express special appreciation to those who made special contributions to the meeting's success.

3. Follow up who's to do what, when.

4. Analyze what worked well and what should have been better... and put the results to work for more effective meetings.

SAFETY TALK TECHNIQUE

For supervisors, the most frequent application of group communication is what's called the "safety talk," "toolbox meeting," "tailgate meeting," or "safety meeting." Done properly, this is very efficient and effective for:

• sharing information with many people quickly

• stimulating group ideas and interaction

• teaching simple concepts and procedures

• giving an inspirational boost

• helping to build a cooperative communication climate.

To get the most out of these meetings, you should do your best to give good safety talks on critical and relevant topics.

Safety Talk Topics

It is important that topics for safety talks be carefully selected, well in advance of the meeting. Careful selection ensures that this important time is given to critical topics rather than the spur-of-the-moment ideas. Each topic selected should directly relate to the people involved — their exposures, their problems, their concerns and their needs. Selection in advance also allows more time for preparation. If talk topics are selected one to three months in advance, a wealth of illustrative material and presentation ideas will unfold in the interval. The Show-and-Tell Talk Tips in *Figure 9-6* show how everyday objects can be used as attention getters for short, to-the-point, safety talks on critical topics.

Five P's For Good Talks

Here is a tried and tested technique that will help you give better safety talks. It is simple; it is effective; it works. It is the "Five P" plan: 1) Prepare, 2) Pinpoint, 3) Personalize, 4) Picturize and 5) Prescribe.

Put these points to work in your safety talks, and they will work for you. To help you do this, let's examine these five P's, one by one and develop guidelines for practical application.

1. Prepare

The person is unique and extremely rare,
Who can give a good talk if he doesn't prepare!

For Heaven's sake, don't wait until the last minute — when you are going to get up in front of your group to give your safety talk — and then say, "Let's see, what should I talk about today?" That would be unfair to your workers, unfair to your company and unfair to you. Most good speakers would as soon think of appearing before an audience half-clothed as half-prepared.

The main ways to prepare are:

• THINK
• WRITE
• READ
• LISTEN
• ORGANIZE
• PRACTICE

Here are a few key concepts you can put into practice for each of these:

• THINK of your own experiences, observations, convictions, ideas and feelings. Choose a topic that you know something about. Remember, you are different from everyone else; no other person has your personality and your perception; you have something special to offer.

• THINK of the company and your department. What are the current problems? What are the current accomplishments? What is being emphasized? What topic will be most timely and helpful?

• THINK of your people; their needs, their backgrounds, their wants, their jobs, their attitudes, their aspirations, their abilities. Pick a subject that will mean something to them.

SHOW-AND-TELL SAFETY TALK TIPS

1 Have each of your workers watch the second hand of his or her watch or **the clock on the wall.** Explain that in the brief span of sixty seconds a full five quarts of blood are pumped through the body and that the loss of just one quart could be fatal. This means, then, a person can bleed to death in just 15 seconds if major blood vessels are cut. Therefore, quick action is a must when an accident victim is bleeding severely; a matter of seconds could make the difference. Once you've proven how important it is to stop severe bleeding, show the crew how it's done (complete instructions can be found in first aid handbooks).

2 The treatment for acid or chemical burns is plain water. It sounds simple, and it is, but there is a catch: it's the volume that counts. Have a **pitcher of water** with you when you give your talk. Explain that when a chemical skin or eye burn occurs you have to act fast. Get water and lots of it. Flush the irritated area continuously for an extended period of time until there is no trace of contaminant left.

3 Many common medications available without prescription bear the warning: "Not to be used while driving or operating machinery. May cause drowsiness." Bring one of the medicine **bottles or boxes** to the meeting, and let everyone read the label. Chances are some of the workers take similar drugs while at work and do not know the danger involved.

4 **Drain cleaner** is potent stuff; so are bleach, furniture polish, disinfectants, insecticides and kerosene. Explain that most (79%, according to one study) household products are at least moderately toxic and will kill in sufficient quantity. Don't be misled by the term "sufficient quantity," - it may be less than a teaspoonful. Remind your listeners that all poisons and all potential poisons must be stored where children cannot reach them.

5 An **ice cube** has many uses for the first aider. But since carrying one into the shop may make for an awfully wet pocket, a block of wood painted white can be used instead. The ice cube can be used as a local anesthetic, a relief from the pain and blistering of burns and to reduce swelling from sprains. Be sure to remind your listeners that first aid is to be practiced off-the-job also.

6 No one would deliberately stand in front of a **rifle range target,** but a worker may be a bull's eye for something as dangerous as a rifle bullet: flying particles from operating machine tools. It is of utmost importance that everyone working near machinery wear protective equipment especially eye protection, and that guards always remain in place.

7 Bounce a **rubber ball,** and explain that the human body, unlike this ball, does not bounce when it hits the ground. Bones break; internal organs rupture. In fact, falls claim almost 20,000 lives every year; the second most frequent cause of accidental death. Remember that trips and slips can be dangerous: so, a clean-up campaign to remove debris from the floor would greatly reduce the danger of a painful or fatal fall. Why not let your talk serve as a kick-off for that campaign?

8 Blow up a **balloon** and let it fly. The air pressure from your lungs is insignificant compared to the 2200+ p.s.i. in a compressed gas cylinder, but the effect of the escaping gas is the same; the container goes flying, sometimes straight through several brick walls. That gas cylinder looks heavy, but safety experts know that if the valve were accidentally knocked off, the unleashed power in the cylinder could cause it to take off, causing tremendous damage and possibly injury or death. Remind your listeners to keep them chained at all times and to use recommended safe practices when moving or handling them.

9 The dangers of **electrical "octopus" outlets** should be known. Explain to your people that every electrical circuit has a definite rated capacity. In most home circuits this rating is 15 amperes (amps). When only two outlets are available from each receptacle, the danger of current overload is minimized. But when an electrical "octopus" outlet is used, the potential current consumed by the appliances plugged into it may easily exceed the safe limit and create overheated wiring, and finally, a fire. Recommend that these devices never be used and that additional permanent wiring should be installed. If this is not possible limit the number of appliances used at one time.

10 Start your meeting by reading a sympathy card and getting your listeners' reactions to it. Discuss how each person can avoid having his or her mate receive one of these prematurely by following the safety advice contained in your remaining comments.

11 Oil will put out a **match,** or so the saying goes. While that is true theoretically, in practice fires can and do start by matches tossed into oil. You can illustrate this by floating a stick in a small pool of oil and placing a candle next to it. Explain that the stick in the oil is like the candle. It catches fire easily and uses the combustible material (wax or oil) around it for its fuel. In the same way, debris lying in oil acts like many wicks. This is an excellent reason for good housekeeping. Remove excess oil and trash promptly.

12 This demonstration is quite effective, and it may save someone from losing a finger in a machinery accident. Fill and **old glove** with plaster of paris and let it harden. Take a hatchet and, in front of your audience, chop off one of the "fingers." This may startle your crew, but they'd be even more startled if they lost a real finger by putting their hands in an unsafe position near moving machinery.

13 Bring a **toy hand grenade** to the meeting, explaining that many work materials are as dangerous as real hand grenades, although many people handle them as if they were toys. They're not. Drums of flammable liquids, aerosol and pressure cylinders and gasoline cans are just a few of the bombs on your job. These, and any other similar materials, should be given the safety attention they deserve.

Figure 9-6

SHOW-AND-TELL SAFETY TALK TIPS

14 By this time your crew has probably heard about two dangers of solvents: fire and toxic fumes, but there is at least one more: skin irritation. Take a **solvent** and a small gob of **grease,** and, in front of the group, show how the solvent dissolves the grease. Then explain that the solvent does the same thing to the human skin. It dissolves its natural oils, causing the skin to become dry and cracked; sores appear and infection can set in. You, yourself, should wear rubber gloves during this demonstration to show your people that they should wear rubber gloves when using solvents. Supervisors note: many toxic chemicals can be absorbed through the skin into the bloodstream, so gloves are really a double protection.

15 Wear, corrosion, kinks, fatigue, drying, overloading, overwinding and mechanical abuse can all deteriorate a wire rope below the safety point. Bring in a **worn wire rope sling** from the shop and teach your workers how to identify defects in the wire rope. A few minutes of this vital instruction could save a life.

16 How would you like your life to be riding on a roll of the **dice?** It may sound preposterous, but it isn't. Every year 115,000 people lose that gamble with death. Certainly some of these people are merely victims of circumstances. But what of the others who deliberately take chances? They're just gamblers who roll for high stakes. And they're gamblers who lose, sooner or later. Your employees can make their own luck if they follow the safety rules. They're made for winners. As you roll the dice, discuss the area of safety most important in your area.

17 This is a bit of basic chemistry that every housewife (and her husband) should know. A chlorinated cleanser when mixed with ammonia will give off deadly chlorine gas. Bring in a **bottle of ammonia and a can of cleaner** so your men will know exactly what you mean, but for heaven's sake, don't mix them. These chemicals are relatively safe when used separately, but together they form a dangerous compound which can cause severe burns of the nose, mouth and lungs or even death.

18 A **dented or scratched hard hat** is enough evidence of its protective value. Show one which has either saved the life of the wearer or has averted a serious injury. If one of your crew has had such an experience, ask him or her to display the hat and tell its story. You might ask the worker his or her opinion of the value of protective equipment, and ask the crew to speculate what would have happened if it had not been worn.

19 A **rabbit's foot** is symbolic of good luck. But since good luck is a poor substitute for good sense, you might bring one of these furry forelegs to the safety meeting, and after discussing the merits of reason over trusting in fate, throw it in the waste basket. Your listeners may not think they trust in luck but they do when they choose to ignore safety rules.

20 Wouldn't it be nice if we could erase pain and suffering like **chalk** from a **blackboard?** List your company's accident statistics (any will do), then erase them with the flip of your wrist. What does it mean? Nothing, and this is the point. The pain and suffering that come with every injury can't be erased unless we stop the accidents themselves. End by listing five safety guideposts to prevent the major accident types your group is experiencing.

21 Any good-sized **daily newspaper** is peppered with accident stories. Bring a paper to your meeting and discuss an accident which is related to the group, either on-the-job or at home. Discuss what happened and how the accident could have been prevented. Be sure to remind your listeners that they too could become a headline (or an obituary).

22 A **jug of water colored with vegetable dye** and a **red stick** can be used to illustrate the danger of storing gasoline in glass containers. The red stick only simulates dynamite, but the power of a gasoline explosion is no fake. One gallon of gas has the explosive power of over 100 sticks of dynamite: something to think about. Indeed, any volatile and explosive solvent stored in glass is a Molotov cocktail waiting to go off. Then, give your workers the facts about safe storage of gasoline and solvents.

23 If you have seen your workers gouged by the mishandling of **screwdrivers,** you may want to show them how to handle one properly. Most people get hurt by holding a part next to the body (on the knee, for example) and pressing the screwdriver firmly into the screwhead. One slip and the screwdriver could pierce the flesh like a knife. If parts are to be held in the hand, show the crew how to position them safely, so that they won't be cut if the screwdriver slips.

24 Years ago, if people wanted to protect their hearing from the deafening noise of heavy machinery, they stuffed some cotton in their ears. It may have been better than nothing, but not much. Show your listeners what hearing protection equipment your firm supplies - **ear muffs or ear plugs.** Explain how these devices are specially designed to prevent hearing damage. Remind everyone to wear hearing protection whenever exposed to loud or constant noises that have been identified as deserving this protection (approximately the noise level at which conversation becomes difficult).

25 How many of your crew know how to handle a ladder safely? Probably not all of them, so why not show them? Cut out a **right triangle from a piece of cardboard** so that the base of the triangle is 1/4 the length of the largest side. The resulting angle of about 75° is difficult to judge. Show your people and tell them that a ladder leaning against a wall should be placed one foot from the wall for every four feet of height.

Figure 9-6, Continued

- WRITE things down. Jot down notes, quotes, ideas, incidents and observations in your day-by-day work, as you go through the workplace. You may want to use a little pocket notebook. (Or use a slip of paper, the back of an envelope, or whatever you carry around in your pocket to write on. But, whatever you use, be sure to put things in writing before they slip away from your thoughts.)

- READ lots of safety material, and other materials, and do it with a selfish viewpoint. Whatever you are reading — whether it's something the safety department sends out, a trade magazine, a technical journal, a book, or the local newspaper — do it selfishly. Say to yourself, "What's in this material that I can use in one of my safety talks (if not this week or next week, sometime)?" You may want to clip it out or take notes and make a deposit in your bank of ideas, information, notes and quotes. This system yields maximum and permanent value from your reading, and helps prepare you to give top-notch safety talks.

- LISTEN carefully to what other people say about safety. Listen to what they complain about and what they praise. Listen to their likes and dislikes. Listen to their problems and suggestions. Listen and learn. You will not only learn more about safety, but also more about the safety ATTITUDES of the people around you. And you'll certainly get many excellent ideas for your safety talks.

- Once you have collected your ideas and information — by thinking, writing, reading and listening — you are ready to ORGANIZE and outline your safety talk. Preparation and organization are real keys to success. Practice improves your timing. (No doubt you have seen the great difference between the disorganized, rambling, beating-around-the-bush speaker and the one who knows what he wants to say and says it, clearly and concisely.) Your outline may be a few key words scratched on a scrap of paper, or a complete outline of key points, supporting facts and examples. But — whatever outline form you use — be ready, know what you are going to say, pay your listeners the respect of giving them a well-organized talk. They, in turn, will respect you for it.

- PRACTICE may make the difference between a "good" safety talk and an "excellent" one. Practice increases your confidence. Practice delivery. But don't memorize a talk — ever! If

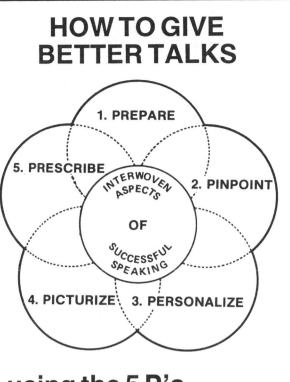

HOW TO GIVE BETTER TALKS

using the 5 P's

PREPARING

- Think about the subject
- Write things down . . . for your idea-bank
- Read related materials selfishly
- Listen to others' ideas and attitudes
- Organize and outline your talks
- Practice

PINPOINTING

- Don't try to cover too much ground
- Zero-in on one main idea . . . that you can state in a single sentence
- Aim for a communication bull's-eye

PERSONALIZING

- Establish common ground with your listeners
- Bring it close to home
- Make it important in their minds
- Make it personal and meaningful to them

PICTURIZING

- Create clear mental pictures for your listeners
- Appeal to both their ears and their eyes
- Help them to really "see what you mean"
- Use visual aids

PRESCRIBING

- In closing your talk, answer the question the listeners always have: "So what?"
- Tell them what to do
- Ask for special action
- Give a prescription

Figure 9-7

you are the type of person who needs notes to jog your thoughts and keep them from rambling all over the place, use them. There is nothing wrong with using notes to keep yourself on the track. But don't memorize your talk. Practice may not make your talks perfect, but it will make them better and better and better. Practice - Practice - Practice.

So much for the first of the five P's...PREPARE. You do it by thinking, writing, reading, listening, organizing and practicing.

2. Pinpoint

The second "P" is to PINPOINT. This simply means, don't try to cover too much ground! Your safety talk is likely to be only five, ten or fifteen minutes. So don't try to cover the whole water-front! If you talk about everything, your listeners will remember nothing.

The main idea in pinpointing is to:

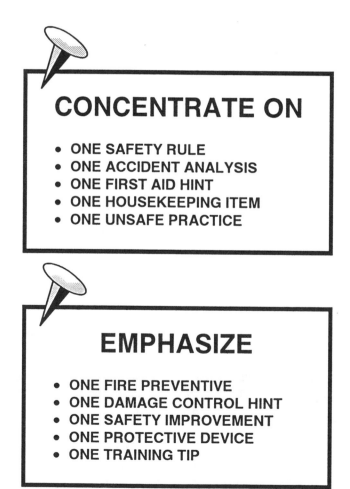

CONCENTRATE ON

- ONE SAFETY RULE
- ONE ACCIDENT ANALYSIS
- ONE FIRST AID HINT
- ONE HOUSEKEEPING ITEM
- ONE UNSAFE PRACTICE

EMPHASIZE

- ONE FIRE PREVENTIVE
- ONE DAMAGE CONTROL HINT
- ONE SAFETY IMPROVEMENT
- ONE PROTECTIVE DEVICE
- ONE TRAINING TIP

Figure 9-8: The Main Idea in Pinpointing

Zero in on one main idea. Avoid the old shotgun approach where you try to pepper the whole target. Use a rifle approach and aim for a bull's-eye (a communication bull's-eye) every time.

3. Personalize

The third of the "Five P's" is PERSONALIZE. This means you must establish common ground with your listeners. Get real interest; bring it close to home; make it mean something to the listeners; make it important to them.

To do this, you relate to their attitudes, abilities and aspirations; their wants, wishes, drives and desires; their jobs; their backgrounds; their interests; their personalities.

In the safety field, you're very fortunate because many of man's strongest instincts are on your side — on the side of safety — powerful desires, for instance, like health, security, comfort, avoidance of pain and even self-preservation itself, the most basic of all.

Appeal to these basic motivations. Make it "personal," not for you, but for your listeners. Make it mean something to them. PERSONALIZE your presentation.

4. Picturize

The fourth "P" is PICTURIZE. This is what you do to create crystal-clear mental pictures for your listeners. Your safety talk is a special type of "communication." Communication is one thing, and one thing only, and that is the process of giving and getting understanding. If your talk doesn't get understanding you don't have communication; you just have noise. For example, if you gave a talk in Greek to people who understood only English, it would be noise, not communication. You must make your safety talk mean something. When you give and get understanding you are really communicating.

Do you want people to "pay attention" to what you say? Do you want them to "understand" what you mean? Do you want them to "remember" your message? If you do, make them use both their ears and their eyes. People understand and remember much better what they both hear and see. So the key point here is to use both sound and sight in your safety contacts; make your presentation both verbal and visual.

Use some combination of:

- demonstrations
- graphs
- discussions
- samples
- displays
- questions
- quizzes
- posters
- charts
- models

- mock-ups
- movies
- booklets
- newspaper items
- photographs
- illustrations
- tools
- drawings
- slides
- actual equipment

You communicate much better when you both TELL and SHOW. You create clear mental images when you use visuals to aid the verbal. You get increased attention, better understanding and improved memory power when you paint vivid mental pictures for your listeners. When you PIC-TURIZE, you help people to really "see what you mean."

5. Prescribe

The fifth and final "P" is PRESCRIBE. In closing your safety talk, answer the questions that your listeners always have in mind... "So what? What does it mean to me? How is it going to help me? What do you want me to do?"

Always think of your safety talk listeners as having these questions in mind... and answer them. Tell them what you want them to do. Ask for some specific action. Give them a prescription.

> You should always get your audience to do something before you finish. It doesn't matter what it is - write your congressman, call your neighbor, consider a certain proposition. In other words, don't leave without asking for the order.
>
> - Lee Iacocca

So What? (Here's What)

Good safety talks don't just happen. They do take some work, but they will lighten your load of responsibility by sharing it with other people. So... start using the "5 P's" this very week.

The sooner you get to work on these techniques, the sooner they will go to work for you. You will soon find that you can easily apply them not only to safety talks, but also to communication contacts on other vital subjects such as quality, productivity, service, job in-

struction and cost improvement.

WORK AT THEM
- **PREPARE**
- **PINPOINT**
- **PERSONALIZE**
- **PICTURIZE**
- **PRESCRIBE**
...and they will
WORK FOR YOU

Figure 9-9: The 5 P's

Effective Talk Outline

The Effective Talk Outline (*Figure 9-10*) can be of great help in preparing and presenting your talks. It may remind you of the old formula: 1) "Tell 'em what you're gonna tell 'em" (INTRODUCTION); 2) "Tell 'em" (BODY); and 3) "Tell 'em what you told 'em" (CONCLUSION).

In the INTRODUCTION, you get their attention by asking a question, telling an appropriate story or anecdote, using an exhibit or otherwise getting them interested. Then you build a bridge of common ground ... tell them why the talk is important to them ... relate to their situation, their kind of people, their world ... make it personally meaningful to them.

Then you pinpoint your message with your topic statement...a short, simple statement that explains your talk in a single sentence. And you complete the introduction with your initial summary, which lets your listeners know the main points around which your talk is organized.

Though it's the biggest part of your talk, the BODY is probably the easiest part. This is where you get down to cases ... give "for instances," examples, explanations ... paint clear mental pictures ... demonstrate and dramatize ... help the audience really "see what you mean" ... develop each of the points you included in your "initial summary."

You should end your talk on a strong note. A strong CONCLUSION includes a restatement of the topic

Effective Talk Outline

- INTRODUCTION -

Attention:

Common Ground (Personalize):

Topic Statement (Pinpoint):

Initial Summary (Organize):

1.

2.

3.

- BODY -

For Instance, Explanation (Picturize):

1.

2.

3.

- CONCLUSION -

Topic Restatement:

Summary Restatement:

1.

2.

3.

Action Step (Prescribe):

Figure 9-10

sentence, a restatement of your initial summary, and a prescription ... a suggestion for action ... what your listeners should think, feel or do.

After you have used the "5P Method" and this "Talk Outline" a few times, your success will lead you to keep on using it. At first it may seem a little awkward, and you may have to force yourself to give it a fair shake. But go ahead and force yourself — you'll be forcing yourself to give better talks! And you won't be the only one to notice your improved ability and results in "group communication" ... your work team and your boss will, too!

PUTTING THE METHOD TO WORK

Examples will help you see how practical this technique is ... how readily you can put it to work. For the first example, suppose that some of your critical safety problems involve portable power tools. In preparing one of a series of safety talks to help solve these problems, your outline might look something like *Figure 9-11*.

Read it completely and carefully, to see how simple it is, how logical it is, how effective it is...and how you might make it even better. Do this right now — before you go on to the next paragraph.

As you probably have decided for yourself, this technique is good not only for your safety talks — but also for talks you give on production, quality, waste control or other important aspects of the job. The same approach (the 5 P's plus the Talk Outline) also works very well for talks you give away from work — for youth groups, church or Sunday School; PTA's and other associations; lodges, clubs and civic groups.

But our emphasis here is the safety talk. *Figure 9-12* is another example of how this technique has been used for safety talks. Once again, for maximum benefit, read the entire example thoroughly. Notice how it follows the time-tested formula:

- **Tell 'em what you're gonna tell 'em**
  (You do this in the Introduction, with your "Topic Statement" and your "Initial Summary")

- **Tell 'em**
  (This is the Body of your talk.)

- **Tell 'em what you told 'em**
  (You do this in the Conclusion, with your "Topic Restatement" and your "Summary Restatement.")

This approach makes excellent use of the teaching and learning power in repetition - repetition - repetition. People are much more likely to remember what has been reinforced in their minds by repetition.

O.K., now you are ready for the third example ... the most practical one ... the one with the real payoff! This is the one where you turn back to *Figure 9-10* and outline your next safety talk. This is the only way to really learn it ... by doing it. You can do it! This is the only way to gain the great benefits ... by doing it. Doing it is the only way to be sure you have the "know-how."

To make it easier, here are some hints on how to go about it, step by step:

- **Pick your subject**
  - choose one important to the group
  - narrow it down

- **State the main idea of the whole talk in a single sentence**
  - I'm going to help you learn how to control severe bleeding.

- **Organize your talk**
  - jot down your main ideas on 3 x 5 cards (see *Figure 9-13*)
  - group your notes into two or three sections or headings, e.g., "Let's discuss it in terms of (1) Direct Pressure, (2) Pressure Points and (3) Tourniquet Precautions."

- **Develop the body of your talk, based on the headings of the initial summary**
  - use evidence, explanations and examples
  - discuss facts and figures
  - present incidents and illustrations
  - demonstrate and dramatize
  - personalize and picturize
  - jot down just the key words or phrases that will keep you on target, trigger the thoughts you want to get across, and remind you of the visual aids you plan to use.

- **Round out the introduction**
  - you already have your Topic Statement and Initial Summary
  - get the listener's attention by asking a question, telling an appropriate story or anecdote, using an exhibit or otherwise creating interest
  - get on common ground by telling the listeners why the talk is important to them; by relating to

Effective Talk Outline

- INTRODUCTION -

Attention:
 This (show portable grinder) can be both a "Lifesaver" and a life taker.
Common Ground (Personalize):
 Every person in this department works with or near these grinders.
Topic Statement (Pinpoint):
 Today we'll review 3 basic safety precautions for portable electric grinders.
Initial Summary (Organize):

1. Use the right tool for the job.

2. Be sure it's in good condition.

3. Use it properly.

- -

- BODY -

For Instance, Explanation (Picturize):

1. Use the right tool for the job.
   - Last week's "near-miss"
   - Wheel marking codes
   - When to discard wheels (Tell & Show)
2. Be sure it's in good condition.
   - Cord-plug-wheel-casing-guard
   - The "shrapnel" incident
3. Use it properly.
   - Exert proper pressure
   - Avoid overheating
   - Keep free of water and oil
   - Set it and store it with care

- -

- CONCLUSION -

Topic Restatement:
 We have reviewed the basic safety precautions for this type of tool (show grinder).
Summary Restatement:

1. Using the right tool for the job.

2. Making sure it's in good condition.

3. Using it properly.

Action Step (Prescribe):
 Check your buddy and yourself on these rules everyday...make them a way of life.

Figure 9-11

Effective Talk Outline

- INTRODUCTION -

Attention:
 Do you think "A miss is as good as a mile?"
Common Ground (Personalize):
 Last Tuesday we all had a "miss" that should make us really think about this!
Topic Statement (Pinpoint):
 Let's see how we can profit from the "near-miss" we had last Tuesday.
Initial Summary (Organize):

1. What happened.

2. The basic causes.

3. Preventing recurrence.

- BODY -

For Instance, Explanation (Picturize):

1. What happened.
   - Discuss and demonstrate the incident (do not reenact it).

2. The basic causes.
   - Maintenance problem
   - Violation of standard job procedure

3. Preventing recurrence.
   - Maintenance log
   - Refresher training in job procedures
   - "Buddy system" on HIPO operations

- CONCLUSION -

Topic Restatement:
 We've looked at some ways we can profit from last Tuesday's "near-miss."
Summary Restatement:

1. We reviewed what happened.

2. We discussed the basic causes.

3. We saw what we must do to prevent recurrence.

Action Step (Prescribe):
 Keep these near-misses more than a mile away — check that log; follow that procedure; use that "buddy system."

Figure 9-12

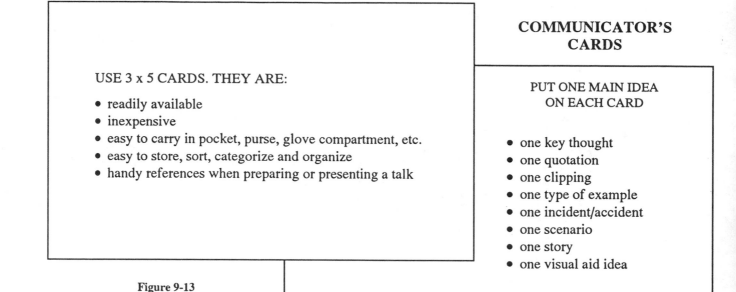

USE 3 x 5 CARDS. THEY ARE:

- readily available
- inexpensive
- easy to carry in pocket, purse, glove compartment, etc.
- easy to store, sort, categorize and organize
- handy references when preparing or presenting a talk

COMMUNICATOR'S CARDS

PUT ONE MAIN IDEA ON EACH CARD

- one key thought
- one quotation
- one clipping
- one type of example
- one incident/accident
- one scenario
- one story
- one visual aid idea

Figure 9-13

their situation, their work, their world; by making it mean something to them.

- **Develop a strong conclusion**
  - restate the Topic and the Initial Summary
  - state the Action Step; answer the listeners' "So what?" questions; tell them what to do; ask them for specific action.

Using *Figure 9-10*, finish your own safety talk outline ... and put it to work.

Getting The Habit

This system is a time-tested, proven pathway to speaking success. It will work for you, if you work at it ... if you make it a habit.

Make a habit of using the 5 P's: PREPARE - PINPOINT - PERSONALIZE - PICTURIZE - PRESCRIBE. Put them to work with these five (practice - practice - practice - practice - practice) and your talks will get better, and better, and better, and better, and better!

Make a habit of using the "Talk Outline."

- Use the INTRODUCTION to get your listeners' attention, establish common ground and "tell 'em what you're gonna tell 'em" (topic statement and initial summary).

- Use the BODY to "tell 'em" — with "for instances," explanations and picturizations of each main point.

- Use the CONCLUSION to "tell 'em what you told 'em" (topic restatement and summary restatement) and give the action step.

By getting the habit of using these tools for good talks, you will be helping your people get the habits of E-S-P: Efficiency - Safety - Productivity.

OTHER TECHNIQUES FOR INTERESTING MEETINGS

One of the most frequently asked questions about group meetings is how to improve employee interest. The simplest answer to that question is to plan interesting meetings. Usually, the most interesting meetings are those with a large amount of group participation. This is quite often the difference between meetings that "fizzle" and those that "sizzle."

Group participation must be honestly desired by the person conducting the meeting or the members will quickly catch on that the techniques to get participation are only "gimmicks." Participation must also be expected by the group leader. This will be indicated in a number of subtle ways, such as how questions are asked and answered. The group leader who expects participation will get far more than the one who doubts that people will really get involved. Also, participation must be encouraged by the structure of the meeting itself. Therefore, it must be planned before the meeting takes place. Some specific techniques to get involvement are:

Accident Imaging. Let one or more employees imagine an accident which could occur in an area and present it to the group to develop preventive measures. The "accidents" thus presented will range from the impossible to the probable, and may include "near-misses" and accidents which have actually occurred but were never reported.

You Are There. For these, the leader will describe to the group an emergency situation, such as a fire in the home or a seriously injured person on the job. The leader will also provide a list of actions which might be taken by one of the persons involved. The group, through discussion, will rank these actions according to which should be done first, second, third, etc. More active discussion can be gained by including potential conflicts in the situation, such as a prize hunting dog in the burning house or an injured employee next to a process which is about to get dangerously out of control.

Problem Solving Meetings. These are very helpful because they produce real solutions to real problems. And they are especially valuable when they tackle problems which can be eliminated or controlled by the participants themselves. Supervisors can contribute a great deal to quality, safety and productivity by holding monthly mutual problem solving meetings with all of their people. The goals and benefits of these meetings include ...

- attaining mutual understanding of common problems and their solutions, by using the group's knowledge and experience.
- promoting commitment to problem correction and control.
- improving performance results through coordinated and cooperative group efforts.

Figure 9-14, Problem Solving Meeting Report, shows the five main aspects of these meetings. Following are some guidelines for supervisors on how to use the system and the form.

1. PROBLEM - As meeting leader, the supervisor writes a brief description of the *specific behavior* which he considers to be a problem (substandard performance) within the group. This may be what people are doing (or are likely to do) that they should not be doing, or what they are not doing that they should be doing. Problem descriptions must be in terms of *actions not attitudes,* in terms of specific, observable, measurable behavior. For example:

- Not wearing eye protection - in the machine shop, on the second shift, only 64% of the workers wore required eye protection last week.
- Moving unsafe loads - last month, in the shipping and receiving area, there were seven recorded incidents in which forklift operators were moving unsafe loads.
- Not following procedures - quality control lab technicians are following only 82% of established Standard Operating Procedures for critical tasks.

The description must tell what it is that the group members are or are not doing that is the problem. And the problem must be one that can be corrected or controlled by a change in their behavior (actions).

This problem description may be given to participants in advance or at the beginning of the meeting.

2. ANALYSIS - as meeting leader, the supervisor lists beforehand the likely reasons and causes behind the behavior. Based on group discussion during the meeting, he or she adds other reasons and causes brought out. Likewise for the solutions... the supervisor lists possibilities beforehand and adds others based on group discussion.

It is essential to encourage, obtain and accept participant input and ideas. This system will not work unless they agree that the problem *is* a problem; unless they feel that it's *their* problem and unless they develop *commitment* to its correction and control. Meaningful participation is the best known way to meet these needs.

3. ACTION - Based on the analysis of reasons, causes and possible solutions, the supervisor helps the group spell out what they agree to do to eliminate or control the problem. If appropriate, the action steps should have specific time frames or deadlines. It can also be helpful to get a commitment (verbal, written, show of hand, etc.) for the action from each person.

4. FOLLOW-UP - Here the supervisor lists all other steps necessary to ensure that the causes are corrected and the actions are carried out. This includes any actions needed to back up commitments made during the meeting, and things he or she and other members of management will do to support participants' behavior changes.

This section of the form can also be used later to record completed follow-up actions. It then becomes a means of communicating follow-up information to all concerned.

PROBLEM SOLVING MEETING REPORT

PLANT: **DEPT.:**   **SUPERVISOR:**   **DATE:**

MEETING PREPARATION	1. PROBLEM — What people are doing (or are likely to do) that they should not do, or are not doing that they should do.

A. Before meeting complete #1 and #2

B. Anticipate changes to be made in #2 as result of meeting

EMPLOYEES ATTENDING

1. ....
2. ....
3. ....
4. ....
5. ....
6. ....
7. ....
8. ....
9. ....
10. ....
11. ....
12. ....
13. ....
14. ....
15. ....
16. ....
17. ....
18. ....
19. ....
20. ....
21. ....

NUMBER EMPLOYEES ATTENDING:

NUMBER EMPLOYEES SUPERVISED:

REVIEWED BY:

NAME
DATE

NAME
DATE

2. ANALYSIS

REASONS AND CAUSES	SOLUTIONS
A.	A. ....
B.	B. ....
C.	C. ....
D.	D. ....
E.	E. ....

3. ACTION — Things we agree to do to eliminate or control the problem.

4. FOLLOW-UP — Steps to ensure that the actions are carried out.

5. OTHER PROBLEMS - ACCOMPLISHMENTS - ACTIONS

Figure 9-14

5. OTHER PROBLEMS, ACCOMPLISHMENTS AND ACTIONS - The meeting should include the opportunity for participants to present other problems of common concern, to share the results of what they have done since the last meeting, and to get feedback from the supervisor on problems and progress. The supervisor should list highlights of these concerns in this section of the form.

Properly completed, the form serves as the minutes of the meeting. It shows where and when the meeting was held, who led it, who attended and summary information under each of the five main sections. It can then be forwarded for required reviews. Copies can be given to each interested person.

This is a system that makes meetings effective; that gets results for quality, safety and productivity.

Other techniques to get involvement and create interest are:

- Have a safety tour with one member of the group and let that person report the findings to the group.
- Let a member pick a film, and introduce, show and explain it. (See *Figure 9-15* on how to get more from your training films.)
- Get ideas from the group about topics for the meetings.
- Give the group advance notification and let them critique the presentation.
- Have a carefully selected member give the safety talk, after some help with its preparation.
- Draw on personal experiences of the group with a safety item.
- Ask participants to prepare written cases, real or potential.
- Ask people for their observations, opinions or reactions.
- Respond positively to conferee questions and comments.
- Use questions, quizzes, paper and pencil tests, verbal tests and performance tests.
- Give individual assignments such as preparing possible quiz items, writing key points on the chalkboard or flip pad, reading portions of written materials aloud for the group, scoring quickie quizzes or doing homework.
- Use buzz groups for case studies; for development of concerns common to the members; for analysis of a viewed movie, videotapes, filmstrip and so on.

- Guide demonstrations and role plays, either with volunteers or by specific assignments.
- Ask participants to practice a procedure or skill ... individually, in pairs or in groups as appropriate for the task.
- Reinforce the good contributions that people make to the meeting.

Also, meetings are more interesting if the group members are doing the same type work and if the visual aids used are items they are familiar with.

AUDIO AND VISUAL AIDS - Properly used, visual and audio aids help both the speaker and the listeners. By analyzing the topic to decide how it can be improved with aids, the speaker gets much more familiar with his or her material, how to organize it, and how to present more in less time. During the talk, aids can also help the speaker by strengthening his or her confidence and poise, providing something useful to do by way of movement and use of hands, and helping to maintain audience contact and rapport.

For the listeners, properly used aids help emphasize the key aspects of good communication:

- Attention
- Interest
- Understanding
- Retention

A good visual aid "is worth a thousand words" because it instantly and vividly portrays things that are nearly impossible to convey verbally; it saves time, creates interest and brings variety; it adds impact and remains in the memory long after the words have been forgotten.

These aids are not a cure-all ... and they do have some disadvantages. Creating them can take a great deal of time and thought. They sometimes divert attention from what is being said. They cost money. If they go wrong, the result can vary from amusement, through mild confusion, to humiliation and catastrophe.

Usually, however, the advantages outweigh the disadvantages. There is no doubt that a good presentation which uses visual (and audio) aids, properly, is much more effective than a good presentation without them. *Figure 9-16* summarizes some of the advantages and disadvantages for various types of aids.

EVALUATION AND FOLLOW-UP

There is no perfect speaker and no perfect meeting. Everyone can do better. Systematic and continuing

How To Get More From Your Training Films

Introducing The Film:

1. Direct the viewer's attention to specific points in the film.
2. Point out the importance, to the viewer personally, of learning from the film.
3. Increase the viewer's anxiety about learning from the film, possibly as it relates to advancement in the organization, performance or by announcing that there will be a test on what was learned.

Conducting A Discussion:

1. Have group discussion of points raised in the film immediately after the film showing.
2. Use the combination of film discussion with techniques that prepare the group for the film they are to see.
3. Perhaps reshow the film to clarify any questions raised in the discussion.

Obtaining Viewer Participation:

1. Instruct the viewers to think of the answers to questions that are asked in the film.
2. Stop the film and have the viewers answer questions out loud or to themselves about the material just presented. Then follow this up with a short discussion, if appropriate.
3. At the end of a film sequence, have the learners practice mentally or mentally review the material they have just viewed.
4. Do not bother with note-taking during the film showing. In most cases it will only interfere with the learning.

Stopping The Film:

1. The film does not have to be run through from beginning to end without stopping just because it was made that way. The film can be stopped at any time for viewer activity.
2. Analyze the film and locate the places where it may be stopped, then plan appropriate discussion at these points.
3. Have the viewer answer questions, discuss material presented in the preceding sequence, and review the points made.

Reshowing A Film:

1. Show the film a second time or schedule a date for later viewing.
2. Make note of the questions which arise after the first showing and make sure they are resolved after the film has been seen twice.
3. Ask trainees to change points of view when seeing the film again. You may want to discuss the underlying meanings and problems the second time.

A Post Meeting Evaluation:

Ask the learner to evaluate the film, the discussion and the presentation in relation to the contribution made to his or her development and job.

Figure 9-15

Audio and Visual Aids

Types	Advantages	Disadvantages
Flip Pads Chart Cards Chalkboards	• Prepared either ahead of time or during presentation • Inexpensive • Easy to use • Good for words, diagrams, charts, symbols, drawings • Often portable • Use in lighted room	• Poor visibility for large groups • Chalkboards tend to be messy
Posters Banners Photos Pictures Drawings Maps	• Inexpensive • Easy to prepare • Easy to use • Use in lighted room • Portable • Easy to file and use again	• Limited to small groups

Boards:
  Flannel
  Magnetic
  Hook & Loop
	• Permit "gradual build-up" and "gradual revelation" techniques
	• Relatively easy to prepare
	• Often portable
	• Use in lighted room
	• Easy to file and use again
		• Poor visibility for large groups
		• Require practice for effective use

Demonstrations Displays Physical Objects Mock-ups Models	• Realistic 3D • Can show many variables and relationships • May show action • May be used indoors or outdoors • Help people really "see what you mean"	• May not be easily portable • May be expensive • Detail visible only to small groups

Audio Aids:
  Records
  Tapes
	• Realistic presentation of interviews, speeches, discussions
	• Realistic sounds of nature, music, machinery, equipment, animals, instruments
	• Easy to use
	• Some equipment very portable and battery operated
		• Require a sound system for large groups
		• Records require professional production

Still
Projectors:
  35mm
  Opaque
  Overhead
	• Good visual impact
	• Depict reality
	• Overhead can be used in lighted room
	• Overhead materials may be prepared ahead of time or during presentation
	• Fairly portable
	• Can be operated either by speaker or assistant
		• Can be costly
		• Often require special preparation
		• Require power source and projection surface
		• 35mm and opaque require darkened room
		• Opaque good only for small groups
		• Require a bit of practice for effective use

Projectors
With Movement
and/or Sound:
  Filmstrips
  Sound-and-
  Slide
  Movies
  Videotape
	• Most realistic
	• Can be adapted to any group size
		• Tend to be expensive
		• Require extensive preparation
		• Require specialized equipment
		• Some equipment not easily portable
		• Require operator training
		• Filmstrips and movies difficult to revise or update

Figure 9-16

improvement requires evaluation of performance (self-evaluation and/or evaluation by others) and application of what's learned from the evaluation, i.e., building on the strengths and overcoming the weaknesses.

Evaluation is easiest and best when it is systematic. *Figure 9-17* is an easy guide for effective analysis of a safety talk (or any other talk), using the 5P system:

- How well did the speaker PREPARE? Did he or she know what to say? ... have the necessary information? ... make a well-organized presentation?

- How well did the speaker PINPOINT? Did he or she concentrate on one main idea? If so, what was the main idea? Did the speaker "stay on the track?"

- How well did the speaker PERSONALIZE? Did he or she hold the audience's attention? ... make it important to them? ... get their participation? ... bring it "close to home?"

- How well did the speaker PICTURIZE? Did he or she use visual aids? ... speak clearly and convincingly? ... get the message across? ... use both sound and sight?

- How well did the speaker PRESCRIBE? Did he or she summarize the main point at the end? ... answer the "so what" question? ... ask for specific action? What was the prescription?

- What one thing would do the most to make it a better talk?

Follow-up of group meetings may involve completing a report such as the one shown in *Figure 9-18*. This information is necessary in evaluating how effectively the investment of supervisory and employee time in group meetings is being used.

CORE CONCEPTS IN REVIEW

Effective leaders use group meetings to help implement important management principles such as the...

1. **The Information Principle:** effective communication increases motivation.

2. **The Distortion Principle:** the more levels a communication goes through, the more distorted it becomes.

3. **The Psychological Appeal Principle:** communication that appeals to feelings and attitudes tends to be more motivational than that which appeals only to reason.

4. **The Utilization Principle:** the sooner and more often an idea or skill is put to work, the better it is learned and remembered.

Group Meeting Leaders

Group meeting leaders who use good learning-and-memory aids get better attention, interest, understanding and retention than those who do not.

1. **Regular planned meetings** help to...
   a. Increase awareness and understanding
   b. Reduce resistance to change
   c. Aid problem identification and analysis
   d. Develop solutions for problems
   e. Stimulate acceptance of policies, practices and decisions
   f. Reinforce desired attitudes and behavior
   g. Reduce injuries and damage - improve safety
   h. Reduce rejects and rework - improve quality
   i. Reduce defects and delays - improve production
   j. Reduce mistakes and waste - improve cost control
   k. Reduce human misery - improve human relations

2. Four key **discussion leading methods** of value to meeting leaders are the...
   a. Lecture and Discussion Method
   b. Question and Answer Discussion Method
   c. Pro and Con Discussion Method
   d. Small Group Discussion Method

3. Effective meeting leaders **apply meeting leadership skills...**
   a. Before the meeting
      (1) Plan: objectives - agenda - actions

"5-P" SAFETY TALK
ANALYSIS SHEET

PREPARE

EVIDENCE OF PREPARATION: _____

_____

SUGGESTIONS FOR IMPROVEMENT: _____

_____

PINPOINT

WAS IT PINPOINTED? ☐ YES ☐ NO
IF "YES", STATE THE MAIN MESSAGE IN ONE SENTENCE: _____

_____

SUGGESTIONS FOR IMPROVEMENT: _____

_____

PERSONALIZE

HOW WAS IT PERSONALIZED? _____

_____

SUGGESTIONS FOR IMPROVEMENT: _____

_____

PICTURIZE

DID THE SPEAKER CREATE CLEAR MENTAL PICTURES?
☐ YES ☐ NO IF "YES", HOW? _____

_____

_____

SUGGESTIONS FOR IMPROVEMENT: _____

_____

PRESCRIBE

WAS A CLEAR PRESCRIPTION (ACTION STEP)
GIVEN IN THE CLOSING PORTION OF THE TALK? ☐ YES ☐ NO IF "YES", WHAT WAS THE PRESCRIPTION? _____

_____

_____

SUGGESTIONS FOR IMPROVEMENT: _____

_____

P.S. – WHAT ONE THING WOULD DO THE MOST TO MAKE IT A BETTER TALK?

_____

_____

Figure 9-17

SAFETY MEETING RECORD

PERSON CONDUCTING:	DEPARTMENT/AREA:		
DATE:	TIME: to	☐ AM ☐ PM	NUMBER ATTENDING:

ATTENDANCE

CONTENT

WHAT WAS THE TOPIC? _____

WHY WAS THIS TOPIC CHOSEN? _____

HOW WAS PARTICIPATION ENCOURAGED? _____

WHAT VISUAL AIDS WERE USED? _____

WHAT SIGNIFICANT QUESTIONS OR CONCERNS WERE EXPRESSED? _____

Figure 9-18

(2) Communicate: purpose - time - place - subjects - expectations

(3) Prepare: meeting place - supplies - equipment - presentation

b. During the meeting

(1) Get it going: start on time - thank attendees - introduce the subject - lay the groundwork

(2) Maintain momentum: promote participation - apply the art of asking questions - deal with sticky situations or problem participants - use repetition, memory aids and audiovisual aids

(3) Bring it to a stop: summarize - highlight action steps - thank participants - end on time

c. After the meeting

(1) Issue minutes and/or reports

(2) Express special appreciation

(3) Follow-up

(4) Evaluate and improve

The 5P method helps supervisors give good safety talks:

1. **Prepare**
2. **Pinpoint**
3. **Personalize**
4. **Picturize**
5. **Prescribe**

An effective talk outline includes...

1. Introduction (**Tell 'em what you're gonna tell 'em.**)
   a. Attention
   b. Topic statement
   c. Common ground
   d. Initial summary

2. Body (**Tell 'em.**)
   a. Explain and exemplify
   b. Demonstrate and dramatize
   c. Personalize and picturize

3. Conclusion (**Tell 'em what you told 'em.**)
   a. Topic restatement
   b. Summary restatement
   c. Action step

Good group **meetings contribute significantly to loss control** by:

1. Using communication time most effectively

2. Reducing communication errors

3. Reducing the losses that result from poor communication or lack of communication

Systematic and continuing improvement of speakers and meetings requires evaluation of performance (self-evaluation and/or evaluation by others) and application of what's learned from the evaluation, i.e., building on the strengths and overcoming the weaknesses.

KEY QUESTIONS

1. What is the main idea in the Information Principle?

2. What are some of the positive purposes of group meetings?

3. What eight words are best to complete the definition, "Communication is..."?

4. What are the four steps of the discussion leading procedure discussed in the chapter?

5. What are the four major discussion leading methods discussed in the chapter?

6. What are the advantages of using the Lecture and Discussion method?

7. What are the advantages of using more participative discussion leading methods?

8. What are several things the meeting leader should do before the meeting occurs?

9. What are the three main parts of the leader's job during the meeting?

10. To ensure best results, what are some things the leader should do after the meeting?

11. What word best completes the following Guide For All Meetings? "To deal with the problems on the table, you must know how to deal with the _____ around it."

12. What are the six basic types of questions discussed under "The Art of Asking Questions"?

13. What are some negative types of meeting participants?

14. What are some positive types of meeting participants?

15. What are some of the advantages and disadvantages of various audio and visual aids?

16. What are the five key words in the "Five P" talk technique?

17. What are the three main parts of the Effective Talk Outline?

18. In the Effective Talk Outline, what are the three parts of the "conclusion"?

19. What are some advantages of using 3 x 5 cards as "communicator's cards"?

20. What are some ways to evaluate talks and meetings for continuing improvement?

PRACTICAL APPLICATIONS SUMMARY

S - For Supervisors
E - For Executives
C - For Safety/Loss Control Coordinators

		S	E	C
1.	Analyze the organization's needs and opportunities for improving group meeting effectiveness.			x
2.	Advise executives on training and development activities to improve speakers and meetings.			x
3.	Advise supervisors on how to cover safety/loss control effectively in meetings.		x	x
4.	Provide information and aids to help supervisors conduct good safety meetings.		x	x
5.	Establish the organization's group meeting performance standards.		x	
6.	Audit performance of groups and individuals to the established standards.			x
7.	Communicate group meeting audit results to all levels of management.			x
8.	Coach meeting leaders for performance improvement.		x	x
9.	Reinforce desired group meeting performance.	x	x	x
10.	Study and use effective meeting leadership skills (for before, during and after meetings).	x	x	x
11.	Use systematic self-evaluation of meeting behaviors for performance management.	x	x	x
12.	Use evaluation feedback from others to improve meeting skills.	x	x	x
13.	Help others improve their speaking and meeting skills by giving them performance feedback.	x	x	x
14.	Use the 5P talk technique.	x	x	x
15.	Practice using the Effective Talk Outline for improving presentations.	x	x	x
16.	Practice "the art of asking questions."	x	x	x
17.	Practice using a variety of discussion leading methods, e.g., Lecture & Discussion, Question & Answer Discussion, Pro & Con Discussion and Small Group Discussion.	x	x	x
18.	Take an active leadership role in safety meetings.	x	x	
19.	Maintain safety/loss control meeting records.	x		x
20.	Motivate people to accomplish safety/loss control results by keeping them informed about matters affecting those results.	x	x	x
21.	Motivate people to accomplish safety/loss control results by giving them opportunities for positive participation in matters affecting those results.	x	x	x
22.	Put the Utilization Principle to work for safety/loss control communication.	x	x	x
23.	Model desired meeting behaviors.	x	x	x

CHAPTER 10

PERSONAL COMMUNICATIONS

"The ordinary human being would like to receive simple and intelligent instruction in what he is expected to do, how it can be done and what constitutes a job well done."
— Lawrence Appley
   Former President,
   American Management Association

INTRODUCTION

A survey of successful executives determined which management activities provided the biggest return on the investment of time. The two activities which led the list (see *Figure 10-1*) were to "listen actively" and to "give effective instructions." Other highly ranked activities were to communicate decisions, speak effectively, explain work, use feedback and write effectively. Thus, more than one-third of the critical management competencies are in communications, and most of these involve communication with individuals.

In the highly influential article, "Factors in Successful Occupational Safety Programs," Alexander Cohen reviewed the relevant research on the important factors in successful safety programs. The two most influential and dominant factors were (1) evidence of a strong management commitment to safety and (2) frequent close contacts between workers, supervisors and members of management on safety matters. Also important was a training emphasis on early indoctrination and follow-up instruction.

The U.S. Bureau of Labor Statistics (BLS) reports that in a recent year 48% of workers injured had been on the job less than one year. New workers are more likely to be hurt because they often lack one vital tool to protect themselves — information. Other accident data by the BLS indicated that of employees...

- hurt while using scaffolds, 27% said they received no information on safety requirements for installing the kind of scaffold on which they were injured

- who suffered head injuries, 71% said they had no instruction concerning hard hats

---

20 CRITICAL MANAGERIAL COMPETENCIES

Importance Rating	Survey Rank & Competency
Super Critical	1. Listen Actively
	2. Give Clear, Effective Instructions
	3. Accept Your Share of Responsibility for Problems
	4. Identify Real Problem
Highly Critical	5. Manage Time, Set Priorities
	6. Give Recognition for Excellent Performance
	7. Communicate Decisions to Employees
	8. Communicate Effectively (Orally)
	9. Shift Priorities, if Necessary
	10. Explain Work
	11. Obtain and Provide Feedback in Two-Way Communication Sessions
Critical	12. Write Effectively
	13. Prepare Action Plan
	14. Define Job Qualification
	15. Effectively Implement Organizational Change
	16. Explain and Use Cost Reduction Methods
	17. Prepare and Use Cost Reduction Methods
	18. Develop Written Goals
	19. Justify New Personnel and Capital Equipment
	20. Participate in Seminars and Read

Figure 10-1

- hurt while servicing equipment, 61% said they were not informed about lockout procedures

- injured while operating power saws, 19% said no safety training on the equipment had been provided.

The purpose of this chapter is to help you communicate with individual workers in five key areas of your day-to-day responsibilities. Specifically, we will look at

- Individual Job Orientation

- Job/Task Instruction

- Planned Personal Contacts

- Key Point Tips

- Job Performance Coaching

The competence gained not only will help you in these important responsibilities, but also will provide a justifiable confidence in handling other situations which require one-to-one communications. This competence is of great importance in the successful handling of many situations where it is not feasible or desirable to get people together in groups. Competence in personal communication skills is every supervisor's best tool for helping his or her people perform profitably.

INDIVIDUAL JOB ORIENTATION

Why Orient?

Numerous safety studies show that new workers are almost twice as likely to have an accident as experienced workers. Also, companies with formal orientation for all new hires have average workers' compensation "modification rates" 25% lower than companies without formal orientation for new hires. Employees who are new to the job and to the work environment, are at an especially dangerous point. Effective supervisors use proper orientation to help new workers get safely through that critical period.

There are also human relations reasons for new employee orientation. Remember when you were brand new on the job? How you felt? How you wanted to "put your best foot forward"? How anxious you were to succeed? How mystifying things seemed to be? The kinds of things you wanted to know about?

Orientation should take these needs and feelings into consideration. Good orientation requires empathy — the ability to put yourself inside the other person's skin, to see things from his or her viewpoint. It should not be a one-sided presentation of company facts and figures. It should be a two-way process of reaching mutual understanding, welcoming the new person into the organization, helping her or him to become familiar with the work environment and laying the groundwork for the desired knowledge, skills and attitudes.

Every supervisor should keep in mind that "first impressions tend to be lasting impressions," and "you never get a second chance to make a good first impression." The orientation process provides a unique opportunity to start building a solid supervisor-worker relationship, to let your behavior show your care and concern for the new employee. Think to yourself, "What kind of mental image do I want this person to have of me?" Then work to establish that image.

The Who Of Orientation

Two key questions here are (1) Who should be oriented? and (2) Who should do the orienting?

Those who should have the benefit of a good orientation are

- The person who is brand new as an employee of the organization

- The employee who just transferred to your plant, office or work site

- The individual who is returning to a type of work she or he has not done for quite some time.

The type and extent of the orientation depend on the situation, the employee's background and the nature of the job. For example, the new employee needs the most complete orientation, while the person returning to the work may need only a refresher.

Who should do the orienting? This depends on the type of orientation and on the organizational structure. Although they sometimes flow together, normally there are two types: (1) Company (general) orientation and (2) Job (specific) orientation. Often, the company orientation is conducted by one or more staff persons (such as Personnel, Safety and Health, Fire Protection and Employee Development) and/or a member of upper management.

However, the *individual job orientation* is where the employee's immediate supervisor can really shine! Here is the opportunity to get the person "started off on the right foot," to show him or her that management cares enough to spend some time just being helpful, to avoid letting wrong ideas and habits get started and to take a giant step toward helping the person do the job safely, efficiently and correctly.

When Should Orientation Occur?

Because the job and the environment are new, probably confusing, and possibly hazardous, orientation should take place before the person starts doing the work. This will reduce the new employee's stress and increase safe, productive performance. The length of the orientation may range from as little as an hour up to several days. It should be long enough to achieve the critical communications, with sessions short enough to be absorbed.

How To Conduct Orientations

The first step is to prepare yourself for the orientation. The values to be gained and the importance of this activity to the new employee fully justify the preparation time. This means setting aside a definite amount of time and arranging for the best possible place. The place may be in your office, in a meeting room, on the shop floor, in the field or any combination of such places. If feasible, it should include a tour of the work area. Preparation includes getting some information about the new employee, notifying others in the work group that a new person will be joining them and getting ready any tools or special equipment which the person will be using. Many companies find it valuable to develop a checklist, such as shown in *Figure 10-2*, as a guide to ensure that important items are not omitted.

The second step is to put the person at ease, by showing your interest in the individual as a human being (not just another tool for getting the job done). If you can do so in an interested, natural, friendly way, get him or her to tell you things such as nickname, family, work experiences and spare time activities. Letting a person talk about himself or herself (a subject he or she is really interested in and knows something about) helps:

- to relax the employee and get two-way communications started

- to show your interest in the employee as a person

- to give you some insight and understanding about the person.

This can be done in a few minutes and is time well spent.

Another important part of preparing the employee for the orientation is to talk about the importance of the job she or he will be doing. Explain where this job fits in, and what contribution it makes to the overall purpose of the organization. Show how it is important to the success of enterprise. This is a first step in building job pride and a feeling of belonging to a team in every new or transferred employee.

The third step is to perform the orientation. It may involve personal presentations, discussions, programmed instruction, reference materials, quizzes, movies, videotapes, sound-and-slides, demonstrations, exercises, exhibits, guided tours and so forth.

Step four is to hold one or more follow-up sessions to check comprehension, retention, questions and suggestions. Some supervisors use the 1-1-1 guide, with planned follow-up contacts one week, one month and one quarter after the initial orientation.

Individual job orientation does take some investment of supervisory time. But, in the long run, nothing will pay you greater dividends than getting every employee started off right. Orientation is a worthwhile investment in improved morale, reduced turnover, greater efficiency and better loss control.

PROPER JOB/TASK INSTRUCTION

Why Instruct?

In 1981, the American Society of Training and Development surveyed over 7,500 supervisors to determine how their employees are trained. *Figure 10-3* shows the results of the study. At least three conclusions can be drawn. One is that a combination of approaches is widely used. The second is that more than half of the supervisors personally provide the training. The third is that a lot of training is done by fellow employees.

ORIENTATION CHECKLIST: SAFETY SECTION
NEW AND TRANSFERRED EMPLOYEES

Employee's Name	Occupation or Job Title	Date

TO BE GIVEN BY PLANT SAFETY PERSONNEL

Items Covered	Initial	Items Covered	Initial
Plant Safety Peformance Past and Present Importance of Employee in the Program		Fire Prevention Program	
Plant Medical Department and Program		How to Report a Fire	
Location of Dispensary		Emergency Alarm Signal	
Workers' Compensation		Location and Use of Fire Equipment	
How to Report Accidents and Incidents		Plant Entrance and Exits (Security - Parking)	
Plant Safety Committees		Traffic Regulations	
Plant Emergency Protection Plan		Locking Out Procedure	
Personal Protective Equipment - Hat, Glasses, Goggles (No Contacts)		Volunteer Emergency Team	
Required Permits - (Entry, Fire, Water, Burning, Vehicular)		Off-The-Job Safety Program	
Hazard Communication Program		Confined Space Entry	

TO BE GIVEN BY SUPERVISION

Items Covered	Initial	Items Covered	Initial
Hazards That Exist In — Department Area		Task Procedures	
Safety Rules For — Department Area		Safety Tools and Equipment	
Fire Prevention Rules For — Department Area		Safe Way to do His/Her Job	
Smoking and No Smoking Areas		Location and Use of Fire Extinguishers	
How to Report Accidents and Incidents		Location and Use of First Aid Equipment	
How to Report Substandard Conditions		Emergency Showers and Water Fountains	
How to Obtain Personal Protective Equipment		Housekeeping	
How to Use Required Personal Protective Equipment		Personal Hygiene and Cleanliness	
Radio Systems & Procedures		Department Safety Promotion	
Standard Operating Procedure Manual			

THE ABOVE NAMED EMPLOYEE HAS THE NECESSARY PERSONAL PROTECTIVE EQUIPMENT AND HAS BEEN INSTRUCTED IN THE SAFETY ITEMS CHECKED ABOVE.

For Plant Safety	Department Supervisor	Recipient of Instruction

Figure 10-2

How supervisors train their employees:

90% have them work along with experienced employees.

57% say "I personally provide the training."

42% provide special training from company training departments.

27% provide training from outside the company.

5% provide no special training.

Figure 10-3

It would be difficult to overstate the importance of the instruction people get in how to do their work properly. Consider the actual case of the eighteen-year-old girl on the first day of her first job after high school. Her ring finger was amputated by the machine she was assigned to operate. Due to inadequate job instruction she will never be able to wear her wedding band on the proper finger. Consider the case of the construction worker who was decapitated his first day on the job when he got too close to a trenching machine and slipped into the trench with it. Again, the basic cause was lack of job instruction. *Figure 10-4* shows the damage done to a 120-ton Wabco, entrusted to a 19-year-old whose previous experience was limited to a five-ton farm truck. The company had decided to eliminate its job training program and hire only "experienced" drivers.

These actual incidents could be multiplied by thousands. They dramatically point up the need for proper job instruction, not only for safety, but also for productivity, cost control and quality. Your effectiveness as a manager/supervisor/leader depends on how well each member of your team understands and carries out his or her job tasks. So, your personal supervisory success is directly related to your skills of teaching-training-instructing.

Figure 10-5, "Proper Job Instruction Problem Sheet," shows four basic areas of job performance and specific problems which might arise in each area as a result of inadequate job instruction. It could be helpful to complete this checklist, to pinpoint some of your problems and identify those which might be solved by Proper Job Instruction. Giving effective instruction may well be your best supervisory technique for helping people perform efficiently, safely and productively.

Figure 10-4: The Cost Of No Instruction

The Who of Job/Task Instruction

Who should receive proper job/task instruction? All people who are assigned work involving tasks that they have not done before, or for which they may need refresher instruction.

Who should be trained in proper job/task instruction technique? The usual answer is "supervisors." And it's true that every supervisor should be an expert in instructing others how to perform critical jobs/tasks efficiently, safely and productively. But they are not the only ones. As shown in the survey results *(Figure 10-3),* a great deal of on-the-job instruction involves workers instructing other workers. To ensure that this job/task instruction is most effective, these worker-instructors also should be well trained in the technique.

What Is The Best Technique?

Proper job/task instruction is "how to get a person to do a job/task correctly, quickly, conscientiously and safely." Notice how individualized this is (**a** person to do **a** job/task). Multiply that by the numbers of people and jobs in your area and you can get *every* person to do all of his or her tasks effectively; you can get *every* job done correctly, quickly, conscientiously and safely. This takes some attention, time and effort... but it's the answer to many of your problems as a supervisor.

Effective instruction is a systematic substitute for trial-and-error learning; a reliable replacement for hit-or-miss instruction. Its two basic goals are

1. To help *motivate* the worker to do the task properly.
2. To make sure the worker knows *how to do* the job properly.

The best technique happens to be an old technique. It goes by many names, e.g., Proper Job Instruction (PJI), Effective Job Instruction, the Four-Step Method of Instruction and Job Instruction Training (or JIT as it was known when it was first developed, at the time of World War II). It was developed to meet the huge training need created when about one-third of our civilian labor force was placed on new jobs, and had to be trained...effectively! It was used in well over 10,000 organizations to train hundreds of thousands of people. It worked. Men and women from all walks of life — farmers, housewives, apartment dwellers — entered shops and factories for the first time in their lives. They effectively learned to do jobs they had never heard of before; jobs involving drill presses, rivet guns, airplane hydraulic systems and so on. The technique has stood the test of time and lived this long for only one reason — it works.

The four steps are easy to remember: Motivate - Tell and Show - Test - Check.

1. MOTIVATE
   - Put learner at ease
   - Find out what the learner knows about the job
   - Position learner properly
   - Build learner's interest
   - Emphasize the importance of the job and the learner's performance

2. TELL AND SHOW
   - Demonstrate the operation
   - Use step-by-step approach
   - Stress key points
   - Instruct clearly and completely

3. TEST
   - Have learner tell and show
   - Have learner explain key points
   - Ask questions and correct or prevent errors
   - Continue until you know the learner knows

4. CHECK
   - Tell learner who to go to for help
   - Put learner on his or her own
   - Follow-up often; answer questions; review key points
   - Reinforce positive parts of performance

Supervisors and others sometimes try to teach a task by simply telling the learner how to do it. But "TELLING is not TEACHING." Most people simply do not learn enough by being told; some tasks are very hard to describe in words; and some work sounds awfully complicated when we hear it described in words. Try, for instance, to teach someone how to tie a necktie just by talking. As reflected in *Figure 10-6,* studies show that the TELLING method is only about 20% effective.

PROPER JOB INSTRUCTION

PROBLEM SHEET

Here are some problems that Proper Job Instruction has helped to solve in production plants. Do you know of similar problems in your departments? Please check in Column 1 those problems you may have observed in your department. In Column 2, check those you feel could be solved or at least helped by good job instruction.

	OBSERVED (Col. 1)	COULD BE SOLVED BY P.J.I. (Col. 2)
PRODUCTION PROBLEMS		
Deliveries delayed because of errors and mistakes by people making the parts	☐	☐
People don't know their jobs	☐	☐
Mix-ups in trucking service	☐	☐
Parts returned by other departments because they were not made properly	☐	☐
Operators have special problems because of engineering changes	☐	☐
Poor planning	☐	☐
People have difficulty in getting up to production on new type of equipment	☐	☐
Aisles too congested	☐	☐
Excessive wear and tear on equipment	☐	☐
SAFETY PROBLEMS		
Safety equipment not used properly	☐	☐
Material not piled properly	☐	☐
Poor shop housekeeping	☐	☐
Don't know safety rules	☐	☐
Employees don't know hazards of their jobs	☐	☐
Employees take unnecessary chances	☐	☐
Minor injuries not reported	☐	☐
QUALITY PROBLEMS		
Meeting inspection standards	☐	☐
Too much scrap or rework	☐	☐
Jigs and gauges not used properly	☐	☐
Not following specifications	☐	☐
Too much left to operator's judgment	☐	☐
PERSONNEL PROBLEMS		
Workers leave for other plants — couldn't "get the hang" of the job	☐	☐
New workers lack experience in mechanical things	☐	☐
Lack of interest in the work	☐	☐
Workers want transfers — think they can "make out" better on other jobs	☐	☐
Claim to have good experience, but don't "come through"	☐	☐
Too much time to get up to production	☐	☐
Instructed improperly	☐	☐
Can't get experienced workers any more	☐	☐
Workers get discouraged learning the job	☐	☐

Most shop supervisors say that somewhere around 80% of their problems could be solved or at least helped if they had a better trained workforce.

Figure 10-5

```
┌─────────────────────────────────────────┐
│  LEARNERS TEND TO REMEMBER...           │
│                                          │
│  10% of what they read                   │
│  20% of what they hear                   │
│  30% of what they see                    │
│  40% of what they see and hear           │
│  70% of what they say as they talk       │
│  90% of what they say as they do a thing │
└─────────────────────────────────────────┘
```

Figure 10-6

Showing alone is not very effective either (only about 30%). The learner may not know what to look for, is likely to see the operation upside down or backwards, does not know what the key points are, and does not know the *why* of things. Still, countless employees may merely be shown ("watch me") how the job is done — then must go through the frustrating and costly trial-and-error process. By itself, "SHOWING is not TEACHING." For example, try to teach someone how to tie a bowline knot just by letting the learner watch you do it.

While learners tend to remember about 20% of what they hear and about 30% of what they see, they tend to remember about 50% of what they both see and hear. So a combination of TELLING and SHOWING gets better results than either alone. But even 50% is not good enough!

```
┌─────────────────────────────────────────┐
│  IF THE LEARNER HASN'T LEARNED,          │
│  THE INSTRUCTOR HASN'T TAUGHT.           │
└─────────────────────────────────────────┘
```

Learners tend to remember about 70% of what they say as they talk in a learning situation, and about 90% of what they say as they do a thing. This is why the TEST and CHECK steps are vital to effective instruction. In the four-step method...

...you *tell* the learner; the learner *hears*

...you *show* the learner; the learner *sees*

...you *demonstrate* and *explain*; the learner *sees* and *hears*

...the learner *explains* to you, and *hears what he or she says*

...the learner *tells and shows*, and hears what he or she *says while doing the task*

In effect, the learner HEARS, the learner SEES, the learner EXPLAINS, the learner DOES, the learner LEARNS.

This technique is easy to learn and to use. Here are four guidelines:

1. **HAVE A PLAN**
   - Knowledge of the job to be taught
   - How much skill you expect the learner to have, and how soon

2. **BREAK DOWN THE JOB**
   - List the important steps
   - Highlight key points
     (Refer to Chapter 7, "Job/Task Analyses, Procedures and Practices," to see how valuable a job breakdown can be as a teaching tool.)

3. **HAVE EVERYTHING READY AND ORDERLY**
   - Proper equipment, materials, supplies and environment
   - Arranged as the employee will be expected to keep things

4. **PRACTICE**
   - Check the effectiveness of your teaching technique
   - Review and refresh your knowledge and skills periodically.

The importance of having things ready and orderly should not be overlooked. By considering the work environment, the tools, machines and all aspects of the task, you can create a "success-prone situation" in which the learner will learn more quickly and begin to achieve job satisfaction much sooner.

PLANNED PERSONAL CONTACTS

Basic Concepts

Whether or not you have planned *group* contacts (e.g., safety meetings, toolbox talks, tailgate sessions), you should have planned *individual* contacts with each employee. Individual contacts are an excellent supplement to group meetings. And they are especially critical when conditions do not permit getting people together for group meetings.

Many personal contacts are spontaneous. They are not planned, but just happen in the normal course of events. These informal contacts provide hundreds of chances to give key point tips and reinforce desired attitudes and behavior. However, these chance contacts should be supplemented with planned personal contacts. Planned individual contacts give you opportunities for:

- personalizing critical aspects of safety, quality, productivity and cost control for each worker

- building better safety awareness and attitudes

- showing each worker your personal concern for proper practices and conditions

- improving your supervisor-worker relationships

They enable you to make best use of the time you invest in direct contact with individual workers.

Using *safety contacts* as an example, a planned personal contact is an intentional get-together of a supervisor and a worker to discuss a critical safety topic related to the employee's work. This enables covering a topic most suitable to the individual, and tailoring the discussion to that person and his or her own work — a specific topic for a specific person doing a specific job in a specific situation.

These contacts should be frequent enough to influence the person's attitudes, knowledge and/or skills. The specific number will vary with the number of employees the supervisor has, how large an area they work in, and similar factors. A contact with each person each week would be good. A minimum standard should be at least one planned contact with each worker each month.

Key Steps For Contacts

Five key steps in conducting a planned personal contact are: (1) pick a critical topic, (2) prepare the contact, (3) make the contact, (4) record the contact and (5) follow-up.

Pick a critical topic - Make it specific. Make it pertinent. It is useless to discuss "safety precautions for chain saws" with someone who does not work around them. To be effective, the topic must relate meaningfully to the person and his or her work. If you pick a safety rule, for example, pick one which is important in the employee's work, one where violations have caused accidents or close calls or one which has significant potential for loss control by that person. In addition to rules and regulations, you can get good leads on topics from your experience and records on inspections, job/task analyses and procedures, investigations, job observations, group meetings and safety promotion campaigns.

Prepare the contact - While it need not take much time, preparation is vital. On 3" x 5" cards, for instance, jot down any key facts or figures you want to use. Pinpoint the main thought you want to emphasize. Decide how to personalize the contact for the individual. Select visual aids if they will help the person to "see what you mean." Think of a key point phrase or prescription to leave in the worker's mind.

Make the contact - Introduce the topic by letting the person know what it is and why it is important. In discussing it, don't just tell but also *ask* and *listen*. Make it truly two-way communication, a mutual discussion. This mutual discussion is vital to the purpose of planned personal contacts. Summarize or conclude by re-emphasizing the main point and giving a prescription for action. Introduce - discuss - summarize.

Record the contact - Simple records can be helpful. They show what you have covered in your planned personal contacts with each person, and when. They serve as a management control tool to ensure meeting the standards for contacts. They enable your analysis of time lapses and topic gaps, to help you plan additional contacts and related communications. (A simple record form is shown in *Figure 10-7*.)

Follow-up - If you should get additional information back to the person, do it as quickly as you can. If you agreed to relay information or suggestions to others, not only do it but also let the worker know that you did it. Use the information from your contacts and records to help guide your ongoing communication and coaching with individuals.

KEY POINT TIPS

"Key points" are those vital bits of information that make or break the job; special tricks of the trade that make the task more efficient; the feel or knack that is the mark of a pro; critical points of quality, productivity, cost control or safety. "Tip" means just what it does in everyday life; a piece of information given in an attempt to be helpful; a small gift; a hint or suggestion. Key point tipping then, is the organized process of giving employees helpful hints, suggestions, reminders or tips about key quality, production, cost or safety points in their work.

PLANNED PERSONAL CONTACTS

DATE	PERSON	TOPIC

DEPARTMENT:
SUPERVISOR:
SIGNATURE:

(Front)

- PLANNED PERSONAL CONTACTS -

1. PICK A CRITICAL TOPIC

- Important to the specific person on the specific job
- A source of actual or potential loss
- A target for improved efficiency - safety - productivity

2. PREPARE THE CONTACT

- Note key facts and figures
- Pinpoint the main message
- Decide how to personalize it
- Prepare to show as well as tell
- Develop a prescription

3. MAKE THE CONTACT

- Introduce: explain what the topic is and why it is important
- Discuss: tell - show - ask - listen
- Summarize: re-emphasize main point and give prescription for action

4. RECORD THE CONTACT

- Keep track of what you have covered, with whom and when
- Use as evidence of accomplishment
- Use in planning additional communications

5. FOLLOW-UP

- Get promised information for the person
- Contact others if necessary to relay information, suggestions or requests
- Tie additional communications in with the contact topic

(Back)

Figure 10-7

Both people and jobs have individual differences. Every person is unique. Every job has its own special hazards, circumstances and problems. You can take maximum preventive action only if you zero in on each specific hazard or problem, face-to-face with the person doing the job — at the job scene - as the job is about to be done. Ask yourself the question, "If this particular person is going to have a serious problem on this particular job, what is it most likely to be?" Reach down into the well of your experience with this job and your knowledge of this person, his or her work habits and experience. Think of the *specific* person, the *specific* task, the *specific* most probable problem and the most important *specific* preventive action. Give that employee the benefit of your knowledge and experience; give a key point tip.

The best tips are short tips. And they should always be given as reminders rather than formal instruction. Here are some examples:

Safety tip - "Jerry, remember to tie in the top of that ladder. I'd hate to see you fall and hurt yourself."

Production tip - "On this set-up, Maxine, it will save you a lot of time and rework if you always follow the pre-operation checklist."

Cost tip - "Frank, I know how you hate to see anything wasted. A key step to waste control here is to use those rods all the way down to one and one-half inches."

Quality tip - "Don't forget, Becky, this batch gets only 0.4% acid additive. Otherwise, it won't meet the specifications you and I both want for this important customer."

Simple isn't it? But it can have a tremendous impact if it is done by *every* supervisor, with *every* worker on *every* critical task. Not only is it another avenue to improved safety, production, cost control and quality, but it's also an excellent human relations tool. If you go back and check each of the examples just given, you will notice that each tip reflects a genuine interest in the attitudes, desires or well-being of the employee.

Key point tipping is a specific, specialized contact technique that...

   ...is easy to learn
   ...takes hardly any time
   ...costs practically nothing
   ...contributes significantly to safe, high quality, injury-free, damage-free production

It gives you another top-notch tool of personal communication. It makes full use of the motivational power of repetition, reminders and reinforcement. It is not a substitute for training, or for any other part of your supervisory job. Rather, it is an added tool in your leadership kit. It can help you get efficiency, safety and productivity while improving employee morale. So make it a spontaneous habit — give a key point tip with every critical task.

JOB PERFORMANCE COACHING

Fundamentals

Job performance coaching is the day-by-day actions you take to help your people perform as well as possible. Effective coaching is "leadership in action" ... motivating, communicating and developing people. It is "management control in action," built on the activities of work identification, standards, measurement, evaluation, correction and commendation. Effective job coaching is an excellent means for building better relationships between you and the members of your work team.

As a supervisor you are, in a sense, a coach for your team of subordinates. Each member of the team has to know what is expected of him or her, how he or she is doing and what he or she should do to improve. They look to you for guidance. The biggest part of your job is to supply that guidance and lead your team to a winning performance...efficient, safe, productive performance.

Remember, the professional coach not only directs field operations on game day, but also tries to improve the knowledge, attitudes and skills of each team member — *every* day of the season. The coach does not get top team performance by complaining about the shortcomings and inefficiencies of the players. The good coach gets winning performances by *coaching* — helping team members overcome their performance deficiencies and make best use of their strong points.

Job performance coaching is based on a simple, basic principle that every employee has a right to know...

- what his or her job is

- the job performance yardsticks

- how he or she is doing

- specific steps to improvement

Just as you want and need to know these things about your job, so do your subordinates about their jobs. When they don't, the consequences are almost always unpleasant. For instance:

- When people don't really know what their jobs are, the results are confusion, wheel-spinning and losses such as waste, damage and injuries.

- When people don't know their performance yardsticks, the results are guesswork, wrong priorities, misdirected energies or hit-and-miss efforts.

- When people don't know how they are doing, the results are low motivation, poor morale and measurement by mind reading.

- When people don't know specific steps to improvement, the results are glittering generalities, procrastination and status quo.

You can get a good start on analyzing how well you coach by searching your conscience for honest answers to the following questions. "How well do I...

...define what is expected?"
...aid performance opportunity?"
...observe and appraise performance?"
...provide performance feedback?"
...take corrective measures?"
...reinforce positive performance?"
...emphasize goals, results and growth?"

Figure 10-8 enables a systematic self-appraisal of 33 aspects of these seven questions.

> You not only can do a helpful self-appraisal of coaching practices by doing the *Figure 10-8* checklist in writing, but also can gain a much greater understanding of the coaching process.

Corrective Coaching

Corrective coaching is what you do to help get employees back on the track; to change from deficiency to proficiency; to solve performance problems. As in any problem solving (see Chapter 13, "Problem Solving Teams and Techniques"), you must first pinpoint the problem and its causes. *Figure 10-9* summarizes the 10-step system for analyzing substandard performance. It includes many aspects of coaching and performance management such as:

- providing performance feedback
- communicating goals and standards
- removing performance obstacles
- providing training and/or guided practice
- transferring or terminating the employee
- re-designing the work
- conducting corrective coaching

The corrective coaching technique has these five steps: (1) get the person's agreement that a problem exists, (2) mutually explore alternative solutions, (3) mutually agree on corrective action, (4) follow-up and measure results and (5) deal with broken contract and/or reinforce desired behavior.

Get the person's agreement that a problem exists - Believe it or not, this step is often bypassed. But it is the most critical step and may involve about half of the coaching discussion time. The supervisor should not assume that the employee recognizes that his or her behavior is a problem. The employee may be doing one thing, but think he or she is doing something else. The employee may not be aware that his or her performance is substandard. Or, the employee may know that he or she is doing something wrong, but not perceive it as a "problem."

The problem will not be solved until the person agrees that there *is* a problem. ("So I'm absent three or four days a month ... what difference does it make?") To be convinced that a problem exists, a person must:

1. *Realize the consequences to others of what he or she is failing to do or is doing wrong.* For example, the worker must perceive that his or her substandard performance interrupts service to customers; requires co-workers to work harder; disrupts work schedules; causes extra costs for temporary help or overtime pay; results in accidents, waste, customer complaints and so on.

2. *Realize what the personal consequences will be if his or her behavior doesn't change.* The worker must perceive the probability of punishment and/or loss of advantages. For example, he or she may be denied preferred work assignments; may not receive a raise; may lose out on promotional opportunities; may be denied participation in prestigious projects; may be transferred, demoted or fired.

JOB PERFORMANCE COACHING PRACTICES
CHECKLIST

1. Poorly: Critical Need For Improvement
2. Fairly Well: Moderate Need For Improvement
3. Very Well: Little Need For Improvement

1. *HOW WELL DO I DEFINE WHAT IS EXPECTED?*

a. Describe job responsibilities and duties?	1 2 3
b. Describe performance goals & standards; measurement yardsticks, results expected?	1 2 3
c. Use appropriate written descriptions to supplement discussions?	1 2 3
d. Model desired behavior?	1 2 3

2. *HOW WELL DO I AID PERFORMANCE OPPORTUNITY?*

a. Ensure effective job instruction and skill training?	1 2 3
b. Delegate duties and responsibilities?	1 2 3
c. Provide proper materials, equipment and environment?	1 2 3
d. Coordinate required services of other people and departments?	1 2 3

3. *HOW WELL DO I OBSERVE AND APPRAISE PERFORMANCE?*

a. Use both informal and planned performance observation?	1 2 3
b. Review records and results?	1 2 3
c. Concentrate on objective, measurable, job-related factors such as attendance, accuracy, quantity and quality of work and other things covered by performance standards?	1 2 3
d. Take notes and use appropriate forms?	1 2 3
e. Evaluate significance of performance variances from standards?	1 2 3
f. Include both plus and minus factors?	1 2 3

4. *HOW WELL DO I PROVIDE PERFORMANCE FEEDBACK?*

a. Provide feedback on performance, problems and progress?	1 2 3
b. Use incidents; get down to cases, discuss performance, not personality?	1 2 3
c. Use questions; ensure two-way communication, learn to listen and listen to learn?	1 2 3
d. Include significant pluses and minuses?	1 2 3
e. Seek basic causes ... reasons for results?	1 2 3
f. Strive for agreement on how the person is doing and why?	1 2 3

5. *HOW WELL DO I TAKE CORRECTIVE MEASURES?*

a. Develop specific improvement plans?	1 2 3
b. Correct by reinstruction, reminders, reviews and refreshers?	1 2 3
c. Use punishment as last resort?	1 2 3
d. Use problem-solving approach?	1 2 3

6. *HOW WELL DO I REINFORCE POSITIVE PERFORMANCE?*

a. Give rewards on the basis of results and improvement?	1 2 3
b. Give immediate recognition for desired (efficient, safe, productive) behavior?	1 2 3
c. Emphasize attention, approval, assistance, success, satisfaction and support?	1 2 3
d. Make a habit of reinforcing positive performance, to make positive performance a habit?	1 2 3

7. *HOW WELL DO I EMPHASIZE GOALS, RESULTS AND GROWTH?*

a. Motivate with goals that ...	
...are specific, clear and communicated?	1 2 3
...are relatively simple and short-range?	1 2 3
b. Motivate with goals that ...	
...are realistically attainable?	1 2 3
...provide challenge or "stretch?"	1 2 3
c. Coach on the basis of significant, verifiable job results?	1 2 3
d. Help employees learn from experience by tracing performance from consequences back to causes?	1 2 3
e. Make my coaching goal "to help people perform as effectively as possible" ...to grow at work?	1 2 3

Figure 10-8

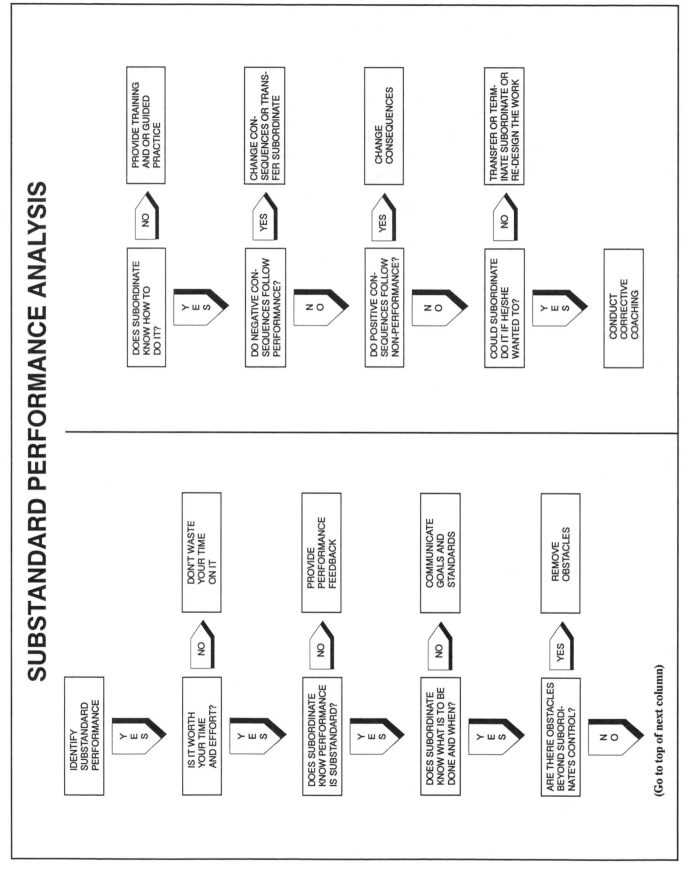

SUBSTANDARD PERFORMANCE ANALYSIS

IDENTIFY SUBSTANDARD PERFORMANCE
— YES →

IS IT WORTH YOUR TIME AND EFFORT?
— NO → DON'T WASTE YOUR TIME ON IT
— YES →

DOES SUBORDINATE KNOW PERFORMANCE IS SUBSTANDARD?
— NO → PROVIDE PERFORMANCE FEEDBACK
— YES →

DOES SUBORDINATE KNOW WHAT IS TO BE DONE AND WHEN?
— NO → COMMUNICATE GOALS AND STANDARDS
— YES →

ARE THERE OBSTACLES BEYOND SUBORDI-NATE'S CONTROL?
— YES → REMOVE OBSTACLES
— NO →

(Go to top of next column)

DOES SUBORDINATE KNOW HOW TO DO IT?
— NO → PROVIDE TRAINING AND OR GUIDED PRACTICE
— YES →

DO NEGATIVE CON-SEQUENCES FOLLOW PERFORMANCE?
— YES → CHANGE CON-SEQUENCES OR TRANS-FER SUBORDINATE
— NO →

DO POSITIVE CON-SEQUENCES FOLLOW NON-PERFORMANCE?
— YES → CHANGE CONSEQUENCES
— NO →

COULD SUBORDINATE DO IT IF HE/SHE WANTED TO?
— NO → TRANSFER OR TERM-INATE SUBORDINATE OR RE-DESIGN THE WORK
— YES →

CONDUCT CORRECTIVE COACHING

Figure 10-9

Getting agreement that a problem exists is more than simply telling the person there's a problem. It is discussing it until the employee actually says something like, "Yes, I agree, that is a problem."

Mutually explore alternative solutions - Supervisor and worker should explore various *specific* solution possibilities. If the problem is "being absent three or four days a month," a proposed solution such as "reduce absenteeism" is worthless. Solutions must be specific, must be behavioral, must indicate *how* the goal will be met. For example:

- Schedule my fishing trips for evenings, holidays or weekends.

- Use a nursery for the one day a week that my spouse cannot be with the children.

- Stop watching the late, late show.

- Schedule my doctor appointments outside of my regular work hours.

- Use the bus rather than the unreliable car pool.

A solution is not "I'll try to do better." Solutions involve specific things the person will do differently to eliminate the problem.

Mutually agree on corrective action - The previous step should have been a free-flowing, brainstorming exploration — unhampered by judgements of the pro's and con's of each idea. Now comes the time to judge and choose. The results should be a mutual agreement on *what* will be done, and *when*. The supervisor should get a clear commitment from the worker.

Follow-up and measure results - Lack of systematic follow-up is an all too common reason why supervisors fail in trying to correct employees' substandard performances. A "promise" of performance is not "performance." Follow-up is simply seeing whether the person is doing what he or she should do — whether performance is up to par. Measurement and documentation of specifics are essential to good follow-up.

Deal with broken contract and/or reinforce desired behavior - If the person has *not* done what he or she agreed to do, by the time it was supposed to be done, take the action that you said you would take. If appropriate, discuss the lack of performance improvement, the reasons for it, and the specifics of a new "contract."

Reinforce the desired behavior as soon as practical after it occurs. Whenever the person's performance *does* improve, even part way toward the goals, recognize the achievement and encourage continued improvement.

If you haven't tried this five-step system of corrective coaching, you are probably enduring performance problems unnecessarily. This is a proven approach to successful corrective coaching. Give it a fair try and you will find that it works.

Developmental Coaching

As a supervisor/leader, you get paid for what your subordinates do. So your most important goal is to help subordinates do the best job they can possibly do. This requires both corrective coaching (just discussed) and developmental coaching. Developmental coaching is what you do to help keep employees on the right track; to maintain optimum performance; to help them learn, grow and make progress. It is personnel development in action at the front line.

Developmental coaching is based on a number of important beliefs, such as the following five.

1. **People want to succeed** - The belief that most people want to do the best job they can; that they want to know how they are doing and what can be done to improve their performance and potential; that people really do not want to fail.

2. **Leadership climate is important** - The belief that most people need and appreciate help in their development, that they do not reach their full potential unless a proper climate is established and assistance is given to their personal development.

3. **Development is personal** - The belief that development is an individual, personal process; that all development efforts should be based on the individual's own specific abilities and needs.

4. **Improving present job performance is basic** - The belief that development is best approached from the standpoint of helping each person do his or her *present* job better; that this is the first step toward increased effectiveness and, coincidentally, preparing the person for greater responsibility.

5. **Communication is vital** - The belief that we all want to know how our supervisor views our performance, and that the supervisor wants to know how we view the situation; that we need to get together

and work out answers to questions such as: What are the *responsibilities* of the job? What *indicators* should we use to measure job performance? How well is the job being done? What improvement *goals* can we agree on? What *action steps* will we take to achieve these goals?

Development coaching centers on these personnel development twins: performance appraisal and performance discussion.

Performance appraisal is simply a systematic evaluation of a person's job performance and potential, made by that person's immediate supervisor. It's a record of how well the individual is doing the job, in the eyes of the supervisor.

Performance appraisals are based on both informal and planned observations and analyses. As a supervisor, you evaluate people's performance through informal observations in your normal, day-to-day contacts with them. You also should have records of your Planned Job Observations (discussed in Chapter 8). And your company may have a planned performance appraisal form (*Figure 10-10* is an example). A good appraisal form can help to review a person's job performance in an orderly manner, and can help to ensure that all appraisers judge performance within the same general framework.

Here are some "appraisal tips" that you may find helpful:

- **Emphasize performance not personality** - Concentrate on the job objectives - job requirements - job performance - job results.

- **Use facts and examples** - Try not to decide on the rating first and then dig up facts to support it! Try for facts and examples first, then the rating.

- **Evaluate typical performance** - Don't over-emphasize one incident, either good or bad. Think of how the person usually performs on the factor being appraised.

- **Avoid ancient history** - Think in terms of how the person has done on the job for the past six months or year, and how she or he is doing *now*.

- **Show the ups and downs** - Keep in mind that a person may do one part of the job well, another part just above average, and still another very poorly. Show the proper spread of performance levels.

- **Don't "Whitewash"** - Show the facts as you see them. It is important to know the individual's

weak points or development needs, as well as his or her strong points.

- **Keep completely confidential** - Appraisal information is every bit as confidential as wage and salary information. Treat it with equal respect.

Performance discussion is a two-way communication between an employee and his or her supervisor regarding: (1) the individual's JOB (responsibilities - indicators - standards), (2) the individual's job PERFORMANCE (not what the person is, but what the person has done), and (3) plans for performance IMPROVEMENT and personal development.

From his book *Effective Psychology for Managers*, here are Mortimer Feinberg's ten most important things to remember for conducting the performance discussion with purpose and tact.

1. **Know the job** - Make sure you and your subordinate agree on the essentials of the job; the responsibilities and the performance standards.

2. **Know the person** - Learn as much as you can about his or her special abilities, needs and values.

3. **Know what race you want the person to win** - Emphasize not trivia, but the things that matter.

4. **Emphasize growth in present job** - Primary satisfaction should stem from one's present accomplishments and full use of abilities. Improving performance on the present job is a giant step in preparing for greater responsibility.

5. **Listen** - Listening both connotes and creates acceptance. Listening to a person talking freely about her or his job, performance, goals and plans is a sure way to learn a lot about that person.

6. **Stress acceptance** - Give recognition for the person's strengths. Discuss weak areas of performance with the attitude of "how can I help bring about the desired improvement?"

7. **Use critical incidents** - Drive home your points with specific significant examples.

8. **Observe limits** - Do not try to be the person's minister, psychologist or psychiatrist. Stay within the limits of job requirements, job performance,

FOLLOW-UP REPORT # 1 ☐ # 2 ☐
ON NEW OR TRANSFERRED EMPLOYEES

NAME _____ CLOCK # _____ POSITION _____

SERVICE DATE _____ TRANSFER DATE _____

REPORT DUE _____ 60 DAY PROBATION EXPIRES _____

SUPERINTENDENT _____ DEPARTMENT _____

PERFORMANCE FACTORS	**PROFILE**	**CODE**
1. GENERAL ABILITY: Mental and physical abillity to do this job well.	E D C B A	E: DEFICIENT Fails to meet minimum requirements
2. JOB PERFORMANCE: Do a fair day's work?	E D C B A	D: FAIR Meets minimum requirements
3. COOPERATION: Attitude toward company, supervisors and fellow workers.	E D C B A	C: SATISFACTORY Meets normal requirements
4. ATTENDANCE: Report on time? Stay on job? Unexcused absences?	E D C B A	B: VERY GOOD Exceeds normal requirements
5. SAFETY AND HEALTH KNOWLEDGE: How well does he or she know general department safety and health rules and practices?	E D C B A	A: OUTSTANDING Far exceeds normal requirements
6. SAFE WORK PERFORMANCE: Observance of rules. Safe work practices. Accident record.	E D C B A	
7. Does he or she use required safety equipment? If not, has he or she been warned?	( )Yes No( )	
8. Has the suggestion system been explained to this person?	( )Yes No( )	
9. Have company and department safety been explained?	( )Yes No( )	
10. Do you think this person will be a safe worker?	( )Yes No( )	
11. Has this report been discussed with the employee? If not, why?	( )Yes No( )	

COMMENTS:

EMPLOYEE'S SIGNATURE: _____ DATE _____

SUPERVISOR'S SIGNATURE: _____ DATE _____

SUPERINTENDENT'S SIGNATURE: _____ DATE _____

Figure 10-10

and performance improvement.

9. **Agree on behavior change goals** - Goals should be mutually acceptable. They should also be specific, realistic, challenging, personalized, time-

bounded, need-fulfilling and measurable.

10. **Set up a timetable** - Deadlines provide the impetus to overcome inertia and the push to overcome procrastination.

CORE CONCEPTS IN REVIEW

No supervisory leadership skills are more important than **personal communication skills** especially when applied effectively to:

1. Individual Job Orientation
2. Job/Task Instruction
3. Planned Personal Contacts
4. Key Point Tips
5. Job Performance Coaching

Individual Job Orientation should be done by the immediate supervisor.

1. Get the person "started off on the right foot."
2. Show him or her that management cares enough to spend some time just being helpful.
3. Avoid letting wrong ideas and habits get started.
4. Take a giant step toward helping the person do the job safely, efficiently and correctly.

Effective Instruction is a systematic substitute for trial-and-error learning; a reliable replacement for hit-or-miss instruction.

Everyone who instructs others on critical tasks, including most supervisors and many workers, should be trained for effective Job/Task Instruction technique. Its goals are

1. To help **motivate** the worker to do the job/task properly
2. To make sure the worker knows **how to do** the job/task properly.

The best known approach is the **Motivate-Tell & Show-Test-Check** technique. This is a direct route to E-S-P (Efficiency-Safety-Productivity).

Planned Personal Contacts involve these five key steps:

1. Pick a critical topic
2. Prepare the contact
3. Make the contact
4. Record the contact
5. Follow-up

"Key Point Tipping" is the organized process of giving employees helpful hints, suggestions, reminders or tips about key quality, production, cost or safety points in their work.

Job Performance Coaching boils down to the day-to-day supervisory actions taken to stimulate a subordinate to improve. You can get a good start on analyzing how well you coach by getting honest answers to the following seven questions: How well do I...

1. Define what is expected?
2. Aid performance opportunity?
3. Observe and appraise performance?
4. Provide performance feedback?
5. Take corrective measures?
6. Reinforce positive performance?
7. Emphasize goals, results and growth?

"Corrective Coaching" is what you do to help get employees back on the track; to change from deficiency to proficiency; to solve performance problems. It involves these five steps

1. Get the person's agreement that a problem exists
2. Mutually explore alternative solutions
3. Mutually agree on corrective action
4. Follow-up and measure results
5. Deal with broken contract and/or reinforce desired behavior.

"Developmental Coaching" is what you do to help keep employees on the right track. It centers on:

1. Performance appraisal (a systematic evaluation of a person's job performance and potential, made by that person's immediate supervisor) and
2. Performance discussion (two-way communication between an employee and his or her supervisor, regarding the individual's JOB, job PERFOR-MANCE and plans for performance IMPROVE-MENT and personal development).

KEY QUESTIONS

1. What are several advantages of two-way communication?

2. Why should new or transferred employees receive an orientation?

3. Name two types of orientation. Which one should the supervisor do?

4. Why is formal follow-up of orientation important?

5. What are the critical things to include in an orientation?

6. Who should receive proper job/task instruction?

7. Who should be trained in effective job/task instruction techniques?

8. Define effective job/task instruction.

9. Name the four key steps of effective job/task instruction.

10. If the learner hasn't learned, the _____ hasn't _____.

11. What is a planned personal contact?

12. What are the five main steps in conducting a planned personal contact?

13. Define key point tipping.

14. Give two or three examples of key point tips.

15. Define job performance coaching.

16. What are the seven major category questions on the Job Performance Coaching Practices Checklists?

17. What is "corrective coaching?" What are its five steps?

18. What is "developmental coaching?"

19. Name the twin factors of personnel development. Define each.

20. List several "appraisal tips."

21. List as many as you can of the ten most important things to remember for conducting an effective performance discussion.

PRACTICAL APPLICATIONS SUMMARY

S - For Supervisors
E - For Executives
C - For Safety/Loss Control Coordinators

	S	E	C
1. Establish performance standards for personal communications such as orientation, job/task instruction, planned personal contacts and job performance coaching.		x	
2. Enable personal communications training for all supervisors.		x	
3. Audit personal communications performance.		x	x
4. Recommend orientation program procedure and content.	x	x	x
5. Help conduct orientations for new and transferred employees.	x		x
6. Conduct orientation follow-ups.	x		
7. Keep records of initial orientations and formal follow-ups.	x		
8. Provide supervisors, and others who instruct, with a written guide to giving good job/task instruction.		x	x
9. Ensure that workers who instruct others on critical tasks are trained, as well as supervisors, in job/task instruction technique.	x	x	x
10. Provide effective instruction for each critical job/task assigned to workers.	x		
11. Use promotional techniques to encourage planned personal contacts and key point tips.		x	x
12. Conduct planned personal contacts with employees.	x		
13. Keep records of planned personal contacts.	x		
14. Give key point tips when assigning critical tasks to workers.	x		
15. Use random sampling to validate the application of planned personal contacts and key point tips.			x
16. Check coaching practices with a systematic self-appraisal.	x	x	x
17. Use "corrective coaching" with subordinates with performance problems.	x	x	x
18. Keep records of corrective coaching cases.	x	x	x
19. Use "developmental coaching" with all subordinates.	x	x	x
20. Keep performance appraisal and discussion records.	x	x	x
21. Reinforce positive applications of personal communication skills.	x	x	x

CHAPTER 11

EMPLOYEE TRAINING

"If you think training is expensive, try ignorance."

WHY TRAIN?

Among the many skills required of you as a manager, the ability to instruct others is of prime importance. By proper training

- Your department will be more efficient.

- Accidents will be eliminated or at least reduced. A properly trained employee knows the job hazards and what to do about them.

- Employee morale and teamwork will improve. Your own and your employees' "job satisfaction" will increase.

- Your own work will be made easier. Less time will be spent correcting mistakes and less supervision of job performance will be required.

- The work force will be more flexible. Employees trained in all phases of their work may readily be transferred from job to job within the group.

- You can meet legal requirements for certain types of training for which management is held responsible.

Many studies show that training is one of the most important factors in successful safety programs. For example, from their study on reducing construction accidents, Levitt and Parker developed seven guidelines, one of which says:

> Managers should provide for the training of newly-hired workers, stressing safety, work-methods and job hazards. Statistics from the study indicate very strongly (99.9% certainty) that such training will significantly reduce accident costs.

Alexander Cohen's review of research on "Factors in Successful Occupational Safety Programs" also highlighted the importance of ...

> ...training practices emphasizing early indoctrination and follow-up instruction in job safety procedures.

As a supervisor you earn your pay by getting your people to do their jobs as well as possible; by helping them produce the products or provide the services profitably. Thus, training is a basic part of your job.

To meet your company's needs (e.g., safety - quality - productivity - cost effectiveness), employees must have certain knowledge, attitudes and skills. Their development cannot be left to chance, to trial-and-error. They require systematic training: the planned process of preparing people to do their work well. This involves techniques that not only develop awareness, information and knowledge, but also develop the "how to" skills through "hands-on" involvement, learning-by-doing and guided practice.

Few people are "born instructors." Most gain this ability as a result of instruction and continued practice. To acquire acceptable skill is not difficult provided you

- Recognize and understand the few fundamentals on which good instruction is based.

- Have a sincere desire to learn these and put them into practice.

Chapter Objectives

1. To orient supervisors to basic principles and techniques for teaching adults.

2. To provide supervisors with a six-step system of employee training.

3. To stimulate supervisors toward continuing improvement in meeting their responsibilities as "managers of learning."

LEARNING/TEACHING GUIDELINES FOR ADULTS

Employees learn, one way or another! They may learn "the hard way," by making mistakes and being corrected, by gradually catching on to what they hear and see others doing. Or, they may learn through a planned process which prepares them to do their jobs well. The big difference between wasteful trial-and-error learning and efficient, effective learning is the way the learning is managed.

Supervisors as Managers of Learning

As a supervisor, one of your many hats is one that says "Manager of Learning." In this capacity, you have a tremendous impact on the learning environment of your workers. The training you do may range from the common situation of giving a few minutes of on-the-job instruction, to serving as a discussion leader or instructor in formal training programs.

If you are among the supervisors who have the help of a specialized training department or individual, you manage the learning of your people by

- Working with the specialist(s)

- Helping to identify the training needs of your people

- Helping to develop training programs to best meet the needs

- Scheduling your people for training

- Serving as a classroom instructor, field instructor and/or on-the-job coach

- Reinforcing trainee application of new knowledge and skills on-the-job

- Evaluating and following up training activities

If you do not have a specialized training department or individual, then you have more complete responsibility for the kinds of critical training activities shown in the above list.

Success as a Manager of Learning requires concentrating on the learners — on their needs; on their knowledge, skills and attitudes; on their job performance. You manage for learning both the knowledge, skills and attitudes associated with job mastery, and their application to achieve job mastery at the level of the experienced worker. If you resist the temptation toward instructor-centered training, and remain learner-centered, you will have taken the biggest steps toward training success. (For additional thoughts along these lines see "Group Meeting Dynamics" in Chapter 9, "Group Meetings").

How Adults Learn

The following basic principles of learning are obvious when they are read. However, they are often ignored, especially in adult learning situations. Their application will make employee training less frustrating and more productive for everyone concerned.

1. **Principle of Readiness** - We learn best when we are ready to learn. You cannot teach someone something for which he or she does not have the necessary background of knowledge, maturity or experience. When people are ready and have sound reasons for learning, they profit from teaching and make progress in learning.

   Readiness also means that the learner is emotionally ready, is motivated to learn. You help to create this readiness by letting learners know how important the training is, why they should take it, and the benefits it should bring them (such as growth, recognition, easier work, variety, challenge, safer work and increased potential). Helping to create the *desire* to learn helps people learn.

2. **Principle of Association** - It is easier to learn something new if it is built upon something we

already know. In training or teaching, it is best to proceed from the known to the new, to start with simple steps (based on what the learner already understands or can do) and gradually build up to the new and more difficult tasks or ideas. Make full use of comparison and contrast, of relationships and association of ideas.

3. **Principle of Involvement** - For significant learning to occur, learners must be actively involved in the learning process. The more senses involved (hearing, seeing, tasting, smelling, feeling), the more effective the learning. The more fully the learners participate in the learning process, the more effectively they learn.

The good instructor gets the *learners* to do the repeating, the practicing, the "learning by doing." The good instructor uses learner involvement tools such as "hands on" training, question and answer, group discussion, audiovisual aids, case problems, role playing, simulations, quizzes and application exercises.

4. **Principle of Repetition** - Repetition aids learning, retention and recall. Conversely, long disuse tends to cause learned responses to weaken and be forgotten. Application and practice are essential. Accuracy should be stressed before speed, to avoid learning a wrong habit that must later be "unlearned." The more often people use what they have learned, the better they can understand or perform it.

5. **Principle of Reinforcement** - The more a response leads to satisfaction, the more likely it is to be learned and repeated. For best results in a teaching/learning situation, accentuate the positive (praise, reward, recognition, success). Also, breaking complex tasks down into simple steps allows the successful learning of one step to help motivate learning the next one. When learning is pleasant and beneficial, people more readily retain what they have learned, and are more likely to want to learn more. Successful learning stimulates more learning.

The effective instructor facilitates learning by creating a warm, participative, positive learning climate. He or she uses feedback to satisfy learners' needs to know that they are doing things correctly and that they are making progress.

Supervisor/Instructor Guidelines

- **Learn to instruct.** Giving instructions, teaching or training effectively are not necessarily "doing what comes naturally." A person may know how to do a job very well, but not know the best way to help someone else learn to do it. Instructing requires preparation, practice, and patience; knowledge of the principles of learning; knowledge of the job to be taught and application of these guidelines.

- **Base training on needs.** If no needs exist, there is no reason to train. You can determine needs by checking the requirements of the job (work objectives, job/task analyses and position descriptions are valuable here) and comparing them with the person's job performance. You might also ask the employees what they think they need to learn.

- **Take the learner's viewpoint.** You get best results when you put yourself in the learner's shoes and orient the instruction to the learner's viewpoint. Keep in mind the learner's goals, abilities, needs, personality and feelings. Keep the instruction at the learner's level.

- **Maximize motivation.** You can lead a person to knowledge, but you can't make that person learn... unless he or she is motivated. You can help bring out people's motivation by working with them to set meaningful goals; by showing personal interest in them; by providing proper incentives for learning and performance; by setting a good example, being a good role model; by using the positive power of praise, reward and recognition; by training effectively.

- **Expect ups and downs.** Typical learning curves show that learning often occurs in spurts. It may advance quite rapidly for a while, then level off a bit, then increase again and so on. Occasionally, there may be a slippage to a lower level of knowledge or skill than the learner already has shown. Both instructor and learner should be prepared to expect these varying rates of progress. Sometimes it may be necessary to find the causes of the slowdown, such as changes of motivation or effort, temporary stress or fatigue or the training method, and take corrective action.

- **Recognize individual differences.** Nearly everyone agrees that each person is unique, but may overlook the importance of the differences. Some of the important factors in training are intelligence, desire to learn, knowledge, aptitudes, interests, motives, attitudes, emotions and learning ability. Trainers should keep these factors in mind and fit the training to the individual.

Don't expect the same method to work equally well with all people or that all employees can learn to perform at the level of the best worker. Good instruction can help the person develop his or her aptitudes to the highest degree, but that potential may not be the same as someone else's.

- **Give frequent feedback.** People usually don't like to play ball unless they know the score. Similarly, learners need to know how they are doing. In fact, some experimental studies have shown that providing systematic knowledge of progress may speed up the learning process by as much as 50 percent. You can give feedback in many ways, such as test results, checklists, charts, graphs and credit for work well done.

- **Remember follow-up.** You must follow up to make sure the training has been effective. This involves special attention until you are certain that the person has learned and is performing properly. (See Chapter 8, "Planned Job Observation," for a systematic approach.) This follow-up should be unobtrusive, patient and helpful — not critical — and can be tapered off to normal supervision when you are sure the person is performing well. Long-range follow-up, an important part of good supervision, may show the need for "refresher" training.

SIX-STEP SYSTEM OF EMPLOYEE TRAINING

Research and experience have shown the importance of these six-steps to successful employee training

1. Pinpoint training needs

2. Set training objectives

3. Decide how best to meet the training objectives

4. Secure and/or develop the training program

5. Do the training

6. Evaluate and follow-up the training.

Let's look at each of them to see how they can guide you to better results through better training.

Pinpoint Training Needs

Apply the professional management Principle of Definition: *A logical and proper decision can be made only when the basic or real problem is first defined.*

Basically, you do this through problem solving — an analysis of existing and potential problems, and their probable solutions. Since not all performance problems indicate a training need, your first big step is to separate training needs from other needs. Performance problem analysis is one systematic way of doing this, as shown in *Figure 11-1*. Systematic analysis of this sort is a good way to ensure that your solutions fit the problems.

Related techniques that help you pinpoint training needs include work analysis, job observation, tests and surveys.

Work analysis involves a complete review of each job in terms of required knowledge and skills. In other words, to do the job well, what must the workers "know" and what must they be "able to do"? You can use a form like the one shown in *Figure 11-2* for a systematic, documented analysis. It's a great tool to help you determine the most critical training needs.

To use *Figure 11-2*, make a list under "Jobs/Tasks" of the ones which your people normally do, or might be called on to do. Use as many pages as necessary. Under "Skills" indicate which skills are required for each task. For instance, the task of building pallets requires skill in operating a radial arm saw; the task of rebuilding wheels for a railcar requires skills in operating an overhead crane and the use of a forklift for various aspects of handling the wheels, as well as skill in the operation of a hydraulic press for removing the wheels from the axles. This systematic analysis of training needs, if properly done, is likely to reveal significant areas of need for training.

The Job/Task Inventory developed in connection with "Job/Task Analyses, Procedures and Practices" (Chapter 7) is a valuable resource. It enables you to direct your training analysis first to the critical jobs — those where lack of knowledge and know-how has serious consequences. Written job/task procedures and practices covering these critical operations give you lots of data on required knowledge and skills. The differences between these requirements and the qualifications of the people who must do the work clearly identify training needs.

Planned Job Observation

Planned Job Observation (Chapter 8) is a good way to evaluate the performance and pinpoint the training needs of a specific person. It gives you a systematic way to compare the person's performance with the

PERFORMANCE ANALYSIS

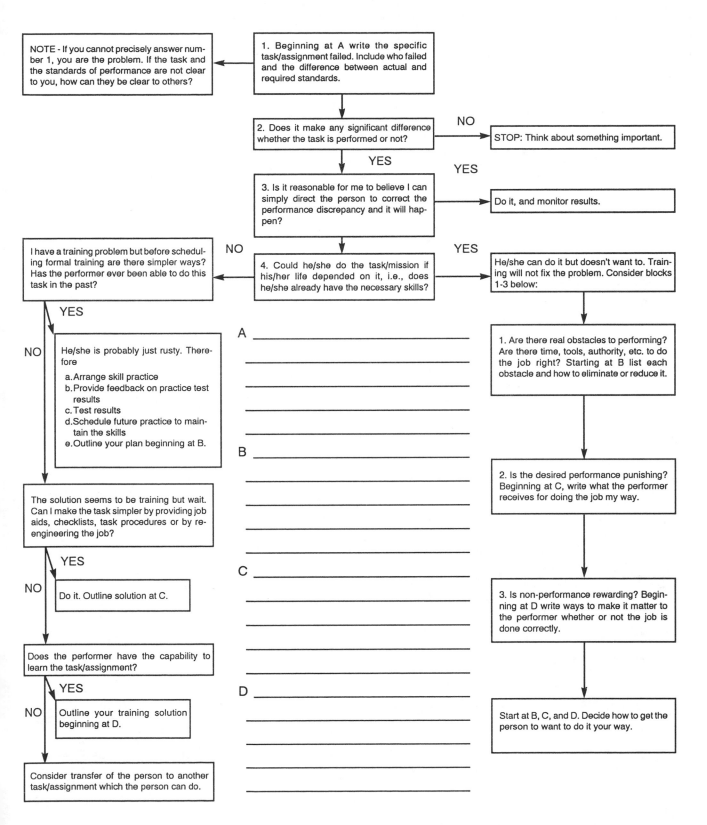

NOTE - If you cannot precisely answer number 1, you are the problem. If the task and the standards of performance are not clear to you, how can they be clear to others?

1. Beginning at A write the specific task/assignment failed. Include who failed and the difference between actual and required standards.

2. Does it make any significant difference whether the task is performed or not?

NO

STOP: Think about something important.

YES

YES

3. Is it reasonable for me to believe I can simply direct the person to correct the performance discrepancy and it will happen?

Do it, and monitor results.

I have a training problem but before scheduling formal training are there simpler ways? Has the performer ever been able to do this task in the past?

NO

4. Could he/she do the task/mission if his/her life depended on it, i.e., does he/she already have the necessary skills?

YES

He/she can do it but doesn't want to. Training will not fix the problem. Consider blocks 1-3 below:

YES

He/she is probably just rusty. Therefore

a. Arrange skill practice
b. Provide feedback on practice test results
c. Test results
d. Schedule future practice to maintain the skills
e. Outline your plan beginning at B.

NO

A _____

_____

_____

1. Are there real obstacles to performing? Are there time, tools, authority, etc. to do the job right? Starting at B list each obstacle and how to eliminate or reduce it.

_____

_____

B _____

_____

The solution seems to be training but wait. Can I make the task simpler by providing job aids, checklists, task procedures or by re-engineering the job?

_____

2. Is the desired performance punishing? Beginning at C, write what the performer receives for doing the job my way.

YES

NO

Do it. Outline solution at C.

C _____

_____

_____

Does the performer have the capability to learn the task/assignment?

_____

3. Is non-performance rewarding? Beginning at D write ways to make it matter to the performer whether or not the job is done correctly.

YES

NO

Outline your training solution beginning at D.

D _____

_____

Consider transfer of the person to another task/assignment which the person can do.

_____

_____

Start at B, C, and D. Decide how to get the person to want to do it your way.

Figure 11-1

SKILL ANALYSIS CHART

JOBS/TASKS	SKILLS										(Add Additional Columns as Needed)
	A	B	C	D	E	F	G	H	I	J	
Date _____ Department _____ Analyst _____ Supervisor _____											
1											
2											
3											
4											
5											
6											
7											
8											
9											
10											
11											
12											
13											
14											
15											
16											
17											
18											
19											
20											
21											
22											
23											
24											
25											
26											
27											

Indicate which skills are required for each job or task by placing an "X" in the appropriate column.

Figure 11-2

standard job procedures and practices.

Tests can also be useful in analyzing the training needs of individuals. These may be knowledge tests (either verbal or written), performance tests or both.

Surveys are often used for identifying training needs. These are usually either structured interviews or written questionnaires. Structured interviews are surveys in which a skilled interviewer finds out what knowledge and skills people feel they need. These interviews yield systematic data that can be recorded, tabulated and analyzed objectively. The information can be anonymous if the purpose is to determine the training needs for a group of employees.

In written questionnaires, employees can identify problems in their jobs, areas in which they wish they had more expertise or their desire for upgrading their skills. *Figure 11-3* is an example from an actual questionnaire used with skilled trades employees. This approach assumes that the individuals know their real needs and will report them honestly. Part of this approach may be a skills inventory or checklist in which people indicate their level of ability in various skills.

Based on one or more of these techniques, a systematic and complete needs analysis enables you to:

- Clearly define training needs by identifying the activity, skill and knowledge components of the work.

Example - Pipe Fitters need training in how to install steel pipe. The major components of the need are to (1) *select* pipe and fittings, (2) *measure* pipe, (3) *cut* and *thread* pipe and (4) *join* pipe.

- Identify the work conditions (e.g., temperature, work space, time pressure, etc.) to consider in the training.

Example - Pipe fitters install new equipment and do repair jobs under all plant conditions (e.g., inside, outside, in temperatures ranging from minus 20 degrees to 95 degrees Fahrenheit and with urgent need to restore operating capability quickly).

- Break the training needs down into specific training topics.

Example - the need to learn how to *cut and thread pipe* requires training in...
...what makes a good joint

1. Purpose of threads
2. Size and type of threads
3. Length of threads
4. Old and new fittings

...use of tools

1. Pipe vise
2. Hand and machine hacksaws
3. Pipe cutter
4. Pipe threader (hand and machine - dies -

21. How adequate, **for the jobs you do**, is your safety knowledge in the following areas?	Completely Inadequate				Completely Adequate		
a. Manual and powered material handling	0	2	4	6	8	10	NA
b. Material storage	0	2	4	6	8	10	NA
c. Hoisting and rigging apparatus	0	2	4	6	8	10	NA
d. Man-lifting equipment	0	2	4	6	8	10	NA
e. Conveyors	0	2	4	6	8	10	NA
f. Ropes, chains, slings	0	2	4	6	8	10	NA
g. Machine and equipment guarding	0	2	4	6	8	10	NA
h. Welding and cutting	0	2	4	6	8	10	NA
i. Hand and portable power tools	0	2	4	6	8	10	NA
j. Electrical hazards	0	2	4	6	8	10	NA
k. Flammable and combustible liquids	0	2	4	6	8	10	NA
l. Fire prevention and control	0	2	4	6	8	10	NA
m. Toxic substances and solvents	0	2	4	6	8	10	NA
n. Workplace carcinogens	0	2	4	6	8	10	NA
o. Ionizing and non-ionizing radiation	0	2	4	6	8	10	NA
p. Personal protective equipment and clothing	0	2	4	6	8	10	NA
q. Personal air sampling monitors	0	2	4	6	8	10	NA
r. Material data sheets	0	2	4	6	8	10	NA
s. Lockout	0	2	4	6	8	10	NA
t. Confined space entry and work	0	2	4	6	8	10	NA

Figure 11-3

ACTION VERBS FOR WRITING OBJECTIVES

ACTIVITY	ASSOCIATED ACTION VERBS			
1. Knowledge	define state list name	write recall recognize label	underline select reproduce measure	relate repeat describe memorize
2. Comprehension	identify justify select indicate	illustrate represent name formulate	explain judge contrast translate	classify discuss compare express
3. Application	predict select explain find	choose assess show perform	construct clarify use practice	apply operate demonstrate illustrate
4. Analysis	analyze identify conclude criticize	justify resolve contrast distinguish	select separate compare examine	appraise question break down differentiate
5. Synthesis	combine argue select compose	restate discuss relate manage	summarize organize generalize plan	precis derive conclude design
6. Evaluation	judge support identify attach	evaluate defend avoid rate	determine attack select plan	recognize criticize choose design
7. Skills	grasp operate bend act	handle reach turn shorten	move relax rotate stretch	position tighten start perform
8. Attitudes	accept challenge judge praise	value select question attempt	listen favor dispute volunteer	like receive reject decide

(From Davies, Ivor K., Industrial Technique, New York: McGraw-Hill Book Company, 1981.)

Figure 11-4

lubricating - cleaning air and oxygen pipe)
5. Chasing threads

You should be especially alert to training needs when you have...

- new employees
- transferred employees
- temporary employees
- promoted employees
- new or revised laws - standards - regulations
- new or remodeled equipment
- new or changed methods or processes
- new or revised procedures and practices

Here are some of the typical topics that many supervisors find necessary to meet employee training needs:

- how to fulfill relevant safety and health laws
- rules education and review
- how to operate equipment properly
- proper use of tools
- effective use of operator's manuals, checklists, forms and required records
- proper work procedures and practices
- proper use of protective equipment
- the "whats" and "whys" of instructional signs and color codes
- safe handling practices for hazardous substances
- what to do in emergency and disaster situations
- fire fighting skills
- proper materials handling techniques
- the "whys" and "hows" of good accident/incident reporting, investigation and correction
- how to contribute to safety meetings
- first aid skills
- techniques and benefits of housekeeping and order
- individual and group problem-solving techniques
- safety habits for on-and-off-the-job

Another step in identifying training needs is to establish priorities. The training needs identified can be ranked according to these criteria:

- What are the consequences if done incorrectly? These may range from minor to catastrophic and the tasks with more serious potential should receive a higher priority.
- How difficult is it to learn? The greater the difficulty, the greater the need for training.
- How often is it done? Tasks done more frequently would rank higher than those seldom done.
- How critical is the response time? Tasks which must be performed immediately when the need arises (i.e., use of a respirator) take precedence over those for which a person will have the time to ask someone for instructions.
- What is the history of deficient performance? Those jobs with a history of "problems" may indicate a high priority for training in how to do them.

Jobs under consideration for training may be ranked from one to five on each of these criteria. The cumulative scores can guide in setting priorities for training.

In the six-step system, then, the first step is to pinpoint training needs, using techniques such as performance problem analysis, work analysis, job observation, tests and surveys. This gives you a list of the major components and specific topics of training to meet the needs.

Set Training Objectives

In the teaching/learning process, nothing is more important than clear, specific objectives. All of the training should aim at the objectives. They encompass the task, the instructor, the learner, the course content and the on-the-job performance.

Objectives are statements of intentions or desired outcomes, prepared in such a way that they guide our problem-solving (or training) behavior, and form the basis for measuring results. They answer two critical questions:

1. What is it that we must teach (that learners must learn)?

2. How will we know when we have taught it (when learners have learned it)?

Objectives should be learner-oriented rather than teacher-oriented. They should describe what the learner is to know and/or be able to do at the end of the training.

As examples, for a course in Machine Shop Practices, here are three of the objectives for a lesson on "Operation of the Power Hacksaw." Trainees must be able to:

1. Describe the operation of the power hacksaw

2. Select and mount a saw blade

3. Operate the power hacksaw safely.

Or, returning to our earlier Pipe Fitting example, it was determined that the training must prepare the learners to:

1. Correctly select new pipe and fittings, using drawing and diagrams.

2. Correctly select replacement pipe and fittings from the use and the physical characteristics of existing, intact piping.

3. Measure, cut, thread and fit all pipe with no spoilage and not more than four percent waste.

4. Make all installations to meet the standard pressure tests on the first trial.

Notice these characteristics of good objectives:

- They are stated in terms of what the learner must know and be able to do following the instruction.

- They use action verbs (describe, select, operate, etc., such as shown in *Figure 11-4*).

- By describing specific terminal behaviors (what the learner can do when the training ends), they make it easier to develop good lesson plans.

- They permit meaningful measurement of training results.

- They reflect the scope of the training and guide the preparation and selection of the training methods, media and materials.

Decide How Best to Meet the Training Objectives

After pinpointing the training needs and setting the training objectives, you examine various training methods, media and materials. Thinking first of *methods*, you should decide how much emphasis to give to (1) instructor-guided training and (2) self-directed training, guided by instructional materials. Then you can make decisions about the use of specific *methods* and *media* such as:

- Aids (audio, visual and combined)
- Apprenticeship
- Assignments
- Buzz groups
- Case studies
- Demonstrations (by the instructor, by an experienced worker, and/or by the learner)
- Discussions
- Exhibits
- Field trips and/or field work assignments
- Four-step method of instruction (motivate - tell & show - test - check & commend)
- Hands-on practice
- Home study materials
- Learning games and simulations
- Lectures
- On-the-job guided experience
- Programmed instruction
- Questions and answers
- Recitation
- Reports (verbal and/or written)
- Role plays and modeling
- Tests, quizzes and feedback
- Videotaping and feedback

The main idea is to pick the training approach that will yield maximum results at minimum cost. This means digging out the best answers to many *who - where - when - what -* and *how* questions. For instance:

WHO are the most knowledgeable people available to help me develop the most effective training? WHO will administer the training program? WHO will serve as instructors (myself - experienced workers - training specialists)? WHO will budget the required investment? WHO will take the training? WHO will evaluate the results? WHO will be responsible for follow-up?

WHERE will the classroom training be conducted? WHERE will the on-the-job or field training be done? WHERE will we get the training equipment, materials and aids?

WHEN will the program start? WHEN will the classroom training be conducted? WHEN will the on-the-job or field training be done? WHEN will the evaluation and follow-up take place?

WHAT written materials are required? WHAT equipment and facilities are needed? WHAT investment is necessary? WHAT are the potential problems to be avoided? WHAT benefits will accrue to the trainees? WHAT benefits will accrue to the organization?

HOW much of the training will be of a "classroom" nature? HOW much will be on-the-job or "field" training? HOW will the trainers be selected and trained? HOW will the trainees be selected? HOW will I (the supervisor) be involved in the program development, implementation and follow-up? HOW will the program be evaluated? HOW will tests (both "knowledge" and "how to") be used? HOW will people be certified, licensed or otherwise designated as trained and qualified? HOW will those who fail to fulfill the requirements be handled? HOW will exceptional performance be recognized and reinforced?

Basically, you should choose instructional methods and media which are both appropriate and practical. They should meet the training needs and objectives; should satisfy as many teaching/learning principles as possible; and should be as functional and economical as feasible. The best methods and media are the simplest and cheapest ones that work.

Secure and/or Develop The Training Program

When you have done the prior three steps well, you will have a good picture of what is needed to do the training job well:

- the lesson plans
- the visual and/or audio aids
- the passouts and study materials
- the facilities
- the tools - machines - equipment

Then you need to answer questions like these: Is a training program already available? If so, where? How feasible is it for our situation? Should we use outside instructors, our own instructors or both? Will we need to train the trainers? What pertinent aids, materials, facilities, tools, machines and equipment do we have within the company? Which should we lease or purchase? Which should we develop ourselves?

Your answers should be based on training effectiveness and cost effectiveness. There is little or no justification for a do-it-yourself program if an outside program will be more efficient and effective. Likewise, there is little or no justification for using an outside program if a do-it-yourself one will do the job better.

You should know something about lesson plans, either to develop your own or to evaluate those developed by other people. Lesson plans are simply guides, outlines or blueprints showing what should happen during the training session. Various instructors prepare them in various forms, two of which are shown in *Figure 11-5*. Whatever their form, good lesson plans bring many benefits. For example, they keep the program focused on the objectives; they help prepare the instructor and build his or her confidence; they arrange the teaching in a logical sequence and permit systematic learning; and they encourage proper management of instructional time.

There are several sources of ready-to-use training programs. Among these are manufacturers, professional developers of training materials, industrial associations, governmental agencies and vocational schools and colleges. These will, of course, need to be carefully evaluated for quality, for being up-to-date and for how well they fit your situation. Some of these will be unusable, some will require modifications and some will "fill the bill" exactly, saving a great deal of preparation time.

The teaching materials you pick for a program may be very simple or very sophisticated. Fairly common ones include:

- PRINTED MATERIALS ... manuals - programmed texts - workbooks - handouts - drawings and wall charts - prepared flip-charts - flannel boards - chalkboards and flip pads.

- AUDIO MATERIALS ... records - tapes - cassettes.

- AUDIO/PRINT MATERIALS ... cassette/workbook - sound page - filmstrip/cassette.

BASIC LESSON PLAN

NAME _____ DATE _____

TITLE OF PRESENTATION _____

OBJECTIVES:

OUTLINE:

LESSON PLAN SUBJECT _____ PAGE

Training Elements Covered	Materials and Equipment

Learning Objectives	Content	Methods	Time Allotted

Figure 11-5

- PROJECTED VISUALS ... slides - filmstrips - 8mm movies (silent) - opaque projections - overhead transparencies.
- PROJECTED AUDIOVISUALS ... 16mm movies - video tapes - sound/slides.
- PHYSICAL OBJECTS ... actual tools, machines, materials - models - simulators.
- HUMAN INTERACTION MATERIALS ... role plays - case studies - demonstrations.

Just as the craftsman selects the right tool for the job, the instructor selects the right teaching method.

Do The Training

Schedule the facilities, the instructors and the participants. Conduct or coordinate the training/learning activities. Use knowledge and proficiency tests to determine the degree to which the training objectives are met. Issue certificates to those who meet the standards for successful completion. Where appropriate, issue a company license or permit (examples are shown in *Figure 11-6*). Among the reasons for a licensing procedure are that it ...

- shows learners that the company is really interested in proper performance.
- serves as evidence that the holder has met specified requirements — a symbol of status.
- motivates continuing attention to proper performance, for maintaining license.
- deters unqualified people from operating expensive, critical equipment.
- facilitates periodic review of qualifications, refresher training and re-issuance of right to operate.

Increase job pride by requiring operators to maintain a high level of proficiency in order to maintain or upgrade the license or permit.

For do-it-yourself classroom training programs, you may find the following key point tips for good instruction helpful:

Prepare Properly

- Know your subject.
- Ensure that all participants know the session's time and place, plus any materials they should bring.
- Make sure the meeting room is big enough.
- Check adequacy of facilities such as chairs, tables, ashtrays (if smoking is permitted), lighting, heating, air conditioning and ventilation.
- See that seating arrangements are optimum. Rather than just rows of chairs, tables and chairs are more comfortable and practical for discussion and notetaking. They should be arranged to permit as much interaction as possible, preferably

EQUIPMENT OPERATOR LICENSE

NAME OF OPERATOR	CLOCK NUMBER
DEPARTMENT/SECTION	
TRAINEE	
TYPE EQUIPMENT	

DATE ISSUED — SIGNATURE OF TRAINING SUPERVISOR

EQUIPMENT OPERATOR LICENSE

NAME OF OPERATOR		CLOCK NUMBER
DEPARTMENT/SECTION		
QUALIFIED TO OPERATE		
TYPE	SIZE/MODEL	TRAINER'S INITIALS

DATE ISSUED — SIGNATURE OF ISSURING AUTHORITY

GOLDEN RULE

- NO RIDERS ON EQUIPMENT

SILVER RULES

- IF YOU AREN'T SURE, ASK FOR INSTRUCTION.
- DRESS SAFELY FOR YOUR JOB.
- INSPECT EQUIPMENT DAILY BEFORE USE.
- SHUT DOWN TO ADJUST AND SERVICE.
- SECURE EQUIPMENT WHENEVER YOU LEAVE IT.

Figure 11-6

with no one's back to anyone else.

- Unless everyone knows everyone else well, ensure that name tags and/or signs are provided.

- Be certain that notebooks or pads and pencils are available for each person.

- Make sure your audiovisual aids and equipment are properly placed and in working order.

- See that your passout materials are stored and organized in order of distribution.

Communicate Clearly

- Speak up so you can be heard.

- Talk not to the floor, ceiling or visual aid... talk to the people.

- Speak at a moderate pace.

- Enunciate clearly.

- Keep language as understandable as possible.

- Use concrete examples to explain and support ideas.

- Use diagrams, sketches, pictures and other appropriate communication aids.

- Frequently get participants' feedback, to check their comprehension and reactions.

Promote Participation

- Recognize signs that people have questions or comments.

- Feed easy questions to non-participative individuals.

- See that no individual monopolizes discussions.

- Protect the right of minority opinion.

- Reward participation with recognition and appreciation.

Reinforce Rapport

- Create a friendly atmosphere.

- Start and end on time.

- Don't ridicule ideas or let participants ridicule one another.

- Be honest... if you don't know, admit it (then try to find and share the answer).

- Don't "play favorites."

- Bring out participants' answers to other participants' questions whenever possible.

- Stick to the subject.

- Don't show off your big vocabulary and technical terminology.

- Compliment good contributions.

- Help people express their thoughts if necessary.

- Thank individuals and the group for their help in the sessions.

Many of these guidelines are also useful for the one-to-one "hands-on" training that supervisors do a great deal of.

Evaluate and Follow-up the Training

All training programs should be evaluated to determine (1) the degree to which the objectives were met, and (2) how the program can be improved. Evaluation can be done at any of three stages: input, throughput or output. In terms of *input*, the costs of training can be assessed, either in comparison with other programs or against a budgeted figure. *Throughput* is usually assessed in terms of the number of people trained in a given period of time. *Output* assessment is harder, but more valuable. It involves four criteria:

1. **Reaction** - measuring the emotional responses of participants to the program. This typically is done with anonymous questionnaires immediately following the program. This feedback should let you know how the learners have received the program, and whether or not they feel they have learned things of value for job performance.

2. **Knowledge** - measuring the knowledge gained by the participants. This usually involves before-and-after tests, oriented to the training objectives.

3. **Behavior** - measuring the skills developed by the training activities. This may involve proficiency tests, direct observation of participants' performance and/or self-reports of skill improvements.

4. **Results** - measuring the organizational effects of training. This is done by direct calculation of changes in accidental losses, waste, quality, productivity and cost effectiveness.

Evaluations enable orderly analysis of factors that helped training effectiveness, factors that hindered it and the program improvements to be made. Knowledge, behavior and results can be assessed before, during and after the training program, and again at follow-up dates. The basic purpose is to find out whether, and to what degree, positive changes occurred — practical, significant changes influenced by the training.

Everyday reality puts much of the responsibility for such measurement and follow-up squarely on the shoulders of supervisors, the ones best able to evaluate on-the-job applications of knowledge and skills. Here are five simple, practical post-training actions for meeting this supervisor responsibility:

1. **Post-training Discussions** - as soon as feasible after the training, have at least one discussion with the employee on the training, on what was learned, and on plans for putting the learning to work.

2. **Job Assignments** - make practical assignments which enable the employee to apply what was learned. For maximum benefit, such assignments should be given soon after the training.

3. **Job Observation** - during both informal and planned performance observations, note evidence of changed behavior related to the training. Contact newly trained people frequently to answer questions and review key points of proper performance. Gradually taper off to the normal amount of supervision.

4. **Performance Feedback** - during performance discussions and coaching contacts, include specific references to newly acquired knowledge and skills. Use constructive coaching and positive behavior reinforcement.

5. **Record and Report** - keep records of the employee's progress and submit reports to higher management. Recommend improvements and/or further use of the training program.

Records aid evaluation and follow-up. You should keep track of who has had various skill training, and who still needs it, with a simple record like that shown as *Figure 11-7*. You should also keep training records on each worker. The Record of Operator Training and Qualification, shown in *Figures 11-8* and *11-9* could be used for a number of types of equipment and vehicles. Good records not only are a sign of good management but also can be invaluable in accident investigation, in the handling of grievances and arbitration cases and in court cases.

Refresher training should also be an ongoing part of training follow-up activities. You should encourage employees to improve and update their knowledge and proficiency. In addition to your informal updating, there should be regular formal refresher training. A good "rule of thumb" is to have refresher training amounting to a minimum of one-half the time of the original training, at least every three years. Successful completion of this retraining should be a condition for maintaining certification or licensing.

COMPARING CLASSROOM TRAINING AND ON-THE-JOB TRAINING

Some training programs take place in "classrooms," some on-the-job and many in both. Let's take a quick look at some similarities and differences between the two.

Differences

Classroom training (CT) and on-the-job training (OJT) have some important differences. For instance:

- CT tends to be for groups; OJT tends to be for the individual.

- The CT environment tends to be "artificial;" the OJT environment is the natural work environment.

- CT tends to have few distractions from learning; OJT tends to have many distractions (such as noise, other equipment and materials, people trying to meet the "production push," etc.).

- CT tends to involve quite a variety of teaching/learning techniques; OJT makes most use of the proper job instruction technique (motivate - tell & show - test - check & commend).

Similarities

Good classroom training and good on-the-job training share some significant features. For example, both ...

SKILL TRAINING RECORD

		SKILLS										
INDIVIDUALS		A	B	C	D	E	F	G	H	I	J	(Add Additional Columns as Needed)
1												
2												
3												
4												
5												
6												
7												
8												
9												
10												
11												
12												
13												
14												
15												
16												
17												
18												
19												
20												
21												
22												
23												
24												
25												
26												

Department _____

Supervisor _____

List each person in the numbered rows. In the lettered columns list the skills required, Use additional columns as needed. Across from the name of each person listed, put an "X" above the dotted line under each skill that person must have. When training in that skill has been accomplished, put the training date under the dotted line.

Figure 11-7

Record of Operator Training and Qualification

Operator Identification

NAME			EMPLOYEE NUMBER	SOCIAL SECURITY NO.
ADDRESS			PLANT	DIVISION
CITY	STATE	ZIP	SECTION	TELEPHONE

Operator Qualification

Type of Equipment/Vehicle	Date Qualified	Basic	Skilled	Type of Equipment/Vehicle	Date Qualified	Basic	Skilled
1				5			
2				6			
3				7			
4				8			

Supervisory Review

The operator qualifications listed above have been verified. The operator has used each type of equipment in which he has qualified or has received refresher training sufficient to maintain skill level. I have voided qualifications which are no longer maintained.

DATE	NAME	SECTION/TITLE	SIGNATURE

Figure 11-8

RECORD OF OPERATOR TRAINING & QUALIFICATION

Training and Evaluations

SUBJECT SESSION	1	2	3	4	5	6	7	8	9	10
USE "X" FOR COMPLETION, "Q" FOR QUALIFICATION TEST, "U" FOR UNQUALIFIED										
PREPARATION										
Personal Protective Equipment										
Issued Operator's Manual										
Physical/Eye Examination										
Employment Orientation										
INSTRUCTION										
Basic Operator Safety Rules										
Protective Equipment Requirements										
Operator Servicing										
Operator Maintenance										
Controls Familiarization										
Pre-Use Inspection/Defect Reporting										
Engine Starting										
Basic Operation/Travel to Work Area										
Guards and Safety Devices										
Accident Reporting										
Work Operations (List Below)										
_____										
_____										
_____										
_____										
_____										
Parking and Securing										
Restrictions on Use										

Figure 11-9

- are designed to satisfy pinpointed needs.
- are focused on specific objectives.
- are learner-centered.
- require proper preparation.
- depend on good communications.
- apply basic principles of learning (such as readiness - association - involvement - repetition - reinforcement).
- include meaningful evaluation and follow-up.
- produce measurable results.

Essence

Safety, quality, productivity and profitability largely depend upon the performance of those who produce the products and provide the services. Their performance depends a great deal on their knowledge, attitudes and skills. These in turn, depend to a large extent on the employee training and development activities provided. You pay for training whether you do the training or not. Whether it's classroom training, on-the-job training or both ... high quality training is a sound investment that provides substantial returns.

SOME SPECIFIC APPLICATIONS

"Employee education and training" is a broad topic and a process of infinite variations. Many of the specific tools and techniques you should use in fulfilling this basic responsibility are covered in Chapter 9, "Group Meetings," and Chapter 10, "Personal Communications," as well as those covered in this Chapter. The specific ones you apply to any given situation depend upon many variables, such as the training topic, the number of people to be trained, the available resources, the time constraints, the organizational climate, and so on. To illustrate the variety, let's look at three examples.

Organizational Rules & Regulations

Education and training regarding rules and regulations extend from new employee orientation to retirement. More specifically, you should be sure to cover this topic at the time of...

- orientation of new or transferred workers.

- initial job training.

- refresher training.

- retraining of transferred workers.

- annual rules review.

- rule changes.

Major sub-topics to cover include (1) General Safety & Health Rules, (2) Job or Craft Rules and (3) Signs, Tags and Color Codes. You may do some of this in "classroom" settings, some in regular group meetings and some in your personal contacts, job instruction and day-to-day coaching.

Here are the major activities to guide your supervisory efforts in this critical area of education and training:

- **Distribute**
  - See that each person has a copy of the rules for the organization as a whole, and for his or her work area.
- **Discuss**
  - Read and explain each rule to the person(s).
  - Use a show-and-tell technique whenever feasible.
  - Give the reasons for the rule.
  - Give examples of how the rule applies to the individual's work situation.
- **Post**
  - See that rules and regulations are posted in positions and places appropriate for reinforcing their message and purpose.
- **Test**
  - Use verbal and/or written tests to check understanding of the rules.
  - Ask the person to explain how the rule applies to his or her work.
- **Enforce**
  - Distribute and discuss the disciplinary policy and procedure as related to rules.
  - Test for understanding.
  - Administer the policy and procedure consistently.
  - Retrain or re-explain as necessary.
- **Reinforce**
  - Let people know how important rules compliance is and why.
  - Commend consistent compliance.
- **Record**
  - Record the forms showing the person's receipt and understanding of the importance of the rules.
  - Record the group training sessions on rules.
  - Record significant violations and related disciplinary actions.
  - Record special commendations.
- **Review**
  - Review relevant rules for each employee at least once a year.
- **Model**
  - Lead the way to rules compliance by your personal example.

Job/Task Procedures

A considerable portion of the training done by supervisors is teaching someone to follow a specific job or task procedure. This type training is covered in detail in Chapter 10, "Personal Communications." *Figure 11-10* shows how a job/task procedure can be used to guide this type of instruction. The first column, "Job Actions," is taken directly from the written procedure. The second column, "Job Information," shows the knowledge that the person must have to do the job/task correctly.

Answers to the following questions will help determine the information required for the second column:

- Are there any safety or health hazards to consider?

- Are there terms which need clarification?

- Does the learner need to know how this part, machine, equipment, etc. is constructed?

- Must the learner understand operating principles of the operation?

- Should he or she know the characteristics and properties of materials used?

- Does the operation involve making calculations?

- Are any measurements taken?

- Will the learner have to read blue prints?

- Does the work involve making sketches?

- Must the learner know the location of the equipment, where to obtain tools, materials, etc.?

- Does the learner lay out the work?

- What job planning is required?

- What forms (records, reports, etc.) are used?

- What is the important reasoning, if any, behind this operation?

- Is it necessary for the learner to know the relationship between his or her department and other departments?

- Are there any important facts (quantities, clearance, tension, rates, capacity, R.P.M., etc.) that the learner must know?

- Are there any other working conditions (rules, regulations, policies, safety practices, procedures, routines, etc.) that the learner should know about?

Mobile Equipment Operator Training

The operation of mobile material handling equipment is often the biggest source of all types of accidents in an organization. Also, the responsibility for training operators often falls on the supervisor. These two factors make it a prime area of supervisory concern. *Figure 11-9,* shown earlier in this Chapter, provides a list of subjects which should be covered in this training as well as a permanent record of how well the trainee did. Any one of those subjects could be broken down into "job actions" and "job information" such as was shown in *Figure 11-10*. These two together would provide an excellent foundation for training by a supervisor.

CORE CONCEPTS IN REVIEW

Development of the knowledge, attitudes and skills required for proper performance is too important to be left to chance — it deserves systematic training activities. Each supervisor should serve as a "Manager of Learning" for his or her workers. The following five primary **principles of learning** are especially important to adult learning:

1. Principle of Readiness
2. Principle of Association
3. Principle of Involvement
4. Principle of Repetition

5. Principle of Reinforcement

Based on these and related principles, here are some practical Supervisor/Instructor guidelines:

1. Learn to instruct
2. Base training on needs
3. Take the learner's viewpoint
4. Maximize motivation
5. Expect ups and downs
6. Recognize individual differences
7. Provide knowledge of progress

"HOW TO TEACH A JOB"

START CENTRIFUGAL PUMP #2 - STEAM DRIVE

POSITION:	UNIT:	JOB NO.
BOILERHOUSE OPERATOR	UTILITIES	3

JOB ACTIONS (WHAT MUST BE DONE)	JOB INFORMATION (WHAT MUST BE KNOWN)
1. Check position of exhaust steam valve to atmosphere	– Location of exhaust steam valve – Why this valve should be in open position – Operating principles of centrifugal pumps and turbine drive – Function of pump No. 2 – Reason for starting up pump – Water pressure to be maintained
2. Open suction valve on water end	– Location of suction valve
3. Open vents on bonnet of pump	– Location of vents – Why vents are opened
4. Open discharge valve on water end	– Location of discharge valve
5. Check lubricating system	– Location of lubricating points – Grade and type of lubricant to use – Amount of lubricant to use – Importance and frequency of lubrication
6. Check cooling water system	– Location of cooling water lines and purpose of cooling system – Importance of keeping lubricating oil from getting hot
7. Open bleed on turbine casing	– Location of turbine casing bleeds – Reason for opening bleeds – Importance of keeping water from turbine casings
8. Check position of overspeed trip	– Location of overspeed trip – How to determine if overspeed trip is in running position – How to put overspeed trip in running position
9. Slowly open steam throttle valve	– Location of steam throttle valve – Reason for opening valve slowly
10. Close bleeds on turbine casing	– When to close bleeds
11. Continue opening steam throttle valve to bring turbine up to desired speed and/or water pressure	– Water pressure required – Maximum turbine speed

Figure 11-10

8. Remember follow-up

Six steps to successful training have been distilled from research and experience:

1. **Pinpoint Training Needs**

    a. Problem analysis
    b. Work analysis
    c. Job observation
    d. Tests
    e. Surveys

2. **Set Training Objectives.** Write statements of intentions or desired outcomes which answer these two questions

    a. What must we teach?
    b. How will we know when learners have learned it?

3. **Decide How Best to Meet the Training Objectives**

    a. Examine various training methods, media and materials
    b. Choose those which are likely to be most efficient and effective for existing needs and objectives
    c. Strive for learner attention, retention, reproduction and reinforcement

4. **Secure and/or Develop the Training Program.** Answer questions like these:

    a. Is a complete training program already available? If so, where?
    b. How feasible is it for our situation?
    c. Should we use outside instructors, our own instructors or both?
    d. Will we need to train the trainers?
    e. What pertinent aids, materials, facilities, tools, machines and equipment do we have within the company? Which should we lease or purchase? Which should we develop ourselves?

Answers should be based on training effectiveness and cost effectiveness.

5. **Do the Training.**

    a. Schedule the facilities, the instructors and the participants.
    b. Conduct or coordinate the training/learning activities.
    c. Use knowledge and proficiency tests to determine how well the training objectives are met.
    d. Issue certificates to those who meet the standards for successful completion.
    e. Where appropriate, issue a company license or permit.
    f. Increase job pride by requiring operators to maintain a high level of proficiency in order to maintain or upgrade the license or permit.

6. **Evaluate and Follow-up the Training**

    a. Determine the degree to which the objectives were met and how the program can be improved.
    b. Evaluate input, throughput and output (reaction - knowledge - behavior - results).
    c. Follow-up by means of post-training discussion, job assignments, job observation, performance feedback, records and reports.
    d. Encourage refresher training.

When properly managed and conducted, employee training yields many benefits. For example, it

1. Transforms unskilled workers into safe, skillful workers in the shortest feasible time
2. Builds workers' self-respect and pride of performance
3. Makes the workforce more flexible
4. Makes your own work easier
5. Reduces scrap, waste, downtime, accidents, injuries and property damage
6. Meets certain legal requirements.

KEY QUESTIONS

1. What are four or five basic benefits of effective employee training?

2. List five or six things supervisors should do as "Managers of Learning."

3. Name and describe five primary principles of learning.

4. True or False? Giving instructions, teaching or

training effectively are usually "doing what comes naturally."

5. True or False? Learning normally occurs in a smoothly accelerating manner.

6. True or False? Knowledge of progress may speed up the learning process by as much as 50 percent.

7. What are the steps in the six-step system of

employee training?

8. True or False? When performance is not up to par, the solution most likely is training.

9. "A logical and proper decision can be made only when the basic or real problem is first defined." This is the Principle of _____

10. Name three or four techniques that help to pinpoint training needs.

11. Define and give an example of a training objective for a specific skill training program.

12. Four vital training dynamics are *attention*, _____, *reproduction*, and _____.

13. The four-step method of instruction is: *motivate*, _____, *test* and

14. What are three or four benefits of good lesson plans?

15. True or False? Tests should not be used in adult training programs.

16. Many key point tips for good instruction are summarized under these four headings: *Prepare Properly*, _____, *Promote Participation* and _____.

17. Why should training programs be evaluated?

18. How should training programs be evaluated?

19. Describe five post-training actions for supervisors in meeting their follow-up responsibilities.

PRACTICAL APPLICATIONS SUMMARY

S - For Supervisors
E - For Executives
C - For Safety/Loss Control Coordinators

	S	E	C
1. Issue training policy, procedures and practices.		x	
2. Recommend changes of training policy, procedures and practices.	x		x
3. Serve as Manager of Learning in own area.	x	x	x
4. Inventory the critical jobs (in own area) for which training is important.	x		
5. Maintain and review the critical job inventory for the whole organization.			x
6. Inventory the training needs of individuals in own area of responsibility.	x		
7. Maintain and review inventory of safety and health training needs for the whole organization.			x
8. Help set training objectives.	x		x
9. Recommend training/learning programs to meet identified needs and objectives.	x		x
10. Assist the development of training/learning programs to best meet the needs and objectives.	x		x
11. Exercise training program approval authority.		x	
12. Schedule employees for training.	x		
13. Serve as instructor (classroom and/or field).	x		
14. Award training certificates, qualified operator permits and/or licenses.	x	x	x
15. Reinforce trainee application of new knowledge and skills to the job.	x		
16. Conduct post-training discussions with employees.	x		
17. Make practical job assignments which enable employees to apply what they have learned.	x		
18. Use constructive coaching and positive behavior reinforcement to "stamp in" learned knowledge and skills.	x		
19. Keep records of employee training progress.	x		x
20. Evaluate training activities and recommend changes and/or further use.			x
21. Audit training management performance and communicate results to all levels of management.			x
22. Establish a management climate that encourages initial training, refresher training and update training.	x	x	x

CHAPTER 12

JOB PRIDE DEVELOPMENT

"The message is clear. They want to be led in a positive, enthusiastic fashion. No one in our country wants to be a loser. They want to work hard. They want to win, and they want to be united in that single purpose. We've got to get excited — get back our pride."
- William J. Weisz, Vice Chairman and
Chief Operating Officer, Motorola, Inc.

INTRODUCTION

Performance Problems

Every decade has its challenges. High on the list of critical challenges during this decade is the need for better quality, safety and productivity. For example, based on U.S. Bureau of Labor Statistics data, notice how poorly we compare in the manufacturing productivity increases for 1970-1980:

Japan	102%
The Netherlands	75%
France	61%
Germany	60%
Italy	59%
UNITED STATES	28%
United Kingdom	26%

The United States and the United Kingdom were outpaced better than two-to-one by Italy, Germany and France; nearly three-to-one by The Netherlands; and approaching four-to-one by Japan.

It may be more than mere coincidence that, in North America, we constantly hear and read about job alienation, apathy and adversary relationships; about people simply "doing their jobs" and looking to other activities for satisfaction; about lack of loyalty to employing organizations; about the lack of pride in performance.

But there also are encouraging signs. For instance, a 1983 social research survey found the percentage of the American work force expressing a strong work ethic (i.e., agreeing with the statement, "I have an inner need to do the best I can regardless of pay") to be more than twice as high as in West Germany and significantly higher than in Japan. The survey also pointed the way to better performance, showing that 75 percent of American workers feel the chief reason they work less than they could is that *managers do not motivate them.*

William James of Harvard found that if motivation is low, employees' performance suffers as much (i.e., 50-70%) as if ability were low. For reasons such as this, motivating is extremely important in supervising - leading - managing.

The American industrial miracle of the past hundred years was largely fueled by *capital investment* and *improved technology.* Today these do not do the trick by themselves. As stated by William J. Abernathy, Harvard Professor and authority on American productivity: "I don't think industrial revitalization has much to do with investment — it has to do with people." In other words, we need greater investment in *human resources development* and applied *behavioral science.* We need to revive and restore job pride.

Functional Definitions

Job pride is a feeling, an attitude, a mainspring that motivates people to do their best. It's the state of mind that says, "I am important, my job is important, I want to do my job as well as possible." Job pride involves self-respect and self-esteem, as well as respect and esteem for the work, the supervisor and the company.

Job pride development is what we do to wind that motivational mainspring, to bring out the best in people. It includes all the things we do to influence, encourage and inspire people toward pride of performance, e.g., orienting - instructing - clarifying goals - delegating - coaching - listening - helping - sharing - collaborating - encouraging - respecting - recognizing - reinforcing.

Job pride development is lifting people up, turning them on, stimulating them to peak performance. It is what we do to develop positive employee attitudes and morale. It is participative leadership in action. It is what we do to help make people proud of their company, their department, their team, their job, their proficiency. Job pride development is a professional management approach to motivation.

Chapter Objectives

The general objective of this chapter is to help supervisors and other managers understand and apply some significant motivational methods that have worked for other people. More specifically:

- To present a five-step system for behavior reinforcement
- To highlight effective leadership skills
- To provide guidelines for applying the core concepts of participative management and QWL (Quality of Work Life).

MANAGEMENT'S MOTIVATIONAL STAGES

There have been three main stages in the development and application of "behavioral science" to the management of human resources: 1) Scientific Management, 2) Human Relations and 3) Participative Management. They are pictured in *Figure 12-1* and summarized as follows:

Stage #1 - Scientific Management

In the early 1900's, Frederick Winslow Taylor, one of the most influential management pioneers, applied the scientific method to the solution of factory problems. He built up orderly sets of principles which could be substituted for the trial-and-error methods then in use. In a meeting of The American Society of Mechanical Engineers in 1903, he said:

It is not only practicable but comparatively easy to obtain, through a systematic and scientific time study, exact information as to how much of any given kind of work either a first-class or an average man can do in a day, and with this information as a foundation...workmen of all classes are not only willing, but glad to give up all idea of soldiering, and devote all of their energies to turning out the maximum work possible, providing they are sure of a suitable permanent reward.

Time study was the big tool. Turning out the maximum work possible was the big objective. The prevalence of "soldiering," or pretending to work while really loafing, was the big assumption behind motivational style. As Taylor said in a 1911 conference, "...almost every workman looks upon it as his duty to do as small a day's work as he can..."

The stop-watch and slide-rule school of scientific management yielded fantastic gains in efficiency, mass production techniques and task specialization. But it also contributed to a caste-like organizational hierarchy, and to making work seem boring, limiting, constricting, mechanical and dehumanized. Management's predominant motivational style was to consider work an impersonal exchange of labor for money — a unit of pay for a unit of work, period.

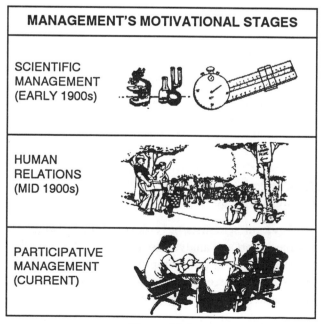

MANAGEMENT'S MOTIVATIONAL STAGES

SCIENTIFIC MANAGEMENT (EARLY 1900s)

HUMAN RELATIONS (MID 1900s)

PARTICIPATIVE MANAGEMENT (CURRENT)

Figure 12-1

Stage #2 - Human Relations

The classic studies for this stage are the well-known "Hawthorne Studies," conducted by Elton Mayo at the

Hawthorne Works of the Western Electric Company in Chicago. The researchers intended to study the relationships between productivity and physical working conditions. However, they concluded that the human element in the work environment had a much greater impact on productivity than the technical and physical aspects of the job.

In a research report entitled, "Behavioral Science: Concepts and Management Application," the National Industrial Conference Board discussed the human relations movement in industry. It summarized:

> Emphasis was on creating a workforce with high morale. It represented an attempt to break down formal or arbitrary boundaries that are part of the fabric of a stratified and bureaucratic organizational structure. Managers trained in "human relations" learned to be "friendly" toward their subordinates, to call them by their first names, and generally to try to keep people content as part of "one big happy family." The attempt to democratize the organization found expression in company-sponsored recreational activities, and in increased emphasis on fringe benefits.

Management's predominant motivational style seemed to be: "be nice," avoid conflict, smooth things over...make them think they are important...make them feel that their ideas are wanted...steer them to the answers and decisions you have already arrived at. Regardless of what the human relations enthusiasts intended, however, this approach to controlling employee behavior was perceived as mollycoddling and manipulative. Something more was needed.

Stage #3 - Participative Management/ Leadership

Behavioral scientists have devoted untold amounts of time, effort and analysis to the matter of motivating people by integrating employees' needs with the organization's needs. Some of the names and ideas that characterize this stage are...

- Douglas McGregor, with his *Theory X* (people are lazy, avoid responsibility, and must be motivated by fear of punishment) and *Theory Y* (work is as natural as play, people can learn to

seek responsibility, and people can be motivated by the rewards of achievement)

- Abraham Maslow, with his *hierarchy of needs* (to stay alive, to be secure, to belong, to "be somebody," to develop potential)

- Frederick Herzberg, with his *hygiene factors* (physical, economic, security and social) versus *motivating factors* (growth, responsibility, achievement and recognition)

- Robert Blake and Jane Mouton, with their managerial grid emphasis on *team management*

- Rensis Likert, with his classic studies showing the results of participative management and *employee-centered supervision.*

Some of the tools and techniques that characterize this stage are job enrichment, management by objectives (goal setting), team building, conflict handling, feedback and psychological "leveling," small group dynamics and positive behavior reinforcement.

There is lots of knowledge, based on research, about these tools for development of job pride. They are not the complete answer, but they are the best we have at this stage of management's motivational styles. Just as the other two stages ("scientific management" and "human relations") developed, grew and held sway for several decades, so will "participative management" influence leadership styles for many years to come.

In a sense, we have come from management by fear (stage 1), through management for contentment (stage 2), to motivational management (stage 3).

DEVELOPING JOB PRIDE THROUGH EFFECTIVE LEADERSHIP

Thousands of studies have been made to determine the skills and abilities of people perceived as good managers, good supervisors and good leaders. You can help crystallize your own thoughts along these lines by taking a few minutes to complete the simple analysis sheet shown as *Figure 12-2.*

1. Use the top portion for the "best" supervisor or best leader in your experience. First, list six *positive* factors of that person's behavior or leadership skills. Then list six *negative* factors (nobody's perfect).

LEADERSHIP ANALYSIS FORM

PLUS (+) FACTORS	MINUS (-) FACTORS
1.	1.
2.	2.
3.	3.
4.	4.
5.	5.
6.	6.
1.	1.
2.	2.
3.	3.
4.	4.
5.	5.
6.	6.
1.	1.
2.	2.
3.	3.
4.	4.
5.	5.
6.	6.

Best Boss

Worst Boss

Me

Figure 12-2

2. Use the middle portion for the "worst" supervisor or leader in your experience. First, list six *negative* factors of that person's behavior or leadership skills. Then list six *positive* factors (everybody has some strengths).

> You will get much more value from this material if you complete the above exercise before reading further. (We will come back to the third part of the exercise later).

Research results support two major conclusions. First, there is no particular personality pattern that distinguishes leaders from others. Successful supervisors-managers-leaders come in all sizes, shapes, types and traits. Second, certain behavioral characteristics are frequently found in successful leaders. Here are some of the skills and abilities that are quite common in such leaders:

- interpersonal skills such as listening, giving feedback, being tactful, coaching, problem solving, demonstrating and generating enthusiasm

- ability to enlist cooperation

- willingness to reason, to work things out, to take a mutual problem solving approach rather than "flying off the handle"

- emphasis on goals - results - achievement

- integrity (being honest, trustworthy, ethical)

- showing the self-confidence that inspires the confidence of others

- use of participative techniques such as asking people for their ideas, suggestions and help

- actively listening and responding to them positively

- giving people encouragement, helping people grow and develop and building pride in people by showing pride in them.

In *A Note On Management Practices,* the Forum Corporation of North America summarizes considerable research on effective leadership practices. They identify nineteen specific managerial behaviors as major factors in establishing and maintaining "high performance climates." The nineteen practices are organized into the following four learning clusters:

1. GOAL AND TASK DEFINITION

- setting challenging and difficult goals and standards for your subordinates

- establishing clear, specific performance goals for your subordinates' jobs

- explaining tasks and projects clearly and thoroughly

- making problems and their causes completely clear, so that subordinates can correct them

2. TEAM BUILDING

- striving to set team or group goals as well as individual goals

- conducting team meetings which help to increase trust and mutual respect among team members

- encouraging subordinates to initiate tasks and projects they think are important

- personally emphasizing and demonstrating goal commitment and persistence in achieving goals

- being supportive and helpful in your daily contacts with your subordinates

3. PERFORMANCE APPRAISAL

- rewarding people for innovation

- sitting down regularly with your subordinates to review their overall individual performance

- using recognition and non-monetary rewards, as well as financial compensation, to reward excellence

- relating the total reward system to the excellence of job performance rather than to other factors such as seniority

4. COACHING AND COUNSELING

- using more recognition than criticism

- communicating high personal standards informally

- building warm, friendly relations with the people who work for you

- expecting subordinates to find and correct their own errors rather than solving problems for them

- allowing subordinates to influence the performance goals that are set

- being supportive and helpful in your daily contacts with your subordinates (this practice appears twice because it is important both to effective team building and to effective coaching).

Going back to your exercise on leadership analysis, *Figure 12-2*, how well did your observations and beliefs agree with the general results of research and writings described above? What key points might you add?

> **If you are tough-minded about your own growth and development, you can gain a lot from completing the bottom portion of *Figure 12-2*. Looking at yourself as a present or potential leader, write in your six most important positive factors (don't be over-modest), and your six most important negative factors. Show courage...do it now. It will help to highlight critical areas in need of improvement, as well as strengths to build on.**

DEVELOPING JOB PRIDE THROUGH BEHAVIOR REINFORCEMENT

The psychological basis for behavior reinforcement is amazingly simple. It is, as shown in *Figure 12-3*, *BEHAVIOR IS INFLUENCED BY ITS EFFECTS. A "negative effect" leads to a low probability of behavior repetition, and a "positive effect" leads to a high probability of behavior repetition. In practical terms, this means that when a specific job behavior results in a negative experience (displeasure, pain, penalty punishment, frustrated desires), that behavior will tend not to be repeated; and when it results in a positive experience (pleasure, reward, recognition, satisfied desires), the behavior will tend to be repeated.*

Behavior reinforcement differs from general, per-

sonal recognition ("You're a good man, Charlie Brown"). It relates clearly to something specific the person has done ("Charlie, I sure do appreciate your

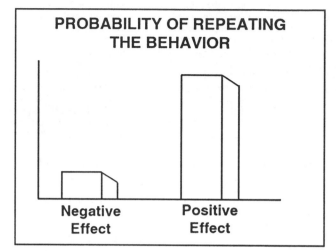

Figure 12-3

attention to eye safety practices...like the way you used those cup goggles today on every job that called for them. Keep it up.") This recognizes the person's behavior. Experiments and experience have shown that this type of reinforcement is a practical, powerful way to influence human behavior.

Figures 12-4 and 12-5 (next page) summarize two actual applications in industry of performance management techniques.

Motivational Balance

We are not saying that you can forget about *negative* motivation, that is, trying to stop undesirable behavior by punishing the offenders with some type of disciplinary action. Indeed, this is one way to influence human behavior (if behavior produces negative effects, that behavior tends *not* to be repeated). But most people overemphasize the negative and some use it as their only approach to motivation. What we *are* saying is that *positive* reinforcement is the other side of the motivational coin. It has been a neglected part of motivational efforts. It offers a relatively untapped reservoir of motivational power. And you should give it *at least as much* attention and application as you give to the negative side of the coin. As depicted in *Figure 12-6*, you should ensure a balanced approach.

Remember, too, that punishment often has undesirable side effects. For instance:

- The person may continue the behavior for which

PERFORMANCE MANAGEMENT PROJECT

I. PROBLEM STATEMENT - In the #3 furnace area the men weren't wearing all the protective clothing they were required to wear by the company regulations and OSHA. They are supposed to wear glasses, asbestos gloves and a smock. The men have been warned about this over and over again. Most of them are usually missing at least one piece of the required clothing.

II. SPECIFIC BASELINE BE-HAVIORS - Once each day I went through the furnace area and counted the number of men wearing all the required clothing. If one piece was missing, I didn't count the man. The behavior I want is wearing all of the required clothing.

III. MODIFICATION ACTION - I had a meeting with the men on my shift in the furnace area. I showed them my baseline data on a graph. I discussed the safety situation with them and asked them where they thought they should be on the graph. They all agreed to try for 100%. Each day when I counted I made some kind of comment to the men who were wearing their clothing. I posted the graph near the door so they could see it each day. They began to get on each other if someone didn't have all of their protective clothing.

IV. EVALUATION - During the 6 weeks of baseline data an average of 22.5% of the men wore all of the required clothing. During the 13 weeks that I had the feedback graph up, the average was 92.3%.

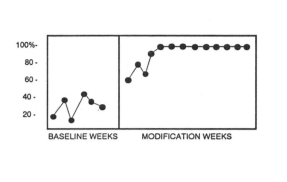

Figure 12-4

PERFORMANCE MANAGEMENT CASE STUDY

Parkdale Mills was experiencing a rate of absenteeism that it considered unacceptable. They began a program to improve the declining rate of attendance. The problem was focused on the second shift in the carding department.

BACKGROUND CONDITIONS

Baseline data on attendance were compiled averaging eighty-six percent for a fifteen-week period. The shift could not operate efficiently at this level of attendance. Carding machines were sitting idle owing to the absence of operators. There were twenty-five employees and one supervisor in this department, and relations between them were satisfactory. The relationships among employees were satisfactory, except for minor, isolated incidents. It was, however, felt that there was a lack of teamwork and shift enthusiasm. Management generally worked toward molding the employees of a shift into a team with accepted goals. It was felt that this had not yet been accomplished on this shift.

During the baseline period, individual absentees were being reprimanded and workers who had good attendance records were not receiving any recognition for their attendance.

A goal was established to reach an average level of ninety-three percent attendance for three weeks.

PROCEDURE

A visual feedback system and social reinforcement were identified as consequences that could be delivered contingent upon improved attendance. A daily attendance chart was placed in the work area. Every employee's name was entered on the chart, and a blue dot was placed on the chart for each day the employee was present and a red dot for each day that the employee was absent. A weekly attendance graph was also posted in the work area to indicate the percent of employees attending each day. The goal of ninety-three percent was indicated on the graph with a horizontal colored line.

Each worker reporting for work was verbally reinforced by the shift supervisor each day. When a worker was absent, he was welcomed back the next day and no reprimand was administered. The supervisor also encouraged each employee to look at the attendance chart and help the department reach its goal of ninety-three percent. The shift supervisor maintained the graph daily.

RESULTS

From the baseline average of eighty-six percent, attendance began to rise immediately after the implementation of the program procedures.

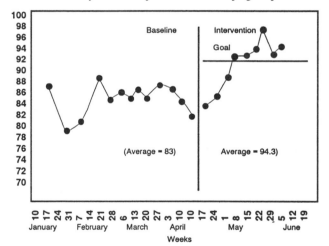

For the following nine-week period, attendance average 94.3 and attained one hundred percent for one week, a record never before attained. The supervisor reported that, in addition to the improvement in the measurable data, the employees were demonstrating a greatly improved enthusiasm and teamwork previously lacking. All the employees had expressed pride in their accomplishment and verbalized their commitment to continue this level of attendance.

The costs of this program were less than ten dollars. This cost was for graph paper and dots for the chart. Parkdale Mills, Inc. estimated that the absence of an employee costs them at least ten dollars per day. The program saved thirty dollars per day using this figure. This would result in an annual savings of approximately $9,000. Additional savings were realized but not computed in operating efficiency and reduced turnover, occurring as a result of the more positive atmosphere and behavior on this shift.

Source: *Behavior Management*, Lawrence M. Miller, © 1978,
Reprinted by permission of John Wiley & Sons, Inc.

Figure 12-5

he or she was punished, and simply try harder not to get caught at it.

- The employee may develop resentment and a "get even" attitude toward those who are responsible for the punishment (i.e., management).

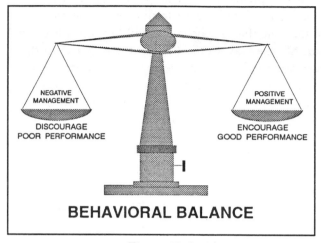

BEHAVIORAL BALANCE

Figure 12-6

- The individual may release his or her frustration through aggression — such as reduced output, substandard quality, waste, damage, fighting with other workers, griping, spreading rumors and running down the boss's reputation.

By contrast, positive motivational efforts not only reap the rewards of more efficient, safe, productive behavior; but also bring the benefits of improved management/employee relations. This positive approach helps to change the employees' image of the supervisor from negative (enforcer, policeman, punisher) to positive (coach, helper, leader).

Five Steps To Behavior Reinforcement Success

You will get most effective results when you apply positive behavior reinforcement systematically. The following steps (shown in *Figure 12-7*) serve as a good guide:

❶ PINPOINT the desired behavior. Be sure it is specific, observable, and measurable. For example...
- the number of safe load lifts per shift, the number of rejects per day or the number of absences per month.
- the percentage of employees returning from break on time, or the percentage of employees wearing the required protective equipment.

- the number of tools or other items left in the wrong place, the number of pallet piles properly stacked, the number of items left blank on accident investigation report forms or the number of inspection items assigned a hazard classification.

❷ RECORD baseline data. Measure and keep a record of the present level of performance on the pinpointed behavior, without calling the attention of the workers to what you are doing. This shows you "what the score is" under present conditions, and enables meaningful comparison with future performance. It enables you to check, compare, and communicate performance changes. You might find, for example...
- the Start of Shift Equipment Safety Check is being made 12% of the times it should be
- tools are left in the wrong place an average of 27 times per week by group Z
- during the six-week baseline period, compliance with the requirement for wearing protective equipment was 22%.

This kind of data also is valuable as a starting point for setting goals that are specific, measurable, realistic and challenging. Setting the performance goals can, itself, be a motivational process - through participative leadership.

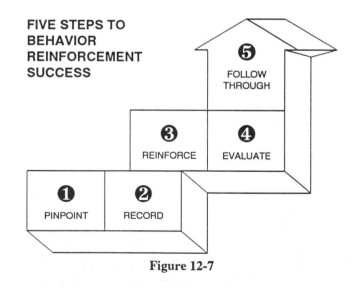

FIVE STEPS TO BEHAVIOR REINFORCEMENT SUCCESS

❺ FOLLOW THROUGH

❸ REINFORCE ❹ EVALUATE

❶ PINPOINT ❷ RECORD

Figure 12-7

❸ REINFORCE specific desired behavior. Remember that the recognition should closely follow the desired behavior. For example...
- "Sam, I sure do appreciate the attention you give to your Start of Shift Equipment Safety Check. Reporting those faulty brakes and get-

ting them fixed this morning eliminated a serious hazard. Nice going!"
- You could post a daily graph for all employees to see, showing the number or percentage of group members who used the checklist properly.
- You could ask workers to make a tick mark on a master roster when they complete the safety check. This would give them immediate reinforcement and enable them to keep track of the group's performance level from shift to shift.

❹ EVALUATE the impact of reinforcement on performance. Measure and keep records of performance. Compare these data with your baseline data. When feasible, convert data into dollar signs. Decide whether or not the experiment or project is worthwhile. Count - chart - compare. For example...
- *Figure 12-4* shows a case with an average of 22% compliance during the six weeks of baseline data counting, and an average of 92% compliance during the thirteen-week modification period. The modification actions included: 1) getting the workers to agree on a compliance goal, 2) daily posting of a compliance graph and 3) verbal reinforcement for compliance.

Essentially then, evaluation involves counting, charting and comparing... as systematically and scientifically as conditions permit.

❺ FOLLOW-THROUGH with appropriate action, based on the facts and your evaluation of these facts. You might want to continue the reinforcement that brought improved results... probably on an intermittent rather than continuous basis. You may also find it effective to change the type of reinforcement, to use the motivational power of variety.

Basically, follow-through involves planning, checking, changing and persisting. You should *plan* the follow-up actions you expect to take. You should *check* (count - chart - compare) the results of your efforts. You should *change* your efforts when your data show that performance levels are slipping — do something more, something less or something different. Above all, you should *persist*. If at first you do not succeed, find the reason and give it another try. If at first you

do succeed, put your successful procedure to work for another desired behavior.

Frequently asked questions about behavior reinforcement are: "How long do I have to keep it up?" and "What happens when I stop the reinforcement?" There is no single answer to fit every situation. Most of the time the new behavior will become a habit or part of "the way we do things around here." In that case taper off the reinforcement and choose another behavior to work on, using these same steps. In a few cases the desired behavior may be difficult or unpleasant. In such cases, it is, of course, wise to look at the situation itself to see if it can be changed in some way so that the difficult or unpleasant behavior is no longer required. If the situation simply cannot be changed then some type of reinforcement may have to be continued indefinitely. There are many jobs where the difficulty of doing them properly becomes a great source of job pride.

> **HABITS ARE FIRST**
> **COBWEBS,**
> **THEN CABLES**

Of course, you can also get results through *informal* use of behavior reinforcement. For instance, pick a person whose performance is variable. For perhaps a month, avoid all temptations to criticize poor performance and, at least once a day, give the person credit for a positive part of his or her performance. Add constructive correction of performance areas in need of improvement, and the result is likely to be better morale and performance. Or, when you are teaching a worker how to perform a new task, make it a point to praise *each step* toward the total desired behavior pattern. Couple this with constructive coaching on the aspects still to be mastered, and you may be surprised at how quickly the learner learns.

You can also apply positive behavior reinforcement to activities such as investigation, inspection and job observation. Rather than concentrating only on the negatives (e.g., parts of the investigation form not filled in properly, unsafe conditions or the poor aspects of performance), also look for and emphasize the *positives* (e.g., the parts of the form that are well done and will be helpful, the good housekeeping and order or the good parts of the person's performance). The results are likely to be positive for both your workers and you.

> When supervisors make a habit of positive behavior reinforcement, employees tend to make a habit of positive behavior.

OTHER MOTIVATIONAL APPROACHES

Quality of Work Life (QWL)

During the first half of this century the term "hired hand" was commonplace. The basic philosophy seemed to be: workers provide the *muscle-power* and bosses provide the *mind-power*. These days, you seldom hear anyone called a "hired hand." There is a growing awareness that we must hire the whole person. Times, conditions and attitudes are different. Today's workers are better educated. They grew up in a far different world than their parents and grandparents did. They have higher expectations. They have a desire for quality, not just quantity, as a life goal.

QWL programs take these current conditions into consideration. They are concerned with qualities such as self-esteem and self-actualization, dignity and development. They involve powerful dynamics such as participation, team building and job enrichment. Many companies and unions are changing from an adversary relationship to a cooperative one. They are making more use of old techniques, and developing new ones, to increase worker involvement and commitment. They are gaining the benefits of various *team* approaches such as labor-management steering committees, productivity improvement teams, problem-solving groups, quality circles and loss control project teams.

The main idea is to put less emphasis on bureaucracy and levels of authority, and more emphasis on "old-fashioned" virtues such as openness, collaboration, trust, equity and self-esteem. Executives and supervisors are finding that by putting these concepts to work they can get better results. Evidence shows that effective QWL programs bring better productivity, higher job satisfaction and greater organizational effectiveness.

Even if your company doesn't have such a program, as a supervisory leader you can do many things to improve the quality of work life for your people. Among the more important ones are to...

- show them that you realize they are not hired hands, but whole human beings with both skills and ideas, with feelings and values, with personal concerns that are not limited to the job they hold... treat each one as a *person*.

- make participation a way of life in your department. Ask your people for their opinions, suggestions, ideas and concerns. Have your personal "open door" (or better yet, open mind) policy.

- let your behavior show that you really are interested, really are listening, really are trying to understand their viewpoints.

- take action on their concerns when you can; explain why when you can't.

- apply team techniques to some of the bigger problems shared by you and your people. Show your respect for their concerns, commitment and creativity by working with them on mutual problem solving teams.

- treat them along the lines that you would like your supervisor to treat you.

Organizational Climate

The job pride, performance and productivity of people are affected by the organization's climate (people's perception of how it feels to work in the organization). A negative climate has negative effects; a positive climate has positive effects. Management's motivational style, reflected in supervisory behaviors, is the major factor which determines whether the climate is negative or positive.

One of the critical aspects of company climate is that it be conducive to growth and development of the individual. This type of climate provides:

O *pportunities* for growth, independent action, creative effort and honest mistakes.

S *timulation* for constant improvement, by maintaining high standards of performance and setting good examples throughout the organization.

C *ounsel* to the individual on job objectives, job

standards, job performance and job improvement.

A *ssistance* to individuals in the form of training programs, on-the-job coaching and instruction, communication, job rotation and time for participating in pertinent out-of-house development activities.

R *ecognition* and reward for superior performance, in terms of praise, pay, status, responsibility and authority.

In the Psychological Corporation's book, *Productivity Gains Through Worklife Improvement*, Edward M. Glaser, Ph.D., defines six significant dimensions of organizational climate, essentially as follows:

RESTRICTIONS - The degree to which employees feel there are too many rules, procedures, policies and practices to which they must conform, rather than being able to do their work as they see fit. Too much "structure," too many restrictions, stifles motivation to achieve.

RESPONSIBILITY - The feeling that employees have a lot of individual responsibility delegated to them — that they can run their jobs pretty much on their own without having to check with the boss every time a decision must be made. This dimension also includes the feeling that management is willing to take some risks in operating the business.

STANDARDS - The emphasis that employees feel is placed on doing a good job. Includes the degree to which people feel that challenging goals are set and that there is appropriate pressure to continually improve personal and group performance.

REWARD - The degree to which employees feel that they are fairly rewarded for good work, rather than only being punished when something goes wrong. A climate which emphasizes punishment tends to cultivate fear-of-failure and demotivates the person who might otherwise be an enthusiastic, success-oriented worker.

ORGANIZATION - The feeling that things are pretty well organized rather than disorderly, confused or chaotic. While too much organization leads to feelings of constraint, too little organization is inefficient.

TEAM SPIRIT - The feeling that general "good fellowship" prevails, that management and fellow employees are warm and trusting and that the organization is one with which people identify and are proud to belong to.

These are some elements of organizational climate that are critical to job pride development.

Here again, the role of the supervisor is very important. For most employees, the immediate supervisory relationship is the most frequent, most personal indication of the "company climate." Supervisors have a great deal to do with whether the climate is perceived as *negative* or *positive*. *Figure 12-8* pictures this and illustrates eleven of the many ways that supervisory behavior can make the big difference.

Work Redesign

You can use work redesign as an important tool for job pride development. This reverses the trend toward work simplification by enlarging the scope of jobs, enriching the content of jobs, and giving employees more control over their work.

Many studies, such as those by Frederick Herzberg and his colleagues at the Psychological Service of Pittsburgh, have shown that workers tend to want:

- meaningful, satisfying work
- some say in planning and carrying out the work
- task variety
- use of various skills
- growth opportunities
- performance feedback (knowledge of results)
- personal impact on results
- recognition for performance.

Work can be redesigned to better fulfill these motivational needs. Techniques for doing this include job rotation, job enlargement and job enrichment.

Job *rotation* involves moving an employee from one job to another during the work day. The tasks usually are closely related to one another, such as various steps required to turn out a part, product or service. Rotation can provide task variety, use of various skills, and a bit of growth opportunity. Thus, it can help to make the work more meaningful and satisfying.

In some ways similar to job rotation, job *enlargement* involves the addition of one or more related tasks to the existing job. The employee learns to perform several steps in the operation required to make a product or provide a service. This is sometimes called

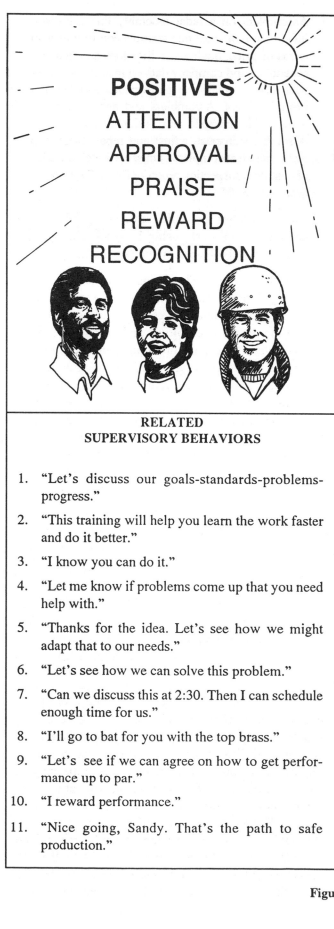

POSITIVES
ATTENTION
APPROVAL
PRAISE
REWARD
RECOGNITION

RELATED
SUPERVISORY BEHAVIORS

1. "Let's discuss our goals-standards-problems-progress."
2. "This training will help you learn the work faster and do it better."
3. "I know you can do it."
4. "Let me know if problems come up that you need help with."
5. "Thanks for the idea. Let's see how we might adapt that to our needs."
6. "Let's see how we can solve this problem."
7. "Can we discuss this at 2:30. Then I can schedule enough time for us."
8. "I'll go to bat for you with the top brass."
9. "Let's see if we can agree on how to get performance up to par."
10. "I reward performance."
11. "Nice going, Sandy. That's the path to safe production."

NEGATIVES
REPRIMAND
WARNING
SUSPENSION
THREAT
FIRING

RELATED
SUPERVISORY BEHAVIORS

1. "I'll do the thinking, you do the work."
2. "Learn it the best you can. Your buddy can help you."
3. "I suppose you'll screw up this job!"
4. "I'll keep looking over your shoulder to make sure you don't goof up."
5. "Your idea won't work here."
6. "I'll nail somebody's hide to the wall for this."
7. "I'm too busy to talk with you now."
8. "There's nothing I can do about it."
9. "Shape up or ship out."
10. "I reward my favorites."
11. "You'll know you are doing O.K. unless you hear from me."

Figure 12-8

"horizontal job loading," because it adds tasks at essentially the same level of difficulty and same organizational level. It makes jobs bigger or broader.

IBM was the first (in the 1940's) to give serious attention to job enlargement. For instance...

- instead of having set-up men lay out the workplace, the operators arranged their own workplaces

- machinists prepared their own specs and sharpened their own tools

- operators who completed jobs no longer set them aside for material handlers to deliver to the next work station; they did it themselves.

Enlarging jobs produced such improvements in output and quality of production that IBM decided to do it on a broad, systematic scale. The operations themselves are engineered to be as simple as possible, but each worker is trained to do as many of these operations as possible.

Job enlargement critics say that adding slightly different tasks of an equally dull, monotonous sort is not really motivational (several boring tasks do not make a "meaningful" job). But proponents have found that job enlargement can help to make work more meaningful and satisfying by increasing task variety, developing various skills and providing growth opportunity.

Job *enrichment* means adding to the basic task some of the planning, organizing and controlling functions usually thought of as managerial. It is sometimes called "vertical job loading." Jobs are considered enriched when the employees participate in planning their work, organizing the work sequence and schedule and controlling the quantity and quality of the work by measuring results against the goals and standards set in the planning phase.

Many companies have benefitted from job enrichment. Among them is Texas Instruments, where it led to a book, *Every Employee A Manager*, by M. Scott Myers. He compares the "traditional" management view of work with "meaningful" (enriched) work. In the traditional view, managers plan, organize, lead and control... and workers *simply* do the work. This division often creates a gap between labor and management, contributing to more or less adversary relationships.

With more meaningful (enriched) work, employees are involved not only in doing the work, but also in planning, organizing and controlling. For example:

Assemblers on a radar assembly line are given information on customer contract commitments in terms of price, quality specifications and delivery schedules, and company data on material and personnel costs, break-even performance and potential profit margins. Assemblers and engineers work together in methods and design improvements. Assemblers inspect, adjust and repair their own work, help test completed units, and receive copies of customer inspection reports. (*Every Employee A Manager*, p. 64.)

Here is another example, involving office work rather than shop work, using both job enlargement (horizontal) and job enrichment (vertical):

Jobs in a large employee insurance section are enlarged horizontally by qualifying insurance clerks to work interchangeably in filing claims, mailing checks, enrolling and orienting new employees, checking premium and enrollment reports, adjusting payroll deductions and interpreting policies to employees. Vertical enlargement involves clerks in insurance program planning meetings with personnel directors and carrier representatives, authorizes them to sign disbursement requests, attend a paperwork systems conference, recommend equipment replacements and to rearrange their work layout. (*Every Employee A Manager*, p. 64.)

These approaches give people some say in planning and carrying out their work, reduce boredom and fatigue by providing task variety, allow people to develop various skills and improve their growth opportunities, provide more specific performance feedback information, increase the realization of personal impact on results and provide better bases for performance recognition. *Figure 12-9* summarizes these work redesign techniques.

There is ample evidence that techniques for QWL, organizational climate, and work redesign can contribute greatly to better quality, safety, productivity and profitability. There also is evidence that they require management leadership skills, especially at the front line, that differ from doing what apparently comes more naturally. The role of the supervisor is critical. For example, Dr. Frederick Herzberg (who coined the phrase "job enrichment" and is recognized internationally as its leading authority) says that supervisory interest, understanding and support are vital; that effective job enrichment requires super-

TECHNIQUES OF WORK REDESIGN

JOB ROTATION	Description - Moving an employee among two or more related jobs or tasks during the work day	Examples: • Type for a while • File for a while • Prepare charts and graphs for a while or • Expedite materials for a while • Operate machine for a while • Package the product for a while
JOB ENLARGEMENT	Description - Adding one or more related tasks to the existing job	Example: Each person does the whole operation, for example, • splicing • soldering • laminating rather than one part of it
JOB ENRICHMENT	Description - Adding to the basic task some of the planning, organizing and controlling functions	Examples: Insurance clerks ... • participate in program planning meetings with personnel directors and carrier representatives • sign disbursement requests • recommend equipment replacements • rearrange their work layout

Benefits

• Greater task variety • Reduced monotony and boredom • Development and application of various skills • Feelings of responsibility - participation - control • Better morale, production, quality and cost effectiveness • Broader base for individual performance feedback and recognition

Figure 12-9

visors with:

- a strong interest in seeing subordinates grow on the job and enjoy high self-esteem from rewarding work.

- a willingness to surrender control to others and thus accept a certain amount of daily ambiguity and anxiety ("I wonder if Joe will get those shipments out without my needling him about them?").

- a tolerance for differences by subordinates in establishing procedures, schedules, communication links, etc.; for people in their individuality aren't necessarily going to program things as the supervisor would.

- a strong orientation toward freedom and results rather than harassment and administrative minutiae.

Experience shows that executives and supervisors can develop the knowledge, skills and attitudes that create the climate for job pride development... but it takes a lot of doing!

JOB PRIDE DEVELOPMENT DYNAMICS

We have discussed these vital aspects of job pride development, effective leadership, behavior reinforcement, quality of work life, organization climate and work redesign. The following four success factors permeate all of them:

- GOAL POWER
- PARTICIPATION
- FEEDBACK
- RECOGNITION

GOAL POWER is the power of performance by objectives - goals - standards. People perform more efficiently and enthusiastically when they have meaningful goals to shoot for... either in sports or at work. To help make sure that goals are meaningful and motivational, make them:

1. *Specific* - Not "We've got to improve productivity," but more like "Increase productivity of the XYZ line 8% by the end of this fiscal period."

2. *Realistic* - When goals are set unrealistically high (such as "Have zero accidents on our 17 construc-

tion sites this year"), they have little or no positive motivational power. People laugh at them, ignore them, or are demoralized by them. Motivational goals are attainable goals.

3. *Challenging* - Goals set ridiculously low have little or no positive motivational power. (Would a high jumper, for instance, really get charged up about a jump with the bar set at four feet?) Goals that provide "stretch" are motivational.

4. *Personalized* - To provide maximum motivational power, goals must be accepted by the individual; their attainment must be controllable by the individual; they must become his or her own goals.

5. *Time-bounded* - People are not positively motivated when goals are too remote. For example, the promise of a gold watch for 30 years of top quality work has no impact on the day-to-day efforts of workers. To motivate people, have goals for this month, this week, this shift and perhaps this hour. Use dates and deadlines.

6. *Measurable* - There must be standards, and indicators which show whether or not the standards are met. Whenever possible, these measures should be in terms of a numerical, percentage, time or other type of figure... they should be quantifiable. (Not "You improved your sales personality," but more like "Your incidence of arguing with prospective customers went from nine per week down to four.")

7. *Need-fulfilling* - As sages have said: to be a successful salesperson, "find a need and fill it." Motivational goals provide incentives that help meet the individual's needs. Remember, each person acts to fill... not your needs... but his or her own needs (such as growth, achievement, responsibility, recognition, affiliation and security).

> **Principle: Motivation to accomplish results tends to increase when people have meaningful goals toward which to work.**

INVOLVEMENT. People have a tremendous need to be involved; to be in on the action; to be part of the team; to participate. The supervisor who asks people for their suggestions and ideas about matters that affect their work, and who truly listens to what they say, develops mutual interest, mutual respect and mutual motivation. There's a world of motivational difference between their goals and our goals; between their program and our program; between their decisions and our decisions. To develop pride of performance, there is no factor that has more power and potential than participation. It is summarized in this principle:

> **Principle: Meaningful involvement increases motivation and support.**

FEEDBACK. For people to learn, to improve, to change, they need feedback that is timely, tangible, focused and frequent. Nobody likes to play ball without knowing the score! Every worker has a right to know these four things:

- what his or her job is
- what the performance yardsticks are
- how well he or she is doing
- the specific steps to improvement

When people don't know what their jobs are, the results are confusion, wheel-spinning, and losses such as waste, damage and injuries. When people don't know their performance yardsticks, the results are guesswork, wrong priorities, misdirected resources and hit-or-miss efforts. When people don't know how they are doing, the results are low motivation, poor morale and measurement-by-mindreading. When people don't know specific steps to improvement, the results are glittering generalities, procrastination, frustration and status quo.

> **Principle: Effective communication increases motivation.**

BEHAVIOR REINFORCEMENT. The need for sincere recognition is one of our most basic, powerful, psychological hungers. Behavior that results in recognition, reward, or reinforcement tends to be repeated — which feeds the hunger again. Leaders are learning to use the motivational power of praise; to give others the awards of attention, assistance and approval; to emphasize support, satisfaction and success; to accentuate the positive; to reap the rewards of reinforcement and recognition.

> **Principle: Behavior with negative effects tends to decrease or stop; behavior with positive effects tends to continue or increase.**

You would have to look long and hard to find any four psychological dynamics that can do more for you in managing performance and developing job pride than these: Goal Power - Participation - Feedback - Recognition. They have been put to work as practical guideposts for many management activities in many companies around the world. As an example, *Figure 12-10* shows how they have been used in industrial foremanship training.

Putting these principles and guidelines to work - month-by-month, week-by-week, day-by-day, hour-by-hour — is your best bet for leading the way to job pride development.

BENEFITS OF JOB PRIDE DEVELOPMENT

When properly applied, job pride development provides significant benefits. Many of these can be measured in tangible terms. Here are some examples:

- Quality, production and safety statistics will improve, depending on the application. These can be measured easily by comparison with prior figures.

- As proper work procedures are followed to a greater degree, and by a larger number of employees, safety performance that controls injuries and property damage will show improvement... and can be measured by comparison with prior figures.

- Available production time will increase, since less time will be spent on "firefighting" a variety of problems caused by poor performance. Encouraging good performance takes less time than discouraging poor performance. Special efforts to "investigate poor quality," "discourage improper work procedures" and "stop growth of unsafe practices" will no longer require so much extra time. Concentration on promoting good quality, proper work procedures and safe practices will achieve more effective results.

SOME DO'S AND DON'TS FOR JOB PRIDE DEVELOPMENT

DO let each person know what is expected; clarify job duties; provide standards, "yardsticks," goals; give clear directions.	DON'T assume that each person sees the job as you see it, don't let them wander aimlessly; don't expect them to be mindreaders.
DO let each person know how he is doing; furnish frequent measures of progress toward goals; help people to "keep score."	"DON'T operate under the philosophy of "they know things are OK unless I tell them otherwise!"
DO instruct, train, guide and follow-up; help people overcome weaker points of performance.	DON'T let people fumble along without help; don't let wrong work habits get established.
DO give each person enough responsibility, authority and freedom for decision-making to challenge and bring out the best in him or her.	DON'T do people's jobs for them; don't SNOOPER-vise.
DO study requirements of each job and abilities and interests of each person; match people and jobs.	DON'T mis-use manpower; don't stifle brainpower; don't destroy job satisfaction.
DO try to understand mistakes; find out what caused them; show real interest in remedies; take action to prevent recurrences.	DON'T expect people to be perfect; don't look for a "scapegoat," don't overemphasize punishment and penalties.
DO base rewards on job results and accomplishments.	DON'T let your own biases, prejudices, or pet peeves control your actions; don't play favorites.
DO encourage friendly, healthy competition on matters such as attendance, punctuality, quality, safety, suggestions and housekeeping.	DON'T dampen the competitive spirit of individuals and groups.
DO admit your mistakes; do have enough courage to say "I don't know, but I'll try to find the answer."	DON'T "pass the buck," try to play superman, or put yourself on a pedestal.
DO solicit, respect, and use the suggestions, opinions and ideas of others; promote active participation; let people help you.	DON'T give the impression that you are aloof, a lone wolf, overly independent, or too self-centered.
DO try to provide working conditions that are clean, safe and pleasant; procedures and tools that are efficient; and work that is well organized.	DON'T take the work environment for granted, don't stop trying to improve the situation.

Figure 12-10

SOME DO'S AND DON'TS FOR JOB PRIDE DEVELOPMENT

DO keep people posted on what is happening within the company, and why; discuss and explain impending changes; nip rumors in the bud; help people "talk things out."	DON'T use a clam or ostrich approach.
DO pay attention to "minor" complaints; have a real "open door" policy; show genuine interest in the other person's problems; correct the situation as soon as you can.	DON'T let "little" problems grow into big ones.
DO make full use of sincere praise; show your appreciation for good work; let your boss know when your employee or your group does outstanding work.	DON'T be a flatterer, a grouch or a chronic fault-finder; don't wait until a person dies, transfers or retires to give him due credit.
DO emphasize the importance of the job; make it meaningful; exlain "the why" of the job; show where the job fits into the total picture; remove monotony and boredom as much as you can.	DON'T let people get the impression that their jobs are meaningless, like digging holes just to fill them up again or like trying to fill a leaking bucket.
DO help to uncover buried abilities of people; develop your men and women; recommend pay increases, transfers and promotions when appropriate; go to bat for your team members.	DON'T "hide their lights under a basket," don't hold people back; don't take the easy way out.
DO provide standards for conduct through reasonable rules and regulations, and enforce them in a fair and consistent manner; give good leadership.	DON'T be a dictator and don't be milquetoast.
DO help people correct their mistakes; be constructive when criticizing, and do it privately; welcome questions and try to answer them in a straight-forward manner.	DON'T make a person feel stupid, cause him to "lose face," or ridicule him.
DO everything within your power to remove sources of conflict, irritation and frustration.	DON'T be a barrier builder.
DO try to analyze your own needs, wants and desires; try to see how others react to you; try to understand and correct your own faults.	DON'T always point your finger toward the other guy.
DO SHOW YOUR INTEREST IN THE INDIVIDUAL; SHOW YOUR RESPECT FOR THE DIGNITY AND UNIQUENESS OF EACH PERSON AND TRY TO UNDERSTAND HIS OR HER VIEWPOINTS AND NEEDS.	DON'T TREAT A PERSON LIKE A MACHINE, A STATISTIC, A "THING" OR A TOOL.

PUTTING PEOPLE-ACTION TO WORK

Figure 12-10 (cont'd)

- Such things as maintenance costs, downtime, delays and purchase expenditures will improve as a reflection of improved work performance and better use of equipment, materials and people.

- Gripes, grievances, and "groaning" will decrease as job satisfaction increases. Employees will develop a sense of pride in connection with their jobs.

These are some examples of the most immediately noticeable benefits. Supervisors are likely to find additional benefits as they gain experience with the application and maintenance of Job Pride Development. Higher management will also find benefit in the fact that foremen and supervisors will be able to devote more of their time to efficient and effective management work, since fewer "crisis" situations will erupt to erode their supervisory time.

In times like these, when productivity and profitability problems are being felt around the world, and craftsmanship threatens to become a thing of the past, Job Pride Development is potentially one of the most valuable tools available to the modern professional manager.

CORE CONCEPTS IN REVIEW

Job Pride Development

1. A professional management approach to motivation holds great potential for contributing to the much needed improvements in quality, safety and productivity.

2. Having moved through the "Scientific Management" era of the early 1900's and the "Human Relations" era of the mid-1900's, we are now in the stage of **"Participative Management."**

3. Behavioral science applications typical of this era include:

   a. **Quality of Work Life** (QWL) programs aim to replace alienation and apathy with identification and enthusiasm. They involve powerful dynamics such as participation, job enrichment, team building and mutual problem solving. They help to fulfill human needs for self-esteem, self-actualization, dignity and development.

   b. **Organization Development** (OD) activities aim to improve the organization's "climate" (people's perception of how it feels to work in the organization). A positive climate provides:
   (1) Growth **opportunities**
   (2) **Stimulation** for improvement
   (3) **Counsel** on job objectives, standards, performance and improvement
   (4) **Assistance** by way of training, communication and career development
   (5) **Recognition** for desired performance

   c. Nineteen specific managerial behaviors have been identified as major factors in establishing and maintaining **high performance climates**, and have been organized into these four learning clusters:
   (1) Goal and task definition
   (2) Team building
   (3) Performance appraisal
   (4) Coaching and counseling

   d. **Work redesign** holds great promise as an effective motivator, as an important impetus to Job Pride Development. It reverses the trend toward work simplification. It makes jobs bigger and better through techniques such as job rotation, job enlargement and job enrichment.

   e. **Positive behavior reinforcement** is the immediate recognition of desired acts. It is based on the simple concept that "behavior is influenced by its effects." In practical terms, this means that when a specific job behavior results in a negative consequence (displeasure, pain, penalty, punishment, frustrated desires), that behavior will tend not to be repeated. But, when it results in a positive consequence (pleasure, reward, recognition, satisfied desires), the behavior will tend to be repeated.

Success steps in using positive behavior reinforcements are:

1. **Pinpoint** the desired behavior

2. **Record** baseline performance data

3. **Reinforce** specific desired behavior

4. **Evaluate** the impact of reinforcement on performance

5. **Follow through** with appropriate action

Four **powerful success dynamics** that permeate all of these methods and techniques are:

1. Goal Power

2. Participation

3. Feedback

4. Recognition

Measurable benefits of Job Pride Development include not only better job satisfaction - attitudes - morale, but also improved quality - safety - productivity.

KEY QUESTIONS

1. What is job pride development?

2. Name and describe the three main historical stages of management motivation.

3. True or False? There is a definite leadership personality pattern.

4. True or False? There are certain behavioral characteristics frequently found in successful leaders.

5. What are the four learning clusters into which 19 different leadership practices have been categorized?

6. What is the psychological basis for behavior reinforcement?

7. True or False? Punishment (negative discipline) should not be a part of a modern motivational system.

8. Name several undesirable side effects of excess emphasis on punishment.

9. What are the five steps to a systematic behavior reinforcement project?

10. What is the main emphasis in Quality of Work Life (QWL) programs?

11. Define organizational climate.

12. Name five important aspects of a company climate that is conducive to growth and development.

13. Work redesign involves _____ the trend toward work simplification.

14. Name several motivational needs that work redesign may help to fulfill.

15. Name and describe three specific techniques involved in work redesign.

16. True or False? Job enrichment involves adding to the "doing" task some of the planning, organizing and controlling functions traditionally thought of as "managerial."

17. Describe the four major job pride development dynamics (success factors).

18. List several benefits of job pride development that can be measured in tangible terms.

PRACTICAL APPLICATIONS SUMMARY

S - For Supervisors
E - For Executives
C - For Safety/Loss Control Coordinators
W - For Workers

		S	E	C	W
1.	Seek suggestions regarding safety policies, procedures and practices.	x	x	x	
2.	Make suggestions regarding safety policies, procedures and practices.	x	x	x	x
3.	Seek suggestions regarding safety program standards and activities.	x	x	x	
4.	Make suggestions regarding safety program standards and activities.	x	x	x	x
5.	Provide opportunities for people to participate in auditing/measuring safety performance.	x	x	x	
6.	Participate in auditing/measuring safety performance.	x	x	x	x
7.	Establish clear, specific performance goals for subordinates' jobs.	x	x	x	
8.	Set team or group goals as well as individual goals.	x	x	x	
9.	Provide frequent feedback on individual and group performance.	x	x	x	
10.	Promote safety program planning teams.	x	x	x	
11.	Serve on safety program planning teams.	x	x	x	
12.	Promote safety problem solving teams.	x	x	x	
13.	Serve on safety problem solving teams.	x	x	x	x
14.	Provide safety and health training.	x	x	x	
15.	Take safety and health training.	x	x	x	x
16.	Actively seek everyone's help in inspection activities.	x	x	x	
17.	Actively participate in inspection activities.	x	x	x	x
18.	Seek suggestions regarding housekeeping and order.	x	x	x	
19.	Actively participate in housekeeping and order activities.	x	x	x	x
20.	Promote total personnel involvement in developing and implementing critical job/task analyses and procedures.	x	x	x	
21.	Assist the development and implementation of critical job/task analyses and procedures.	x	x	x	x
22.	Promote the positive, problem solving approach to accident/incident investigation.	x	x	x	
23.	Provide training and coaching in accident/incident investigation.	x	x	x	
24.	Participate actively in accident/incident investigations to find causes, not culprits.	x	x	x	x
25.	Follow-up the implementation of remedial actions resulting from investigations.	x	x	x	
26.	Promote the reporting and investigation of "close calls."	x	x	x	
27.	Report "close calls."	x	x	x	x

	S	E	C	W
28. Investigate "close calls" and take appropriate action to prevent recurrence.	x	x	x	x
29. Use positive behavior reinforcement in feedback from planned job observations.	x	x	x	
30. Provide coaching, training, and constructive correction of performance problems noted in planned job observations.	x	x	x	
31. Seek suggestions regarding emergency action plans and programs.	x	x	x	
32. Make suggestions regarding emergency action plans and programs.	x	x	x	x
33. Promote participation in rules development, enforcement and reinforcement.	x	x	x	
34. Help to develop, enforce and reinforce rules and regulations.	x	x	x	x
35. Provide accident/incident analysis feedback to all levels of the organization.	x	x	x	
36. Help identify the need for skill training programs.	x	x	x	x
37. Provide skill training programs.	x	x	x	
38. Take skill training programs.	x	x	x	x
39. Seek suggestions regarding personal protective equipment programs.	x	x	x	
40. Make suggestions regarding personal protective equipment programs.	x	x	x	x
41. Provide first aid training for all levels.	x	x	x	
42. Take first aid training.	x	x	x	x
43. Provide supervisory training in job orientation, job instruction, coaching and tipping techniques.	x	x	x	
44. Apply modern techniques of job orientation, job instruction, coaching and tipping.	x	x	x	
45. Provide training in how to hold good group meetings.	x	x	x	
46. Conduct good group meetings.	x	x	x	
47. Contribute to good group meetings as a participant.	x	x	x	x
48. Seek suggestions for safety promotion activities.	x	x	x	
49. Make suggestions for safety promotion activities.	x	x	x	x
50. Promote safety with contests and awards which require people to learn, do and/or remember something for safety.	x	x	x	
51. Participate in safety contests and awards programs.	x	x	x	x
52. Use more recognition than criticism.	x	x	x	x
53. Seek suggestions regarding work redesign techniques.	x	x	x	
54. Make suggestions regarding work redesign techniques.	x	x	x	x
55. Set the safety leadership example.	x	x	x	

CHAPTER 13

PROBLEM SOLVING

Life is a problem-solving experience...an unending series of problems — problems which must be decided... And for leaders, these problems and their decisions have added significance, because leaders are responsible for others...
- Earle S. Hannaford, Ph.D.

INTRODUCTION

As a practical philosopher once said: "Almost anyone can steer the ship if the sea is calm." But getting through troubled waters is something else! As a manager-supervisor-leader, you earn a healthy portion of your pay by how well you guide your part of the organization through the turbulence of problems that must be solved.

Problems, problems everywhere, and hardly time to think! Supervisors and executives constantly face people problems, equipment problems, materials problems, quality problems, cost problems, safety and loss control problems. Accident investigation is a prime example of a problem solving process. Inspections often identify problems to be solved. Effective problem solving helps to separate the *professional* manager from the amateur.

The primary objectives of this chapter are:

- To stimulate application of a seven-step system of problem solving for loss control
- To pinpoint the dynamics of success for problem solving groups
- To encourage analysis of *potential* problems as a loss prevention tool

A SEVEN STEP SYSTEM FOR PROBLEM SOLVING

The following seven steps form a fundamental framework for effective problem solving:

R	ECOGNIZE THE PROBLEM
A	NALYZE THE PROBLEM
I	DENTIFY POSSIBLE CAUSES
D	EVELOP POSSIBLE SOLUTIONS
E	VALUATE POSSIBLE SOLUTIONS
R	EACH A DECISION
S	TIMULATE ACTION

The best way to illustrate this system is to apply it, step by step, to an actual problem. This will enable you not only to learn the system, but to see the reasons for each step and the benefits to be gained.

Step 1 - Recognize the Problem

The most critical element in any problem solving system is RECOGNITION. After all, we can't begin to solve a problem until we realize we have one! While this may seem all too obvious, the fact is that companies have been forced out of business by problems they didn't know they had — until it was too late — and supervisors have been replaced for failure to solve problems they weren't even aware existed.

How can this happen? How can people be unaware of major problems in their own area of responsibility? How can a truly serious problem be missed or overlooked?

In almost every case, the answer can be found in lack of appropriate standards for the situation or operation involved. Standards tell us what we can expect, or what "should be" in such areas as work performance, safety, costs, production rates or quality levels. Without standards we have no way of telling if things are as they should be, or if something is wrong. In fact, for our purposes, we can define a problem as *a deviation from a standard for which the cause is not known.*

The best, and perhaps only dependable way to avoid "missing" or "overlooking" a problem is to 1) have standards for our work, 2) measure all performance against those standards and 3) note all deviations from these standards. It is difficult to imagine any acceptable alternative to this procedure.

There are many sources of written standards such as governmental agencies, standards setting groups such as American National Standards Institute and Canadian Standards Association, manufacturers of chemicals and machinery and, of course, in-plant written standards and data sheets. There are also un-written standards which have grown up over a period of time and which are widely accepted as the way things are supposed to be.

Let's assume we have the elements required for problem recognition (standards and measurements against those standards). What types of problems might be revealed? Here are some typical examples:

1. Throughout the main plant, water spray pressures in the personnel showers have dropped about one-third in the last two weeks.

2. Injuries recorded in the OSHA log of our assembly plant are five times as high as they were a year ago.

3. In the main plant, hand injuries have increased sharply. To date there have been 14 injuries compared to 3 for the same period last year.

4. Grinding hours are up 12% in the Fabrication Department over the same period last year. This is not a prohibitive increase, but it is unusual since the time required for grinding generally does not fluctuate.

5. Productivity in the shearing operation has increased by almost 18% in the last four months.

Each of these situations involves a "deviation from some accepted standard for which the cause is not known." In most cases, the standard is simply some baseline established by past performance. Item five, it should be noted, is not something that we would normally consider a problem. But it is a deviation from a standard for which the cause is not known. By recognizing and analyzing this positive deviation (this good news) and determining its causes, we may be able to do more of it.

Let's use these situations, or problems, to work our way through the problem solving system. Taking an appropriate problem and tracking it through the system, step by step, is probably the best way to learn just how the system works and the benefits it offers.

Step 2 - Analyze The Problem

The situation shown in *Figure 13-1* isn't very funny in everyday life. Too often it leads to doing the wrong thing, right now! Sometimes it's better to do nothing at all than to do everything wrong. Doing *something* may be the worst possible action. Analyzing and doing the effective things is the best approach.

Figure 13-1

Having recognized the five problems above, and having defined them in terms of their degrees of deviation from standards, we are ready for the second step in our system — ANALYSIS.

In this step, we examine each problem to determine its severity and/or urgency. In brief, we want to ask how bad it is and how urgent the need is for solution. Each situation must be evaluated in terms such as:

- How serious is it at present?
- Will it get more serious if left unattended?
- How *quickly* can it become more serious (overnight, next week, next year, etc.)?
- Is it a problem worth our time and effort (not all are)?

Our intent in this analysis is to ensure we are working on the *right* problem. With limits on the time and money we can devote to problem solution, this is a critical step. In addition, some problems are so serious that any delay in their solution can jeopardize life or health, or even survival of the business. For these reasons, we cannot afford to work on the wrong problem. Keeping all this in mind, let's look at each of our five problems and see if closer analysis can help determine action priorities.

1. The drop in the water spray pressure in the personnel showers is due to the installation of water-saver washers promoted by the Department of Natural Resources to conserve water and energy. The resulting water spray appears adequate to do the job.

2. Almost all of the injuries recorded in the OSHA log of the assembly plant are "foreign body in the eye." These go up quite a bit in the summer months when large floor fans are in use. The new plant manager, just to be on the safe side, sends affected employees to a doctor to have the foreign objects removed. He is under the impression that because a doctor does it, even though it is a first aid procedure, it has to be recorded. While the problems created by the floor fans should not be ignored, the "increase" in recordable accidents is not as serious as it first appeared.

3. Hand injuries have averaged less than one per year over the last ten years. The workforce and activity level during that time have not varied significantly. Twelve of the fourteen hand injuries this year oc-

curred within the last three months. All were cuts of varying severity. Two of the last twelve resulted in lost work days.

4. While total grinding hours are up 12%, their distribution appears uneven. All of the increase appears to occur regularly every fourth week in a period of three to four days. This will be followed by just over three weeks of normal grinding hours and then another sharp increase for a little less than a week. The pattern extends over the last three months. The surge has caused some shipping delays.

5. The productivity increase in the shearing section has apparently been achieved through some minor scheduling changes and the installation of new shear knives that allow four weeks between required knife changes as opposed to two weeks with the old equipment.

While Items 3 and 4 both qualify as bona fide problems, it is fairly clear that Item 3 is the most severe and needs the most immediate attention. While Item 5 is not a problem in the normal sense, it should be analyzed more closely when time permits to determine the exact causes of the productivity increase. This will enable the increase to be sustained and allow consideration of applications in other areas.

Problem Solving Worksheet

Now that the top priority problem has been determined, it must be analyzed in greater detail. An aid in this systematic evaluation is the "Problem Solving Worksheet" shown as *Figure 13-2*. This form can serve as a detailed record of problem solving efforts. Its use also aids the thorough, step by step, procedure required in professional problem solving.

Column 1 - *Description of Problem* - In this column, the particular problem being addressed should be stated as clearly and concisely as possible. This step, along with the others given below, helps us to apply the Principle of Definition - "a logical decision can be made only if the real problem is first defined." Often as not, decisions are made about problems without anyone having a clear statement of the problem to be solved. The description should include the degree of deviation from accepted performance levels. In our example, the problem is described as:

PROBLEM SOLVING WORKSHEET

1. PROBLEM Be as specific as possible. Include deviation from applicable standards	2. PRIORITY	3. LOCATION(S) Where is problem occurring? Dept., Function, Process, Task Involved.	4. TIMING When did it first occur? Is it continual? Interval, if any, between occurrences.	5. DEGREE How many? How much? How bad is it right now? How bad can it be? Is it getting worse? At what rate?	6. PROBLEM CAUSE(S) List major cause(s) most likely to be main contributors to problem. Define relationship of cause to problem as exactly as possible.

Figure 13-2

PROBLEM SOLVING WORKSHEET

7. CORRECTIVE ACTION	8. FOLLOW-UP	9. STATUS
Describe steps to be taken to resolve problem. Include not only steps taken, but how they are intended to correct deviation.	Monitor and measure the results of corrective action. How well is the problem solved? Give measures that show the effects of corrective action. Be specific.	Is project done? Will it be checked later? Is additional action to be taken? When? By whom?

Figure 13-2 (Continued)

Fourteen hand injuries in the last 12 months, compared to an average of less than one such injury per year for the preceding ten years. Last year there were three hand injuries. The injuries in the last 12 months have all been cuts of varying degrees of severity.

Column 2 - *Priority* - A priority is assigned to the described problem or problems to help assure that they are dealt with on a "worst first" basis. This is an application of another fundamental problem solving principle - the Principle of the Critical Few - "In any given group of occurrences, a small number of causes will tend to give rise to the largest proportion of results." Use of this principle helps us separate the "critical few" major problems from the "trivial many" minor problems. The priorities used here are:

1. A problem likely to cause permanent disability, loss of life or body part and/or extensive loss of structure, equipment, material or quality.

2. A problem likely to cause serious injury or illness, resulting in temporary disability and/or property, material, equipment or quality loss that is disruptive but less severe than "1."

3. A problem likely to cause minor (non-disabling) injury or non-disruptive property, material, equipment or quality loss.

The purpose of these categories is to allow the ranking or classification of problems by their potential severity. The categories given here are quite similar to those in the Inspections chapter. However, you should not feel bound by them. If you want five priority levels, or even ten, feel free to develop them. But be sure that they allow adequate classification of problems *you* must contend with, and that they stimulate dealing with the "worst first". The priority for our hand injury problem will be "1," based on severity and rate of increase.

Column 3 - *Location* - Here we define as closely as possible where the problem is occurring. This lets us "zero in" on the proper area rather than spread our attention over the entire plant. It also helps us narrow down the sources of possible causes for the problem. In the hand injuries case, twelve of the fourteen injuries in the last year have occurred in the assembly area during installation of stabilizer bars on a fabricated assembly. This is the final task performed prior to sending the completed assemblies to shipping.

Column 4 - *Timing* - The purpose of this section is to pinpoint, as closely as possible, the exact time the problem appears to have started or was first noticed, and when it occurs. Every effort should be made to determine whether or not the problem occurs continually, sporadically or at some discernible intervals.

The sharp increase in hand injuries began thirteen weeks ago. They seem to happen in "spurts" of two or three injuries every third or fourth week since that time. The pattern seems to be two or three hand injuries in a two or three-day period followed by 19 or 20 days without injury before the cycle repeats itself.

Column 5 - *Degree* - Here we define the degree of deviation from standard and, where possible, its trends. State exactly how severe the problem is, how severe it can become, and, where appropriate, how rapidly it can worsen. Also, note whether the problem is static or becoming more severe.

The hand injuries over the last twelve months (14) represent a 1400% increase over the average injuries per year for the preceding ten years. Nearly 86% of these injuries (12) have occurred in the last three months. They appear to be increasing in severity, and the last two have resulted in lost workdays. In both of these cases, overtime was required to avoid production delays. Should the injuries continue at this rate and this severity, the associated costs alone would be prohibitive, not to mention the pain, suffering and effect on employee morale.

Step 3 - Identify Possible Causes

With all the information in Columns 1 through 5 of the worksheet gathered and recorded, we are ready to identify possible causes. This is a critical step and requires caution. Whenever a situation needs correcting, there tends to be pressure for quick results. But, if the first piece of plausible evidence is labeled as *the* cause, and action is taken, the result is likely to be frustration and further loss. The systematic problem solver resists the temptation to jump to conclusions and take hasty action.

Notice again the title of this step - Identify Possible Causes (plural). It is important to keep in mind the Principle of Multiple Causes: "Problems are seldom, if ever, the result of a single cause." A common mistake in problem solving is to look for *the* cause and then to attempt to solve the problem on that basis.

One important question to ask in uncovering causes is, "What is *distinctive* about this situation?" How does the problem situation differ from similar situations which do not have this problem? What is being done to, or with, the problem situation that is not being done to or with others? What is true (unique features, attributes, uses, etc.) about the problem situation that is not true about others?

A second important question deals with *change*. What, if anything, has changed in any of the distinctive features? When did the change take place? What event took place around or preceding the appearance of the problem? What is there about the change that could cause the problem? Putting together the answers to these two questions will almost always point to the causes of the problem.

Such a review of the facts gathered about our case problem reveals the following:

1. The increase in hand injuries began at about the same time that the new longer-life shear knives were installed in the shearing area.

2. The hand injuries are occurring when stabilizer bars are added to an assembly as part of a larger assembly process. The stabilizer bars are cut to length in the Shearing Department and are sent directly to the Assembly Department with no intermediate processing or inspection.

3. A review of accident investigation reports reveals the hand injuries are cuts caused by "edge droop" on the stabilizer bars after they have been sheared. "Edge droop" is normally caused by dull shear knives. It also tends to be more prevalent with "mild" (or softer) grades of steel such as that used in the stabilizer bars.

4. There is an approximate correlation between the hand injuries and grinding costs in that they seem to increase at about the same intervals. Closer investigation shows that this results from the stabilizer bars being sent to grinding for removal of the "fins" or edge droop whenever injuries occur. The grinding step is continued for about one to one-and-a-half weeks before it is stopped, because the fins disappear from the sheared bars. The cycle repeats in about three weeks.

From the information available, at this point it appears the fins or edge droop on the stabilizer bars (which are the source of the hand injuries) are a result of extended use of the new shear knives. They apparently become dull enough in the fourth week of use to produce the fins on the stabilizer bars. At the end of the fourth week they are changed, as part of the routine maintenance, and the problem disappears. The problem may be aggravated by the mild grade of steel being used in the bars. Column 6 of the worksheet (*Figure 13-2*) can be used for listing the causal information.

Step 4 - Develop Possible Solutions

The next step in our system is the development of possible solutions for the problem. Notice that we say solutions (plural)... not *the* solution. It is important to list all possible solutions, without attempting to judge which is best. That selection will be made later.

In *The Art of Problem Solving*, Edward Hodnett reflects the thinking of many when he says:

> The more choices you have, the better your solution to a problem is likely to be. As you start your attack on a problem, therefore, you keep asking, not merely, "Is there another alternative?" You ask, "How many more alternatives are there?" The difference between the fair problem solver and the first-rate one shows up here. The superior problem solver is not thrown off by three or four possible solutions, even when they are good. The presence of any number of good answers does not mean that the best has yet been turned up. Standard practice for all problem solving, then, is to list *all* the possible alternatives before making a decision.

The change catalysts shown as *Figure 13-3* are intended as thought joggers for developing possible solutions.

For our case problem, major possible solutions are:

1. Go back to the old style shear knives that are replaced every 8 to 10 days.

2. Add an inspection step to the production process after shearing, and send any bars that require grinding to the grinding department.

3. Send all stabilizer bars directly from shearing to grinding before they go to assembly.

4. Issue abrasion and cut resistant gloves to all employees in assembly who handle the stabilizer bars.

CHANGE CATALYSTS

ADAPT?	What else is it like? What other ideas does it suggest? Does the past offer a parallel? What might be "copied"? How can we put it to your use?
COMBINE?	Can you blend it or use an assortment? Can you combine purposes, appeals, goals, or ideas? Package in larger units? Put "this" and "that" together?
MAGNIFY?	What can we add to it? Can we make it bigger? Longer? Fatter? Heavier? Faster? More useful?
MINIFY?	What can be removed from it? How might we reduce it? Can we make it shorter? Thinner? Lighter? Slower? Less hazardous? Can we break it up? Eiminate it altogether?
MODIFY?	Can you change color? Meaning? Motion? Odor? Sound? Shape? Size? Feel? Can you make it more attractive? Easier? Safer? Unique?
REARRANGE?	Can you interchange the present components? Use another sequence? Change pace or schedule?
REVERSE?	Can we use opposites? Turn it backwards? Turn it upside down? Change it from right to left? Left to right? Use a mirror image?
SUBSTITUTE?	Another ingredient? Another material? Another tool? Another piece of equipment? Another location? Another surrounding? Another person? Another group?
SIMPLIFY?	Make it more understandable? Give it fewer parts? Fewer operations? Fewer levels or steps? Use standardization? Use mechanization? Use automation? Use humanization? Make it easier to operate?

Add your favorite below:

Figure 13-3

5. Change the steel used for the stabilizer bars to a "harder" grade (one with a higher carbon content), that will be less likely to develop "fins" during shearing.

6. Change the new shear knives more frequently, perhaps at three-week intervals rather than four. (This seems to be about the time they become significantly duller.)

7. Combine #5 and #6 above.

While these solutions may not represent all possibilities, they do represent the most practical steps presently available. It is often helpful in developing possibilities to also develop lists of "musts" and "wants." "Musts" are those criteria which a solution absolutely must meet to be acceptable. For instance:

- Must not cost more than $25,000
- Must not involve any layoffs
- Should be implemented within three months
- Should not damage morale

If an alternative does not meet a "must," it is discarded. This screens out the impossibilities and reduces your alternatives to the relevant few. "Wants" are things that it would be nice to have but which, by themselves, would not disqualify a solution.

Step 5 - Evaluate Possible Solutions

In this step, each possible solution is carefully evaluated for both positive and negative potential. A straightforward, common sense approach is all that is required. Look at each possible solution in terms of the good effect(s) it might have and any undesirable side effects it could also have. List both effects for every solution. This will allow you to remember, later, why you chose a particular course of action *and* why you rejected another.

In our example, such an evaluation produces the following results:

1. *Go back to the old style shear knives that are replaced every 8 to 10 days.*
   + would probably eliminate "fins" since they never occurred with this style shear knife
   - would lose productivity gains realized
   - would increase maintenance costs and downtime associated with shear knife changes

2. *Add an inspection step to the production process after shearing and send bars that require grinding to the Grinding Department.*
   + would reduce chances for hand injuries in assembly by removal of "fins" before pieces are received
   - would introduce possibility of hand injuries during inspection process since such inspection (visual) would require handling of stabilizer bars by inspectors
   - would increase costs by requiring an additional step in production process
   - would introduce some degree of delay in production time because of additional handling
   - would still involve costs of grinding

3. *Send all stabilizer bars directly from shearing to grinding before they are given to assembly.*
   + would assure "fins" would be removed before pieces arrive in assembly, thereby reducing risk of hand injuries
   - would add a handling step to the production process with associated costs and delays
   - would still involve costs of grinding
   - would require substantial unnecessary handling of material since most bars would probably not require grinding. This would cause additional delay time

4. *Issue abrasion and cut resistant gloves to all employees in assembly who handle the stabilizer bars.*
   + would reduce employee exposures to the "fins" and minimize chances of hand injuries
   - would add some degree of discomfort for employees, since gloves are rather heavy and stiff
   - would make assembly operation somewhat more difficult because of less finger dexterity
   - would allow others (customers as an example) to be exposed to "fins" and possible hand injury. In case of a third party, this could involve liability

5. *Change the steel used for the stabilizer bars to a "harder" grade (one with higher carbon content) that will be less likely to develop "fins" during shearing.*
   + would probably reduce or eliminate "fins" since harder steel does not form shear droop under normal circumstances

- harder steel would reduce the life of the shear knives - they would become dull much quicker and require more frequent replacement with associated costs and delay time
- Breakage would increase since harder steel is more brittle and prone to breakage during shearing. This would increase material costs
- harder steel would probably cost more than that currently in use

6. *Change the new shear knives more frequently, perhaps at three-week intervals rather than four. (This seems to be about the time they become significantly duller.)*
   + would minimize or eliminate "fins" with corresponding reduction of hand injuries
   + would allow retention of as much as half the increased productivity realized by installation of the new shear knives since they could still be used nearly twice as long as the old knives
   - would involve some loss of productivity due to one week reduction in life of shear knives from present level

7. *Combine #5 and #6 above.*

   + would further reduce or totally eliminate the "fins" and the resulting hand injuries for reasons already given in "5" and "6"
   - could require more frequent shear knife changes because of harder steel, wiping out any remaining productivity increase from the new knives
   - would increase material cost, maintenance and downtime for reasons previously noted

Each of the possible solutions offers a way to control or eliminate hand injuries, but each has its own cost for achieving this. We want the solution with the best cost-to-benefit ratio that will still solve our problem.

Step 6 - Reach A Decision

If the preceding steps in our problem solving system have been done properly, this will not be an overwhelmingly difficult decision. This does not mean the "best" solution will always stand out sharply from all the others. It does mean "good" solutions will normally be easily distinguished from "bad" ones. Being forced to choose one solution from two or three good ones is not a bad situation to be in.

The right decision is the one that gets the most done with the fewest adverse consequences. One of the biggest mistakes is wishing for the perfect solution. Typically, there is none. In making important decisions, you have to do a delicate balancing act. Peter Drucker says it like this:

> ... there is no "perfect" decision. One always has to pay a price ... one always has to balance conflicting objectives, conflicting opinions, conflicting priorities. The best decision is only an approximation — and a risk...(p. 479)

But, if you have done the prior steps well — have recognized and analyzed the problem, have identified causes, have developed and evaluated solution alternatives — then making the decision (selecting a solution) is rational and relatively simple.

In our example, the selection is fairly easy. Possible solution #6 seems noticeably better than the alternatives. It will allow retention of a significant amount of the increase in productivity realized with the new shear knives and still reduce the problem of the hand injuries. Implementation costs should also be minimal compared to the other solutions. Also, it does not introduce any additional variable such as a new type of steel. This will make the effect of the change procedure easier to measure since any improvement realized can be connected solely to the more frequent shear knife replacement.

The solution to be used, "change the new shear knives more frequently ... at three-week intervals rather than four," should be entered under "Corrective Action," Column 7 on the Problem Solving Worksheet (*Figure 13-2*).

However, making the decision is not the final phase of the process. Frequently, there is a huge gap between "making the decision" and "carrying it out", between intention and implementation! Which leads us to the final step of the problem solving process.

Step 7 - Stimulate Action

Making a good decision is one thing, but transforming it into a specific *action plan* is another. As Peter Drucker puts it ("The Effective Decision" chapter of *Management*):

> ... no decision has been made unless carrying it out in specific steps has become someone's work assignment and responsibility. Until then, there are only good intentions ... converting a decision into action requires answering several distinct questions.

- Who has to know of this decision?
- What action has to be taken?
- Who is to take it?
- What does the action have to be so that the people who have to do it *can* do it?

A good action plan serves you in much the same way that a road map serves the automobile traveler — it's your *operational map*. Your plan should specify:

- the steps or actions required
- the sequence in which these should be carried out
- the responsibilities of the various people involved
- the provisions for follow-up and control

Another important part of effective implementation is *communicating* the decision and action plan to those directly and indirectly affected. People are certain to have questions like these:

- What is the reason for the decision
- Whom will it affect and how
- What benefits are expected for individuals, for departments and for the company
- Specifically, what is each person's role in implementing the decision
- What adjustments will be required in terms of how the work will be done
- When does the action called for by the decision go into effect

By communicating the answers to these kinds of questions, you can head off many difficulties and aid effective implementation of your decision.

Follow-up and feedback round out the problem solving process. Once the solution for a problem has been implemented, the results should be regularly evaluated to document the effectiveness of the solution. Attention should also be given to any other aspects that might be unintentionally affected by the solution. We want to be sure we don't create other problems with the solution to our subject problem.

In our case study, for instance, we want to closely watch the effect the more frequent shear knife changes have on productivity and delay times. While some decrease can be expected in shear department productivity, it should be minimized... and perhaps even compensated for... in the assembly area by the resulting absence of hand injuries and their associated costs. In the same vein, the average number of grinding

hours can be expected to drop and this should be measured as another result of the solution.

To consider the effects of our solution only in terms of reduced hand injuries would ignore many of the potential benefits. Documenting all these effects also aids in calling to management's attention the real cost of injuries. Too often, injuries are considered only in light of the immediate pain, suffering and inconvenience. While these certainly are not to be ignored, they are only a part of the effect produced. The long range effect of the costs associated with injury accidents can seriously damage a company's profitability. By measuring and reporting on the reduction or elimination of these costs, supervisors can continually remind higher management of their contribution.

Columns 8 (Follow-up) and 9 (Status) of the Problem Solving Worksheet (*Figure 13-2*) can help you to manage for feedback and follow-up...a mark of the truly effective problem solver.

BITS AND PIECES

Perhaps the process seems involved and difficult. Take heart! You don't have to learn it all at once, and you don't always have to use the whole thing. As Edward Hodness says:

Learning to solve problems is like learning to play baseball. You learn to throw, to catch, to bat, to make plays and to execute all sorts of refinements of these basic skills. You do not learn to play baseball. You learn these basic skills separately, and you put them together in new combinations every game ... You learn the skills, and you combine them to play the game as circumstances dictate. (*The Art of Problem Solving*, p. 194)

If the best solution is obvious, it would be foolish to go through all seven steps! You may go from problem recognition directly to action, as in these examples:

Problem	Action
Water gushing from broken pipe	Close shutoff valve
Worker does not know how to perform the new task	Give proper job instruction

- Person bleeding from open wound
- Apply direct pressure and related first aid
- Open flywheel presents severe hazard to equipment operator
- Install guards

But for many problems the solutions are not so simple and obvious. Problems like these, for instance:

- Excess turnover or absenteeism
- Lift trucks lasting only three-quarters as long as they should
- Workers violating rules and safe practices
- Lack of cooperation between safety and maintenance
- Loss of materials is costing $100 per day
- We are injuring three or four people every week

TIME may be a critical variable in problem solving. Sometimes there isn't much of it; seldom does there seem to be enough. The professional manager gauges the time available and uses it most efficiently to recognize and analyze the problem, identify causes, develop and evaluate solution alternatives, reach a decision and stimulate action. Problem solving knowledge and skill help to avoid "snap judgments" and "quick and dirty" decisions.

There is no special virtue in slavishly following every step in the entire process if a brief, informal use of the ideas can result in an effective solution of the problem. In fact, the better you know the whole process, the better you can single out the parts that are most appropriate to the problem at hand... and the better prepared you will be to use the entire process when it is appropriate.

PROBLEM SOLVING TEAMS

The 1980's brought acute awareness of the need for increased productivity, greater profitability and more efficient and effective performance. Along with this awareness came considerable emphasis on Quality of Work Life, Organization Development, Participative Management, Job Enrichment and a host of related team building and performance improvement techniques such as shown in *Figure 13-4*.

VARIATIONS ON THE TEAM THEME

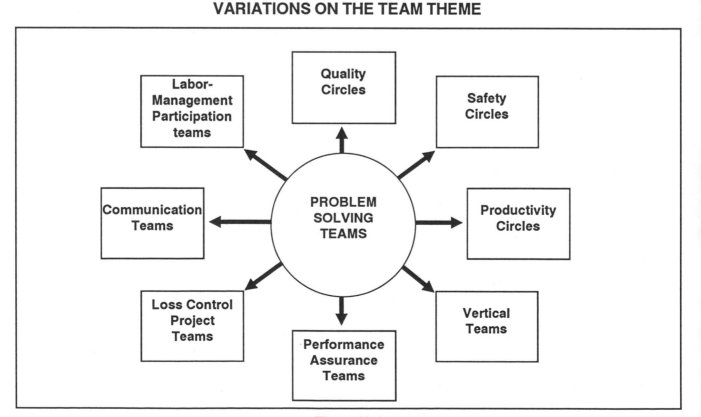

Figure 13-4

Quality Circles

Due largely to Japanese applications and accomplishments, the spotlight of attention focused on QUALITY CIRCLES. Let's look at them as a prototype of problem solving teams.

BASIC DESCRIPTION - They are small groups, often 7-10 people who do similar work. They meet voluntarily on a regular basis (such as one hour each week) to:

- discuss their work quality problems
- work together on fact finding and cause analysis
- recommend solutions to management
- implement solutions within their scope

STRUCTURE - Circle *members* are non-management employees who work directly in production, maintenance, service and support functions. Members of a specific circle normally do the same or similar jobs and thus, all are familiar with the same work, environment and problems. The circle *leader* usually is the Foreman or Supervisor of the members. Middle and upper *managers* support and assist the circle concepts and activities. The *facilitator* is a person responsible for training members, leaders and managers in how to make circles successful, and for coordinating circle activities throughout the organization.

CIRCLE SUCCESS FACTORS - Following are the types of factors that contribute to successful circles:

- Management commitment and support
- Common goals for managers and workers
- Voluntary participation
- Clear goals, roles, procedures and relationships for participants
- A people-building philosophy
- Climate of trust - respect - caring - sharing
- Adequate training
- Recognition for accomplishments

A special comment about "adequate training" is appropriate here. Too often, managers expect people to automatically know how to make Quality Circles successful. However, experience shows that training is critical. Successful circle training may include all or some of these tools and techniques: 1) elementary quality control techniques (such as sampling, data gathering, recording and charting); 2) thinking skills (such as rational problem solving, cause-and-effect

analysis and brainstorming; 3) group dynamics (such as group leadership, group participation, constructive confrontation and team building; and 4) how to make effective presentations.

FAILURE FACTORS - Following are the types of factors that contribute to circle failures:

- Inadequate training
- Lack of leadership and/or management support
- Management overemphasis on short-term results and short-term profits
- Supervisors/managers threatened by perceived loss of "authority" and/or "status"
- Non-participative climate
- Adversary employee-management relationships
- Lack of reinforcement for accomplishments

RESULTS - Successful Quality Circles yield an excellent return on investment. Here, for instance, are some examples quoted from the February 21, 1980 *Wall Street Journal* ("U.S. Firms, Worried by Productivity lag, Copy Japan In Seeking Employees' Advice"):

- An assembly-line circle at the solar-turbines division of International Harvester found a way to simplify the production of a compression disc for a turbine. As a result, several production steps were eliminated and $8,700 a year was saved.

- The group at American Airlines maintenance and engineering center in Tulsa came up with a savings of $100,000 a year by simply replacing old hand grinders with new, more efficient tools.

- At Northrop's aircraft plant in Hawthorne, California, a quality circle of mechanics assembling the F5 military fighter found that workers kept breaking expensive drill bits when they bored into the titanium on the tail of the aircraft. After a lengthy analysis, the angle of the drill was changed slightly, resulting in fewer broken bits and savings of $28,000 a year.

- The circle at a GM plant in Michigan decided it should do something about the large number of automobiles leaving the assembly line with flat tires. Their analysis eventually traced the problem to a defective tire stem. The part was replaced, and the company's annual saving turned out to be $225,000.

> **PRINCIPLE OF INVOLVEMENT:**
> Meaningful involvement increases motivation and support.

Team Variations

Many project teams, task forces, committees and related problem solving groups differ significantly from Quality Circles. For instance, a "Vertical Team" is quite common. This type includes people from various levels in the organization — people with unique experience, education or expertise for solving the specific problem at hand. Upper management selects the team leaders and assigns the problem to the team. Some members may volunteer, some may be appointed. The team has considerable freedom concerning when and how to meet; and freedom of access to information in various parts of the organization. The team is dissolved when the problem is solved.

No one type of problem solving team is best for all situations, i.e.: PARTICIPATION may be either voluntary or assigned; MEMBERS may represent one level or many levels; PROJECTS may be self-determined or assigned; FACILITATORS may or may not be used; the group's SCOPE may encompass a single problem or multiple problems; MEETINGS may be regularly spaced or "as needed"; KNOWLEDGE & SKILL may be aided by special training, or may be based on prior training and experience.

Teams can be designed to fit the situation. They can concentrate on problems of safety - quality - productivity - cost control — or combinations thereof. A good example is the one detailed in the "Property Damage and Waste Control" chapter of this book. Informal problem solving teams can be established to deal with a variety of problems. A supervisor, working with a group of knowledgeable employees, can lead the group through the seven problem solving steps discussed above.

Key Considerations

No matter what you call them — circles, teams, task forces, committees, groups, etc. — problem solving teams have proven to be effective and adaptable to various situations. Experience has shown the following factors to be key elements for success:

- Management commitment, support and involvement
- Climate of collaboration and team building
- Emphasis on participative identification, analysis and solution of problems
- Shared goals - shared experiences - shared learning - shared benefits
- Provision of personal growth opportunities through team projects
- Providing the twin ingredients of self-esteem
  - Feeling that "I am important"
  - Feeling that "my work is important"
- Adequate training in problem solving and team techniques
- Positive recognition and reinforcement

Problem solving teams bring benefits not only of better knowledge, skills and attitudes, but also better safety, quality, productivity and cost control.

POTENTIAL PROBLEM ANALYSIS

> **"An ounce of prevention is worth a pound of cure."**

Among the most rewarding, profitable actions any professional manager can take are those he or she takes to *predict* problems, then to...

- take action to *prevent* these potential problems from coming to pass
- take action to *minimize* the effects in case the problems do occur

However, many managers do far less potential problem analysis than they should. Could the following be among the common reasons for this?

- They are so busy correcting today's problems they don't take time to prevent tomorrow's
- Raises and promotions tend to go to those who show the best record of solving current problems
- They tend to feel that their decisions and actions are correct, and to overlook their problem-causing possibilities

- In spite of Murphy's Law (if anything *can* go wrong, it *will*), they sometimes find it difficult to ask the question, "What *could* go wrong?"

Kepner and Tregoe *(The New Rational Manager)* describe Potential Problem Analysis as an attitude, an orientation towards the future, and a systematic thinking process. They emphasize managing the future:

Potential Problem Analysis is a procedure that enables us to walk into the future, see what it may hold, and then return to the present to take action now — when it can do the most good... It is a protective process through which we ensure that the future will be as good as we can make it...(p. 140)

A pertinent application is the accident imaging ("What if...?") analysis described further in the chapter on "Incident Recall."

Figure 13-5 is a simple diagram showing the main aspects of Potential Problem Analysis. The following seven key questions can serve as a general guide to this process:

1. WHAT COULD GO WRONG? Consider, at least, these six sources of potential problems:
   - Where you are trying something new, complex or unfamiliar
   - When your deadlines are tight
   - When a sequence is critical or has impact on others
   - When an alternative is missing
   - When things involve more than one person, function or department
   - Where responsibility is hard to assign, or is outside your area

2. WHAT, SPECIFICALLY, IS EACH POTENTIAL PROBLEM? Tell *what* it is, *where* it will occur, *when* and in what *degree*.

3. HOW RISKY IS EACH POTENTIAL PROBLEM? Potential Problem Analysis is a systematic process in which you identify and deal with problems that are reasonably likely to occur and are worthy of attention. Set priorities in terms of how *serious* it will be if it happens, and how *probable* it is that it might happen. Consider categories along these lines:

   - Would be *fatal*; *must prevent* at all costs

- Would be *harmful*; *want to control* as much as possible
- Would only be *annoying*; *can ignore* as calculated risk

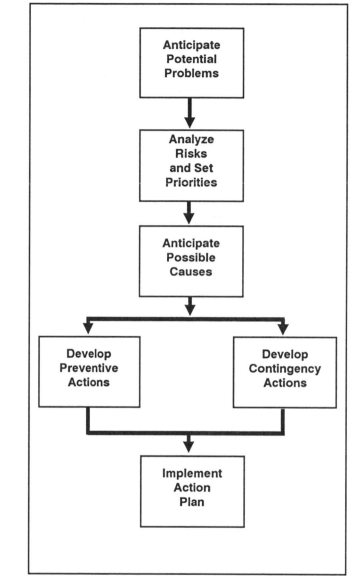

Figure 13-5

4. WHAT ARE THE POSSIBLE CAUSES OF EACH PROBLEM? Use your experience and judgment to develop a list of all possible causes.

5. HOW PROBABLE IS EACH POSSIBLE CAUSE? Estimate the probabilities. Set priorities for attention and action.

6. HOW CAN EACH SIGNIFICANT POTENTIAL CAUSE BE PREVENTED, OR ITS PROBABILITY REDUCED? Plan preventive actions that completely remove the potential cause or reduce the probability of its occurrence.

7. WHAT CONTINGENCY ACTIONS ARE IN ORDER? For serious potential problems, develop fail-safe actions to offset or minimize the effects the problem could produce. For potential problems for which there are no preventive actions, develop contingent actions to minimize the effects of the potential problem. Establish early warning signals that will alert you to the problem and trigger your contingency actions.

Take the actions that give the most results for the least cost and effort. Preventing a problem is usually better than having to take contingency action; and preventive actions are usually the least expensive.

You may find it helpful to structure your analysis of a potential problem around a simple form such as shown in *Figure 13-6*.

Potential Problem Analysis is positive, preventive and professional. It reflects a positive attitude of "I *can* foresee the future to some degree, and *can* change it for the better." While analysis of current and past problems is *afterthought* - after the loss; analysis of POTENTIAL PROBLEMS is *forethought* - before the loss - preventive. Potential Problem Analysis is the mark of the management "pro."

CORE CONCEPTS IN REVIEW

Problem solving is one of the most critical and challenging aspects of work as a manager-supervisor-leader. It requires both analytical and creative thinking. It can be summarized as shown in *Figure 13-7*.

Team effort often plays a vital role in problem solving. "Quality Circles" are a good example. They are small groups (often 7-10 people) who do similar work. They meet voluntarily on a regular basis (such as one hour each week) to:

1. Discuss their work quality problems

2. Work together on fact finding and cause analysis

3. Recommend solutions to management

4. Implement solutions within their scope

The circle leader usually is the Foreman or Supervisor. Middle and upper managers support and assist the circle concepts and activities. A facilitator is responsible for training members, leaders and managers in how to make circles successful; and for coordinating circle activities throughout the organization.

Other types of successful problem solving groups have other characteristics. For example:

1. Participation and projects are assigned rather than voluntary.

2. Members come from various functions and levels rather than one.

3. They do not use a facilitator.

4. The group works on a single problem rather than many.

5. Participants receive no special training for the assignment, but rely on existing knowledge and skills.

The supreme problem solving skill is **Potential Problem Analysis.**

1. This involves a systematic analysis to **predict** problems.

2. Take action to **prevent** the potential problems from becoming real.

3. Take contingent action to **minimize** the effects (losses) in case the problems do occur.

The following questions form a framework for this analysis:

1. What could go wrong?

2. What, specifically, is each potential problem?

3. How risky is each potential problem?

4. What are the possible causes of each problem?

5. How probable is each possible cause?

6. How can each significant potential cause be prevented or its probability be reduced?

7. What contingency actions are in order?

Potential Problem Analysis is pre-contact (pre-loss) control at its best...**the mark of the master manager.**

ANALYSIS OF POTENTIAL PROBLEM

What: _____

Where: _____

When: _____

Extent: _____

Possible Causes	Probability	Preventive Actions	Residual Probability	Contingent Actions

Figure 13-6

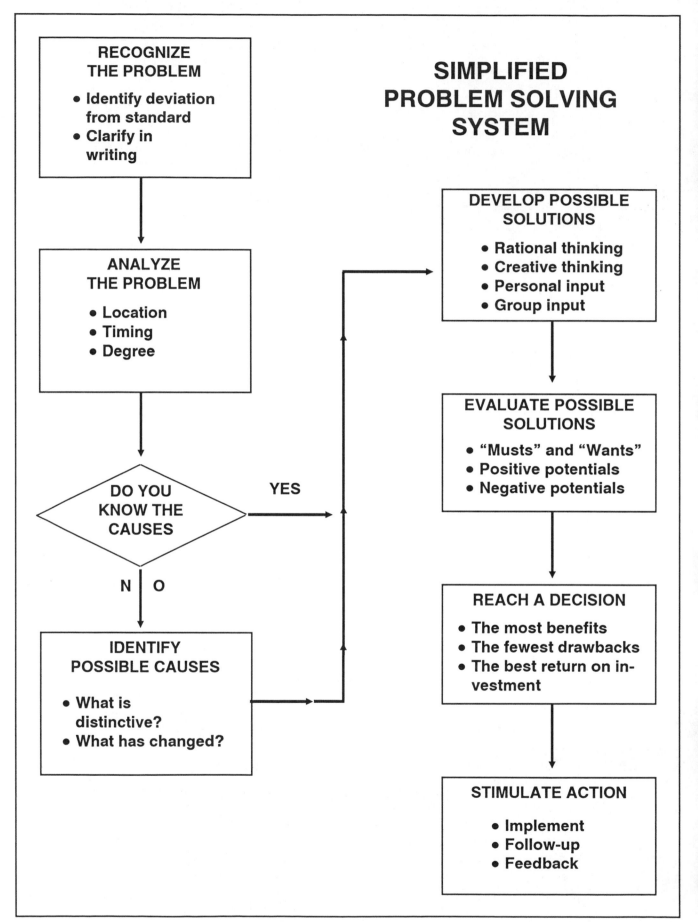

SIMPLIFIED PROBLEM SOLVING SYSTEM

RECOGNIZE THE PROBLEM
- Identify deviation from standard
- Clarify in writing

ANALYZE THE PROBLEM
- Location
- Timing
- Degree

DO YOU KNOW THE CAUSES

YES

N | O

IDENTIFY POSSIBLE CAUSES
- What is distinctive?
- What has changed?

DEVELOP POSSIBLE SOLUTIONS
- Rational thinking
- Creative thinking
- Personal input
- Group input

EVALUATE POSSIBLE SOLUTIONS
- "Musts" and "Wants"
- Positive potentials
- Negative potentials

REACH A DECISION
- The most benefits
- The fewest drawbacks
- The best return on investment

STIMULATE ACTION
- Implement
- Follow-up
- Feedback

Figure 13-7

KEY QUESTIONS

1. What are the seven steps (R-A-I-D-E-R-S) of the systematic problem solving process?

2. At which step of problem solving is "brain-storming" most useful?

3. What are several of the change catalyst questions?

4. True or False? To properly recognize (identify) a problem you should reduce it to writing?

5. What is the Principle of Definition?

6. A problem can be considered to be a _____ from a performance standard for which the cause is not known.

7. Why is it important to clarify the solution criteria (MUSTS and WANTS)?

8. True or False? The professional problem solver keeps going until he or she finds the perfect solution.

9. What are three important aspects of implementing a solution?

10. What are some distinctive features of Quality Circles as compared with other types of problem solving teams?

11. What are the circle success factors?

12. What are the circle failure factors?

13. What kinds of return on investment have been reported for Quality Circles?

14. What is the Principle of Participation?

15. Why is Potential Problem Analysis critical?

16. What are the seven key questions that serve as a guide to Potential Problem Analysis?

17. Potential Problem Analysis is _____ control at its best.

PRACTICAL APPLICATIONS SUMMARY

S - For Supervisors
E - For Executives
C - For Safety/Loss Control Coordinators

	S	E	C
1. Establish a participative problem solving climate throughout the organization.		x	
2. Establish an organizational climate receptive to both analytical reasoning and creative thinking.		x	
3. Enable training in problem solving and group dynamics.		x	
4. Clarify the goals, roles, procedures and relationships of problem solving team members, leaders and advisors.		x	
5. Lead problem solving teams.	x	x	
6. Establish a climate that recognizes "problem preventers" as well as problem solvers.	x	x	
7. Advise and assist problem solving teams.		x	x
8. Be aware of the human perceptual pitfalls that can prohibit effective problem solving.	x	x	x
9. Take training in problem solving and group dynamics.	x	x	x
10. Train others in problem solving and group dynamics.	x	x	x
11. Separate symptoms from basic problems and basic causes.	x	x	x
12. Use both analytical reasoning and creative thinking.	x	x	x
13. Personally practice participative problem solving.	x	x	x
14. Serve as a member of problem solving teams.	x	x	x
15. Use a systematic approach to Potential Problem Analysis.	x	x	x
16. Advise and assist others in applying systematic Potential Problem Analysis.	x	x	x
17. Recognize and reinforce problem solvers.	x	x	x
18. Recognize and reinforce problem preventers.	x	x	x

CHAPTER 14

MANAGING THE TROUBLED EMPLOYEE

"At least 85% of all work accidents are caused by the inability to cope with emotional distress."
- E. M. Gherman, *Stress and the Bottom Line*

INTRODUCTION

A troubled employee is anyone whose personal problems, including substance abuse, interfere significantly with job performance. Personal problems include problems from marriage and family, finances, mental or physical health, job situations or other aspects of a person's life which create difficulties for that person. Substance abuse includes addiction to alcohol and other drugs as well as misuse of over-the-counter or prescription medication. While anyone may experience difficulties in these areas at one time or another, it is at the point where they interfere significantly with job performance that a person becomes a "troubled employee."

One of the biggest mistakes management can make about troubled employees is to assume they do not employ any. Of the 110 million people in North America who use alcoholic beverages, it is estimated that 8 million, or about 1 in 13 (7.7%), have a drinking problem. About four and one-half million of these people are employed. On the basis of numerous studies, it has been determined that 5% of the employees in any industry will have a drinking problem. Problem drinking ranks third among the four most serious disorders (the others are heart disease, cancer and mental illness). It is a disease which strikes at all levels of society and all levels of a firm's personnel. Among the alcoholics who have publicly admitted their illness are federal legislators, religious leaders and corporate executives.

Management Concerns

An extensive survey of recent research done on the prevalence of persons with emotional problems was presented in a 1978 Task Panel Report to the President's Committee on Mental Health. Findings from 28 studies done in Canada, the U.S. and Europe indicated that 20% of the populations studied suffered from some type of mental disorder. Yet only one-fourth of these persons were receiving any type of treatment. A 1960 survey, entitled "Americans View Their Mental Health," indicated that 25% of those surveyed experienced problems for which mental health treatment would be helpful. Yet, only 14% of those with such problems had sought help. These figures indicate that slightly more than 20% of Americans are experiencing problems which they regard as serious enough to require mental health treatment, but are not receiving any treatment from mental health professionals, clergymen or physicians. In addition, there is a large number of persons struggling with family, health, job and financial problems which are creating significant levels of stress.

A loss of $16-20 billion a year in North America has been attributed to work time lost through the behavioral problems of these employees in business, industry and government. The kinds of losses cover the spectrum of management concerns, e.g., safety, absenteeism, morale, productivity, turnover, legislation and humanitarian concerns.

SAFETY is one of these concerns. Safety experts agree completely that emotional upset plays a significant role in accident causation. Their convictions are based on personal experience and research such as the following.

University of Texas — "The vast majority of accidents contain a substantial human factor, often irrational or irresponsible action, indicating the involvement of mental or emotional duress in accident causation."

A consulting psychiatrist — "Twenty percent of those reporting for treatment were, to some degree, emotionally disturbed. Moreover, these individuals had a forty percent higher serious injury experience than other plant employees."

Survey of industrial nurses — "It is estimated that eighty to ninety percent of all accidents are of emotional origin."

An emotionally disturbed employee is a potential hazard. More than half of all traffic fatalities involve persons under the influence of alcohol or other drugs. There is increasing evidence that emotional upset is a major contributing factor in a large percentage of traffic accidents. On and off-the-job, the emotionally disturbed person is seven times more likely than other persons to meet with a fatal accident. Distracted by inner concerns, he or she may walk right into traffic. Under the influence of alcohol or other drugs, even prescription or over-the-counter drugs whose warning labels have been ignored, a person may stick his or her hand, or head, into a piece of moving machinery. High anxiety may lead to unsafe shortcuts and ignoring crucial safety procedures. Unreasonable fear of a mistake may lead to exactly the mistake that is feared, or one even worse. The person who is absorbed in private problems rather than the task at hand, whose thoughts are muddled, or whose reaction time is slowed by the influence of alcohol or other drugs, is a good candidate for an accident.

ABSENTEEISM, and the accompanying costs of workers' compensation, wage continuation, replacement employees, decreased production, overtime, increased supervisory time and other indirect costs, is also a concern. A troubled employee will have 2.5 to 5.5 times the number of absences that other employees have. Also costly is "on-the-job absenteeism," in which the employee is physically present but mentally absent.

MORALE is another concern. Troubled employees do not work in a vacuum. A person who is emotionally upset or under the influence of alcohol or other drugs can easily spoil morale by unpredictable behavior and the "acting out" of inner problems, or by taking out real or imaginary grievances on other employees. The efforts of the group may be sabotaged as an expression of anger. Supervisors, unwise or untrained in coping with troubled employees, can also add to the morale problem by leaving themselves open to charges of either favoritism or witch hunting.

TURNOVER among troubled employees is unusually high, either because the employee has to be discharged or because job instability is one aspect of the troubled personality. Replacement costs include recruiting, hiring and training. However, establishing an effective level of performance is by far the biggest cost. These costs have been analyzed by Lawrence R. Zeitlin. A tabulation of his findings is shown in *Figure 14-1*.

REPLACEMENT COSTS

Job Classification	Indirect Costs
Semi-Skilled Personnel	1/2 year's salary
Supervisors and First-Line Managers	1 year's salary
Policy- and Decision-making Level Executives	2-3 year's salary
Top Level Executives, such as President or Head of Major Division	So high as to make estimate meaningless

Figure 14-1

PRODUCTIVITY is certainly hampered, for the reasons above, or simply because the troubled employee has so little room on his or her emotional agenda for the goals of the organization, or even realistic personal goals. An employee with a broken spirit is just as disabled as one with a broken leg. Defects in thinking and judgment can be very costly, especially with key employees.

In both the public and the private sector, it costs the equivalent of twenty-five percent of the annual wage of each troubled employee to cover lateness and absenteeism; judgment errors; recruiting, placement, and training experience; skills and knowledge loss; spoilage of materials; group dissension; additional time by management; clerical and medical involvement; and increased accidents and overtime. To get a rough but conservative estimate of how much troubled employees cost your organization, use the formula in *Figure 14-2.*

HOW MUCH DO TROUBLED EMPLOYEES COST YOUR ORGANIZATION?

In using this formula, remember that emotional and addiction problems are no respecters of social standing, education or income. For problem drinkers only, about 30% will be manual workers, 25% white collar workers, and 45% professional and management personnel. Therefore, you should include in your figures all levels of your organization, from top management on down.

To compute the number of troubled employees in your organization, divide the total number of your employees... by 10 (10%). Enter that number. _____(A)

To compute the cost per affected employee, take the average wage (total payroll divided by total employees) _____ and divide that figure by 4 (25%). Enter that amount.. $____(B)

Multiply (A) times (B) to arrive at a rough, but conservative, estimate of how much troubled employees cost your organization each year. $____

Figure 14-2

RECENT LEGISLATION in the United States regards alcoholism and drug addiction as illnesses. It prohibits the discharge of employees for those reasons alone. Persons affected are now protected by the same provisions which apply to handicapped employees. Legal guidelines and requirements will likely include mental illnesses and emotional disturbances under the same categories.

HUMANITARIAN CONSIDERATIONS are another concern. That business and industry must be concerned for employees as persons in their own right, and not just as means to an end, is an idea whose time has come. Today's management is increasingly concerned not only with lost production, but also with lost weekends. The insensitivity of the past is yielding to

a new insight into the human cost of the troubled employee.

One can approach the problem with a tough-minded concern for profits, or with a humanitarian concern for people. Either approach leads eventually to the same conclusion: the problem of the troubled employee is too costly to be ignored.

CAUSES OF TROUBLED EMPLOYEES

A big mistake frequently made by managers is to believe that their only recourse with troubled employees is to either endure them or fire them. An understanding of the causes of troubled employees can go far toward correcting this assumption.

In keeping with modern loss control thinking, basic causes can be divided into two categories: personal factors and job factors. Let's look at each of them.

Personal Factors

Personal factors include stress producing events or situations (stressors) in the life of the employee. Some life events, in order of the amount of stress produced, are given in *Figure 14-3.* This list was developed by Dr. Thomas H. Holmes, a professor of psychiatry. It was based on a study of more than 5,000 hospital patients. The person who in the previous year acquired fewer than 150 stress points has only one chance in three of serious illness in the next two years. Score 150 to 300, and there's a 50-50 chance of serious illness; over 300 units, the likelihood is almost 90 percent.

Notice that not all of the events are negative. Some are ordinary and positive events; family events, economic events, vacation, retirement, etc. The common factor is that each involves changes in one's lifestyle that require adaptive or coping behavior. If the stress is too intense, or lasts too long, behavior can break down and errors and accidents may occur. Perhaps at this point a note to the reader is indicated. If you have acquired a large number of stress points in the past year, you can reduce your chances of hospitalization or other problems by such simple measures as making sure your diet is balanced and controlled, getting appropriate exercise and adequate rest and finding someone with whom to "talk it out" in confidence.

Actual mental illness may be another basic cause of

LIFE EVENTS RANKED BY RESULTANT STRESS

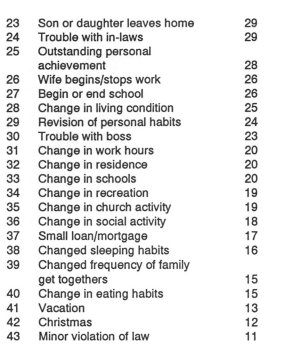

RANK	LIFE EVENT	STRESS POINTS	RANK	LIFE EVENT	STRESS POINTS
1	Death of spouse	100	23	Son or daughter leaves home	29
2	Divorce	73	24	Trouble with in-laws	29
3	Marital separation	65	25	Outstanding personal achievement	28
4	Jail sentence	63	26	Wife begins/stops work	26
5	Death of a family member	63	27	Begin or end school	26
6	Personal injury/illness	53	28	Change in living condition	25
7	Marriage	50	29	Revision of personal habits	24
8	Fired from job	47	30	Trouble with boss	23
9	Marital reconciliation	45	31	Change in work hours	20
10	Retirement	45	32	Change in residence	20
11	Family member illness	44	33	Change in schools	20
12	Pregnancy	40	34	Change in recreation	19
13	Sex difficulties	39	35	Change in church activity	19
14	Gain of new family member	39	36	Change in social activity	18
15	Business readjustment	39	37	Small loan/mortgage	17
16	Change in financial state	38	38	Changed sleeping habits	16
17	Death of close friend	37	39	Changed frequency of family get togethers	15
18	Change of line of work	36	40	Change in eating habits	15
19	Change in number of arguments with spouse	35	41	Vacation	13
20	Mortgage signed over $10,000	31	42	Christmas	12
21	Foreclosure of loan	30	43	Minor violation of law	11
22	Change in work responsibility	29			

Figure 14-3

problems on the job. Mental illness may result from too much stress, or it may be caused by an imbalance in the delicate chemistry of the brain, growths on the brain, physical damage to the brain, reaction to drugs or impaired circulation of blood in the brain from a variety of reasons.

Another basic cause may be physical illnesses. Some of these may be chronic problems, such as high blood pressure, diabetes, migraine or emphysema. Others may be failing eyesight or hearing. Any physical illness can, and often does, influence behavior and performance on the job. Many persons suffer from chronic pain, which can be a continuing source of stress and emotional upset.

Addiction problems may result from stress, from emotional disturbance, from physical illness or from a combination of these. The addiction or dependence may be to alcohol or other chemical substances, either prescription or non-prescription. It is the source of a large number of behavioral problems in the workplace.

Job Factors

Job factors include adjustment to a job transfer, assignments calling for new skills, replacement by a machine, change in supervisors or approach of retirement. The threat of failure can create stress. Among the causes here are inability to meet quotas, failure to get a promotion, discharge or demotion, or promotion to a job beyond abilities.

The aftereffect of accidents can create emotional problems, particularly if the employee feels, or is made to feel, at fault; or if someone was seriously injured; or if the potential for injury was great. Often the employee will mentally "replay" the accident, becoming so absorbed in thought about what he or she did or did not do that the person becomes a hazard to self or others. At times, people are so fearful after an accident that, in becoming overly cautious, they actually "back into" another accident.

Job conditions can also be stressors. Excessive noise and heat can cause declines in performance, especially with complicated tasks. For some people, working in high locations, or dark or cramped quarters, can stir up such irrational fears that they become completely immobilized. Under some circumstances, aspects such as information overload, isolation, cold, rain, accelerated work pace, fatigue, inadequate lighting or erratic working hours can also create problems. When work seems to be punishing or purposeless, employees will sometimes escape into daydreams or otherwise occupy their minds with something beside the task at hand. People may actually create problems to relieve monotony or reduce tension. All of these causes are aggravated when accompanied by lack of physical or mental ability for the job assignment, inadequate motivation and feedback in job performance, or being required to work with unsafe tools or equipment.

Inadequate supervision is another source of difficulties among employees. A supervisor who does not know his or her job creates feelings of insecurity and causes employee dissatisfaction. Improper job planning causes confusion and decreases incentive. Giving persons assignments that are not matched by their qualifications is a source of stress, whether the employee is over-qualified or under-qualified. Orders that do not match the employee's level of experience or which are given in the wrong tone of voice cause problems. Delegating supervision to an unqualified person so that employees are incompetently supervised by a "straw boss" is a source of resentment. Inadequate or improper training leaves employees feeling hopeless and helpless about performing properly. Supervisors who ignore safety hazards are a source of dissatisfaction and stress to workers who resent the unnecessary risks involved in doing their jobs. If new or transferred employees are poorly indoctrinated, they are likely to experience high levels of stress. Failure to provide proper tools and materials is an insult to employees' intelligence and a cause of stress. Neglect in letting an employee know where he or she stands leads to doubt and wrong assumptions.

Multiple Causes

An important management principle, "The Principle of Multiple Causes," states that problems which impair the efficiency of an organization seldom, if ever, have a single cause. This principle certainly applies to the causes of troubled employees. Often it is a combination of *personal* and *job* factors: a high work location with a person unusually afraid of heights; a noisy work area for an employee who has a very cramped and noisy home life; or an unguarded machine and preoccupied employee. Most accidents are the result of an almost chance combination of time, place, person, equipment and attitude. Often the elimination, change or control of any one of those factors can prevent the accident and the loss. The following account of an actual accident illustrates the principle of multiple causes.

The accident occurred in a canning operation in which a chain conveyed cans along stainless steel guides. Suddenly the machine jammed, and the operator turned it off. Bill, age 45, with 25 years with the company and 8 years on his job, was operating a machine further down the line. When the line stopped, Bill came up to discover the reason for the delay. The operator explained that the machine had jammed and went to report the matter to his supervisor. While he was gone, Bill decided to "investigate." He started the machine, and, although the motor ran, nothing happened because the chain was jammed. Bill then got under the conveyor, where he saw the chain hanging slack over the sprockets. When he pulled the chain over the sprocket with his fingers, the chain suddenly moved forward. It caught his right hand between the chain and the sprocket, amputating all four fingers at the knuckles.

An investigation revealed that the chain had jammed because one of the links had worked loose. The chain was repaired, and a guard was placed under the sprocket. Also, all employees were instructed in the importance of, and the procedures for, locking out machinery for cleaning, repairing, oiling and adjusting. During the investigation, Bill's supervisor recalled that prior to the accident, Bill was becoming increasingly "touchy," particularly when he was approached about his increasing absences and spoilage of materials.

Bill was compensated for his mutilated right hand and given another job because he could no longer perform his old one. During the process of physical therapy and rehabilitation, Bill talked to a counselor. He related his boredom with his job, his need for more money as his children entered college, the lack of promotional opportunities and the almost desperate feeling that life and opportunity were passing him by. Also, less than two months prior to the accident, Bill discovered that his wife was emotionally involved with another man. His confidence in himself was shattered. Partially out of boredom, and partially to prove his "real worth," he attempted to repair the machine.

The accident cost Bill the effective use of his right hand and a permanent loss of earning power. It cost the company the management time and production delay in the confusion after the accident, the time of the supervisor who accompanied Bill to the hospital and stayed with him while surgery was done, the continuation of Bill's wages during rehabilitation, the loss of Bill's experience on the job and the training of someone else to do it.

That particular accident could have been prevented by a guard under the sprockets or by the operator locking out the machine before leaving it. But it is quite possible that Bill would have had a different accident. If Bill's supervisor had been alert to the warning symptoms of Bill's increasing absenteeism and material spoilage, and had either provided Bill a listening ear to his real concerns or had insisted that Bill talk with someone else, it might have prevented any accident involving Bill. There may have been promotional or job enrichment possibilities that Bill was unaware of. At the very least, he could have "gotten it off his chest" by talking out rather than acting out his inner turmoil. He could have clarified his thoughts and feelings and gotten a better perspective on himself and his problems.

Many accidents are caused by distraction. Most of us can recall an accident or near-accident we had while driving because we were "lost in thought." That accident potential is magnified when people have almost overwhelming personal, financial, family or health problems on their minds.

It should be emphasized that the concern expressed here is not just for "accidents." Also included are losses such as:

(1) The executive who, under the influence of alcohol, makes costly decisions;

(2) The secretary who has far too many "off" days, when it seems impossible to do anything correctly;

(3) The shipping clerk who steals from the company to support a drug habit;

(4) The salesperson who alienates clients because his or her breath smells like alcohol;

(5) The employee with two jobs who depends on drugs to stay awake; and

(6) The machine operator whose production remains below standard because her boyfriend works the second shift and the only time they can be together is after midnight.

APPROACHES TO THE TROUBLED EMPLOYEE

Three common approaches to the troubled employee are: (1) the cover-up approach, (2) the limited approach and (3) the comprehensive approach.

The Cover-Up Approach

The unwritten policy of the cover-up approach is: "We will help you hide your problems as long as possible, but when they can no longer be covered up we will fire you." This approach is the most costly to both the organization and the employee. Delays in facing up to the problem usually make it that much harder to deal with when it can no longer be evaded. This frequent approach indicates that many managers do not know what else to do.

The Limited Approach

The limited approach deals only with alcoholism or drug abuse. It has the advantage of being more focused than a comprehensive approach. Alcoholism and drug abuse are often more concrete and observable. There is less tendency with this approach to disguise these problems, as has been done in the past, and more tendency to deal forthrightly with them. However, the problem drinker or drug abuser often has other problems, which may in fact be the basic cause of the substance abuse problems. Also, there are many other employee problems which impair job performance, but which express themselves in ways other than alcoholism and drug abuse.

The Comprehensive Approach

The comprehensive approach, also called the "broadbrush" approach, takes into account other job impairment factors such as emotional disturbance, family disruption, illness in the family and financial and occupational stress. Many alcohol and drug abuse programs grow into more comprehensive programs. However, this approach may lead to more difficult collective bargaining and grievance problems. It can be misunderstood and even abused by supervisors. It has met with some resistance from unions, who sometimes view it as an open-ended device for management control of practically any form of dissent.

Despite possible problems, there are four primary reasons for adopting the comprehensive approach.

1. The same humanitarian and profit-oriented concerns that require an alcoholism and drug abuse program also require a program for emotional and other problems. There is no convincing reason to help alcoholics and drug addicts but not help those people whose problems are expressed through different symptoms.

2. The management procedures for both types of programs are the same.

3. The purpose of comprehensive programs, and one of the reasons for their success, is that they can identify problems early, thus providing a better chance of successful treatment. Among employees who develop alcoholism, performance and/or attendance problems will usually appear long before on-the-job signs of "a drinking problem" become apparent. Therefore, the "broadbrush" approach may well be the most helpful to the alcoholic employee by confronting him or her with the problem earlier.

4. In a comprehensive program, the supervisor need not determine if the employee's problems are or are not caused by abuse of alcohol or other drugs before referring the employee to someone else. Also, the employee need not admit to a drug or drinking problem prior to referral to a counselor or program coordinator.

The following cases show the effectiveness of comprehensive programs in dealing with the problems of troubled employees:

Bill was a pressman in a large packaging company. He was both well trained and highly skilled. Replacing him would have been a major expense. Yet, his unpredictable absences were causing costly delays. Bill was referred to a program coordinator who persuaded him to contact the local alcohol and drug abuse clinic. Not only have Bill's absences dramatically decreased, but his work is of even better quality.

Hank, a 29-year-old order filler with a wife and three children, had been on his present job for two years. His supervisor's opinion that Hank was highly promotable had been confirmed by tests at the personnel office. However, Hank's bills were piling up. The day after he had gotten two strong letters from creditors, Hank slipped down a ladder, injuring his legs. After the accident Hank's supervisor talked to him. Hank related his problem of keeping his mind on his job, especially with his financial pressures. His supervisor told Hank of the promising test results and assured him that he was in line for the next opening as assistant supervisor. He referred Hank to the community counseling service which, in turn, referred him to a financial planning service. Hank soon showed more interest in his work and had no more accidents.

Barbara had been a machine operator for twenty years. It was her only job since starting work at 18. Because of a large order, she had been recently transferred to a new machine, the only one she had not worked on previously. She had been a rapid learner on each of the other machines, but just could not get the knack of this one. As her production fell further behind, something which had never happened before, she became increasingly upset and her reject rate went up sharply. When her supervisor looked to see why everyone had stopped work, she saw Barbara, her head on her arms, crying. In conversation with her supervisor, Barbara related that her husband had lost his job because of his drinking, leaving Barbara the only support for the family. Barbara was referred to the local counseling agency and became involved in Alanon. Although her husband had not yet solved his drinking problem, Barbara was better able to cope with it. Her productivity is back to its former high level.

Joel was a welder who worked in the confined interior of small steel tanks. Several times he had bruised his head and body by bumping into the

HOW A "TROUBLED" EMPLOYEE BEHAVES

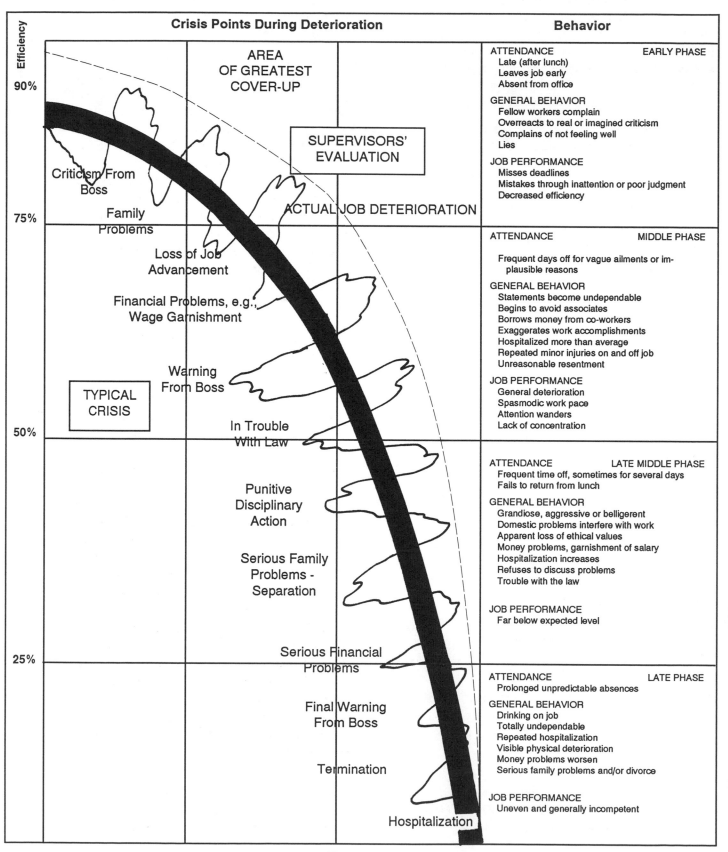

Figure 14-4

manhole frame when leaving his work. Once his foreman noticed him, for no apparent reason, making an unusually hurried exit. When the foreman asked Joel about it, he said that at times while working in the tank he was overcome by panic at being in such a close place. When the foreman asked why he had not requested outside work, Joel replied that he did not want anyone to think he was "chicken." At the first opportunity, Joel was transferred to outside work and had no more accidents.

THE SUPERVISOR'S ROLE

The front-line supervisor is the point of management control for managing troubled employees. No one else is as familiar with the employees' work record. Better than anyone else, supervisors know the individuals concerned, their leave records, work habits, conduct and appearance on the job. Also, the monitoring of employee performance, which is crucial to program success, is an integral and accepted part of a supervisor's responsibilities. Second only to the troubled employee, it is the supervisor who has the most to gain from effective management of the troubled employee. There are six very practical guidelines for supervisors in doing this:

(1) Recognize the importance of the supervisory role
(2) Identify the symptoms of developing problems
(3) Document the patterns of performance
(4) Discuss performance with the employee
(5) Learn to listen; listen to learn
(6) Know when to refer an employee to a counselor.

1.   Recognize Role

Supervisors should recognize the importance of their supervisory role. They have a unique place in the lives of their employees, who look to them for leadership and example, often imitating the way they do things. Supervisors who help their employees do their jobs with ESP (Efficiency, Safety and Productivity) help them succeed in a crucial area of their lives. This contributes to their sense of security, self-respect, confidence and identity. Not even ministers, physicians, or family members, as important as they are, make the same kind of contribution a good supervisor can make. Supervisors do not have to be psychologists to help troubled employees; they just need to be good supervisors.

Supervisors are authority figures and a part of management. They have the authority to say "yes" or "no" to requests, to give or withhold approval and attention and to make recommendations concerning their employees. Supervisors are coaches and guides. As such, they have the opportunity and obligation to observe and act upon job performance. Supervisors have legitimate concerns for total job performance which they, as part of management, have every right to expect. These legitimate concerns include attendance, timeliness, productivity, cooperation, safety, morale and costs. Supervisors who ignore or attempt to cover up performance problems do their employees a disservice. The longer treatment is delayed, the more difficult it is — and the more deeply ingrained the substandard work practices become.

2.   Identify Symptoms

Supervisors should identify the symptoms of developing problems. These symptoms include behavior changes, emotional distress, health problems, and performance changes.

BEHAVIOR CHANGES. Uncharacteristic behavior should raise a warning flag: the usually quiet employee who is suddenly outspoken; the usually talkative employee who is suddenly silent; the normally passive employee who becomes demanding; the "good mixer" who begins to avoid fellow workers; the usually neat person who neglects personal appearance; the alert employee who becomes unusually slow; or the employee who develops money problems, complains about pay shortages or borrows from other employees.

EMOTIONAL DISTRESS. Obvious emotional distress is a symptom that an employee's problems are at or over the threshold limit of ability to cope with them. Emotional agitation shows in uncontrollable fears, angry outbursts or extreme excitability. When an employee is jumpy, easily rattled, inattentive or prone to abrupt, erratic movements; when she or he seems not to "hear" or "see," or their thoughts do not seem to be related to what they are doing; they are likely to be troubled about something. Excited talking and gesturing, startled reactions to sound, trembling, talking to oneself and/or nervous conversation with another person may also be symptoms of emotional agitation.

A person who is depressed seems to be withdrawn to an inner world. He or she tends to behave mechanically, based on past habit rather than attention to the work situation. They also seem not to "see" or "hear" because of their preoccupation with thoughts, worries or nameless anxieties. Sometimes they are mentally "out of this world." Avoidance of co-workers, outbursts of tears or unusually slow movements may also be symptoms of depression.

HEALTH PROBLEMS. It almost goes without saying that management must be alert to the health problems of employees. Some problems may be chronic, such as high blood pressure, diabetes, migraine, epilepsy, emphysema or chronic pain. Signs of physical distress are nausea, headaches, dizziness, slurred speech, disorientation, pain or cramps. Ulcers or repeated gastritis may also indicate underlying problems.

PERFORMANCE CHANGES. Changes in job performance should also alert a supervisor. Among the aspects to look for are declines in productivity, quality or cooperation; increases in absenteeism, tardiness or clashes with other employees; and safety problems, such as rule violations, unsafe behavior and accidents. Since monitoring job performance is a critical supervisory management responsibility, each supervisor should be alert to deviations from standard performance.

3. Document Performance

Supervisors are responsible for recording facts about an employee's performance and conduct in the work environment. They should document the patterns of declining performance, but not their opinions as to what the basic cause or causes might be. If the problem results in arbitration proceedings, the supervisor's qualifications for attempting such diagnosis will certainly be challenged and his or her case weakened. Many of the basic causes have identical or similar symptoms. Often, highly specialized training is required to make an accurate diagnosis of the true cause. Even if a supervisor had this training, these diagnostic and interpretive functions are not a part of his or her job.

Proper documentation requires a written record of specific aspects of the employee's performance that do not meet established minimum standards. Since documentation should FOCUS on performance problems, proper documentation should be...

...**F** - Filed in the employee's service jacket or personnel folder, not on "secret" notes. There are laws which prohibit the collection of "secret" information about employees.

...**O** - Objective. It should contain facts that are observable or measurable, not subjective opinions. It should state what a person did or said, or facts about their appearance or performance.

...**C** - Clear and easily understood. It should be easily readable by another person, and should be clear as to exactly what is being documented.

...**U** - Used to identify patterns of behavior and performance. Supervisors should refer to written records rather than relying on memory.

...**S** - Systematic and done at regular intervals. It should be done on every occasion of a problem and not on a hit-or-miss basis. Notes should be dated and signed without fail by the person making them. Inadequate documentation is a major reason why supervisors are often unable to justify their disciplinary decisions.

Documentation is necessary to identify patterns of deterioration in job performance such as the following:

ABSENTEEISM. Patterns of absenteeism vary with each person. The following are some general patterns: unauthorized leave; excessive sick leave; Monday and/or Friday absences; repeated absences of 2-4 days or 1-2 weeks; excessive tardiness, especially on Monday mornings or in returning from lunch; leaving work early; peculiar and increasingly improbable excuses for absences; and a higher absenteeism rate than other employees. Usually any excess absenteeism or increases in absenteeism should be noted.

ON-THE-JOB-ABSENTEEISM. This includes continued absences from the work station more than the job requires, frequent trips to the water fountain or bathroom, long coffee breaks and physical illness on the job.

ACCIDENT REPEATER BEHAVIOR includes accidents on the job, frequent trips to the nurse's office, accidents off the job which affect job performance, unsafe behavior and violation of safety rules.

DIFFICULTY IN CONCENTRATION may be indicated when work requires great effort, jobs take more time than normal or there are hand tremors when concentrating.

CONFUSION may be marked by difficulty in recalling instructions or details, in handling complex assignments or in recalling one's own mistakes.

SPASMODIC WORK PATTERNS include alternate periods of very high and very low productivity.

RELUCTANCE TO CHANGE JOBS may present a threat because control of the present job allows hiding low job performance.

COMING TO WORK OR RETURNING FROM LUNCH IN AN OBVIOUSLY ABNORMAL CONDITION is a clear sign of performance deterioration.

GENERALLY LOWERED JOB EFFICIENCY includes such things as missed deadlines, mistakes due to inattention or poor judgment, material wastes, bad decisions, customer complaints or improbable causes for poor job performance.

POOR HUMAN RELATIONS. Friction in human relationships, including supervisor-employee relationships, usually results in decreased job performance. The following behaviors affect job performance and may indicate a problem: over-reaction to real or imagined criticism, wide swings in morale, money problems with co-workers, complaints from co-workers, unreasonable resentments and avoidance of associates.

DISCUSSIONS AND JOB COUNSELING SESSIONS. Documentation should cover not only the patterns mentioned above, but should also summarize the content of the discussions, your remarks and the employee's remarks. Note the actions taken to correct the employee's deficiencies as well as the result of such actions.

Remember, all employees, including managers, exhibit some of these performance problems occasionally. It is a *pattern* of performance problems over a period of time that should be recognized and documented.

4.   Discuss Performance

Supervisors should discuss with the employee substandard behavior or declining performance. Some behavior, such as violation of important rules, is serious on the first occasion. Other substandard behavior or performance problems become serious when repeated. To discuss these effectively, these seven steps should be followed in sequence:

a. Prior to the discussion, the supervisor should outline the points he or she intends to discuss and the action desired from the employee. These points must be properly documented.

b. In the interview, based on documentation, describe the problem; evaluate performance, not the person. Some examples are:

NOT - "You sure have been grouchy lately."

BUT - "You lost control of your temper three times this week."

NOT - "Don't you believe in safety rules?"

BUT - "That's the third time this week you've been in that area without your hard hat."

NOT - "You seem to have trouble showing up for work."

BUT - "You've been absent four days this month and tardy on six other days."

c. Get agreement that there is a performance problem.

d. Get agreement on what will be done to correct the problem. Be specific.

e. Set a time for a follow-up discussion to review progress.

f. Do the follow-up interview. In the meantime, give positive support and reinforcement for improvements.

g. If, by the follow-up session, the problem has not been dealt with, deal with the employee on the basis of not keeping the commitments made.

However, it may be that the employee wants to talk about the performance problem or the personal problems behind it. In such cases...

5.   Listen and Learn

Be a good listener - "tap the awesome power of the listening ear." More than 4,000 years ago, the prime minister to the Pharaoh of Egypt wrote these words to his son and successor in office:

> **Be calm as you listen to a petitioner's speech. Do not refuse him before he has swept out his body, or said that for which he came. It is not necessary that all his requests should be granted; but a good hearing is a soothing of the heart.**

It is equally true today. Modern psychologists tell us that listening is probably the most simple and effective single technique for helping troubled people. Effective listening can be learned. The key is one's desire to understand what is really bothering the person. Listening enables the employee to "get it off his (or her) chest," clarify thoughts and feelings, reduce tension, and "blow off steam." Sometimes just having someone who listens will enable a person to deal with the problem. At other times, listening can avert serious results, at least temporarily, until the more basic problems can be identified and helped.

There is an old expression, "Never judge a brave until you have walked for a moon in his moccasins." To truly listen is to walk in the moccasins of another person, to see the situation as he or she sees it.

The ARROWS of listening can help get to the heart of the matter. These arrows are:

A - Accept the speaker
R - Restate content
R - Reflect feeling
O - Open-ended questions
W - Wait for clarification
S - Summarize the conversation

ACCEPT THE SPEAKER - Neither condemn nor condone - merely accept what is being said.

For example:
"Uh-huh."   "Tell me more."
"I see."   "That's interesting."
"I understand."

Accepting what the employee says reduces his or her need for self-defense. It avoids a conversation in which each speaker begins with, "Yes, but...." Let the employee state his or her case. Listen positively and attentively.

RESTATE CONTENT - Restate in your own words the meaning of what the person is saying. For example:

Employee -   "Every time I get that machine up to production speed, something breaks down on it."
Supervisor - "Production is down because of the poor condition of the machine."

Restating lets the employee know that you are listening. Thus it encourages him or her to explore further. It also provides an opportunity for correction of misunderstandings. It keeps you both on the same path.

REFLECT FEELING - Reflection is similar to restating in that you "mirror" back what you heard. However, in reflecting, feelings or emotions are reflected rather than ideas.
For example:

Employee -   "Sam just keeps on needling me until I get to the point where I explode."
Supervisor - "Sam's needling makes you very angry."

It has been demonstrated repeatedly that emotions hide and distort facts. Like in strip mining, the only way to expose the ore is to remove the overburden. Allowing the employee to ventilate feelings enables you both to eventually "strike it rich," in terms of facts and understanding.

OPEN-ENDED QUESTIONS can further the conversation. These are questions that cannot be answered with a "yes" or "no." Usually they begin with "what," "why" and "how." How do you feel about that? What can I do to help? Why do you think that is so? What suggestions would you make? Open-ended questions encourage the flow of information.

WAIT FOR CLARIFICATION - The pause is one of the most powerful communication tools. Waiting for clarification is asking without words. In effect, it says, "I'm willing to wait for you to collect your thoughts." Short pauses are useful after the other person has said something. They silently say, "If you have more to add I am willing to listen." Pauses are also helpful when you have asked a question. Instead of rushing in to clarify what you have said, your pause silently says, "Take your time, I am willing to wait." Rushing in too quickly is like playing both sides of a tennis match. Wait for the employee to answer. If the person is not certain of the question, he or she will ask you to repeat it.

SUMMARIZE - At the end of the conversation, a brief summary of what has been said is an excellent communications tool. It assures the employee that you really did listen. And it provides an immediate opportunity for the correction of any misunderstanding.

The ARROWS of effective listening go a long way toward keeping supervisory efforts on target. They are effective for dealing with a large number of problems — behavioral, health and performance. They are useful after an accident to allow an employee an opportunity to relive the experience without blame and thus to integrate it into his or her self-image. They also provide guidance on when to refer the employee to someone else.

6. Know When to Refer

Supervisors should know when to refer an employee to someone else. When an employee's work performance is unacceptable or deteriorating for no apparent reason, or when the employee knows the reason but is unable to cope with it, he or she should be referred to someone else. A resource person should be available to help the employee find the specific help needed. That person might be in the personnel office, the counseling service, medical department or community mental health service. It is not the supervisor's responsibility to make specific referrals such as family counseling, alcoholism counseling or addiction counseling. Specific referral requires a diagnosis, which is beyond the supervisor's role. If the employee is a danger to himself or others, he or she should be escorted (not sent) to the personnel department, the medical department, the hospital or home; depending on the circumstances, your organization's policy and your supervisor's guidance.

The employee who does not accept this referral, and whose overall work performance continues below established minimum requirements, should be given a firm choice between seeking assistance or accepting the consequences — the appropriate administrative or disciplinary action which must be initiated. Sometimes this alone will be sufficient to improve work performance. If so, and if performance really has improved (not just been covered up), you need not take further corrective action unless the performance again deteriorates.

UPPER MANAGEMENT'S ROLE

Starting a company program is not a complex management maneuver. The same principles apply here as for any other new company program — define the problem, get the best and latest information on how to handle it, work out a solution tailored to company structure, and plan how the program can be introduced smoothly and economically into existing company procedures.

The role of upper management here is the same as in any other area: planning, organizing, leading and controlling. The planning stage may involve the use of an outside consultant experienced in occupational programs. The programs should be presented to managers and, if unionized, to union representatives. The presentation should show the problem in terms of its financial and human cost; the need for supervisors to be able to deal effectively and constructively with related performance problems; and related personnel policies.

At the second stage, "organizing," upper management designates the persons responsible for implementation and support, appoints a program coordinator and establishes a tentative time frame for the remaining steps of implementation. The persons responsible for implementation review the company's health-medical insurance coverage for its coordination with the program. They develop a written policy (such as the one shown in *Figure 14-5*), designate the official diagnostic-referral services and begin implementation of the policy and programs. Also, the program coordinator establishes liaison with the diagnostic-referral services if these are outside the organization.

The "leading" stage involves management orientation and supervisory training. Since supervisors are the "hinge" of the program, special training sessions must be provided for them. The program coordinator should make individual contact with the supervisors from time to time to discuss specific problems they might be having. Also, there should be employee orientation and family notification. Continuing awareness among employees can be gained by a brochure, in new employee orientation, follow-up training for supervisors, the posting of educational visual aids on bulletin boards and similar actions publicizing the program.

Management "control" is maintained through continuing measurement, evaluation and improvement. Measurements can be made of *program performance*. This includes the number of referrals made, the employee level of those making referrals, the percentage of employees in the program, the amount and quality of information communicated about the program, the degree to which confidentiality is maintained, the demonstration of support by top management, the amount of initial and follow-up training given to supervisors and the amount of supervisory input into program evaluation.

Measurements can also be made of *program results*. These include the percentage of self-referrals, the degree to which the characteristics (age, sex, marital status, employment level) of those in the program match the characteristics of the total employee population, reductions in turnover and absenteeism and number of employees restored to satisfactory job performance.

The Occupational Program Consultant in your state's or province's Alcohol and Drug Abuse Commission can help establish both limited and com-

VIII. COMPREHENSIVE POLICY STATEMENT

Certain employees of the _____ as well as members of their families may experience behavioral-medical problems, which not only affect their personal lives, but often result in substandard job performance. It is our policy to help employees whose poor job performance is a result of this type of problem, possibly avoiding discipline which could result from such behavior. To accomplish this, we will provide assistance to these persons within _____ .

The following shall be our policy:

I. The _____ recognizes alcoholism, drug abuse and other mental conditions as illnesses that can be successfully treated.

II. The purpose of this policy is to assure that all employees with these illnesses will receive the same consideration and opportunity for treatment that is given to employees with other illnesses.

III. The social stigma often associated with these illnesses is improper and unfair. We believe that a company-wide positive attitude and realistic acceptance of these illnesses will encourage our employees to voluntarily seek and accept available treatment.

IV. Our concern is not limited to the effects of alcohol and drug abuse on the employee's job performance, but includes all behavioral-medical problems that affect an individual's job performance.

    A. Alcoholism - An illness in which an individual's drinking seriously and repeatedly interferes with his or her health or job performance.

    B. Mental Illness - Behavior which seriously and repeatedly interferes with job performance.

    C. Drug Abuse - Use of drugs which seriously interferes with job performance or health, or being under the influence of a drug that is not under the valid medical direction of a licensed physician.

V. Implementation of this policy is the responsiblity of all division directors, department heads and supervisors. They will enforce procedures to assure that no employee with alcohol, mental health or drug problems will have his or her job security threatened by submitting themselves for diagnosis and treatment.

VI. It is recognized that department heads and supervisors are neither qualified nor expected to make professional judgments as to whether or not an employee is addicted to alcohol or drugs; just as they are neither qualified nor expected to diagnose any other illness.

VII. The employee is responsible to comply with referrals for diagnosis and to cooperate with the prescribed remedial programs.

VIII. An employee's refusal to accept diagnosis and treatment, or continued failure to report for and/or respond to treatment, will be handled in the same way that similar refusals are handled for other illnesses.

IX. We hope that through this policy, employees who suspect that they have an alcohol, mental health or drug problem, even in its early stages, will be encouraged to seek diagnosis and follow through with the prescribed treatment.

X. The confidentiality of records kept on "alcohol/mental illness/drug-involved employees" is necessary and will be preserved, as with all confidential medical-insurance records.

XI. Expenses incurred for treatment and/or hospitalization are those provided under the group health insurance program.

XII. The Personnel Division is responsible for implementation of this policy, for coordination with department heads and employee organizations and for ensuring the training of referral coordinators.

APPROVED: _____

Figure 14-5

prehensive programs for all types of troubled employees. These persons can also be of great assistance in selecting which particular agency in your location to work with. In some areas, it will be the mental health center, in others the local alcohol and drug abuse commission. In yet other areas there may be other public or private agencies to work with. The state Occupational Program Consultant is also a good source for films and literature dealing with troubled employees. The National Clearinghouse for Alcoholism Literature and Information (NCAAI), Box 2345, Rockville, Maryland 20852, is the source for a free "Dictionary of Occupational Program Consultants."

In Canada, each province has an alcohol and/or drug abuse center which may be contacted for assistance.

PROGRAM BENEFITS

Organizations which have adopted a management approach to troubled employees similar to the one outlined in this chapter have reported benefits such as these:

1. The satisfactory rehabilitation of a large group of people with problems. These employees have valuable experience, knowledge and job training. Employees who enter treatment programs as outlined above have a remarkably high rate of successful treatment and recovery. Experience has shown recovery rates of 60% to 80% or more. Programs which allow early intervention and referral, while the employee still has a viable job, home and family, have far greater chances of success than do other types of programs. The incentive of holding onto one's job remains a powerful motivator in treatment programs.

2. The strengthening of important supervisory skills, particularly as supervisors become more effective at monitoring, measuring, coaching and counseling the job performance of their employees.

3. Significant improvement in overall work performance of the employees involved.

4. A substantial improvement in loss control and cost control. For example, including coverage for alcoholism in a comprehensive family health insurance policy has been shown to reduce benefit payments for other kinds of health care, both for the alcoholic and for other family members.

5. The solution of many strained personnel problems.

6. Improved employee relations.

7. The saving of considerable supervisory time, formerly spent in solving related problems.

8. Improved public relations, developed through the demonstration of positive human behavior.

Many large corporations have adopted comprehensive approaches to the troubled employee. Also, a growing number of smaller firms are using outside consultants and counselors to assist them in setting up their own programs. These companies feel that their investment in time, attention and services is well returned by the benefits of their programs.

CORE CONCEPTS IN REVIEW

Virtually every organization has **troubled employees** — those whose personal problems interfere significantly with job performance.

1. Studies show that just one type, problem drinkers, make up about 5% of industrial employees.

2. All types together make up about 10% of the work force.

Management interest in this situation is motivated by vital factors such as safety, absenteeism, morale, productivity, turnover, legislation, humanitarian concerns and costs. **The additional costs of a troubled employee is likely to be about 25% of his or her annual wages.** Both the economic costs and the human costs are too great to be ignored. There are many contributing causes of troubled employees:

1. **Personal factors** (stress-producing)
   a. Family problems
   b. Financial problems
   c. Medical problems
   d. Marital problems
   e. Mental problems
   f. Legal problems

2. **Job factors** (stress-producing)
   a. Reorganization
   b. New performance requirements
   c. Fear of being replaced or laid off

d. Demotion
e. Promotion
f. Hazardous surroundings
g. Boredom
h. Inadequate supervision

Three **common management approaches** to the troubled employee problem are:

1. The **cover-up approach** — we will make believe the problem doesn't exist, until it gets so bad we have to fire you.

2. The **limited approach** — we will try to do something about alcoholism/drug abuse, but not about other kinds of employee troubles.

3. The **comprehensive approach** — we will try to help troubled employees, no matter what the causes are.

The **role of supervisors** in managing troubled employees is summarized in these six steps:

1. Recognize the importance of the supervisory role

2. Identify the symptoms of developing problems

3. Document the patterns of performance

4. Discuss performance with the employee

5. Learn to listen; listen to learn

6. Know when to refer an employee to a counselor

Upper management's role in a company program for dealing with troubled employees is the same as its role in any other company program: **planning, organizing** and **leading** the way with policy, procedures, practices and personal commitment. Management **control** comes by:

1. Identifying the necessary work to be done and who is to do it

2. Setting program standards

3. Measuring and evaluating how well the program meets the standards

4. Motivating continued improvement through constructive correction of substandard performance and commendation of good performance.

Companies with effective programs for managing troubled employees gain many benefits, such as:

1. Rehabilitation of many people with personal and performance problems

2. The strengthening of important supervisory skills

3. Substantial improvements in loss control and cost control

4. Solution of many critical personnel problems

5. Significantly improved employee and public relations

6. Savings of supervisory time formerly spent in dealing with the effects of troubled employees

7. A significant bottom-line return on investment.

KEY QUESTIONS

1. It has been determined that about what percent of employees have a drinking problem?

2. Define a troubled employee.

3. What are management's concerns with troubled employees?

4. A troubled employee is likely to cost the organization about what percent of his or her annual wage?

5. Name three life events that create a high level of stress.

6. What are the three common management approaches to the troubled employee?

7. Why is the "broadbrush" approach recommended?

8. Why is the front-line supervisor the "point of management control" for troubled employees?

9. What are some symptoms of developing problems?

10. What are some guidelines for performance discussion with employees?

11. What do the "ARROWS of listening" stand for?

12. When should the supervisor refer a troubled employee to someone else?

13. What is upper management's role in a troubled employee program?

14. What are some benefits of a well-managed troubled employee program?

PRACTICAL APPLICATIONS SUMMARY

S - For Supervisors
E - For Executives
C - For Safety/Loss Control Coordinators

	S	E	C
1. Establish costs to the organization of troubled employees.			x
2. Establish a comprehensive policy for statement on troubled employees.		x	
3. Publicize the organizational policy for troubled employees.			x
4. Establish liaison with helping agencies.			x
5. Provide management training in managing troubled employees.			x
6. Communicate and publicize the program.		x	
7. Develop appreciation of role in dealing with troubled employees.	x	x	x
8. Identify the symptoms of developing problems.	x	x	
9. Document patterns of declining performance.	x	x	
10. Discuss with subordinate substandard behavior or declining performance.	x	x	
11. Learn to be a good listener.	x	x	x
12. Make referrals to program coordinator.	x	x	
13. Make referrals to outside helping agencies.			x
14. Evaluate the program on the basis of reduced costs, self-referrals and representative participation.			x
15. Communicate program evaluation to appropriate persons.			x
16. Develop corrective actions to overcome any problems encountered.	x	x	x

CHAPTER 15

PROPERTY DAMAGE AND WASTE CONTROL

"... exclusive concentration on injury-causing accidents is also the chief obstacle to further big steps toward their prevention. In the light of all this, it is scarcely an exaggeration to designate damage control as a 'modern key to safety,' in tune with the technological advances of the second half of the 20th century."
- Dr. S. Laner

INTRODUCTION

There is an unending list of raw materials, equipment, products and facilities that are damaged or destroyed by accident every day. Thousands upon thousands of items are crushed, dented, cracked, strained or broken by undesired happenings — items such as jars, tubes, boxes, clothing, wires, cans, vehicles, guardrails, doors, windows, counters, columns, tables, machines, fixtures, tires, spindles, frames, floors and walls. The damage is there. You can identify, evaluate and control it once you are "tuned in" to it.

The purpose of this chapter is twofold. First, to present the size and scope of the problem. Second, to clearly define practical steps which almost any organization can take to control this major source of loss.

THE SIZE AND SCOPE OF THE PROBLEM

While there are extensive statistics concerning the frequency and costs of accidental injuries, there is no single source of comprehensive cost data for accidental property damage. Some insight into the size of the problem can be gained by evaluating the statistics presented in *Accident Facts*, published by the National Safety Council. A recent issue reveals that 200,000,000 workdays were lost by persons with non-disabling injuries and by persons with no injuries who stopped to help the injured or discuss the accidents. Common sense tells anyone who has ever worked in industry that there are many more property damage accidents than injury accidents, causing much more lost time and related dollar losses.

It staggers the imagination to estimate what the actual total cost of property damage may be if we consider that the "other costs" related to injuries reported in the NSC publication are presented as $14,000,000,000. This includes the monetary value of time lost by workers other than those injured, who are directly or indirectly involved in accidents; and the time required to investigate the accidents, write the reports and so on. It is logical to assume that "other costs" of property damage would be much greater than those involved with injuries. Several examples from specific industries emphasize this point:

- An automotive truck-manufacturing plant manager reported the direct costs of property damage in the previous 12 months to be $4,605,000. This figure was approximately 10 times the cost of workers' compensation.

- An oil company reported general property damage costs of $5,740,700, compared to $60,500 for injuries. Motor vehicle damage costs were listed separately and represented $276,000 in additional property damage losses. This shows a damage-to-injury cost ratio of 99-to-one.

- A mining company's records show 892 reported property damage accidents for the year, costing $615,750, compared to 157 reported injuries, costing $37,562. Damage-to-injury cost ratio: 16-to-one.

- A steel plant's records indicate reported property damage costs for 12 months at $928,544. Its workers' compensation costs were less than $100,000. Ratio: nine-to-one.

- A heavy machinery manufacturing corporation executive reported the total costs of accidents (including general property damage) to exceed 10 million dollars during the year analyzed. While not revealing the costs of injuries, he indicated they were *less than 20%* of the total accident costs.

In one recent year there were 148,857,145 freight damage claims paid by Class I railroads alone, according to an editorial in *Materials Handling Engineering Magazine*. In addition, records of the Federal Railroad Administration indicate that over 5,000 railroad derailments serious enough to require reporting occur annually, with costs exceeding $100,000,000.

An executive of a New York department store reported that from 30 to 40 percent of all furniture gets damaged somewhere between the time it is made and the time it rests in your living room.

Other information available from professional associations, insurance companies and the U.S. Department of Transportation, shows that motor fleet, marine, rail and air transportation cargo damage alone substantially exceeds the total costs of injuries in the U.S. The size of this prevalent problem of property damage and waste is reinforced by the reports of hundreds of supervisory personnel contacted annually in management training conferences.

These data fully support the estimates that in business and industry as a whole the ledger costs of property damage range, conservatively, from five to 50 times the insured costs of injuries. This startling information is portrayed in the "cost iceberg," *Figure 15-1*. Notice that the $1 at the top of the iceberg is the *insured* costs (hospitalization and workers' compensation) of injuries and illnesses. The $5 to $50 is the ledger (actual) costs of *uninsured* property damage, over and above the damage covered by insurance. Another important point is that this estimated ratio is for business and industry as a whole. Some highly capital-intensive operations have reported actual figures as high as 100 to one.

The total costs of *waste* in industry are perhaps even more staggering than the enormous figures on property damage. For example, the Federal Energy Information Office reports that Americans use 70.924 quadrillion BTU's per year. Industrial and transportation activities account for about 65% of the total energy consumption. When the President asked all Americans to cut back 5%, many businesses found that they could do even more. Waste is often the result of long-unquestioned plant practices that, upon analysis, are shown to have no effect on employee performance or product dependability. Energy used for heating represents about 18% of the nation's energy consumption. The National Bureau of Standards estimates that approximately 40% of the energy used for heating is wasted. NBS research also indicates that energy requirements for cooling can be reduced 30% with little sacrifice to comfort, and that energy for illumination can be effectively reduced 15% in most existing buildings simply by turning off lights when not needed.

There is unbelievable waste in the utilization of many sources of energy, such as compressed air, gas and raw water. Comments on energy control and other waste-related areas will be made throughout this chapter. It is sufficient to indicate at this point that there is little doubt that the costs of waste in industry at least equal, and probably exceed, the costs of

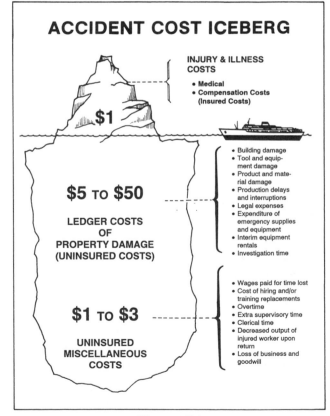

Figure 15-1

property damage. However, these costs, as enormous as they are, are not the only reason for concern.

RELATIONSHIPS OF PROPERTY DAMAGE AND PERSONAL HARM

As a general rule, organizations which are not in control of property damage are also not in control of injuries and illnesses of people. There are several reasons why this is so. One is that most property damage accidents have high *potential* for personal injury or illness. Once the sequence of events in an incident gets under way, it is often a matter of chance whether the result is a near-miss, property damage or personal harm. The difference may be only fractions of an inch or milliseconds of time.

Another reason is that property damage accidents and personal injury accidents tend to have the same causes. If an employee does not know how to operate a piece of equipment properly, there will be accidents. Some will damage property, some will injure people, some will do both. However, the basic cause is the same. Another example: inadequate maintenance on overhead cranes will cause accidents. Whether people are injured, property is damaged or both, the basic cause is the same.

A third reason is that the study of all accidents (injury/illness/property damage) yields more information about accident causation than the study of only one type. The ratio study shown in *Figure 15-2* clearly reveals that there are nearly three times as many property damage accidents as there are injury accidents. In other words, an organization which investigates and analyzes only injury accidents is using only 27% of the accident data it should be using. The systematic study of *all* accidents, whether or not they resulted in personal injury, will yield far more information about accident causes and controls.

Yet another relationship between property damage control and personnel safety is that of attitudes. An organization which ignores property damage communicates to its people that safety is not very high on its agenda of concerns. The message is subtle, but it is very real and can affect any statements to the contrary. Employees are not likely to take property damage and waste any more seriously than the organization does. This cannot help but create situations and attitudes which will eventually result in injuries. People like to work for a company which "cares." And, as Hugh M. Douglas, former corporate safety director for Imperial Oil, once said, "We take better

care of our people when we take better care of our business."

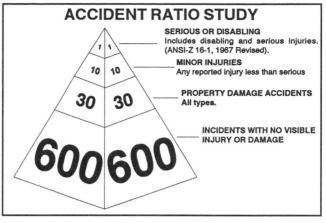

Figure 15-2

WHY PROPERTY DAMAGE ACCIDENTS HAVE BEEN NEGLECTED

The question arises as to why management has not been motivated to inquire more deeply into the nature and extent of this accident element and its economics. Research shows that safety programs throughout the world have tended to emphasize only injury-type accidents in their organized accident reporting, investigation and analysis.

Philosophically, there is nothing new about damage control as an important element in the overall accident prevention effort. Safety measures are on record as early as the middle 1800's, when explosive powder mills were built with exceedingly heavy masonry walls on three sides, a light wooden roof, and a light fourth wall facing a river. In case of an accidental explosion, the force would then be directed toward the river, with less chance of injury to employees from debris that would otherwise have blown about. Organized efforts to eliminate unsafe practices or conditions — and prevent accidents that could result in personal injury or property damage - are as old as the safety movement itself. But while injury-type accidents have been emphasized, damage-type accidents have been neglected.

Why, then, were the costly accidents that could cause extensive harm and expensive production losses not included in the organized safety program? Why has the term "accident" continued for so many years to be deeply entrenched in the minds of safety specialists, and others, as a word with only one synonym: "injury"?

Part of the answer is that early compensation laws so

increased the cost of occupational injuries that employers were forced to find methods of reducing the injuries. The accident prevention movement thus was greatly advanced by means of the injury cost sheet—and much more rapidly than it would otherwise have been. With insurance rates based on injury experience and costs, it was natural that the newly introduced safety director, following management's specific request, directed all efforts to the injury-associated accident.

Therefore, costs unrelated to injuries were buried in the general plant operating costs. There was no stimulus to broaden remedial efforts similar to those provoked by the compensation laws. So, in practice, the term "accident prevention" really meant "injury prevention," not only to operating management but also to safety personnel.

With the tremendous strides taken in specific areas of accident prevention in the Space Age, it seems paradoxical that the same basic safety rules (those requiring employees to report all accidents resulting in injury) have generally remained unchanged in the great majority of operations. This exclusive, formal emphasis on the injury-type accident has been continued to the present day in the accident investigation and analysis procedures of many safety programs. Regardless of the injury *potential* and the tremendous dollar losses, these programs generally include no requirement for the investigation of an accident unless it terminates in injury.

It is true that some companies do force periodic attention to select near-injury accidents because of the nature of their occurrence and their potential severity. While of significant value to the overall safety programming effort, the sometime inclusion of these accidents does not begin to compare with the value of establishing an integrated method for the reporting, investigating, analyzing and remedying of *all* accidents.

It is interesting to note that certain motor transport fleets (both bus and freight lines), a number of utility companies with large motor fleet operations and members of the air transportation industry have incorporated property damage accidents into certain phases of their overall safety programs. This exception to the rule again points out the important role that identified costs have played in the growth and development of safety programs. For many years, insurance companies have established transport coverage rates on a combination of property damage and injury experience. Companies with major investments in transportation equipment have been forced, because of escalating costs, to take a close look at property damage as well as personal injury accidents. It is well known that a bad property damage experience in this industry can lead to a crippling loss of insurance coverage.

In most states and provinces, passenger car drivers are very much aware of the attitude of insurance companies toward the individual whose driving record is marred consistently by property damage accidents. Even if the costs paid by the carrier are less than the premium paid by the driver, continuing insurance coverage may be denied or made prohibitively expensive. Insurance carriers have long recognized that the same habits that cause minor accidents are potentially more costly risks for major accidents, including serious or fatal injury.

Most states and provinces require a driver to report promptly any accident in which property damage exceeds a certain value (for example, $100). Analysis of these accidents provides the basis for remedial action to avert continued highway accident costs and, more importantly, the associated injuries and deaths.

The typical occupational safety program has neglected the property damage element for reasons such as these:

1. The industrial safety movement was originally fostered by, and still is guided by, the important humane aspects of injury-type accidents.

2. Worker compensation laws have focused management's attention on the identified costs associated with lost-time injuries.

3. Accidental injury records, for treatment and insurance record purposes, have long been the source of control for maintaining injury investigation programs.

4. Industry has experienced little or no pressure, from within or without, to deal with accidents involving property damage.

5. There has seemed to be no immediately available source of property damage accident facts and figures.

6. Historical precedence has created the managerial attitude that safety people have no business "snooping" into the business.

7. Safety specialists and other members of the management team have been plagued by the ever-

present resistance to change.

8. Even where major damage cost problems exist, they are frequently buried in general maintenance and purchasing costs. And there they lie, unrecognized as preventable accident expenses.

EVOLUTION TOWARD TOTAL ACCIDENT CONTROL

Starting in the 1950's, Lukens Steel Company led the way to industrial property damage control. After about a decade of development and success, the program was published in 1966 by the American Management Association as the book, *Damage Control,* by Bird and Germain. Billing it as "a new horizon in accident prevention and cost improvement," the AMA said:

Damage Control is the first book published on a totally new approach to plant safety that places the emphasis on *all* accidents — not just those resulting in injury. It describes a practical injury and cost reduction program developed by the Lukens Steel Company to reduce potential injuries, correct causes of accidents, eliminate production tie-ups, improve product quality and heighten employee morale.

Visits, speeches, articles and seminars followed. Interest spread to many companies in many countries. In recent years, the escalating costs of repairing and replacing damaged tools, machines, materials and facilities have motivated even greater management interest and involvement in total accident control. Today, damage control is recognized as a vital part of safety/loss control by leading organizations around the world. As shown in *Figure 15-3*, it serves as a solid bridge from the injury-oriented safety program to the

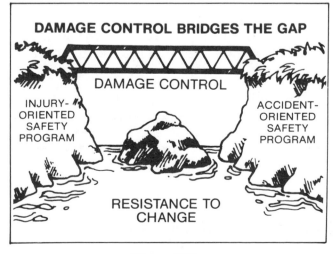

DAMAGE CONTROL BRIDGES THE GAP

DAMAGE CONTROL

INJURY-ORIENTED SAFETY PROGRAM

ACCIDENT-ORIENTED SAFETY PROGRAM

RESISTANCE TO CHANGE

Figure 15-3

accident-oriented safety program. Many modern managers have bridged the gap and have put to practical use the definition: "An accident is an undesired event that results in harm to people, damage to property or loss to process."

The basic framework for damage control is the same as for any other aspect of loss control: *identification/evaluation/control.*

IDENTIFICATION OF ACCIDENTAL PROPERTY DAMAGE

The first step toward control of accidental property damage is to recognize, identify and inventory the specific items being damaged. Many organizations use a standard such as the following to guide their efforts in this direction:

Any damage incident that is considered outside the standards established or desired for fair wear and tear by the most knowledgeable persons will be considered accidental and included in the reporting system.

There are three major ways to identify critical items damaged: 1) by personal observation, 2) by management directive and 3) by systematic audit.

Identification by Personal Observation

Any member of management can spot damage during his or her normal contacts on the work floor, in the field, in the shop or wherever the bulk of operating and maintenance activities occur. In some cases, the damage from the single incident will obviously be great enough to classify it as a critical item. In other cases, it may be necessary to get answers to a few questions like these:

- How often does this type of damage occur?
- How much dollar loss does this type of incident usually cause?
- What is the cumulative loss during a meaningful budget period (e.g., month, quarter, or year)?

A significant number of critical damage items can be identified by this personal observation and follow-through. However, since this approach tends to be superficial, it should be supplemented by more systematic methods.

Identification by Management Directive

In this approach, the chief operating executive issues

a directive requesting department heads, with the help of their supervisors, to identify their own items of damage and waste. This request should follow suitable "mind preparation" so that everyone is thoroughly familiar with the purpose of the exercise. The staff safety/loss control coordinator, along with the top official, can be a critical figure in this process. For example, he or she may do most of the research and provide information to the executive for use in the communication and promotion activities. He or she may also use the information submitted by the department heads to compile a company-wide inventory of critical damage items.

This approach has great appeal because it enables managers to identify their own problems in their own way. This reduces the resistance to change which might come from having outsiders identify the items. It also obtains total management involvement, emphasizes the need for everyone's involvement and makes everyone aware of top management's interest in accident control.

Identification by Systematic Audit

While a majority of managers may feel more comfortable getting the information by directive, many items will not be voluntarily identified. This does not necessarily indicate dishonesty. It does mean that the whole picture is not revealed. Though one reason may be intentional cover-up, the biggest reason is a lack of awareness that some of the problems *are* property damage and waste problems. Whatever the reasons, the systematic audit will help to uncover many items subject to the bias of people with vested interests.

For best results, the systematic audit should be very well planned, including thorough explanations of the program to all levels of management. Special efforts should be made to assure the free exchange of all related information. Often there is subtle resistance by subordinates to revealing information that could reflect negatively on the boss. This loyalty and the resultant resistance to change should be recognized, and efforts made to minimize it.

An essential part of preparation is to list every supervisor in direct charge of any repair shop, area or location where anything damaged ultimately goes for repair, replacement, salvage or disposal. This list must ensure that no areas or sources of damage information are omitted. Remember that many things are repaired in the field as well as in the shop, and that some

damaged items are sent outside for repair.

In addition to the names of the front-line supervisors for each of these locations, put the names of their department heads on the list. You now have the locations to audit and the names of the people who probably have the greatest knowledge of what comes into the area, what's done to it and what it costs.

Then, arrange a meeting with each front-line supervisor in his or her shop or area. If possible, the department head (or assistant) should also be there. This provides an additional source of management information, and exerts a significant motivational influence for full cooperation of the front-line supervisor. The possibility that the supervisor may "clam up" on vital information which might otherwise have been shared is outweighed by the overall value of this manager's presence. The information the department head gains in this exercise may also be of great value in future activities to control property damage losses. Make every effort to help each person recognize the importance of taking the time necessary to do this audit properly. Choose a time for the meeting that best meets participants' needs.

The "auditor" asks the supervisor to recall items of damage or waste that have come into his or her area within the last year or so. It usually helps to tour the area with the supervisor and to ask lots of questions about the nature of activities in the area. List each item identified, with information on unit cost and the estimated number damaged or wasted per year.

A worksheet like the one shown in *Figure 15-4* is helpful in developing the damage inventory. In column 1, list *all* items discovered. Put the unit costs (per item, pound, kilowatt, gallon, etc.) in column 2. Enter the estimated number damaged or wasted per year in column 3 and multiply it by the number in column 2 to get the estimated costs for column 4. Later investigation should reveal actual costs, to be listed in column 5.

Frequently, front-line supervisors are quite accurate about numbers and costs. After all, they may order the replacement parts, they schedule the workers who do the repairs and their information on what comes through the area should be as accurate as anyone's.

The audit exercise must be carried out in each shop or area. If conducted with patience, perseverance and a positive attitude, it will provide an abundance of valuable data for damage control.

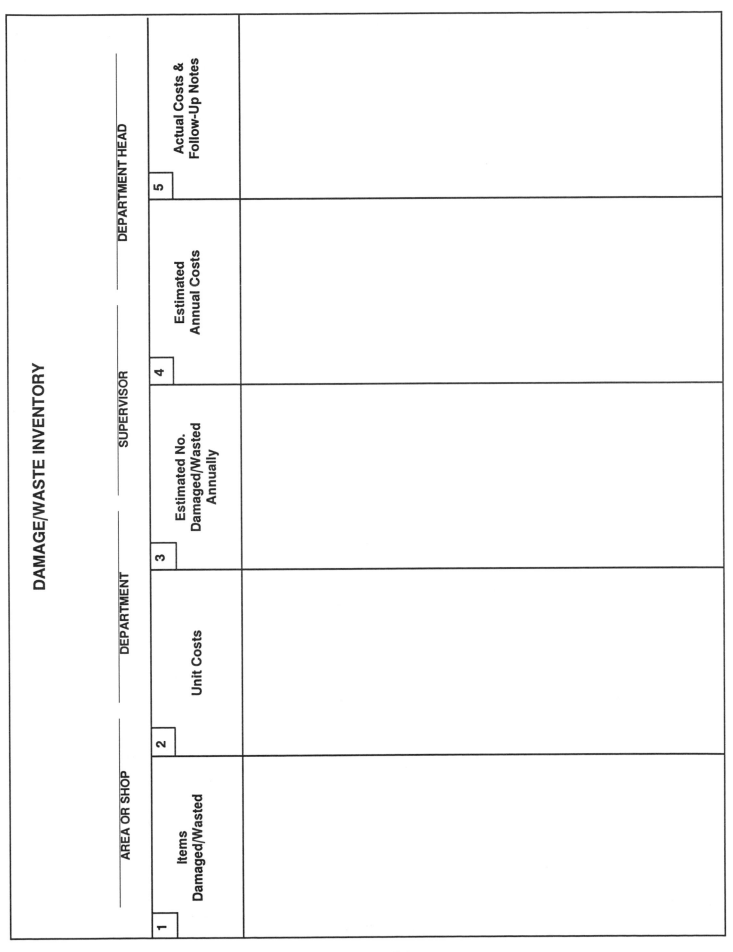

DAMAGE/WASTE INVENTORY

AREA OR SHOP

DEPARTMENT

SUPERVISOR

DEPARTMENT HEAD

1. Items Damaged/Wasted

2. Unit Costs

3. Estimated No. Damaged/Wasted Annually

4. Estimated Annual Costs

5. Actual Costs & Follow-Up Notes

Figure 15-4

EVALUATION OF PROPERTY DAMAGE PROBLEMS

The purpose of evaluation is to determine the critical items of damage and set priorities for action. This is another area where the "Pareto Principle" or "Principle of the Critical/Vital Few" holds true:

The majority (80%) of any group of effects is produced by a relatively small (20%) number of causes.

The critical damage items are the relatively few that produce the bulk of the dollar losses. These losses include not only the costs of repair and replacement, but also the costs of related downtime, quality problems, materials and product spoilage, loss of customer good will and orders and so on.

It is important to identify as many items of waste and damage as possible. However, not every item will be "critical." Some will be so minor in cost or occur so infrequently that the expense to do anything about them would cost more than the savings to be realized. The "Damage/Waste Inventory" form discussed earlier (*Figure 15-4*) provides not only a convenient way of listing the items but also of computing their annual costs. These annual costs are key considerations in determining critical items and action priorities. For instance, let's say column 4 has these dollar entries:

$$\begin{array}{r}
\$ \ \ 5,200 \\
\$ \ \ 1,800 \\
\$ 90,000 \\
\$ \ \ \ \ 500 \\
\$ 68,500 \\
\$ \ \ 3,700 \\
\$ \ \ \ \ 150 \\
\$ \ \ 8,300
\end{array}$$

It's easy to evaluate the relative severity of the eight items and put them in priority order-ranging from $90,000 down to $150.

Critical items are not always the expensive but rare items of major damage. Many critical items cost relatively little to repair or replace each time, but have such a high frequency of repair or replacement that their annual cost is critically high. *Figure 15-5* shows how this was true in a program of small tool and equipment conservation in one tool crib of a mine. Notice, for instance, the "spray paint" item—a two dollar item, but with savings of $19,528!

SMALL TOOLS & EQUIPMENT
CONSERVATION/WASTE CONTROL PROGRAM

CONSUMPTION

IDENTIFICATION	COST	1981	1982	1983 (Nov.8)		SAVINGS
12" Crescent Wrench	$ 15.75	1,221	1,005	536	(- 469)	469 x $ 15.75 = $ 7,386.75
Punch Lock	$140.00	256	199	107	(- 92)	92 x $140.00 = $12,880.00
2 ½ Lb. Axe	$ 10.50	334	212	106	(- 106)	106 x $ 10.50 = $ 1,113.00
Swede Saw	$ 10.50	209	167	40	(- 127)	127 x $ 10.50 = $ 1,333.50
14" Pipe Wrench	$ 23.00	195	222	80	(- 142)	142 x $ 23.00 = $ 3,266.00
18" Pipe Wrench	$ 34.00	359	173	63	(- 110)	110 x $ 34.00 = $ 3,740.00
Square Shovel	$ 12.50	509	349	155	(-194)	194 x $ 12.50 = $ 2,425.00
Cable Cutter	$ 77.60	143	86	46	(- 40)	40 x $ 77.00 = $ 3,104.00
Hack Saw	$ 7.30	667	422	210	(-212)	212 x $ 7.30 = $ 2,547.50
Swede Saw	$ 10.20	1,022	1,080	429	(-651)	651 x $ 10.30 = $ 6,640.20
Speed Wrench	$ 10.50	183	212	87	(-125)	125 x $ 10.50 = $ 1,312.50
8-Lb. Hammer	$ 16.50	281	113	64	(- 49)	49 x $ 16.50 = $ 808.50
6" Crescent Wrench	$ 9.00	203	121	92	(- 29)	29 x $ 9.00 = $ 261.00
8" Crescent Wrench	$ 10.00	184	116	83	(- 33)	33 x $ 10.00 = $ 330.00
Spray Paint	$ 2.00	12,785	14,670	4,906	(-9.764)	9.764 x $ 2.00 = $19,528.00
1-Gal. Plastic Pail	$ 2.50	523	536	380	(- 156)	156 x $ 2.50 = $ 390.00
Knock-Off Blocks	$ 16.20	303	502	227	(-.275)	275 x $ 16.20 = $ 4,455.00
C.I.L. Testers	$ 31.90	273	300	164	(-136)	136 x $ 31.90 = $ 9,338.40
#3 Padlocks	$ 5.80	774	586	654	(- 70)	0
Fire Nozzles	$ 13.00	114	178	93	(- 85)	85 x $ 13.00 = $ 1,105.00
10' Measuring Tape	$ 5.50	164	254	225	(- 29)	29 x $ 5.50 = $ 159.50

$ 81,123.85

CONTROL METHOD

1. First one issued free.
2. Exchange - free:
   (if broken, worn, empty and any part returned)
3. No return - user charged

Figure 15-5

The severity of the problem is not the only consideration. The costs of the damage and/or waste must be weighed against such factors as:

- What kinds of control measures are possible?
- To what degree can the losses be controlled?
- How much will the controls cost?

CONTROL TECHNIQUES

Two things often happen as a result of the preceding activities. One is a reduction in the problem, because of increased awareness. However, this will only be temporary and may not affect the most critical items or deal with the basic causes. The second outcome is that the identified losses are significant enough to further motivate upper management - to improve safety and "the bottom line."

There are two main approaches to systematic control of property damage. One is the Problem-Solving Team approach, which can produce significant loss reductions in six months or less. The other is the long-range approach, which integrates damage and waste control into every facet of the safety/loss control program - for lasting results. Most managers are also interested in long-range management control and program continuity. There is no instant solution to basic causes of property damage, such as improper motivation, inadequate design and inadequate work standards. These require the long-range, integrated approach. Both approaches have their place and both are needed for effective results-immediate *and* long-range.

The Problem-Solving Team: For Fast Results

The project team is a proven technique for obtaining the fast results that most managers want. After the critical items have been identified and evaluated, the appropriate executive sets up a team to analyze a high-priority problem, determine the basic causes, develop solution alternatives and recommend the best solution.

Experience shows that it is usually good to pick a person at the department head level to lead the team. A person at this level tends to be close enough to the "action" to contribute innovative and creative thinking about the problem, and yet is high enough in the organization to make fairly important decisions. And if it can be the department head whose budget must absorb the damage costs, so much the better! As the Principle of Vested Interest says, "A manager is predominantly interested in those economic considerations affecting his or her own budget." This vested interest motivates the manager to pick a good team and work for maximum results.

Team members should represent those who are most familiar with the problem situation, and those most likely to have meaningful input toward analysis and solution. This usually includes the employee who operates or uses the critical damage (or waste) item, and the immediate supervisor of the activity. Maintenance people, repair center supervisors, engineers, purchasing personnel and supplier representatives may be valuable sources of information and potential team members. But remember, the team not only should be large enough to provide information upon which to act, but also small enough to move ahead efficiently (typically from 3-7 members). Keep in mind that those with valuable information need not be regular team members. They can simply be invited to one or more meetings for their information and ideas.

Prior to the actual operation of the teams, it may be helpful to give brief training in team leadership, small group dynamics and problem-solving skills.

While team success does not stand or fall on the use of forms, experience has proven that a minimum number of good forms are of great value in managing the program. They strengthen and maintain effective communication for everyone and provide easy-access documents for useful analysis and records of results. The forms shown in this chapter illustrate the type that can be helpful in maintaining a good management system. In practice, they may have to be modified to the specific needs of a given industry or organization. A brief description of the forms and their intended uses gives additional insight into the operation of the Problem-Solving Team technique.

General Information Form (Figure 15-6) - This should be completed as early as possible because it serves as a starting point and general guide for team operation. Its completion requires causal analysis and objective setting, which set the stage for a management-by-objectives approach to the project. It is a good source of information for any new team chairperson, advisor or member. This form should be updated periodically (e.g., quarterly, semi-annually, or yearly) for ongoing projects.

Cost Analysis Form (Figure 15-7) - It is absolutely necessary to establish a valid measurement of the team's results for each critical item of damage or waste. When told that the damage is decreasing, ex-

DAMAGE/WASTE CONTROL PROJECT
GENERAL INFORMATION FORM

1. Project No.	2. Subject		3. Report No.	4. Date
12	Grinder Damage		1	Feb. 15, 19__

5. Project Leader	6. Project Adviser	7. Frequency of Progress Reports
D. J. Brown	Ray Slider	Quarterly

8. Purpose of Project

To determine the cause of spindle fracture and stator burn-outs since the cost constitutes over 78% of grinding repair costs and is believed to be substantially outside the parameters of fair wear and tear.

9. Most Frequently Damaged Item or Injured Body Part	10. Main Accident Type Involved
Spindles and Stators	Unknown

11. Departments or Areas Involved	12. Supervisory, Staff or Technical Personnel Involved
All grinding areas, Purchasing, Maintenance shop, Maintenance cost control	D. J. Brown Paul Martin B. J. Lowery Park Dague

13. Equipment and Related Products Involved	14. Occupations, Jobs and Crafts Involved
B & D Portable Hand Grinder Model 20	Grinder

15. Maintenance Centers Involved	16. Sources of Additional Information
General Maintenance Shop	Black & Decker representative R. Bunter

17. What Conditions or Practices Apparently Resulted in the Losses

Not accurately known at present. Based on early studies it is believed that striking the locking nut by the grinder in order to loosen it is causing crystalization that results in fracture under load. It is also felt that improper grinder practice is resulting in burn-outs since formal job observations apparently bring about substantial reductions during the periods of observations.

18. Project Objectives with Target Date for Progress and Control

To reduce grinding maintenance cost 15% by July 25, 19— and 35% by December 25, 19__ through engineering and/or grinder behavior controls.

19. Methods for Achieving Objectives

1. Design new wrench to provide proper torque on nut - May 15, target date.
2. Establish positive controls for operator grinding behavior - June 1, target date.

20. Additional Comments or Recommendations

The above methods for achieving objectives are based on early studies of this problem but are believed to possess excellent potential for control.

Figure 15-6

DAMAGE/WASTE CONTROL PROJECT
COST ANALYSIS

1. Date Established	2. Project Leader	3. Project Adviser

4. Clearly Describe Method Used to Compute and Measure Costs

The number and cost of stators and spindles burned out or broken will be related to the number of grinding hours for the month. A frequency in number and severity in cost per thousand hours of grinding can be determined by multiplying the number (in determining frequency) or the total cost (severity rate) by 1,000 and dividing by the hours worked for the month.

Cost of replacing spindle including labor and parts $ 19.50

Cost of replacing stator including labor and parts $ 21.75

5. Show Mathematics Involved with Computation

Example involved 200 burned-out stators for month

$$\frac{200 \text{ stators} \times 1000}{4,500 \text{ grinding hours for month}} = \begin{array}{l} \text{stators per 1,000} \\ \text{grinding hours} \end{array}$$

$$\frac{200 \text{ stators} \times 21.75 \text{ (cost est.)} \times 1000}{4,500 \text{ grinding hours}} = \begin{array}{l} \text{loss per 1,000} \\ \text{grinding hours} \end{array}$$

6. Who Decided and/or Agreed Upon this Method of Computation

7. List All Sources of Cost Information

M. J. Brown, Maintenance Control
B. I. Lowery, Purchasing Agent

8. What Potential Annual Costs Savings Are Indicated

2,100 stators and 1,825 spindles were replaced in 19__ at a cost of $81,262.50. Based on the best judgment and data it is believed that the cost can be cut at least 35% during the coming year through the LIP system. This prediction is based on the best information available on the expectant life of stators on the nature of spindle fracture.

Figure 15-7

DAMAGE/WASTE CONTROL PROJECT
TEAM PROGRESS FORM

Project No.: 12   Subject: Grinder Damage   Report No.: 3

Date: July 1, 19__   Project Leader: D. J. Brown   Project Adviser: R. Slider

Report should include: 1. What has been accomplished since last report? 2. How was it accomplished and who did it? 3. What new recommendations and/or improvements have been made? 4. What are the results?

Jack Bumer has received six band wrenches now in use in building three. These wrenches have been in use for about 2 months. The grinders were properly instructed in their use and all open-end wrenches were collected. According to the daily log in the repair shop, replacement of spindles has dropped off at least 35%. Since actual man-hours are not known at this time, this figure is a conservative estimate. Based on this early response, D. J. Brown has ordered another 12 band wrenches to equip all grinders in the shop.

Job Observations were made of 5 grinders in June by O. J. Tober each day for 10 workdays. They were generally found to be following their T.J.A. Of particular interest, however, was the fact that burned-out stators during the month of June dropped down $500 per thousand grinding hours. There seems to be a good possibility that standard grinder practice is not being followed in the absence of a grinder foreman. D. J. Brown has requested formal job observations on 5 grinders in building #1 and frequent informal observations on all grinders during the next two weeks to diagnose this problem.

Figure 15-8

ecutives are likely to ask questions such as: "How much?" - "How do you know?" - "What is it costing us?" - "What's the net bottom line?"

Just as with an injury frequency rate, the costs involved with any critical item must be related to an accepted base of exposure hours or units accepted as best for the purpose by members of the project team. The information from the individual cost analysis forms should be used to compute results not only for each critical item, but also for the overall program. (The formulas for figuring various rates are shown in *Figure 15-11*.)

As with the General Information Form, the input for this Cost Analysis Form should be obtained as soon as possible after the project team is formed.

Team Progress Report (*Figure 15-8*) - Routine progress reports from teams can take many forms. A fairly simple one is the informal newsletter style. This simple format permits easy coverage of important information such as...

- What has been accomplished since the last report?
- How was it accomplished and who did it?
- What new recommendations and/or improvements have been made?
- What are the results?
- What new or revised goals have been set?

Summary Form (Figure 15-9) - This form summarizes the results of the team activity for all of its projects. It should be designed to be as simple as possible. Words can be abbreviated. Every waste or damage project should be given a different number, which is retained throughout its life. Additional information on any project is always easy to obtain through this numbering system. A form in this type of style should be sent to members of upper management at least quarterly.

DAMAGE/WASTE CONTROL PROJECT
SUMMARY FORM

Period	Project Leader		Loss Control Coordinator		Year

No.	Project	Project Start Date	Primary Action Taken	Fiscal Year Results	Total Project Results
	Total # Projects		FYTD Results	Period Results	

Figure 15-9

Program Integration: For Long-Range Control

When used properly, Problem-Solving Teams do yield fast, sometimes dramatic, results. But they are not enough. Thorough, long-range control of damage can be maintained only by integrating it into every facet of the safety/loss control program. Following are some suggestions for doing this:

• *Leadership and Administration* - The safety/loss control policy statement should show a concern for property damage control as well as the safety and health of people. Guidance to management in dealing with this critical area should be included in the program reference manual. Management responsibilities for damage control should be defined in their position descriptions. Managers should be required to establish organizational and departmental objectives for damage control and should be actively involved in damage/waste control Problem-Solving Teams.

• *Management Training* - In management training programs, the integration of property damage control must be so complete that managers do not think of accidents as injuries, but as undesired events which result in personal injury, property damage or process loss. Training in team leadership, small group dynamics and problem solving techniques will help equip managers to lead and serve effectively on Problem-Solving Teams.

• *Planned Inspections* - Supervisors and other inspectors should look not only for "unsafe conditions" but also for property damage. Perhaps each quarter they could give special attention to developing a damage inventory. Pre-use equipment checklists should require damage notations.

• *Job/Task Analysis & Procedures* - When analyzing the "potential problems" for each step of the task, supervisors should be alert to actions that could result in damage or waste, as well as injuries, production delays and quality problems. Control measures in the resultant job/task procedures should include damage/waste control measures.

• *Accident/Incident Investigation* - It usually requires only a small change in the typical investigation report form to allow it to be used to report property damage investigations. The form shown in Chapter 4 can serve as a guide for form design. That chapter also has helpful guidelines for determining which incidents to investigate. In essence, *all* accidents and incidents should be investigated, at least enough to determine their *potential* frequency and severity. Those with high potential should then be thoroughly investigated.

To stimulate upper management involvement in damage investigations, it is necessary to establish what is "major damage loss" for that organization. One food-processing company uses $500 or more, many organizations use $1,000, and one aviation manufacturer uses $50,000. A key to selection is that point at which management feels it justifies additional investigative attention. However, once the criterion has been established, it should apply both to those events which *actually* result in that amount of loss and to those with the realistic *potential* to do so. This criterion also permits the use of frequency rates for "major property damage accidents." In addition, it helps to avoid the impractical requirement for thorough investigation of every little bit of damage discovered (e.g., small dents in pieces of equipment). It is far more practical to handle damage items with small individual, but great cumulative, costs as a critical item for a Problem-Solving Team. In effect, these teams are an additional investigative tool.

Supervisors play a key role in property damage investigations as in other investigations. One vital aspect of this role is in getting property damage accidents reported so they can be investigated in a timely manner. They can improve damage reporting if they understand and overcome the common reasons for not reporting it - reasons such as: fear of discipline ... "nobody seems to care" ... "the company can afford it" ... "it's too little to fuss about" ... "why rock the boat?" Supervisors can overcome these factors when the management system helps them to show employees this attitude:

- We are just as serious about damage accidents as we are about injury accidents.

- We will be tougher on you for not reporting damage than we will for causing the damage.

- We are taking a positive approach to reporting and investigation; a mutual problem-solving approach.

- Employees stand to gain significant benefits, such

as 1) preventing recurrence of damage accidents that are likely to harm people next time and 2) ensuring that equipment and facilities are kept in good, safe working condition.

• *Planned Job Observations* - When making job observations and giving performance feedback, supervisors should be sure to include appropriate emphasis on property damage and waste control.

• *Rules and Practices* - Simple changes are all that is needed in existing rules related to injury-type accidents. The two rules below have been adopted by hundreds of companies:

- Report immediately to your foreman or supervisor any condition or practice you think might cause injury to employees, *damage to property or loss to process.*
- Whenever you or the equipment you operate is involved in personal injury *or damage to property*, regardless of how minor, you must immediately report it to your foreman or supervisor.

The only change that was required was the addition of the phrase "or damage to property" (shown in italics above).

As rules, job procedures and standard practices are published or revised, care should be taken to ensure that they cover behavior which prevents property damage and waste.

Properly administered discipline, as a last resort, is an essential part of any good safety/loss control program. It is important to use discipline more in established cases where accident information was volunteered. Some companies have adopted a policy of automatic discipline for individuals found to be involved in property damage who failed to report it. A dramatic comparison of accident reporting before and after a program of strict enforcement of the reporting rule is shown in *Figure 15-10*. The values that can come from increased reporting, investigation, causal analysis and remedial action are quite evident.

• *Accident/Incident Records, Analyses, and Reports*-Along with the periodic (e.g., monthly) injury information, damage frequency and severity rates should be circulated. Maintenance records should identify accidental damages. Repetitive and significant items of damage should be added to the "critical few" list regularly. Damage costs should be determined and communicated for the entire organization and for each department. Managers should use Problem-Solving

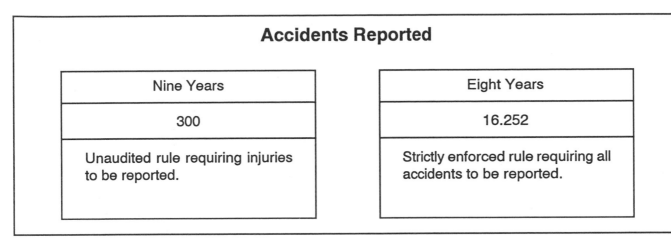

Accidents Reported	
Nine Years	**Eight Years**
300	16.252
Unaudited rule requiring injuries to be reported.	Strictly enforced rule requiring all accidents to be reported.

Figure 15-10

Team reports for effective damage/waste cost-control purposes.

• *Skill Training* - A major percentage of the property damage of most companies involves materials-handling equipment. It accounts for 60-85% of the damage in most industrial environments.

While not a panacea in the control of property damage, few factors are more important than adequate skill training of equipment operators, followed up with adequate emphasis on damage control in planned observations, coaching, communication and motivation activities.

Here are some specific steps which will not only reduce property damage, but will also make skill training more effective in general:

A. Adequate formal training should be given to every equipment operator before assigning him or her to the job.

B. A special form indicating critical items to review with a new or transferred operator should be completed by the supervisor when first assigning any operator.

C. A complete training manual (designed to include the development of awareness of the importance of property damage control as well as the techniques involved) should be utilized in training, and a copy should be given to each operator.

D. Operator safety rules and related job procedures should be part of the training manual, but should also be issued separately for individual reference as independent items.

E. Operators should be licensed or certified as part of their training program, with cards and identifica-

tion badges or decals worn in a prominent position. The holding of a license should be contingent upon a good operating record.

F. Desired performance of operators following training should be properly recognized, with recorded commendations made when appropriate. Consistent violations of rules and procedures should be handled in accordance with the company's enforcement procedures.

G. A minimum of six planned job observations of each operator should be made annually, with forms completed and proper discussions with operators conducted.

H. Rules and job procedures should be reviewed frequently, but not less than annually, in a formal manner with all operators. Oral or written testing should be an important part of this important exercise, to learn what the operator knows.

I. Provision for recognition of operators who meet desired standards of performance is considered helpful by most supervisors of equipment operators. It is suggested that a total evaluation of personal injury and property damage records, commendations, violations, observations, testing results, etc., be considered in determining those eligible for such recognition.

• *Purchasing and Engineering Controls* - Significant amounts of property damage occur as a result of improper purchasing and engineering. Equipment fails because it does not meet the requirements of the operation. Fires and explosions occur because of improper design or inadequately identified materials. Machines break down because they do not have the proper load limits.

Purchasing personnel are highly cost-conscious. However, they may be penny wise and pound foolish unless they have information about *all* of the costs, including damage and waste, traced back to certain purchased items. There should be close coordination between the safety/loss control function and the purchasing function. They should share information about legislative requirements, safety specifications for purchased materials and equipment and effective control of hazardous substances. They should develop a simple system (e.g., the purchase order number followed by "A" for accident) for identifying purchases made to replace items destroyed by accidents. Coupled with similarly identified "service requests" or "work orders," these provide valuable data for effective damage cost control.

No opportunity to minimize property damage is more important than the integration of safety/loss control into the conception and design stages of new construction and the redesign of operating facilities. This is the prime opportunity to control the exchange of energy involved in damage accidents. Any experienced executive knows how much more difficult it is to obtain an additional expenditure to eliminate, segregate or protect a building, product line or equipment installation once construction has begun — and especially after it has been completed. Total accident control coordination must become a habit at the earliest stages.

- *Personal Communications* — Property damage and waste control should be included in the orientation of new and transferred employees, both in their initial session and the follow-up sessions. Supervisors should include the subject, where appropriate, when giving job instruction. They also should adequately emphasize damage and waste control in their coaching and safety tipping contacts.

- *Group Meetings* - The relationships of property damage and waste control to safety, quality and productivity should be integrated into the meetings regularly held at all levels of the organization. Materials distributed to supervisors to help them prepare for their safety/loss control meetings with workers should include items on damage and waste control.

- *General Promotion* - Promotion programs can add to the development of safety awareness, including awareness of the role of damage and waste control. Safety/loss control leaders have long maintained that the safety-conscious worker, working in a hazardous environment, will have fewer accidents than the worker, even in a relatively hazard-free environment, who lacks safety awareness.

Effective promotion can create an atmosphere of interest and awareness, helping to communicate that a safety and conservation program exists, and that it should be a major concern of everyone. Well prepared property damage and waste control messages should be included in newsletters to equipment operators, newspapers and magazine articles, posters and bulletin board notices, and special promotional contests and campaigns. Circulated safety statistics and informational reports should include facts and figures on damage/waste control. Protection of people and protection of property should be constant companions in general promotion activities.

- *Regular Repair Center Audits* - Safety program coordinators know the value of the dispensary or first aid area as a control point for measuring the result as of an injury control program. Injuries and illnesses reported to this area provide statistics on the frequency of occurrence and enable measurement of the effectiveness of investigation. Likewise, repair centers are primary "first aid" locations for damaged equipment and material. The information that can be obtained from these areas forms a point of control for the entire damage control program. Checks of these locations should be regular and systematic. A program should be designed to include an effective, yet simple, system for repair center personnel to regularly report all damaged items.

USING PROPERTY DAMAGE MEASUREMENTS

Since accidental property damage occurs more often than injuries and results in much greater dollar losses, logic says that for control purposes we must give attention to damage rates just as we do to injury rates. Progressive organizations calculate and communicate rates such as those shown in *Figure 15-11* as one way of showing losses and savings, problems and progress. The Major Property Damage rates are roughly equivalent to the Disabling Injury rates and the Serious Property Damage rates to the Recordable Injury rates.

"Major" property damage is that which reaches or exceeds a locally established value. While this figure varies greatly from one organization to another (i.e., from a ten-person machine shop to a ten thousand-person aerospace company), a commonly used figure is

$1,000. "Serious" property damage is that which is serious enough to require a formal detailed investigation. This cut-off point is also set by management and must be specific and constant.

The kinds of costs to be included in the costs of accidental property damage should be established by a committee of operating people, since the rates are kept for their benefit. Some organizations will choose to include only repair and/or replacement costs. Others will include downtime and investigation time, etc. Whatever is to be included should be clearly agreed upon so that everyone is "playing by the same rules."

The number of Critical Property Damage items is an absolute number rather than a rate. It shows the number of items listed on the damage waste inventories (*Figure 15-4*) above the dollar costs established as critical. The total costs of these items is also recorded and translated into a rate as shown in *Figure 15-11*.

MEASUREMENTS OF PROPERTY DAMAGE

Major Property Damage Frequency Rates

$$\frac{\text{Number of major p.d. accidents} \times 200,000}{\text{Man-hours worked}}$$

Major Property Damage Cost Rate

$$\frac{\text{Total costs of major p.d. accidents} \times 200,000}{\text{Man-hours worked}}$$

Serious Property Damage Frequency Rate

$$\frac{\text{Total costs of serious p.d. accidents} \times 200,000}{\text{Man-hours worked}}$$

Serious Property Damage Cost Rate

$$\frac{\text{Total costs of serious p.d. accidents} \times 200,000}{\text{Man-hours worked}}$$

Critical Item Cost Rate

$$\frac{\text{Total costs of critical items} \times 200,000}{\text{Man-hours worked}}$$

Figure 15-11

These rates are based on 200,000 work hours, which represents the hours worked in one year by 100 employees (100 employees x 40 hours per week x 50 weeks per year). They could also be based on other meaningful indices, such as tons or units of production, barrels of throughput, sales, etc., by substituting those figures for 200,000.

DAMAGE/WASTE CONTROL IN SMALLER OPERATIONS

Smaller organizations most likely will choose a less formal approach to solving damage and waste problems. They may have very few managers. Their property damage and waste may cost proportionately more than that of larger organizations, because they have fewer resources to absorb the losses. For instance, it is not unusual for building materials outlets to lose $100 a day just in damaged inventory. Many small warehouses have to repair their building walls and storage racks quite regularly. Grain elevators and feed mills experience damage from vehicles banging into doors at the ends of pits; damaged grain spouts, conveyors and bagged materials; dust-clogged bearings and gears; and kinked car-puller cables. Retail stores have damaged goods, shelves, equipment and fixtures. Many smaller organizations have maintenance shops. Often items brought in for repair are damaged further. Tools and equipment may be used by many different people, with varying levels of skill, and damaged as a result. The list could go on almost indefinitely. The problems are there.

The smaller organization can build its efforts around these four fundamentals: education/identification/evaluation/control.

Education

Do everything possible to drive home, for every person, what an accident really is: "an undesired event that results in harm to a person, damage to property or loss to process." The "damage to property" can be just as important as the "harm to a person" - not only because damage accidents are very expensive, but also because they have the *potential* for harming people. Also, the basic causes and controls for accidents are the same, whether they caused personal harm, damage or both.

Identification

The identification of damaged items in smaller organization may simply involve the senior manager sitting down with the person or persons responsible for maintenance and developing a list. Since this same manager may sign all purchasing requests, it should be fairly easy to review those also. Or, the senior manager may assign someone else to make the survey. Periodically, a safety meeting can be devoted to gaining employees' help in the identification process. The regular inspection program can also be helpful if inspectors look not only for hazards, but also for property damage. Accident investigators can identify all damage and waste resulting in accidents.

All three ways of identifying critical items of damage may be used (personal observation, management directive and systematic audit), but they will be done in ways that simplify and suit them to the smaller organization.

Evaluation

Since managers in smaller operations are usually extremely busy people, probably "wearing many hats," it is essential that they invest their resources in the activities with the greatest potential payoff (i.e., the "critical few"). Converting damage into dollars permits easy evaluation. The most critical items are those involving the most dollars of loss - both actual and potential loss.

Control

Depending on the magnitude and complexity of the corrective action, one or more persons may be appointed to study the problem and recommend corrective action. The same person or persons will follow up to ensure that solutions have actually been implemented. If the item of damage or waste is critical enough, the top manager may chair the Problem-Solving Team, with other managers as members. Fewer or different forms may be used than are used in larger organizations.

As in larger organizations, maximum long-range results require damage/waste control integration into all aspects of the safety management system - however many or few those aspects may be. In the smaller organization they most likely will include critical activities such as: management directives/ inspections/ investigations/rules and practices/personal communications/group meetings/basic general promotion techniques.

WASTE CONTROL

Related to Safety/Loss Control

Waste control is a vital part of loss control. It also relates to safety, since waste can contribute to accidents, injuries and damage. Gas leaks, for example, not only waste expensive gas but can also harm people and damage property. Steam leaks are not only wasteful, but can also injure people and damage materials. The fire extinguisher that has been wasted in horseplay, or to cool a drink, is not available to put out the fire. Wasted materials contribute to disorder, clutter and accidents.

While waste control can and should extend substantially beyond its relationship to safety, it is a natural companion. A typical pattern of program development is for the company to grow from injury control to accident (injury and damage) control, then to loss control (with waste control as one of its many elements).

Another connection between damage control and waste control is that the steps involved are the same for each recognition, evaluation and control. Both the long-range and the short-range programs described above may be as readily applied to waste as to damage. In waste control, as in damage control, management example is critical. *Figure 15-12* shows a large number of ways that supervisors can control waste.

PROGRAM BENEFITS

The potential of property damage and waste control to safety, quality, productivity and profitability is enormous. *Figure 15-13* shows, for example, one company's vast loss reduction/profit improvement through their total accident control program. Benefits such as these are common:

- Increased awareness of the value of tools, materials, equipment, supplies and facilities.
- A safety plant environment, with fewer serious injuries.
- Reduced damage, downtime and delays.
- Lower costs and higher profitability.

It's the best of both organizational worlds - the economic and the humane.

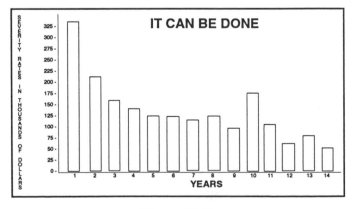

Figure 15-13

158 WAYS SUPERVISORS CAN CONTROL WASTE

Control Waste of Energy/Utilities

- Increase energy utility cost awareness in your employee orientations, your group meetings, and your regular worker contacts.
- Request prompt repairs of leaky valves, pipes and fittings for gas, water, steam hydraulic systems and pneumatic systems.
- Avoid unnecessary use of large, energy-hogging machines for small work.
- Promote energy utility conservation with posters and signs (e.g. "if this switch is on just five extra minutes per shift, it wastes $3,649 per year).
- Schedule work to provide adequate time for preventive maintenance.
- See that powered machines and equipment are not running unnecessarily.
- Where possible, use cold water chemical cleaners rather than steam.
- Request proper insulation on pipes, ducts, ceilings and walls.
- Where a turn-off procedure for lights is appropriate, let everyone know what the procedure is and why.
- Check air system leakage regularly.
- Check water-wasting practices regularly, re-use water for machine cooling, boiler feedwater, rinse tanks and sanitary systems.
- Cut heating and cooling costs from excess exhaust by:
  ...scrubbing and returning air from grinding, buffing and plating
  ...running booth exhausts only when needed
  ...inspecting for "short circuits" between air heaters and exhaust ducts
  ...using fast electric door closers for large doors in materials handling areas
- See that local ventilating systems are operated and maintained properly.
- Use participative problem solving teams for critical energy utility problems.

Control Waste of Materials & Supplies

- Include materials and supplies conservation in:
  ...the orientation of new and transferred employees
  ...planned job observations
  ...coaching and key point tipping
- Give proper job instruction with each assigned task.
- Discuss with workers the monetary value of materials and supplies.
- Make sure that employees get the proper materials and supplies for each job.
- Use the "turn in the old to get the new" system for tools and supplies.
- Make sure that blueprints, sketches and instruction sheets are clear and legible.
- Make sure that machines and equipment are properly adjusted, properly calibrated and in good working order.
- Make sure that your orders and instructions are clearly understood.
- Enforce compliance with standards for conservation of materials and supplies.
- Reinforce conservation of materials and supplies with adequate recognition.
- Use medical services to see whether eyesight or other health problems are causing mistakes and waste.
- Make sure that people are qualified and trained for the work they must do.
- Order no more materials and supplies than needed, return excess materials and supplies to stock.
- See that materials and supplies are properly piled - stored - dispensed.
- Maintain quality checks from beginning to end of the work process, to detect and correct potential problems and waste as soon as possible.
- Prohibit personal use of company tools, materials and supplies.
- Monitor the materials and supplies check-out and security systems.
- Whenever practical, salvage rather than scrap.
- Set the example for materials and supplies conservation.

Control Waste of Machines & Equipment

- Study and teach the uses and capacities of all critical machines and equipment.
- Avoid using unnecessarily large machines and equipment for small work, and vice versa.
- Plan and schedule the work to make full use of available machines and equipment.
- Determine which parts or items will create the biggest problems if they don't operate properly and establish an inspection program to ensure proper operation.
- Use start-of-shift or pre-use inspections to prevent potential accidents and downtime.
- Ensure adequate lubrication, cleaning and preventive maintenance.
- Monitor housekeeping practices (cleanliness and order) to prevent accidents and protect both people and property.
- Protect idle machines and equipment from dirt, dust, rust, fumes and damage.
- Secure needed repairs promptly.
- Prohibit makeshift repairs by workers.
- Balance the need for production with the needs for safety, quality and cost control.
- Provide adequate instruction on the proper operation and care of machines and equipment.
- Monitor the speeds and feeds that operators use.
- Use standard enforcement and behavior reinforcement to prevent abuse and misuse of machines and equipment.
- Listen to and learn from workers about the problems and conditions of machines and equipment.
- Develop with workers a sense of pride in the care and use of machines and equipment.
- Carefully consider all costs when deciding whether to repair, salvage, sell or scrap machines and equipment.
- Keep informed on new developments regarding machines and equipment for your type of work.

Control Waste of Peoplepower

- Make every effort to match worker abilities and work requirements.
- Conduct effective job orientations for new and transferred people.
- Contact new and transferred workers frequently for coaching, tipping and orientation follow-up.
- Communicate clear standards of performance to each employee, clarify job duties and performance expectations.
- Correct substandard performance and commend good performance.
- Show your concern for the safety of each person.
- Emphasize proper procedures and practices.
- Give proper job task instruction, guidance and follow-up.
- Encourage training for employee growth and development.
- In reviewing performance with each person, base the discussion on specific, observable, measurable facts and behaviors (i.e., performance, not personality).
- Furnish frequent measures of progress toward goals, help people to "keep score."
- Give full credit where credit is due.
- Promote and upgrade qualified people whenever possible
- Train and develop an understudy.
- Admit your mistakes to workers, and use them as learning experiences.
- When assigning work to people, consider their physical problems, health problems and other problems you know of.
- Read and understand company policies so you can interpret them to your people.
- In dealing with other departments and with higher management, stick up for your people.
- In dealing with workers, avoid thoughtless criticism of company management, policies, procedures and goals.
- Follow up every absence to determine the reason; stress the importance of attendance.
- Set an example by your own attendance and punctuality.
- Keep your promises.
- Make maximum use of positive discipline and constructive coaching.
- Avoid playing favorites among your people.
- Encourage friendly, healthy competition on matters such as attendance, punctuality, quality, safety, suggestions and housekeeping.
- Use the power of participation for good group communications and mutual problem solving.
- Do everything you can to provide your people with good working conditions, efficient organization and proper tools, machines and equipment.
- Try to solve minor complaints before they become major grievances.
- Emphasize the importance of people's jobs; explain the "why" of the job and where it fits into the total picture.
- Do everything within your power to remove sources of conflict, irritation and frustration.
- Deal sensibly with gossip and tale-bearing.
- Show your interest in each individual, your respect for the dignity and uniqueness of each person, and your desire to understand his or her values and viewpoints.

Control Waste of Ideas

- Ask workers for their opinions and suggestions.
- Ask for advice and information from other departments (e.g., Purchasing, Engineering, Personnel, Safety & Health).
- Listen to suggestions and ideas with a receptive mind.
- Thank people for their ideas - interest - input.
- Implement good ideas from other people, with full credit.
- Follow-up implemented ideas and communicate their benefits.
- When rejecting ideas, explain why and encourage continuing participation.
- Tap the fresh experience and viewpoints of new workers from other organizations.
- Establish mutual problem solving teams.
- Conduct "brainstorming" sessions with workers.
- Participate in "brainstorming" sessions with peers and others.
- Encourage people to think of how to change things: adapt - combine - magnify - minimize - modify - rearrange - reverse - substitute - simplify.
- Encourage full use of the suggestion system.
- Hold participative meetings.
- Read and study as much and as widely as possible.
- Build up "idea folders" (e.g., each idea on a 3x5 card).
- Dare to do the different.

Control Waste of Space

- Practice and preach this concept of "order": a place is in order when there are *no* unnecessary things about and *all* necessary things are in their proper places.
- Ensure proper piling - shelving - stacking - storage of raw materials, supplies and products.
- Keep passageways clear.
- See that machines and permanent equipment are placed for the best balance of space utilization and efficient operation.
- Consider space utilization and efficiency in the placement of lockers, washrooms, toolrooms and supply rooms.
- Make maximum safe use of "vertical" space as well as "horizontal" space.
- Order no more materials and supplies than needed.
- Return excess items to stockrooms - storerooms - toolrooms - warehouses.
- Provide adequate and properly placed scrap bins/waste containers.
- Send unuseable tools, machines and equipment to scrap yard, salvage yard or dump.
- Discard obsolete and unnecessary papers and files.
- Ensure efficient routing of materials through the facility.
- Prohibit unnecessary items at work stations.
- Request repairs of roofs, floors, doors and walls to permit maximum use of space.
- Enforce compliance with housekeeping standards and reinforce good housekeeping practices.

Control Waste of Time

- Communicate clear performance standards (a fair day's work).
- Correct and commend performance to maintain compliance with standards.
- Plan work properly, to keep workers from waiting for materials or waiting between jobs.
- Establish priorities for your work and your group's work.
- Schedule work and workers to avoid excess people and excess overtime.
- Be sure you understand orders, instructions and requests received.
- Delegate the right tasks to the right people.
- Get feedback to be sure that others thoroughly understand your orders, instructions and requests received.
- See that tools, supplies, materials and portable equipment are kept in their proper places.
- See that people have the proper tools, supplies, equipment and materials for every job.
- Analyze tasks to eliminate unnecessary steps.
- Analyze how you and your people spend time.
- Promote efficient performance by training and coaching workers properly.
- Give the employment department adequate notice of needs for layoffs or for more people.
- Write requisitions, records and reports intelligibly.
- Submit requisitions, records and reports promptly.
- Keep well organized files; discard obsolete contents.
- Make decisions promptly.
- Request repairs and preventive maintenance to avoid excess downtime.
- Eliminate unnecessary materials handling.
- Teach, preach and practice that "time is money" (e.g., at $10 hr. three minutes wasted each hour equals $1,020/yr. wasted).
- Plan and use agendas for your meetings.
- Prevent procrastination.
- Set a good example for time utilization.

Control Waste of Paperwork

- Train employees on the benefits and costs of paperwork.
- Train employees on how to complete required paperwork properly.
- See that communications equipment is efficiently operated and well maintained.
- Issue enough paper work for adequate information and documentation, but avoid unnecessary and overlapping paperwork.
- Don't use paper if a local phone call will do the job.
- Ensure that written materials are clear and legible.
- Consolidate several report forms into one (e.g., one investigation report form for injuries, occupational illnesses, property damage, near-misses and other loss incidents).
- Keep the frequency of records and reports at the minimum required to meet their basic purposes.
- Distribute copies to those who use them, and *only* to those who use them.
- Every four to six months, attach a brief form to each report, requesting information on the report's value and useability. Delete from the distribution list those who don't respond or don't use it.
- Minimize supporting details (K.I.S.S.).
- Meet required deadlines for required letters, memos, reports and records.
- Post retention times on file materials; periodically move older contents from active files to storage files; discard obsolete materials.
- Use an organized filing system and see that everyone who needs to use it knows the system.
- Date and sign all paperwork you issue.
- Enter basic data on forms only once (e.g., leave space between hazard entries on inspection report forms; add follow-up information in those spaces on a copy; avoid rewriting all other information on the form).
- Issue clear written job/task procedures.
- Use computers and data processing equipment effectively.
- Monitor the use of copy machines.

WASTE COSTS BILLIONS EACH YEAR, MOST OF IT CAN BE STOPPED BY POSITIVE ACTIVE LEADERSHIP AND COOPERATION

Figure 15-12

CORE CONCEPTS IN REVIEW

Damage and waste are all around us. Once we identify them we can evaluate and control them. While there is no single source of comprehensive cost data for accidental property damage, conservative estimates peg it at from five to fifty times as much as the costs of injuries.

Three of the major reasons why damage control is a **vital part of safety** are:

1. The basic causes and controls are the same for injury accidents as for damage accidents.

2. Many property damage accidents also injure people, and most of them have the potential to do so.

3. Being concerned with all accidents, rather than a limited category, vastly increases the base for effective control.

Control of property damage and waste involves:

1. **Identification** of the specific items being damaged by other than normal wear and tear. This may be done by personal observation, by management directive and/or by systematic audit of items repaired, replaced, salvaged or disposed of.

2. **Evaluation,** i.e., determining the critical items of damage and setting priorities for action. The critical items are the relatively few that produce the bulk of the dollar losses. Other evaluation considerations include the kinds of control measures that are possible, the degree to which losses can be controlled and how much the controls will cost.

3. **Application of control techniques.** For fast results, the Problem-Solving Team technique has proven successful. The appropriate executive sets up a team to analyze a high-priority item, determine the basic causes, develop solution alternatives and recommend the best solution. This approach can yield significant, measurable loss reduction in just a few months.

For long and lasting results, property damage control must be integrated into every facet of the safety/loss control program.

Waste control is a vital part of loss control. Often, it is also an integral part of safety. Meaningful, profitable targets of a war on waste include time/ideas/materials and supplies/machines and equipment/space/people power/energy and utilities/paperwork. Here are five damage and waste control measures:

1. **Investigation** at the scene and upper management review meeting of **major losses.**

2. **Investigation** at the scene and upper management review of analyses of **serious losses.**

3. **Identification of the critical few items** of damage and waste, with project team problem-solving.

4. **Inclusion of damage and waste control thinking** in every program activity.

5. **Property damage measurements** used in addition to injury measurements.

Effective control of property damage and waste brings enormous benefits, in both economic and human terms- better profitability, better productivity, better quality and better safety.

KEY QUESTIONS

1. True or False? There is no single source of comprehensive cost data for accidental property damage.

2. Conservative estimates indicate that property damage costs range from _____ to _____ times the insured costs of injuries.

3. Give at least three reasons why organizations which lack control of property damage also tend to lack control of occupational illnesses and injuries.

4. Give at least four of the eight listed reasons why the typical occupational safety program has neglected the property damage element.

5. The American Management Association published the *Damage Control* book in: a)1946, b)1956, c)1966, d)1976.

6. What is the vital link by which damage control bridges the gap from an injury-oriented safety program to an accident-oriented safety program?

7. The basic framework for damage control is: r_____, e_____, and c_____.

8. Name three ways to identify critical items of damage.

9. Why should you get an estimate (e.g., from repair shop supervisors) of the annual cost of damaged items?

10. What is the primary criterion for evaluating the criticality of items damaged?

11. True or False? Items with low unit costs of damage should not be on the critical item list.

12. Name two major approaches to systematic control of property damage.

13. What are two or three reasons why a department head may be a good person to lead a team working on a critical damage item?

14. Why should damage control team activities and accomplishments be documented?

15. What is the formula for figuring the "major property damage frequency rate"? The "major property damage cost rate"?

16. List at least seven of the safety/loss control program elements into which damage control must be integrated for long-range results.

17. What can supervisors do to help get property damage reported?

18. Just as medical and first aid areas can serve as control points for measuring the effectiveness of injury reporting, so can _____ _____ serve as control points for measuring the effectiveness of damage reporting.

19. What are the four fundamentals around which smaller organizations can build their damage/waste control efforts?

20. True or False? Waste control is a vital part of loss control.

21. True or False? Waste control often is vitally related to safety.

22. List at least four of the eight discussed categories for waste control.

23. How many activities are included in the Figure showing ways in which supervisors can control waste? a)118, b)138, c)158, d)178.

24. Name several significant benefits of effective property damage and waste control.

PRACTICAL APPLICATIONS SUMMARY

S – For Supervisor
E – For Executives
C – For Safety/Loss Control Coordinators

	S	E	C
1. Include property damage control in the company loss control policy.		x	
2. Issue letters of endorsement for the program, or similar written evidence of commitment.		x	
3. Establish organization and departmental objectives for damage control.		x	
4. Expand accident reporting rules to include not only injuries but also damage.	x	x	
5. Expand hazard reporting rules to include not only those that could cause injury but also those that could cause damage.	x	x	
6. Apply current disciplinary practices to the failure to report property damage.	x	x	
7. Keep managers informed of damage/waste control state-of-the-art.			x
8. Obtain signed slips from all employees, signifying receipt and understanding of revised rules, including property damage aspects.	x	x	
9. Notify and seek cooperation of labor relations department and union leaders on all steps of the damage/waste control program.		x	x
10. Issue Standard Practice for Accident/Incident Investigation, including property damage.		x	
11. Revise Accident/Incident Investigation form to accommodate injury/illness, damage and other incidents.		x	x
12. Establish dollar figures for "serious" and "major" property damage losses.		x	
13. Include damage frequency and severity rates in the regularly issued accident information.	x	x	x
14. Establish a system to accumulate all related costs on major property damage accidents.	x	x	x
15. Maintain regular contacts with repair and maintenance personnel.	x	x	x
16. Ensure that repair forms and records permit identification of accidental property damage costs.	x	x	x
17. Consider use of "Caution - Defective" tag system to provide useful damage information on all items sent to repair shops.	x	x	
18. Photograph all major property damages.	x		x
19. Maintain files of property damage photographs and related cost data.			x
20. Issue periodic reports regarding property damage losses (costs and actual or potential injuries).		x	x

	S	E	C
21. Include property damage accidents in major accident announcements and accident management review meetings.		x	
22. Establish problem-solving teams for critical damage items.	x	x	
23. Give a good balance to injury and damage information in all safety/loss control written communications.		x	x
24. Include damage control in employee orientations, job instructions, and day-to-day coaching and tipping.	x		
25. Emphasize relationships of waste control to loss control and safety.	x	x	x
26. Establish problem-solving teams for critical items of waste.	x	x	
27. Integrate property damage and waste control into all facets of the safety/loss control program.	x	x	x
28. Recognize and reinforce good performance on reporting and controlling damage and waste.	x	x	x

CHAPTER 16

OCCUPATIONAL HEALTH

"Occupational health is devoted to the anticipation, recognition, evaluation and control of those factors or stresses, arising in and from the workplace, which may cause sickness, impaired health and well-being or significant discomfort and inefficiency."

INTRODUCTION

Occupational health hazards pose some of the most significant management challenges of this decade. New research into old problems and the additional exposures created by new technology combine to create an ongoing series of situations to deal with. Frontline managers are in an ideal position to help reduce or otherwise control occupational health hazards because of their relationship with workers, their management skills and their knowledge of the work done within their areas of responsibility. However, some specialized knowledge is needed.

Good judgment and the natural senses can often be counted on to identify mechanical and physical hazards. But dusts, vapors, fumes, temperature extremes and noises are not always as easily recognized. In fact, many vapors and fumes are colorless and odorless. Some, such as benzene or hydrogen sulfide, are so toxic that if they can be smelled, the permissible exposure has already been exceeded.

The intent of this chapter is to take some of the mystery out of occupational health by presenting critical information in a useful and understandable way. Also, specific management techniques for frontline managers are given to help them in the identification, evaluation and control of occupational hazards.

TYPES OF OCCUPATIONAL HEALTH HAZARDS

Recognizing the exposure, evaluating its origin and potential to produce loss, and controlling potential loss exposure are the three basic elements of any successful occupational health program. With this in mind, it will be helpful to become familiar with some of the more common occupational health hazards. They are usually divided into four categories (illustrated in *Figure 16-1*):

1. **Chemical** - chemical hazards include mists, vapors, gases, fumes, dusts, liquids and pastes whose chemical composition can create problems.
2. **Physical** - physical hazards include noise, radiation, temperature extremes, barometric pressure and humidity extremes, illumination, vibration, microwaves, lasers and infrared and ultraviolet radiation.
3. **Biological** - biological hazards include insects, mold, fungi, bacteria, viruses, rickettsia, gastro-intestinal parasites and other agents.
4. **Ergonomic** - ergonomics is the science of people at work. It is concerned with making the interface of the man/machine/environment as safe, efficient and comfortable as possible. Typical concerns include work station design, work posture, manual materials handling, workrest cycles and seating. Both the psychological and the physiological aspects of the workplace are important.

The following sections discuss each of these four types of hazards in greater detail.

CHEMICAL HAZARDS

Each year about 6,000 new chemicals are created and many of these find their way into the workplace. A significant number of these, in addition to the many chemical substances already in use, have the potential to create major health problems unless they are

---

THE FORMS OF POSSIBLE HEALTH "STRESS"

CHEMICAL

MIST - suspended liquid droplets

VAPOR - gaseous form of liquid

GAS - formless matter

SMOKE - solid/liquid particles of combustion

DUST - solid particles, also fibrous

AEROSOL - fine liquid/solid matter

FUME - particles in heated gaseous state

PHYSICAL

NOISE - unwanted sound

TEMPERATURE - high/low extremes

ILLUMINATION - level of intensity

VIBRATION - motion condition

RADIATION - Ionizing - cell damaging

RADIATION - Non-ionizing - heat producing

PRESSURE - atmospheric (high/low)

BIOLOGICAL

BACTERIA - VIRUS - FUNGUS

PARASITE - Plant/Animal

ERGONOMIC

MONOTONY - repeated motion

WORK PRESSURE - worry/fatigue

OVERLOAD - perceptual/mental

BODY POSITIONS - lifting/twisting/straining

METABOLIC CYCLES - overtime/shift/rotation

PSYCHOSOCIAL - relationships/feelings

Figure 16-1

---

properly used. At this point it will be helpful to understand the difference between toxic and hazardous. *Toxic* refers to the *ability* of a material to produce harm to a living organism. *Hazard* refers to the *probability* that a substance in a particular situation will produce harm. If administered in a certain manner and in sufficient dosage, practically any substance can be harmful. Some substances are not highly toxic but have high potential hazard because of their potential for fire or explosion. Some materials, such as cyanide, arsenic and mercury or beryllium compounds are highly toxic, or capable of producing significant harm in small amounts. However, all materials can be handled safely if the proper precautionary measures are taken. The toxicity of a material remains constant - the degree of hazard is controllable.

Method of Entry Into the Body

The route of entry into the body sometimes changes the whole toxicity mechanism. For instance, trichlorethylene poisons the system when it is ingested, while acute inhalation mainly causes anesthesia. Three routes by which chemical substances can enter the body are: inhalation (breathing), absorption (through the skin), and ingestion (swallowing). A fourth and far less common route of entry is by injection with needles, nails, glass or by the force of compressed air or pressurized liquid such as hydraulic fluid.

Inhalation. Inhaled chemicals can be rapidly absorbed into the bloodstream and carried to all parts of the body. The surface area of the lungs ranges from 300 square feet at rest to about 1000 square feet during inspiration. This large surface area (the size of a small house) provides toxic agents with a large surface for absorption. In fact, this area is up to 35 times the surface area of the skin. Because of the very thin membranes in the lungs, the flow of blood is much closer to the air contaminant here than anywhere else in the body. With this in mind, it is understandable why approximately 90% of all industrial poisonings (other than dermatitis) are due to inhalation.

Many air contaminants, instead of being absorbed and carried throughout the body, remain in the lungs and cause irritation. This irritation causes pulmonary (lung) inflammation, which, in turn, causes pulmonary scarring. This scarring and its related effects have many names (anthracosis, byssinosis, siderosis, silicosis, asbestosis), but the underlying cause is the same: pulmonary irritation and scarring due to air contaminants.

Absorption. Absorption of toxic chemicals through the skin is usually a slower process. However, where cuts or scratches have broken the skin, it can be very rapid. Some chemicals are readily absorbed through the skin and hair follicles. An outer coating of sebum, sweat and keratin usually provides a small amount of protection, but is readily washed away by soap and water and many organic solvents and bases. It is not uncommon for some chemicals to even be absorbed through leather-soled shoes and into the bottom of the foot. Chemicals readily absorbed through the skin include: benzene, toluene, nitroglycerine, lead, mercury and arsenic. When body oils have been removed by degreasers such as gasoline, kerosene or other solvents, skin absorption is greatly enhanced. In hot environments absorption is also enhanced.

Ingestion. Normally, adults do not knowingly eat or drink toxic chemicals for anything other than pleasurable experiences. However, eating, smoking or drinking in areas where toxic chemicals exist may cause problems. Many chemicals are easily absorbed into the bloodstream during digestion. From the digestive tract, the blood flows directly to the liver and other parts of the body. Careful and thorough washups before eating and at the end of the work shift are necessary to prevent ingestion of toxic substances.

Air Contaminants

Inhalation of air contaminants is the number one cause of occupational illnesses (excluding dermatitis). The reasons for this were mentioned earlier, e.g., large surface area and plentiful blood supply. Since air contaminants are such a common source of exposure, they must be carefully evaluated and understood. In measuring the concentration of substances in the air, the following terms are important:

1. ppm (parts per million) - parts of vapor or gas per million parts of air at room temperature and pressure.

2. mg/m^3 - milligrams of a substance per cubic meter of air.

The length of exposure must also be considered to properly evaluate an occupational health exposure. This is because the dose one receives is a function of the concentration of the contaminant and the length of exposure. It is assumed that, for most substances, there is a safe or tolerable level of exposure below which there will be no significant adverse effects. This tolerable level is referred to as the threshold limit value (TLV). TLV's are determined by laboratory research and actual cases of occupational exposures. TLV's are published yearly by the American Conference of Government Industrial Hygienists (ACGIH).

Several points should be noted concerning TLV's. TLV is a trademark of the ACGIH and should not be used when referring to the values published by other organizations. Some regulatory agencies have taken the TLV guidelines and adopted them as standards called Permissible Exposure Limits (PEL).

Four categories of threshold limit values used by the ACGIH are:

1. Time-weighted average (TLV-TWA) is the average concentration for a normal 8-hour workday or 40-hour work week to which nearly all workers may be repeatedly exposed, day after day, without any adverse effect.

2. Short-term exposure limit (TLV-STEL) is the maximum concentration to which workers can be exposed for a short period of time (typically 15 minutes) without suffering irritation, chronic or irreversible tissue change or sufficient narcosis (mental depression leading to stupor or unconsciousness) to increase accident proneness, impair self-rescue or materially reduce work efficiency. The STEL should be considered a maximum allowable concentration, or absolute ceiling, not to be exceeded at any time during a continuous 15-minute period. No more than four 15-minute exposure periods per day are permitted, with at least 60 minutes between each exposure period, provided that the daily TLV-TWA is not exceeded.

3. Ceiling (TLV-C) is the concentration that should never be exceeded, even instantaneously.

4. TLV-Skin indicates substances which can add to the overall exposure by being absorbed through the skin (including mucous membranes and eyes) as well as by other means.

It should be made clear that TLV's are guidelines only. No two persons are alike. Individual variations exist in mental health, physiological makeup, metabolism and past exposures, to name a few. A concentration of a contaminant equal to the TLV will not bother most employees while a few individuals may become ill. Other variables to consider when evaluating the risk associated with exposure to chemical substances include the length of exposure, other concurrent chemical exposures, such as medications or chemicals associated with other aspects of the job, previous experiences, and the route of exposure. *Figure 16-2* is a partial list of variables to consider when evaluating the degree of hazard of an occupational health exposure.

HEALTH HAZARD VARIABLES

- CHEMICAL CONCENTRATION
- ROUTE OF EXPOSURE
- LENGTH OF EXPOSURE
- INDIVIDUAL VARIATION (AGE, SEX, RACE, ETC.)
- FREQUENCY OF EXPOSURE
- PREVIOUS WORK EXPERIENCES
- DRUG INTERACTIONS
- CHEMICAL FORMULATION
- CONTROLS IN USE
- ENVIRONMENT (TEMPERATURE, HUMIDITY, ETC.)

Figure 16-2

Whenever a supervisor has any doubts concerning the exposure and reaction of any employee to a toxic substance, he or she should seek the advice of qualified experts.

Air contaminants are divided into the categories of dusts, fumes, smokes, mists, gases and vapors.

Dusts

Dusts are solid particles generated by crushing, grinding, handling, rapid impact, detonation, drilling and decrepitation (breaking apart by heating). Dust particles are measured in micrometers. A micrometer, or micron, as it is often called, is 1/1000 of a millimeter, or 1/25, 400th of an inch. Dust particles range in size from .1 to 25 microns. Those from .5 to 5 microns are deposited deep in the lung and cause most dust-induced illnesses. Larger particles tend to be filtered by the hairs in the nose or settle in the nose, pharynx, throat or bronchi before reaching the alveoli (air sacs) deep in the lungs. A person with normal eyesight can see a 50-micron particle. Smaller dust particles cannot be seen individually, but may appear as a haze when light shines through them.

In determining the hazard presented from dust contamination, four critical factors to consider are:

- Type of dust
- Length of exposures
- Concentration of dust inhaled
- Size of dust particles.

As with all types of occupational health exposures, variations among persons must also be considered when evaluating the hazard.

Type of Dust. Dust can be classified into two categories, organic and inorganic. Organic dusts originate from living material; e.g. cotton and grain. Inorganic dusts originate from non-living matter; e.g., minerals and metals. Since the body reacts in different ways to different types of dust, one must know the type of dust to know what type of illness can be caused.

Length of Exposure. Some problems such as anthracosis and silicosis may be evident only after several years' exposure. Toxic metal dust exposures from lead and manganese cause problems in a much shorter time (several days to several weeks). Dusts causing allergic reactions often need only very brief exposures (e.g., seconds) to cause a reaction. The length of exposure must be considered when assessing the degree of hazard.

Dust Concentration. The importance of knowing how much of a particular type of dust is in the air cannot be overemphasized. The use of time-weighted averages, short-term exposure limits, and ceiling concentrations are critical in evaluating the existence of a health hazard.

Particle Size. Dust particles 10 microns or less are considered respirable. Since dust ranges in size from .1 micron to 25 microns, most dust is not respirable. Larger particles are more easily filtered and settle more readily than smaller particles. However, smaller particles have a proportionately larger surface area than larger particles. Therefore, small particles present more of an opportunity for toxic chemicals to contact the surface of the lungs and be absorbed.

Free Silica and Asbestos. The two major pathogenic (disease-producing) dusts in industry are free silica and asbestos. Free silica causes a lung disease called silicosis. Free silica is present in mining operations, glass manufacturing, foundries (from the use of sand), granite quarrying and sand-blasting operations.

The inhalation of asbestos fibers causes asbestosis. Asbestos is used in fireproofing material, insulation, shingles, home siding, brake linings and battery casings. Handling, cutting, processing or abrasion of asbestos may generate respirable fibers. *Figure 16-3* is a highly enlarged picture of asbestos fibers.

Fumes

Fumes are solid particles created by condensation of a substance from a gaseous state. Fumes generally

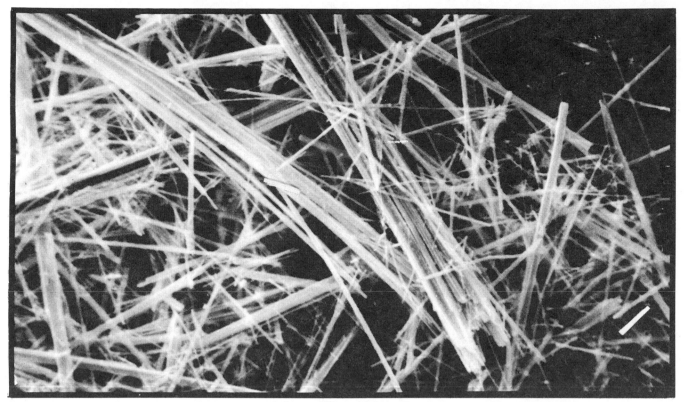

Asbestos Fibres (Enlarged)

Figure 16-3

occur after a molten metal changes from a liquid to a vapor or gas and is condensed in the air. This process usually produces "oxides" when the vaporized metal reacts with the air. All metal fumes and dusts are irritating. However, some cause more harm than simple irritation when inhaled. Fumes and dusts are produced in operations such as smelting, gas cutting, abrasive cutting, grinding and welding. Major metals (or their compounds) posing a health hazard are: antimony, arsenic, beryllium, cadmium, chromium, cobalt, copper, iron, lead, manganese, mercury, selenium, tellurium, thallium, uranium and a few others.

Lead is the source of a major metal fume and dust contaminant. Today, severe cases of lead poisoning are rare. However, exposures to lead must continually be controlled to prevent moderate symptoms. Lead is accumulated in the body and symptoms appear only when a sufficient amount has been accumulated. It may take months for toxic levels of lead to build up in the body, but the symptoms of poisoning may appear overnight. Airborne concentration of lead must be kept at very low levels (TLV = .15 mf/m^3), good housekeeping must be practiced and all employees with significant exposures should be included in a medical surveillance program which includes monitoring of blood and urine for lead levels.

The fumes of zinc and its oxides, if inhaled, can cause a disease called metal fume fever. Symptoms usually disappear within one day. Zinc oxide fumes are the most common cause of metal fume fever, but inhalation of magnesium, copper and other metal fumes may also cause the same syndrome. Common sources of zinc fumes include welding, brazing or cutting of zinc or galvanized surfaces. Because workers in brass foundries often contract this disease (brass is composed of zinc, copper and lead), it is often called "brass ague."

Beryllium dust or fumes are highly toxic substances which can cause localized pulmonary and/or systemic disease. It is so toxic that several cases of poisonings have occurred from wives handling their husbands' contaminated clothing. Toxic beryllium dust or fumes originate from metallic beryllium but not from mining beryllium ore.

Smokes

Smokes are produced by the incomplete combustion of organic materials such as wood, coal, petroleum products and plants. In general, smoke is considered to consist of particles less than .1 micron and, therefore, smaller than dust particles in size. Smoke generally contains gases, droplets and dry particles.

Mists

A mist is composed of very small liquid particles suspended in air. A mist is created by condensation from a gas to a liquid or by dispersing liquid into very small particles. This dispersion can be accomplished by splashing, foaming, spraying, atomizing (mechanically breaking up a liquid into very small particles) and other processes.

Hazards associated with mists often occur during the use of acids. Chromic, hydrochloric, hydrofluoric, nitric and sulfuric acids are often used in a diluted form for pickling, cleaning and electroplating operations. These acids are frequently used in huge tanks with large surface areas or they are sprayed in large cabinets where mists may be easily formed. Tanks and spray cabinets should be equipped with adequate ventilation to carry away any toxic mist that might develop. All acid mists are serious lung irritants if inhaled.

Some acids (such as nitric) can form poisonous gases when they react with metal, and the mist of chromic acid can cause painful ulcers when it comes in contact with the skin.

Proper ventilation and personal protective equipment, such as respirators, should be used whenever acid mists exist.

Gases

Gases are formless fluids which occupy whatever space is available to them. Gases diffuse; that is, they spread widely throughout a structure. Gases can be changed to a liquid or solid state by an increase in pressure and a decrease in temperature. Gases can be produced by arc welding, combustion, decomposition of burned organic matter and other chemical reactions. Some examples of gases are ordinary air, methane, carbon dioxide, carbon monoxide and sulfur dioxide.

Different gases react in different ways in the lungs. Some gases do not affect the lungs at all, but are dissolved into the blood and exert their toxic effects at some other area of the body. One example of this type of gas is carbon monoxide. Carbon monoxide is a toxic gas commonly found in industry. It is responsible for more deaths by asphyxiation and more dangerous exposures than any other single gas. Carbon monoxide is most often produced by incomplete combustion of petroleum products in internal combustion engines. It passes into the blood without disturbing the lungs. Hemoglobin, the chemical that transports oxygen throughout the body, has a difficult

time doing it when carbon monoxide is present. Thus, a person can easily die due to lack of oxygen in the blood.

Some gases produce adverse reactions directly in the lungs. An example is phosgene gas, a product of some solvents when they are decomposed by heat or radiation. Phosgene gas is very irritating and causes fluid to form in the lungs. An individual can literally drown in these fluids.

Hydrogen sulfide gas is often encountered in the petroleum industry. It is very irritating to the lungs. Because of this irritation, fluid accumulates in the lungs, resulting in difficult breathing. The central nervous system is also affected by the gas, causing respiratory paralysis and resulting in asphyxiation. Hydrogen sulfide is extremely toxic and must be monitored very closely when the possibility of its presence exists. Other gases that can be extremely hazardous include nitrogen oxides, chlorine and fluorine.

It is important to know the characteristics of the particular gas you are dealing with before you can properly evaluate the potential problems that may be presented through its use.

Vapors

Vapors are the gaseous forms of substances which are normally in liquid or solid states at room temperature and pressure. Vapors can be expected to be present wherever their liquid sources are found. Vapors also diffuse. Concentrations of vapors can be found when using organic solvents, paint thinner, spot removers, cleaning agents and drying agents. Knowing the vapor pressure of liquids (the pressures exerted by vapor above the liquid being vaporized) can help determine the relative amount of vapor present and, therefore, the severity of a vapor hazard. The higher the vapor pressure, the greater the amount of vapors released from a liquid.

The use of solvents creates the most common vapor hazards. Solvents are generally used for cleaning purposes or to dissolve materials. Some commonly used solvents are mineral spirits, alcohol, trichloroethylene, xylene and methylene chloride.

Solvent vapors usually gain entrance to the body through inhalation and to a much lesser extent from skin absorption. Solvents also present fire and explosion hazards. Each solvent must be evaluated on an individual basis to determine the hazards it presents, and to determine proper handling, storage, disposal and emergency procedures needed. Anyone handling solvents should be familiar with:

1. The solvent itself and its properties.

Flash Point - The lowest temperature at which enough vapor is given off to form a mixture with air that is ignitable. If this temperature is above 100F (37.8C) the liquid is called combustible. If it is below 100F, it is called flammable.

Flammable (Explosive) Range - Anyone familiar with gasoline engines knows that if there is too little gas in the fuel-air mixture (too lean) the engine will not run. Also, if there is too much gas (too rich) the engine will not run. The range between these two points is called the flammable, or explosive, range. This range includes all the concentrations of a vapor between the lower explosive limit (LEL) and the upper explosive limit (UEL). *Figure 16-4* lists various flammable and combustible liquids based on each liquid's flash point.

Vapor Pressure - The pressure exerted by the solvent's vapors in the area above the solvent. The higher the vapor pressure the greater the amount of vapor present.

Vapor Density - The density of the solvent's vapors relative to atmospheric air. If the vapor density is greater than 1, it sinks to the floor; if the vapor density is less than 1, it remains suspended in air.

2. The type and method of application.

3. The type and length of worker exposure.

4. The temperature at which the solvent will be used.

5. The exposed surface area of the solvent.

6. The evaporation rate (this relates to vapor pres-

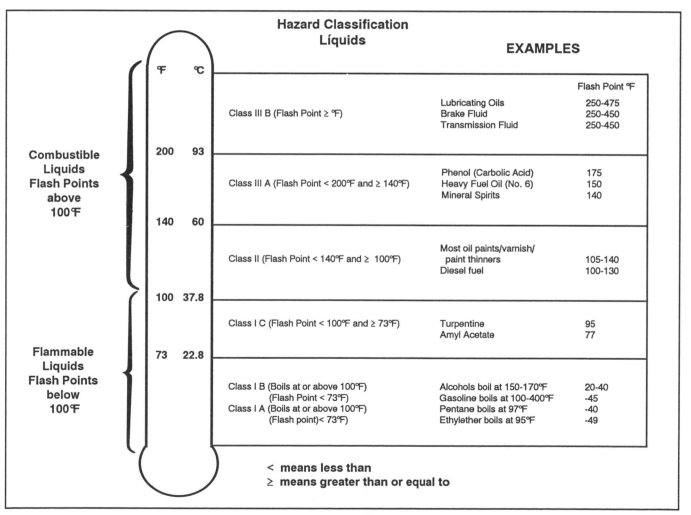

Figure 16-4

sure).

7. The toxic properties (PEL, TLV).

8. The ventilation provided (general, local).

9. The pattern and direction of airflow in the work area.

10. The expected vapor concentration.

11. The proper storage procedures.

12. The proper labelling procedures.

13. The proper disposal procedures for both solvent and solvent contaminant materials.

These considerations show that much more than the toxicity of a solvent, i.e., the ability of a material to produce harm, must be considered when evaluating the existence of an occupational health hazard. To implement an effective occupational health program, every condition of a solvent's use must be analyzed.

It is not simply the larger and more extensive applications that produce solvent hazards. Large tank operations or spraying processes using solvents are more likely to be identified as problems and be protected with ventilation fans, hoods and similar protective devices. It is the smaller "one-shot" or infrequent applications that often produce the greatest hazards. At times an individual may feel there can be no real hazard in the use of a particular solvent, since it is used infrequently or only in small amounts. The degree of the hazard is too often associated with the amount of solvent used. This is not a safe assumption! People have died from using less than four ounces of carbon tetrachloride during a cleaning operation in an extremely confined area. The explosion hazard presented by the vapors from one cup of gasoline staggers the imagination.

A frequently overlooked method of controlling vapor hazards is the proper labeling of solvents. Labels should provide information on the existence of a hazardous substance (i.e., its chemical name and its concentration); the nature of the hazard (i.e., fire, explosion, skin irritant, caustic, etc.); the hazard signal word (danger, warning or caution); handling and storing precautions (i.e., store away from heat or sparks, keep container sealed, use adequate ventilation, use proper protective equipment); emergency treatment and clean-up instructions; and date dispensed and date to be discarded (if applicable). A sample label and the information it should contain is shown in *Figure 16-5*. Solvents should never be taken from properly labeled containers and placed in

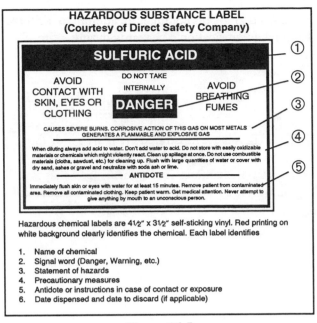

HAZARDOUS SUBSTANCE LABEL
(Courtesy of Direct Safety Company)

Hazardous chemical labels are 4½" x 3½" self-sticking vinyl. Red printing on white background clearly identifies the chemical. Each label identifies

1. Name of chemical
2. Signal word (Danger, Warning, etc.)
3. Statement of hazards
4. Precautionary measures
5. Antidote or instructions in case of contact or exposure
6. Date dispensed and date to discard (if applicable)

Figure 16-5

smaller unmarked containers. If labels do not give all the desired information, the manufacturer should be contacted immediately to provide proper labels and provide the user with a material safety data sheet.

A supervisor should have a good working knowledge of commonly used hazard identification systems and symbols. Many substances present more than one type of hazard. The hazard identification system diamond, illustrated in *Figure 16-6*, is often seen on labels. The diamond provides health, fire, reactivity and specific hazard data on various substances.

Fire, health and reactivity data found on the diamond

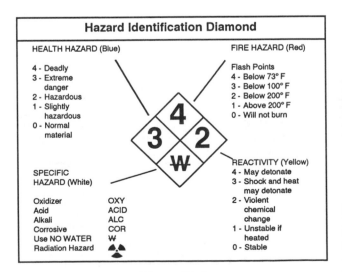

Figure 16-6

are coded 0 to 4. This coding is an attempt to facilitate the quick identification of hazards during a fire. *Figure 16-7* provides a further explanation of these classifications.

Internationally standardized or universal sets of symbols are being used more and more on labels to identify occupational health hazards. Sample standardized symbols are illustrated in *Figure 16-8*. Various shapes convey important information.

Figure 16-9 illustrates five standardized shapes and explains their meaning. The use of particular colors has come to mean specific things. The following is a list and explanation of colors and what they represent.

Red - indicates danger or heat: an immediate hazard; also identifies firefighting equipment and emergency controls.

Green - indicates safety; safe to work or proceed; also identifies rescue locations and medical equipment.

Yellow - indicates a potential hazard; indicates a changing condition that could present an energy contact.

Orange - indicates a dangerous point of a hazard, or an abnormal aspect of a hazard; also means "under repair."

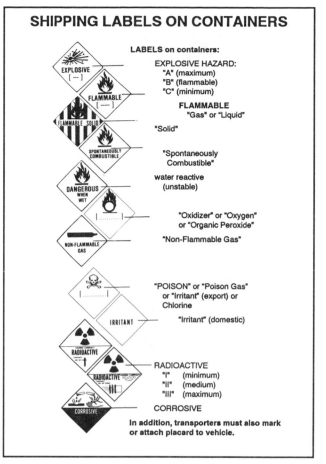

Figure 16-8

Identification of the Fire Hazards of Materials					
Identification of Health Hazard Color Code: BLUE		Identification of Flammability Color Code: RED		Identification of Reactivity (Stability) Color Code: YELLOW	
Type of Possible Injury		Susceptibility of Materials to Burning		Susceptibility to Release of Energy	
Signal		Signal		Signal	
4	Materials which on very short exposure could cause death or major residual injury even though prompt medical treatment is given.	**4**	Materials which will rapidly or completely vaporize at atmospheric pressure and normal ambient temperature or which are readily dispersed in air and which will burn readily.	**4**	Materials which in themselves are readily capable of detonation or of explosive decomposition or reaction at normal temperatures and pressures.
3	Materials which on short exposure could cause serious temporary or residual injury even though prompt medical treatment is given.	**3**	Liquids and solids that can be ignited under almost all ambient temperature conditions.	**3**	Materials which in themselves are capable of detonation or explosive reaction but require a strong initiating source or which must be heated under confinement before initiation or which react explosively with water.
2	Materials which on intense or continued exposure could cause temporary incapacitation or possible residual injury unless prompt medical treatment is given.	**2**	Materials that must be moderately heated or exposed to relatively high ambient temperatures before ignition can occur.	**2**	Materials which in themselves are normally unstable and readily undergo violent chemical change but do not detonate. Also materials which may react violently with water or which may form potentially explosive mixtures with water.
1	Materials which on exposure would cause irritation but only minor residual injury even if no treatment is given.	**1**	Materials that must be preheated before ignition can occur.	**1**	Materials which in themselves are normally stable, but which can become unstable at elevated temperatures and pressures or which may react with water with some release of energy but not violently.
0	Materials which on exposure under fire conditions would offer no hazard beyond that of ordinary combustible material.	**0**	Materials that will not burn.	**0**	Materials which in themselves are normally stable even under fire exposure conditions and which are not reactive with water.

Figure 16-7

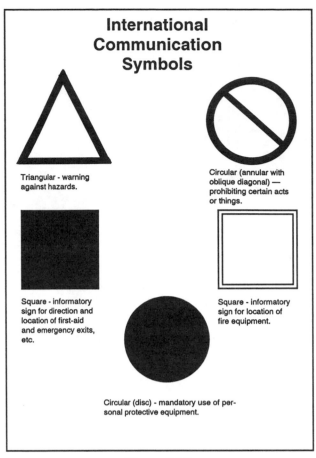

International Communication Symbols

Triangular - warning against hazards.

Circular (annular with oblique diagonal) — prohibiting certain acts or things.

Square - informatory sign for direction and location of first-aid and emergency exits, etc.

Square - informatory sign for location of fire equipment.

Circular (disc) - mandatory use of personal protective equipment.

Figure 16-9

Blue - indicates information; also cold temperature.

Every container in use should be labeled. Extra labels for identifying "working containers," i.e., those containers used for dispensing chemicals, can be ordered from suppliers. A homemade label may be a tag, an adhesive-backed sheet of paper, or information that is stenciled or painted directly on the hazardous material container.

When hazardous materials are used, a placard quite often facilitates the communication of important safety information. A placard carries the same information as the label plus fire, reactivity, health and fire extinguishing instructions. Placards should supplement, but not replace, labels.

Control of Air Contaminants

When designing a system to control air contaminants, consider the nature of the agent, its physical properties, the degree of exposure and the nature of the work process. Some common control methods are:

Substitution or Replacement. Replacing toxic substances with a relatively harmless substitute is often feasible. Abrasive blasting need not be done with sand if steel particles, nut-shells or other non-silica products can be satisfactorily substituted. Dolomite gravel may be substituted for free silica in certain metal casting operations. Benzene may be replaced by the less toxic xylene or toluene. To make an intelligent decision in this regard, you must know the properties of both the substance in use and its potential substitute. Many chemical substitutes can do the job equally well but with a fraction of the original hazard potential.

Isolation of Operation. Often a process can be isolated in a booth or other enclosure to prevent the contamination of the surrounding air. At times the process can be mechanized so that no employee has to be in the booth at the time of the operation.

Elimination or Reduction of Employee Exposure. A work area generating significant amounts of contaminated air can often be isolated from the general work area. The isolated area should have self-closing doors, no windows and a slightly negative pressure relative to the general work area to prevent contamination of the general work area. Many operations do not require continuous employee monitoring. By restricting employees from this hazardous area at times other than those required, exposures can be minimized. It may be possible to completely enclose an operation with workers controlling the function from outside.

Change in Process or Operation. The amount of contamination can frequently be controlled or minimized by changing the process or operation involved. For example, a dip tank cleaning process might release less solvent vapor than spraying or swabbing. An automated spray paint booth enables the worker to avoid toxic vapors or mists.

Local Exhaust. Air contaminants can often be trapped at their source and exhausted from the building or immediate area by hoods and fans as permitted by environmental laws. The collection system should be mounted as close as possible to the point of generation. An ideally designed system from the standpoint of worker protection would completely enclose the hazardous operation and exhaust the contaminants out of this closed system. In fact, the method many engineers use to design an exhaust system is to visualize it completely enclosed, then "cut holes" in this imaginary box to permit worker accessibility. Care must be taken to ensure that the exhaust system not only removes harmful air contaminants, but is practical to use as well. In other operations, local exhaust (high velocity, low volume) can be used to effectively capture and remove dust, fumes and vapors away from the breathing zone of employees. Local exhaust systems must be designed to be used very close to the point of the operation where the contaminant is released to be effective.

Ventilation. It is unusual for significant health hazards to be completely controlled by a general ventilation system. However, where the sources of a contaminant are numerous, widely distributed, and/or not highly toxic, general ventilation may be the best solution. General ventilation usually involves opening windows and doors and turning on fans to relieve hazardous conditions. This can be effective, but oftentimes it aggravates problems and recirculates settled contaminants.

Wetting-Down Methods. Wetting-down methods are particularly useful with dust hazards. Using water or other suitable agents will often greatly reduce or eliminate the amount of dusts generated. Cutting, drilling, grinding, mixing and foundry molding all lend themselves to this type of control. Dust may be reduced by as much as 75% by properly utilizing wetting-down procedures. This method of control is widely used to minimize airborne asbestos fibers during removal of insulation materials containing asbestos.

Housekeeping. Air contaminants can often be effectively controlled or eliminated simply by good housekeeping. Keeping lids on stored solvents, cleaning up spilled materials and quickly removing dust as it accumulates (before it can become dispersed in the air again) can greatly minimize hazards.

Personal Protective Equipment. When other control methods do not completely eliminate the hazard and no other practical means exist for effectively controlling it, respirators may be used. They are a "last resort" control measure and should rarely be considered as a first line of defense. Care must be taken to ensure that the proper type of respirator is used for the hazard involved. Respirators must be properly fitted, maintained and worn in order to be effective. The subject of respirator use is discussed in more detail in the section entitled "A Supervisory Program for Occupational Health Hazards." Other protective equipment may range from clothing, gloves, coveralls, etc., to completely enclosed "space suits."

Personal Hygiene. With proper attention to personal hygiene, the chance of accidental ingestion or skin absorption is reduced. Places for eating, drinking or smoking must be some distance from working areas. Washing facilities with hot and cold water and soap should be conveniently placed. When a contaminant can be carried on or in clothing, change rooms and showers are needed. An emergency shower should be available whenever and wherever the chance of accidental chemical contamination exists.

Air Monitoring. Air monitoring is necessary to identify an air contaminant and to evaluate the effectiveness of established control measures. Some instruments take a direct reading which is indicated visually or audibly. Others take samples which are later analyzed in a lab. The measuring equipment may be attached directly to the worker or placed in the work area depending on the type of measurement needed.

Skin Irritants

The skin provides many vital bodily functions. It protects the body; it conserves fluid; it synthesizes vitamins; it fights infection; it helps to regulate body temperature; it is a sensory organ; it can regenerate itself; it keeps bacteria out; and when hung on the right skeleton, it can be quite attractive. Death can easily occur if enough skin is damaged. It is the first line of defense against exposures to many toxic chemicals. There are many processes, procedures, materials and situations that can contribute to the development of skin diseases. Surveys have indicated that as many as 25% of all workers have exposure to some type of skin irritant. The majority of compensation claims filed are a result of occupational skin diseases.

As with all other organs of the body, the susceptibility of the skin to the effects of toxic exposure is greatly dependent on individual variation. Age, sex, race, previous exposure, personal hygiene, amount of hair and many other factors also contribute to an individual's response to skin irritation.

Skin problems can be caused by mechanical agents (e.g., friction, pressure, trauma); physical agents (e.g., temperature extremes, electricity, ultraviolet light, ionizing radiation); biological agents (fungal, bacterial, plants, insects); and chemical agents. Since chemical agents induce most cases of occupational dermatitis, we will deal primarily with them.

Acids, solvents and strong bases are the primary causes of occupational dermatitis. Nitric acid, sulfuric

> ## Some guidelines for
> ## CHEMICAL HANDLING
>
> **KEEP INFORMED** of
> hazardous chemicals:
>
> - Read labels for warnings, precautions, first aid.
> - Follow "Material Safety Data Sheets" for your area.
>
> **FOLLOW PROCEDURES:**
>
> - Wear personal protecion equipment and monitoring devices when required
> - Follow good housekeeping. Keep emergency and traffic areas clear. Remove unused chemicals.
> - Wash up after using and before eating. Keep food, drink and smoking away from chemical areas.
> - Store chemicals in limited quantities, in proper containers, in separate/secure areas.
> - Dispose of waste chemicals per procedure in proper drains or containers — only.
> - In case of hazardous spill or exposure, know and follow emergency procedure. Get medical care right away.

Figure 16-10

acid and sodium hydroxide are among the substances that can cause chemical burns and contact dermatitis by direct action on the skin and are referred to as *primary irritants*. Other chemicals are considered sensitizers because the substance may not produce noticeable irritation or damage to the skin on an initial contact, but may cause the skin to have a very strong reaction on subsequent future contacts. Once an individual is sensitized, the skin may react in areas other than those exposed to the chemical and the worker may "break out" all over. The hardeners used in many "two-part" paints are often sensitizers for many people. Other chemicals can sensitize the skin to light so that a worker exposed to sunlight may develop sunburn more easily than someone not exposed to the chemical.

A major problem with dermatitis is that many people fail to seek treatment at the first indication of a problem. There is a tendency to wait and see if it goes away. Unfortunately, this allows time for additional contact with the irritant, prolonging the exposure and further aggravating the condition. With chemical agents in particular, the workers may inadvertently spread the exposure by wiping away perspiration or touching other areas of the body while the irritant is on their hands or clothes. They can expose others by not washing their hands or exposed parts of their bodies regularly. Their contaminated clothing can also expose others who come in contact with it.

Methods of Preventing and Controlling Industrial Skin Diseases

The first step in the prevention and control of industrial skin diseases is recognition. Supervisors should be thoroughly familiar with all substances in their areas that might cause skin irritation and the operations in which they are used. Supervisors should ensure that all possible precautions are taken to minimize exposure to these substances and that all workers are aware of the potential hazards. Many methods of control are available to prevent or minimize incidents of occupational dermatitis. Several are similar to those discussed under Controls of Air Contaminant Hazards.

Substitution. Whenever possible, non-irritating or less irritating substances should be substituted for irritants. Consideration should be given to the substance selected as well as the form in which it is supplied. For example, dry sodium hydroxide and potassium hydroxide are now available in a virtually dust-free form. Many other products may be available as prills (beads), pellets, granules or solutions which will do an adequate job.

Engineering Controls. Enclosures, temperature controls, automated handling devices, exhaust hoods and process changes are all engineering controls that can be used to reduce exposures to irritating substances.

Standard Practices. Detailed and accurate labelling of known irritant substances and strictly enforced standard practices for their handling and use are excellent controls that the supervisor can influence. Proper labelling procedures were discussed earlier in this chapter. Many problems can be avoided by making employees aware of the hazards associated with these materials and the precautions to be taken in their use.

Standard practices should include personal hygiene practices required for the job. Regular cleaning procedures should also be part of the standard practice in any area with an exposure hazard from irritants. All aspects of cleanliness should be emphasized, ranging from the worker and his or her clothing, to the floor and the machinery sitting on it.

Personal Protective Equipment. Personal protective equipment, such as gloves and special clothing, can be effectively used to avoid or minimize exposure to skin irritants. When selecting gloves, aprons, boots, and sleeves, special attention should be given to how the irritant reacts with the piece of protective equipment. For example, products composed of natural rubber soon deteriorate after exposure to a strong alkali. Synthetic rubber, such as neoprene, is more resistant to alkaline solutions and solvents than natural rubber, but may be adversely affected by solvents containing chlorinated hydrocarbons. A wide variety of inexpensive, disposable clothing is available and is very convenient to use.

Protective ointments and creams (often called barrier creams) are available for use with specific skin irritants. These creams protect the skin from exposure and can be washed off after a job is completed, thereby removing any irritants that might contact the skin. In general, barrier creams are ineffective as the sole means of protection, but can be used to supplement the use of personal protective equipment.

Pre-Employment or Pre-Placement Consideration

All workers should be screened prior to placement on a job with any degree of exposure to skin irritants. Care should be taken in placing persons with allergies or a history of pre-existing skin disease on jobs that could aggravate these conditions. Employees should be informed, before performing a job, of the materials involved and any possible irritants that might be encountered. An informed employee is much better prepared to provide the supervisor with information regarding improper exposures or adverse reactions to certain chemical substances.

PHYSICAL HAZARDS

The second category of occupation health hazards is physical agents. Physical agents include noise, vibration, ionizing radiation, illumination, temperature and pressure extremes, lasers and microwaves. Supervisors need to be aware of these physical agents because of their potential to produce harmful immediate or cumulative effects.

Noise

Noise can be defined as any unwanted sound. What may be noise to one person is music to another. Exposure to noise has many adverse effects on workers, ranging from physical stresses to psychological imbalances. Noise contributes to accidents by making it difficult to hear warnings. It is estimated that 14 million workers in the U.S. alone are exposed to hazardous noise.

Excessive noise can destroy one's ability to hear. The amount of damage noise produces depends on how loud the noise is and how long it is heard. The frequency or pitch also has some effect in that high-pitched sounds are more damaging than low-pitched sounds.

Hearing loss may range from a tiring or fatiguing of the inner ear, causing a temporary hearing loss, to a permanent loss of hearing. Typically, the worker with a temporary hearing loss will have difficulty understanding conversation at the end of the work shift, with normal hearing returning by the beginning of the next shift. Permanent hearing loss results from destruction of the cells of the inner ear which will never be repaired or replaced. People with a permanent hearing loss never recover normal hearing. They typically say, "I can hear you, but I can't understand you." Usually the ability to hear high-pitched sounds is lost first, which means a person can still hear some sounds but speech or other sounds may be unclear or distorted. It is interesting to note that hearing aids may make speech louder, but cannot make it clearer. This is why hearing aids are rarely a cure for hearing loss.

Other adverse effects of noise include increased heart rate, increased blood pressure and narrowing of blood vessels which, over a period of time, place an added burden on the heart and contribute to various cardiovascular diseases. Noise also stresses other parts of the body; causing abnormal hormonal secretions, muscle tension, nervousness, sleeplessness and fatigue. These can lead to reduced job performance, high rates of absenteeism, increased accident rates, poor morale, high labor turnover and increased compensation claims.

Some basic concepts must be understood before a noise problem can be properly managed. The amount of pressure created by sound waves is measured in units called decibels (dB). If the level of sound is increased by 5dB, it seems to the ears as if the sound intensity has doubled. If decreased by 5dB, it seems to be reduced by half. The frequency of a sound wave is the number of vibrations per second, measured in Hertz (Hz). Young people can hear sound ranging from 20Hz to 20,000Hz. Sound composed of frequencies higher than 20,000Hz is called ultrasound and usually cannot be heard by humans.

Certain instruments measure the level of sound (dB) on an "A" scale which is a scale of the frequencies heard by the human ear. Measurements done on this scale are referred to as dB(A). *Figure 16-11* illustrates various sounds and their corresponding dB(A) readings.

Readings taken with sound level meters should be taken as near as possible to the ear of the worker, and that ear should be the ear closest to the source of the noise. Often noise cannot be localized and/or the worker moves during the job, so this may be impossible to do. If this is the case, it may be possible for an audio-dosimeter to be worn by the worker to provide a more accurate measurement of noise exposure.

Instruments for measuring sound levels and sound properties include sound-level meters, octave-band analyzers, and personal audio-dosimeters. To accurately measure noise and determine the nature and extent of a noise problem, one should receive special training in this area. Training is available through instrument manufacturers, governmental agencies and private institutions.

It should be remembered that noise does not have to produce discomfort or distraction to be harmful. The fact that workers do not appear to be bothered or do not complain about the noise level is no guarantee that a noise problem does not exist. Loss of hearing can and does occur without discomfort. A gradual loss of hearing can occur without an individual being aware of it. A person does not get used to excessive noise - he gets deaf. *Figure 16-12* contains some non-technical rules of thumb for recognizing noise problems.

Methods of Controlling Noise Exposures

The first method for controlling noise exposures which usually occurs to the untrained supervisor is the blanket application of personal protective equipment, such as earmuffs or earplugs. This should rarely be the first control method used. While personal protective equipment can be helpful, there are often more effective ways of dealing with the problem. The following approaches to noise control should be considered in the order in which they are given.

Reduction of noise at its source. Often machines are allowed to deteriorate due to lack of maintenance.

	Sound intensity ratio	Sound level in dB(A)	Sound source
Harmful range	1000 000 000 000 000	140	Jet engine
	10 000 000 000 000	130	Riveting hammer
THRESHOLD OF FEELING			
	1 000 000 000 000	120	Propeller aircraft
Critical Zone	100 000 000 000	110	Rock drill
	10 000 000 000	100	Plate fabrication shop
	1 000 000 000	90	Heavy vehicle
Safe range	100 000 000	80	Very busy traffic
	10 000 000	70	Private car
	1 000 000	60	Ordinary conversation
	100 000	50	
	10 000	40	Soft music from radio
	1 000	30	Quiet whisper
	100	20	Quiet urban dwelling
	10	10	Rustle of a leaf
THRESHOLD OF HEARING	1	0	

Figure 16-11

Non-Technical Rules of Thumb to Help Supervisors Recognize Noise Problems

1. A noticeable, though temporary, loss of hearing after leaving an area of noise where an extended period of exposure existed.

2. Employee complaints of headaches or a "ringing in the ears" (tinnitus) during or after the work day.

3. Difficulty in verbal communication in an area as demonstrated by the fact that it is hard to be heard or understood at close distances.

4. Accidents occurring because warnings were not heard.

5. Comments or complaints related to some degree of hearing loss.

If any of these symptoms exist, a more detailed survey of the area should be conducted.

Figure 16-12

This deterioration creates noise problems where none should exist. The establishment of a regular maintenance program frequently eliminates or significantly reduces the noise from poorly maintained equipment. In other cases, a muffler or other type of baffle may solve the problem. Substitutions of processes is another alternative (such as spot welding rather than riveting, or use of a vibrating marking tool in place of stamping).

Reduction of noise transmitted. In cases where noise produced by a machine or process cannot be controlled at the source, the transmission of that noise can often be significantly reduced. Vibration mounting, padding, altering frequencies, reducing turbulence can all be used to reduce the amount of noise transmitted. Administrative practices such as worker rotation or the decision to construct "quiet rooms" where workers can periodically get away from the noise can also be used to control noise hazards.

Personal protective equipment. When other methods have not satisfactorily controlled the noise problem, effective noise attenuation can often be achieved through the use of personal protective equipment (such as a variety of earmuffs or earplugs). Considerable attention should be given to proper fit, application and usage. Regulations requiring hearing protection should be strictly enforced after the need for such protection and its purpose have been fully explained to all workers affected.

Vibration

Noise and vibrations often originate from the same source and for this reason are frequently associated with each other. However, the adverse effects from noise and vibration are quite different.

There are two types of vibration. The first is "whole body" vibration such as that which occurs while sitting on a tractor seat. The second is "segmental" vibration, like that transmitted to your hands while operating a chain saw. Whole body vibration can lead to increased oxygen consumption, increased respiratory rate, increased cardiac output, abnormal posture (probably due to nerve damage), altered brain activity, altered visual acuity and certain biochemical changes.

Segmental vibration, usually resulting from the use of certain hand tools, may cause constriction of blood vessels, leading to "white fingers" as seen in Raynaud's Syndrome. It can also lead to inflammation and degeneration of nerves, causing paralysis and decreased sensitivity to touch and temperature, deformation of the bones of the wrist and a shrinking of muscles. Vibration in the range of 40 to 125Hz is most frequently implicated in reported cases of vibration disorders.

Methods of controlling vibration hazards are isolation, dampening and source reduction. Isolation involves separating the source of the vibration from the surface which radiates it. Separation can be accomplished by using flexible piping connectors, conduit or ductwork and/or anchoring housings to the floor instead of the machine. Dampening reduces the ability of the radiating source to vibrate by coating it with a "deadener." Reduction at the source involves reducing impacts, reducing sliding or rolling friction and/or reducing imbalance. Solutions to vibration problems can often be found by using a common sense approach. If a single, simple answer is not obvious, vibration measurements can be used to show what progress is being made and to indicate future steps for correction.

Temperature Extremes

There are a number of variables to be considered when evaluating the hazards presented by temperature extremes. Individual variation, length of exposure, type of work, wind speed, humidity, wet bulb temperature (temperature considering the cooling effects of evaporation), dry bulb temperature (temperature not considering the cooling effects of evaporation) and other factors should be taken into consideration when identifying and evaluating hazards presented by temperature extremes.

Common sense can go a long way in solving many problems associated with temperature extremes. However, professional help from physicians or industrial hygienists must often be sought to provide effective solutions. Extreme cold can cause tissue damage from hypothermia and frostbite with little discomfort or warning. Extended exposures to low temperatures may, of course, cause death. Heat stress, the body's response to stresses brought about by excess heat, strains the cardiovascular system, causes cramps, heat exhaustion, heat stroke and even death.

Compounding the dangers of temperature extremes is the fact that employees are often unaware of any problem or threat to their health until it is too late. Employees say they can "take it" or are not "bothered" by the environment, but this is no guarantee that they are indeed safe. It should be kept in mind that exposure to high temperatures can dangerously raise the body's core temperature while the worker is totally unaware of any discomfort, and that frostbite can occur with little or no pain at all.

Once a problem caused by temperature extremes has been recognized and properly evaluated, there are several possible methods of control. The methods used depend on the type and degree of exposure.

Cold Environments

Some suggested controls for exposures to cold are:

Proper Clothing. The dead air space between the warm body and the outside air is critical. Clothing is worn to keep warmth in and cold out. Oftentimes several layers of relatively light clothing are more protective than a single heavy garment because additional dead air space is created. Clothing should be adequate for warmth, but not so heavy as to cause excessive perspiration or energy expenditure. If several layers of clothing are worn, then, as exertion increases, some clothing can be removed to prevent perspiration. Wet skin is damaged much more rapidly than dry skin, and greatly increases the hazard to the worker.

Good Physical Condition. Workers in good physi-

cal condition are better able to adapt to temperature extremes by making full use of the body's own adaptive abilities, e.g., good cardiac and pulmonary reserves.

Buddy System. In areas of extreme cold (such as storage or refrigeration vaults), workers should never work alone. Loss of consciousness in such areas could be fatal in a short period of time.

Hot Environments

Control of heat stress from hot environments includes engineering controls, administrative procedures, acclimatization, proper clothing and personal protective equipment.

Engineering controls. Some engineering methods used to control heat-induced stresses include:

Ventilation. Both general ventilation and spot cooling are used to reduce the heat present in the work environment. Local exhausting of hot air can effectively control an excessively hot environment. Personal cooling fans can facilitate evaporation of perspiration and removal of environmental heat. Care must be taken to avoid circulating very hot air since this will only serve to increase worker heat stress. Evaporative cooling or mechanical refrigeration techniques can also be used to reduce air temperatures.

Equipment and process changes. Sometimes heat-producing equipment and processes can be isolated, redesigned, relocated or substituted in order to reduce the amount of heat generated. Some examples include covering steaming tanks, hot water drains and hot water pipes to reduce the heat released into the air.

Work-saving devices. Try to make better use of power tools and lifting aids to reduce normal labor. The resulting reduction of work load on employees will result in less heat stress.

Heat shields or barriers. Workers can be protected from radiant heat by reflective shields of aluminized material or insulating boards. Use of such barriers can significantly reduce exposures and might preclude the need for personal protective equipment.

Administrative Practices. Some effective administrative control measures utilized to reduce heat stress include:

Selection and periodic examination of workers. A worker's past performance in hot environments is perhaps the most reliable criterion to predict future performance under similar conditions. New employees without previous heat exposures should be screened by procedures such as standard physical fitness and heat tolerance tests. Periodic employee examinations, particularly for older employees, should be made with particular attention given to chronic impairments or progressive diseases of the various body systems, e.g., circulatory, pulmonary, genito-urinary and endocrine systems.

Work controls. Work controls include: a work-rest schedule to reduce stress peaks, work distribution over a maximum period of time, strenuous work scheduled during coolest part of the day and distribution of heavy work to several employees.

Worker training. Workers should be taught the basics of how to prevent heat illness as well as its symptoms, causes and treatment.

Replacement of body fluids. Workers in hot environments should increase their intake of fluids and electrolytes (minerals) to replace those lost from perspiration evaporation. A normal diet usually provides an adequate amount of salt intake. If an increased amount of salt intake is needed (and this is highly unlikely, considering that most North Americans consume ten to fifteen times the amount of salt necessary) it should be done at meal time by salting one's food. Drinking water should be kept cool (40-60F) to encourage its consumption. Drinking small quantities of water at frequent intervals should be encouraged.

Acclimatization. In hot environments, a person acclimated to heat will have a lower heart rate, lower body temperature, higher sweat rate and a more diluted sweat (containing less salt) than an unacclimated person. Working in heat for about two hours a day for seven to fourteen days will essentially result in complete acclimation to that particular situation. Acclimation is usually achieved by maintaining environmental conditions at a relatively constant level and by gradually increasing the amount of work done (over a week). Lack of water or salt will reduce the speed of acclimation. Once acclimatization is achieved, it is lost slowly; but a measurable amount can be lost in just a few days.

Personal protective equipment. The type and amount of clothing workers wear significantly affects their ability to cope with heat stresses. Clothing should be loose enough to allow proper air and blood circulation, but not loose enough to be caught by moving machinery or equipment. Aluminized or reflective clothing can be used to protect workers from radiant heat generated in steel mills, foundries and other hot metal industries. Adequate protective equipment varies greatly from job to job. Information on available equipment can be found in scientific and quasi-scientific literature.

Ionizing Radiation

Once limited to medical research, diagnosis and treatment, ionizing radiation is now increasingly used in industry. Non-destructive testing of pipelines and castings is commonly done with X-ray devices. Radioactive gauges are used in quality control, where critical tolerances must be maintained. Radioactive trace elements are used in analytical chemistry.

Because it cannot be seen, heard, felt or tasted, it gives no advance warning of the damage it is causing. In fact, it may be days, weeks, months or even years before the effects of overexposure can be detected. The effects of overexposure are often very difficult to attribute to an overdose of ionizing radiation. It usually damages rapidly reproducing cells first, such as in the intestinal tract, bone marrow (where blood cells are produced), hair follicles, the base of the fingernails, etc.

The use of ionizing radiation requires strict control procedures (usually provided by the government), and a full knowledge of the subject by the supervisor. Adequate training and education are a must for supervisors of jobs with ionizing radiation hazards. Radiation protection is a highly technical field and should be undertaken only by a fully trained person.

A primary precautionary measure when exposed to ionizing radiation hazards is to closely monitor radiation exposures. Ionizing radiation monitoring can be accomplished through the use of film badges, film rings or pocket dosimeters. Pocket dosimeters give a continuous reading of ionizing radiation present whereas film badges must be removed and processed to determine the dose of ionizing radiation received. The worker will not know if the exposure was excessive until after the film is developed. A pocket dosimeter is preferable, especially on critical jobs with a high likelihood of ionizing radiation exposure, because of its ability to provide instantaneous reading. Some workers mistakenly think that film badges provide protection from ionizing radiation. *Pocket badges do not protect,* they simply measure the degree of exposure. Instruments do exist which give a warning signal whenever certain levels of radiation are exceeded.

Non-Ionizing (Electro-Magnetic) Radiation

Non-ionizing radiation, in the form of infrared, ultraviolet, microwaves and lasers, cause personal harm in ways other than ionizing radiation. Non-ionizing radiation can burn the skin or underlying structures, and microwaves may cause deep internal damage. The first step in controlling non-ionizing radiation hazards is to recognize their possible existence.

1. **Infrared radiation.** Some typical industrial sources of infrared radiation are the drying and baking of paints, inks or varnishes; heating of metal parts for shrink fittings; forging; thermal aging; dehydrating of meats, vegetables and pottery; and the smelting and refining of ores. Radiant heat raises the temperature of the surface it falls on and not the air through which it travels. Therefore, ventilation and air movement do not help to control this type of hazard. Radiant heat shields and reflective clothing are commonly used to protect against radiant heat. Protective eyewear with appropriate infrared filters should also be used.

2. **Ultraviolet radiation.** A common source of ultraviolet radiation is sunlight. Industrial sources of ultraviolet radiation include arc welding and ultraviolet lamps used for inspection purposes and/or for sterilization. Welding flash, or flash burn, is a common complaint of welders who inadvertently look directly at a welding arc without proper eye protection (in the form of the correct filter lens). Appropriate clothing is a primary method of control. Welders should always wear long-sleeved shirts, buttoned at the cuff and the collar. Use of a welder's mask with a proper filter lens is also necessary. Unnecessary exposure to welding should be avoided.

3. **Microwaves.** Microwave radiation is being increasingly used for cooking, drying in wood-gluing operations, freeze-drying and medical diathermy. Microwaves produce heat inside a material and present a serious health hazard to humans. Excessive exposure to microwaves can cause cataracts and damage to the reproductive organs. Control of hazards associated with microwave use is achieved by proper shielding, minimizing exposures, sound job procedures and a good maintenance program. Government agencies and manufacturers provide exposure criteria for microwave users.

4. **Lasers.** The laser (light amplification by stimulated emission of radiation) is composed of parallel light waves traveling in the same direction. In recent years, lasers have found applications outside of research in the areas of communication, welding, curing, surveying, mechanical measuring, dimensional holography and in the field of surgery. The intensity of laser waves may be such that serious injury can result if they are handled improperly. Reflections from lasers are just as hazardous as the direct beams. The eye is the most vulnerable part of the body, because the lens focuses the laser to a tiny spot on the retina. This increases the laser's intensity on the retina, causing serious injury and even blindness. Safe exposure limits have not been clearly defined and for this reason, exposures to lasers should be avoided if at all possible. Laser technology is highly sophisticated. Consultation with qualified professionals for guidance in this area is recommended. ANSI-136-1, "Standard for the Safe Use of Lasers," may provide some helpful information in this area.

Illumination

Man, a few fish, and some birds are the only species to enjoy polychromatic vision - the ability to see things in "living color." Without proper lighting, this precious gift is wasted; also, readily apparent hazards are both overlooked and created. Illumination is so simple and so fundamental that it is often slighted. A brief tour through many facilities, often even those that pride themselves on their safety and health programs, will reveal many of the following hazards related to illumination:

1. Burned-out bulbs in seldom-used halls, stairways and storage areas.

2. Fluorescent light fixtures with one or more fluorescent tubes burned out or not functioning properly.

3. Light fixtures covered with dirt, grease or oil.

4. Little or no provision for emergency lighting.

5. Unlighted or dimly lighted exits and intersections.

6. Temporary (and usually inadequate) lighting that, over time, has become permanent.

7. Poorly placed lighting sources that cast shadows in the employee's work area.

8. Windows so dirty as to reduce the amount of light entering.

Terms often used in the design and evaluation of lighting are:

1. **Footcandle** - a unit of illumination. The illumination at a point on a surface one foot from, and perpendicular to, a "standard" candle.

2. **Glare** - any brightness that causes discomfort, annoyance, interference with vision or eye fatigue.

3. **Illumination level** - the amount of light falling on a surface, measured in footcandles (if square feet) or lux (if square meters).

4. **Intensity** - how much light a source emits in a given direction. The unit of measurement is the candela, sometimes referred to as "candlepower."

Standards of recommended illumination levels are available for certain areas, tasks and locations.

If it is felt that an illumination problem exists, light levels should be measured with an appropriate light meter. These readings should then be compared to applicable standards. If no standard can be found, discussion with employees will often provide some solutions.

Increasing illumination levels, changing the location of light sources, or even painting an area brighter or with more reflective colors usually provides significant improvements.

Remember, the most common lighting problems are listed in the first part of this section. It makes sense to rule these causes out before looking elsewhere for sources of illumination problems.

BIOLOGICAL HAZARDS

Bacteria, viruses, fungi, rickettsia, arthropods (insects), protozoa, helminths (worms), animals and plants can all present biological hazards. Too often attention is focused on infectious agents such as bacteria and viruses only to forget about the meter reader fighting off the crazed killer named "Fido" in Mrs. Smith's backyard, or the lineman that gets bitten by the poisonous snake or the groundkeeper who suffers from hay fever or poison ivy.

In general, biological hazards do not present as many hazardous exposures as other types of occupational health hazards. However, there are certain occupations with a significant number of exposures. Occupations involving food or food processing, plants and animals, laboratory personnel, hospital personnel, physicians, veterinarians and research personnel all have a high level of exposure to biological hazards. Miners and farmers are also at a greater risk because of their contact with the soil. A number of diseases are easily transmitted from animals to man (zoonotic diseases), and are of great concern to meat packers, laboratory researchers and veterinarians. Some of these diseases are leptospirosis (Weil's disease), brucellosis (undulant fever), tuberculosis, psittecosis and others.

Supervisors should identify all exposures to biological hazards that exist in their operation. Once they have been identified, qualified medical personnel, industrial hygienists and/or reference texts should be consulted to evaluate the severity of the hazard. Once the hazard has been evaluated, steps to control it should be established. Some commonly used methods of control include good personal hygiene procedures; insect control; personal protective equipment, such as filtration masks and protective gloves; adequate job procedures; proper sanitary facilities; employee education; monitoring; and good housekeeping.

ERGONOMICS

The fourth category of occupational health hazards is ergonomics. The term comes from two words which mean "work" and "law." Thus, ergonomics deals with the laws of work. It studies the relationship of man with machine by designing the work environment to "fit" the physical and mental characteristics of the work. Its use enables the design of jobs that not only increase a worker's skill and productivity but also safeguard the person from overexertion and stress. Ergonomic solutions to problems may be as simple as adding a footrest to a workbench, providing an adjustable stool or raising the work surface to a comfortable level. Or it may be as complicated as redesigning a hand tool to fit the worker's grip or altering material handling operations to avoid lifting, stooping or bending. Some major ergonomic concerns are:

Lifting

Improper lifting techniques and poor workplace design are the source of many thousands of needless back injuries each year. Back injuries account for approximately 33% of all compensation claims.

Poor workplace design contributed to the fatigue of these women, shown embossing shoe leather in 1919. It's a safe bet that whoever designed these workstations never had to work at them.

Figure 16-13   *Photo courtesy of Job Safety and Health*

Several lifting methods have been developed and taught to workers. The key factor in any lifting technique is to bend the knees when lifting. By doing this, back muscle and intervertebral disc strain is reduced. Other aspects of proper lifting, such as feet apart, load in close, etc., tend to be done automatically when a person bends the knees to lift.

Supervisors who teach their employees to bend their knees when they lift, who specify which lifts must be done by two or more people and who encourage their employees to use available lifting aids will significantly reduce their back injury cases. Even greater reductions can be achieved by designing out the need for lifting, particularly from awkward positions.

Fatigue

Many industries commonly work extended shifts, in which fatigue can become a problem and rotating shifts, which can create stress from disrupted bodily rhythmic cycles.

Fatigue can result from any number of factors, including monotony, excess noise, worry, poor eating habits, working too hard, working too long and others. Symptoms of chronic fatigue include an inability to sleep or rest and chronic substandard performance. Fatigue symptoms may include drowsiness and lack of stability while walking or moving; but the most common symptoms are forgetfulness, loss of self-control, distress, anxiety, irritability and emotional instability. The sufferer of chronic fatigue will be unable to focus attention on detail and may be unaware of substandard performance.

Metabolic Rhythm

An individual's bodily functions and activities vary throughout a 24-hour cycle as a person becomes adjusted to a day-work and night-rest cycle. The term "circadian rhythm" is sometimes used to describe this cycling of bodily functions and other metabolic phenomena that occur in people during a 24-hour period. When this cycle is disturbed by changes in a work shift, altered sleeping habits, travel across time zones, etc., substandard acts increase and efficiency decreases. An altered metabolic rhythm generally results in a downgrading of performance in the first 24-hour period after a change occurs, a critically poor performance the second 24-hour period, followed by gradual improvement over the next 5 days. After one week, an individual's metabolic rhythm becomes adjusted to near the previous efficiency.

Recent research indicates that if the shifts are rotated forward (with the clock) that there is less stress than if they are rotated backward (to an earlier shift). Some organizations have found it worthwhile to offer sufficient shift differentials to eliminate the need for rotating shifts.

A wise supervisor will take both fatigue and altered metabolic rhythm into account when making work assignments, particularly complicated work assignments with a high potential for serious loss.

Psychosocial Hazards

Psychosocial hazards are better known as employee stress. A great deal of research is currently being done in this area. Early indications are that worker stress is a major problem in industry today. Causes include working under unreasonable conditions, poor relationships with supervisors and co-workers, boredom and a sense of helplessness regarding control over one's own life. This latter cause of stress, i.e., helplessness regarding one's own destiny, appears to be the number one cause of stress in the workplace today.

Stress is more than just a "psychological imbalance." It often surfaces as a number of physical ailments. Hypertension and its consequences, cardiac failure, peptic ulcers, bowel disorders, headaches and other disorders are directly attributable to stress. Stressors (anything causing stress), if uncontrolled, may also lead to the excessive use of alcohol, tobacco and other drugs. These drugs, in turn, may cause disease, aggravate a pre-existing disease, or increase a worker's susceptibility to other occupational health disorders. Alcohol, for example, induces many liver enzymes to convert a relatively harmless substance into a potent toxin. Chronic alcohol abuse can cause liver failure or reduce the liver's ability to carry out normal bodily functions. With this reduced capacity to detoxify chemicals, exposure to an even slightly toxic substance may cause severe illness.

The cost of stress-related problems in terms of early retirement, absenteeism, labor turnover, accidents, decreased productivity, etc., is staggering. This area is rapidly emerging as a major concern and it behooves an alert employee, supervisor or manager to recognize excessive stress and take measures to control it.

Other sources of ergonomic stress are poorly designed work stations and controls/displays. Many work stations were designed with little consideration for the people who would be working there. Consequently, the jobs require unnecessary reaching, bending, and stretching, which lead to excessive fatigue and contribute to back and other problems. Supervisors are usually not consulted in the initial design of work stations. However, they may be involved in modifications. An excellent source of information for this is the people who do the work. It can often be an amazingly inexpensive way to increase safety, quality and productivity.

Improperly designed controls and displays are often confusing, especially in emergency conditions. For instance, most display needles and controls move to the right to indicate an increase and to the left to indicate a decrease. Having controls and displays which violate this principle is just asking for trouble. Also, color coding for controls (red for stop, green to start) should be consistent.

This entire area of ergonomics is still fairly young, but will have increasing impact in the years to come as more work is done in this area. Some simple changes (such as the angle of the handles on tools) have already made significant contributions to improved health and safety.

HAZARD COMMUNICATION (STANDARD 1910.1200)

In the United States, employers must be in compliance with the provisions of 1910.1200, including initial training for all current employees, by May 25, 1986. The standard applies to "...any chemical which is known to be present in the workplace in such a manner that employees may be exposed under normal conditions of use or in a foreseeable emergency." It requires "...comprehensive hazard communication programs, which are to include container labelling and other forms of warning, material safety data sheets and employee training." Similar requirements also exist in other countries.

Labels and Other Forms of Warning

Among other requirements, the standard requires employers to ensure that each container of hazardous chemicals in the workplace is labeled, tagged or marked with the following information:

- Identity of the hazardous chemical(s) contained therein
- Appropriate hazard warnings.

The employer may use signs, placards, process sheets, batch tickets, operating procedures or other such written materials in lieu of affixing labels to individual stationary process containers, as long as the alternative method identifies the containers to which it is applicable and conveys the required information. The written materials must be readily accessible to the employees in their work area throughout each work shift.

Material Safety Data Sheets

The employer must maintain copies of the required sheets for each hazardous chemical in the workplace, and must ensure that they are readily accessible during each work shift to employees in their work areas.

Material safety data sheets may be kept in any form, including operating procedures, and may be designed to cover groups of hazardous chemicals in a work area where it may be more appropriate to address the hazards of a process rather than individual hazardous chemicals.

Employee Information and Training

Employers must provide employees with information and training on hazardous chemicals in their work area at the time of initial assignment, and whenever a new hazard is introduced into their work area. Employees must be informed of:

- The requirements of 1910.1200
- Any operations in their work area where hazardous chemicals are present
- The location and availability of the written hazard communication program.

Employee training must include at least the following:

- Methods and observations that may be used to detect the presence or release of a hazardous chemical in the work area

- The physical and health hazards of the chemicals in the work area
- The measures employees can take to protect themselves from these hazards, including specific procedures the employer has implemented
- The details of the hazard communication program developed by the employer.

A SUPERVISORY PROGRAM TO MANAGE OCCUPATIONAL HEALTH HAZARDS

Recognition

How can the front line supervisor recognize potential occupational health hazards? What are some practical tools to help identify occupational health exposures? The following pointers should prove helpful:

1. **Use Material Safety Data Sheets.** Material Safety Data Sheets *(Figure 16-14)* are readily available from manufacturers and suppliers. A safety/loss control program should have written standards requiring suppliers to provide data sheets with the purchase of hazardous substances. These data sheets are usually kept on file in the purchasing department, at shipping and receiving or in the safety and health office. A review of these data sheets often identifies many chemical substances used in day-to-day operations.

   Hazardous materials data sheets aren't worth the paper they are printed on if they aren't used. Data sheets or information from them should be properly circulated between purchasing, receiving, safety and health/loss control, supervisory personnel and all other appropriate departments and personnel. Proper coordination is a critical part of any successful program. They can also be the topics of short talks at safety meetings.

2. Know the work processes. Occupational health hazards can be both purchased and produced. The Material Safety Data Sheet addresses exposures from purchased chemicals. How can a frontline manager recognize hazards produced during the work process? The answer is, "Know your work process." The frontline manager should become familiar with the by-products produced during the work process. It is not suggested that supervisors become organic chemists. However, they should possess a fundamental knowledge of the work oc-

Material Safety Data Sheet

Manufacturer's Name	Emergency Telephone No.
Address	Other Information Calls
Signature of Person Responsible for Preparation	Date Prepared

SECTION 1 - IDENTITY

Common Name (used on label) (Trade Name & Synonyms)	Case No.
Chemical Name	Chemical Family
Formula	

SECTION 2 - HAZARDOUS INGREDIENTS

Principal Hazardous Component(s) (chemical & common names)	Threshold Limit Value (units)

SECTION 3 - PHYSICAL & CHEMICAL CHARACTERISTICS (Fire & Explosion Data)

Boiling Point	Boiling Specific Gravity (H^{2}O=1)	Vapor Pressure (mm Hg)
Percent Volatile by Volume (%)	Vapor Density (Air = 1)	Evaporation Rate (_____ = 1)
Solubility in Water	Reactivity in Water	
Appearance and Odor		

Flash Point	Flammable Limits in Air % by Volume	Lower	Upper	Extinguisher Media	Auto-Ignition Temperature

Special Fire Fighting Procedures

Unusual Fire and Explosion Hazards

Figure 16-14

SECTION 4 - PHYSICAL HAZARDS

Stability	Unstable ☐ Stable ☐	Conditions to Avoid

Incompatibility
(Materials to Avoid)

Hazardous
Decomposition Products

Hazardous Polymerization	May Occur ☐ Will Not Occur ☐	Conditions to avoid

SECTION 5 - HEALTH HAZARDS

Threshold
Limit Value

Signs and Symptoms of Exposure	1. Acute Overexposure

2. Chronic
Overexposure

Medical Conditions Generally
Aggravated by Exposure

Chemical Listed as Carcinogen or Potential Carcinogen	National Toxicology Program	Yes ☐ No ☐	I.A.R.C. Monographs	Yes ☐ No ☐	OSHA	Yes ☐ No ☐
OSHA Permissible Exposure Limit	ACGIH Threshold Limit Value		Other Exposure Limit Used			

Emergency and
First Aid Procedures

1. Inhalation

2. Eyes

3. Skin

4. Ingestion

SECTION 6 - SPECIAL PROTECTION INFORMATION

Respiratory Protection
(Specify Type)

Ventilation	Local Exhaust	Mechanical (General)	Special	Other

Protective Gloves	Eye Protection

Other Protective
Clothing or Equipment

SECTION 7 - SPECIAL PRECAUTIONS AND SPILL/LEAK PROCEDURES

Precautions to be Taken
in Handling and Storage

Other
Precautions

Steps to be Taken in Case
Material is Released or Spilled

Waste Disposal
Methods

IMPORTANT
Do not leave any blank spaces. If required information is unavailable, unknown or does not apply, so indicate

Figure 16-14 (continued)

curring in their operations in order to identify occupational health hazards produced there. A frontline manager should know that when lead fittings are welded together lead fumes are generated; that unvented salamanders and certain blast furnaces produce carbon monoxide gases; that certain electroplating operations involve hydrogen cyanide and that if acid is combined with this chemical, hydrogen cyanide gas is produced. Many other examples could be given to make the point. Frontline managers must know their operations before they can begin to identify any chemical hazards involved.

3. Inspections. Simple walk-through inspections of a work area can readily identify many occupational health hazards. In many cases, using one's natural senses may be all that is needed. For example, if during an informal walk-through inspection of a production area a colleague who is standing three feet away from you cannot hear what you are saying unless you shout, the area probably presents a noise hazard with sound levels approaching 85-90dB(A). Another example might involve a walk-through tour of a maintenance shop. As you entered the shop you noticed a fruity odor even though you are nowhere near any degreasing operation. You also notice that even though every light in the place is turned on you still had a difficult time seeing that grease spot you just slipped and fell on. Even without knowing the concentration of that organic solvent you smelled or the exact foot-candles of light present in the work area, you have just identified several hazardous occupational health exposures and poor housekeeping procedures. Many chemicals have known odor threshold values given in parts per million. If an individual happens to smell a chemical, it can be assumed that a concentration equal to or greater than the odor threshold exists. Knowing the odor threshold often provides a rough estimate of the chemical concentration in a given area. However, it should be cautioned that this is a very imprecise approach and that there may be hazards that are not smelled.

4. Review job/task analyses. A review of existing job/task analyses often identifies exposures to occupational health hazards. Conducting new job/task analyses and reviewing previously completed job/task analyses should also provide ideas on how to control identified occupational health exposures.

5. Recalling past experiences. Recall previous conversations with employees and the complaints that were expressed. Have there been complaints of headaches, tinnitus (ringing in the ears), muffled hearing when the work shift ends, sore eyes, itching skin? Comments of this nature may indicate existing occupational health hazards. Complaints are often indicators of near-misses and could point to areas needing additional attention.

6. Review old accident investigation reports. Previous accident investigations often contain information on past occupational health hazards. As an old history professor once said, "Whoever said that history repeats itself is nuts. It doesn't. But the lessons that can be learned from studying our predecessors' mistakes should help us solve present and future challenges." This adage applies to the review of old accident reports. The basic causes which were identified may help to solve existing problems, as well as prevent the repetition of old mistakes.

7. Utilize available professional support. Occupational health specialists, industrial hygienists, sampling technicians, medical personnel, etc., may be available to help you. Their training and expertise is usually strong in areas where the frontline manager is weak. They are more familiar with chemical reactions and by-products from those reactions and they have the technical qualifications to conduct sound level measurements, air monitorings, light meter readings, etc. They are able to translate the medical and scientific jargon often found on data sheets and other specific documents into understandable terms. They can evaluate the results of their testing and formulate a plan for corrective actions.

8. An occupational health hazard survey sheet or checklist can be a good tool used by frontline managers or professional support personnel to identify occupational health exposures. *Figure 16-15* is a sample occupational health survey form. It deals specifically with raw materials and by-products encountered on the job. It can be easily modified to include physical and biological exposures that may also be encountered on a job.

Evaluation

Once the existence of an occupational health exposure has been recognized, it must be evaluated to determine the potential effects it will have on the

OCCUPATIONAL HEALTH SURVEY

Operation _____

Surveyed by _____

Date _____

Direction _____ Date _____

Direction _____ Date _____

Data Sources _____

OCCUPATION	NATURE OF JOB/TASKS	OCCUPATIONAL HEALTH HAZARDS	CONTROL MEASURES									COMMENTS AND EXPLANATION
			ELIMINATE OR SUBSTITUTE	LOCAL EXHAUST	GENERAL VENTILATION	WET DOWN	PPE	SHIELDING	ISOLATION	ADMINISTRATIVE PRACTICE	WORK PRACTICE	

Figure 16-15

employee, machinery and/or equipment. Oftentimes, people think of a hazard evaluation as simply monitoring of the degree of employee exposure. It is recognized that monitoring is an important part of the evaluation process, but most front line managers are simply not qualified to take air, water, sound or illumination measurements. However, the evaluation process involves much more than simply monitoring exposures and there is quite a bit that the frontline managers can do to evaluate and/or recognize occupational health hazards on their operations.

When evaluating an occupational health hazard, one must consider the concept of toxicity vs. hazard. *Toxicity* is the *ability* of a substance to produce harm once it reaches a susceptible site in or on the body. *Hazardous* refers to the likelihood that it will produce harm. It is the use of a substance as much as the degree of toxicity that determines the hazard. For example, chromates are extremely toxic to the skin and respiratory tract. They are widely used in low concentrations as pigments in paints. If paint containing chromates is brushed on (not sprayed) and if there is no skin contact then there is a low hazard situation (i.e., low concentration, no skin contact, little chance for inhalation) with a highly toxic material.

On the other hand, freons (halogenated hydrocarbons) are relatively non-toxic but can pose a significant hazard if used in an enclosed space where they might displace oxygen or where open flames can cause toxic decomposition products (i.e., deadly phosgene gas).

Only when all pertinent data on the degree or dosage of the exposure concentration, the frequency of the exposures, the length of exposure and the toxicity of the particular agent involved have been collected can the degree of hazard that exists be evaluated. Many factors interrelate to produce a given hazard. Factors such as dosage, route of exposure, type of chemical formulation, humidity, temperature, individual variation, length of exposure, frequency of exposure, drug interactions and more should all be evaluated when assessing the degree of hazard presented by a particular occupational health agent. (Refer to *Figure 16-2.*)

The Material Safety Data Sheet can be of great help in evaluating occupational health hazards. Data sheets identify whether or not any one of 30 materials, e.g., asbestos, silica, benzene, etc., are components of the chemical compound being used. Data sheets provide a large amount of information needed to evaluate the possible hazard or hazards presented by a particular

chemical. Other sources of information are the American Industrial Hygiene Association's Hygienic Guide series; the American Conference of Governmental Industrial Hygienist - TLV data booklet; various journals; and a number of texts, including the National Fire Protection Association's handbook, Patty's Industrial Hygiene and Toxicology texts, National Safety Council's Fundamentals of Industrial Hygiene, Sax's Dangerous Properties of Industrial Materials and many more.

The supervisor should recognize that, in many situations, the evaluation of an occupational health hazard should be deferred to specially trained and qualified personnel.

Control

The frontline manager should be aware of the various techniques used to control occupational health hazards. *Figure 16-16* shows several techniques com-

---

CONTROL

General methods of controlling harmful environmental factors or stresses include the following:

Engineering Controls include eliminating the hazard altogether, substituting a less hazardous process, isolation or enclosure, local exhaust, general ventilation, wetting-down process, shielding, shock, or vibration mounting and machinery or workplace redesign.

Work Practices involve activities such as worker education and training, good housekeeping, labeling, proper storage, personal hygiene, rules compliance and behavior reinforcement.

Administrative Controls involve the scheduling of workers to minimize hazardous exposures and the installation of warning and alarm systems to notify workers when they have received a maximum allowable exposure.

Personal Protective Equipment should be used as a last resort.

Figure 16-16

monly used. Many of these controls fall outside the realm of the supervisor's responsibilities and authority; however, many do not. Good housekeeping, personal hygiene, employee education, the use of personal protective equipment, the establishment of and conformity to job/task procedures, the assurance that all chemical hazards are properly labeled and stored and the initial recognition of occupational health hazards all depend heavily on frontline managers. Without their help and guidance in these areas, safety and industrial hygiene control will be of little value.

Three methods of control strongly influenced by the frontline manager, but not often discussed in detail, are proper use, storage and maintenance of personal protective equipment, including such items as gloves, protective footwear, aprons, eye protection, ear protection, head protection, respirators, barrier creams and protective lotions. A critical part of any personal protective equipment program is the proper use, storage and maintenance of respirators. Respirators should be used only under four conditions:

1. To reduce exposures while other controls are being implemented.

2. To supplement other control measures.

3. To provide protection during activities such as maintenance and repairs when other controls are not feasible.

4. To provide protection during emergencies.

Respirators do not in any way affect the source of an exposure and by themselves may not provide adequate protection. Therefore, respirators should rarely be considered as a primary means of controlling any hazard.

The flowchart in *Figure 16-17* should provide guidance for the selection of an appropriate respirator. The supervisor's primary job in a respiratory protection program is to ensure that all respirators are properly used, stored and monitored. The selection of an appropriate respirator should often be deferred to qualified personnel.

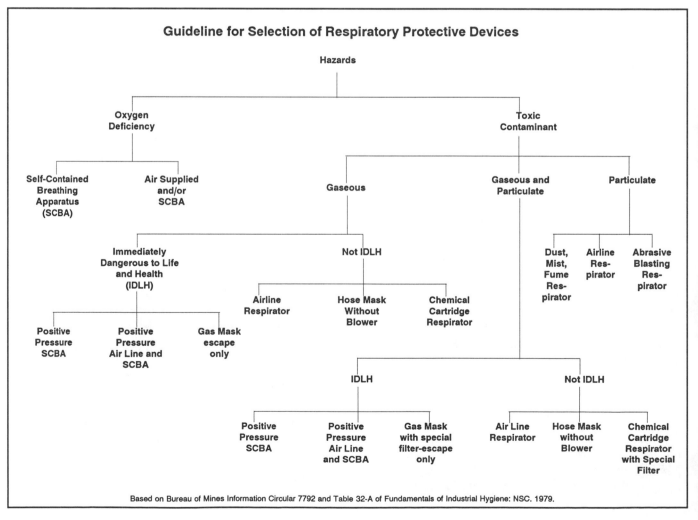

Guideline for Selection of Respiratory Protective Devices

Based on Bureau of Mines Information Circular 7792 and Table 32-A of Fundamentals of Industrial Hygiene: NSC. 1979.

Figure 16-17

Respirators should be stored in such a way as to be protected against dust, sunlight, heat, extreme cold, excessive moisture and damaging chemicals. Respirators for emergency use should be quickly accessible at all times and should be stored in compartments built specifically for this purpose. When stored, the respirator's facepiece and exhalation valve should rest in normal position so as not to distort the elastomer. When inspecting the respirators, check for cracks in the facepiece, inflexibility and normal function of the exhalation valves. Also, inspect the headbands, connecting tubes, fittings and canisters/cartridges to ensure that they are working properly. The cartridge or canister should be replaced when: 1) it has been used for its specified lifetime; 2) when vapors can be smelled inside the mask; 3) when breathing becomes difficult; or 4) when the canister's shelf life has expired (whichever comes first).

Respirators assigned to an individual should be cleaned daily. The facepiece should be stripped of cartridge and washed in warm water with a mild detergent and then either hand or air dried.

Special problems such as glasses or facial hair often emerge and confound the supervisor's efforts to manage a successful respirator program. Special full-face respirators are designed to accommodate the wearing of glasses beneath them. The problems associated with facial hair aren't so easily resolved. Facial hair prevents the respirator from obtaining a proper seal, thus reducing its effectiveness. Companies have resolved this problem by forbidding facial hair if it interferes with the function of the respirator. This doesn't mean that the entire beard, sideburn or mustache must be removed. Oftentimes part of the facial hair can be trimmed to allow a proper seal. If this policy is not possible at your plant, then a pressure-demand self-contained breathing apparatus or positive pressure air-line system may be used. These systems apply a constant positive pressure within the face-mask of a full-face respirator and prevent the inhalation of contaminants. A poor seal will decrease the efficiency of this system, however, and this decreased efficiency should be considered when formulating a respiratory protection program.

The third area, especially amenable to control by the frontline manager, is the proper storage of hazardous materials. Hazardous materials for the purposes of this discussion include acids, caustics, flammable and combustible liquids. A proper storage area should exist for storing hazardous materials. This storage area should be isolated, yet conveniently accessible. The walls and floor should be constructed of impermeable material (e.g., concrete). Good drainage should exist to facilitate easy clean-up of spills. The storage area should be well ventilated (a minimum exhaust of one cubic foot per minute per square foot of floor area, but not less than 150 cubic feet per minute). The National Fire Prevention Association's Standard No. 251 presents specifications for building and construction materials when designing a hazardous material storage room. Proper electrical grounding must exist for all electrical exposures in the storage area.

An approved storage cabinet is supposed to limit the internal temperature to a maximum of 325F when exposed to fire for ten minutes. Approved storage cabinets must also be labeled FLAMMABLE - KEEP FIRE AWAY. No more than 120 gallons of Class I, Class II or Class III A (flash points at or above 140F but below 200F) materials are permitted to be stored in a single cabinet, and no more than three such cabinets are allowed in one area unless they are separated by at least 100 feet. No more than 60 of the 120 gallons stored in approved cabinets can be Class I and II liquids. The National Fire Prevention Association Standard No. 30, "Flammable and Combustible Liquids Code," and various regulatory agencies established conditions and procedures for safe storage of flammable and combustible liquids.

Other suggestions for proper chemical storage include: properly label all chemicals; chemicals should be dispensed by authorized personnel only; store highly toxic chemicals in containers distinctively shaped; never stack drums containing more than 30 gallons on top of one another; practice good housekeeping; allow at least 24 inches between sprinkler heads and stored items; do not block or obscure fire alarms, electrical switch boxes, emergency lighting and first aid equipment; consider storing flammable and corrosive material on trays; and keep incompatible chemicals segregated.

This last point, keeping incompatible chemicals segregated, is very important. When certain chemicals are combined, explosions or the formation of highly toxic and/or flammable substances may occur. Certain water-sensitive substances such as potassium, sodium, lithium, calcium and others liberate explosive hydrogen gas when contacted with water vapors. Chemicals such as nitrides, sulfides, arsenides and others release volatile flammables when contacted with moisture. Some chemicals called oxidizers release oxygen when exposed to heat, moisture or other chemicals. These chemicals provide their own source of oxygen in the event of a fire and are very difficult to extinguish. Some examples of oxidizers are peroxides, organic nitrates, nitrites, chlorates, perborates and permanganate. *Figure 16-18* lists various chemicals and their incompatible counterparts. A good reference on incompatible chemicals is the NFPA Pamphlet 491 M found in the NFPA's Fire Protection Guide on Hazardous Material.

A successful occupational health program needs support and commitment from all levels of management. If employees feel that management lacks commitment to the occupational health program or simply doesn't care about the employee's well-being, then employee cooperation will be minimal. True concern and honest intent can overcome many structural deficiencies in an occupational health program, but the most comprehensive program cannot overcome managerial or employee indifference.

CORE CONCEPTS IN REVIEW

New research into old problems, plus additional exposures created by new technology, combine to create tremendous management **challenges regarding occupational health**. Managers at all levels, especially frontline, are in ideal positions to control occupational health hazards. To do so, some of the "mystery" must be removed from the field by means of information/communication/education. Four common categories of occupational health hazards are:

1. **Chemical**
   (mist/vapor/gas/smoke/dust/aerosol/fume).

2. **Physical** (noise/temperature/illumination/vibration/radiation/pressure).

3. **Biological** (bacteria/virus/fungus/parasite).

4. **Ergonomic** (monotony/work pressure/overload/body positions/metobolic cycles/psychosocial hazards).

The following are important **variables to consider when evaluating the degree of hazard of an occupational health exposure**:

1. Chemical concentration
2. Route of exposure (inhalation, ingestion, absorption)
3. Length of exposure
4. Individual variation (age, sex, race, etc.)
5. Frequency of exposure
6. Previous work experience
7. Drug interactions
8. Chemical formulation
9. Controls in use
10. Environment (temperature, humidity, etc.)

The use of **solvents creates the most common vapor hazards**; not only health hazards but also fire and explosion hazards. Anyone handling solvents should be familiar with:

1. The solvent's flash point, flammable range, vapor pressure and vapor density
2. The type and method of application
3. The type and length of worker exposure
4. The temperature at which the solvent will be used
5. The exposed surface area of the solvent
6. The evaporation rate
7. The toxic properties
8. The general and local ventilation provided
9. The pattern and direction of airflow in the work area
10. The expected vapor concentration
11. The proper storage procedures
12. The proper labeling procedures
13. The proper disposal procedures for both solvent and solvent contaminant materials

The **common methods for control** of various occupational health hazards are:

1. **Air Contaminants**

   a. Substitution or replacement
   b. Isolation of operation
   c. Elimination or reduction of employee exposure
   d. Change in process or operation
   e. Local exhaust
   f. Ventilation
   g. Wetting-down methods
   h. Housekeeping
   i. Personal protective equipment
   j. Personal hygiene
   k. Air monitoring

2. **Industrial Skin Diseases**

   a. Substitution of substances

INCOMPATIBLE CHEMICALS

THESE CHEMICALS	SHOULD NOT BE CONTACTED WITH →	THESE CHEMICALS
Acetic acid	Chromic acid, ethylene glycol, hydroxyl-containing compounds, nitric acid, perchloric aid, permanganates and peroxides	
Acetone	Bromine, chlorine, nitric acid and sulfuric acid	
Acetylene	Bromine, chlorine, copper, mercury and silver	
Alkaline and alkaline earth metals such as calcium, cesium, lithium, magnesium, potassium and sodium.	Carbon dioxide, chlorinated hydrocarbons and water	
Aluminum and its alloys (particularly powders)	Acid or alkaline solutions, ammonium persulfate and water chlorates, chlorinated compounds, nitrates and organic compounds in nitrate/nitrite salt baths	
Ammonia (anhydrous)	Bromine, calcium hypochlorite, chlorine, hydrofluoric acid, iodine, mercury and silver	
Ammonium nitrate	Acids, chlorates, chlorides, lead, metallic nirates, metal powders, finely divided organics or combustibles, sulfur and zinc	
Ammonium perchlorate, permanganate or persulfate	Combustible materials: oxidizing materials such as acids, chlorates and nitrates	
Aniline	Hydrogen peroxide or nitric acid	
Barium peroxide	Combustible organics, oxidizable materials and water	
Barium rhodanide	Sodium nitrate	
Bismuth and its alloys	Perchloric acid	
Bromine	Acetone, acetylene, ammonia, benzene, butadiene, butane and other petroleum gases, hydrogen, finely divided metals, sodium carbide and turpentine	
Calcium carbide	Moisture (in air) or water	
Calcium hypochlorite	(Activated) ammonia or carbon	
Calcium oxide	Water	
Carbon, activated	Calcium hypochlorite	
Chlorates	Acids, aluminum, ammonium salts, cyanides, phosphorous, metal powders, oxidizable organics or other combustibles, sugar, sulfides and sulfur	
Chlorine	Acetone, acetylene, ammonia, benzene, butadine, butane and other petroleum gases, hydrogen, metal powders, sodium carbide and turpentine	
Chlorine dioxide	Ammonia, hydrogen sulfide, methane and phosphine	
Chromic acid	Acetic acid (glacial), acetic anhydride, alcohols, combustible materials, flammable liquids, glycerine, napthalene, nitric acid, sulfur and turpentine	
Copper	Acetylene, hydrogen peroxide	
Cumene hydroperoxide	Acids (mineral or organic)	
Cyanides	Acids or alkalies	
Fluorine	Most materials	
Hydrocarbons such as benzene, butane, gasoline, propane, turpentine, etc.	Bromine, chlorine, chromic acid, flourine, hydrogen peroxide and sodium peroxide	
Hydrocyanic acid or anhydrous hydrogen fluoride	Alkalies and nitric acid	
Hydrogen peroxide (3%)	Ammonia (anhydrous or aqueous)	
Hydrogen peroxide (30% or 90%)	Chromium, copper, iron, most metals or their salts. Same as 3% hydrogen peroxide plus aniline, any flammable liquids, combustible materials, nitromethane and all other organic matter	
Hydrogen sulfide	Fuming nitric acid or oxidizing gases	
Iodine	Acetylene, ammonia (anhydrous and aqueous) and hydrogen	
Lithium	Acids, moisture in air and water	

THESE CHEMICALS	SHOULD NOT BE CONTACTED WITH →	THESE CHEMICALS
Lithium aluminum hydride	Air, chlorinated hydrocarbons, carbon dioxide, ethyl acetate and water	
Magnesium (particularly powder)	Carbonates, chlorates, heavy metal oxalates or oxides, nitrates, perchlorates, peroxides, phosphates and sulfates	
Mercury	Acetylene, alkali metals, ammonia, nitric acid with ethanol and oxalic acid	
Mercuric oxide	Sulfur	
Nitrates	Combustible materials, esters, phosphorous, sodium acetate, stannous chloride, water and zinc powder	
Nitric acid (concentrated)	Acetic acid, aniline, chromic acid, flammable gases and liquids, hydrocyanic acid, hydrogen sulfide and nitratable substances	
Nitric acid	Alcohols and other oxidizable organic material, hydroiodic acid (hydrogn iodide), magnesium or other metals, phosphorous and thiophene	
Nitrites	Potassium or sodium cyanide, ammonium salts	
Nitro paraffins	Inorganic alkalies	
Oxalic acid	Mercury or silver	
Oxygen (liquid or enriched air)	Flammable gases, liquids, or solids such as acetone, acetylene, grease, hydrogen, oils and phosphorous	
Perchlorates	See chlorates	
Perchloric acid	Acetic anhydride, alcohols, bismuth and its alloys, grease, oils or any organic materials and reducing agents	
Peroxides (organic)	Acids (mineral or organic)	
Phosphorous	Chlorates and perchlorates, nitrates and nitric acid	
Phosphorous (red)	Oxidizing materials	
Phosphorous (white)	Air (oxygen) or other oxidizing materials	
Phosphorous pentoxide	Organic compounds or water	
Picric acid	Ammonia heated with oxides or salts of heavy metals and friction with oxidizing agents	
Potassium	Air (moisture and/or oxygen) or water	
Potassium chlorate or perchlorate	Acids or their vapors, combustible materials, especially organic solvents, phosphorous and sulfur	
Potassium permanganate	Benzaldehyde, ethylene glycol, glycerin and sulfuric acid	
Silver	Acetylene, ammonium compounds, nitric acid with ethanol, oxalic acid and tartaric acid	
Sodium amide	Air (moisture and oxygen) or water	
Sodium carbide	Moisture (in air) or water	
Sodium chlorate	Acids, ammonium salts, oxidizable materials and sulfur	
Sodium hydrosulfite	Air (moisture) or combustible materials	
Sodium nitrate	Ammonium nitrate or other ammonium salts, antimony, cyanides	
Sodium nitrite	Ammonium nitrate or other ammonium salts, cyanides	
Sodium oxide	Water, any free acid	
Sodium peroxide	Acetic acid (glacial), acetic anhydride, alcohols, benzaldehyde, carbon disulfide, ethyl acetate, ethylene glycol, fufural, glycerine, methyl acetate and other oxidizable substances	
Sulfur	Any oxidizing materials	
Sulfuric acid	Chlorates, perchlorates and permanganates	
Water	Acetyl chloride, alkaline and alkaline earth metals, their hydrides and oxides, barium peroxide, carbides, chromic acid, phosphorous oxychloride, phosphorous pentachloride, phosphorous pentoxide, sulfuric acid and sulfur trioxide, etc.	
Zinc (particularly powder)	Acids or water	
Zinc chlorate	Acids or organic materials	
Zirconium (particularly powder)	Carbon tetrachloride and other halogenated hydrocarbons, peroxides, sodium bicarbonate and water	

Reprinted by permission from: THE SAFETY HANDBOOK, Exxon Research and Engineering Company

Figure 16-18

b. Engineering controls
c. Standard practices
d. Personal protective equipment
e. Personnel placement

3. **Noise**

a. Reduction at its source
b. Reduction of noise transmitted
c. Personal protective equipment
d. Administrative procedures

4. **Vibration**

a. Source reduction
b. Isolation
c. Dampening

5. **Cold**

a. Proper clothing
b. Good physical condition
c. Buddy system

6. **Heat**

a. Ventilation
b. Equipment and process change
c. Work-saving devices
d. Heat shields and barriers
e. Selection and periodic examination of workers
f. Work controls such as schedules and rest periods
g. Worker training
h. Replacement of body fluids
i. Acclimatization
j. Personal protective equipment

7. **Radiation**

a. Education and training
b. Exposure monitoring
c. Heat shields and reflective clothing
d. Personal protective equipment
e. Proper job procedures
f. Effective maintenance

8. **Illumination**

a. Measure light levels; meet lighting standards
b. Use brighter, more reflective colors
c. Maintain lighting systems (fixtures, bulbs, etc.)
d. Keep windows, bulbs, etc., clean
e. Place lights properly

9. **Biological Hazards**

a. Employee education

b. Monitoring
c. Personal hygiene
d. Insect control
e. Proper job procedures
f. Personal protective equipment
g. Proper sanitary facilities
h. Good housekeeping

10. **Ergonomics**

a. Design and engineering
b. Education and training
c. Administrative controls (such as shift scheduling)
d. Labor-saving devices

11. **Psychosocial Hazards**

a. Management/Supervisory/Leadership training
b. Coaching/Counseling/Employee Assistance Programs
c. Positive behavior reinforcement

Supervisory management of occupational health hazards boils down to: **recognition, evaluation and control.**

1. **Recognition** of potential problems requires that supervisors:
   a. Use Material Safety Data Sheets
   b. Know the work processes
   c. Conduct effective inspections
   d. Prepare and review job/task procedures
   e. Recall past incidents
   f. Review existing investigation reports
   g. Use available professional support
   h. Use a health hazard survey sheet or checklist

2. **Evaluation** includes monitoring and measuring air samples, water samples, sound levels, illumination, etc., and is usually done by trained specialists. Supervisors can provide valuable information about the workplace environment, employee experiences and the work processes that could affect hazard levels.

3. **Control** techniques which depend heavily upon supervisors include:
   a. Good housekeeping
   b. Personal hygiene
   c. Employee training
   d. Proper job procedures
   e. Proper job instruction
   f. Job observation
   g. Rules compliance

h. Protective equipment compliance
i. Proper posting and labeling
j. Proper storage of hazardous materials
k. Group communications
l. Personal safety and health contacts

KEY QUESTIONS

1. List five similarities between an occupational health program and a safety program.

2. What are the three steps in dealing with an occupational health hazard?

3. Give the four major categories of occupational health exposures and give several examples of each.

4. List 10 techniques for controlling occupational health hazards.

5. Define these terms in your own words: dust, fumes, vapor, gas, mist and smoke. Know where to look for specific scientific definitions (e.g., a good reference text).

6. List three criteria that must be considered when evaluating a hazard.

7. What is the difference between ionizing and non-ionizing radiation? Give two examples of each.

8. What are some typical illumination hazards found in general industry?

9. What is the difference between hazardous and toxic?

10. What do PEL, TLV-C, STEL, TLV-TWA stand for? Explain their meaning.

11. What is noise?

12. When should the use of personal protective equipment be considered?

13. List three situations that should tip you off to a noise problem in your working area.

14. What is the key to any proper lifting technique?

15. What are four causes of stress in the work environment and what are five consequences of this stress?

16. What are six techniques a supervisor can use to help identify his or her occupational health exposures?

17. Discuss what tools a supervisor should use in evaluating his or her health hazard.

18. What information should all good labels contain? List five items.

19. Assuming that you have a proper storage area for your hazardous materials, list ten factors that must be considered before you stock this area.

PRACTICAL APPLICATIONS SUMMARY

S – For Supervisors
E – For Executives
C – For Safety/Loss Control Coordinators

	S	E	C
1. Issue a policy statement indicating management's support for, and commitment to, an occupational health program.		x	
2. Ensure that the policy statement is circulated to everyone in the organization.		x	
3. Ensure that occupational health subjects are part of management meetings.		x	
4. Periodically participate in safety and health tours of the facilities.		x	
5. Review all major loss occupational health incidents.		x	
6. Ensure that occupational health is part of the management audit program.		x	
7. Maintain a safe and healthful work environment.	x	x	x
8. Instruct and guide employees.	x		
9. Enforce proper housekeeping.	x		
10. Prevent the consumption of food, beverages and tobacco in unauthorized work areas.	x		
11. Inform the appropriate departments of hazardous conditions or operations.	x		
12. Inform medical personnel of hazardous exposures and send employees involved to medical facility.	x		
13. Ensure proper use of personal protective equipment.	x	x	x
14. Administer disciplinary action for rules violations.	x		
15. Ensure that all toxic materials used in the work area are properly labelled.	x		
16. Ensure that all toxic materials used in the work area are properly stored.	x		
17. Ensure adequate monitoring and measuring of occupational health hazards.	x	x	x
18. Include occupational health subjects in group safety and health meetings and personal contacts.	x		
19. Coordinate educational, purchasing, engineering, safety, occupational health, supervisory and enforcement activities.			x
20. Provide educational material.			x
21. Conduct surveys and audits.			x
22. Recommend program improvements.	x	x	x
23. Reinforce and recognize good performance for safety and health.	x	x	x

CHAPTER 17

FIRE LOSS CONTROL

"Is fire friend or foe? It can be either. The difference is *control*. Just as our ancestors learned to control fire well enough to put it to work for the betterment of human society, so must each of us do our individual part — every day of our lives — to control fire as a friend and to prevent fire a a foe."
— Global Guardian

INTRODUCTION

Frontline supervisors have a very important role in fire prevention and control. They may sometimes believe the bulk of this responsibility rests with engineers who design facilities and methods with an eye to fire prevention, or with professional firefighters, or even with fire inspectors who recommend installation of portable fire extinguishers or sprinkler systems. Such is not the case. A key person in any effective fire loss control program is the frontline supervisor. Here are some reasons why:

- Engineers can design work methods and workplaces to facilitate fire loss control efforts. They can use fire retardant materials, provide adequate means of exit, minimize hazards from inadequate wiring or heating systems and design methods for fire control. Such things are helpful in reducing the risk of fire loss, but they are not enough. Only the supervisors have the day-to-day knowledge of the materials manufactured, used or stored within the facility or the hazards created by day-to-day conditions, practices and changes. Only the supervisors can manage the operation for ongoing fire prevention and control.

- Professional firefighters are invaluable in controlling loss from fire. They are trained in fire extinguishment and control, but usually are involved only *after* a fire has started. Their effectiveness depends on the type of fire, the fuel available for the fire, accessibility to the area of the fire and the length of time the fire has been burning before they arrive. They have little or no control over these variables. But supervisors do!

- "Outside" fire inspectors from governmental or insurance agencies can make periodic inspections for visible or apparent fire hazards. They are trained experts in their field, but they do not know all the details of the operation or the hour-by-hour conditions. They may visit the facility two, three or four times a year, but they do not spend every day there — as supervisors do. Only supervisors are in a position to manage the daily processes, procedures, practices and potential hazards.

For reasons such as these, supervisors are a key to any effective fire loss control program. They are in the best position to manage for meeting the prime objective — *fire prevention*.

THE NATURE OF FIRE

The behavior of fire from its inception through the complete burning process is entirely predictable. It follows well-defined patterns, often referred to as the "Nature of Fire." Fire itself is a chemical reaction, known as combustion, in which combustible material is oxidized rapidly. This causes a release of energy in the form of heat and light. For many years this was graphically depicted as a triangle consisting of oxygen, fuel and heat (*Figure 17-1*). Recently, a

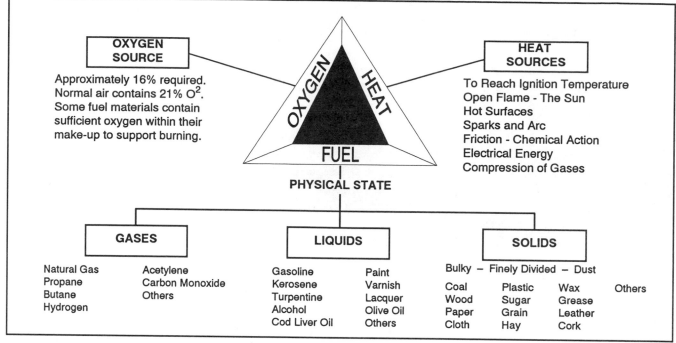

OXYGEN SOURCE
Approximately 16% required. Normal air contains 21% O^2. Some fuel materials contain sufficient oxygen within their make-up to support burning.

HEAT SOURCES
To Reach Ignition Temperature
Open Flame - The Sun
Hot Surfaces
Sparks and Arc
Friction - Chemical Action
Electrical Energy
Compression of Gases

OXYGEN HEAT FUEL

PHYSICAL STATE

GASES

Natural Gas	Acetylene
Propane	Carbon Monoxide
Butane	Others
Hydrogen	

LIQUIDS

Gasoline	Paint
Kerosene	Varnish
Turpentine	Lacquer
Alcohol	Olive Oil
Cod Liver Oil	Others

SOLIDS

Bulky – Finely Divided – Dust

Coal	Plastic	Wax	Others
Wood	Sugar	Grease	
Paper	Grain	Leather	
Cloth	Hay	Cork	

Figure 17-1

refinement has developed which promotes better understanding of both burning and extinguishment. In this new concept the triangle has been replaced by a four-sided geometric figure called a "tetrahedron" or triangular pyramid (*Figure 17-2*). One side is known as the chemical chain reaction. Thus the four sides are oxygen, fuel, heat and the chain reaction. Removal of any one of these elements rapidly extinguishes the fire.

- *Fuel* - This element is defined as any material that can be oxidized rapidly, such as wood, paper, oil, grease, certain metals, dust, gases and so forth. Fires are classified according to the type of fuel involved (as discussed later).

- *Oxygen* - Fire needs only 16% oxygen to burn. The air we breath includes 21% oxygen. So fuel is normally surrounded by plenty of oxygen to support burning. The more oxygen available, the more intense the fire becomes. Perhaps the best example of this is the familiar welding torch which combines acetylene gas with pure oxygen to produce extremely hot temperatures. The oxygen makes it burn much hotter than it would by itself. Some fuels contain sufficient oxygen within their make-up to support burning and, therefore, may burn in an oxygen-free environment.

- *Heat* - Often confused with temperature, heat is a type of energy said to be in "disorder," while temperature is a measure of that disorder. The heat of a fire may start at a low temperature, may rise rapidly as the fire continues to consume fuel, and may reach several thousand degrees. Heat can also reignite a fire that has been "put out" if the extinguishing agent has not cooled it sufficiently.

- *Chemical Chain Reaction* - This reaction begins very early in the burning process and grows in intensity, feeding the fire. As the fire begins,

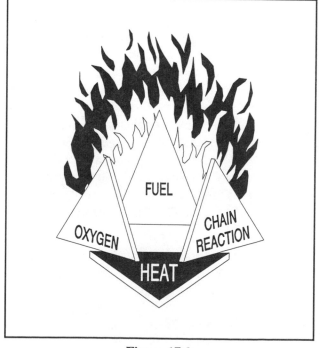

Figure 17-2

"atomic molecules" or "free radicals" are thrown off and immediately drawn back into the base of the fire, as pictured in *Figure 17-3*. These preheated atoms intensify the blaze by providing additional fuel, gases and oxygen. Under the old triangle concept of fire, it was felt that the fuel itself did not burn, but was heated until it gave off a gas — which burned so close to the fuel that it *appeared* the fuel was burning. Under the newer pyramid concept, this has been revised. It is now felt that the fuel is initially heated, putting off a gas or vapor that is ignited; but as the fire sets up the chain reaction, the fuel itself begins to burn, and may continue until it's all consumed. While the action depicted in this process seems like a step-by-step process, it is not. For all practical purposes, it all occurs instantaneously.

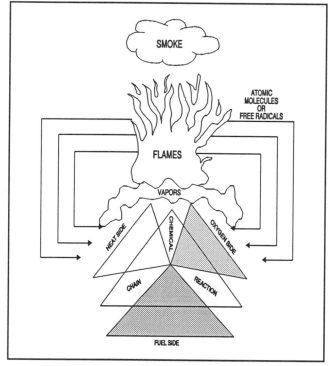

Figure 17-3: The Chemical Chain Reaction

FIRE EXTINGUISHING METHODS

The best method of stopping a fire depends on its size and the type of fuel involved. Some fires are best fought by attacking the supply of oxygen. With others it is more practical to remove the fuel or heat. Certain types of fires (such as in petroleum storage tanks, rail-car tankers or boat cargos) require very detailed plans that combine several techniques like cooling, oxygen depletion and dilution of the fuel, all in sequential steps. The danger of explosions must also be considered, since some fuels will react violently to some extinguishing agents. An example is water applied to burning liquids or metals.

Planning an effective method of combating fires requires understanding of these four extinguishment methods

1. Remove the fuel
2. Exclude the oxygen
3. Reduce the heat
4. Interrupt the chain reaction.

Remove the Fuel

Removal of fuel to extinguish fire is very effective, but is not always practical or even possible. Methods of fuel removal include turning off fuel supply valves, pumping flammable liquids from a burning tank or removing unburned portions of solid combustibles. Removal of fuel can also be accomplished by diluting some liquid materials, such as ethyl alcohol, which is soluble in water. Foam or other surface-active agents can be used to float on the surface of flammable liquids to contain the flammable vapors and so remove fuel from the combustion process.

Exclude the Oxygen

Smothering extinguishes fires by separating or excluding the oxygen from the other elements that make a fire. A common example of this is extinguishing a grease fire in a frying pan by placing a cover on the pan. Smothering is often an easy method of extinguishment. However, some fires cannot be put out by smothering. Examples include some plastics such as cellulose nitrate, metals like titanium, and certain other fuels that do not depend on external oxygen to burn.

Since the air we breath contains 21% oxygen and a fire needs only 16% to burn, we must recognize that most fuels are surrounded by sufficient oxygen for burning. So, to some extent, the exclusion of oxygen should be considered for proper control of all fires. It's also important to recognize that while a fire needs 16% oxygen to burn freely, it may burn slowly and smoulder for a long time when less oxygen is available. In the case of smouldering in an area such as a tightly closed closet, a fire may smoulder and slowly heat the available fuel — then virtually explode into a ferocious fire when the door is opened, providing a new source of oxygen.

Reducing the Heat

Reducing or removing the heat is a widely used method of fire extinguishment. It is often referred to as cooling and quenching the fire. This is actually controlling the temperature of the fire to the point where the fuel is not hot enough to give off the gas vapors which burning requires. Heat itself travels away from the fire in several ways, through the processes of convection, conduction and radiation. Cooling is actually a form of heat travel or transfer, since the heat is absorbed by the cooling agent, such as water. Of all the extinguishing agents, water absorbs more heat per volume than any other agent. Typically, it is also readily available. Therefore, it is the most widely used fire extinguishment agent.

Interrupt the Chain Reaction

The fourth method of fire extinguishment is the interruption or inhibition of the chain reaction in which the atomic molecules or free radicals that have been preheated are thrown off from the blaze and drawn back into the base of the fire, rapidly increasing the fire's intensity. Scientists have found that the simultaneous formation and consumption of certain atoms are the key to the chain reaction which produces the flame itself. Certain chemical substances can break up this reaction. When introduced into the fire in the proper amounts, these substances inhibit the atoms and prevent the flame from burning. The most commonly used substances are the Halon gases such as Halon 1301, Halon 1211, and Halon 2402. Halon is an odorless, clear gas that quickly replaces the free radicals or molecules. In its pure form, it is toxic. Thus, due care must be taken before using it in a closed environment containing people. Normal usage is not dangerous, since the gas dissipates very quickly and settles to floor level. Halon has very poor cooling ability and is further reduced in efficiency by wind or ventilation. But used properly, Halon is among the most effective extinguishing agents. It requires no cleanup, causes no corrosion and can suppress an explosion even after is has started.

CLASSIFICATION OF FIRES AND EXTINGUISHERS

Fires are classified by the type of fuel that is involved in producing the fire. Consequently, extinguishing agents are designated according to the type of fire they will eliminate or control. *Figure 17-4* shows common markings for extinguishers containing the agents recommended for each major fire classification. Ex-

tinguishers suitable for more than one class of fire may be identified by multiple symbols. Markings should be on the front of extinguishers and of a size and form to give easy legibility at a distance of three feet. When applied to walls and panels near extinguishers, they should be easily legible from fifteen feet.

Class "A" Fires and Extinguishers

Class "A" fires are the most common type in North America. They involve ordinary combustible materials such as wood, paper, rubber, dust, most plastics and materials that combine these solids. Water is the most often used extinguisher, exerting a cooling or quenching effect to reduce the heat of the burning material. Other agents used to combat Class "A" fires are usually a water-based combination of chemicals to increase the efficiency. Dry powders also will reduce the Class "A" fire under some conditions, due to smothering effects. Halon will interrupt the chain reaction and quickly snuff out the blaze. But neither of these has the cooling capacity of water, so water is most often used.

Class "B" Fires and Extinguishers

Class "B" fires are those involving flammable liquids, greases and gases. Examples are gasoline,

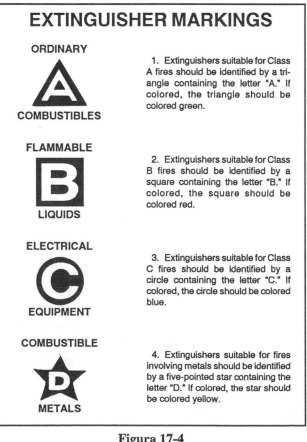

Figura 17-4

motor oils, acetylene, methane and so on. The normal method of extinguishment involves the smothering effect in which oxygen is excluded from the fire. Foam is often used to float on the surface and cut off the oxygen. Other methods involve removal of the fuel through draining or other measures. Water should never be used on a Class "B" fire unless it is specially treated with chemicals and/or used as a very fine spray.

Class "C" Fires and Extinguishers

This classification involves the presence of electrical energy, such as faulty wiring or electrical appliances and tools. Once the electricity is removed, the fuel remaining will constitute either a Class "A," "B" or "D" fire. First consideration in fighting the Class "C" fire is to use an extinguishing agent which is non-conductive and will not shock the user. The safest procedure with these fires is to first cut off or de-energize the source, then treat the fire as "A," "B" or "D," depending on the specific fuels burning. Several different types of powder and carbon dioxide agents are available. Most popular today are the extinguishers known as "multi-purpose" which will handle several classes of fires.

Another way to remember these first three classes of fires is:

A =	Material leaving ASH	
B =	Material that may BOIL	
C =	Equipment operated by electrical CURRENT	

Class "D" Fires and Extinguishers

Perhaps the most dangerous of the four classifications is the Class "D" — the burning of combustible metals such as magnesium, titanium, zirconium, sodium and potassium. Selection of extinguishing agents is critical, since burning metal may explode violently if the wrong agent is used or if it contains moisture. The extremely high temperature of the metals makes most of the commonly used agents ineffective or even dangerous. Most burning metals must be extinguished by smothering the fire. There is no agent available that will control fires in all combustible metals. Each metal must be analyzed and a specific agent selected. Extinguishing agents may include Potassium Bicarbonate (Purple K), Potassium Carbonate (Monnex) or Potassium Chloride (Super K). Some burning metals may also be extinguished with dry sand.

LEGISLATIVE REGULATORY REQUIREMENTS

Regarding legal requirements or legislative regulations for fire prevention, several governmental levels must be considered. The U.S. federal government has taken the lead in specifying the basic requirements, as incorporated into the Occupational Safety and Health Act of 1971. Managers should also check with city, county and state authorities which may have additional requirements. Also, many of the federal regulations refer to what they call "the authority having jurisdiction," which means that the federal regulations can be superseded by some local measures. In Canada, primary guidance will be found in the various provincial regulations and those of the various safety organizations.

Most of the guidelines in these regulations are the type that good business and good management would dictate to be included in any loss control program anyway. Some are stated briefly below, based on the OSHA manual, as very basic considerations in managing an ongoing Fire Loss Control Program. Many of the items listed here are discussed more fully later in this chapter.

Emergency Action Plans: Must be in writing (unless there are less than 10 employees) and must cover all perceived emergencies, such as fire, storm, flood, explosions, bomb threats, etc. As a minimum, the plan must include the following:
1. Method of reporting emergencies
2. Alarm systems
3. Evacuation plans
4. Training of employees
5. A written fire plan, consisting of:
   a. identification of hazards
   b. methods of hazard control
   c. housekeeping procedures
   d. names and titles of personnel who will combat fires in the workplace
   e. training of employees
6. Provision of more sophisticated firefighting equipment if employees do more than fight fire in the incipient stage. Portable fire extinguishers must also be provided.
7. Maintenance of equipment
8. Marking and control of exits
9. Control of specific hazards and cut-off valves
10. Fire brigades - the company must determine whether or not to have a fire brigade. If one is

organized, the guidelines specify the type of training and the required equipment. It is generally felt that if a company is more than 10 minutes from the arrival of a fire department, it should have a fire brigade. But the choice is left to industry.

ELEMENTS OF THE FIRE LOSS CONTROL PROGRAM

Because of the constant and catastrophic threat to the work environment, fire loss control management is among the critical aspects of business. To varying degrees, the law demands it, and good business dictates it. And it must be accomplished in conjunction with the management of production, quality, cost and safety. It cannot survive as a viable practice if the operation has to stop in order for fire safety to be accomplished. Like all other elements of a loss control program, it must be a functioning part of the management system.

Keep in mind that the primary purpose of a Fire Loss Control Program is the *prevention* of fires — to keep them from starting in the first place. However, we must never become so complacent as to think that no fires will occur! Despite our best efforts, we still have fires. So the management program must provide both for preventing fires and for minimizing losses when fires do occur. Following are seven important elements of such a Fire Loss Control Program:

1. Hazard Inventory
2. Written Fire Plan
3. Training Program
4. Inspection Program
5. Regular Fire Drills
6. Fixed Responsibility and Accountability
7. Management Involvement

1. Hazard Inventory

Identification and evaluation of all fire potentials are vital to program success. All fire loss exposures must be identified and management decisions, based on sound principles and understanding of the nature of fire as it pertains to those risks, must be made. When the option exists, management should always eliminate the hazard through a modification, an engineering process or perhaps substitution of a process or material that reduces the degree of risk. Management must decide: Will the risk be terminated? Treated? Tolerated? Transferred?

The hazard inventory should be as complete as possible, considering factors such as:

- all physical hazards concerned with the facility and its construction
- the procedures or processes used to produce the products or services
- the materials used in every aspect of the business
- the tools, equipment and forms of energy used in the work
- the likelihood of the workplace environment changing in the future

Purchasing and Engineering departments play a key role in control of both incoming hazards and hazards that might be built into new or modified facilities.

2. Written Fire Plan

A well-designed fire plan will contain most of the items listed below:

- A list of the major workplace fire hazards and their proper handling; storage procedures; potential ignition sources (such as welding and smoking) and procedures for their control; and the type of fire protection equipment or systems to be used for control.
- Names or regular job titles of people responsible for maintenance of equipment and systems installed to prevent or control fires
- Names or regular job titles of people responsible for control of fuel source hazards
- Written housekeeping procedures that will enable the employer to control accumulations of flammable and combustible waste materials and residues so they do not contribute to a fire emergency.
- Training requirements which ensure that employees receive training in four defined areas:
  - Awareness of the fire hazards of the materials and processes they are exposed to
  - Knowledge of those parts of the fire prevention plan needed to protect themselves in case of emergency
  - Review of the plan whenever it is changed, and at least annually
  - Training in the use of fire extinguishers provided in the workplace
- Procedures for regular maintenance of installed firefighting equipment, items which might be sources of ignition and all fire extinguishers located in the facility.

- Proper marking and control of exits to prevent their blockage at any time. As part of the training of employees, each one must physically walk the route of evacuation so there is no misunderstanding about it in emergency situations.
- Proper identification and marking of emergency cut-off valves. Persons designated to perform shut-down operations must be clearly identified and properly trained in their emergency roles.

3. Training Program

The items and areas listed here should be considered in addition to those highlighted above. In both cases, training should be based on prepared lesson plans. This aids consistent and ongoing training, which is necessary because new employees must be trained and all employees must have an annual update.

Supervisors should be well trained in the "Nature" and how it applies to their own environment. They should also receive detailed training in the specific hazards of the workplace. Management will find a system of *hot-work permits* valuable for controlling fires (see *Figure 17-5*).

Care must be taken to train all supervisors, including those who work in the administrative areas, even though the threat of fire may not be as great for them. Keep in mind that all fires start small.

Employee training, discussed earlier, includes such things as the specifics of fire potentials in their work procedures; department and plant rules which relate to fire loss control; emergency preparedness; and first aid training for burns.

4. Inspection Program

While many of the areas of concern — such as Housekeeping and Critical Parts Inspections — are part of the regular facility inspection program, it is important that fire be given some special considerations. In addition to the areas included in regular monthly inspections and daily informal walkarounds, special hazards should be covered in separate fire inspections. Things that must be checked should be shown on a checklist. A checklist that includes all the things and areas that supervisors should check is one of the best ways to ensure adequate inspection, detection and correction — before fires occur.

The fire inspection may be done quarterly, monthly or even daily, depending on the hazards involved. Periodic fire inspections are a wise move because they offer the opportunity to zero in on specifics that might otherwise be overlooked. The inspection should begin with a thorough understanding of the layout of each building and each process utilized in the operation. Questions as to the degree of authority the inspector has should be settled before the inspection begins. The inspector must have access to every room, closet, "cubbyhole," private office or any other area, regardless of who is in charge of these areas.

Start the inspection with the roof and walk all the way around the periphery, looking down at the ground areas and the surrounding buildings. Many hazards have a habit of occurring in vacant lots or seldom utilized areas. After checking the roof, proceed to the top floor, starting at one side and working all the way around until every area has been thoroughly inspected. Then repeat the process on the next floor. Continue working down through the building, including basement areas.

Every building and facility should have one person who is accountable for fire protection in that building. If possible, this person should accompany the inspector. As a bare minimum, the inspector and the accountable person should meet after the inspection to discuss the findings.

Every supervisor should be trained in the specifics of what to look *at* and what to look *for* — whether it is a fire inspection or regular monthly inspection. A small sample of such areas and items is given below:

- Brooms, pipes and other debris stacked around or against circuit breakers.
- Containers of paint or solvent left unsealed and/or next to heat sources.
- Collections of flammable debris (such as rags, papers, boxes and wood) that could become ignited or supply fuel to a fire starting from some other source.
- Loose, frayed or temporary wiring that could serve as an ignition point for fire.
- Non-explosion-proof lighting, fixtures, switches, etc. in areas where flammable vapors or dusts could accumulate and ignite.
- Fire extinguishers that are inoperable or cannot be reached because of materials blocking access.
- Unmarked and/or blocked fire exits or means of escape from an area in event of a fire.
- Exit doors that open inward, so that passage from the area is more difficult — or even impossible

CUTTING & WELDING PERMIT

Applies Only to Area Specified Below

Date _____

Building _____ Floor _____

Nature of the job _____

_____

The above location has been examined. The precautions checked below have been taken to prevent fire.

PRECAUTIONS

The supervisor must inspect the proposed work area and check precautions taken to prevent fire.

GENERAL PRECAUTIONS

☐ Sprinklers and/or fire hose in service.
☐ Cutting and welding equipment in good repair.
☐ Area supervisors notified.

PRECAUTIONS WITHIN 50 FEET OF WORK

☐ Floors swept clean of combustibles.
☐ Combustible floors wet down, covered with damp sand or metal or fireproof sheets.
☐ No combustible materials or flammable liquids.
☐ Combustibles and flammable liquids protected with fire-proof tarpaulins or metal shields.
☐ All wall and floor openings covered.
☐ Fireproof tarpaulins suspended beneath work to collect sparks.

WORK ON WALLS OR CEILINGS

☐ Construction noncombustible and without combustible covering or insulation.
☐ Combustibles moved away from opposite side.

WORK ON ENCLOSED EQUIPMENT
(Tanks, containers, ducts, collectors, etc.)

☐ Equipment cleaned of all combustibles.
☐ Containers purged of flammable vapors.
☐ Adequate air flow through enclosed equipment to be provided while cutting and welding is done.

FIRE WATCH

☐ To be provided during and for 60 minutes after each operation.
☐ Supplied with extinguishers or small hose.
☐ Trained in use of equipment and in sounding alarms.

I have personally examined the above area and certify that the checked precautions have been taken.

Signed _____
Supervisor

Permission is granted for this work.

Permit expires _____
Date   Time

Signed _____
Superintendent

Time started _____ Time finished _____

FINAL CHECK-UP

Work area and all adjacent areas to which sparks and heat might have spread (such as floors above and below and on opposite side of walls) were inspected for at least 60 minutes after the work was completed and were found fire safe.

Signature _____
Supervisor

After signing, return permit to person who issued it.

Figure 17-5

if groups of employees converge upon them in panic during a fire.

- Combustible materials stored near flame or spark-producing operations (such as grinding, gas cutting or welding).
- Fuel and oxygen lines that are unmarked or improperly identified, allowing them to be mistaken for water or air lines.
- Absence of "No Smoking" signs in areas where flammable liquids, vapors, gases or other highly-combustible materials are stored or used. Use of spark-producing tools or equipment in such areas.
- Inadequate ventilation in areas where painting, solvent cleaning or other operations are performed that produce flammable vapors or gases.
- Fire extinguishers that are located in areas where they are not readily visible.
- Fire extinguishers that are not appropriate to the type of hazard in the area.
- Fittings that could allow pneumatic tools to be inadvertently connected to fuel or oxygen lines.
- Flammable liquids in unmarked or improperly identified containers.

This list is by no means complete. Each work area and facility is different. This list itself must be an extension of the supervisor's detailed knowledge of the work being done, the material used, the tools, the personnel and the physical plant itself.

5. Regular Fire Drills

The purpose of a fire drill is to verify the organization's readiness to handle a fire emergency effectively. It should include the entire facility and is best done unannounced. However, this is not always possible or practical. It may be necessary to hold the drills by department or section. Alarms normally used should be included, but possibly altered so the employees will know it is only a dry run.

Each member of management should have specific responsibilities during an emergency, and be required to carry them out during the drill. As an example, a manager may be responsible to ensure that all people in a particular area are evacuated, then close the doors and walk the evacuation route to watch for people who have strayed or become disabled.

Routes of evacuation and exits are normally depicted in the Fire Plan in the form of a diagram with arrows showing the routes out of the plant or office. These

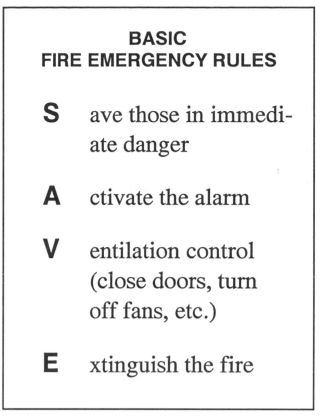

Figure 17-6

should also be posted in the workplace.

6. Fixed Responsibility and Accountability

Many Fire Plans do not adequately treat this vital area. Some hardly touch it, assuming that good managers do not have to be told what to do. But for the program to function properly, each person must know specifically what he or she is responsible and accountable for.

SUPERVISORS: KEYS TO MANAGEMENT CONTROL - All levels of management must play a part in the program to control and prevent fires. However, the front-line supervisor is widely recognized by professionals as the key person. Many supervisors feel they have little or no responsibility beyond the occasional participation in fire drills. While there is no doubt of the importance of the Fire Inspector and the Safety/Loss Control specialist, their efforts will be ineffective unless the front-line supervisor is active in the program. Supervisors have the most control over the variables that affect both the prevention and the proper control of emergencies. Supervisory control extends to:

- The primary causes of fires
- Fuel availability for fires to start
- Early reporting of fires
- Accessibility of fire areas
- Evacuation of employees
- Resources for fighting incipient fires

Also, supervisors have broad knowledge of the products, materials, machines, equipment, processes, buildings, storage and day-to-day hazards of the work. This magnitude of involvement makes supervisors critical to the management of the fire program. They should be given the responsibility for all the fire hazards and equipment in their areas, such as fire extinguishers and hot-work permits. They should also receive a copy of the Fire Plan and be thoroughly trained in its execution.

RESPONSIBILITY FOR FACILITIES - Each building or area should be assigned to a specific person, who clearly understands that he or she is responsible for the building and accountable for all aspects of the Fire Plan. This includes fire inspections and the execution of those items listed in the inspection checklist or as a part of general planned inspections or critical parts inspections. Supervisors must also accept responsibility for the work processes, tools and equipment being used by the employees. If the facility is especially large, a supervisor may be assigned a specific part of it, but there should be one person who has overall responsibility for the entire building.

OTHER MANAGERIAL RESPONSIBILITIES - Every manager should have some specific responsibility, if only in the execution phase of the plan. Purchasing and Engineering managers, for instance, could be responsible for ensuring that processes, materials and equipment are considered for their potential fire hazards before they are introduced into the workplace. Janitorial managers, who often work other than "normal" work hours, can be held accountable for the actions of their personnel and be required to make their own fire inspections.

The key to responsibility and accountability is that it not be left to chance or to assumptions. It must be clearly spelled out in detail to every manager and employee. People have to be *told*, *trained* and *audited* to ensure that there is no misunderstanding of the role they play in this important area.

7. Management Involvement

As indicated earlier, management involvement starts at the top and goes to the very bottom. Top management must be active in setting policy, establishing procedures, approving the written plan and actively participating in all fire drills and inspections. Management must also insist that fire inspection results be reported regularly in management meetings, to emphasize the importance of fire prevention to the whole management team. Special activities, such as National Fire Prevention Week or a housekeeping contest, offer unique opportunities for increased participation by all levels of management.

The effectiveness of the program will depend directly on the attention and participation of the upper levels of management. In essence, executives must be more than just concerned; they must be committed and involved for effective fire loss control. They must recognize that the program's success depends in large measure on their own involvement. Failure to do so can mean that they are gambling with the lives of employees and with the business itself, which cannot exist in the long term without effective control of fire hazards.

CORE CONCEPTS IN REVIEW

Fire can be friend or foe, depending on how well it is managed. Front-line supervisors have a very important role in **fire prevention and control**.

1. They have the day-to-day knowledge of the materials manufactured, used or stored within the facility.

2. They know the hazards created by day-to-day conditions, practices and changes.

Knowing the basics of the nature of fire helps in understanding how to prevent and control it. The **fire** tetrahedron aids this knowledge by providing a mental picture of fire's four necessary components:

1. **Fuel**
2. **Oxygen**
3. **Heat**
4. **Chain reaction**

This leads, naturally, to four major methods of combating fires:

1. **Remove** the fuel.

2. **Exclude** the oxygen.

3. **Reduce** the heat.

4. **Interrupt** the chain reaction.

Four classifications of fires and extinguishers are:

1. **Class A** (ordinary combustibles)

2. **Class B** (flammable liquids)

3. **Class C** (electrical equipment)

4. **Class D** (combustible metals)

It is vitally important to use the appropriate extinguisher.

Effective fire loss control management requires awareness of the legal requirements or legislative regulations, at federal, state or provincial and local levels.

Seven components of a **fire loss control management program** are:

1. Hazard inventory
2. Written fire plan
3. Training program
4. Inspection program
5. Regular fire drills
6. Fixed responsibility and accountability
7. Management involvement

One need not be a fire expert to properly manage fire loss control activities. There are plenty of experts available who can be called upon for any needed assistance. But, since fire can literally destroy the entire organization and its people, **it is critical that fire loss control be expertly managed**.

KEY QUESTIONS

1. This chapter is devoted to the _____ of fire (a. science; b. management; c. fighting; d. awareness)

2. True or False? Most people who successfully manage fire loss control are fire or safety engineers.

3. Why must supervisors fill such a key role in fire loss control?

4. What are the four components of the fire tetrahedron? Why are they important?

5. List four major fire extinguishment methods.

6. The air we breath contains 21% oxygen. A fire needs _____% to burn.

7. What is the most widely used fire extinguishment agent?

8. Name several examples of a Class A fuel for fire.

9. What are Class B fires?

10. How do you treat a Class C fire after the electric energy is cut off?

11. What are Class D fires?

12. True or False? The Occupational Safety and Health Act of 1971 includes considerable emphasis on fire prevention.

13. It is generally felt that if a company is more than _____ minutes from the arrival of a fire department, it should have a fire brigade.

14. A fire loss control program must provide both for p_____ and for m_____ losses when fires do occur.

15. Name seven important elements of a fire loss control management program.

16. List several items that should be included in a written fire plan.

17. What are some critical items of training for supervisors? For workers?

18. True or False? There should be fire inspections, in addition to the informal inspections and the regular planned inspections.

19. Professionals widely recognize the _____ as the key person in fire loss control management.

20. How can responsibility and accountability be clearly established?

21. Name several ways that upper managers can be actively involved in fire loss control.

PRACTICAL APPLICATIONS SUMMARY

S – For Supervisors
E – For Executives
C – For Safety/Loss Control Coordinators

		S	E	C
1.	Include fire loss control in a policy statement reflecting management's positive attitude and commitment to safety/health/loss control.		x	
2.	Appoint a coordinator to administer the overall emergency action plan.		x	
3.	For each building or area, assign overall fire loss control responsibility to a specific person.		x	
4.	Assign specific fire loss control responsibilities to every member of management.		x	
5.	Issue detailed emergency instructions for each department, building or area.	x	x	
6.	Identify and evaluate all fire potentials.	x	x	x
7.	Issue a written fire plan.		x	
8.	Provide adequate fire loss control educational material and training aids.	x	x	x
9.	Include fire prevention and control in day-to-day managing activities.	x	x	x
10.	Provide adequate fire warning and extinguishment systems and devices.		x	
11.	Keep abreast of legal requirements or legislative regulations for fire prevention.	x	x	x
12.	Ensure appropriate marking and control of exits.	x	x	x
13.	Organize and train fire brigades where appropriate.	x	x	x
14.	Give adequate emphasis to the specific fire loss control responsibilities of the Purchasing and Engineering departments.		x	x
15.	Train employees in fire hazard awareness, fire prevention techniques, emergency actions, proper use of fire extinguishers and first aid skills.	x	x	x
16.	Ensure training of supervisors in the nature of fire and the specifics of fire loss control for their areas.		x	x
17.	Ensure proper preventive maintenance and inspection of firefighting equipment.	x	x	
18.	Ensure proper identification and marking of emergency cut-off valves.	x	x	
19.	Establish standards for fire inspections.		x	
20.	Participate in fire inspections.	x	x	x
21.	Include fire prevention in informal and regular planned inspections.	x	x	x
22.	Participate in regular fire drills.	x	x	x
23.	Participate in special activities such as National Fire Prevention Week.	x	x	x
24.	Include fire prevention and control in both on-the-job and off-the-job safety promotion activities.	x	x	x
25.	Ensure adequate audits of the fire loss control management program.		x	x

CHAPTER 18

OFF-THE-JOB AND FAMILY LOSS CONTROL

Of disabling injuries from work and home accidents, over 60% happen at home. Nearly twice as many people are killed in home accidents as in work accidents. When it comes to accidents, there's no place like home.

INTRODUCTION

There are two major groups of reasons why every company and every supervisor should be interested and involved in off-the-job safety — humane reasons and business reasons. On the humane side, no supervisor wants his or her people, or their family members, to be killed, disabled or otherwise harmed. Whether accidents occur on the job or off the job makes no difference in terms of the resulting pain, suffering and tragedy. As members of the human race, we feel even more for anyone with whom we have a special relationship — such as those on our work team.

On the business side, there are many additional reasons for being interested and involved in off-the-job safety. For instance:

- quality and production suffer when knowledgeable, skilled workers are absent or disabled because they were injured off the job

- job performance is downgraded when workers are absent or distraught because family members were killed or disabled by off-the-job accidents

- the dollar costs of medical treatment, poor quality, production losses, absenteeism, waste and mistakes that result from off-the-job accidents are intolerable

- in some countries worker's compensation covers employee injury and illness whether or not it occurred on the job.

The objectives of this chapter are to show managers/supervisors/leaders why they should be committed to off-the-job (as well as on-the-job) safety; to show how off-the-job safety can be emphasized on the job; and to present the framework for a systematic family safety leadership program.

OFF-THE-JOB ACCIDENT PROBLEMS AND LOSSES

Illustrative Cases

The following cases illustrate a few of the many ways that off-the-job accidents can adversely affect any operation:

Case No. 1

A first-class machine operator fractured his pelvis when he fell from a ladder while painting his home. Since the craftsman's prolonged absence from work was involved, the machine shop foreman requested that a temporary employee be hired to operate one of the less complicated machines, in order to free a more experienced operator to replace the injured man. The supervisor spent several days helping the new employee and his reassigned machinist adjust to their jobs. In the meantime, he sent the department superintendent a memo to explain the expected drop in machine tool production during the adjustment period.

Case No. 2

A parts inspector reported off to be at his wife's bedside, as she had suffered a ruptured spinal disc when she fell while standing on a chair in the kitchen. The date of his return remained indefinite until he could arrange for a "live-in" baby sitter for a six-month-old infant and a two-year-old child. The inspection supervisor hoped that his temporary overtime arrangements, necessitated by this man's absence, could be discontinued soon enough to avoid hiring and training an inspector-trainee.

Case No. 3

The plant nurse called the supervisor of a line crew to report that an electrical repairman had been to the dispensary five times during the past two days with a headache and an upset stomach, which she felt could be associated with the hospitalization of his three-year-old daughter for accidental oral poisoning. The nurse was concerned about the employee's mental state on the job, as she felt that he had an above-average exposure to high potential loss situations.

While these cases are hypothetical, they are nonetheless typical of a large group of incidents which cost employers as much, if not more, than on-the-job incidents. Further, the cases clearly illustrate that off-the-job incidents cannot be isolated from an organization's loss control program, as the effect of such incidents has great impact on any organization's operations.

Human Losses

In our society we hear huge numbers all the time, so much so that the phrase "gee-whiz figures" has been coined to cover this staggering statistics phenomenon. But when the figures reflect broken arms, blindness, deafness, paralyzed legs, lung disease, brain damage and dead mothers, fathers, wives, husbands, daughters, sons and other loved ones — we cannot have the "gee-whiz" attitude! We're talking of *people*, flesh and blood, other beings essentially like us.

What accidents do to people is tragic. For example, *Figure 18-1* shows the death and disabling injury figures for the United States and Canada in 1989. They show that three out of four worker deaths, and nearly 60% of the disabling injuries suffered by workers, occurred off the job. Expanding the view beyond workers to everyone, off-the-job accidents caused 79% of the disabling injuries and 88% of the deaths. With numbers like these, there should be no doubt regarding the need to do much more for off-the-job safety.

Figure 18-2 puts this information into a form that may be easier to relate to. Notice that work accidents kill a person every 51 minutes and disable a person every 19 seconds. That's horrible. But look at accidents to workers *off the job*: a death every 14 minutes and a disabling injury every 11 seconds; 101 deaths and 7,700 disabling injuries every day, 365 days a year! In Canada there is an off-the-job death every 2-1/2 hours and a disabling injury every 2 minutes; nearly 10 deaths and 750 disabling injuries every day of the year!

And it's not always "somebody else" or somebody else's family!! Every one of us should be concerned with, and committed to, off-the-job safety.

Family problems such as accidents affect employees both on and off the job. Responses include:

- Presence desired at home for seriously injured member of family.

- Emergency presence necessitated at home in cases of critically injured family members.

ON-THE-JOB AND OFF-THE-JOB COMPARISONS

	U.S.			CANADA		
	Workers On The Job	Workers Off The Job	Everyone Off The Job	Workers On The Job	Workers Off The Job	Everyone Off The Job
Deaths	10,400	36,900	84,100	980	3,560	8,120
Disabling Injuries	1,700,000	2,800,000	7,300,000	167,000	274,000	709,000

Figure 18-1

- Temporary presence necessitated at home to care for family members in absence of injured homemaker.

- Presence required at home in case of accidental death to family member.

- Emotional upset of anxiety, on the job and off the job, due to concern for injured family member.

It would be reasonable to assume that the last item would involve most — if not all — employees each time a serious family accident occurs.

In light of available statistics on the frequency of accident occurrence and the volume of research data available on the effects of emotional upset, it is obvious that family accidents can:

1. Constitute a major cause of absenteeism
2. Adversely affect employee morale
3. Decrease employee efficiency
4. Increase the probability of accidents from human error, on and off the job

Dollar Losses

The cost of off-the-job accidents to employers and employees is staggering. As reflected in *Figure 18-3*, of the conservatively estimated 148.5 billion dollars (9.4 billion in Canada) of accident losses in 1989, only 33% resulted from work accidents. The other 67% resulted from public accidents, home accidents and motor-vehicle accidents.

Some of the costs of off-the-job accidents are paid directly, in the form of wages to absent employees and the cost of hiring and training replacements. But a significant portion of it is hidden. For example, the skilled craftsman, technician or supervisor injured off the job may not be replaced immediately. Such a temporary absence of an employee with special knowledge and ability can result in added costs due to lower production, late deliveries, use of overtime and related factors. The permanent loss of an employee, through death in an off-the-job accident, can result in company-borne costs involving insurance settlements

Accidents: The Grim Reaper

Class of Accident	Severity	One Every —	No. per Hour	No. per Day	No. per Week	Total 1989
All accidents	Deaths	6 minutes	11	259	1,820	94,500
	Injuries	4 seconds	1,030	24,700	173,100	9,000,000
Motor-vehicle	Deaths	11 minutes	5	128	900	46,900
	Injuries	19 seconds	190	4,700	32,700	1,700,000
Work	Deaths	51 minutes	1	28	200	10,400
	Injuries	19 seconds	190	4,700	32,700	1,700,000
Workers off-job	Deaths	14 minutes	4	101	710	36,900
	Injuries	11 seconds	320	7,700	53,860	2,800,000
Home	Deaths	23 minutes	3	62	430	22,500
	Injuries	9 seconds	390	9,300	65,400	3,400,000
Public nonmotor-vehicle	Deaths	28 minutes	2	52	370	19,000
	Injuries	13 seconds	270	6,600	46,200	2,400,000

Source: Accident Facts. National Safety Council, 1990

Figure 18-2

Costs of accidents in 1989

Accidents in which deaths or disabling injuries occurred, together with noninjury motor-vehicle accidents and fires, cost the nation in 1989, at least

$148.5 billion

(billion)

Motor-vehicle accidents .... $ 72.2

> This cost figure includes wage loss, medical expense, insurance administration cost and property damage from moving motor-vehicle accidents. Not included are the cost of public agencies such as police and fire departments, courts, indirect losses to employers of off-the-job accidents to employees, the value of cargo losses in commercial vehicles and damages awarded in excess of direct losses. Fire damage to parked motor-vehicles is not included here but is distributed to the other classes.

Work accidents .... $ 48.5

> This cost figure includes wage loss, medical expense, insurance administration cost, fire loss and an estimate of indirect costs arising out of work accidents. Not included is the value of property damage other than fire loss, and indirect loss from fires.

Home accidents .... $ 18.2

> This cost figure includes wage loss, medical expense, health insurance administration cost and fire loss. Not included are the costs of property damage other than fire loss, and the indirect cost to employers of off-the-job accidents to employees.

Public accidents .... $ 12.5

> This cost figure includes wage loss, medical expense, health insurance administration cost and fire loss. Not included are the costs of property damage other than fire loss, and the indirect cost to employers of off-the-job accidents to employees.

Source: Accident Facts. National Safety Council, 1990

Figure 18-3

and the cost of selecting, hiring and training a replacement. Also, in the future, it may be covered by workers' compensation, as is now done in New Zealand. The kinds of costs involved in off-the-job accidents are summarized in *Figure 18-4*.

The enormous size of this off-the-job accident problem on a national basis affects very real costs that are hidden even deeper, with a major impact on insurance costs, taxes and welfare contributions by individuals and organizations.

While an increasing number of companies are keeping records on their off-the-job injury experience, very few maintain accurate cost information. Even fewer are aware of all the costs that arise from accidents to members of employees' families. It boggles the mind to consider the total impact that off-the-job and family accidents have on an organization's operations and profit picture, when added to the huge costs of on-the-job accidents.

Both in terms of human losses and dollar losses, off-the-job and family safety is a relatively untapped area for making an enormous contribution to both organizations and fellow human beings.

CONTROL GUIDELINES

While the use of basic rules of common sense by the employee and his or her family cannot rightfully be considered our total responsibility, we are nonetheless in a position to instill a loss control "consciousness." This originates with top management, is implemented by supervisors and safety coordinators and is passed on to employees. They, in turn, become the loss control leaders in their family units. Thus, there are large numbers of people in our communities who could be affected by this "filter" process.

Based on the experience of pioneers in off-the-job and family loss control, the following six guidelines are suggested.

Guideline No. 1

The program should be family-oriented, rather than aimed at the employee alone. Not only does management frequently pay for the insurance costs of accidental injury to family members, but these injuries are also a major indirect source of absenteeism and on-the-job anxiety to the employees, all of which become areas of loss for the employer.

OFF-THE-JOB COST CATEGORIES

(Every one of these costs will not arise in connection with every off-the-job accident, but each is a potential cost, and during a period of time, many or all of them will arise

1. **Direct**
   Wages paid to injured workers while off the job.

2. **Indirect (disabling)**

   a. Wage cost due to decreased output of injured worker after he returned to work.

   b. Personnel cost of hiring replacement workers.

   c. Wage cost of supervisors for time spent in training replacement workers.

   d. Wage cost due to lower output of replacement workers during break-in period.

   e. Products, materials, tools, etc., spoiled by replacement workers during break-in period.

   f. Wage cost of time lost by other workers who were delayed getting started because injured worker was a member of a team, his output was needed or other workers discussed the accident.

   g. Wages paid during time spent by noninjured workers for visiting the injured, attending funerals.

3. **Indirect (nondisabling)**
   This cost arises in connection with the following (many

workers will lose some hours from work even though they do not lose a full day at any one time):

   a. Wages paid during time lost by workers for doctor or dispensary visits.

   b. Wage cost due to decreased output of worker because of his injury.

   c. Wage cost of other workers who may be slowed down, either because the injured worker was slow, temporarily absent or needed help of other workers.

   d. Spoilage of product or materials due to less efficient work because of the injury.

4. **Insurance**
   Each company can determine its own insurance cost covering off-the-job accidents. Generally this will be included in some form of health and accident coverage, and the insurance company will be able to state that portion of the premium which is for the accident portion of the policy. While this cost is not as flexible as others listed above, most policies do provide for some form of credit for improved experience.

Reprinted from DATA SHEET 601, Revision A, National Safety Council

Figure 18-4

Guideline No. 2

The problem deserves a broad loss control approach. Fire, traumatic injury, illness or injury from exposure to toxic substances, and loss associated with theft and vandalism are some of the major interrelated areas of potential loss for employee, their families and their employers. By referring to our effort as "Family Loss Control," we focus attention on all these important items and create the avenue to inclusion of additional problem areas as the program expands.

Guideline No. 3

A well-organized program produces best results. Posters, slogans and safety messages are only one small part of the overall program. All major areas of control used in an on-the-job program must be suitably incorporated into a family loss control program to produce best results.

The form shown in *Figure 18-5* is important for two reasons. First, it provides a source of statistical information to show the initial size of the problem and improvements made. Second, it gives an indication of the causes of accidents so that efforts can be specifically targeted.

The off-the-job disabling injury frequency formula (called for by the form) is based on 312 exposure hours per employee per month. It is based on the following

assumption:

The average employee works eight hours a day, five days a week. If eight hours for sleeping are excluded, there remain eights hours a day, or 40 hours during the work week, in which the employee is exposed to injury off the job. In addition, he has two days each weekend, of 16 exposure-hours each. These 72 exposure hours each week, multiplied by four and one-third weeks per month, total 312 exposure hours per employee per month. Since overtime is offset by holidays, vacations and other absences, no special allowance is provided for it.

An off-the-job disabling injury frequency rate is computed as follows:

$$\frac{\text{Number of OTJ disabling injuries} \times 200{,}000}{312 \times \text{number of employees} \times \text{number of months}} = \begin{array}{l}\text{OTJ Disabling}\\\text{Injury Rate}\end{array}$$

Guideline No. 4

Family-based loss control leadership must be provided on an ongoing basis. Just as the first-line supervisor within the company is a key to the systematic planning, leading, organizing and controlling efforts that assure program continuity and success on the job, someone within the family group must accept the full responsibility to lend this special leadership

OFF-THE-JOB SAFETY SUMMARY

REPORTING UNIT _____   MONTH OF _____

LOCATION _____   APPROVED BY _____

	CURRENT MONTH	ACCUMULATED YEAR TO DATE
AVERAGE NUMBER OF EMPLOYEES		
EXPOSURE HOURS AT 312 HOURS/EMPLOYEE/MONTH		
NO. OF OFF-THE-JOB DISABLING INJURIES		
NO. OF FATALITIES		
OFF-THE-JOB DISABLING INJURY FREQUENCY RATE*		

LOCATION - CAUSE - SEVERITY - ANALYSIS

(Indicate Fatalities by Superscripts)

TRANSPORTATION	No.	Work-days Lost	HOME	No.	Work-days Lost	PUBLIC	No.	Work days Lost
AUTO/TRUCK			FALLS AND SLIPS			ANIMAL OR INSECT		
a. collision			a. on steps			EXPOSURE-HEAT/COLD		
b. pedestrian			b. icy surfaces			FALLS, SLIP		
c. working on			c. walking surfaces			FIREARMS		
d. miscellaneous			d. ladders and scaffolds			FIRE		
RAILROAD			e. miscellaneous			EXPLOSION		
BUS			ELECTRICITY			FIGHT AND ASSAULT		
BICYCLE			FIRE OR EXPLOSION			RECREATION		
MOTORCYCLE			MACHINERY OR TOOLS			SPORTS		
OTHER TRANSPORTATION			TOXIC MATERIALS			OTHER CAUSES		
			IMPROPER LIFTING					
			HOT OBJECTS					
			STRUCK BY OBJECTS					
			SHARP OBJECTS					
			OTHER CAUSE					
Totals This Month			Totals This Month			Totals This Month		
YEAR TO DATE			YEAR TO DATE			YEAR TO DATE		

Observations: _____

_____

_____

* Number of off-the-job disabling injuries to employees, times 200,000, divided by (312 times the number of employees times the number of months)

Figure 18-5

and motivation to the family loss control program. One or both parents can fill this role. The employee is usually in the best position to learn the proper techniques used by the employer.

Guidelines No. 5

Overall direction must be provided by a coordinating organization with the professional knowledge and experience to guide the program effectively. The average family unit needs outside help and guidance in developing and maintaining an effective loss control program. Many aspects of a good loss control program require highly specialized professional knowledge not readily available to everyone. The first-line supervisor (representing the employer) is in an excellent position to serve as a link with employees, communicating know-how and specialized knowledge of loss control in regular on-the-job contacts.

Guideline No. 6

There is a need to provide individual program leadership within public groups outside the family unit. Family members spend an increased amount of time in educational, leisure and recreational activities. Leadership in loss control should be provided at these points of contact to make the program totally effective. Leadership support must come from every organization involved with these away-from-home influences.

SUPERVISORY ACTIONS

These guidelines highlight the important role that first-line supervisors must play to effectively manage the family loss control program. They are in the best position to prepare members of their work group for leadership roles in their individual family units. By an organized cooperative effort on the part of all supervisors, an effective family loss control program can be developed and maintained for an entire employee population and for their families.

An enormous contribution to human happiness, well-being and economic stability could be made by the combined effort of management groups, if these proven concepts were applied in an organized manner throughout the world. Organizations such as the Industrial Accident Prevention Association of Ontario in Canada and the National Safety Council in the United States are facing the challenge of organizing the business world for such a program. The first and most important step in such a worthy project is providing the individual supervisor with the training necessary to organize the program at the work-unit level.

The potential benefits of a well-planned, properly executed family loss control effort are great enough for the individual supervisor that careful thought should be given to ways and means of finding the time to introduce and maintain an effective ongoing program.

Listed below are several specific approaches to teach and motivate employees at various stages of the program's implementation. Experience has proved that, as the program grows and matures, the supervisor increases the number of communication avenues used.

Group Communications. Off-the-job and family safety can become a regular part of group safety meetings in at least two ways. Most job-related topics have at least one off-the-job application. Subjects such as machine guarding, hand tools, ladders, chemical handling, electrical safety, etc., have off-the-job applications. References to these will increase worker understanding of the material and may well enhance their application *on the job*. Certainly, it will communicate the vital message that safety is a way of life and not just a company rule. In addition, a certain number of group meetings each year can be devoted to off-the-job subjects. Sample topics are shown in *Figure 18-6*.

Personal Communications. References to off-the-job applications when giving job instruction and key point tips provide another avenue of understanding the importance and application of what is being taught.

Rule Education and Job Procedures. Every opportunity to teach or review on-the-job rules or standard job procedures is a good time to associate applicable off-the-job and family loss control measures. Supervisors who consistently blend their on-the-job training with off-the-job applications have grasped the real key to developing a total loss control attitude within their people.

Annual Family Protection Conference. This is a one-day conference for employees and their spouses, devoted entirely to loss control subjects of vital concern to everyone. Selected speakers present subjects that will strengthen the leadership skills of the family members in attendance. Public relations departments usually see these events as outstanding opportunities to promote the company image and will give them appropriate publicity. Distributors of loss control equipment and devices can be invited to exhibit during the day, adding an atmosphere that is usually well-received.

SAMPLE OFF-THE-JOB SAFETY TOPICS

HOME

Accidental Poisoning
Artificial Respiration
Avoiding Falls
Back Injury Prevention
Burglar-proofing
Carbon Monoxide
Child Safety
Control of Severe Bleeding
Disaster Drills
Electric Hazards
Fire Checklist
Fire Escape Plan
Fire Prevention
Fire Extinguishers
Gardening Mishaps
Holiday Hazards
Home Fire Extinguishers
Ladder Safety
Moving Things Safely
Mower Safety
Oral Poisoning
Order
Prevent Vandalism
Protect Your Hands
Relieving Choking
Safe Storage & Piling

Slips and Trips
Smoke Detectors
Snow-Thrower Safety
Storage of Flammables
Summer Heat Hazards
Swimming Pool Safety

MOTOR VEHICLE

Automobile Inspection
Backing Accidents
Changing Tires
Defensive Driving
Drinking and Driving
Drive Like A Pro
Driving in the Dark
Hydroplaning
Ice and Snow Hazards
Know Your Roads
Mystery Crash
Night Driving
Pedestrian Safety
Safe Seeing Habits
Seat Belt Safety
Turnpike Safety
Two-Car Crashes
Watch That Child
Winter Driving

RECREATIONAL

ABC's of Water Safety
Baby Sitting Safety
Bicycle Safety
Camping Hazards
Careless Smoking
Chemical Hazards
Do-It-Yourself Accidents
Drug Abuse
Fishing Safety
Gun Safety
Hand Tool Safety
Home Workshop Accidents
Hunting Safety
Machine Tool Safety
Power Boating Safety
Power Tool Safety
Pressurized Cans
Safe Storage
Safe Swimming
Safety at the Pool
Slips and Falls
Small Craft Safety
Sports Safety Tips
Storage of Chemicals
Water Safety

Figure 18-6

Family Incident Reports. If properly approached, employees can participate in the spirit of the program by completing Family Incident Reports (*Figure 18-7*) to share their hard-won experiences with their fellow workers. Emphasis must be placed on the complete anonymity of these reports and that their only purpose is to help fellow employees prevent a similar incident occurring to them or their families. It might also be stressed that this is just a way of sharing with a wider group of people what they already share with their immediate circle of friends.

Enlisting Aid of Community Groups. As Guideline 6 pointed out, loss control leadership must be provided through those organizations that have frequent contacts with employees and their family members. Nearly every supervisor belongs to a social or service organization, club, fraternity, fire department, PTA or other similar type of group. Each of these organizations should have someone who is designated as chairperson of its safety or loss control promotion committee to sponsor and promote functions that encourage safety and health.

Other community organizations that can play an important role in promoting safety and loss control include churches and Sunday Schools, hospitals and auxiliaries, private and public educational institutions, American Red Cross, St. John's Ambulance, law enforcement agencies, civic clubs, sports organizations, professional associations and service clubs.

It is also important to remember that the skills and attitudes acquired in off-the-job safety efforts are of great value in on-the-job leadership by these same people.

Because of supervisors' special training, knowledge and appreciation of these values of loss control, they can promote the importance of such community involvement in those organizations and with those group leaders they contact through their off-job personal associations. Many of these groups could be interested in organizing special community-wide programs and projects. Others will want to include information on this vital subject in their bulletins and publications. Some typical projects or programs successfully conducted by various organizations have been:

FAMILY INCIDENT REPORT

EXPLANATION: Employees are invited to share information on any unfortunate incident that resulted in personal physical harm or property loss to them or members of their family. Circumstances regarding this incident can then be shared with fellow employees, i.e., give them information that could be helpful in preventing a similar occurrence to them or their family. The only purpose of this program is loss prevention for everyone. Names of individuals need not be given, nor will names ever be used if you place them on this report. If you desire to cooperate with the family loss control program, please fill in the information on this form. Thank you for sharing information that could help someone else prevent personal injury or property damage.

IDENTIFICATION

COMPANY OR BRANCH Portland Container Corp.		DEPARTMENT Assembly Department			
EXACT LOCATION basement stairway – home	DATE OF OCCURRENCE 2-10-19—		TIME 5:30 ☐ AM ☒ PM		DATE REPORTED 2-12-19—

PERSONAL INJURY		PROPERTY DAMAGE		OTHER INCIDENT	
PERSON(S) INJURED (CHECK) WORKER_____ SPOUSE X CHILDREN_____		PROPERTY DAMAGED		PERSON REPORTING INCIDENT	
NUMBER INJURED 1	INJURED PART(S) OF BODY right hip	ESTIMATED COSTS $	ACTUAL COSTS $	OCCUPATION	COST IF APPLICABLE $
NATURE OF INJURIES broken hip		NATURE OF DAMAGE		NATURE OF INCIDENT	
OBJECT/EQUIPMENT/SUBSTANCE INFLICTING INJURY basement floor		OBJECT/EQUIPMENT/SUBSTANCE INFLICTING DAMAGE		OBJECT/EQUIPMENT/SUBSTANCE	

INCIDENT DESCRIPTION

DESCRIBE CLEARLY WHAT HAPPENED:

My wife was going down the stairs to the basement to get a jar of fruit when she stepped on a small box of bottle caps or a bundle of newspapers, we are not sure which it was. She lost her balance and fell off the side of the stairs landing on her right side. We both knew that these things should have been stored someplace else. Martha also feels that the bulbs in the center of the basement doesn't throw enough light over on the stairs and I agree with that.

PREVENTION ADVICE

WHAT SPECIAL ADVICE OR INFORMATION CAN YOU SHARE THAT COULD HELP OTHERS AVOID SIMILAR INCIDENTS?

I think that everyone should check their basement stairs and any others in their homes to see that they do not have anything stored on them, even if it is on the side. Another thing to check is to see if a light should be placed right at the stairs so that anyone can see good enough to prevent them from falling. Most important I think is to make sure that railings are placed on every stairway outside the house as well as inside.

Figure 18-7

- Hunting or Gun Safety Courses
- First Aid Courses
- Life Saving and Water Safety Courses
- Boating Safety Courses
- Bicycle Rodeos and Safety Inspections
- Baby Sitting Courses
- Annual Safety Banquets

In addition to the sponsorship of major programs, many of these organizations would quickly recognize the value of having speakers address their regular meetings on loss control subjects. Every such program offered to the public provides reinforcement for both the on-the-job and family loss control programs.

There is no limit to the number and variety of ways that the important fundamentals of family loss control can be communicated to employees and the public. As safety and loss control become a way of life with supervisors, they find it increasingly difficult to distinguish between on-the-job and off-the-job loss control training. When they reach this point in the development of their total safety awareness, they seldom need to search for separate ways to get the message across. They occur in the natural course of hour-by-hour contacts with people, on and off the job, in all avenues of life.

PRACTICAL SUGGESTIONS FOR TRAINING FAMILY SAFETY LEADERS

Both logic and experience say that the tools and techniques for achieving optimum results in family safety are the same ones that get optimum results within the company. Two major factors which determine the successful transfer of on-the-job techniques to off-the-job situations are 1) the individual employee's interest in the safety and well-being of his or her family and 2) each supervisor's ability to communicate, educate and motivate employees toward safety as a way of life.

Safety depends on human K-A-S-H, on the

$\boxed{\text{K}}$ nowledge

$\boxed{\text{A}}$ ttitudes

$\boxed{\text{S}}$ kills and

$\boxed{\text{H}}$ abits

of people... be it on the job, off the job, anywhere, everywhere. Supervisors are in a key position to influence the safety knowledge, attitudes, skills and habits of every employee in their area of responsibility. Supervisors have the opportunity to transfer some of their own leadership ability (as used on the job) to employees who then can use it off the job; in their leadership role with the family. Supervisors have the challenge of helping workers see how to apply these techniques in the home and family environment, under circumstances somewhat different from the work situation. Following are some ideas of various ways this can be done.

Inspections

Help your people see the tremendous importance of inspection as a before-the-loss activity. Emphasize the values of informal inspections, pre-use inspections and special planned inspections at home and in other off-the-job situations. Use examples such as these:

- Whenever any family member uses a motor-vehicle, they should automatically invest a few seconds in a safety check of critical items such as tires that look low on pressure, lights, brakes and oil pressure. Conduct more complete inspections before major trips.
- Before using any hand tool, power tool, mowing machine, etc., check to see that it is in good, safe working condition.
- Train every family member to identify and correct potential hazards, such as chemicals and drugs within reach of youngsters and improper storage or use of gasoline, paints, solvents, garden sprays and other dangerous, flammable, explosive materials.
- Periodically conduct a family "team inspection" for a critical factor such as fire hazards. Use guidelines such as shown in *Figure 18-8.*
- Conduct periodic inspections of your home's heating system (filters, screens, valves, grates, stovepipes, etc.) and electrical system (fuses, plugs, cords, outlets, etc.)
- Use day-to-day informal inspection and periodic planned inspection for good housekeeping (cleanliness and order). Train every family member to practice this definition: a place is in order when there are *no* unnecessary things about, and *all* necessary things are in their proper places.

In addition to discussing how to inspect and what to look for in the home, you can invite each member of your work unit to make on-the-job planned inspections with you — with the specific purpose of teaching what to look for off the job. Throughout the inspection, make frequent references to similar conditions and problems at home, on the highway, in recreational

HOME FIRE SAFETY CHECKLIST

Do we...   Yes   No

- Prevent accumulation of rubbish, paper, discarded clothing, lint and other flammable materials? ☐ ☐
- Quickly wipe up spilled grease and liquids? ☐ ☐
- Prevent accumulation of grease and spilled materials under stove burners and in the oven? ☐ ☐
- Turn pot handles to the back of the stove so that small children cannot grab them? ☐ ☐
- Check pilot light and other potential problems when gas burner doesn't light within four seconds? ☐ ☐
- Open windows and doors for ventilation when we smell gas? ☐ ☐
- Keep curtains, towels, hot mitts, etc. away from the stove burners? ☐ ☐
- Avoid multiple socket electrical connections? ☐ ☐
- Keep electric light bulbs away from walls, curtains and other flammable materials? ☐ ☐
- Ensure that electric cords do not hang over nails or pipes and are not behind radiators, across walkways, hidden under rugs or passed through door jambs? ☐ ☐
- Avoid coin slugs or over-capacity fuses? ☐ ☐
- Use weatherproof electrical outlets, cords and connections for outdoor lighting and equipment? ☐ ☐
- Repair or replace frayed electrical wires, loose sockets or plugs and faulty appliances? ☐ ☐
- Periodically clean and lubricate motors on tools and appliances? ☐ ☐
- Have the heating system checked each year? ☐ ☐
- When leaving the ironing board, disconnect the electric iron and place it on its stand? ☐ ☐
- When drying clothes and other items, make sure they hang at a safe distance from stoves, heaters and other sources of fire? ☐ ☐
- Keep the clothes dryer free of lint? ☐ ☐
- Use only flameproof cleaning products? ☐ ☐
- Absolutely avoid storing oily rags; containers of wax, fuel or paint; and other flammable, explosive materials in the dwelling unit without proper metal containers and cabinets? ☐ ☐
- Store fuel for power mowers, boat motors, etc., in approved metal safety cans? ☐ ☐
- Use a flashlight, rather than matches, when checking for possible fuel leaks of vehicle, water heaters, stoves, furnaces and so on? ☐ ☐
- Avoid smoking in bed, while lying down on the sofa, and in similar "resting" situations? ☐ ☐
- Use ashtrays designed to prevent contents from accidentally falling out? ☐ ☐
- Double check to make sure cigarettes, cigars and pipe ashes are completely out before putting them into waste containers? ☐ ☐
- Keep matches and lighters out of the reach of youngsters? ☐ ☐
- Teach our children the fundamentals of fire prevention? ☐ ☐
- Avoid accumulation of dry grass, boards and other flammable items near buildings? ☐ ☐
- Clean up scrap, wood and sawdust after each job? ☐ ☐
- Have the fire department number prominently posted at each phone extension? ☐ ☐
- Have adequate fire extinguishers, escape ladders and early warning fire detector/alarm devices? ☐ ☐
- Keep each responsible household member adequately trained for when and how to use fire extinguishers? ☐ ☐
- Have periodic emergency evacuation drills? ☐ ☐

Figure 18-8

activities and so on. This powerful combination of leadership example and personal participation can be among your best bets for helping to develop safety as a way of life for each of your people, both on and off the job.

Task Analysis and Procedures

Help your people realize how basic and vital proper procedures are to safety and cost control, both at work and at home. Emphasize that performing jobs or tasks properly saves time and money; minimizes injuries, damage and waste and produces the best results. When you have written procedures for tasks, discuss how they can be adapted and applied to off-the-job activities.

The task analysis and procedures process provides another excellent opportunity for a collaborative, participative approach. Get your people to work with you in analyzing tasks and in developing new or revised procedures. Ask them, for instance, to jot down their thoughts about a critical task they perform — using a piece of paper divided into three columns along these lines:

KEY STEPS	LOSS EXPOSURES	PRECAUTIONS

Figure 18-9 - Task Analysis Worksheet

Encourage workers to train all family members to make full use of the recommended safe operating procedures that usually accompany any power tool or piece of mechanical equipment. These procedures are provided by manufacturers and by organizations such as the U.S. Consumer Product Safety Commission (see *Figure 18-10* for an example). Suggest that they keep a folder, a file or a notebook of these important papers, so they can be referred to as needed. Keep them in a handy place that all household members know about.

Remember, too, this includes not only equipment such as mowers, chain saws, weed eaters, circular saws and drills, but also equipment such as vacuum cleaners, washers, clothes dryers, hair dryers, stoves and microwave ovens.

Work with them in developing this information into a standard procedure or work practice. In your discussions, emphasize related off-the-job applications. Show them how they can easily do this type of thing with family members for critical tasks in home and recreational activities.

Accident/Incident Investigation

Encourage family leaders (employees) to investigate the cause of each off-the-job accident and close call; and to develop (with family members) corrective and preventive measures. Consider using an on-the-job reporting system for off-the-job incidents. The Family Incident Report form shown earlier (*Figure 18-7*) could be filled out voluntarily by the employee as soon as possible after the incident. Information from these reports could provide excellent material for safety meetings and group discussions. You could use these meetings and discussions not only to promote off-the-job safety for all of your people, but also to relate the consequences, the causes and the controls right back to the work situation In effect, you could "kill two birds" (off-the-job accidents and on-the-job accidents) "with one stone" (effective investigation).

Suggest that employees encourage their family members to share their accident and near-accident experiences with the rest of the family. This can help to put everyone on guard against suffering the consequences of similar incidents; can help to get at basic causes and corrections; and can provide the helpful data needed for the previously mentioned Family Incident Report. Discuss the importance of avoiding the blame-fixing attitude, and of using the mutual problem-solving approach.

Analyze Family Incident Reports to determine your employee's critical off-the-job loss problems. Use classification categories such as those included in the summary form shown earlier as *Figure 18-5*. Use the analysis information as a guide to your special emphasis program activities.

Emphasize with your workers (family leaders) how important it is for their investigations to focus on *causes*, not culprits; and to get at *basic* causes, not just the symptoms (unsafe acts and conditions). Use lists such as those shown in *Figure 18-11* to help in training them to focus on basic causes — the only effective avenues to effective control.

SPOT THE DANGERS
ALL AROUND YOU AND YOUR FAMILY

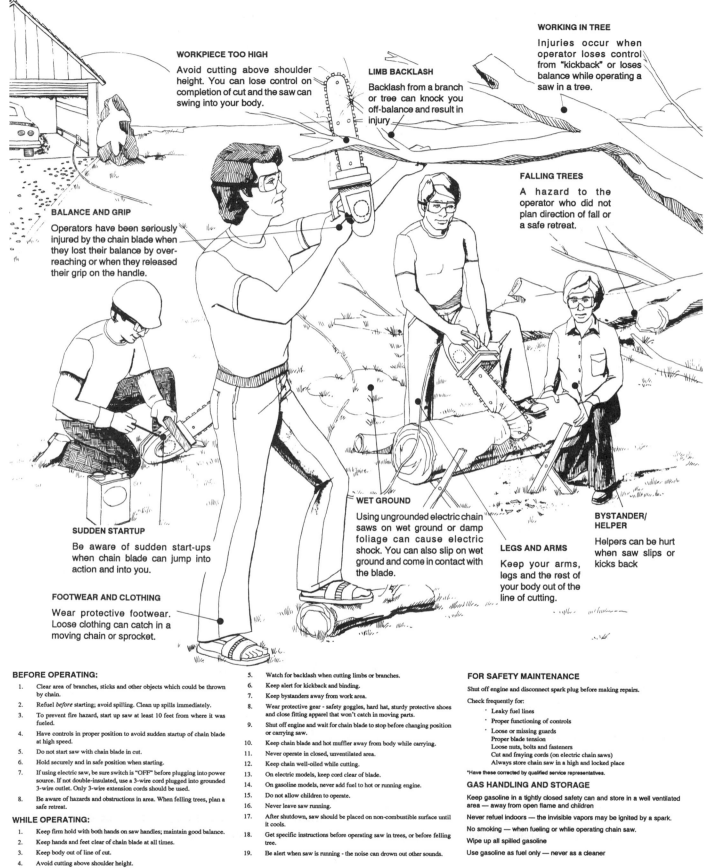

WORKPIECE TOO HIGH

Avoid cutting above shoulder height. You can lose control on completion of cut and the saw can swing into your body.

LIMB BACKLASH

Backlash from a branch or tree can knock you off-balance and result in injury

WORKING IN TREE

Injuries occur when operator loses control from "kickback" or loses balance while operating a saw in a tree.

BALANCE AND GRIP

Operators have been seriously injured by the chain blade when they lost their balance by over-reaching or when they released their grip on the handle.

FALLING TREES

A hazard to the operator who did not plan direction of fall or a safe retreat.

SUDDEN STARTUP

Be aware of sudden start-ups when chain blade can jump into action and into you.

FOOTWEAR AND CLOTHING

Wear protective footwear. Loose clothing can catch in a moving chain or sprocket.

WET GROUND

Using ungrounded electric chain saws on wet ground or damp foliage can cause electric shock. You can also slip on wet ground and come in contact with the blade.

LEGS AND ARMS

Keep your arms, legs and the rest of your body out of the line of cutting.

BYSTANDER/ HELPER

Helpers can be hurt when saw slips or kicks back

BEFORE OPERATING:

1. Clear area of branches, sticks and other objects which could be thrown by chain.
2. Refuel *before* starting; avoid spilling. Clean up spills immediately.
3. To prevent fire hazard, start up saw at least 10 feet from where it was fueled.
4. Have controls in proper position to avoid sudden startup of chain blade at high speed.
5. Do not start saw with chain blade in cut.
6. Hold securely and in safe position when starting.
7. If using electric saw, be sure switch is "OFF" before plugging into power source. If not double-insulated, use a 3-wire cord plugged into grounded 3-wire outlet. Only 3-wire extension cords should be used.
8. Be aware of hazards and obstructions in area. When felling trees, plan a safe retreat.

WHILE OPERATING:

1. Keep firm hold with both hands on saw handles; maintain good balance.
2. Keep hands and feet clear of chain blade at all times.
3. Keep body out of line of cut.
4. Avoid cutting above shoulder height.

5. Watch for backlash when cutting limbs or branches.
6. Keep alert for kickback and binding.
7. Keep bystanders away from work area.
8. Wear protective gear - safety goggles, hard hat, sturdy protective shoes and close fitting apparel that won't catch in moving parts.
9. Shut off engine and wait for chain blade to stop before changing position or carrying saw.
10. Keep chain blade and hot muffler away from body while carrying.
11. Never operate in closed, unventilated area.
12. Keep chain well-oiled while cutting.
13. On electric models, keep cord clear of blade.
14. On gasoline models, never add fuel to hot or running engine.
15. Do not allow children to operate.
16. Never leave saw running.
17. After shutdown, saw should be placed on non-combustible surface until it cools.
18. Get specific instructions before operating saw in trees, or before felling tree.
19. Be alert when saw is running - the noise can drown out other sounds.

FOR SAFETY MAINTENANCE

Shut off engine and disconnect spark plug before making repairs.

Check frequently for:
- Leaky fuel lines
- Proper functioning of controls
- Loose or missing guards
  Proper blade tension
  Loose nuts, bolts and fasteners
  Cut and fraying cords (on electric chain saws)
  Always store chain saw in a high and locked place

*Have these corrected by qualified service representatives.

GAS HANDLING AND STORAGE

Keep gasoline in a tightly closed safety can and store in a well ventilated area — away from open flame and children

Never refuel indoors — the invisible vapors may be ignited by a spark.

No smoking — when fueling or while operating chain saw.

Wipe up all spilled gasoline

Use gasoline as fuel only — never as a cleaner

Figure 18-10

DON'T STOP WITH THESE "SYMPTOMS"

UNSAFE ACTS	UNSAFE CONDITIONS
• Operating equipment without authority • Failure to warn • Failure to secure • Operating at improper speed • Making safety devices inoperable • Removing safety devices • Using defective equipment • Using equipment improperly • Not using personal protective equipment • Improper loading • Improper lifting • Improper position for task • Servicing equipment in operation • Horseplay • Under the influence of alcohol and/or other drugs	• Inadequate guards or barriers • Inadequate or improper protective equipment • Defective tools, equipment or materials • Congestion or restricted action • Inadequate warning system • Fire and explosion hazards • Poor housekeeping; disorder • Hazards such as gases, dusts, smokes, fumes and vapors • Noise exposures • Temperature extremes • Inadequate or excess illumination • Inadequate ventilation

CORRECT THESE "BASIC CAUSES"

PERSONAL FACTORS	JOB FACTORS
• Lack of aptitude (innate capacity) • Lack of knowledge • Lack of skill • Improper or inadequate motivation • Fatigue and stress • Physical problems • Mental problems • Inaccurate perception • Misjudgment • Reaction time too fast or too slow • Inattention - distraction - boredom	• Inadequate design • Inadequate communication • Inadequate training - coaching • Inadequate inspection of purchased items • Inadequate maintenance • Inadequate task planning • Inadequate task analysis and procedures • Lack of guided experience • Inadequate incentives • Inadequate direction • Lack of discipline • Wear and tear; deterioration • Lack of leadership example

Figure 18-11

Teach employees to do effective off-the-job investigations by having them help you do on-the-job investigations. Each time you conduct an investigation in your department, ask one (or several if it's appropriate) of your people to be on your investigation team. In your discussions with these team members, include emphasis on the techniques that are adaptable or directly applicable to their off-the-job investigations. You not only will develop better human relations and get more effective accident investigations, but also will contribute significantly to the development of positive safety knowledge, attitudes, skills and habits in your workers and their families.

Job/Task Performance Observation

Encourage family loss control leaders to make frequent spot observations of family members as they perform critical activities with significant potential for accident/injuries/damage/waste. Activities that quickly come to mind as examples are the use of a power mower or weed-eater, the driving of a motor vehicle and activities involving ladders or lifting. Discuss with your people how these performance observations can help them to:

- learn more about the work habits of their family members
- pinpoint practices that could cause accidents and related losses — before the losses occur
- check on the adequacy of instructions they have given
- spotlight specific behaviors for recognition and reinforcement
- determine specific needs for coaching
- give appropriate on-the-spot constructive correction
- show real interest in helping their loved one perform their tasks efficiently and safety

Show your employees the importance and effectiveness of job/task performance observation through *your* observation, both informal and planned, of their performance — and the resulting constructive correction, recognition and reinforcement. Share your leadership skills with them through the example you set. This helps prepare them to do the same with their family members.

Emergency Preparedness

Train employees to transfer pertinent aspects of emergency preparedness from work to home. Emphasize critical concerns that are common to on-the-job and off-the-job emergency preparedness. Use areas and examples such as the following:

EQUIPMENT - Discuss and promote the needs for and the benefits of equipment such as smoke alarms, fire extinguishers, security warning systems, swimming pool rescue devices and security checks to protect vital records and valuables from fire, smoke and water damage.

UTILITY CONTROLS - Urge family loss control leaders to make sure that everyone in their home knows where the control valves and switches are for water, gas and electricity — and how to turn them off and on properly in case of emergency.

TELEPHONE NUMBERS - Stress the need for prominent posting of emergency numbers at each telephone extension. These could include numbers for fire department, police, hospital, doctor, poison control center and ambulance service. These are critical not only for babysitters but also for members of the household. In an emergency, there is no time to search for telephone numbers.

TRAINING AND DRILLS - Train employees to train family members. They should know, for instance, how to respond to various types of emergencies, such as fires, storms, floods, hurricanes, tornadoes, robberies and serious injuries. They should have exit drills so they will know how and where to get out of various areas of the home in case of fire. Drivers should be trained for various emergencies, such as how to change a flat tire out in the "boondocks." They should be trained to handle the emergencies most likely to occur in their recreational activities (e.g., hiking, camping, swimming, boating, fishing, skiing, snowmobiling and various sports).

FIRST AID - This is probably the easiest and most basic area for you to show your people the commonality of on-the-job and off-the-job safety/loss control tools and techniques. When you give first aid training, or discuss it with employees, you automatically are in an area where the knowledge and skills are equally applicable at work, at home, in sports, on vacation, anywhere. Promote first aid training for workers and their families.

The *payoff* also is both off the job and on the job. As *Figure 18-12* explains in more detail, people trained in first aid have fewer accidents than those who are not trained; the accident reduction occurs both on and off the job; the accident frequency may be reduced as much as 30 percent; and each dollar invested in first aid training for employees produces an accident cost

---

Project FACTS

Heralded Breakthrough: Proven Reduction in Accident Incidence

Projects FACTS 1 and 2 speak for themselves.

Their message, translated from the technical language used by expert statisticians who assessed results of the two break-through programs carried out over the past four years in Orillia and Cambridge-Guelph:

There is a positive, statistically discernible relationship between reduced accident rates and First Aid Training.

Project FACTS 1, carried out in Orillia, had as its goal saturation Emergency First Aid Training for all residents of the community. Project FACTS 2, which covered the Cambridge-Guelph industrial area, concentrated on providing First Aid Training for as many employees as possible of business and industries in the two communities. The effects of both projects on the incidence of injuries were evaluated by statisticians from York University. The Industrial Accident Prevention Association provided bursaries to finance the research.

Among their conclusions:
- First Aid Training is positively related to reduction in accidents;
- First Aid-trained employees have fewer accidents than those who are not trained;
- In Cambridge-Guelph's Project FACT 2, where conditions permitted a more detailed analysis based on study of comparable trained and non-trained subjects, those with First Aid Training had half the number of accidents as those without training;
- First Aid training has been shown to reduce accident frequency, on and off the job, by as much as 20 to 30 percent;
- Taking into account that indirect costs of an industrial accident are four times the direct, readily-discernible costs of such occurrences (Heinrich formula), dollar investment in First Aid Training results in substantial savings for participating firms - an estimated $6.97 for each dollar invested based on the Cambridge-Guelph Project FACTS 2 analysis.

Project FACTS 1 in Orillia was a joint undertaking of St. John Ambulance and The Workers' Compensation Board, Ontario, with the former responsible for the training programs.

Figure 18-12

saving estimated at nearly seven dollars. It's the best of both worlds: economic and humane.

Personal Protective Equipment

In some of your group and personal communications regarding personal protective equipment, include discussion about its application off the job as well as on. Eye protection, for instance, is important when using rotary mowers, in some avocational construction and repair activities, when using certain chemicals and when operating some home workshop equipment. Activities that may call for respiratory protection include those such as plowing, cultivating, threshing, sanding, painting and working with chemical sprays and dusts. Hearing protection should be used when shooting guns and operating noisy equipment such as some weed-eaters and mowing machines. Foot protection is a good precaution when using rotary mowers, working with timber or carrying heavy objects. Hand protection is important when working with solvents, cleaners, chemicals, cutting devices and materials with rough edges or splinters. Everyone should use seat belts for personal protection in motor vehicles.

Family safety leaders should be taught to teach their family members, by both education and example, the importance of personal protective equipment. It is just that — PERSONAL — regardless of whether the person is at work, at home or at play.

Personal Communication

It is difficult to think of any supervisory leadership skills that are more important than the personal communication skills of effective instruction, coaching and key point tipping. And supervisory leaders can help their workers realize the importance of such skills for family safety leaders.

EFFECTIVE INSTRUCTION - If there is one leadership skill that is more useful than all the others, this is it. Supervisors should stress this with family loss control leaders. They can apply the "motivate/tell & show/test/check" technique (summarized in *Figure 18-13*) directly to their off-the-job situations.

It's valuable at home — for teaching someone how to operate a new washing machine, decorate a cake, repair a leaky faucet, build a deck, paint the woodwork, prepare a meal, plant a flower bed or a thousand other tasks. It's valuable for driver training — whether the person is learning to drive the family car, truck, bicycle, motorcycle, snowmobile, tractor or boat. It's valuable in sports activities — for teaching family members various aspects of golf, tennis, baseball, football, basketball, soccer, water skiing, snow skiing, scuba diving, hunting, fishing or other games and sports.

COACHING AND KEY POINT TIPPING - These skills supplement effective instruction skills, and can be applied easily to home safety situations. Coaching covers the day-to-day actions a person takes to help another person improve. Key point tipping is a specialized aspect of coaching. It's the organized process of giving people helpful hints, suggestions, reminders or tips about key quality, productivity, cost or safety points in their performance.

By demonstrating and discussing these personal

EFFECTIVE JOB INSTRUCTION

TO PREPARE FOR EFFECTIVE JOB INSTRUCTION

1. HAVE A PLAN

a. Knowledge of the job to be taught
b. How much skill you expect the learner to have, and how soon

2. BREAK DOWN THE JOB

a. List the important steps
b. Highlight key points

3. HAVE THINGS READY AND ORDERLY

a. Proper equipment, materials, supplies and environment
b. Arranged as the employee will be expected to keep things

4. PRACTICE

a. Check the effectiveness of your teaching technique
b. Review and refresh your knowledge and skills periodically

ESSENTIAL ELEMENTS OF EFFECTIVE JOB INSTRUCTION

MOTIVATE

- Put learner at ease
- Find out what learner knows about the job
- Position learner properly
- Build learner's interest

TELL & SHOW

- Demonstrate the operation
- Use step-by-step approach
- Stress key points
- Instruct clearly and completely

TEST

- Have learner tell & show
- Have learner explain key points
- Ask questions and correct or prevent errors
- Continue until you know the learner knows

CHECK

- Tell learner whom to go to for help
- Put learner on his own
- Follow up often; answer questions; review key points
- Taper off to normal amount of supervision
- Reinforce positive parts off performance

Figure 18-13

communication skills with workers, supervisors can contribute significantly to the carryover of these vital skills into the employee's homes and other off-the-job situations. This adds greatly to the knowledge, attitudes, skills and habits that make safety a way of life.

Group Communications

Rather than conducting regular "group loss control meetings," it is more likely that family leaders will conduct "table talks" or informal discussions when there is something worthwhile to talk about. You can help them learn how to improve these group communications. By doing this, you not only will help them be more effective in teaching their loved ones but also will help them develop communication skills that are valuable in all aspects of life, both on and off the job.

One good way of providing a significant teaching/learning experience is to give each employee an opportunity to present a planned talk to his or her on-the-job work group on a key loss control subject. The full value of this experience is gained only when you first teach your group the principles to use, then follow each presentation with analysis and feedback of performance to the individual. *Figure 18-14* shows one set of principles that has been used by thousands of supervisors. But whether you use this one or some other one, use some specific principles or guidelines for making your group presentations — and teach those same principles or guidelines to your people as family safety/loss control leaders.

General Promotion

Although family safety leaders may not use general promotion techniques just as they are used in business and industry, you can suggest how they can adapt some of them for effective safety promotion at home. For instance, while homes do not have safety bulletin boards, many do have cork and/or chalkboards for grocery lists and phone messages. Or they use magnets for attaching messages to the refrigerator. These boards and magnets could be used occasionally to post a safety cartoon, a clipping from the local newspaper or a bit of safety information which the family leader obtained at work. Such postings are likely to stimulate questions, comments and discussions, thereby focusing attention on the subject and helping to stamp safety into people's minds.

As a supervisor, you might also reproduce and dis-

EFFECTIVE TALK ANALYSIS GUIDE

1. How well did he **prepare**? Did he know what he was going to say?... have the information he needed?... make a well-organized presentation?

2. How well did he **pinpoint**? Did he concentrate on one main idea? If so, what was the main idea? Did he stay "on the track?"

3. How did he **personalize**? Did he hold the audience's attention?... make it important to them?... get participation from them?... bring it "close to home"?

4. How well did he **picturize**? Did he use visual aids?... speak clearly and convincingly?... get his message across?... use both **sound** and **sight**?

5. How well did he **prescribe**? Did he summarize his main point at the end?... answer the "so what" question?... ask for specific action? What was his "prescription"?

6. What **one thing** would do the most to make it a better talk?

Good for all kinds of talks

Figure 18-14

tribute to your group facts, figures and articles related to off-the-job safety. For example, information such as shown in *Figure 18-15* could give family safety leaders lots of help for critical topic safety promotion. In this sense, critical topics are those that are the greatest source of home fatalities — such as falls, fires and poisoning. Then, family leaders could use follow-up information and checklists (such as shown in *Figure 18-16*).

If your company sends newsletters or magazines containing safety/loss control information to the homes of employees, you have another good opportunity to encourage safety promotion by family leaders. Refer to that safety information in your group meetings and personal contacts with workers. Discuss how they can use it to promote greater off-the-job safety awareness and action.

Leadership Training

A "Loss Control Leader's Club" is a good way for several supervisors to team up and to share in the direction of an off-the-job monthly club meeting activity, devoted entirely to teaching and learning the skills involved with family loss control leadership. This type of activity is ideal for presentation and teaching of leadership subjects by supervisors, who share each important activity to be incorporated into the family program. Business organizations are usually happy to lend support by providing a meeting room.

A "Loss Control Leader's Course" involves organizing a 10-12 hour course on "Family Protection Leadership," spread over several meetings. The time and place could be scheduled to provide interest within the work group and gain the participation of as many husband and wife teams as possible. While it does require a great deal of special preparation, it is quite surprising how many supervisors thoroughly enjoy an off-the-job opportunity to meet with employees and their spouses. This approach is probably the best way to teach systematic loss control leadership. It should include presentation of distinctive certificates in appropriate ceremonies.

Leadership Example

Your most powerful tool for teaching others to be safety leaders is the example you set. As the supervisor, the on-the-job leader, your actions shout so loudly that people may not hear what your words are saying. Your teaching will command the respect it deserves only when you practice what you teach.

THE MORE YOU SHARE YOUR LEADERSHIP SKILLS THE MORE EFFECTIVE YOUR LEADERSHIP WILL BE

BENEFITS OF FAMILY LEADERSHIP IN OFF-THE-JOB SAFETY

Approaches such as those discussed in this chapter have a host of potential values and benefits. The following list is not complete, but representative:

- Spreading sorely needed leadership skills more fully throughout society

- Developing safety and loss control knowledge,

How people died in home accidents, 1989

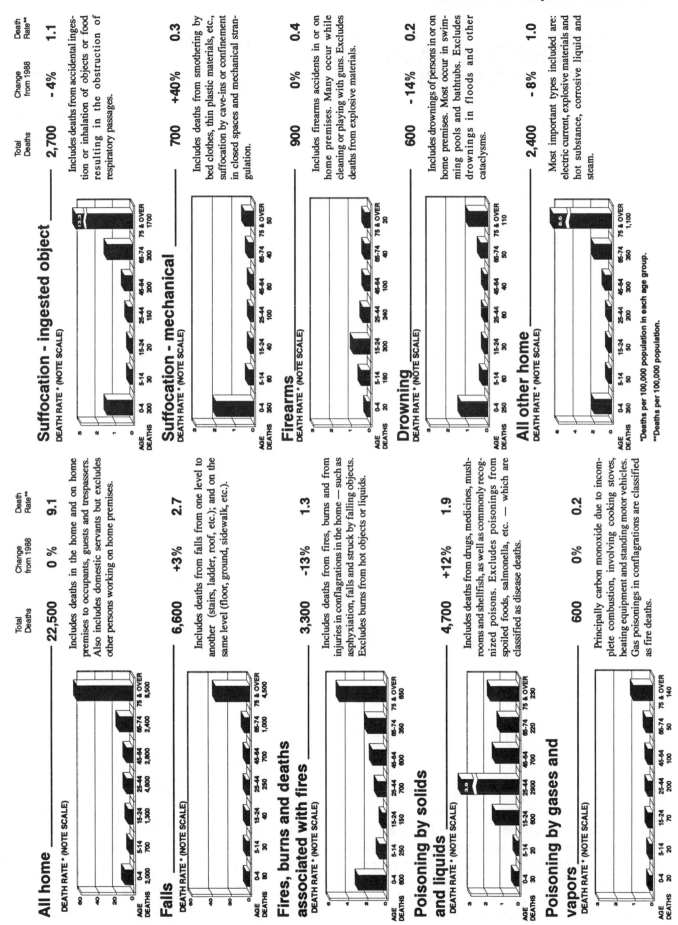

Figure 18-15

Source: National Safety Council, Accident Facts, 1990 edition.

Promote With Questionnaires
such as
"Take Fall Safety Home"

Only motor vehicle accidents kill more people than accidents in the home. And the leading cause of accidental deaths in the home is *falls*. You and your loved ones may profit greatly from checking your habits at home. Here are some of the sorts of things you should check as potential slip/trip/fall hazards.

	No	Yes

Outside

1. Do we return yard and garden tools to their storage racks quickly after use? ____ ____
2. Do we fill in yard holes and repair broken walks and driveways promptly? ____ ____
3. Do we keep swings, slides and other outdoor play equipment maintained in safe condition? ____ ____
4. Do we keep ladders in safe condition? ____ ____
5. Do we follow prescribed safety practices when using ladders? ____ ____

Garage/Workshop/Basement/Utility Room

6. Do we have them well-lighted, with switches at the doors? ____ ____
7. Do we keep their contents orderly (i.e., in their proper places)? ____ ____
8. Do we clean up spills promptly? ____ ____

Living Room/Family Room/Bedroom

9. Do we have hallways and heavy traffic areas well lighted? ____ ____
10. Do we have convenient night lights(especially in bedrooms of children and the elderly)? ____ ____
11. Do we keep traffic areas and exits clear of furniture, obstructions and tripping hazards? ____ ____
12. Do we have nonskid backing on small rugs and avoid using them at the top of stairs? ____ ____

Bathroom/Kitchen

13. Do we use nonskid mats, decals or textured surfaces in tubs and showers? ____ ____
14. Do we have bathroom night lights for children and elderly persons? ____ ____
15. Do we habitually use a step stool or utility ladder when getting at high light fixtures, cupboards or shelves? ____ ____
16. Do we promptly clean up all spills? ____ ____

Stairways

17. Do we have well-lighted stairs, with switches at the top and bottom? ____ ____
18. Do we have sturdy handrails for both outside steps and inside stairways? ____ ____
19. Do we have sturdy bannisters on open stairs, stairwells and balconies? ____ ____
20. Do we avoid using stairways for storage (even "temporarily")? ____ ____
21. Do we keep children from playing on stairs? ____ ____
22. Do we keep treads and stair coverings in good repair? ____ ____
23. Do we avoid carrying vision-blocking loads? ____ ____

Congratulations on your "yes" practices. Now work on the others. The life or well-being of a loved one may depend on it.

Figure 18-16

attitudes, skills and habits for people in all walks of life

- Reducing the tragic toll of accidental deaths and disabling injuries

- Reducing the huge cost of absenteeism and inefficiency caused by accidents

- Reducing the huge financial drain — on individuals, families and companies — of accident costs for insurance, medical care, lost work and repair or replacement of damaged items.

- Developing better participation, morale, human relations and employee-management collaboration

- Making a significant contribution to family life and the quality of life, both on and off the job

CORE CONCEPTS IN REVIEW

The two major groups of reasons why every company and every supervisor should be interested and involved in **off-the-job safety** are:

1. Humane reasons which focus on people

2. Business reasons which focus on performance and economies.

Three out of four worker deaths, and nearly 60% of the disabling injuries suffered by workers, occur off the job. Only about one-third of identified accident costs result from work accidents. Nearly two-thirds result from public accidents, home accidents and motor vehicle accidents.

The following six guidelines for **off-the-job programs** are based on the experience of pioneers in this field.

1. Programs should be family-oriented, rather than aimed only at employees

2. The problems deserve a broad loss control approach (traumatic injury, illness due to hazardous exposures, fire, theft, damage, waste, etc.)

3. Well organized programs produce best results

4. Family-based loss control leadership must be provided on an ongoing basis

5. Overall direction must be provided by a coordinating organization with the professional knowledge and experience to guide the program effectively

6. There is a need to provide program leadership within public groups outside the family unit

The tools and techniques for achieving optimum results in **family safety/loss control** are the same ones that get optimum results in company programs. The following are examples of **critical program elements** for both on and off the job:

- a. Inspections
- b. Task analyses and procedures
- c. Accident/incident investigation
- d. Job/task performance observation
- e. Emergency preparedness
- f. Personal protective equipment
- g. Personal communications
- h. Group communications
- i. General promotion
- j. Leadership training
- k. Leadership example

Among the **significant benefits of family safety leadership and off-the-job safety** are:

1. Spreading sorely needed leadership skills more fully throughout society

2. Developing safety and loss control knowledge, attitudes, skills and habits for people in all walks of life

3. Reducing the tragic toll of accidental deaths and disabling injuries

4. Reducing the huge cost of absenteeism and inefficiency caused by accidents

5. Reducing the huge financial drain — on individuals, families and companies — of accident costs for insurance, medical care, lost work and repair or replacement of damaged items

6. Developing better participation, morale, human relations and employee-management collaboration

7. Making a significant contribution to family life and the quality of life, both on and off the job

KEY QUESTIONS

1. Name the two major types of reasons why supervisors should be interested and involved in off-the-job safety.

2. _____ out of four worker deaths, and nearly _____ percent of the disabling injuries suffered by workers, occur off the job.

3. List several ways that family problems (such as accidents) can affect employees on the job.

4. True or False? Dollar losses from work accidents are considerably greater than from non-work accidents.

5. List four or five categories of company costs that may arise in connection with off-the-job accidents.

6. Six program guidelines have emerged from the experience of pioneers in off-the-job and family safety/loss control. List as many of them as you can.

7. Name eight to ten community groups that could sponsor and promote functions which encourage safety and health.

8. Which management group has the greatest potential and ongoing impact for off-the-job safety emphasis? a) Upper management; b) Middle management; c) Frontline management.

9. True or False? The tools and techniques for achieving optimum results in family safety are essentially the same ones that get optimum results within the company.

10. What are the four aspects of safety K-A-S-H?

11. Give several examples of items in and around the home that should be inspected.

12. How can supervisors help to train employees for...

    a) Off-the-job inspection activities?
    b) Task analysis and procedures?
    c) Accident/incident investigation techniques?
    d) Job/task performance observation?
    e) Group communications at work and at home?

13. List five or six basic causes of accidents in the category of "personal factors," and five or six in the category of "environmental factors."

14. Name three or four home/family applications of emergency preparedness.

15. True or False? Research shows that first aid training tends to reduce accidents.

16. List several off-the-job activities that call for personal protective equipment.

17. It is difficult to think of any leadership skills that are more important than the personal communication skills of effective i_____, c_____ and key point t_____.

18. Name the four essential elements of effective job instruction.

19. What are the five P's of the effective safety talk technique?

20. Explain the concepts of...

    a) a Loss Control Leader's Club
    b) a Loss Control Leader's Course

21. The more you share your l_____ skills, the more effective your l_____ will be.

PRACTICAL APPLICATIONS SUMMARY

S – For Supervisors
E – For Executives
C – For Safety/Loss Control Coordinators

	S	E	C
1. Include off-the-job and family safety in the organization's safety/loss control policy and/or directives.		x	
2. Keep the management group informed of state-of-the-art practices regarding off-the-job and family safety/loss control.			x
3. Establish a system for collecting, analyzing and communicating off-the-job and family accident information.		x	
4. Keep track of the company's costs for off-the-job and family accidents.		x	x
5. Provide leadership trainer training for frontline supervisors.		x	x
6. Coordinate ongoing activities within the company for off-the-job and family safety/loss control.		x	x
7. Coordinate and/or participate in special emphasis and ongoing safety activities within the community.	x	x	x
8. Use on-the-job safety/loss control activities to help train employees as off-the-job safety leaders.	x		
9. Use employee involvement in on-the-job inspections as a springboard to off-the-job inspections for family safety/loss control.	x		
10. Relate worker participation in task analysis and proper procedures to their off-the-job activities, as well as on the job.	x		
11. Train workers in proper investigation techniques, use them in on-the-job investigations and relate their knowledge and experience to off-the-job accident/incident investigation.	x		
12. Coach workers regarding off-the-job applications of the job/task performance observation and feedback techniques used on the job.	x		
13. Train employees to transfer pertinent aspects of emergency preparedness from work to home.	x		
14. Relate on-the-job personal protective equipment applications to off-the-job applications.	x		
15. Show employees the values of good personal communications (e.g., effective job instruction, coaching, key point tipping) for both on and off the job.	x		
16. In group safety meetings, include emphasis on how to have effective family group discussions for safety/loss control.	x		
17. Use company safety promotion activities to promote off-the-job and family safety/loss control.	x	x	x
18. Provide supervisors with the information, incentives and aids to help them train and motivate employees to live safely both on and off the job.		x	x

CHAPTER 19

SPECIAL PROBLEM SOLUTIONS

"It is the problems of life that create the greatest opportunities." - Anonymous

INTRODUCTION

This chapter briefly answers some of the common questions asked by supervisors in safety/loss control training sessions around the world. The answers are based on analysis of tools and techniques that have proven helpful through the years. To the old-timer who has learned these through experience, most of the suggestions will not seem to be new or unique — they will seem to be "common sense." To the relatively new supervisor, as well as the experienced one facing new challenges related to these problems, the suggestions should be valuable. Hopefully, these answers will help to make "common sense" more common.

There is no magic formula or secret solution that guarantees success in leading the way through these problems. The suggestions give some guidelines that others have been able to use successfully. They do, however, require effort and the application of supervisory management skills. If you work at them, they should work for you.

WHAT CAN I DO TO SELL AND PROMOTE SAFETY?

Some say the first law of selling is: "sell yourself first." People "buy you" before they buy your product. To sell yourself best, you must know yourself. How do you come across to your people? Do they believe you? Do they trust you? What are your strengths? Your limitations? Do you think safety, believe safety, live safety? Do you treat safety on a par with quality, production and cost control? Does your behavior speak loudly for safety?

Every good salesperson learns everything he or she can about the product. In this case, the "product" is safety. To sell and promote it best, you must keep your safety knowledge as complete and current as possible: think about it — read about it — write about it — talk about it — do something about it.

You need to know enough about safety not only to understand it yourself, but also to help other people understand it. You should have a good grasp of critical aspects such as:

- Implications of the modern definition: safety is control of accident losses.
- The updated accident cause-and-effect (domino) sequence.
- The vital differences between "symptoms" and "basic causes."
- The ISMEC concept of control.
- The differences between the post-contact, contact and pre-contact stages of control — and the main actions to take for each stage.
- The ratio of major injuries to minor injuries, to property damage accidents, to near-accidents — and what this means for accident prevention and control.

- The place of communication, training and motivation in safety programs.
- How and why safe behavior reinforcement works.
- The content of your organization's safety/loss control policy, procedures, practices, rules and regulations.
- The "whys" and wherefores" of program elements such as orientation, inspection, job/task analysis and procedures, investigation, planned job observation, proper job instruction, safety meetings, coaching and tipping.

For successful selling, you also must know your customers — in this case, your employees. People buy things and do things for their own reasons. Not your reasons, *their* reasons. This means you need to know as much as you can about people in general, and about your workers in particular. Then you can do the best job of relating safety to *their* needs, *their* desires, *their* goals, *their* work, *their* viewpoints, *their* families, *their* attitudes, *their* well-being.

Promote Safety In Meetings

Meetings provide excellent opportunities for selling/promoting safety. They may be orientation meetings, training meetings, problem-solving meetings, informational meetings or regular safety meetings. All of these give you a good chance to show your concern not only with production, quality and costs, but also with safety.

You can get better and better results from your meetings by applying the meeting leadership skills discussed in Chapter 9, *Group Meetings*.

Promote Safety with Individuals

As a supervisor, you are a key person in the work life of each of your workers. They look to you for leadership. They learn from you. Through individual contacts, each one gets to know you better and you get to know him or her better. Use these contacts to emphasize safety, as well as other things. The primary purpose of the contact may be:

- job orientation
- job assignment
- proper job instruction
- job/task analysis
- planned job observation
- incident investigation
- project follow-up
- planned personal contact

- rules review
- performance feedback

But whatever the primary purpose is, every such contact is a natural opportunity for promoting safety.

Promote Safety in Print

Printed materials such as bulletins, posters, statistical reports, booklets, magazines and newsletters can be used effectively to promote safety and health. They can both supplement and reinforce your other promotional activities. Following are some hints on how to make them most effective.

Bulletins and Posters — Be the first to know the content of current posters and bulletin board materials. Encourage your people to read them. Stimulate interest by referring to them in your group meetings and personal contacts. Ask people what they think the message is, what it means, and why it is important. See that posters and bulletin boards are kept neat and up-to-date.

Magazines and Newsletters — These usually reach a large majority of employees and their families, contain safety and health items, report unusual accidents and lessons learned from them and tell what is being done to promote safety and healthful work conditions.

Here are 4 R's as tips for using these materials effectively: read/refer/reproduce/reinforce. *Read* them, note highlights and figure out how they apply to your operation. *Refer* to them in talking with your people. Stimulate others to read them. *Reproduce* portions of materials that relate to your operation. Underline, circle or highlight key points. Distribute them to each person. *Reinforce* written materials by discussing them, by asking others to read and comment on them by working them into your personal contacts and group meetings.

Statistical Reports - Polish dull safety statistics into shining examples of effective communication. Convert numbers and percentages into dollars and human beings. Relate to flesh and blood, to fathers, mothers, sons, daughters, brothers, sisters, grandparents and grandchildren. Discuss specific accidents behind the figures. Ask people to think and talk about what effects a given case may have had upon the family. Use aids to create clear mental pictures of what the losses mean in terms of people, property, production and profits.

Promote Safety with Awards and Recognition

Recognition and reinforcement are powerful promoters of safe behavior. Incentive programs, contests, awards and special presentations can be effective tools in your safety promotion kit.

Contests which require people to *learn, do* or *remember* something for safety can be effective promotional tools. They help to keep interest high, focus attention on critical areas, encourage learning and stimulate improvement. As a supervisor, you can do a lot to help make contests successful. For example, you can:

- Be well informed of the nature of contests and their rules.
- Pass out and collect contest materials on time.
- Encourage your people to read the materials and participate in the contests.
- Prevent coverup of injuries and property damage.
- Ask your people for suggestions about what should be promoted.
- Share your group's ideas with those responsible for preparing contests.
- Give adequate recognition to your people who win. Make the awards special and meaningful.
- Let your enthusiasm show. Help make safety fun.

Safety suggestion campaigns may be helpful promotional tools. With proper planning, organization, publicity and follow-up, these campaigns can bring forth many excellent ideas from the people closest to the hazards — the workers themselves. And they can stimulate a lot of thinking about safety.

You can help by suggesting special campaigns, encouraging people to make suggestions, assisting them in brainstorming and developing their ideas, giving your people credit for their participation and doing your part in the program in a timely and willing manner.

There are quite a few safety recognition clubs for those who have avoided death or serious injury through the use of personal protective equipment. Examples are the Shield of Safety Club, Wise Owl Club, Half Way to Hell Club, Golden Shoe Club, Kangaroo Club, Gold Cap Award, Ten-On-Two Club and Crown Club. When workers qualify for these awards, you have an excellent opportunity for safety promotion.

Awards presentations can be like frosting on a cake — and make a tremendous difference. Awards serve as incentives, help build good will, maintain interest and provide opportunities for publicity and recognition. Presentation of awards should be done in some special way. Often it's a good idea to include the winner's boss, family, co-workers and/or others such as top executives and community dignitaries at the presentation. Pictures and publicity help, too. As a supervisor, you should make sure that your workers who earn awards get adequate recognition in an appropriate presentation ceremony. This is an investment in positive motivation that pays great dividends.

Promote Safety by Personal Example

Safety promotion leadership for your area is in your head (what you think), in your heart (what you believe) and in your hands (what you do). The importance of your personal example is reflected in this little poem by Forrest H. Kirkpatrick:

> The eye's a better student and more willing than the ear;
>
> Fine counsel is confusing, but example's always clear;
>
> And the best of all the preachers are the men who live their creeds,
>
> For to see the good in action is what everybody needs.
>
> I can soon learn how to do it if you'll let me see it done;
>
> I can watch your hands in action, but your tongue too fast may run;
>
> And the lectures you deliver may be very wise and true,
>
> But I'd rather get my lesson by observing what you do.
>
> For I may not understand you and the high advice you give,
>
> But there's no misunderstanding how you act and how you live.

Summary Principles and Promotion Aids

Five primary principles are threaded through all we have said about supervisory safety promotion. They are the principles of Information, Involvement, Mutual Interest, Behavior Reinforcement and Utilization. *Figure 19-1* includes descriptions of these principles nestled among 125 promotion and thought-joggers.

PROMOTION PRINCIPLES

THE INFORMATION PRINCIPLE
EFFECTIVE COMMUNICATION INCREASES MOTIVATION

THE INVOLVEMENT PRINCIPLE
MEANINGFUL INVOLVEMENT INCREASES MOTIVATION AND SUPPORT

THE MUTUAL INTEREST PRINCIPLE
PROGRAMS AND IDEAS ARE BEST SOLD WHEN THEY BRIDGE THE WANTS AND DESIRES OF BOTH PARTIES

THE BEHAVIOR REINFORCEMENT PRINCIPLE
BEHAVIOR WITH NEGATIVE EFFECTS TENDS TO DECREASE OR STOP; BEHAVIOR WITH POSITIVE EFFECTS TENDS TO CONTINUE OR INCREASE

THE UTILIZATION PRINCIPLE
THE SOONER AND MORE OFTEN AN IDEA OR SKILL IS PUT TO WORK, THE BETTER IT IS LEARNED AND REMEMBERED.

PROMOTION AIDS: A to Z

ANECDOTES
ANNOUNCEMENTS
AUDIO TAPES
AUDIT
AWARDS

BADGES
BALLOONS
BANNERS
BOOKLETS
BULLETIN BOARDS

CAMPAIGNS
CARTOONS
CHALK BOARDS
CHARTS
COACHING
COMMENDATIONS
COMMITTEES
CONTACTS
CONTESTS
COUNSELING

DEMONSTRATIONS
DIAGRAMS
DISCIPLINE
DISPLAYS
DRAWINGS

EQUIPMENT
EXAMPLES
EXHIBITS

FEEDBACK
FILMSTRIPS
FIRST AID COURSES
FLANNEL BOARDS
FLIP CHARTS

GRAPHS
GUARDS
GROUP MEETINGS

HANDBOOKS
HANDOUTS
HOUSEKEEPING

INSPECTION
INSTRUCTION
INVESTIGATION

JOB ANALYSIS
JOB INSTRUCTION
JOB OBSERVATION
JOB ORIENTATION

KANGAROO CLUB
KEY POINT TIPS
KITS
KUDOS

LEADERSHIP
LEAFLETS
LETTERS

MACHINES
MAGAZINES
MOBILES
MOCK-UPS
MODELS
MOTIVATION
MOVIES

NEWSLETTERS
NEWSPAPERS
NOTICES
NOVELTIES

PROMOTION AIDS: A to Z

ORDER
ORIENTATION

PAINTINGS
PERSONAL CONTACTS
PERSONAL EXAMPLE
PICTURES
POCKET CARDS
POLICIES
POSTERS
PROCEDURES
PROJECTORS
PROTECTIVE EQUIPMENT

QUESTIONNAIRES
QUIZZES
QUOTATIONS

RADIO
RECOGNITION
RECORDS
REGULATIONS
REINFORCEMENT
REMINDERS
REPORTS
REWARDS
RULES

SAFE JOB PRACTICES
SAFETY CLUBS
SAFETY TALKS
SAFETY TIPS
SCHEMATICS
SIGNS
SLIDES
SLOGANS
STANDARDS
SYMBOLS
SUGGESTION SYSTEMS
SUPERVISION

TAGS
TEAMS
TELEVISION
THEME PROGRAMS
TOOLS
TOURS
TRAINING
TRANSPARENCIES

UNDERLYING CAUSES
UNDERSTANDING

VARIETY
VIDEOTAPES
VIGILANCE
VISUAL AIDS
VITAL STATISTICS

WALLET CARDS
WARNINGS
WISE OWL CLUB
WORKSHOPS

X-RAYS

YARNS
YOURSELF

ZEAL
ZEST
ZING

Figure 19-1

HOW CAN I OBTAIN AND MAINTAIN COMPLIANCE WITH RULES AND REGULATIONS?

Violation of established rules and regulations is one of the most common causes of accidents. But there are organizations, and individual supervisors, who manage to keep this cause under control. The ways they do this are summarized here in terms of 1) Preparation, 2) Presentation, 3) Enforcement, 4) Reinforcement and 5) Leadership Example.

Preparation of Rules

When called upon to assist in developing rules that affect your people, use guidelines such as the following.

Apply the Principle of Involvement - "Meaningful involvement increases motivation and support." Find out what rules your workers think are needed. Get their ideas and suggestions. Tap the positive power of the "our rules" attitude. People are much more likely to live up to rules they helped to create.

Keep Rules at a Minimum - Don't try to cover everything with rules. Emphasize practices and conditions that could result in major loss. Keep these four key questions in mind:

- Is there a real need?
- Does this rule meet the need?
- Is it practical?
- Is it enforceable?

People are much more likely to comply with rules when they are important and few.

Apply the "Kiss" Principle - "Keep It Short and Simple." Avoid complicated details that make rules hard to understand and remember. People are much more likely to follow rules that are short/ simple/clear/understandable.

Keep Rules as Practical as Possible - Rules that require people to replace easy, convenient, normal behavior with difficult, inconvenient, unusual behavior invite non-compliance. For example:

- If compliance takes more time than non-compliance, people will tend to break the rule — to save time.
- If compliance requires more effort (work) than non-compliance, people will tend to break the rule — to save the effort.
- If compliance is less comfortable than non-compliance, people will tend to break the rule — to avoid discomfort.

People are much more likely to live up to rules based on "normal" human behavior.

Give Reasons for Rules - There should be good reasons for all rules. If there is no good reason, there should be no rule. Print the reason with the rule. People are much more likely to comply with rules when they understand the reasons for them.

Presentation of Rules

Following are some practices you can use to stimulate good understanding and retention when covering rules with workers.

Suggest Worker Preview - Make sure each person as his or her own copy of the rules. Ask people to get familiar with them, to note their questions and comments. This prepares them for a good rules discussion with you.

"Show & Tell" During the Discussion - Use visual aids to increase attention, retention and understanding. Demonstrate what the rule means and why it is important. Use pertinent tools and equipment, pictures, slides, flip pads, transparencies and so on. Ask workers to highlight or underline key words in their printed materials. Use both sound and sight. Help people to both hear and see what you mean.

Test Their Knowledge of Rules - Get feedback. Find out how well they know the rules and the reasons for them. Resist the temptation to assume that they understand what you have presented only once. Give written and/or verbal tests (see a simple example in *Figure 19-2*). Discuss the test results as a summary and wind-up for your presentation.

Enforcement of Rules

Equitable, consistent enforcement of rules encourages compliance. This requires clear communication of the rules, the reasons and the related disciplinary policy and procedures. It also requires good records, such as:

- A rule discussion record, preferably signed by the worker, when the rules were received and discussed.
- Records showing which rules were emphasized in group meetings, and when.

```
┌─────────────────────────────────────────────┐
│                                             │
│        SAMPLE QUESTIONS FOR RULE            │
│          EDUCATION AND REVIEW               │
│                                             │
│  1.  What action should you take when you are │
│      not sure about how to do the job?      │
│      (Ask for Proper Job Instruction)       │
│                                             │
│  2.  Report immediately to your foreman or  │
│      supervisor any _____ or      │
│      _____ you think might cause  │
│      injury to employees or damage to equip-│
│      ment.                                  │
│      (condition)  (practice)                │
│                                             │
│  3.  Why should you keep your work area     │
│      clean and orderly?                     │
│                                             │
│      (Dirt and disorder cause injury, damage,│
│      waste, etc.)                           │
│                                             │
│  4.  Use the right _____ and      │
│      _____ for the job; use them  │
│      in a _____ manner.           │
│                                             │
│      (tools) (equipment) (safe)             │
│                                             │
│  5.  What should you do when you or the     │
│      equipment you operate are involved in an│
│      accident that results in injury or damage?│
│      (Report it immediately to your foreman or│
│      supervisor; get first aid promptly.)   │
│                                             │
│  6.  True or False? Every employee is ex-   │
│      pected to use, adjust, alter and repair│
│      equipment.                             │
│      (False... "only when authorized.")     │
│                                             │
│  7.  What types of personal protective equip-│
│      ment must be worn at all times in plant│
│      operating and maintenance areas?       │
│      (Approved head, eye and foot protection.)│
│                                             │
│  8.  Why should there be no horseplay on the│
│      job?                                   │
│      (It distracts people from their work,  │
│      causes accidents, injures people,      │
│      damages property, etc.)                │
│                                             │
│  9.  What is the first thing to remember about│
│      proper lifting?                        │
│      (Bend your knees.)                     │
│                                             │
│  10. General safety rule number 10 says to  │
│      obey all specific _____, _____ and │
│      _____.                       │
│                                             │
│      (rules) (signs) (instructions)         │
│                                             │
└─────────────────────────────────────────────┘
```

Figure 19-2

- Records of rules reviews and refresher training.
- Records of individual violations and related disciplinary actions.
- Records of group or individual commendations for rules compliance.

Enforcement is an example of your "management control" function at work: identifying desired behavior, setting standards, evaluating what you observe and measure and improving compliance through commendation/correction/coaching.

Reinforcement of Rules

You can reinforce the importance of rules, and gain greater compliance, by referring to them frequently in both formal and informal, individual and group contacts.

Group Meeting Discussions - A major rule can be an excellent topic for a short safety meeting. Examples of accidents and near accidents caused by rule violations serve as excellent motivational material for helpful discussions.

Personal Contact Reminders - Rules should be emphasized and highlighted when giving proper job instruction (PJI) or informal tips for improved job performance.

Behavior Reinforcement Contacts - A positive program of reinforcement for specific rules can be implemented by following the behavior reinforcement technique discussed in Chapter 12, *Job Pride Development*.

Reference to Postings - General safety and health rules should be posted in positions and places that reinforce their message and purpose. Verbal reference to these postings is another way to reinforce their importance — and to stimulate compliance.

Basis for Contest Awards - A knowledge and understanding of specific rules can be the required preparation for award eligibility in promotion programs and contests.

Formal Review - All rules should be reviewed with all employees (using techniques mentioned under "Presentation of Rules") not less than once each year.

Leadership Example

The question at the beginning of this section was "How Can I Obtain and Maintain Compliance with Rules and Regulations?" Perhaps the most important answer is "by the leadership model you demonstrate, the personal example you set for your people." Now and then, look into your mental mirror to see what kinds of answers are reflected back for questions like these:

- How often do I ignore rules violations?
- How often do I recognize people for their good job of rules compliance?
- How well do I follow the rules myself?
- How well does what I *do* support what I say about rules?

People are much more likely to follow the rules when they have the best example to follow in their leader.

WHAT'S THIS THING CALLED "CONSTRUCTIVE CORRECTION" OR "POSITIVE DISCIPLINE"?

Basic Definition

When most people think of "discipline" they think in terms of scolding, threatening, reprimanding and punishing. But this is just one side of the coin — the negative side.

The positive or constructive side should be considered more often. The word *discipline* comes from the same root as the word *disciple* and means "to teach so as to mold." True discipline involves assisting, guiding and training people; it encourages self-development and self-control; it is constructive rather than destructive; it emphasizes correction rather than punishment. The positive discipline process is the coaching process at its finest.

Reasons for Corrective Discipline

Corrective discipline comes to mind when people break rules, violate required work practices or otherwise fail to meet performance standards. In other words, we think of discipline as a solution to a performance problem. But how often is "punishment" the best solution?

One of the most basic truths in problem solving is that we must concentrate not on symptoms but on causes. What are the causes behind violations? Why do people fail to meet performance standards? Why

don't employees do what they are supposed to do? Clear answers come from experience and research. For example, in his book *Coaching For Improved Work Performance*, Ferdinand Fournies discusses his survey of 4,000 managers, from foremen to presidents. Responses to "Why don't subordinates do what they are supposed to do?" were as follows:

WHY SUBORDINATES DON'T DO WHAT THEY ARE SUPPOSED TO DO

1. They don't know what they are supposed to do.
2. They don't know how to do it.
3. They don't know why they should.
4. There are obstacles beyond their control.
5. They don't think it will work.
6. They think their way is better.
7. Not motivated; poor attitude.
8. Personally incapable of doing it (personal limits).
9. Not enough time for them to do it.
10. They are working on wrong priority items.
11. They think they are doing it (no feedback).
12. Poor management.
13. Personal problems.

The majority of reasons do not call for punishment. They call for better management/supervision/leadership. They call for communication, motivation and training. They call for coaching.

The Corrective Discipline Process

Most supervisors are familiar with this four-stage disciplinary approach: 1) oral warning, 2) written warning, 3) time off without pay and 4) discharge. This is a fairly common, almost traditional, approach — the negative approach. But it need not be the *only* way! In fact, some companies have replaced it with a positive approach.

Figure 19-3 compares the punitive and positive approaches. Though they both can end in discharge, the psychological impact of the two approaches is vastly different. The punitive approach relies almost totally on warnings, reprimands, threats and other forms of punishment. In contrast, the positive approach is one of helping, coaching and mutual problem solving. Even the discharge can hardly be considered as punishment when the prior help has been given, the paid time off has been provided and the choice has been made by the employee.

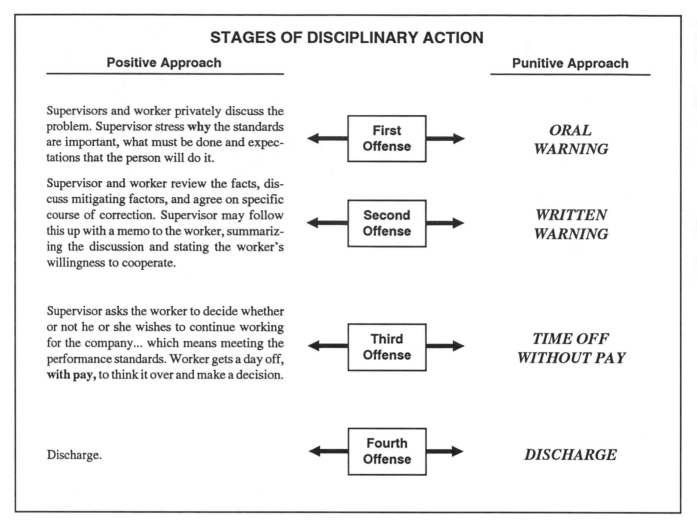

Figure 19-3

With either of the two approaches, you don't always go through all four stages. Some offenses automatically result in discharge the first time. Others may be serious enough that you start at the second or third step. But even in these cases, your approach can be either punitive or positive — and can make a huge difference. In other words, you can administer *corrective* discipline in a *constructive* manner. The way you do it and how you explain it are what make the difference. Your words and actions say either:

"I'm punishing you because I care, I'm concerned about your performance, and I want to help you meet required standards."

-or-

"I'm punishing you because the system calls for it, or because I want to get even with you."

Preventive Discipline

"An ounce of prevention is worth..." Whether it be in matters of physical health, mental health, delinquency, crime, traffic or safety — *preventive measures* are most important, most valuable, most satisfying. The same is true regarding organizational discipline.

Preventive discipline means that we try, at all times, to prevent violations of rules and standards from occurring so that corrective discipline won't be necessary. Here are a few pointers on how to prevent violations:

1. Be sure that *you* know what the company's rules and standards are, and why they are necessary.
2. Be sure that your employees know what the company's rules and standards are, that they understand them and that they know why they are necessary.
3. Emphasize why and how observance of the rules and standards is in the workers' best self-interests.
4. Instruct your people in the proper work methods and practices.
5. Give simple, clear, understandable assignments

and get feedback to make sure they are understood.

6. If an employee definitely cannot be taught to do a particular job, consider whether he or she might be able to do some other job. Don't just wait for the chance to terminate the person — try to save him or her.

7. If you have reason to believe that an employee is going to violate a rule or standard, don't sit back and wait for your chance to "nail" him or her. Don't be like a cop waiting behind a billboard with your motorcycle engine running. Try to get the employee on the right road before he or she is in trouble.

8. Before you take punitive action against a worker, ask yourself this question: "Have I given this person every consideration and help that I would believe was fair if I were in his or her shoes?"

It also helps to analyze cases where punitive action was taken and see what really happened and how it might have been prevented. In each case, you can ask yourself "What could I have done to *prevent* this offense?" and "What can I learn from this case to help me *prevent* similar violations in the future?" Look especially for conditions and contributing factors such as:

- person placed in wrong job
- inadequate training
- failure to create a positive work atmosphere
- failure to provide motivational incentives and reinforcement
- poor communication
- poor working conditions
- failure to detect early warning signs of a troubled employee
- excessive tolerance of substandard performance
- poor instructions
- playing favorites or displaying prejudices
- treating people like machines

If one or more of these, or similar management weaknesses, were involved, something *can* and *should* be done about it. After all, the most successful punitive action can't do any more than mop up the already spilled milk. The real leadership talent is to keep it from spilling in the first place.

PITFALLS AND PRECAUTIONS IN DISCIPLINARY DISCUSSIONS

PITFALLS	PRECAUTIONS
Flying off "half-cocked."	Take the time to get the facts.
"Seeing red."	Count to ten. Cool off. Keep emotion down and problem-solving logic up.
Assaulting and insulting the person or personality.	Concentrate on behavior — specific actions — performance.
Being a "bulldozer."	Ask for the other person's version, explanations and suggestions. Listen actively.
"Skimming the surface."	Search for the basic causes of the problems. Treat the disease, not the symptoms.
"Blowing off steam" in public; humiliating the individual and yourself.	Discuss violations and problems in private.
"Running hot and cold."	Deal promptly and fairly with all violations. Enforce standards consistently.
Being "too soft" or "too hard."	Make the corrective action fit the violation and the circumstances. Be both firm and fair.
Leaving mental pictures "fuzzy."	Carefully discuss the standard, the violation and the corrective action. Get feedback which shows mutual understanding.
Threatening and "bluffing."	Clarify and specify consequences of future violations. Follow through as promised.
Negativism	Give credit for the person's performance pluses. Express confidence in his or her ability to improve. Praise progress.

Figure 19-4

HOW CAN I GET PROPER USE OF PROTECTIVE EQUIPMENT?

Since the use of protective equipment is usually covered by rules and practices, most of the earlier comments on gaining compliance with rules and regulations apply to this subject as well. In addition, there are specific potential problems regarding protective equipment that deserve special attention. This section briefly describes the factors believed to have the greatest effect upon the success or failure of a protective equipment program: 1) advance promotion of need, 2) selection of equipment, 3) proper personal fitting, 4) sensitivity to individual problems, 5) period of adjustment, 6) sanitation and waste control, 7) continuous promotion, 8) behavior reinforcement, 9) follow-through and 10) showing the way.

Advance Promotion of Need

Few people like to be surprised, unless the surprise is pleasant. Well in advance of any formal program or requirement, you should begin a well-organized effort to promote the real need for the equipment. Every time you demonstrate specific values to be received and needs to be met by the equipment, you help prepare people to cooperate.

Selection of Equipment

Whenever practical, representatives of those who will have to wear the equipment should have their say in selection decisions. For example, when several models all meet required specifications, you should give workers the chance to express their preferences. Apply the Principle of Involvement: "Meaningful involvement increases motivation and support." When your people participate in the selection of personal protective equipment, they will be more likely to wear it willingly.

Proper Personal Fitting

The majority of complaints about protective equipment involve physical discomfort. Nearly every protective item has certain features that can be adjusted or regulated to best adapt it to the individual user. You should thoroughly explain to the individual every feature that could affect proper use and comfort. Certain features, such as a respirator seal, are critical to the worker's safety and health. To save time and avert major problems that could be caused by ignorance, you should become familiar with all important features concerning proper fit. By making sure that workers are fitted properly and thoroughly understand the use and care of the equipment, you will have taken a giant step toward the prevention of problems.

Sensitivity to Individual Problems

You should quickly and clearly identify those few people with real or alleged problems, and systematically work to resolve them. It is generally best to assume that all problems are real. There usually are several practical solutions to each problem which will not sacrifice program standards. These standards should always be maintained during problem-solving exercises.

Experience shows that the success or failure of a program frequently hinges on the supervisor's ability to resolve the relatively few problems that can be expected to accompany any program. Solutions invariably come from positive, persistent efforts to find answers.

Period of Adjustment

A certain amount of resistance and negative response to wearing or using something that feels "different" or seems to be inconvenient is a natural thing with any group. You can handle this best with an understanding attitude of encouragement and positive reinforcement during the early period of adjustment. In due time, most resistance and negative response will disappear and be replaced by pride in group conformance.

Sanitation and Waste Control

Providing a means, when needed, to clean and sanitize equipment could affect its acceptance and use. As a supervisor, you may not be responsible for some of the details of such a program, but you should be aware of its mechanics to see that it is carried out to meet the real needs of your people. Teaching workers the proper care and use of their equipment has two major benefits: 1) it helps to assure that people will use equipment properly and 2) it minimizes the need to replace costly articles misplaced or damaged through negligence.

Many organizations with better programs loan personal protective equipment to workers, with the understanding that they must replace it if they lose it. A simple card-file system requires a signature or initial by the worker for each item received. This record also serves as a reference to analyze whether usage is normal or abnormal. This type of effort encourages good stewardship on the part of workers and promotes their respect for and proper use of protective equipment.

Continuous Promotion

Most supervisors quickly recognize that an effective level of protective equipment performance is much more likely when every available opportunity is used to reinforce desired behavior. Group meetings and personal contacts provide excellent opportunities for promoting proper use of equipment through positive reinforcement.

A pair of safety glasses that saved a worker's eye and a hard hat that prevented serious injury are excellent examples of items widely used by supervisors around the world to maintain interest and keep their programs effective. It is not uncommon for people to give personal testimonials on the value of such equipment during meetings or other contacts. Keeping the group well-informed of its level of performance in the proper use of equipment can also be a very strong motivational tool. Group recognition for attaining a desired level of performance over a specified period of time is another good supervisory technique. The most important thing to realize is that your promotional efforts must be continuous and your techniques varied to hold everyone's interest.

Behavior Reinforcement

Application of the principles of behavior reinforcement described earlier can have special values in maintaining an effective equipment program. One special application deserving mention is the use of behavior reinforcement with workers who have been identified as non-conformers to required standards. You should devote as much (or more) effort to giving positive reinforcement when you observe conformance by the person with the problem as you give to correcting his or her non-conformance.

Behavior reinforcement is one of the most powerful tools you can use, especially with workers who use special equipment only on infrequent occasions. Maintenance of standards in this type of situation presents one of the greatest challenges, since the individual's awareness and judgment are the primary control factors. Written commendations from supervisors for workers who consistently comply with protective equipment standards in this type of situation are especially suitable for reinforcing desired practices.

Follow-Through

With an effective program of continuous education and promotion, and an organized effort to solve problems as they occur, you should have little need for punishment in your program of enforcement. As a last resort, you should be prepared to use it as described earlier under "constructive correction."

Showing the Way

There is no area of your loss control work in which the personal example you set is more important than it is for personal protective equipment — an area of high visibility behaviors. By being the model, by personally complying with all protective equipment requirements at all times, you give your group a powerful and positive promotional influence.

WHAT CAN I DO TO MOTIVATE GOOD HOUSEKEEPING PRACTICES?

Here are some choice statements attributed to leading executives:

- "Order is the first step in doing anything right, and if you cannot manage the order of your operation, you cannot manage your operation."

- "There isn't anything that will waste all three things that we use (TIME, ENERGY and MATERIALS) like disorder."

- "You must stop assuming that it costs money to keep plants and offices in order. IT COSTS MONEY NOT TO KEEP THEM IN ORDER."

- "You should manage your plant or office in such a way that you have order at all times. If you wait until the work turn is over to get orderly, WHAT GOOD HAS ORDERLINESS DONE YOU ON THAT WORK TURN?"

- "If you allow yourself and your operation to become dirty and disorderly, you may require janitorial services to remove the accumulation of dirt. BUT PREVENTING THAT ACCUMULATION IS GOOD MANAGEMENT."

- "A program of orderliness — carried out by supervision and individual employees — can bring big reductions in accidents, stores inventories and wasted time and energy."
- "The sure result of order is greater and safer production of better products at lower costs. Improved production and costs mean increased business and prosperity for any organization and its employees."

As a supervisor, you probably feel that benefits such as these are well worth the investment of some time and effort. The following seven suggestions should help to make your investment most profitable: 1) Know the difference between "cleanliness" and "order", 2) Teach "cleanliness" and "order" to others, 3) Conduct an "operation order" campaign, 4) Encourage an "orderly" attitude, 5) Set up a system to recover unnecessary items, 6) Use the power of positive recognition and 7) Apply personal observation/decision/action.

Know the Difference Between "Cleanliness" and "Order"

Before you can motivate desirable practices in others, you need a clear picture of what it is you are attempting to motivate. Many supervisors think of good housekeeping only in terms of cleanliness and, by so doing, miss the whole meaning of *order*. While cleanliness is an important part of housekeeping, it is only one part. The old slogan, "A clean plant is a safe plant," has led to acceptance of another widely-used slogan, "A place for everything, and everything in its place." Both of these slogans relate to the "clean" aspect of housekeeping — but may miss the whole point of "order." For example, a four-foot piece of 2x4 lumber or a six-foot piece of 1-1/2" iron pipe, neatly placed on a shelf will appear to reflect good housekeeping (as suggested in the above slogans). But if the board belongs in the carpenter shop and the pipe in the pipe shop, they are not in "order" by the definition stated in *Figure 19-5*.

While their placement on the shelf looks "clean and neat," their absence from the proper place for storage could cost this organization money. In fact, when one considers an entire organization and all of the possible items that might not be in their proper places, one begins to gain a perspective of the cost of disorder. Efficiency experts have estimated that an average company loses at least $50.00 per year, per employee, because of "pack rats." They cause un-

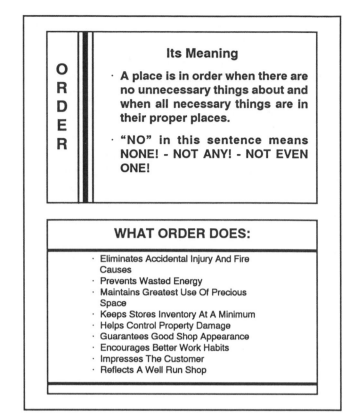

Figure 19-5

necessary purchasing of items that are on the premises but not where they are needed — because of the disorderly habits of people. In addition to the millions of dollars lost in business each year from this type of disorder, many organizations allow expensive materials and equipment to occupy valuable operating-area floor space. These are items that should be moved to locations where they could be readily used, or should at least be stored in their proper places to make valuable floor space available for operations.

Housekeeping, then, includes both cleanliness and orderliness. Cleanliness usually requires janitor-type clean-up work, but orderliness requires the application of management skills. The supervisor who conveys the message of orderliness as well as cleanliness to each member of the work team is taking giant steps toward improved efficiency while eliminating many problems that have potential for accidents and related losses.

Teach "Cleanliness" and "Order" to Others

Most workers want to contribute to the team effort and require only the necessary knowledge to make their contribution count. Here are some of the better ways to teach them the meaning and values of good housekeeping.

Explain the meaning of order and its benefits to everyone. Print the definition shown in *Figure 19-4* on a large card, and the benefits on the reverse side. Discuss these as a major subject in one of your group meetings. Follow up with added comments in your individual contacts.

Select special items of disorder for discussion purposes. Be positive by pointing out the costs your group can control through a program of order regarding those items.

Conduct an "Operation Order" Campaign

Give each worker a pocket-sized copy of the definition of order and its values. Challenge your people to put forth an extended effort for 30 days to maintain order every day, throughout the day. Let them know you will evaluate the overall campaign at the end of 30 days to determine how it has benefited everyone. Check with each team member daily during the 30 days to reinforce the program. At the end of the period, get each person's opinions on how order benefited him or her. Check the group's overall results in safety, quality and production for the month so that major changes in these areas can be reported. Make your report to the group and send a copy to the boss. The results will invariably produce many additional ideas for future direction.

Encourage an "Orderly" Attitude

Develop the habit of asking two key questions about anything that appears to be unnecessary:

1. Is this item necessary?
2. Is it in its proper place?

By your example, both words and deeds, teach others to develop the attitude and actions that will correct disorder before it causes accidents and losses.

Set Up a System to Recover Unnecessary Items

Start your system with the request that each worker clean out his or her shelves and storage places and return all unnecessary items of value to a point for inventory and value assessment. Make the program positive by keeping the group appraised of the inventory value recovered. Follow up by announcing a system for the return of anything of value deemed unnecessary by the responsible individual. Keep everyone informed periodically on the value of the program.

Use the Power of Positive Recognition

Just as behavior reinforcement can be a tool to motivate compliance with rules and protective equipment requirements, it can also be applied to individual housekeeping efforts, both cleanliness and order. Personal recognition of the orderly arrangement of the individual's tools and equipment, for instance, will soon develop a personal pride in *order* that people will wear like a badge of honor. Recognition can be utilized in any one of the many forms that have been mentioned throughout this book. For example, the wallet card shown in *Figure 19-6* can be given to deserving people during your formal and informal inspections.

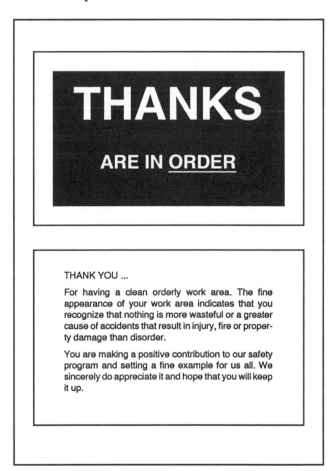

Figure 19-6

Apply Personal Observation/Decision/Action

With better understanding and new insight of what housekeeping is really all about, you are better equipped to get many things done in the interest of general efficiency and loss control. In this "new light," you will be more likely to see the existing disorder as you make your formal and informal inspections (described in Chapter 6).

Make full use of the power of observation for preventing accidents, inefficiency, waste and related losses. For better order in your operation, use your daily opportunities to look around, to examine things, to ask questions. When making inspection tours, observe conditions that are questionable. Seek answers to questions. Does it belong here or not? Is it useable? Is it suitable for scrap or salvage? If it shouldn't be here, where should it be? What is it for? Shall I keep it, or see that it gets where it belongs? Careful thinking and analysis should give you good answers, enabling good decisions. After you have observed something, thought about it and decided what is to be done, take the action you think is best to improve the situation.

HOW CAN I INCREASE CONSERVATION AWARENESS REGARDING EQUIPMENT AND MATERIALS?

Escalating costs and lack of availability of many common items have increased the need to encourage conservation habits within work groups. While excessive use or abuse of things sometimes seems difficult to measure, factual results of a good conservation program can be measured by comparing experience before and after special efforts. Higher management looks more and more to front-line supervisors as a forward wall of defense, to control waste and loss through continuous efforts to create good conservation habits within their work groups. Positive actions in the following four areas should help you accomplish this important goal: 1) Use group meetings to increase conservation awareness, 2) Use a suggestion system to increase conservation awareness, 3) Use personal contacts to increase conservation awareness and 4) Use special projects to increase conservation awareness.

Use Group Meetings to Increase Conservation Awareness

If you are like many other supervisors, you are always looking for ways to add VIM (Variety/Interest/Motivation) to your group meetings. Emphasis on specific items for conservation can help you do this. You might do it as simply as selecting one item each week to highlight for one minute in your meeting. Mention how much the item is used by the group, its unit cost and the total cost of usage for a specific period of time. Extend a positive challenge for team cooperation on greater conservation regarding this item. Let the group know that you will keep them informed on the results of their efforts.

The keys to results from a simple, direct approach are 1) the positive use of factual data, 2) the follow-up and feedback, to measure results and keep people informed and 3) giving full credit where credit is due. With good leadership, a program of this type can bring big savings for any organization over a period of time.

Use a Suggestion System to Increase Conservation Awareness

As cost awareness develops, you can also encourage suggestions for conservation from the group. Many organizations have suggestion systems that offer awards and other types of recognition for good ideas. Supervisors serve as significant catalysts to enlist the thinking of their people in this important area for action. Three questions that help to stimulate thinking in any program of conservation are:

1. Is it necessary?
2. Is it best suited for the job?
3. Is there a less costly substitute?

Of course, we must always be wary that our enthusiasm for conservation and cost reduction does not diminish our efforts to accomplish all these desirable objectives with the highest practical level of safety and health considerations.

As program efforts move along, you may decide to meet with a small group of your people to "brainstorm" with them on ways and means to conserve particular items. It is often quite surprising how many good suggestions come out when we simply solicit people's help in an organized way, under conditions that encourage a free flow of ideas. Meeting with the group in an office, for a short talk over a cup of coffee, will bring benefits extending far beyond the program of conservation.

Some supervisors prefer to involve their entire team in this type of exercise by meeting with three or four workers at a time in several meetings. The overall benefits to be gained far outweigh the costs involved. Of course, such meetings should be held in a businesslike manner and restricted to a designated period of time.

Use Personal Contacts to Increase Conservation Awareness

Supervisors frequently are involved in the control of replacement items or the issuance of new ones.

This control may be direct (such as approving a requisition which goes to someone at a disbursing point) or it may be indirect (where supervisors check and investigate to determine whether or not practices are out of control). In either case, you can exert a positive influence by creating a desire in the person who actually handles the distribution of items to tactfully question workers about conservation.

People quite frequently discard items before their full use has been achieved. Also, workers may request a greater number of items than they need at the time. This does not mean that they don't care; their conservation habits may be poor because they have not been made aware of how much it "really matters." In most cases, a new item has some slight advantages over a partially-used one. In the worker's mind, these advantages seem to offset the seemingly small waste involved. A spirit of stewardship must be instilled in each worker, so that he or she will treat all items as if they were his or her own — and had to be paid for out of his or her own pocket. Each supervisor plays a big part in creating this spirit of stewardship through persistent efforts to convey the clear message that:

- management does care
- conservation means increased benefits for everyone
- the worker is the key to conservation control

No better way exists to do this than through the day-to-day personal relationships between you and the members of your team.

Use Special Projects to Increase Conservation Awareness

It's often said that improvement in any area of loss control will result from any systematic effort to produce improvement. Accepting this truism, you could direct your organized effort into any area showing lack of control in conservation, and could produce positive results. But, since your time and resources are limited, you should concentrate your efforts on the items that will produce the greatest returns for the time and effort invested. In keeping with the professional management "Principle of the Critical/Vital Few," it is likely that about 20% of the items produce about 80% of the waste and loss. Doesn't it make sense to identify those "critical few" and concentrate on them?

The following nine steps can serve as your guide in selecting conservation projects and taking specific improvement actions:

1. With the help of workers, list all items that should possibly be considered for attention in a conservation program. Include items as varied as tools, machines, supplies, raw materials, products, protective equipment, utilities and power sources.

2. Gather information from knowledgeable people. Analyze the facts about each item. Consider the nature and frequency of usage and the unit and total costs involved.

3. Select the "critical few" targets for projects — those items for which conservation can make the greatest cost savings.

4. Perform an "efficiency check" on critical items (see Chapter 7, *Job/Task Analysis, Procedures & Practices*, for more details). Talk to the most knowledgeable people in your organization to determine whether or not the item being used is the most suitable for the job, whether or not it is the optimum price and whether or not it is being used in the best way.

5. Share the results of your investigation with your workers and others. Make suggestions to your supervisor on changes indicated by your efficiency check. Reinforce important suggestions in writing.

6. Establish new standards, procedures or practices for most effective use of the item.

7. Manage control of your standards for proper usage. Make sure that your communication, education and motivation efforts regarding conservation of the "critical few" items are persistent. Continually correct substandard usage and commend proper usage.

8. Document results. Keep written reports of your efforts and results simple and to the point, but adequate for use as records and references.

9. Keep people informed. Communicate upward as well as downward. Give feedback. Get feedback. Use the power of sharing, caring and teamwork to further develop and reinforce conservation awareness.

Whether you decide to concentrate your efforts on specific conservation problems, or adopt routine emphasis on good conservation habits in all normal work activities, or both, you can't go wrong. The resulting cost reduction and increased efficiency will benefit you, your work group and the whole organization — and will indicate to upper management the professional level of your supervisory management skills.

CORE CONCEPTS IN REVIEW

What can I do to sell and promote safety?

1. Know yourself, your product (safety) and your customers (workers).

2. Take advantage of every opportunity to **promote safety:**
   a. In meetings
   b. With individuals
   c. Through printed materials
   d. With awards and recognition
   e. By personal example

3. Apply the principles of:

   a. Information
   b. Involvement
   c. Mutual Interest
   d. Behavior Reinforcement
   e. Utilization
   to your safety promotion activities

How can I obtain and maintain compliance with rules and regulations?

1. In the **preparation** of rules:
   a. Get employee participation
   b. Keep rules short and simple
   c. Keep rules as practical as possible
   d. Give the reasons for the rules

2. In the **presentation** of rules:

   a. Suggest worker preview
   b. Show and tell during the discussion
   c. Test people's knowledge of the rules

3. In the **enforcement** of rules:

   a. Communicate the rules, the reasons for them and the related disciplinary policy and procedures
   b. Show consistency
   c. Keep good records

4. For **reinforcement** of rules, refer to them frequently in both formal and informal, individual and group contacts.

5. Perhaps most important of all, set the best **leadership example.**

What's this thing called "Constructive Correction" or "Positive Discipline"?

It means **to teach so as to mold.** It recognizes that most of the real reasons for substandard performance call for coaching rather than punishment.

1. The **punitive** approach to corrective discipline relies almost totally on:
   a. Warnings
   b. Reprimands
   c. Threats
   d. Other forms of punishment

2. The **positive** approach is one of:

   a. Helping
   b. Coaching
   c. Mutual problem solving

Preventive discipline involves the communication, training and motivation activities that enable people to comply with the rules and meet the performance standards.

How can I obtain and maintain proper use of protective equipment?

1. Promote the need for the equipment and the benefits it brings.

2. Let people participate in selecting personal protective equipment.

3. Ensure proper personal fitting, sanitation and waste control.

4. Show sensitivity to individual problems with specific equipment items.

5. Allow a period of adjustment to newly-acquired equipment.

6. Consistently enforce compliance with requirements for protective equipment.

7. Recognize and reinforce proper use of the equipment.

8. Serve as a living model of proper usage.

What can I do to motivate good housekeeping practices?

1. Know the difference between "cleanliness" and "order."

2. Teach "cleanliness" **and** "order" to others.

3. Conduct an "operation order" campaign.

4. Encourage "orderly" attitudes and habits.

5. Set up a system to recover items that are unnecessary where they are and return them to their proper places.

6. Use the power of positive recognition for good housekeeping.

7. Apply your powers of personal observation, decision and action for cleanliness and order — every day.

How can I increase conservation awareness regarding equipment and materials?

1. Emphasize conservation in group meetings.
2. Use a suggestion system to increase conservation awareness.
3. In your personal contacts, share ideas and information about equipment and materials conservation.
4. Use special projects for conservation of critical items.

KEY QUESTIONS

1. "Sell yourself first." How does this relate to safety promotion by supervisors and safety professionals?

2. List four or five basic approaches to safety promotion.

3. How can you breathe a bit of life into routine safety statistics?

4. To increase safety contest effectiveness, make sure they require people to l_____, d_____ or r_____ something for safety.

5. Describe five or six things supervisors can do to help make safety contests successful.

6. Name five professional management principles which apply to safety promotion.

7. True or False? Employees should have a say in the development of rules governing their own behavior.

8. True or False? In general, the more rules you have the better it is.

9. Why should supervisors use the "show and tell" technique when presenting rules to workers?

10. How often should supervisors review relevant rules with each employee?

11. List several ways in which supervisors can reinforce the importance of rules.

12. The word "discipline" comes from the same root as the word "disciple" and means _____.

13. What is the purpose of punishment? How effective does it seem to be?

14. Describe the *positive* counterpart of the *punitive* (oral warning/written warning/time off without pay/discharge) disciplinary approach.

15. What's the difference between "corrective" discipline and "preventive" discipline?

16. Describe five or six things supervisors can do as preventive discipline.

17. Describe five or six precautions to take in disciplinary discussions.

18. True or False? Whenever practical, representatives of those who will have to wear the protective equipment should have their say in selection decisions.

19. The majority of complaints about protective equipment involve p_____ d_____.

20. Why should we keep track of the personal protective equipment issued to each employee?

21. How do "cleanliness" and "order" differ?

22. Give the exact definition of "order."

23. Name four or five benefits of "order."

24. Efficiency experts have estimated that an average company loses at least $_____ per year, per employee, because of "pack rats."

25. What are two key questions to ask about anything that appears to be unnecessary?

26. Describe four different ways to increase conservation awareness regarding equipment and materials.

27. How does the Principle of the Critical/Vital Few apply to equipment and materials conservation projects?

PRACTICAL APPLICATIONS SUMMARY

S – For Supervisors
E – For Executives
C – For Safety/Loss Control Coordinators

		S	E	C
1.	Provide adequate bulletin boards for safety and health promotion purposes.		x	
2.	Keep posters and bulletin board materials neat and current.	x		
3.	Reinforce posted materials by referring to them in meetings and personal contacts.	x	x	x
4.	Issue safety and health program facts and figures.			x
5.	Use issued safety and health program facts and figures in group meetings and personal communications.	x	x	x
6.	Implement critical safety subject theme campaigns and/or contests.		x	x
7.	Promote active employee participation in theme campaign and contests.	x	x	x
8.	Present safety awards to individuals and groups.	x	x	
9.	Suggest safety and health information for company publications.	x	x	x
10.	Issue written rules and regulations for safety and health.	x	x	
11.	Orient new workers to safety and health rules and regulations.	x	x	
12.	Review relevant rules with each worker at least once a year.	x		
13.	Issue a written disciplinary policy as a guide to handling rules violations.		x	
14.	Consistently enforce safety and health rules and regulations.	x	x	x
15.	Recognize and reinforce rules compliance.	x	x	x
16.	Maintain proper balance between punitive and positive discipline.	x	x	
17.	Issue written standards regarding required protective equipment.		x	
18.	Provide proper personal protective equipment for all employees on all jobs.	x	x	
19.	Keep records of protective equipment issued to each employee.	x		
20.	Instruct employees in the proper fitting, use and maintenance of personal protective equipment.	x		
21.	Consistently enforce compliance with protective equipment requirements.	x	x	x
22.	Recognize and reinforce consistent, proper use of personal protective equipment.	x	x	x
23.	Resolve problems of specific individuals regarding specific items of protective equipment.	x		
24.	Promote proper usage of protective equipment through group meetings, individual contacts and personal example.	x	x	x

	S	E	C
25. Educate all employees on the difference between "cleanliness" and "order" in housekeeping.	x	x	x
26. Participate in "operation order" campaign.	x	x	x
27. Implement a system to recover items that are unnecessary where they are and move them to their proper places.	x	x	
28. Apply positive behavior reinforcement to individual employees and work groups for their contributions to good housekeeping (cleanliness and order).	x	x	x
29. Emphasize conservation of equipment and materials in group meetings with workers.	x	x	
30. Include conservation of equipment and materials in group meetings with workers.	x	x	
31. Solicit employee suggestions regarding targets and techniques of equipment and materials conservation.	x	x	
32. Carry out special projects for conservation of critical items.	x	x	

Bibliography

A Note on Management Practices. Long Beach , CA: The Forum Corporation of North America, 1980.

Accident Facts. Chicago: National Safety Council, 1984.

Accident Prevention Manual for Industrial Operations. 8th Edition, Vol. 1, Engineering and Technology. Vol. 2, Administration and Programs.

AEP, *Manual for Instructors.* American Electric Power Service Corporation. 1978.

Allen, Louis A. *The Management Profession.* New York: McGraw-Hill Book Company, 1964.

Allison, W. W. *Profitable Risk Control.* Chicago: American Society of Safety Engineers, 1985.

Bell, Chip and Fredrick Margolis. *A Preventer's Guide to Conferences.* Madison, WI: American Society for Training and Development, 1980.

Bird, Frank E., Jr. *Management Guide to Loss Control.* Loganville, GA: Institute Publishing, 1974.

Bird, Frank E., Jr. and George L. Germain. *Damage Control.* New York, American Management Association, 1966.

Bird, Frank E., Jr. and Harold E. O'Shell. "Incident Recall," *National Safety News,* October, 1969.

Bird, Frank E., Jr. and Robert G. Loftus. *Loss Control Management.* Loganville, GA: Institute Publishing, 1974.

Bittel, Lester R. *Improving Supervisory Performance.* New York: McGraw-Hill Book Company, 1976.

Blake, Robert R. and Jane Srygley Mouton. "Principles of Behavior for Sound Management," *Training and Development Journal,* October, 1979.

Broadwell, Martin M. *The Supervisor as an Instructor.* Reading, MA: Addison-Wesley Publishing Company, Inc., 1978.

Broadwell, Martin M. *The Supervisor and On-the-Job Training.* Reading, MA: Addison-Wesley Publishing Company, 1975.

Burson, James L. W. H. Spain. "Safety and Health Management: Professional Development of the Staff." *Professional Safety,* 1985.

Chapanis, Alphonse. *Research Techniques in Human Engineering.* Baltimore: The Johns Hopkins Press, 1959.

Clayton, George D. and Florence Clayton. *Patty's Industrial Hygiene and Toxicology, Volume I, General Principles,* 3rd Rev. Edition. New York: John Wiley & Sons, 1978.

Cohen, Alexander. "Factors in Successful Occupational Safety Programs," *Journal of Safety Research,* December, 1977.

Cohen, Deborah Shaw. "Why Quality of Work Life Doesn't Always Mean Quality," *Training/HRD,* October, 1981.

Cralley, Lester and Lewis Cralley, editors. *Patty's Industrial Hygiene and Toxicology Volume III. Theory and Rationale of Industrial Hygiene Practice.* New York: John Wiley & Sons, 1979.

Cribbin, James J. *Leadership.* New York: AMACOM, 1981.

Crosby, Philip B. *Quality is Free.* New York: New American Library, 1979.

Crowe, M. Joan and Hugh M. Douglas. *Effective Loss Prevention.* Toronto: Westprint, 1976.

Cullen, James G., Steven Sawzin, Gary R. Sisson and Richard A. Swanson. "Training, What's It Worth," *Training and Development Journal,* August, 1976.

Daniels, Aubrey C. and Theodore A. Rosen. *Performance Management.* Atlanta: Performance Management Publications, Inc., 1983.

Davies, Ivor K. *Instructional Technique*. New York: McGraw-Hill Book Company, 1981.

Deegan, Arthur X., II. *Coaching*. Reading, MA: Addison-Wesley Publishing Company, 1983.

Drake, John D. *Counseling Techniques for the Non-Personnel Executive*. New York: Drake-Beam & Associates, Inc., 1974.

Drucker, Peter F. *Managing In Turbulent Times*. New York: Harper & Row, Publishers, 1980.

Eastman Kodak. *Ergonomic Design for People at Work*. Vol. I. Toronto: Lifetime Learning Publications, 1983.

Encyclopedia of Occupational Health and Safety. Vols. I and II. 3rd Edition. Geneva: International Labor Office, 1983.

Eninger, M. U. *Accident Prevention Fundamentals*. Pittsburgh: Normax Publications, 1972.

Ferry, Ted S. *Readings in Accident Investigation*. Springfield, IL: Charles C. Thomas, Publisher, 1984.

Findlay, James V. *Safety and the Executive*. Loganville, GA: Institute Publishing, 1979.

Findlay, James V. and Raymond L. Kuhlman. *Leadership in Safety*. Loganville, GA: Institute Publishing, 1980.

Findlay, James V. and Richard G. Morrison. *Supervisory Control of Absenteeism*. Loganville, GA: Institute Publishing, 1977.

Fournies, Ferdinand F. *Coaching for Improved Work Performance*. New York: Van Nostrand Reinhold Company, 1978.

Fundamentals of Industrial Hygiene. 2nd Edition. Chicago: National Safety Council, 1981.

Germain, George L. *Safety Performance Management*. Loganville, GA: Institute Publishing, 1981.

Gilbert, Thomas F. *Human Competence*. New York: McGraw-Hill Book Company, 1978.

Gilmore, Charles. *Accident Prevention and Loss Control*. New York: American Management Association, 1970.

Glaser, Edward M. *Productivity Gains Through Worklife Improvement*. New York: Harcourt Brace Jovanovich, 1976.

Gordon, Thomas. *Leader Effectiveness Training*. New York: Wyden Books, 1977.

Grimaldi, John V. and Rollin H. Simonds. *Safety Management*. 4th Edition. New York: Irwin, 1984.

Hackman, J. Richard and Greg R. Oldham. *Work Redesign*. Reading, MA: Addison-Wesley Publishing Company, Inc., 1980.

Haddon, William, Jr. "On the Escape of Tigers: An Ecologic Note," *Technology Review*. May 1970.

Harless, J. H. *An Ounce of Analysis*. McLean, VA: Harless Performance Guild, Inc., 1975.

Hayes, Robert H. "Why Japanese Factories Work," *Harvard Business Review*. July-August, 1981.

Heinrich, H. W., Dan Peterson and Nestor Roos. *Industrial Accident Prevention*. 5th Edition. New York: McGraw-Hill Book Company, 1980.

Henrick, Kingsley. *Improving Performance for Safety and Health*. New York: Garland STPM Press, 1982.

Howell, Denny L. and George L. Germain. "Foreman/Worker Talks Yield Mutual Benefits," *Plant Operating Management*. March, 1971.

Jay, Antony. *Effective Presentation*. London: Management Publications, Limited, 1970.

Johnson, William G. *MORT Safety Assurance Systems*. Chicago: National Safety Council, 1980.

Johnson, Spencer and Larry Wilson. The One Minute Sales Person. New York: William Morrow and Company, Inc., 1984.

Juran, J. M. *Upper Management and Quality*. 4th Edition. New York: Juran Institute, 1982.

Kepner, Charles H. and Benjamin B. Tregoe. *The New Rational Manager*. Princeton, NJ: Princeton Research Press, 1981.

Key, M. M., A. Henschel, J. Butler, R. Ligo and I. Tabershaw, editors. *Occupational Diseases: A Guide to Their Recognition*. Washington, DC: U.S. Department of Health, Education & Welfare, DHEW (NIOSH) Publication No. 77-181, 1977.

Kuhlman, Raymond L. *Professional Accident Investigation.* Loganville, GA: Institute Publishing, 1977.

Laird, Dugan. *Approaches to Training and Development.* Reading, MA: Addison-Wesley Publishing Company, Inc., 1978.

Laird, Dugan and Ruth House. *Training Today's Employees.* Boston: CBI Publishing Company, Inc., 1983.

Lambie, H. K. "Accident Control Through Motivation," *Selected Readings in Safety.* Macon, GA: Academy Press, 1973.

Levitt, Raymond E. and Henry W. Parker. "Reducing Construction Accidents — Top Management's Role," *Journal of the Construction Division.* ASCE, September, 1976.

Levy, Seymour. *A Guide to Counseling.* New Rochelle, NY: Martin M. Bruch, Ph.D. Publishers, 1976.

Lowrance, William A. *Of Acceptable Risk.* Los Altos, CA: William Kaufman, Inc., 1976.

Luthans, Fred and Robert Kreitner. *Organizational Behavior Modification.* Glenview, IL: Scott, Foresman and Company, 1975.

Mackie, J. B. and Raymond L. Kuhlman. *Safety and Health in Purchasing.* Loganville, GA: Institute Publishing, 1981.

Mager, Robert F. and Kenneth M. Beach, Jr. *Developing Vocational Instruction.* Palo Alto, CA: Fearon Publishers, 1967.

Mager, Robert and Peter Pipe. *Analyzing Performance Problems.* Belmont, CA: Fearon Publishers, 1970.

Making Prevention Pay: Interagency Task Force Report. Washington: National Technical Information Service, 1981.

McCormick, Ernest J. *Human Factors in Engineering and Design.* 4th Edition. New York: McGraw-Hill Book Company, 1976.

McKinnon, Gordon P. editor. *Fire Protection Handbook.* 14th Edition. Boston: National Fire Protection Association, 1984.

Metz, Edmund J. "The Verteam Circle," *Training and Development Journal.* December, 1981.

Miller, Lawrence M. *Behavior Management.* New York: John Wiley & Sons, 1978.

Mills, Ted. *Quality of Work Life: What's in a Name?* Washington, DC: General Motors Corporation, 1978.

Myers, M. Scott. *Every Employee a Manager.* New York: McGraw-Hill Book Company, Inc., 1957.

Ouchi, William. *Theory Z.* Reading, MA: Addison-Wesley Publishing Company, 1981.

"Performance Management Pays Off for 3M Canada," *Training/HRD.* January, 1979.

Peters, Thomas J. and Nancy Austin. *A Passion for Excellence.* New York: Random House, 1985.

Peters, Thomas J. and Robert H. Waterman, Jr. *In Search of Excellence.* New York: Harper & Row, Publishers, 1982.

Peterson, Dan. *Human-Error Reduction and Safety Management,* New York: Garland STPM Press, 1982.

Peterson, Dan. *Safety Management,* Englewood, JR: Aloray Publisher, 1975.

Peterson, Dan. *Analyzing Safety Performance.* New York: Garland Publishing, Inc. 1980.

Pope, William C. "Systems Safety Management, Principles of Organization and Management of Risk Control." Alexandria, VA: National Safety Management Society.

Proctor, Nick H. and James P. Hughes. *Chemical Hazards in the Workplace.* Philadelphia: J. B. Lippincott Co., 1978.

Safety and Production, An Engineering and Statistical Study of the Relationship Between Industrial Safety and Production. New York: Harper and Brothers Publisher, 1928.

Sanderson, Michael. *The Supervisor's Personal Guide to Identifying and Solving Problems Quickly.* New York:

Executive Enterprises Publications Co., Inc., 1981.

Sax, N. Irving. *Dangerous Properties of Industrial Materials*, 6th Edition. New York: Van Nostrand Reinhold Co., 1984.

School of Human Biology, Guelph, Ontario. Industrial *Ergonomics: The Industrial Application of Ergonomics.* Toronto: Industrial Accident Prevention Association, 1981.

Smith, Michael J., Harvey H. Cohen, Alexander Cohen and Robert J. Cleveland. "Characteristics of Successful Safety Programs," *Journal of Safety Research.* Spring, 1978.

Snell, Frank. *How to Hold a Better Meeting.* New York: Cornerstone Library, 1974.

Tarrants, William E. *The Measurement of Safety Performance.* New York: Garland STPM Press, 1980.

The Industrial Environment - Its Evaluation and Control. Washington: National Institute for Occupational Safety and Health, 1973.

"The New Industrial Relations," *Business Week.* May 11, 1981.

The Off-the-Job Safety Program Manual. Chicago: National Safety Council, 1984.

Vervalin, Charles H., editor, *Fire Protection Manual for Hydrocarbon Processing Plants.* Vol. 1, 3rd Edition. Houston: Gulf Publishing Company, 1985.

Walters, R. W. and Associates. *Job Enrichment for Results.* Reading, MA: Addison-Wesley Publishing Company, Inc., 1975.

Williams, Philip E. and James L. Burson. Industrial *Toxicology: Safety and Health Applications in the Workplace.* New York: Van Nostrand Reinhold Company, 1985.

Zemke, Ron. "What's Good for Japan May Not Be Best for You and Your Training Department." *Training/HRD.* October, 1981.

Subject Index